'Magisterial, rich and suggestive ... MacMillan is a wry and humane chronicler of this troubled world.' Christopher Clark, *London Review of Books*

'*The War that Ended Peace* tells the story of how intelligent, well-meaning leaders guided their nations into catastrophe. These epic events, brilliantly described by one our era's most talented historians, warn of the dangers that arise when we fail to anticipate the consequences of our actions. Immersed in intrigue, enlivened by fascinating stories, and made compelling by the author's own insights, this is one of the finest books I have read on the causes of World War I.' Madeleine Albright, former Secretary of State

'Among the cascade of books arriving for the anniversary, this work truly stands out.' *The Times*

'Vivid, gripping and scholarly' Piers Brendon, *Independent*

'[An] excellent, elegantly written book ... as fine an assessment of the reason peace failed as any yet written.' Saul David, *Evening Standard*

'Once again, Margaret MacMillan proves herself not just a masterly historian but a brilliant storyteller. She brings to life the personalities whose decisions, rivalries, ambitions, and fantasies led Europe to "lay waste to itself" and triggered decades of global conflict. Hers is a cautionary tale of follies a century in the past that seem all too familiar today.' Strobe Talbott, President, Brookings Institution

'Immensely readable account ... an impressive feat' *Prospect*

'One of the strengths of *The War That Ended Peace* is MacMillan's ability to evoke the world at the beginning of the twentieth century ... MacMillan's portraits of the men who took Europe to war are superb ... The logic of MacMillan's argument is such that even now, as she leads us day by day, hour by hour through the aftermath of the assassination of Archduke Franz Ferdinand in Sarajevo on June 28, 1914, we expect some statesman or other to jump on the lighted fuse.' *New York Times*

'Magnificent ... *The War that Ended Peace* will certainly rank among the best books of the centennial crop.' *Economist*

MARGARET MACMILLAN is the author of *Women of the Raj* and international bestsellers *Nixon in China* and *Peacemakers: The Paris Conference 1919 and its attempt to end the war*, which won the 2002 Samuel Johnson Prize. Her most recent book is *Uses and Abuses of History*, also published by Profile. The past Provost of Trinity College at the University of Toronto, she is now the Warden of St Antony's College and a Professor of International History at Oxford University.

Margaret MacMillan

THE WAR THAT ENDED PEACE

How Europe Abandoned Peace for the First World War

P
PROFILE BOOKS

This paperback edition published in 2014

First published in Great Britain in 2013 by
PROFILE BOOKS LTD
3A Exmouth House
Pine Street
London ECIR OJH
www.profilebooks.com

10 9 8 7 6 5 4 3 2 1

Printed and bound in Great Britain by
CPI Group (UK) Ltd, Croydon CRO 4YY

A CIP catalogue record for this book is available from the
British Library.

ISBN 978 1 84668 273 5
eISBN 978 1 84765 416 8

To my mother Eluned MacMillan

Contents

Maps

Europe, 1914

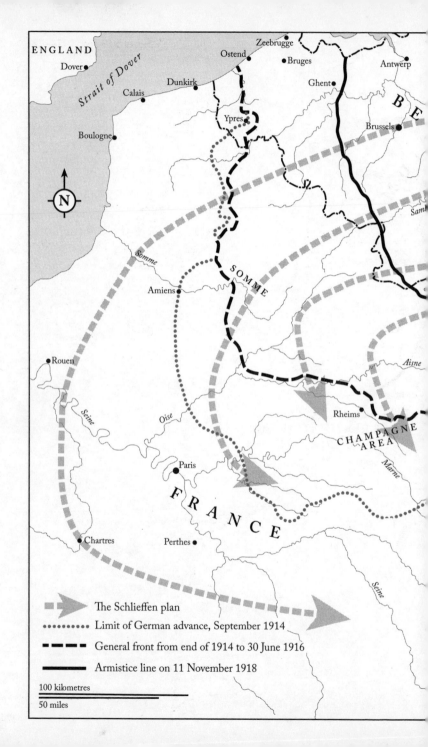

ENGLAND

Dover

Strait of Dover

Calais

Dunkirk

Boulogne

Ostend

Zeebrugge

Bruges

Ghent

Antwerp

Ypres

Brussels

B E

Somme

Amiens

SOMME

Sam

Rouen

Seine

Oise

Aisne

Rheims

CHAMPAGNE
AREA

Paris

Marne

F R A N C E

Chartres

Perthes

Seine

N

The Schlieffen plan

Limit of German advance, September 1914

General front from end of 1914 to 30 June 1916

Armistice line on 11 November 1918

100 kilometres

50 miles

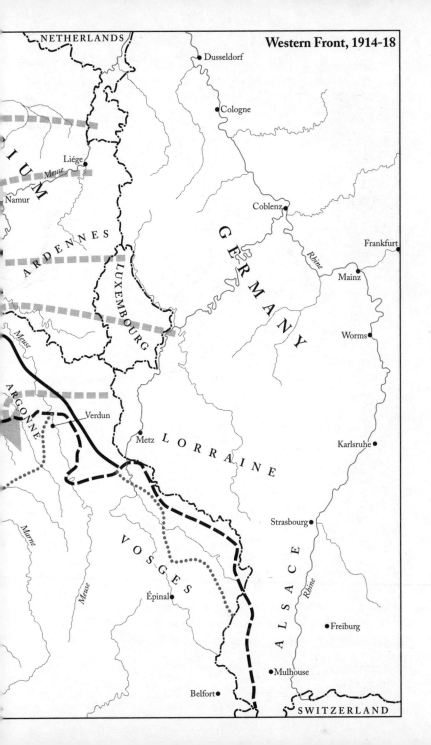

Western Front, 1914-18

NETHERLANDS

Dusseldorf

Cologne

BELGIUM

Liége

Meuse

Namur

Coblenz

ARDENNES

GERMANY

Frankfurt

LUXEMBOURG

Rhine

Mainz

Worms

Meuse

ARGONNE

Verdun

Metz

LORRAINE

Karlsruhe

Marne

Meuse

VOSGES

Strasbourg

Épinal

ALSACE

Rhine

Freiburg

Belfort

Mulhouse

SWITZERLAND

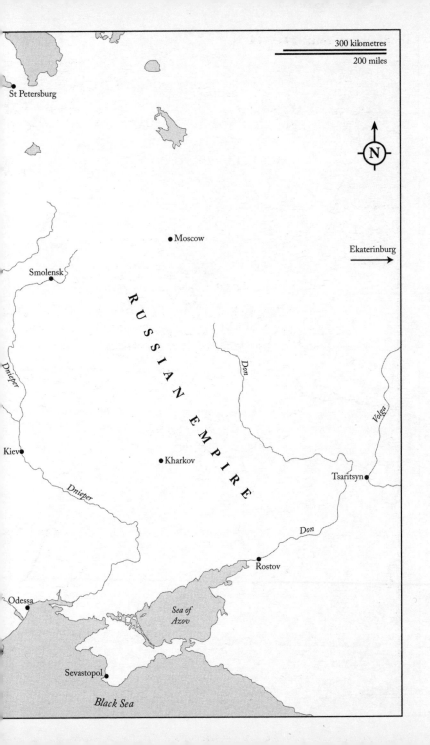

300 kilometres

200 miles

N

St Petersburg

Moscow

Ekaterinburg →

Smolensk

R U S S I A N   E M P I R E

Dnieper

Don

Volga

Kiev

Dnieper

Kharkov

Tsaritsyn

Don

Rostov

Odessa

Sea of Azov

Sevastopol

Black Sea

The Balkans, 1912-14

RUSSIA

Vienna
Bratislava

Ipel

Budapest

Tisza

Danube

Drava

N

AUSTRIA – HUNGARY

Sava

ROMANIA

Prut

Siret

Olt

Argeş

Bucharest

BOSNIA

Belgrade

Danube

Sarajevo

SANJAK

Novi Bazar

Morava

SERBIA

Nis

Danube

MONTENEGRO

Cetinje

Sofia

BULGARIA

Adriatic Sea

Skopje

Vardar

Marita

Adrianople

ALBANIA

Salonika

Taranto

ITALY

Vlorë

Dardanelles

GREECE

Aegean Sea

OTTOMAN EMPIRE

Ionian Sea

Athens

—··— Frontiers in 1913

------ Frontiers in 1912

150 kilometres

150 miles

Introduction: War or Peace?

> There have been as many plagues as wars in history;
> yet always wars and plagues take people equally by surprise.
> —Albert Camus, *The Plague*

> Nothing that ever happened, nothing that was
> ever even willed, planned or envisaged, could seem
> irrelevant. War is not an accident: it is an outcome.
> One cannot look back too far to ask, of what?
> —Elizabeth Bowen, *Bowen's Court*

Louvain was a dull place, said a guidebook in 1910, but when the time came it made a spectacular fire. None of its inhabitants could have expected such a fate for their beautiful and civilised little town. Prosperous and peaceful over many centuries, it was known for its collection of wonderful churches, ancient houses, a superb Gothic town hall and a famous university which had been founded in 1425. The university library, in the distinguished old Cloth Hall, held some 200,000 books including many great works of theology and classics as well as a rich collection of manuscripts which ranged from a little collection of songs written down by a monk in the ninth century to illuminated manuscripts over which the monks had toiled for years. In late August 1914, however, as the smell of smoke filled the air, the flames that destroyed Louvain could be seen from miles away. Much of the town, including its great library, went while its desperate inhabitants, in scenes that would become all too familiar to the twentieth-century world, struggled out into the countryside carrying what belongings they could.

Like much of Belgium, Louvain had the misfortune to be on the route of the German invasion of France in the Great War that broke out in the summer of 1914 and which was to last until 11 November 1918. The German war plans called for a two-front war with a holding action against Russia, the enemy in the east, and a rapid invasion and defeat of France in the west. Belgium, a neutral country, was meant to acquiesce quietly as German troops marched through on their way southwards. As with so much of what later happened in the Great War, those assumptions turned out to be very wrong. The Belgian government decided to resist, which immediately threw the German plans out, and the British, after some hesitation, entered the war against Germany. By the time the German troops arrived in Louvain on 19 August they were already resentful at what they saw as an unreasonable Belgian resistance and they were nervous about being attacked by Belgian and British troops as well as by ordinary civilians who might decide to take up arms.

For the first few days all went well: the Germans behaved correctly and the citizens of Louvain were too afraid to show any hostility to the invaders. On 25 August new German troops arrived, retreating from a Belgian counter-attack, and rumours spread that the British were coming. Shots were fired, most likely by the nervous and perhaps drunken German soldiers. Panic mounted among the Germans, who were convinced that they were under attack, and the first of the reprisals started. That night and in the next days civilians were dragged out of their houses and a number, including the mayor, the head of the university, and several police officers, were shot out of hand. By the end some 250 out of a population of around 100,000 were dead and many more had been beaten up and insulted. Fifteen hundred inhabitants of Louvain, from babies to grandparents, were put on a train and sent to Germany where the crowds greeted them with taunts and insults.

The German soldiers – and their officers frequently joined in – sacked the town, looting and pillaging and deliberately setting buildings on fire. Eleven hundred of Louvain's 9,000 houses were destroyed. A fifteenth-century church went up in flames and its roof caved in. Around midnight on 25 August, German soldiers went into the library and poured petrol about. By morning the building was a ruin and its collection no longer existed, although the fires smouldered on for several days afterwards. A local scholar and priest talked to the American ambassador to Belgium a few days later; the Belgian was calm as he described the destruction in the city, the friends shot, the pathetic refugees, but when he got to the library he put his head on his arms and wept.[1] 'The centre of the city is a smoking heap of ruins,' reported a professor who returned. 'An oppressive silence everywhere. Everybody has fled; at the windows of cellars I see frightened faces.'[2]

This was only the start as Europe laid waste to itself in the Great War. The 700-year-old Rheims Cathedral, the most beautiful and important of the French cathedrals and where most French kings had been crowned, was pulverised by German guns shortly after the sack of Louvain. The head of one of its magnificent sculptured angels was found lying on the ground, its beatific smile still intact. Ypres, with its own superb Cloth Hall, was reduced to rubble and the heart of Treviso in the north of Italy destroyed by bombs. Much although by no means all of the destruction came at the hands of Germans, something which had a profound impact on American opinion and which helped to propel the United States towards entering the war in 1917. As a German professor said ruefully at the war's end: 'Today we may say that the three names Louvain, Rheims, *Lusitania*, in almost equal measure have wiped out sympathy with Germany in America.'[3]

Louvain's losses were small indeed by what was to come – the more than 9 million soldiers dead and another 15 million wounded or the devastation of much of the rest of Belgium, the north of France, Serbia or parts of the Russian and Austrian-Hungarian Empires. Yet Louvain came to be a symbol of the senseless destruction, the damage inflicted by Europeans themselves on what had been the most prosperous and powerful part of the world, and the irrational and uncontrollable hatreds between peoples who had so much in common.

The Great War started on the other side of Europe from Louvain, in Sarajevo in the Balkans with the assassination of Archduke Franz Ferdinand, heir to the throne of Austria-Hungary. Like the fires that raced through Louvain, that act set in motion a conflict which grew to encompass most of Europe, and many parts of the world beyond. The greatest battles, and the greatest losses, were on the Western and

Eastern Fronts but there was fighting too in the Balkans, in the north of Italy, throughout the Middle East and in the Caucasus, as well as in the Far East, the Pacific and Africa. Soldiers from around the world also poured into Europe, whether from India, Canada, New Zealand or Australia in the British Empire or from Algeria or sub-Saharan Africa in the French. China sent coolies to transport supplies and dig trenches for the Allies while Japan, also an ally, helped to patrol the world's waterways. In 1917, the United States, stung beyond endurance by German provocations, entered. It lost some 114,000 soldiers and came to feel that it had been tricked into joining a conflict in which it had no stake.

Peace, of a sort, came in 1918, but to a very different Europe and world. Four great empires had fallen to pieces: Russia, which had ruled over many subject peoples from Poles in the west to Georgians in the east; Germany with its Polish and overseas territories; Austria-Hungary, the great multinational empire at Europe's centre; and the Ottoman Empire, which still included pieces of Europe as well as today's Turkey and most of the Arab Middle East. The Bolsheviks had seized power in Russia with dreams of creating a new communist world and that revolution had set in motion a train of others, in Hungary, Germany, or later in China. The old international order had gone for ever. Weakened and poorer, Europe was no longer the undisputed master of the world. In its colonies nationalist movements were stirring and new powers were rising on its periphery, to the east Japan and to Europe's west the United States. The Great War was not the catalyst for the rise of the Western superpower – that was already happening – but it sped up the coming of America's century.

Europe paid a terrible price in many ways for its Great War: in the veterans who never recovered psychologically or physically, the widows and orphans, the young women who would never find a husband because so many men had died. In the first years of the peace, fresh afflictions fell on European society: the influenza epidemic (perhaps as a result of churning up the rich microbe-laden soil in the north of France and Belgium) which carried off some 20 million people around the world; starvation because there were no longer the men to farm or the transportation networks to get food to the markets; or political turmoil as extremists on the right and the left used force to gain their ends. In Vienna, once one of the richest cities in Europe, Red Cross workers saw typhoid, cholera, rickets and scurvy, all scourges they thought had disappeared from Europe. And, as it turned out, the 1920s and 1930s were only a pause in what some now call Europe's latest Thirty Years War. In 1939, the Great War got a new name as a second world war broke out.

The Great War still casts its shadow both physically and in our imaginations. Tons of ordnance are still buried in the battlefields and every so often someone – an unlucky farmer ploughing in Belgium, perhaps – is added to the casualty lists. Every spring after the ground has unfrozen, units of the Belgian and French armies have to gather up the unexploded shells that have been heaved up. In our memories too the Great War, thanks in part to an extraordinary outpouring of memoirs and novels and paintings, but also because so many of us have family connections to it, remains that dark and dreadful chapter in our history. Both my grandfathers fought in the war; one in the Middle East with the Indian Army, the other a Canadian doctor in a field hospital on the Western Front. My family still has the medals won then, a sword given by a grateful patient in Baghdad, and a hand grenade which we played with as children in Canada until someone realised that it had probably not been disarmed.

We also remember the Great War because it is such a puzzle. How could Europe have done this to itself and to the world? There are many possible explanations; indeed, so many that it is difficult to choose among them. For a start the arms race, rigid military plans, economic rivalry, trade wars, imperialism with its scramble for colonies, or the alliance systems dividing Europe into unfriendly camps. Ideas and emotions often crossed national boundaries: nationalism with its unsavoury riders of hatred and contempt for others; fears, of loss or revolution, of terrorists and anarchists; hopes, for change or a better world; the demands of honour and manliness which meant not backing down or appearing weak; or Social Darwinism which ranked human societies as if they were species and which promoted a faith not merely in evolution and progress but in the inevitability of struggle. And what about the role of individual nations and their motivations: the ambitions of the rising ones such as Germany or Japan; the fears of declining ones such as Great Britain; revenge for France and Russia; or the struggle for survival for Austria-Hungary? Within each nation too there were the domestic pressures: a rising labour movement, for example, or openly revolutionary forces; demands for votes for women or for independence for subject nations; or conflict between the classes, between the believers and the anti-clericals, or between the military and civilians. How did these all play their part in keeping Europe's long peace or moving it towards war?

Forces, ideas, prejudices, institutions, conflicts, all are surely important. Yet that still leaves the individuals, not in the end that many of them, who had to say yes, go ahead and unleash war, or no, stop. Some were hereditary monarchs with great power – the Kaiser of Germany, the tsar of Russia or the emperor of Austria-Hungary; others – the President of France, the Prime Ministers of Britain and Italy – were embedded in constitutional regimes. It was Europe's and the world's tragedy in retrospect that none of the key players in 1914 were great and imaginative leaders who had the courage to stand out against the pressures building up for war. Somehow any explanation of how the Great War came must balance the great currents of the past with the human beings who bobbed along in them but who sometimes changed the direction of the flow.

It is easy to throw up one's hands and say the Great War was inevitable but that is dangerous thinking, especially in a time like our own which in some ways, not all, resembles that vanished world of the years before 1914. Our world is facing similar challenges, some revolutionary and ideological such as the rise of militant religions or social protest movements, others coming from the stress between rising and declining nations such as China and the United States. We need to think carefully about how wars can happen and about how we can maintain the peace. Nations confront each other, as they did before 1914, in what their leaders imagined was a controlled game of bluff and counter-bluff. Yet how easily and how suddenly Europe went from peace to war in those five weeks after the assassination of the archduke. During previous crises, some as bad as the one of 1914, Europe had not gone over the edge. Its leaders – and large parts of their people had supported them – had chosen to work matters out and to preserve the peace. What made 1914 different?

Let us start by imagining a landscape with people walking through it. The ground, the vegetation, the hills, the streams, these are all Europe's key components, from economies to social structures, while the breezes are the currents of thought that were shaping European views and opinions. Assume that you are one of the walkers. You will have choices ahead of you. The weather is fine although you can see a few small clouds in the sky. The way lies easy ahead across an open plain. You know that you have to keep moving because the exercise is good for you and because you eventually want to reach a safe destination. You also know that as you go along you may have to take some care. There might be unfriendly animals about, there are streams to be forded and there may be steep cliffs ahead. It does not occur to you though that you could possibly go over one of them to your doom. You are too sensible and too experienced a walker.

Yet in 1914 Europe did walk over the cliff into a catastrophic conflict which was going to kill millions of its men, bleed its economies dry, shake empires and societies to pieces, and fatally undermine Europe's dominance of the world. The photographs of cheering crowds in the great capitals are misleading. The coming of war took most Europeans by surprise and their initial reaction was disbelief and shock. They had grown used to peace; the century since the end of the Napoleonic Wars had been the most peaceful one Europe had known since the Roman Empire. True there had been wars, but these had been far-off colonial ones like the Zulu wars in southern Africa, on the periphery of Europe like the Crimean War, or short and decisive like the Franco-Prussian War.

The final lurch towards war took just over a month between the assassination of the Austrian archduke at Sarajevo on 28 June and the outbreak of a general European war on 4 August. In the end, the crucial decisions of those weeks which took Europe to war were made by a surprisingly small number of men (and they were all men). To understand how they acted as they did, however, we must go further back, to look at the forces that had shaped them. We need to understand the societies and institutions of which they were the products. We must try to comprehend the values and ideas, emotions and prejudices, which informed them as they looked at the world. We also have to remind ourselves that, with one or two exceptions, they had very little idea of what they were getting their countries and the world into. In that they were very much in tune with their times; most Europeans thought a general war was either impossible, improbable, or bound to end quickly.

As we try to make sense of the events of the summer of 1914, we must put ourselves in the shoes of those who lived a century ago before we rush to lay blame. We cannot now ask the decision-makers what they were thinking about as they took those steps along that path to destruction, but we can get a pretty good idea from the records of the time and the memoirs written later. One thing that becomes clear is that those who made the choices had very much in mind previous crises and earlier moments when decisions were made or avoided.

Russia's leaders, for example, had never forgotten or forgiven Austria-Hungary's annexation of Bosnia and Herzegovina in 1908. Moreover, Russia had failed to back its protégé Serbia when it confronted Austria-Hungary then and again in the Balkan wars in 1912–13. Now Austria-Hungary was threatening to destroy Serbia. What would it mean for Russia and its prestige if it stood by yet again and did nothing? Germany had not fully backed its ally Austria-Hungary in those earlier confrontations; if it did nothing this time, would it lose its only sure ally? The fact that earlier and quite serious crises among the powers, over colonies or in the Balkans, had been settled peacefully added another factor to the calculations of 1914. The threat of war had been used but in the end pressures had been brought to bear by third parties, concessions had been made, and conferences had been summoned, with success, to sort out dangerous issues. Brinkmanship had paid off. Surely this time in 1914 the same processes would start to work. Only this time brinkmanship did not work. This time Austria-Hungary did declare war on Serbia with Germany's backing; Russia decided to support Serbia and so went to war with Austria-Hungary and Germany; Germany attacked Russia's ally France; and Britain came in on the side of its allies. And so they went over the edge.

The outbreak of war in 1914 was a shock but it did not come out of a clear blue sky. The clouds had been gathering in the previous two decades and many Europeans were uneasily aware of that fact. Images of thunderstorms about to break, dams about to burst, avalanches ready to slide, these were quite common in the literature of the time. On the other hand, they had, many of them, leaders and ordinary citizens alike, a confidence that they could deal with the threats of conflict and build better and stronger international institutions to settle disputes peaceably and make war obsolete. Perhaps the last golden years of prewar Europe are largely a construct of later generations, but even at the time the literature also had images of the rays of sunlight spreading across the world and humanity marching towards a more prosperous and happy future.

Very little in history is inevitable. Europe did not have to go to war in 1914; a general war could have been avoided up to the last moment on 4 August when the British finally decided to come in. Looking back, we can of course see the forces that were making war more likely: the rivalries over colonies, economic competition, ethnic nationalisms which were tearing apart the failing empires of Austria-Hungary and the Ottomans, or the growth of a nationalist public opinion which put new pressures on leaders to stand up for their nation's perceived rights and interests.

We can see, as Europeans did at the time, the strains in the international order. The German question, for example. The creation of Germany in 1871 had suddenly presented Europe with a new great power at its heart. Would Germany be the fulcrum around which the rest of Europe would turn or the threat against which it would unite? How were the rising powers outside Europe – Japan and the United States – to be fitted into a world system dominated by Europe? Social Darwinism, that bastard child of evolutionary thinking, and its cousin militarism, fostered the belief that competition among nations was part of nature's rule and that in the end the fittest would survive. And that probably meant through war. The late nineteenth-century's admiration of the military as the noblest part of the nation and the spread of military values into civilian societies fed the assumptions that war was a necessary part of the great struggle for survival, that it might indeed be good for societies, tuning them up so to speak.

Science and technology which had brought so much benefit to humankind in the nineteenth century also brought new and more dreadful weapons. National rivalries fuelled an arms race which in turn deepened insecurities and so added yet more impetus to the race. Nations looked for allies to make up for their own weaknesses and their decisions helped to bring Europe closer to war. France, which was losing the demographic race with Germany, made an alliance with Russia in part for its huge reserves of manpower. In return Russia got French capital and French technology. The Franco-Russian alliance, though, made Germany feel encircled; it tied itself closer to Austria-Hungary and in so doing took on its rivalries with Russia in the Balkans. The naval race which Germany intended as a means of forcing Britain to be friendly instead persuaded the latter not only to outbuild Germany but to abandon its preferred aloofness from Europe and draw closer to France and Russia.

The military plans that came along with the arms race and the alliances have often been blamed for creating a doomsday machine that once started could not be stopped. In the late nineteenth century every European power except Britain had a conscript army, with a small proportion of their trained men actually in uniform and a far larger number back in civilian society as reserves. When war threatened huge armies could be called into being in days. Mass mobilisation relied on detailed planning so that every man reached his right unit with the right equipment, and units were then brought together in the correct configurations and moved, usually by rail, to their designated posts. The timetables were works of art but too often they were inflexible, not allowing, as in the case of Germany in 1914, partial mobilisation on just one front – and so Germany went to war against both Russia and France rather than Russia alone. And there was a danger in not mobilising soon enough. If the enemy was on your frontiers while your men were still struggling to reach their units or board their trains, you might have lost the war already. Rigid timetables and plans threatened to take the final decisions out of the hands of the civilian leaders.

Plans are at one end of a spectrum of explanations for the Great War; at the other are the nebulous but nevertheless compelling considerations of honour and prestige. Wilhelm II of Germany modelled himself on his great ancestor Frederick the Great, yet he had been mocked as Guillaume le Timide for backing down in the second of the two crises over Morocco. Did he want to face that again? What was true of individuals was also true of nations. After the humiliation of defeat by Japan in 1904–5, Russia had a pressing need to reassert itself as a great power.

Fear played a large role too in the attitudes of the powers to each other and in the acceptance by their leaders and publics of war as a tool of policy. Austria-Hungary feared that it was going to disappear as a power unless it did something about South Slav nationalism within its own borders and that meant doing something about the magnet of a South Slav and independent Serbia. France feared its German neighbour, which was stronger economically and militarily. Germany looked apprehensively eastwards. Russia was developing fast and rearming; if Germany did not fight Russia soon it might never be able to. Britain had much to gain from a continuation of the peace but it feared, as it had always done, a single power dominating the continent. Each power feared others but also its own people. Socialist ideas had spread through Europe and unions and socialist parties were challenging the power of the old ruling classes. Was this a harbinger of violent revolution, as many thought? Ethnic nationalism as well was a disruptive force, for Austria-Hungary but also in Russia and in Britain where the Irish question was more of a concern to the government in the first months of 1914 than foreign affairs. Could war be a way of bridging divisions at home, uniting the public in a great wave of patriotism?

Finally, and this is true of our own times as well, we should never underestimate the part played in human affairs by mistakes, muddle, or simply poor timing. The complex and inefficient nature of both the German and the Russian governments meant that the civilian leaders were not fully informed about military plans even when these had political implications. Franz Ferdinand, the Austrian archduke who was assassinated in Sarajevo, had long stood out against those who wanted war to solve Austria-Hungary's problems. His death, ironically, removed the one man who might have been able to prevent his country from declaring war on Serbia and thus setting the whole chain reaction in motion. The assassination came at the start of the summer holiday period. As the crisis mounted, many statesmen, diplomats and military leaders had already left their capitals. The British Foreign Secretary, Sir Edward Grey, was bird watching; the French President and Prime Minister were on an extended trip to Russia and the Baltic for the last two weeks of July and frequently out of contact with Paris.

Yet there is a danger in so concentrating on the factors pushing Europe towards war that we may neglect those pulling the other way, towards peace. The nineteenth century saw a proliferation of societies and associations for the outlawing of war and for the promotion of such alternatives as arbitration for settling disputes between nations. Rich men such as Andrew Carnegie and Alfred Nobel donated fortunes to promote international understanding. The world's labour movements and socialist parties organised themselves into the Second International, which repeatedly passed motions against war and threatened to call a general strike should one break out.

The nineteenth century was an extraordinary time of progress, in science, industry, and education, much of it centred on an increasingly prosperous and powerful Europe. Its peoples were linked to each other and to the world through speedier communications, trade, investment, migration, and the spread of official and unofficial empires. The globalisation of the world before 1914 has been matched only by our own times since the end of the Cold War. Surely, it was widely believed, this new interdependent world would build new international institutions and see the growing acceptance of universal standards of behaviour for nations. International relations were no longer seen, as they had been in the eighteenth century, as a game where if someone won someone else had to lose. Instead, all could win when peace was maintained. The increasing use of arbitration to settle disputes among nations, the frequent occasions when the great powers in Europe worked together to deal with, for example, crises in the decaying Ottoman Empire, the establishment of an international court of arbitration, all seemed to show that, step by step, the foundations were being laid for a new and more efficient way of managing the world's affairs. War, it was hoped, would become obsolete. It was an inefficient way of settling disputes. Moreover, war was becoming too costly, both in terms of the drain on the resources of the combatants and the scale of the damage that new weapons and technology could inflict. Bankers warned that even if a general war were to start, it would grind to a halt after a few weeks simply because there would be no way of financing it.

Most of the copious literature on the events of 1914 understandably asks why the Great War broke out. Perhaps we need to ask another sort of question: why did the long peace not continue? Why did the forces pushing towards peace – and they were strong ones – not prevail? They had done so before, after all. Why did the system fail this time? One way of getting at an answer is to see how Europe's options had narrowed down in the decades before 1914.

Imagine our walkers again. They start out, like Europe, on a broad and sunlit plain but they reach forks where they have to choose one way or another. Though they may not realise the implications at the time, they find themselves passing through a valley which gets narrower and may not lead to where they want to go. It might be possible to try to find a better route, but that would require considerable effort – and it is not clear what lies on the other side of the hills hemming in the valley. Or it is still possible to reverse one's steps, but that can be expensive, time consuming and possibly humiliating. Could the German government, for example, have admitted to itself and the German people that its naval race with Britain had been not only misguided but a colossal waste of money?

This book traces Europe's path to 1914 and picks out those turning points when its options narrowed. France's decision to seek a defensive alliance with Russia as a counterbalance to Germany was one, Germany's decision in the late 1890s to start a naval race with Great Britain another. Britain cautiously mended fences with France and then, in time, with Russia. Yet another key moment came in 1905–6, when Germany tried to break up the new Entente Cordiale in the first crisis over Morocco. The attempt backfired and the two new friends drew closer together and started to hold secret military talks which added another strand to the ties linking Britain to France. Europe's subsequent serious crises – the Bosnian crisis of 1908, the second Morocco one in 1911, and the Balkan wars of 1912 and 1913 – added to the layers of resentments, suspicions, and memories which shaped the relations among the great powers. That is the context in which decisions were taken in 1914.

It is possible to break free of the past and start again. Nixon and Mao, after all, decided in the early 1970s that both their countries would benefit from an end to over twenty years of hostility. Friendships can change and alliances can be broken – Italy did so at the start of the Great War when it refused to fight beside its Triple Alliance partners of Austria-Hungary and Germany – but as the years pass and the mutual obligations and the personal links build up it becomes more difficult. One of the compelling arguments that supporters of British intervention used in 1914 was that Britain had led France to expect its help and that it would be dishonourable to back out. Nevertheless there were attempts, some as late as 1913, by the powers to cut across the two alliance systems. Germany and Russia talked from time to time about settling their differences, as did Britain and Germany, Russia and Austria-Hungary or France and Germany. Whether through inertia, memories of past clashes or fear of betrayal, whatever the reasons, the attempts came to nothing.

Still, we come in the end in to those few generals, crowned heads, diplomats or politicians who in the summer of 1914 had the power and authority to say either yes or no. Yes or no to mobilising the armies, yes or no to compromise, yes or no to carrying out the plans already drawn up by their militaries. The context is crucial to understanding why they were as they were and acted as they did. We cannot, however, play down the individual personalities. The German Chancellor, Theobald von Bethmann Hollweg, had just lost his much-loved wife. Did that add to the fatalism with which he contemplated the outbreak of the war? Nicholas II of Russia was a fundamentally weak character. That surely must have made it more difficult for him to resist his generals who wanted immediate Russian mobilisation. Franz Conrad von Hötzendorf, the chief of staff of the Austrian-Hungarian armies, wanted glory for his country but also for himself so he could marry a divorced woman.

The war, when it finally came, was so frightful that a search for the guilty started which has continued ever since. Through propaganda and the judicious publication of documents every belligerent country proclaimed its own innocence and pointed its finger at the others. The left blamed capitalism or the arms manufacturers and dealers, the 'merchants of death'; the right blamed the left or Jews or both. At the Peace Conference in Paris in 1919 the victors talked of bringing the guilty – the Kaiser, some of his generals and diplomats – to trial, but in the end nothing came of it. The question of responsibility had continuing significance because if Germany was responsible, then it was right that it should pay reparations. If not, and this of course was the general view in Germany and increasingly in the English-speaking world, then reparations and the other penalties Germany had suffered were deeply unfair and illegitimate. In the interwar years the prevailing view came to be, as David Lloyd George put it: 'The nations slithered over the brink into the boiling cauldron of war without any trace of apprehension or dismay.'[4] The Great War was nobody's fault or everybody's.

After the Second World War, several bold German historians, led by Fritz Fischer, took a second look at the archives to argue that Germany was indeed culpable and that there was a sinister continuity between the intentions of Germany's last government before the Great War and Hitler. They have themselves been challenged and so the debate goes on.

The search will probably never end and I will myself argue that some powers and their leaders were more culpable than others. Austria-Hungary's mad determination to destroy Serbia in 1914, Germany's decision to back it to the hilt, Russia's impatience to mobilise, these all seem to me to bear the greatest responsibility for the outbreak of the war. Neither France nor Britain wanted war, although it might be argued that they could have done more to stop it. In the end, though, I find the more interesting question to be to how Europe reached the point in the summer of 1914 where war became more likely than peace. What did the decision-makers think they were doing? Why didn't they pull back this time as they had done before? Why, in other words, did the peace fail?

CHAPTER I

Europe in 1900

On 14 April 1900 Emile Loubet, the President of France, talked approvingly about justice and human kindness as he opened the Paris Universal Exposition. There was little kindness to be found in the press comments at the time. The exhibitions were not ready; the site was a dusty mess of building works; and almost everyone hated the giant statue over the entrance of a woman modelled on the actress Sarah Bernhardt and dressed in a fashionable evening dress. Yet the Exposition went on to be a triumph, with over 50 million visitors.

In style and content the Exposition partly celebrated the glories of the past and each nation displayed its national treasures – whether paintings, sculptures, rare books or scrolls – and its national activities. So where the Canadian pavilion had piles of furs, the Finnish showed lots of wood, and the Portuguese decorated their pavilion with ornamental fish. Many of the European pavilions mimicked great Gothic or Renaissance buildings, although little Switzerland built a chalet. The Chinese copied a part of the Forbidden City in Beijing and Siam (today Thailand) put up a pagoda. The Ottoman Empire, that dwindling but still great state which stretched from the Balkans in southern Europe through Turkey to the Arab Middle East, chose a pavilion which was a jumble of styles, much like its own peoples who included Christians, Muslims and Jews and many different ethnicities. With coloured tiles and bricks, arches, towers, Gothic windows, elements of mosques, of the

Grand Bazaar from Constantinople (now Istanbul), it was fitting that the overall result still somehow resembled the Hagia Sophia, once a great Christian church that became a mosque after the Ottoman conquest.

Germany's pavilion was surmounted by a statue of a herald blowing a trumpet, suitable, perhaps, for the newest of the great European powers. Inside was an exact reproduction of Frederick the Great's library; tactfully the Germans did not focus on his military victories, many of them over France. The western facade hinted, though, at a new rivalry, the one which was developing between Germany and the world's greatest naval power Great Britain: a panel showed a stormy sea with sirens calling and had a motto rumoured to be written by Germany's ruler, Kaiser Wilhelm II, himself: 'Fortune's star invites the courageous man to pull up the anchor and throw himself into the conquest of the waves.' Elsewhere at the Exposition were reminders of the rapidly burgeoning power of a country that had only come into existence in 1871; the Palace of Electricity contained a giant crane from Germany which could lift 25,000 kilos.

Austria-Hungary, Germany's closest friend in Europe, had two separate pavilions, one for each half of what had come to be known as the Dual Monarchy. The Austrian one was a triumph of Art Nouveau, the new style which had been catching on in Europe. Marble cherubs and dolphins played around its fountains, giant statues held up its staircases and every inch of its walls appeared to be covered by gold leaf, precious stones, happy or sad masks, or garlands. A grand reception room was set aside for members of the Habsburg family which had presided for centuries over the great empire stretching from the centre of Europe down to the Alps and Adriatic, and the exhibits showed off the work of Poles, Czechs, and South Slavs from the Dalmatian coast, only some of the Dual Monarchy's many peoples. Next to the Austrian pavilion and separating it from that of Hungary stood a smaller one, representing the little province of Bosnia, still technically part of the Ottoman Empire but administered since 1878 from Vienna. The Bosnian pavilion, with its lovely decorations by craftsmen from its capital of Sarajevo, looked, said the guide published by Hachette, like a young girl being brought out into the world for the first time by her parents.[1] (And they were not particularly happy ones at that.)

1. In the 1899–1902 war between the British Empire and the two independent Afrikaner (or Boer) republics in South Africa, the sympathy of much of the world was with the Afrikaners. Lord Kitchener was the target of particular international condemnation for his brutal policy of breaking Afrikaner resistance by destroying their farms and livestock and forcing their women and children into concentration camps.

The mood of the Hungarian pavilion was strongly nationalistic. (Austrian critics said sourly that the folk art on display was vulgar and its colours too bright.) The exhibits also included a reconstruction of the great citadel of Comorn (Komárom) in the north which stood in the way of the Ottomans in the sixteenth century as they stretched northwards into Europe. Much more recently, in 1848, it had been held by Hungarian nationalists in the revolt against the Habsburgs but had fallen to Austrian forces in 1849. Another room was dedicated to the Hussars, famous for their bravery in the wars against the Ottomans. The exhibits paid less attention though to the millions of non-Hungarian peoples, Croatians or Rumanians, for example, who lived within Hungary's borders.

Italy, like Germany a new country and a great power more by courtesy than in reality, had built what looked like a vast, richly decorated cathedral. On its golden dome stood a giant eagle, its wings outstretched in triumph. Inside it was filled with art from the Middle Ages and the Renaissance, but the glories of the past could weigh heavily on a poor young country. Britain, by contrast, chose to be low key even though it still dominated much of the world's trade and manufacturing and had the world's biggest navy and largest empire. Its exhibit was housed in a cosy country house designed by rising young architect Edwin Lutyens in the half-timbered Tudor style and consisted mainly of English paintings from the eighteenth century. Some private British owners had refused to lend their works because Britain's relations with France, traditionally difficult, were particularly strained in 1900.[2]

Russia had pride of place at the Exposition as France's favoured ally. The Russian exhibits were huge and scattered in several different locations, ranging from a massive palace in the style of the Kremlin dedicated to Siberia to a richly decorated pavilion named in honour of the tsar's mother, Empress Marie. Visitors could admire, among much else, a map of France made in precious stones which the tsar, Nicholas II, had sent as a present to the French and marvel at the sheer extent of the Romanovs' possessions. The French themselves did not have their own pavilion; the whole Exposition was after all designed to be a monument to French civilisation, French power, French industry and agriculture, and French colonies, and room after room in the different special exhibits was devoted to French achievements. The French section of the Palais des Beaux-Arts was, said the guide, naturally a model of good taste and luxury. The Exposition marked the reassertion by France that it was still a great power, even though only thirty years previously it had been utterly defeated as it had tried to prevent Germany coming into existence.

The Universal Exposition was nevertheless, the French declared, a 'symbol of harmony and peace' for all of humanity. Although the more than forty countries exhibiting in Paris were mainly European, the United States, China, and several Latin American countries also had pavilions. As a reminder though of where power still lay, a large part of the Exposition was given over to colonies where the European powers showed off their possessions. The crowds could marvel at exotic plants and beasts, walk by replicas of African villages, watch craftsmen from French Indochina at their work, or shop in North African souks. 'Supple dancing girls', said an American observer severely, 'perform the worst forms of bodily contortions known to the followers of Terpsichore.'[3] Visitors came away with a comfortable assurance that their civilisation was superior and that its benefits were being spread around the globe.

The Exposition seemed a suitable way to mark the end of a century which had started with revolutions and wars but which now stood for progress, peace and prosperity. Europe had not been entirely free of wars in the nineteenth century but they had been nothing to compare with the long struggles of the eighteenth century or the wars of the French Revolution and later those of Napoleon which had drawn in almost every European power. The wars of the nineteenth century had generally been short – like the one between Prussia and the Austrian Empire which had lasted for seven weeks – or colonial wars fought far from European soil. (The Europeans should have paid more attention to the American Civil War which not only lasted for four years but which gave an early warning that modern technology and the humble barbed wire and spades were shifting the advantage in war to the defence.) While the Crimean War in the middle of the century had involved four European powers, it was the exception. In the Austro-Prussian War, the Franco-Prussian, or the Russo-Turkish the other powers had wisely stayed out of the conflict and had done what they could to build peace again.

In certain circumstances war was still seen as a reasonable choice for nations if they could see no other way to obtain their goals. Prussia was not prepared to share control of the German states with Austria and Austria was determined not to concede. The war that followed settled the issue in Prussia's favour. Resorting to war was costly but not excessively so. Wars were limited both in time and in their scope. Professional armies fought each other and damage to civilians and to property was minimal, certainly in light of what was to come. It was still possible to attack and win decisive victories. The Franco-Prussian War of 1870–71, though, like the American Civil War, hinted that armed conflict was changing: with conscription, armies were bigger, and better and more accurate weapons and increased firepower meant that the forces of the Prussians and their German allies suffered large casualties in the opening attacks on the

French. And the surrender of the French army at Sedan did not end the fighting. Instead the French people, or large sections of it, chose to fight on in a people's war. Yet even that had finally ended. France and the new Germany had made peace and their relations had gradually mended. In 1900 the Berlin business community sent a message for the opening of the Exposition to the Paris Chamber of Commerce, wishing success to 'this great undertaking, which is destined to bring the civilized nations of the world nearer to one another in the labours common to them all'.[4] The large numbers of German visitors who were expected to go to Paris would, so many in Germany hoped, help to build better relations between the peoples of their two countries.

All the peoples of the earth have worked on the Exposition, said the special Hachette guide: 'they have accumulated their marvels and their treasures for us to reveal unknown arts, overlooked discoveries and to compete with us in a peaceful way where Progress will not slacken in her conquests'. The themes of progress and the future ran throughout the Exposition, from the new moving pavements to the cinema in the round. At one of the pavilions, the Château d'Eau, with its cascading waterfalls, shooting fountains, and coloured lights playing on the waters, the centrepiece in a giant basin was an allegorical group which represented Humanity led by Progress advancing towards the Future and overthrowing the rather odd couple of Routine and Hatred.

The Exposition was a showcase for individual countries but it was also a monument to the most recent extraordinary achievements of Western civilisation, in industry, commerce, science, technology, and the arts. You could see the new X-ray machines or be overwhelmed, as Henry James was, by the Hall of Dynamos, but the most exciting discovery of all was electricity. The Italian Futurist artist Giacomo Balla later called his daughters Luce and Elettricità in memory of what he saw at the Paris Exposition. (A third daughter was Elica – Propellor – after the modern machinery he also admired.) Camille Saint Saëns wrote a special cantata in praise of electricity for the Exposition: *Le Feu céleste* with orchestra, soloists and choir was performed at a free concert. The Palace of Electricity was ablaze with 5,000 light bulbs and high on the summit of its roof stood the Fairy of Electricity in her chariot drawn by a horse and dragon. And there were dozens more palaces and pavilions devoted to the important activities of modern society, among them machinery, mining and metallurgy, chemical industries, public transportation, hygiene, and agriculture.

There was still more, much more. The second modern Olympic Games took place nearby in the Bois de Boulogne as part of the Exposition. Sports included fencing (where the French did very well), tennis (a British triumph), athletics (American dominated), cycling and croquet. At the Exposition Annexe in Vincennes you could examine the new motorcars and watch balloon races. Raoul Grimoin-Sanson, one of the earliest film directors, went up in his own balloon to film the Exposition from above. As the Hachette guide said, the Exposition was 'the magnificent result, the extraordinary culmination of the whole century – the most fertile in discoveries, the most prodigious in sciences, which has revolutionized the economic order of the Universe'.

In light of what was to come in the twentieth century such boasting and such complacency seem pitiful to us, but in 1900 Europeans had good reason to feel pleased with the recent past and confident about the future. The thirty years since 1870 had brought an explosion in production and wealth and a transformation in society and the way people lived. Thanks to better and cheaper food, improvements in hygiene, and dramatic advances in medicine, Europeans were living longer and healthier lives. Although Europe's population went up by perhaps as much as 100 million to a total of 400 million, it was able to absorb the growth thanks to increased output in its own industry and agriculture and imports from around the world. (And emigration acted as a safety valve to avoid an even more dramatic increase – some 25 million Europeans left in the last two decades of the century for new opportunities in the United States alone and millions more went to Australia or Canada or Argentina.)

Europe's cities and towns grew as people moved from the countryside in increasing numbers in search of better opportunities in factories, shops and offices. On the eve of the French Revolution in 1789, Paris had some 600,000 inhabitants; by the time of the Exposition, 4 million. Budapest, the capital of Hungary, showed the most dramatic increase: in 1867 it had 280,000 inhabitants and by the time of the Great War, 933,000. As the numbers of Europeans making a living from agriculture went down, the industrial working classes and the middle classes grew. Workers organised themselves into unions, which were legal in most countries by the end of the century; in France the number of workers in unions went up fivefold in the fifteen years before 1900 and was to reach 1 million just before the Great War. In recognition of the increasing importance of the class, the Exposition had exhibits of model houses for workers and organisations for their moral and intellectual development.

Alfred Picard, the engineer who organised the Paris Exposition, recommended that visitors start with the Palace of Teaching and Education. Education, he said, was the source of all progress. The palace showed curriculums and methods of instruction from infant schools to university in France as well as other countries. The United States exhibit was worth a visit, said the Hachette guide, to see the curious teaching methods favoured by the Americans. (It did not specify what those might be.) There were also special displays for technical and scientific education and adult evening classes. As Europe's economy changed, governments and business alike had realised that they needed a better-educated population. The late nineteenth century saw the spread of universal education and literacy. On the eve of the Great War, even Russia, widely regarded as the most backward power in Europe, had almost half of the children who lived in cities and towns in elementary school and 28 per cent of those in the countryside – and the goal was to make that 100 per cent by 1922.

The increase of public libraries and adult education classes encouraged reading and publishers responded to the new mass markets with comic books, pulp fiction, thrillers, and adventure stories such as Westerns. The mass newspaper, with its big splashy headlines and lavish use of illustrations, made its appearance. In 1900 the *Daily Mail* in London had a circulation of over 1 million. All this contributed to widening the horizons of Europeans and also to making them feel part of larger communities than their ancestors would have done. Where once most Europeans would have seen themselves as members of their village or town, they now increasingly felt themselves to be German or French or British, part of something called a nation.

There were no exhibits in Paris devoted to the art of government itself but there were many which showed the increasing number of things that governments did, from public works to the well-being of their citizens. Governing in the new Europe was more complicated a task than it had been even thirty years previously because society was more complicated. The spread of democracy and the extension of voting rights also meant that an expanding public demanded more. No government wanted large numbers of disgruntled citizens. The memories of Europe's many revolutions were all too fresh. Moreover, the move by all of Europe's armies, except the British, to conscripting young men for a limited number of years meant that the ruling classes had to depend on the co-operation and goodwill of the masses. As Prince Yevgeny Trubetskoy, one of the more intelligent Russian aristocrats, said, 'it is impossible to govern against the people when it is necessary to turn to it for the defence of Russia'.[5]

Governments were finding that they had to provide more than basic security for their populations. This was partly in hopes of avoiding social conflict but also because a healthier and better-educated workforce was better for the economy and for the military. Germany's great Chancellor, Otto von Bismarck, pioneered the modern welfare state with such things as unemployment insurance and old-age pensions in Germany in the 1880s, and his example was followed throughout Europe. Governments also realised that they needed better information – statistics became an important tool in the late nineteenth century – if they were to govern efficiently. Governing now required trained servants. The old amateurish ways in armies or bureaucracies, where young men were chosen on the basis of family and connections, no longer were good enough. Officers who could not read maps or who did not understand tactics or logistics could not manage the increasingly large modern armies. Foreign offices could no longer provide congenial refuges for gentlemen who liked to dabble in foreign affairs. And the arrival of the new and unpredictable factor of public opinion meant that governments could no longer manage their foreign affairs with a free hand.

Better communications, including the new fast and cheap public post offices and the telegraph, not only brought Europeans into contact with each other and fostered nationalist feeling but also made them aware of what was going on in other countries. Cheaper and easier travel also helped. In the cities the horse-drawn vehicles were gradually giving way to newer forms of transportation such as electric trams. The first branch of the Paris Métro opened in time for the Exposition. (And the first Métro pickpockets started their activities too.) Railway and canal networks spread out across Europe and the steamship lines criss-crossed the oceans. In 1850 there were only 14,000 miles of railway track in the whole continent; by 1900, over 180,000. The visitors to the Paris Exposition came from all over Europe and even further afield like the thousands of Americans who were in Paris that summer. A new phenomenon had appeared: mass tourism. Where once travel for pleasure was only for the rich and leisured – think of the Grand Tours that young noblemen would make in the eighteenth century – it was now within reach of the middle classes and even the prosperous working classes. In the 1840s an enterprising Englishman, Thomas Cook, started to use the new railways to organise outings for temperance societies. By the end of the century, Thomas Cook and Son was organising travel for thousands of tourists a year. In 1900, inevitably, the firm laid on a special programme of visits to Paris and the Exposition.

Europe was starting to look more like the world we know. Cities were getting rid of their old slums and narrow laneways and building more spacious roads and public spaces. In Vienna, the government opened up for development the swathes of land that had protected the approach to the old city walls. The Ringstrasse with its huge public buildings and elegant apartment blocks became the symbol of the new modern city. And Vienna, like other European cities, was cleaner and more salubrious by the end of the century, brighter too as electric lights replaced the old gas ones. You were surprised and delighted whenever you revisited one of the great European cities, recalled Stefan Zweig, the famous Austrian writer, in his autobiography. 'The streets were broader and finer, the public buildings more imposing, the shops more elegant.'[6] Prosaic improvements such as better drains, indoor bathrooms and clean water supplies meant that the old diseases such as typhus and cholera which had once been commonplace began to vanish. At the 1900 Exposition the Palais de l'Hygiène showed off new systems of heating and ventilation for public buildings such as hospitals and one room, devoted to the conquest of disease, gave a bust of the great Louis Pasteur the place of honour. (A Canadian visitor said she would have enjoyed those exhibits more 'had there not been so many horrid Frenchmen about'.)[7]

In another exhibit, for fabrics and clothing, the French showed off the work of their best couturiers but also the ready-made clothes which were bringing fashion within the reach of the middle-class consumer. New consumer goods – bicycles, telephones, linoleum, and cheap newspapers and books – were becoming part of everyday life, and the big new department stores and catalogue shopping were making them available to everyone who could afford them. And that was an increasing number of Europeans. Thanks to mass production, what had been luxury goods were now affordable by ordinary households. In the 1880s German factories were producing 73,000 pianos a year. Public entertainments and amusements were both cheaper and more elaborate. The new medium of film stimulated the building of special cinema theatres, often beautifully decorated. The French also had their café-concerts where for the price of a drink or a coffee patrons could watch a singer or two, perhaps a comic, even dancers. In Britain, the public houses, with their bright lights, shining brass, overstuffed chairs and embossed wallpaper brought a touch of glamour to an evening outing for members of the lower classes.

Europeans were also eating much better. One of the palaces at the Exposition showed the glories of French agriculture and foods (as well as a colossal sculpture of the apotheosis of a bottle of champagne) but others such as the Palais de l'Horticulture Étrangère showed foodstuffs from around the world. Europeans were becoming accustomed to pineapples from the Azores, mutton and lamb from New Zealand or beef from the Argentine, brought in the new refrigerator ships or packed into tins. (Campbell's tinned soup won a gold medal at the Paris Exposition.) Improvements in farming and the opening up of new agricultural lands around the world as well as cheaper and faster transportation brought a drop in food prices by almost 50 per cent in the last third of the century. Life was good, especially for the middle classes.

Stefan Zweig, who was nineteen in 1900, has left a picture of his carefree youth. His family were prosperous and indulgent and let him do whatever he pleased at the university in Vienna. He did a minimum of academic work but read widely. He was just starting on his career as a writer, publishing early poems and his first articles. In the last thing he ever wrote, *The World of Yesterday*, he chose to call the time of his youth before the Great War 'the Golden Age of Security'. For the middle classes in particular, their world was just like the Habsburg monarchy, seemingly stable and permanent. Savings were secure and property was something to be passed down safely from one generation to the next. Humanity, particularly European humanity, was clearly moving onto a higher plane of development. Societies were not only increasingly prosperous and better organised but their members were also kinder and more rational. To Zweig's parents and their friends the past was something to be deplored while the future was increasingly bright. 'People no more believed in the possibility of barbaric relapses, such as wars between the nations of Europe, than they believed in ghosts and witches; our fathers were doggedly convinced of the infallibly binding power of tolerance and conciliation'.[8] (At the start of 1941 Zweig, by now in exile in Brazil, sent his manuscript to his publisher. A few weeks later he and his second wife committed suicide.)

His Golden Age of Security and the evidence of progress before the Great War were greatest in western Europe (including the new Germany) and in the developed parts of Austria-Hungary such as the German and Czech lands. The great powers, combining wealth, territory, influence and military power, were still all European: Britain, France, Germany, Austria-Hungary and Italy, and, on Europe's eastern edge, Russia, a nation which had always been seen as not quite European, was starting its dramatic rise to world power. Still considered by many in the West to be stuck somewhere in the sixteenth century, Russia was in fact on the verge of an economic take-off – and perhaps a political one as well. The Russian displays at the Paris Exposition included the obligatory homage to the glories of Russian history and civilisation but they also showed locomotives, machines, and weapons. In the special pavilion devoted to Russia in Asia, visitors could sit in railway carriages which rocked gently to and fro to give the illusion of movement while a painted panorama showing the vast new lands of the Russian east rolled past. The message was that a dynamic Russia was acquiring new colonies, linking them with the Trans-Siberian Railway, and bringing them the benefits of modern civilisation including the technology to develop their rich natural resources.

This was not just wishful thinking on the part of the Russians. From the 1880s onwards Russia's development by most measures had been extraordinary. Like later success stories, the Asian Tigers after the Second World War, for example, it was shifting from a primarily agricultural economy to an industrial one. Russia's growth rates – an average of 3.25 per cent per year – matched or exceeded those of world leaders such as Great Britain and the United States when the latter two had been at a similar stage. Although the war with Japan and the subsequent revolutionary upheavals in 1905 set Russian development back, it picked up again rapidly in the last years before the Great War. By 1913 Russia was the biggest agricultural producer in Europe and in industry was catching up fast with the other industrial powers. On the eve of the war, it was fifth among the world's nations in industrial production.[9] And there was evidence, mixed to be sure, that Russian society and politics were moving in a more liberal direction.

What would have happened to Russia if the Great War had not come? Or if Russia had somehow managed to stay out? Would there have been a revolution in 1917? Without the war and the collapse of the old regime, would the Bolsheviks, that revolutionary splinter group, ever have been able to seize power and impose their rigid and doctrinaire policies? We will never know but it is not difficult to imagine a different, less bloody and less wasteful path for Russia into the modern age. And it is tempting to imagine a different future for Europe as well. It had so much to celebrate in 1900 and so did its other great powers. Britain still was secure and prosperous even though it had rivals around the world and in Europe. France seemed to have put its decades of revolutions and political upheavals behind it and had recovered from its humiliating defeat by Prussia and its German allies in the war of 1870–71. Germany had Europe's fastest-growing economy and was rapidly spreading its influence east and south through trade and investment. It looked set to become the powerhouse at Europe's core – and without any need to use its powerful army; as it had at last done in the late twentieth century. Austria-Hungary had survived, which was a triumph in itself, and its many nationalities enjoyed the benefits of being part of a larger economic and political unit. Italy was gradually industrialising and modernising.

The colonial displays at the Exposition hinted too at the extraordinary power that a very small part of the world had amassed in the course of the previous centuries. Europe's countries dominated much of the earth's surface whether through their formal empires or by informal control of much of the rest through their economic, financial and technological strength. Railways, ports, telegraph cables, steamship lines, factories around the world were built using European know-how and money and were usually run by European companies. And Europe's dominance had increased dramatically in the nineteenth century as its scientific and industrial revolutions gave it, for a time at least, an edge over other societies. The first Opium War at the end of the 1830s between Great Britain and China saw the British using an armour-plated steamship (appropriately named the *Nemesis*) against a Chinese navy still equipped with the junks that had served China well for centuries. In 1800 before the gap in power opened up, Europe had controlled approximately 35 per cent of the world; by 1914 that figure was 84 per cent.[10] True, the process had not always been a peaceful one and European powers had come close to war several times over the spoils. By 1900, however, the tensions caused by imperialism seemed to be subsiding. There was not much left to divide up in Africa, the Pacific or Asia, and there was, or so it seemed, a general agreement that there should be no sudden land grabs in such declining states as China or the Ottoman Empire, tempting though their weakness made them to imperialists.

Given such power and such prosperity, given the evidence of so many advances in so many fields in the past century, why would Europe want to throw it all away? There were many Europeans, like Stefan Zweig's parents, who thought that such recklessness and folly was simply impossible. Europe was too interdependent, its economies too intertwined, to break apart into war. It would not be rational, a quality greatly admired at the time.

The march of knowledge throughout the nineteenth century, in so many fields from geology to politics, had, it was widely assumed, brought much greater rationality in human affairs. The more humans knew, whether about themselves, society, or the natural world, the more they would make decisions based on the facts rather than on emotion. In time, science – including the new social sciences of sociology and politics – would uncover everything we needed to know. 'The history of mankind is part and parcel of the history of nature,' wrote Edward Tylor, who was one of the fathers of modern anthropology, 'and our thoughts, wills, and actions accord with laws as definite as those which govern the motions of the waves, the combination of acids and bases, and the growth of plants and animals.'[11] Tied to this faith in science – or positivism, as it was usually referred to at the time – was an equal faith in progress, or, as Europeans often wrote, Progress. Human development was, so it was assumed, linear, even if not all societies had reached the same stage. Herbert Spencer, in his time the most widely read British philosopher, argued that the laws of evolution applied as much to human societies as they did to species. Moreover, progress was generally seen to be across the board: advanced societies were better in all respects from the arts to political and social institutions to philosophy and religion. European nations were manifestly in the lead (although there was room for disagreement about rankings among them). Other nations, the old, white dominions of the British Empire being promising examples, would eventually follow along. At the Exposition there was considerable interest in the Japanese exhibits since, said the guide, Japan had adapted with marvellous rapidity to the modern world. And Japan was now a player in international relations, if not globally then certainly in Asia.

The other challenge that was unfolding to Europe's dominance came to its west, from the New World. When the United States was left out initially from the row of important foreign pavilions along the Seine, its chief representative to the Exposition, a rich Chicago businessman, explained why this would not do: 'The United States have so developed as to entitle them not only to an exalted place among the nations of the earth, but to the foremost rank of all in advanced civilization.'[12] By 1900 the United States had recovered from the Civil War. Its government had crushed the last Indian resistance and American domination of its land mass was complete. Immigrants were pouring to work in its farms, its factories and its mines and the American economy was expanding rapidly. Where Britain had led the first industrial revolution in the early nineteenth century based on coal, steam power and iron, the United States with its grid of electricity and its seemingly limitless ability for technological innovation was in the forefront of the second at the end of the century. By 1902, American plants produced more iron and steel than Germany and Great Britain together. American exports, from cigarettes to machinery, tripled between 1860 and 1900. By 1913 the United States had 11 per cent of the world's trade and that share was increasing annually.

At the Exposition, the American pavilion, which did end up in a prime location by the river, was a model of the Capitol in Washington, with, on its dome, a giant sculpture showing Liberty drawn by four horses in the Chariot of Progress. The correspondent for the *New York Observer* described the American exhibits for his readers: the superb works by American sculptors such Augustus Saint-Gaudens, the magnificent displays of jewels from Tiffany and Company, or the watches and clocks which were the equal of any from Switzerland. Only a couple of displays from London and Paris, he said dismissively, 'approached the perfection of the gold and silver work which was displayed by the United States'. And there were samples of American technology – Singer sewing machines, typewriters, vast electrical dynamos – and of the raw materials – copper, wheat, gold – which were pouring out on to the world's markets. 'Enough was done', he reported complacently, 'to make a profound impression upon the millions of visitors, of the power, wealth, resources and ambition of the United States.'[13] And in his view the Paris Exposition paled by comparison with the Chicago World's Fair of 1893.[14] His was the voice of a new American self-confidence and a growing American nationalism with ambitions to play a greater part in the world.

The time had now come, so historians such as Frederick Jackson Turner argued, to move beyond American shores and spread American influence to nearby islands and to other countries. Talk of the United States' manifest destiny in the world found many eager listeners, from businessmen searching for new markets to evangelicals looking for souls to save. While Americans did not see their expansion as imperialist – unlike that of the European powers – the United States did somehow still acquire both territory and spheres of influence. In the Pacific it established a presence in both Japan and China and gathered up a series of tiny islands whose names – Guam, Midway, Wake – were going to become famous in the Second World War. In 1889 the United States got involved in a complicated dispute with Germany and Britain over the sharing out of the Samoan islands and in 1898 annexed the Hawaiian islands. As a result of the Spanish–American War in the same year, the United States found itself in control of the Philippines, Puerto Rico and Cuba. Central America and the Caribbean became an increasingly important backyard as American investment flowed southwards. By 1910 Americans owned more of Mexico than the Mexicans themselves. To the north, Canada remained a temptation to annexationists.

The growing American world presence brought what was at first the unwelcome realisation that the United States was going to have to spend money on a modern navy and one, moreover, which could operate in both the Atlantic and the Pacific. In 1890, at a time when even little Chile had a stronger navy than the United States, Congress reluctantly approved the first three modern American battleships. The gradual building of American military power was accompanied by an increasing willingness on the part of the United States to assert its rights against other powers. In 1895 the new Secretary of State, Richard Olney, raised the rank of American representatives abroad to that of ambassador so that they could talk as equals with their fellow diplomats. The same year the headstrong and pugnacious Olney intervened in Britain's dispute with Venezuela over its borders with the British colony of Guiana (today Guyana) to warn off Salisbury, the British Prime Minister. 'Today the United States is practically sovereign on this continent and its fiat is law upon the subjects to which it confines its interposition,' wrote Olney, adding that 'its infinite resources combined with its isolated position render it master of the situation and practically invulnerable as against any or all other powers'. Salisbury was annoyed but Britain had enough troubles elsewhere and so he was content to let the dispute go to arbitration. When the United States seized Cuba and Puerto Rico from Spain in the war of 1898, Britain again did nothing. In the succeeding years, the British renounced any interest in building a canal across the isthmus of Panama and moved their Caribbean Fleet back into home waters, thus effectively conceding dominance in the region to the United States.

The man who best exemplified the new mood in the United States was Theodore Roosevelt, whose first and most successful project was himself. A sickly, unprepossessing child from an old Establishment family, he made himself through sheer will into a bold swashbuckling cowboy, explorer, outdoorsman and hunter (the Teddy bear was named after him). He was also a hero of the Spanish–American War for the charge at San Juan Hill, although his many critics noted that his memoirs gave the impression that he had won the war single-handed. Henry James talked about 'the mere monstrous embodiment of unprecedented and monstrous noise' and nicknamed him Theodore Rex. Roosevelt was driven by ambition, idealism and vanity. As his daughter famously remarked: 'My father always wanted to be the corpse at every funeral, the bride at every wedding, and the baby at every christening.' In September 1900, he became President when an anarchist shot President William McKinley. Roosevelt loved the office – 'the bully pulpit' – and took particular pleasure in managing American foreign policy.[15]

Like many of his compatriots he believed that the United States ought to be a force for good in the world, promoting the spread of democracy, free trade and peace, which he saw as intertwined. In his first message to Congress in 1901 he said, 'Whether we desire it or not, we must henceforth recognize that we have international duties no less than international rights.' He also made it clear that, under his leadership, the United States would back up its good intentions with muscle and that meant having a strong navy. 'No one point of our policy, foreign or domestic, is more important than this to the honor and material welfare, and above all to the peace, of our nation in the future.' Roosevelt had always been fascinated by ships and the sea (not unlike his contemporary Kaiser Wilhelm II of Germany) and he made good his word. The American navy, which had eleven battleships in 1901, when Roosevelt became Vice-President, had thirty-six by 1913 and was the third largest in the world after those of Germany and Great Britain. The economic growth of the United States and its growing military power worried the Europeans. While the British chose accommodation, Kaiser Wilhelm talked from time to time of the need to bring the European powers together to face the challenges he saw coming from Japan and the United States, perhaps separately or perhaps together. Since the Kaiser was notably inconsistent, he also talked on other occasions of working with the United States against Japan. The prospect that the United States itself might increasingly intervene in Europe's affairs in the coming century and, moreover, not once but twice take part in Europe's great wars would have seemed fantastical to the Kaiser, as it would to most Europeans, and to the Americans themselves.

Surely the evidence of the century that had just passed showed that the world, especially the European world, was moving away from war. With a few exceptions the great powers had come together since the end of the Napoleonic Wars in the Concert of Europe to manage Europe's international affairs. The leading statesmen of the powers had got into the habit of consulting each other and committees made up of their ambassadors had met frequently to deal with pressing issues, such as the debts owed by the Ottoman government to outside interests. The Concert had worked with success to sustain Europe's long peace since 1815, guaranteeing treaties, insisting on respect for the rights of nations, encouraging the peaceful resolution of disputes, and, where necessary, calling smaller powers to order. The Concert of Europe was not a formal institution but it was a well-established way of dealing with international relations which served several generations of Europeans well.

Progress had gone hand in hand with peace so that the Europe of 1900 was a different one from that of a century before, infinitely more prosperous and apparently much more stable. The meetings which took place in the Congress Palace during the Paris Exposition reflected widespread hopes that the future would be even brighter. There were over 130 different events including discussions on the condition and rights of women, socialism, fire-fighting, vegetarianism, and philosophy.[16] The 9th Universal Peace Congress which was held there won the Exposition's Grand Prize for its work. 'There was a wonderfully carefree atmosphere abroad in the world,' wrote Zweig, 'for what was going to interrupt this growth, what could stand in the way of the vigour constantly drawing new strength from its own momentum? Europe had never been stronger, richer or more beautiful, had never believed more fervently in an even better future ...'[17]

We now know, of course, that such faith in progress and reason was sadly misplaced, that the Europeans of 1900 were heading towards a crisis in 1914 that they failed to manage, with dreadful consequences: two world wars and a host of smaller ones, the rise of totalitarian movements on both the right and the left, savage conflicts between different nationalities, and atrocities on an unimaginable scale. It was the triumph not of reason but of its opposite. Most of them, though, did not know they were playing with fire. We must try to separate that knowledge of what was to come and remember that the Europeans of the time did not, for the most part, realise that they and their leaders were making decisions and taking steps which narrowed their options and which in the end destroyed their peace. We must attempt to understand those people of a century ago. We need to get at, as much as we can, what was in their minds: what they were remembering, fearing, or hoping. And what were their unspoken assumptions, the beliefs and values they did not bother to talk about because everyone shared them? Why did they not see the dangers which were gathering about them in the years leading up to 1914?

To be fair to that lost world of 1900, not all Europeans shared the general confidence about either the future of humanity or its rationality. The Paris Exposition may have celebrated those two pillars of late nineteenth-century thought, the belief in progress and positivism with its faith that science could solve all problems, but such assumptions were under attack. Increasingly the claims of science to lay bare a universe in which everything worked according to orderly laws were being undermined. The work of Albert Einstein and his fellow physicists into atomic and sub-atomic particles suggested that unpredictability and random occurrences lay beneath the visible material world. Reality was not the only thing being called into question. So too was rationality. Psychologists and the new sociologists were showing that humans were more influenced by unconscious forces than had been assumed. In Vienna, the young Sigmund Freud was inventing the new practice of psychoanalysis to delve into the human unconscious and in same year as the Exposition he published *The Interpretation of Dreams*. Gustave Le Bon's work on how people can behave in unexpected and irrational ways when they are in groups made a deep impression at the time and is still being used today by, among others, the American military. His book on the psychology of the crowd, which came out in 1895, was a popular success and was almost immediately translated into English.

The Paris Exposition also celebrated material progress but there were doubts as well about that. Although Karl Marx welcomed the creative destruction of capitalism as it swept away old societies and brought new social organisations and new industrial methods of production which would ultimately benefit the downtrodden and poor, many on both the left and the right deplored the process. The great French sociologist Emile Durkheim worried about the loss of the old stable communities as people moved into the big cities. Others like Le Bon worried about whether reason and humanity could survive in mass society. Part of the reason Pierre de Coubertin, the founder of the modern Olympics, valued sport so much was that he saw it as developing the individual and arming him or her against the levelling and dulling effects of modern, democratic civilisation.[18] And was life

perhaps getting too fast? Doctors had discovered a new illness, neuras-
thenia, a nervous exhaustion and collapse, which they blamed on the
hectic pace and the strains of modern life.[19] An American visitor to the
Exposition was struck by how many of the new motorcars there were
in Paris; 'they fly along the roads, and whiz through the streets like
lightning, and threaten to take the place of carriages, especially for
heavy traffic'.[20] At the Exposition itself visitors stepped gingerly on and
off a moving pavement and crowds gathered to watch the frequent
tumbles.

And was European society really superior to all others? Scholars
familiar with the history of India or China, for example, challenged the
assumption that Europe was in the forefront of civilisation and pointed
out that both had achieved great heights in the past yet had apparently
declined. So progress might not be linear at all. Indeed, societies might
instead go through a cyclical process of advance and decay and not
necessarily get better. And what was civilisation anyway? Were the
values and achievements of the West really superior to those of other
parts of the world and other ages? The guide to the Exposition was
patronising about the small exhibit of Japanese art which showed, it
said, how Japanese artists stuck doggedly to their traditional styles but
a new generation of European artists found inspiration in the arts of
other, non-European cultures. When Vincent van Gogh used the styles
of Japanese prints in his paintings or Picasso drew on African sculpture
they and other European artists did not see these as charmingly primitive or old-fashioned but as different and containing insights that
European art lacked. When Count Harry Kessler, an urbane and cultivated German, visited Japan in the 1890s he saw Europe in a new and
unfavourable light: 'We have the greater intellectual, and perhaps also
– although I doubt it – stronger moral force, but regarding true, inward
civilization the Japanese are infinitely ahead of us.'[21]

The Paris Exposition had warning signs, easier to see in retrospect,
of the tensions which were shortly going to tear European civilisation
apart. The colonial and the national exhibits which were, after all, about
showing off hinted at the rivalries among the powers. A famous German
art critic of the day mocked French pretensions to lead European civilisation. 'France', he reported on his visit to the Exposition, 'did not take
the slightest part in those enormous changes, which commerce and

industry created in other countries, especially in its constantly danger-ous neighbours, England and Germany.'[22] The French for their part had a large building dedicated entirely to Captain Jean-Baptiste March-and's expedition across Africa two years earlier which had nearly led to a war with Britain, and Loubet, the French President who had talked about justice and human kindness at the opening, had decided to have the Exposition in 1900 in part to forestall the Germans who had been planning their own one for Berlin.[23] The Paris Exposition, said Picard, the chief organiser, would not only reflect the genius of France but 'show our fair country to be, today as yesterday, in the very vanguard of Progress'.[24]

And some of that progress was in the military arts. The Palace of Armies and Navies (in a building resembling a mediaeval fortress) showed, said the guide, the great advances of the past decade in making weapons more destructive. It pointed out as a desirable counterbalance that the capacity for defence had also grown with things such as stron-ger armour plate. In the sections set aside for foreign countries, the British had built a Maison Maxim, its facade decorated with artillery shells and cannon, devoted to the eponymous new machine gun. The Russians brought some of their new weapons and the German emperor sent a display of his favourite uniforms. Outside, a separate pavilion built by the French company Schneider displayed its artillery. War was, said the official catalogue of the Exposition, 'natural to humanity'.[25]

The Exposition also contained harbingers of the system of alliances which was going to push the European powers into choosing sides in the years before 1914. The day of the opening, the French President also opened a new bridge over the Seine, named after the late Tsar Alexan-dre III. After all, the Russian government, said the guide, had exerted itself enormously to collaborate in the Exposition, 'this great work of peace'. The Franco-Russian alliance was new – signed only in 1894 – and still a tricky one, made as it was between the Russian autocracy and a republican France. It was understood to be defensive, although its details were secret. Nevertheless it made Germany uneasy, even though it had its own defensive alliance with Austria-Hungary. The new chief of the German army's general staff, Count Alfred von Schlieffen, began to make plans for a two-front war, against Russia on Germany's eastern frontiers and France in the west.

The greatest power of all, the British Empire, had no alliances with anyone and up to this point that had not caused it concern. But 1900 was not a good year. The British had gone blithely into a war in South Africa the year before against two much smaller Afrikaner republics: the Orange Free State and the Transvaal. The odds – the whole British Empire against two tiny states – should have made the outcome a foregone conclusion, but the British had in fact done very badly in what was called at the time the Boer War. Although the Afrikaners were on the run by the end of the summer, they did not finally concede defeat until the spring of 1902. Equally worrying, the war showed just how unpopular the British were in much of the world. In Marseilles, locals gave a warm reception to a party from Madagascar on its way to the Exposition whom they mistook for Afrikaners. In Paris, an enterprising fashion house made a hat in grey felt, *à la Boer*. At the Exposition itself the modest Transvaal pavilion with its flag flying proudly, drew a large crowd, eager, said the Hachette guide, 'to show their sympathy for the heroic little nation which is defending its independence in the south of Africa'. Piles of flowers dedicated to 'the hero', 'the patriot' or 'the lover of freedom' surrounded the bust of Paul Kruger, its former President.[26]

That sympathy mixed with pleasure when British forces suffered one defeat after another was echoed throughout Europe. Commentary on the Continent made much use of the image of David and Goliath. The German weekly *Simplicissimus* had a cartoon of a dead elephant being pecked by carrion birds as ants swarmed towards it with the comment 'the harder they fall ...' There was also shock at the brutal tactics the British used to deal with Afrikaner guerrilla warfare. General Kitchener, who took over command, had local women and children rounded up and placed in concentration camps so that they could no longer feed and shelter their fighters. Through yet more British incompetence, the camps became places of disease and death. A French cartoon had Kitchener as a great toad squatting on Afrikaner corpses and obscene cartoons circulated of Queen Victoria. Her son and heir, Prince Edward, as a result refused to visit the Exposition.[27]

Great powers depend on their prestige and the perception of others that they are powerful as much as material factors such as their military and their economies. In 1900 Britain was looking weaker and dangerously alone. In a move that was entirely defensive, it started to mend fences with the other powers and to look for allies. Yet this can also be seen as one of the many steps towards the outbreak of the Great War. Europe was going to drift into an alliance system which divided it into two camps, increasingly suspicious of each other and increasingly well armed. And there were those, a minority to be sure, who did not shrink from the prospect of war, or indeed even welcomed it, because they saw it as noble, necessary, an inevitable part of human history, or as a way of solving their nation's internal problems. On the other side stood all those Europeans, including many of their leaders, who thought that a general war was simply inconceivable in the modern world. That confidence was also dangerous for it led to the assumption that all crises could be safely managed and, in the case of Great Britain, that it could remain detached, as it had always preferred, from the Continent.

CHAPTER 2

Great Britain and
Splendid Isolation

———

T hree years earlier, in 1897, as it celebrated sixty years of Queen Victoria's reign, Britain had never appeared so powerful. The Diamond Jubilee was marked around the world by events ranging from marching schoolchildren to fireworks to military reviews, in Canada, Australia, the Cape Colony in southern Africa, India, Ceylon, in all the many places the British flag flew. In Rangoon, 600 prisoners were released and at Port Said there was a Venetian fête with water sports. Addresses and telegrams of congratulation poured into London from every part of the empire. It was, said the *Spectator*, 'as if one roar of acclaim and loyalty were coming up from the whole earth'. The *New York Times* correspondent said that Americans shared in the general admiration for the queen and should take pleasure in the fact that relations between the United States and Britain were now so cordial.[1]

Manufacturers made sure there were plenty of souvenirs: playing cards, mugs, plates, scarves, commemorative medals, bibles. In Britain itself the cities and towns outdid themselves with banquets and balls and 2,500 bonfires blazed from one end of the country to the other. In Manchester 100,000 children were invited to a special breakfast and in London Alexandra, the Princess of Wales, held Diamond Jubilee feasts at which anyone, no matter how poor or shabby, could dine on roast beef and beer. Four hundred thousand Londoners turned up. The churches held special services while choirs sang Sir Arthur Sullivan's special jubilee hymn 'O King of Kings'.

Following the suggestion of the energetic new Colonial Secretary, Joseph Chamberlain, the queen and her Prime Minister, Lord Salisbury, decided that the Jubilee should show off the empire. So while European monarchs were not invited, Prime Ministers from the self-governing colonies and princes from India were. (This also avoided having as a guest the queen's difficult grandson Wilhelm II of Germany, who, it was feared, would only make trouble.) The Prince of Wales gave a special dinner for the colonial premiers and on 21 June the queen, showing impressive stamina for her seventy-eight years, presided over a state banquet at Buckingham Palace. She sat between the heirs to the Italian and Austrian-Hungarian thrones, the future Victor Emmanuel III and Archduke Franz Ferdinand, only one of whom would live to succeed. Twenty-four chefs from Paris were brought in for the occasion and the centrepiece was a crown taller than a man made of 60,000 orchids gathered from every part of the empire.

The next day, Tuesday 22 June, a huge parade wound its way for six miles through London from Buckingham Palace to St Paul's Cathedral. 'Of unparalleled grandeur', said *The Times*, it was designed to celebrate both Victoria's long reign and her vast empire. It was an impressive display of British power. A newsreel, one of the first made, shows rank after rank of sailors, marines, mounted cavalry, and soldiers. The Canadians led the empire section which included Indian lancers, the Rhodesian Horse, the Trinidad Light Horse, and the Cape Mounted Rifles.

Open carriages brought members of the royal family and foreign princes and grand dukes, most of them related to each other and to the queen herself. And finally came the state carriage drawn by eight cream horses with the tiny figure of Victoria, dressed as she had been since the death of her beloved Albert thirty-six years before, in black with a black bonnet. She had not always been popular with her subjects but this day she received loud and fervent cheers. In her journal that night the queen wrote: 'No one ever, I believe, has met with such an ovation as was given to me, passing through those 6 miles of streets ... The cheering was quite deafening & every face seemed to be filled with real joy. I was much moved and gratified.'[2] The service, which included a Te Deum composed by the dead Albert, was held outside because the queen could

2. By the end of the nineteenth century the European powers had seized much of the world for their empires and at times imperial rivalries had brought them close to war. China, where the declining Manchu dynasty was struggling to keep control, looked like their next prey. As the Europeans perch on the egg called China, Japan, which was now dreaming of building its own empire on the mainland of China, and the United States, which opposed imperialism and tried to insist on an 'Open Door' policy in China, look uneasily on.

not manage the steps to the cathedral and had refused to be carried up them. (She also refused to contribute towards the Jubilee's costs.)

The greatest spectacle of all, and the most impressive display of British power, was the naval review at Spithead the following Saturday. In the sheltered waters of the Solent, between the south coast of England and the Isle of Wight, 165 ships – among them 21 battleships, 53 cruisers, and 30 destroyers – lay in rows. Public enthusiasm was intense. Spectators had come from all over England, jamming the local towns, lining the shores, and hiring scores of sightseeing boats.[3] German steamers brought over crowds of Germans who were fascinated by this display of naval power. Over 200 reporters were present and the Admiralty for the first time laid on an official press boat.[4] Japan and the United States, both fledgling naval powers, each sent a warship in greeting. Germany sent an obsolete battleship. 'I deeply regret that I have no better ship to place at your disposal,' Kaiser Wilhelm wrote to his brother, an admiral, 'while other nations shine with their fine vessels.'[5]

As the royal yacht carrying Edward, the Prince of Wales, who was representing his mother, entered its waters, the fleet fired a great salute. The *Victoria and Albert* made its way slowly along the fleet, followed by yachts with his guests, the Admiralty yacht, *Enchantress*, and steamers for members of the House of Commons and the Lords.[6] The prince, dressed in an admiral's uniform, took the salute from the thousands of sailors lining the decks above on the naval ships. There was a sudden flurry of excitement when the inventor Charles Parsons cheekily turned up in his new ship, the *Turbinia*. With its special fast steam turbine, it darted up and down at high speed, well out of the reach of the slower navy ship sent to catch it. (The Admiralty were forced to look at his invention and his turbines were later going to power its huge dreadnoughts.) Rudyard Kipling, who was present for the review, said he 'never dreamed that there was anything like it under Heaven. It was beyond words – beyond any description!'[7] When the sun went down, the ships flashed into view again, outlined with the new electric lights while their searchlights played on the fleet and on the spectators still massed on the shores. As the Prime Minister had said when the Diamond Jubilee was being planned, 'a great naval review would be a most fitting mode of celebration'.[8]

If Queen Victoria stood for longevity and order and the Royal Navy for British power, her Prime Minister, Robert Cecil, the third marquess of Salisbury, appeared the epitome of calm self-confidence, both that of his country and of the British landowning classes. For centuries ownership of agricultural land had been the chief source of wealth and influence in virtually all European countries. In Britain some 7,000 families, from the minor gentry with estates of 1,000 acres or more to the great aristocrats with estates of more than 30,000 acres, owned most of the agricultural land and often urban land, mines, and industries as well. For all the gradations of wealth among them, collectively they made up the polite society which Jane Austen and Anthony Trollope described so well. With their wealth and status came power. The upper levels of the civil service, the Church, the armed forces, the House of Commons, and of course the House of Lords were all dominated by the landed classes. Even in 1897, after successive reforms had widened the franchise and brought new sorts of men into politics, 60 per cent of Members of Parliament still came from those classes. Men such as Salisbury felt it was right that they should. 'Every community has natural leaders', he wrote in an article in the *Quarterly Review* in 1862, 'to whom, if they are not misled by the insane passion for equality, they will instinctively defer. Always wealth, in some countries birth, in all intellectual power and culture, mark out the men to whom, in a healthy state of feeling, a community looks to undertake its government.' And the privileged had an obligation to take on the governing of their less fortunate fellows.[9]

Salisbury was more prey to doubts than this might indicate. His childhood had been loveless and spartan even by the standards of his class. Sent to his first boarding school at the age of six, he later described it as 'an existence among devils'. Eton was not much better; he was savagely bullied and his father eventually took him away and had him privately tutored. Perhaps as a result of his early experiences he was deeply pessimistic about human nature and its propensity to do evil. He also suffered throughout his life from 'nerve storms', attacks of depression which would lay him low for days on end.[10]

As compensation, life gave him brains, character and a head start as a member of the ruling class of the most powerful country in the world. When he decided that politics was his métier, his connections ensured him a place in the House of Commons. (He did not have to bother with the effort of electioneering since his seat was not contested.) He also had a long and successful marriage to a woman who was his equal both intellectually and in strength of character. Visitors to Hatfield, his country house, found a happy domestic scene with rambunctious children who, unlike many Victorian children, were encouraged to speak up.

While he was bored by smart society and frequently forgot names, he was nevertheless courteous in an absent-minded way. At a dinner for party supporters, he made sure to talk to each guest about his particular interests but said to his private secretary with concern at the end, 'there was someone I have not identified who, you said, made mustard'.[11] He did not bother much with the usual pastimes of his peers such as shooting or hunting. Horses to him were merely a means of getting about and an inconvenient one at that. In his later years he took up riding a tricycle for his health. Dressed in a purple velvet poncho, he would cycle near Buckingham Palace or, at Hatfield, along the special paths that had been made for him. There, a young footman would push him up the hills and then jump on behind for the run down. (His grandchildren were fond of lying in wait for him with jugs of water.)[12]

He was at once deeply religious and fascinated by science. Hatfield already had a chapel; he now built a laboratory for his experiments. His wife, said their daughter Gwendolen, 'shared in the painful experiences familiar to relatives of self-educating chemists'. He once fainted at Lady Salisbury's feet after inhaling the chlorine gas he had just made. On another occasion, there was a loud explosion in the laboratory. Salisbury appeared 'covered with blood and severely cut about the face and hands to explain to his terrified family – with evident satisfaction at the accurate working out of chemical laws – that he had been experimenting with sodium in an insufficiently dried retort'.[13]

The family were relieved when he turned to electrical experiments although again the results were not always happy. Hatfield had one of the first private electrical systems in Britain and the first fatal electrocution when an estate worker touched a live cable.[14] For a time the family and their guests at Hatfield had to eat dinners in the glare of a pair of early arc lights. Those were followed by a series of the latest innovations. 'There were evenings', remembered Gwendolen Cecil, 'when the household had to grope about in the semi-darkness, illuminated only by a dim red glow such as comes from a half-extinct fire; there were others when a perilous brilliancy culminated in miniature storms of lightning, ending in complete collapse.' When the first phones appeared, Hatfield's guests had to step cautiously over the wires lying across the floors. The devices were primitive and could only pick up phrases enunciated clearly and slowly. Salisbury's voice echoed around the house, said Gwendolen, as he 'reiterated with varying emphasis and expression, "Hey diddle diddle, the cat and the fiddle; the cow jumped over the moon"'.[15]

With his long beard and imposing bulk, Salisbury looked, some thought, like his contemporary the famous Victorian cricketer, W. G. Grace. Others compared him to 'one of Michelangelo's versions of God'.[16] Salisbury himself was generally indifferent as to what others thought of him. He refused, when he was Prime Minister, to live in Downing Street. When his father had complained that he was marrying a social inferior and would be shunned by society, Salisbury had merely replied: 'The persons who will cut me because I marry Miss

Alderson are precisely the persons of whose society I am so anxious to be quit.'[17]

After all he was a Cecil, from one of England's great families. One of his most famous ancestors William Cecil, the first Lord Burghley, was the close adviser of the first Queen Elizabeth during most of her reign. And his son, Robert, was Secretary of State both to her and to her successor James I. Over the centuries the family accumulated wealth and titles. James I made Robert the Earl of Salisbury, and gave him the royal palace at Hatfield. Robert promptly tore it down and used the bricks to build the great rambling house which is still there today. King George III made the title even grander in the time of Salisbury's grandfather, with only one stipulation: 'Now my lord, I trust you will be an English marquess and not a French marquis.'[18] The first marquess's son married a young and very rich heiress and so assured the family's continuing fortunes. Although he cared little for comfort and was a notoriously shabby dresser (he was once turned away at the door of the Casino in Monte Carlo),[19] Salisbury, with an income of between £50,000 and £60,000 per year, was a very rich man. And Hatfield House, while it was not on the scale of Blenheim Palace or Chatsworth, was a very grand house with its Long Gallery, its Marble Hall, its library, drawing rooms, and dozens of bedrooms. In addition he had a London house with its own ballroom and a Chalet Cecil just outside Dieppe.

Unconventional though he may have been, Lord Salisbury was to both his compatriots and to foreigners a true representative of one of the most admired and envied classes in the world. All over Europe, the upper classes imported English nannies and grooms, wore tartans, and ate marmalade at breakfast. In Miklós Bánffy's novel *They Were Divided*, set among the Hungarian upper classes before the war, a young nobleman who has loved England from afar finally gets the chance to go to London. He tells his ambassador he wants only one thing, to become a temporary member of the most exclusive men's club in London, the St James's. And so, for two weeks, he sits in the window of the club. 'It was a heavenly feeling.' No matter that he does not see anything else of London or that he cannot speak to anyone because his English is too poor.[20]

The prestige of the British aristocracy was also partly a matter of wealth. The great families in Britain were as rich as the richest Germans or Russians and there were more of them. Moreover, prosperity spread downwards into smaller landowners and sideways to the rising new industrial and commercial classes. As Queen Victoria's daughter, the mother of the future Wilhelm II, wrote to her mother from Germany in 1877: 'You know how small fortunes are in Germany and how little people are accustomed to luxury and *train du grande monde.*' At the same time, though, the upper classes across Europe, particularly those whose income came mainly from their rural estates, were feeling a chill as the world changed around them. Industrialisation and the spread of European power around the world combined to make agriculture in Europe less important and less profitable. Cheap food from the Americas and such parts of the world as Australia was good for the working classes and their employers, not so good for landowners. Incomes from agriculture in Europe fell precipitously in the last two decades and the value of agricultural land dropped correspondingly.

Landowners were sometimes fortunate enough to own urban property, which was going up in value. Salisbury derived only a quarter of his income from agricultural land; the rest came from urban property or investments. The bigger among them also saved themselves by opening businesses or investing in industry or by marrying money outside their own circles as the French Prince de Polignac did with the heiress to the Singer sewing-machine fortune. An increasing number did not survive. Chekhov's *The Cherry Orchard* or Miklós Bánffy's Transylvanian trilogy depicting estates mortgaged to the hilt and old families going under reflected the reality.

In the decades before the Great War, the landed aristocracy and the lesser gentry were not only losing ground economically as classes; in many parts of Europe they were also losing in other ways. The rising middle and working classes and the new men of wealth now challenged their privileges and competed with them for power. The old classes were no longer as socially dominant as they had once been. The owners of fortunes made from commerce and industry – think of the friends of King Edward VII with names such as Rothschild, Lipton and Cassels – could match them with beautiful houses and lavish entertainment. In politics and government too the landed interests no longer counted as much as they had once done, even in countries such as Germany. The extension of the franchise – in Britain the number of those voting doubled from 3 million to nearly 6 million in the reforms of 1884 and 1885 – and the redrawing of voting boundaries broke apart many of the cosy old arrangements where seats in Parliament were in the gift of local magnates.[21]

Salisbury did not like the changes even though he was clearly one of the more fortunate ones. 'Things that have been secure for centuries,' he said, 'are secure no longer.' Mass democracy was undermining the traditional upper classes and this was bad for society. 'He thought and fought for his order,' said his fellow politician Lord George Hamilton, 'not to ensure to them privileges or exemptions, but because he believed their maintenance did supply the best material for sound and reliable government.' Salisbury sought office, so Hamilton believed, solely for the promotion of his country's welfare.[22]

If so, he sought with success. By the time of the Diamond Jubilee Salisbury had been Prime Minister three times, Foreign Minister three times, and Secretary of State for India twice. Fortunately, he had a great capacity for hard work and an equally important ability to cope with pressure. He did not lose sleep over worry, he told a niece, and when he had to make decisions, he told his family, he simply did his best even if it was something as trivial as trying to decide whether to take an overcoat for a walk. 'I feel it is exactly the same way, but no more, when I am writing a despatch upon which peace or war may depend. Its degree depends upon the materials for decision that are available and not in the least upon the magnitude of the results which may follow. With the results I have nothing to do.'[23]

When he became Prime Minister for his last time in 1895 he chose, as he had done before, to be his own Foreign Minister. 'Our first duty', he told an audience a few months after the Diamond Jubilee, 'is towards the people of this country, to maintain their interests and their rights; our second is to all humanity.' Since he believed that British hegemony in the world was generally benevolent, the two goals were not in his mind incompatible. His strategy in foreign affairs was a simple one: to protect Great Britain, its interests and its position in the world, preferably without unnecessary complications – such as alliances and secret agreements. He did not like what he described to the queen as 'active measures'.[24] Perhaps he was referring obliquely to his great rival William Gladstone and his Liberal Party, who did believe in intervening in

Europe and, if necessary, for humanitarian reasons. At best, Salisbury thought, Britain should use its influence to prevent its neighbours from 'flying at each other's throats' because that was generally bad for everyone.[25] And he was prepared, where he felt British interests were at stake, to be firm, even to the point of threatening military action. With the opening of the Suez Canal, Egypt became of crucial importance to British links with India and the Far East. Britain had to control it whatever other nations thought and, as a further safeguard, the upper reaches of the Nile as well. At the end of the 1890s, Salisbury was to find himself in a military confrontation with France there.

Like so many of his countrymen, Salisbury tended to assume that foreigners were more selfish and less reliable than the British and, in the case of the Latins, more emotional. The Greeks were 'the blackmailers of Europe' and when the French moved in on Tunisia, it was 'well within the French code of honour as habitually practised'.[26] When Britain and Germany competed for influence in East Africa in the 1880s, Salisbury warned a young consul who was being sent to the island of Zanzibar: 'The whole question of Zanzibar is both difficult and dangerous, for we are perforce partners with the Germans whose political morality diverges considerably from ours on many points.'[27] Although he could muse about the 'vanity' of expanding the empire, he was determined that Britain should have its share of whatever was going: 'the instinct of the nation will never be content without a share in the booty which it sees its neighbours greedily dividing'.[28]

He does not seem to have disliked any one nation more than another – except for the United States. He found in Americans everything he disliked about the modern world: they were greedy, materialistic, hypocritical, and vulgar and believed that democracy was the best form of government. During the Civil War he was a passionate supporter of the Confederate side, partly because he thought that Southerners were gentlemen and Northerners were not. In addition, though, he feared the growth of American power. As he wrote gloomily in 1902: 'It is very sad, but I am afraid America is bound to forge ahead and nothing can restore the equality between us. If we had interfered in the Confederate War it was then possible for us to reduce the power of the United States to manageable proportions. But *two* such chances are not given to a nation in the course of its career.'[29]

His views on foreigners did not prevent Salisbury, when he was in charge of foreign affairs, working for specific ends with other powers. He made agreements, for example, with Italy and Austria at the end of the 1880s to maintain the status quo in and around the Mediterranean. To keep Egypt safe from the French, who had not forgiven Britain for taking over its management in 1882, he kept on good terms with Germany. At times, although he disliked the growing importance of public opinion in foreign affairs, he found it useful in refusing unwanted commitments and alliances. In the 1890s, when the Germans suggested a common front against the French, Salisbury regretted that his hands were tied: 'Parliament and people would not be guided in any degree by the fact that the Government had some years before signed a secret agreement to go to war.'[30] He also made the further argument, easier perhaps with an unwritten constitution, that Great Britain was constitutionally barred from making peacetime agreements that could lead to war.[31] More importantly, the Royal Navy – the largest in the world – and the geographical advantages that came from being an island, meant Britain had the freedom to choose to remain relatively independent in world affairs.

While he did his best to keep Britain free of entanglements, Salisbury also tried to prevent strong blocs coalescing against it. As he explained in a speech at Caernarvon in 1888, nations should behave like sensible householders with their neighbours.

> If you wish to get on with the people with whom you are living, you must not be looking for perpetual opportunities of getting a little advantage over them; you must view your own claims and theirs in a just and neighbourly spirit, – on the one hand never sacrificing any important and genuine right in respect to which you think that oppression or encroachment is being attempted, – and, on the other hand, abstaining from erecting small controversies into envenomed disputes and treating every difference as a matter of vital principle.

Those who are not careful to behave in a reasonable and neighbourly fashion, he went on, 'will find that they are opposed by a combination of those neighbours …'[32]

If there were to be combinations, Salisbury felt, and this reflected a long-standing British policy, it was better that they should be two or more and against each other rather than Britain. Britain's relations with Europe usually worked best when Britain was on as friendly a footing with as many of the other powers as possible and when there was a rough balance of power on the Continent which enabled Britain to manoeuvre among the different groupings. Salisbury managed to convince himself, if not the other European powers, that Britain was in this way contributing to the greater good of all. As he put it in his Caernarvon speech, 'There is all the difference in the world between good natured, good humoured effort to keep well with your neighbours, and that spirit of haughty and sullen "isolation" which has been dignified by the name of "non-intervention". We are part of the community of Europe and we must do our duty as such.'[33]

Although Salisbury disliked what he called 'jargon about isolation',[34] that is how his foreign policy has come to be characterised. When Queen Victoria protested in January 1896 that Britain seemed somewhat isolated, Salisbury replied sharply that isolation 'is much less danger than the danger of being dragged into wars which do not concern us'. It was a view shared by his Conservative colleagues. 'Our isolation', Lord Goschen, the First Lord of the Admiralty, told a Conservative gathering in 1896, 'is not an isolation of weakness, or of contempt for ourselves; it is deliberately chosen, the freedom to act as we choose in any circumstances that may arise.'[35] In the same year first a Canadian politician and then Joseph Chamberlain added the adjective 'splendid' and the term spread with surprising rapidity. 'Splendid isolation' and Britain's skilful manipulation of the balance of power were, so it was argued, not only a deliberate policy choice but one sanctified by tradition at least as far back as the great Queen Elizabeth I herself as she manoeuvred between her rivals of France and Spain to ensure Britain's safety. 'A balance of power on the Continent', said an historian of her reign, 'was what suited her, as it has generally suited this country.'[36] Montagu Burrows, the Chichele Professor of Modern History at Oxford, vested it with almost mystical significance as 'the Balance' and quoted Edmund Burke with approval as saying that Britain was of all powers the most suited to look after it. 'It is not too much say', he said proudly, 'that it has been the saving of Europe.'[37]

In retrospect, how complacent it seems. Even at the time there was something defiant about it all. In 1897, as it celebrated the Diamond Jubilee, Britain was indeed isolated but its position in the world was not all that splendid. It had no secure friendships in Europe. It was engaged in a number of disputes and rivalries around the world, with the United States over Venezuela, with France in several parts of the world, with Germany in Africa and the Pacific, and with Russia in Central Asia and China. The empire itself was a mixed blessing. To be sure it brought Britain prestige and it gave British manufacturing protected markets and in theory it brought greater power as well. A cartoon in *Punch* at the time of the great naval review showed an old British lion rowing four young lions – Australia, Canada, New Zealand and the Cape – out to see the fleet.[38] Yet the young lions did not always show much enthusiasm for taking on the burden of defending themselves, much less the empire as a whole.

And the empire kept growing as Britain took on still more colonies and protectorates around the world, partly in an attempt to protect what it already had. As other powers joined in the scramble for territory its empire became increasingly vulnerable. Sir Thomas Sanderson, the Permanent Undersecretary at the Foreign Office, said a few years later: 'It has sometimes seemed to me that to a foreigner reading our Press the British Empire must appear in the light of some huge giant sprawling over the globe, with gouty fingers and toes outstretched in every direction which cannot be approached without soliciting a scream.'[39] The term 'imperial over-stretch' had not yet been coined but Britain was suffering from it by the 1890s. Kipling's poem 'Recessional', which he wrote just after he saw the great naval review at Spithead, contained a warning:

> *Far-called our navies melt away –*
> *On dune and headland sinks the fire –*
> *Lo, all our pomp of yesterday*
> *Is one with Nineveh and Tyre!*
> *Judge of the Nations, spare us yet,*
> *Lest we forget – lest we forget!*

While Britain was still the world's leading manufacturer, its industries were being overtaken by newer and more dynamic ones in Germany or the United States, which were also cutting into its overseas markets. The stories that toy soldiers for British children were made in Germany may not have been true but they reflected a growing anxiety – including about Britain's ability to defend itself.

Because it was an island, Britain had been able to get away with having a tiny army and relying on its navy for its own defence and that of its empire. The advances in technology meant that navies were increasingly expensive and the burden on the budget correspondingly greater. 'The weary Titan,' said Joseph Chamberlain, 'staggering under the too-vast orb of his fate.'[40] Moreover, there were worries that the global commitments of the Royal Navy left the British Isles themselves underprotected. Pessimists in the military had been warning since the late 1880s that the French, if they chose, could easily sweep aside a British naval force in the Channel and land an invasion force in England. Salisbury himself sketched out a scenario in 1888 in a memorandum to the Cabinet in which he envisaged the French, led 'by the kind of soldier who comes to the top in a revolution', landing on a Saturday night when the British were enjoying the weekend. With the help of 'two or three Irish patriots', the invaders could cut the telegraph wires and make their way to London before anyone in the British military could react.[41] The prospect – and how much he really believed in it is questionable – did not stop him, however, from continuing to take his holidays in France.

The poor relations with France remained to trouble Salisbury's last government; indeed, there was to be another quite serious war scare in 1898. The new and developing friendship between France and another rival for empire, Russia, was also worrying. Salisbury's preference for working with the Triple Alliance of Germany, Austria-Hungary and Italy no longer seemed an adequate counterbalance. How little it could be depended upon was demonstrated by the Armenian massacres during the mid 1890s in what is today the eastern part of Turkey.

These unfortunate Christian subjects of the Ottoman Empire were being slaughtered by their Muslim neighbours and the government, either deliberately or through sheer incompetence, did nothing to prevent the atrocities. British policy had for much of the century been to prop up the Ottomans as a way of keeping the waters leading from the Black Sea into the Mediterranean out of the hands of the Russians.

Self-interest, however, did not always fit well with British public opinion, which found much to outrage it when the Ottoman Empire treated one or other of its Christian communities badly. Gladstone indeed had fought a whole election campaign on the Bulgarian atrocities and the need for the international community to do something. For all that he disliked meddling in the internal affairs of other nations, Salisbury had always taken a dim view of the Ottomans and would have been happy to abandon them earlier if Britain had not needed a friend at the eastern end of the Mediterranean. In 1895 he tried to find partners – possibly Austria or Italy, perhaps Germany, even Russia – to put pressure on the Ottomans to stop the attacks on the Armenians but no other power was willing to act. Salisbury had sleepless nights over the matter but was forced to accept that there was nothing Britain could do. He also came to the conclusion that he would have to look for other ways to safeguard British interests in the Mediterranean and the crucial Suez Canal link to India than propping up the moribund and corrupt Ottoman Empire. The question, which was to remain open for the next few years, was how. Increased (and expensive) military strength in Egypt and in the Mediterranean? An alliance with another power with interests in the region such as France or Russia? Neither seemed likely given the rivalries elsewhere.

The Ottoman Empire was worrying in another way, for the temptations it offered in an age of imperialism. The powers, and their publics, measured their importance in the world in terms of the number of colonies they possessed but the supply of unclaimed land was running out. Africa had been pretty much divided up by the 1890s, as had the Far East and the Pacific islands. That left the parts of the world where the old orders were collapsing: China, for example, Persia or the Ottoman Empire. In 1898 Salisbury made a speech in the Albert Hall in London which became famous. 'You may roughly divide the nations of the world as the living and the dying,' he told his Conservative audience. 'On the one side you have great countries of enormous power growing in power every year, growing in wealth, growing in dominion, growing in the perfection of their organisation.' On the other side, were their natural victims, dying of the diseases of corruption and misgovernment. The process which Salisbury saw as likely to occur was a potentially dangerous one. 'The living nations will gradually encroach on the territory of the dying, and the seeds and causes of conflict among civilised nations will speedily appear.'[42]

They already were appearing. Britain and France had quarrelled over Egypt, still nominally part of the Ottoman Empire, in the 1880s and the French and Italians were rivals in Tunis. The Ottoman government floundered like a fish in a net and the strings grew ever tighter; loans from European governments and banks and then more outside control over its finances; concessions to European interests to build railways, good for commerce but also a way of extending European influence; European interference in the name of humanitarianism with its treatment of its Christian subjects; and European demands for reforms. Further down the road, when the Ottomans could no longer cope, their territories, which included parts of the Balkans and the Arab Middle East, would surely be up for grabs.

The spread of the Russian Empire southwards and east brought Persia into the Great Game between the Russians and the British in Central Asia. The Russians were increasingly influential in the north while the British tried to consolidate their position in the south and along the Indian Ocean and both wooed the Shah of Shahs. The game played on in Afghanistan, which now stood between Russian territory and British India, in Tibet, and further east in China.

In Asia, the European powers found China, with its evident weakness, almost irresistible. They were joined by the United States even though opposition to imperialism had deep historical roots there; Grover Cleveland, President in the mid 1880s and then again between 1893 and 1897, and a leading opponent of the United States acquiring colonies, famously said in his first inaugural address that his country would remain true to its revolutionary origins and that it had no ambitions towards other continents. Yet the United States was already predisposed to intervene in its own backyard in the Caribbean and was shortly to take over the Philippines, Hawaii and Puerto Rico. Where China was concerned, American administrations maintained that the only right course was an Open Door policy with access for all nations to China's territory in place of exclusive spheres of interest.

To the Westerners' surprise and considerable admiration, Japan, which had seen off the threat of becoming another colony by a rapid adaptation to the new forces in the world, showed that it too had imperialist ambitions in China. The powers forced concession after concession out of the moribund regime in Beijing: treaty ports where foreigners could live and work under the protection of their own laws and their own governments; railways, of course – and in China these were protected by foreign troops; and exclusive rights to mining and trade in particular areas. The Chinese rightly saw a pattern emerging where their country would be carved up like a melon.

Britain was comfortably dominant in trade and commerce in China, particularly along the Yangtze valley, and did not particularly want to acquire pieces of China along with the burden of having to administer them. But could it stand back and watch as other powers moved in on China, perhaps annexing territory? When Salisbury took office in 1895, Russia was already challenging British interests in the northern part of the country. And the competition for influence in China was about to heat up as other players including Germany joined in.

To add to Salisbury's worries, relations with the United States, always tricky, were in a particularly bad phase. The long-running dispute between Britain and Venezuela over the latter's borders with British Guiana had suddenly been taken up by the Grover Cleveland administration. In July 1895, a month after Salisbury took office, the Secretary of State, Richard Olney, issued his belligerent note saying that the United States had the right to intervene in the dispute. He cited the authority of the Monroe Doctrine, that wonderfully vague and infinitely elastic statement which warned outside powers against interfering in the New World. There was uproar in the press on both sides of the Atlantic. The American ambassador in London read out a long dispatch to Salisbury in which his government supported the claims of Venezuela to a substantial piece of British Guiana and demanded that the British agree to arbitration. Salisbury took four months to answer. He refused to accept that the Monroe Doctrine gave the United States any authority over British possessions in the New World and suggested that the Americans had 'no apparent practical concern' in a boundary dispute between a British possession and another country. Cleveland said he was 'mad clean through' and there was much excited talk of war in both Britain and the United States. The British had enough on their plate elsewhere and had no inclination to fight and opinion in the United States was divided. Eventually, a compromise was reached; Salisbury stopped objecting to the American extension of the Monroe Doctrine and some minor changes were made to the border in an arbitration in 1899. Venezuela, which the American ambassador in London, dismissed as 'a mongrel state', got very little. (The Venezuelan President Hugo Chavez claimed the disputed land until his death, and his successors continue to do so.)[43]

Salisbury made concessions in other disputes as well. When in 1896 the French annexed Madagascar, where Britain had extensive interests, he let it go by without a protest. He still resisted, though, any suggestions that Britain look for more permanent relationships. He refused as he had always done to worry unduly about every corner of the globe. He preferred to concentrate on the areas of vital importance to the British Empire. As he said to Sir Evelyn Baring (later Lord Cromer), the proconsul in Egypt, when there was a scare about security in the Red Sea: 'I would not be too much impressed by what the soldiers tell you about the strategic importance of these places. If they were allowed full scope they would insist on the importance of garrisoning the moon in order to protect us from Mars.'[44] His colleagues worried that he was a bit too unconcerned and that he did not have a clear foreign policy. Or if he did he was not about to reveal it; Salisbury's penchant for secrecy grew more pronounced with age. Lord Curzon, who worked as his Undersecretary at the Foreign Office, later described him as 'that strange, powerful, inscrutable, brilliant, obstructive deadweight at the top'.[45] Curzon felt that Salisbury too often resorted to throwing bones to dogs, who then, as was so evident with France and Russia, only bayed for more. While not all his colleagues were as critical, most worried that Salisbury was no longer up to the work involved in being Prime Minister as well Foreign Minister. He was showing his age by the late 1890s and he was depressed by the drawn-out illness of his wife which ended with her death in 1899.

Even before he formally stepped down as Foreign Minister in 1900, Salisbury was already ceding a large role in foreign affairs to his nephew Arthur Balfour, who was Leader of the House of Commons, and his Colonial Secretary, Joseph Chamberlain. The two men could scarcely have been more different. Balfour was Salisbury's nephew and so part of that cosy interrelated circle at the apex of British society. As an oldest son of a rich man, he had extensive estates in Scotland. He was handsome, clever, and charming, although many found him cold and elusive.

His smile, said one acquaintance, was 'like moonlight on a tombstone'.[46] It was said that his heart was broken when the woman he loved died of typhoid fever but a close friend suspected that he had 'exhausted his powers in that direction' and preferred the ease of affairs with safely married women. His great passion was philosophy and, curiously, he was to develop an enthusiasm for Zionism during the Great War. Although he worked hard, he tried not to show it. He drifted out of the House of Commons to play golf and drifted back in for late sittings in his evening clothes. He lay back on the bench 'as if to discover', said *Punch*, 'how nearly he could sit on his shoulder blades'.[47]

He found Chamberlain interesting but unsympathetic. 'Joe, though we all love him dearly,' he wrote to a favourite mistress, 'somehow does not absolutely or completely mix, does not form a chemical combination with us.'[48] Chamberlain was a self-made industrialist, one of the new men whose rise Salisbury had so deplored. Born into a middle-class family, he had left school at sixteen and ended up working in a family business in Birmingham which made metal screws. Unlike Balfour, he had married – three times. His first two wives died giving birth to sons, the first Austen and the second Neville, who was going to become famous or infamous as the appeasing Prime Minister of the late 1930s. His third wife, who was about half his age, was an American, the daughter of the Secretary of War in the administration of President Cleveland. It was by all accounts a very successful marriage.

Energetic, driven and ambitious, the young Chamberlain had built the business into the biggest of its kind in England and retired a very rich man at the age of thirty-six. He did not like sports and had few hobbies save an unlikely passion for orchids, which he raised in special greenhouses. (He always wore one in his buttonhole.) He took up politics with the same drive as he had business and became mayor of Birmingham. He worried about primary education for all, about drains and clean water, slum clearance and the provision of libraries. Even when he went to the House of Commons as a Liberal he remained the city's undisputed ruler. In Parliament he surprised his colleagues by not being a wild demagogue but a highly polished debater making concise and pointed speeches. 'The performance', according to the British journalist, J. A. Spender, 'was, if anything, too perfect. "It is all very nice, very nice, Mr. Chamberlain," said an old member whose advice he sought, "but the House would take it as such a great compliment, if now and again you could manage to break down."[49]

Chamberlain remained a radical, advocating social reforms, and attacked such privileged institutions as landlords and the established Church of England. Yet he also developed a passionate attachment to the British Empire which he believed was a force for good in the world. That conviction led him to break with the Liberals in 1886 when they proposed Home Rule for Ireland; Chamberlain and his supporters argued that it would undermine the unity of the empire. In time, the Liberal Unionists, as they were known, moved towards the Conservative Party.[50] Chamberlain never defended himself to his former colleagues. He simply moved on. He had, said Spender, 'a deadly concentration' on what he was doing and that was mainly politics: 'Everything to his vision was black or white, with clear-cut outlines and no half-tones.'[51]

In his first years as Colonial Secretary as he grappled with challenges and crises from cod in Newfoundland to gold in southern Africa, Chamberlain was made acutely aware of how isolated Britain was and how vulnerable. Moreover, public opinion, that new and unpredictable force in foreign affairs, was demanding action to shore up British interests around the globe. Isolation, he argued, was no longer serving Britain well and Balfour was coming to agree with him. France would not do as an ally, given the current tensions over Africa and the two countries' historical rivalry. As for Russia, as Chamberlain said in a speech in 1898, 'when you sup with the devil, take a long spoon'. Increasingly his thoughts turned to Germany, with which Britain had relatively few disputes. Nor was he alone; other key figures, Cabinet ministers, admirals, officials in the Foreign Office, influential writers, were coming to think along the same lines.[52]

With Salisbury's half-hearted approval, Chamberlain started discussions with the German ambassador in London about a possible treaty. In 1899 he had friendly conversations with the Kaiser and his Foreign Secretary, Bernhard von Bülow, at Windsor Castle, which encouraged Chamberlain to think that an alliance, perhaps including the United States as well, might be feasible. The day after the German party left Britain, he made a public speech at Leicester sketching out 'a new Triple Alliance between the Teutonic race and the two great trans-Atlantic branches of the Anglo-Saxon race which would become a potent influence on the future of the world'.[53] There were some other promising signs. In 1898, Britain made an agreement with Germany over Portugal's colonies of Mozambique, Angola and Timor, which, given the nearly bankrupt state of their owner, were likely to be coming on the world market. The two signatories (Portugal was not consulted) agreed that they would keep outsiders at bay and divide up the Portuguese Empire between themselves. The following year the British ended an absurd quarrel with the Germans over the Samoan islands in the South Pacific by conceding control of the main island to them.

By 1901 Chamberlain, as he told a member of the German embassy in London, was in favour of closer co-operation with Germany and perhaps Britain's becoming a member of the Triple Alliance with Germany, Austria-Hungary, and Italy.[54] Balfour agreed. It seemed to him that Britain's most likely enemy was the alliance of France and Russia. 'It is a matter of supreme moment to us that Italy should not be crushed, that Austria should not be dismembered, and, as I think, that Germany should not be squeezed to death between the hammer of Russia and the anvil of France.'[55]

The Germans were not averse to the idea but were in no hurry to conclude a full-blown agreement or see Britain become a member of the Triple Alliance, especially since it seemed to them that the British needed them more than the other way round. The Boer War, which broke out in October 1899, just two years after the triumphal Diamond Jubilee, had severely damaged British prestige and confidence. In the first months, as one humiliating defeat followed another, there was real fear in Britain that France would take the opportunity to invade or that France and Russia might threaten Britain's position in the Indian Ocean.[56] In January 1901, Queen Victoria died, perhaps another sign that the old order was passing.

Inquiries after the war showed that British commanders had been incompetent, that forces had been sent into combat without clear orders, proper maps or sufficient intelligence, and that equipment had been completely inadequate. Leo Amery, who was a reporter in the field for *The Times*, wrote, for example, of the disaster at the Battle of Spion Kop: 'No effort was made beforehand to ascertain the shape of the position to be occupied, or to furnish the officers entrusted with its capture with such information. No sufficient effort was made by the officers themselves to discover the shape of the summit before intrenching.'[57] The war led to widespread reforms in the military but it was to take some time before these could have an impact.

To make matters worse in those years at the end of the century, the situation in China remained unstable, which threatened Britain's extensive interests there. In 1897, Germany had used the excuse of two murdered missionaries to force the weak Chinese government to give it a concession including a port at Tientsin (Tianjin) and railways in the Shantung (Shandong) peninsula. This had set off what looked like the start of a serious scramble for China. Russia unilaterally seized a warm-water port, named after a British naval lieutenant, William Arthur, at the southern end of Manchuria. The Cabinet considered sending ships from its China squadron north to expel the Russians but thought better of it for fear of what Russia's ally France might do. A few months later, Russia grabbed another port just to the north-east of Port Arthur and forced the Chinese government to sign away its rights to both for twenty-five years.

With cries coming from the press and from his colleagues such as Chamberlain, that Britain do something, indeed anything, Salisbury said gloomily "'the public" will demand some territorial or cartographic consolation in China. It will not be useful, and will be expensive; but as a matter of pure sentiment, we shall have to do it.' And so Britain demanded a port at Weihaiwei on the northern side of the Shantung peninsula and to the south of the Russian ports in Manchuria. (In the end it was useless as a port but did have a nice sandy beach for swimming.)[58] In 1900, and this at least appeared to be good news, Germany and Britain came to an agreement in China in which both undertook to use their influence for an Open Door policy in China which would allow free access for all the powers. In British minds at least, this was really directed against Russia in Manchuria; the last thing Germany, which had a long land frontier with Russia in Europe, wanted was a conflict with its neighbour. This became clear in the aftermath of the Boxer Rebellion.

In 1900, a movement which had initially started against the Manchu dynasty was adroitly turned by them against the foreigners from overseas. All over north China Western missionaries, diplomats and businessmen were attacked and, in Beijing, foreign diplomats were besieged in the summer of 1900. An international relief force was hastily cobbled together by the great powers, which for once had reason to act together. The Boxer Rebellion was put down, Beijing was sacked, and the Chinese government was forced to pay a large indemnity and accept even more foreign interference in its affairs. The Russians took the opportunity to move forces into Manchuria and when the rebellion was over found excuses not to leave. Rumours spread that Russia was negotiating a deal with China for the permanent occupation of Manchuria. When the British government asked the Germans for support, as they tried to find ways to get the Russians to back down, the answer was very clear. Bülow got up in the Reichstag on 15 March 1901 to say that the Anglo-German agreement on China 'was in no way concerned with Manchuria'.[59]

It was all too clear that Germany was not prepared to help Britain with its imperial interests at the cost of causing trouble for itself in Europe. And, as a number of British were asking themselves, did Britain really want to get drawn into German disputes with France and Russia in Europe? The Germans, however, still thought the British would come round when they eventually saw that friendship with Germany was their best option. 'We ought not to show any uneasiness or anxious haste,' Bülow said to his subordinate Friedrich von Holstein in October 1901. 'We must let hope shimmer on the horizon.'[60]

Lord Lansdowne, who had by now replaced Salisbury as Foreign Secretary, tried to keep the discussions alive with the Germans but failed. He also made desultory, equally unproductive, overtures to the Russians. Nevertheless he was convinced, as were many of his colleagues, that Britain could not go back to Salisbury's policy of detachment from Europe. Lord George Hamilton, by now Secretary of State for India, reported a gloomy conversation with Balfour that summer of 1901:

He said the conviction was forced upon him that we were for all practical purposes at the present moment only a third-rate power; and we are a third-rate power with interests which are conflicting with and crossing those of the great powers of Europe. Put in this elementary form the weakness of the British Empire, as it at present exists, is brought home to one. We have enormous strength, both effective and latent, if we can concentrate ... but the dispersion of our Imperial interests ... renders it almost impossible.[61]

That autumn Lord Selborne, the First Lord of the Admiralty, pointed out to his colleagues in the Cabinet that Britain only had four battle-ships in the Far East while Russia and France together would soon have nine.[62]

By this stage, however, public opinion in both countries was becoming a significant factor. In the autumn and early winter of 1901–2, for example, a silly public dispute between Bülow, now German Chancellor, and Joseph Chamberlain stirred up anger in both countries. Chamberlain made a speech in Edinburgh in which he defended British troops against accusations that they were treating the Afrikaner civilians excessively harshly. Chamberlain went on to say that the other nations had behaved much worse, Prussia for example in the Franco-Prussian War. Nationalists in Germany seized on what they saw as a serious insult and Bülow insisted on a formal protest to the British Foreign Office. The British tried to explain the remarks away but refused to make a formal apology. Bülow then chose to appeal to German opinion with a defiant speech in the Reichstag in January 1902. To cheers, he quoted a famous phrase of Frederick the Great to the effect that anyone who dared criticise the German army would find he was 'biting on granite'. Three days later Chamberlain spoke to equal enthusiasm in his stronghold of Birmingham: 'What I have said, I have said. I withdraw nothing. I qualify nothing. I defend nothing. I do not want to give lessons to a foreign minister and I will not accept any at his hands.' Privately he said to Baron Hermann von Eckardstein of the German embassy in London, 'I have had enough of such treatment and there can be no more question of an association between Great Britain and Germany.'[63]

The British government had already come to the conclusion that it needed to look elsewhere. With an increasingly weary Salisbury's acquiescence, it was investigating the possibility of a defensive alliance with Japan. This was not as extraordinary as it seemed. Japan was an up-and-coming power; in the 1890s it handily defeated China in a war. Curzon, who knew Asia well, wrote to Salisbury in 1897: 'If European Powers are grouping themselves against us in the Far East we shall probably be driven sooner or later to act with Japan. Ten years hence she will be the greatest naval Power in those seas ...'[64] That last appealed to the British naval industry, always a powerful lobby, who liked the orders which the Japanese navy kept placing. In 1898, Admiral Charles Beresford, who had taken time out from his naval career to become a Member of Parliament and head of the Navy League, told the annual dinner of the Japan Society of London: 'there is much affinity between our two nations and an alliance between them would tend greatly to the peace of the world'.[65] Moreover, Japan's interests were conveniently confined to the Far East. There was not therefore the same danger as there would have been with Germany of an alliance dragging Britain into a war in Europe. Britain could use Japan to counter Russia, in particular in China, and perhaps make its rival empire think twice before advancing further in Central Asia towards India.

From the Japanese perspective, Britain was the friendliest of the great European powers. In 1895, at the end of the Sino-Japanese War, Russia, Germany, and France had combined against Japan to force it to give up some of what it had gained from China, notably in Manchuria. Shortly afterwards Russia had made its own move and seized the two southern ports in Manchuria and started to build a short cut for the Trans-Siberian Railway across the north. During the Boxer Rebellion Britain and Japan had worked well together. Japan, like Britain, had explored its alternatives through talks with Russia and Germany. Like Britain it came to the conclusion that these were going nowhere.

Just before Christmas 1901, Prince Ito Hirobumi, one of the elder statesmen who had overseen Japan's transformation after 1868, stopped in London on his way from Russia. Like Salisbury, he had been Prime Minister of his country three times. (Unlike Salisbury, he was also a notorious womaniser.) It was given out that he was visiting Britain purely for the sake of his health. Nevertheless he was received by Edward VII, who gave him the Grand Cross of the Order of the Bath. The Lord Mayor of London gave a large banquet in his honour. When he rose to reply to the toast, Ito, according to *The Times*, was greeted 'with prolonged cheers'. In his speech Ito talked about the long and friendly relations, 'almost a century', between Japan and Britain and his own happy memories of a country where he had come to study as a young man. 'It is only natural in me', he went on, 'to entertain a sincere hope as to the further continuation of our friendly feelings and mutual sympathies in the future, that these friendly feelings and mutual sympathies which have existed between us in the past shall be daily more strongly cemented in the future. (Cheers).'[66] He visited Salisbury at Hatfield and Lansdowne at his country house of Bowood and had particularly interesting conversations with the latter.

On 30 January, the Anglo-Japanese Alliance was signed. Although the British had hoped that it might cover India as well, the Japanese had insisted that it remain restricted to China. The two countries promised to follow an Open Door policy (although Japan's particular interest in Korea was conceded); to remain neutral if attacked by a third party; and to come to each other's aid if two or more powers attacked. There was also a secret clause covering naval power in the region. The British and the Japanese navies were going to start talking to each other about co-operation against potential enemies in the Pacific such as France or Russia. News of the treaty was greeted with considerable excitement in Japan, where there were public demonstrations in support of it. In Britain the reaction was more muted and the government preferred it that way.

Britain had abandoned a policy which, if not strictly speaking was either one of isolation or centuries old, had served it well. For much of the nineteenth century it had been able to comfortably build its trade and its empire without worrying too much about combinations of powers against it. The world had changed though and France and Russia together now made a formidable opponent. New powers such as Germany, the United States, and Japan itself were also undermining British global hegemony. Its treaty with Japan was a way of testing the waters, to see if it wanted to plunge further into the entanglements of alliances. In 1902, things were looking up for Britain. The Boer War had finally ended in May and Transvaal and the Orange Free State were now part of the British Empire. And hopes that Germany could be made into a firmer friend had certainly not gone away completely. In Germany, the reaction initially was one of mild pleasure. By allying itself with Japan, Britain was a step closer to a confrontation with Russia in Asia and possibly with France as well. When the British ambassador in Berlin informed the Kaiser about the new treaty, Wilhelm's initial reaction was: 'the noodles seem to have had a lucid interval'.[67]

CHAPTER 3

'Woe to the country that has a child for King!' Wilhelm II and Germany

'It *almost breaks* my heart', wrote Queen Victoria in the spring of 1859 to her uncle Leopold, the king of the Belgians, '*not* to witness our *first grandchild* christened! I don't think I *ever* felt *so* bitterly disappointed *about anything* as about this! And then it is an *occasion* so gratifying to both *Nations*, which brings them *so much* together, that it is *most* peculiarly mortifying!'[1] The child, born in Prussia to her oldest daughter Victoria, was the future Wilhelm II of Germany and the proud grandmother's hopes for both it and the future friendship between their peoples promised to come true.

A British–German partnership made a lot of sense. Germany was a great land power, Britain a sea one. Germany's interests lay mainly in Europe, Britain's overseas. Until the 1890s while Bismarck was still in control, Germany was content to be a continental power so the two countries were not rivals for empire. It helped too that they had a common enemy in France and shared an apprehension about French ambitions. After all, Prussia and Britain had fought side by side to defeat Napoleon. When Prussia, under Bismarck's skilful leadership, united the German states into the new Germany in 1870, Britain watched with

3. Otto von Bismarck, the Iron Chancellor, was a consummate Prussian statesman who, through a mix of skilful diplomacy and force, had brought about the creation of Germany in 1871. In the succeeding decades he had made Germany the centre of European politics, playing one nation off against another and ensuring that France, Germany's bitter foe, remained isolated. Wilhelm II, who became Kaiser in 1888, resented Bismarck's dominance and, in 1890, dismissed him with the result that Germany's foreign policy fell into less skilled hands.

benevolent neutrality. The great intellectual Thomas Carlyle (who wrote an admiring biography of Frederick the Great) spoke for many of his peers when he said publicly: 'That noble, patient, pious, and solid Germany should be at length welded into a nation, and become Queen of the Continent, instead of vapouring, vain-glorious, gesticulating, quarrelsome, restless, and over-sensitive France, seems to me the hope-fullest public fact that has occurred in my time.'[2] Germany's growing prosperity, later the subject of concern in prewar British circles, was initially welcomed as trade between the two countries increased.

Surely the similarities between the German and English peoples too demonstrated that both were part of the Teutonic race, sharing the same sensible and sober values, as perhaps they had always done. Some historians argued that both – the continental and the island branches – had stoutly resisted the Roman Empire and had developed their own sound political and social institutions over the centuries. Religion, which still counted for much in the nineteenth century, was another link, at least if you were among the majority of Protestants in each country. Moreover, in both countries the elites were largely Protestant.[3]

Each found much to admire in the other. For the British, it was German culture and science. German universities and higher technical schools became models for British educators. British students in such fields as medicine had to learn German in order to read the latest scientific work. Germans dominated the important fields of biblical scholarship and archaeology, and German history, with its stress on archival work, the amassing of facts, and the use of evidence was felt to show the past 'as it really was'. For their part Germans admired English literature, especially Shakespeare, and the British way of life. Even during the Great War, the Cecilienhof at Potsdam, built for the crown prince, took as its model an English Tudor house. Its bookshelves to this day are filled with the works of popular British authors from P. G. Wodehouse to Dornford Yates.

At the personal level there were many links, from the business communities in each other's cities to marriage. Robert Graves, that most English of poets, had a German mother. Eyre Crowe, later famous in the Foreign Office as a firm opponent of Germany, was born to a mixed couple in Germany and educated almost completely in German. Higher up the social scale, English women such as Evelyn Stapleton-Bretherton, born in Sussex, married Prince Blücher, a descendant of the great Prussian marshal, and Daisy Cornwallis-West of North Wales became Princess of Pless, wife of one of the richest men, from one of the oldest families, in Germany. At the very top were the royal families themselves. Queen Victoria was descended from two German royal families, the Hanoverians and, through her mother, the Saxe-Coburgs. She then married a Saxe-Coburg cousin, Prince Albert. Between them they were related to virtually every ruling family in Germany (and most throughout Europe as well). In 1858, when their daughter married the future heir to the Prussian throne, it appeared that another important strand had been added to the web that connected the British and the Germans.

Why did things go so badly wrong? Political scientists might say that the fact that Germany and Britain found themselves on opposite sides in the Great War was foreordained, the result of the clash between a major global power feeling its advantage slip away and a rising challenger. Such transitions, they argue, are rarely managed peacefully. The established power is too often arrogant, lecturing the rest of the world about how to manage its affairs, and too often insensitive to the fears and concerns of lesser powers. Such a power, as Britain was then, and the United States is today, inevitably resists its own intimations of mortality and the rising one is impatient to get its fair share of whatever is on offer, whether colonies, trade, resources or influence.

In the nineteenth century, Britain had the world's largest empire and dominated the seas and world trade. Understandably perhaps, it showed little sympathy for the aspirations and concerns of other nations. As Winston Churchill, always a statesman with a strong sense of history, wrote shortly before the Great War:

> We have engrossed to ourselves, in a time when other powerful nations were paralysed by barbarism or internal war, an altogether disproportionate share of the wealth and traffic of the world. We have got all we want in territory, and our claim to be left in the unmolested enjoyment of vast and splendid possessions, mainly acquired by violence, largely maintained by force, often seems less reasonable to others than to us.

Moreover, Britain frequently irritated the other European powers with its confident assumption of superiority, for example, to the institutions and politics on the Continent, by its reluctance to uphold the Concert of Europe, and the way in which it carefully intervened in conflicts only when it saw a clear gain for itself. In the scramble for colonies, British statesmen tended to claim that they were taking on more territory merely for the security of their existing possessions or perhaps out of benevolence towards the subject peoples, while other nations were motivated entirely by greed.

Germany by contrast showed both the insecurities and the ambitions of a rising world power. It was sensitive to criticism and endlessly concerned that it was not being taken seriously enough. It was a big country at the heart of Europe, and economically and militarily stronger, as well as more dynamic, than its largest neighbours of France, Russia and Austria-Hungary. Yet in its gloomier moments it saw itself as being encircled. Its trade was soaring around the world and increasingly cutting into Britain's share but that was not enough. It did not have the colonies, along with the concomitant naval bases, coaling stations, and telegraph junctions which were held to be the mark of a global power. Moreover, when it tried to take territory overseas, in Africa or the South Pacific, Britain invariably appeared to raise objections. So when the new Foreign Secretary, Bernhard von Bülow, gave a stirring speech to the Reichstag in 1897 in which he talked about Germany demanding its place in the sun, it was well received by his countrymen.

Britain, like other dominant powers before and since, was aware that the world was changing and that it faced new challenges. Its empire was too big and too spread out – which prompted arguments from imperialists at home to take even more territories to protect existing ones and the crucial shipping and telegraph routes. Its industrial output, while still great, was less in terms of the world's total as new powers such as Germany and the United States were catching up fast and older ones such as Japan and Russia were entering the industrial age at high speed. And being first can lead to problems in the long run. Britain's industrial infrastructure was old and not being renewed quickly enough. Its education system was turning out too many classicists and not enough engineers and scientists.

Yet the question still remains: why did Britain find itself with Germany as its main enemy when there so easily could have been others? Germany was after all only one among several threats to Britain's world dominance. Other powers wanted their equivalent of a place in the sun. In the years before 1914, there could have been a war over colonial issues between Britain and the United States, Britain and France, or Britain and Russia – and in each case there nearly was. Those potentially dangerous relationships, though, were managed and the main sources of conflict dealt with. (We have to hope today that the United States and China will be as sensible and as successful.)

True, there were strains in the relationship between Britain and Germany over the years, a tendency to suspect the motives of the other, and to take offence too readily. The Kruger telegram of 1896 when the Kaiser impetuously dispatched his congratulations to the President of the little independent Transvaal on the Afrikaners' success in holding off the Jameson Raid (a gang of British adventurers had tried to seize control of the Transvaal) led to angry comment in Britain. 'The German Emperor has taken a very grave step', said *The Times*, 'which must be regarded as distinctly unfriendly to this country.'[4] Salisbury was at a dinner party when he received the news and is reported to have said to his neighbour, one of Queen Victoria's daughters, 'What cheek, Madame, what cheek!'[5] British public opinion was enraged. Wilhelm had recently been made honorary colonel of the Royal Dragoons; his fellow officers apparently cut up his portrait and threw the pieces into the fire.[6] Paul Hatzfeldt, the German ambassador in London, reported to Berlin: 'The general feeling was such – of this I have no doubt – that if the Government had lost its head, or on any ground wished for war, it would have had the whole public behind it.'[7] On the eve of the Great War, Sir Edward Goschen, the British ambassador in Berlin, said to a colleague that in his view the Kruger telegram was the start of the division between Britain and Germany.[8]

Even when agreements were reached, the process left behind a residue of bitterness and mistrust. When Britain made difficulties in 1898 in the negotiations over the Portuguese colonies, the Kaiser wrote an irate memorandum: 'Lord Salisbury's conduct is quite Jesuitical, monstrous and insolent!'[9] The British for their part deeply resented the way the Germans exploited Britain's preoccupation with the deteriorating situation in southern Africa to make Britain negotiate in the first place. Salisbury, who did not share Chamberlain's enthusiasm for a broad alliance with Germany, told the German ambassador, 'You ask too much for your friendship.'[10]

The following year Germany threatened to withdraw its ambassador from London when Salisbury balked at giving way to German demands over the Samoan islands. The Kaiser impetuously sent an extraordinarily rude letter to his grandmother criticising her Prime Minister. 'This way of treating Germany's interests and feelings has come upon the people like an electric shock, and has evoked the impression that Lord Salisbury cares no more for us than for Portugal, Chile or the Patagonians.' And he added a threat: 'If this sort of high-handed treatment of German affairs by Lord Salisbury's Government is suffered to continue, I am afraid that there will be a permanent source of misunderstandings and recriminations between the two nations, which may in the end lead to bad blood.'[11] The old queen, after consulting Salisbury, replied very firmly indeed: 'The tone in which you write about Lord Salisbury I can only attribute to a temporary irritation on your part, as I do not think you would otherwise have written in such a manner, and I doubt whether any Sovereign ever wrote in such terms to another Sovereign, and that Sovereign his own Grandmother about their Prime Minister.'[12]

The Boer War produced fresh tensions. The German government actually played a helpful role in refusing to join a coalition of powers to force Britain to make peace with the two Boer republics. Germany did not receive as much credit as it might have done in part because of the condescending and high-handed tone Bülow among others adopted with Britain. As Friedrich von Holstein, the effective head of the German Foreign Office, said later: 'By acting in friendly manner and speaking in an unfriendly one, we fell between two stools (for "we" read "Bülow").'[13]

Moreover, the fact that the German public, from the empress down, was largely pro-Boer confirmed the perception in Britain that Germany was working actively for British defeat. Rumours circulated that German officers were enlisting in the Boer armies when in fact the Kaiser had forbidden them to take part. In the opening months of the war, Britain seized three German mail steamers suspected, wrongly as it turned out, of carrying war materiel to the Boers. (One, according to the German diplomat Eckardstein, had nothing more dangerous than boxes of Swiss cheese.) When the British were slow to release the ships, the German government charged Britain with violating international law and used threatening language. Bülow, who wanted to keep the talks with Chamberlain alive for the time being, wrote to the then Chancellor Gottfried von Hohenlohe: 'The acuteness and depth of Germany's unfortunate dislike of Britain are most dangerous to us. If the British public clearly realized the anti-British feeling which dominates Germany just now, a great revulsion would occur in its conception of the relations between Britain and Germany.'[14] In fact the British public were aware of the feeling in Germany because the British press reported it in detail. The establishment Athenaeum Club in London had a special display of German cartoons and anti-British articles.[15]

While it is difficult to measure in an age before opinion surveys, it does seem as though elite opinion in each country, whether in foreign offices, parliaments, or the military, was hardening against the other by the start of the twentieth century.[16] And there was a new and, for many in ruling circles, disconcerting factor in the growing importance of public opinion. 'The least ill humour toward us prevails in the higher circles of society, perhaps also in the lower classes of the population, the mass of the workers,' Count Paul Metternich, who succeeded Hatzfeldt as German ambassador in London, reported to Berlin in 1903. 'But of all those that lie in between, and who work with brain and pen, the great majority are hostile to us.'[17] Loud public demands for the German government to do something about Britain or that the British government stand up to Germany not only put pressure on the decision-makers but limited how far they could go in working with the other country.

Samoa, for example, was a crisis that need not have happened because no great national interests were at stake. Yet it proved unnecessarily difficult to resolve because of public agitation, especially in Germany. 'For even though the great majority of our pothouse politicians did not know whether Samoa was a fish or a fowl or a foreign queen', said Eckardstein, 'they shouted all the more loudly that, whatever else it was, it was German and must remain forever German.'[18] The German press suddenly discovered Samoa to be essential for national prestige and security.[19]

Yet public opinion is often volatile. Think of the sudden change in the United States in 1972 when President Nixon went to Beijing and China went from being a bitter enemy to a new friend. When Queen Victoria had her last fatal illness, the Kaiser rushed to her side even though the Boer War was still on and his government feared that he might meet a hostile reception. He held her in his arms for two and a half hours as she died and later claimed that he helped his uncle, now King Edward VII, lift her into her coffin. She was, he remembered, 'so little – and so light'.[20] The *Daily Mail* called Wilhelm 'a friend in need' and *The Times* said he would have an 'abiding place in their memories and affections'. The *Telegraph* reminded its readers that he was half-English: 'We have never lost our secret pride in the fact that the most striking and gifted personality born to any European throne since Frederick the Great was largely of our own blood.' At a lunch before he left, Wilhelm made a plea for friendship: 'We ought to form an Anglo-German alliance, you to keep the seas, while we would be responsible for the land; with such an alliance not a mouse could stir in Europe without our permission.'[21]

Economic competition, a troubled relationship with mutual suspicions and occasional open hostility, the pressures of public opinion, all these help to explain why the Kaiser's wishes did not materialise and why Germany and Britain followed diverging paths before 1914. Yet if Germany and Austria-Hungary had become enemies again (as they had been until 1866) or if Britain had gone to war with France, it would be just as easy to find similar factors at work. And if Germany and Britain had formed an alliance, it would be as easy to find explanations for that. So, when all that is said, the question remains. Why did Germany and Britain become such antagonists?

Part of the explanation lies in the way Germany was governed, which gave too much power to the complicated and bewildering character who sat at its summit from 1888 until 1918 when he was forced to abdicate. Wilhelm II was blamed in Allied propaganda for starting the Great War and indeed the victorious allies at Paris for a time contemplated bringing him to trial. That was probably unfair: Wilhelm did not want a general European war and in the crisis of 1914 as well as previous ones his inclination was to preserve the peace. Count Lerchenfeld, the perceptive representative of Bavaria in Berlin before the Great War, believed that he was well intentioned – 'Kaiser Wilhelm erred but he did not sin' – but that his violent language and outrageous statements gave observers the wrong impression.[22] Nevertheless, he made a crucial contribution to the steps by which Europe turned into two heavily armed hostile camps. When he decided to build a navy to challenge British sea power, he drove a wedge between Germany and Britain and from that much else followed. Moreover, Wilhelm's erratic behaviour, his changeable enthusiasms and his propensity to talk too much and without thinking first helped to create an impression of a dangerous Germany, a maverick that would not play the international game and which was bent on dominating the world.

Emperor of the Germans, the king of Prussia, first among his fellow German monarchs, the descendant of the great warrior-king Frederick the Great, and grandson of his namesake Wilhelm I in whose reign Germany came into being, Wilhelm II wanted to dominate not just the

German but the world's stage. He was naturally restless and fidgety, his features animated and his expressions changing rapidly. 'To have a conversation with him', said Baron Beyens, the Belgian ambassador in Berlin before the Great War, 'means to play the part of a listener, to allow him time to unfold his ideas in lively fashion, while from time to time one ventures upon a remark on which his quick mind, flitting readily from one subject to another, seizes with avidity.'[23] When something amused him Wilhelm laughed loudly and when he was annoyed his eyes flashed 'like steel'.

He was handsome, with fair hair, soft fresh skin and grey eyes. In public he played the part of ruler quite well, in his variety of military uniforms and his flashy rings and bracelets and with his erect soldier's bearing. Like Frederick the Great and his grandfather, he barked out orders and scribbled terse and often rude comments – 'stale fish', 'rubbish', 'nonsense' – on documents. He composed his features into a stern mask and his eyes were cold; the famous moustaches with their aggressive tilt were fixed into place every morning by his personal barber. 'We ask ourselves', remarked Beyens, 'with a touch of anxiety, whether the man we have just seen is really convinced of what he says, or whether he is the most striking actor that has appeared on the political stage of our day.'[24]

Wilhelm was an actor and one who secretly suspected that he was not up to the demanding role he had to play. The long-serving French ambassador in Berlin, Jules Cambon, felt that 'H.M. had to make a great effort, and a very great effort, to maintain the severe and dignified attitude befitting a sovereign and that it was a great relief to him when the official part of the audience was over, to relax and indulge in agreeable and even jocose conversation which he believed to be much more in common with H.M.'s real nature.'[25] He had, thought Albert Hopman, a naval aide who was usually inclined to be sycophantic, 'somewhat a feminine tilt to his character, because he is lacking logic, businesslike manner, and a true inner manly hardness'.[26] Walther Rathenau, the highly intelligent and perceptive German industrialist, was amazed at the contrast between the private and the public man when he was first introduced to the Kaiser. He saw a man trying hard to show a forceful dominance which did not come naturally: 'a nature directed against itself, unsuspecting. Many have seen this besides me: neediness, softness, a longing for people, a childlike nature ravished, these were palpable behind the athletic feats, high tension and resounding activity.'[27]

In that, Wilhelm was also like Frederick the Great. Both men had gentle, sensitive, and intellectual sides which they felt their circumstances obliged them to smother. While Wilhelm did not have Frederick's exquisite taste, he loved designing buildings (admittedly rather ugly and grandiose ones). In his later years he developed a passion for archaeology and dragged his unfortunate court off for weeks on end to Corfu, where he had a dig. On the other hand he did not like modern art or literature. 'That's a nice snake I've reared in my bosom,' he exclaimed after the first Berlin performance of Richard Strauss's *Salome*.[28] The Kaiser's taste ran rather to loud and brassy music.[29]

He was intelligent with an excellent memory and liked to engage with ideas. 'Again and again one cannot help wondering', wrote a long-suffering official in his household, 'at the remarkable closeness with which the Emperor watches every modern tendency and all progress. Today it is radium; tomorrow it will be the excavations in Babylon; and perhaps the next day he will discourse on free and unprejudiced scientific research.'[30] He was also a good Christian and gave sermons when the mood took him, full, said Hopman of one effort, 'of mysticism and crass orthodoxy'.[31] Wilhelm had a tendency, largely unchecked because of who he was, to know it all. He told his uncle, Edward, how the British should conduct the Boer War and sent sketches for battleships to his Navy Office. (He also gave the British navy much unsolicited advice.)[32] He told conductors how to conduct and painters how to paint. As Edward said unkindly, he was 'the most brilliant failure in history'.[33]

He did not like being contradicted and did his best to avoid those who disagreed with him or wanted to give him unwelcome news. As the diplomat Alfred von Kiderlen-Wächter said to Holstein in 1891, 'He just talks himself into an opinion ... Anyone in favor of it is then quoted as an authority; anyone who differs from it "is being fooled".'[34] For the most part, those who were part of Wilhelm's court and his closest official advisers learned to humour their master. 'The higher we go the worse this intriguing and servility naturally become,' said Count Robert Zedlitz-Trützschler, for seven years the Controller of the Kaiser's

Household, 'for it is at the top that one has most to fear and most to hope. Everybody in the immediate neighbourhood of the Emperor in time becomes, to all intents and purposes, his slave.'[35]

His servants also had to keep their master amused and endure his practical jokes. Throughout his life, Wilhelm's sense of humour remained that of an adolescent. He made fun of physical oddities, teasing, for example, the representative of the state of Baden in Berlin about his bald head.[36] On his annual summer cruises in the North Sea, Wilhelm forced his fellow passengers to turn out for morning exercises and found great amusement in pushing them over from behind or in cutting their braces. He deliberately shook hands too hard with his strong right hand, its fingers festooned with sharp rings, poked people in the ribs, and pulled their ears.[37] When he struck Grand Duke Vladimir of Russia a 'resounding blow' with his field marshal's baton, it was of course, said Zedlitz, a joke. 'No one could help noticing that this kind of *nonchalance* was far from pleasant to these royal and imperial personages, and I cannot help fearing that the Emperor has seriously displeased not a few crowned heads by such horseplay, which they can scarcely be expected to find to their taste.'[38] Indeed, the king of Bulgaria, a country which Germany hoped to make an ally of, once left Berlin 'white-hot with hatred' after the Kaiser smacked him on the bottom in public.

Although he was prudish when women were present, in the company of his male companions Wilhelm loved rude stories and slapstick, and thought it was the height of comedy to have hefty soldiers dressed up as women. 'I have done the Dwarf,' said Kiderlen after one outing with Wilhelm, 'and turned out the lights to the Kaiser's vast delectation. In an improvised sing-song, I did the Chinese twins with C.; we were connected by an enormous sausage.' In 1908 the head of his Military Cabinet died of a heart attack while he was dancing dressed in a tutu and feather hat.[39]

There have always been rumours that Wilhelm was homosexual, partly because of his great friendship with Philip Eulenburg who was certainly so, but it seems doubtful. In his youth he had several affairs with women and appears to have been devoted to his wife, the German duchess Augusta Victoria, or, as she was usually known, Dona. Yet when she died, after the Great War, he promptly married again. Dona was strongly anti-British, extremely conservative and rigidly Protestant; she would not, for example, have Catholics in her household. Nor would she allow anyone about whom there was the slightest murmur of scandal to appear at court. Berlin grew accustomed to the sight of the royal party leaving theatres when Dona felt that she had spotted something indecent on the stage. Beyens, the Belgian ambassador in Berlin, said unkindly but accurately: 'Her great aim is to make the family life in the royal residences as cosy and homelike as that of a humble Prussian squire.'[40] And despite all Wilhelm's attempts to make her more elegant by choosing her clothes and lading her with expensive and showy jewels, she herself looked like the wife of a Prussian squire. When she wore a gold dress with a red sash to a court ball, said one observer unkindly, she looked 'like a cheap party cracker'.[41] Dona adored Wilhelm and gave him seven children but she did not entertain him. For that he turned to his cruises and his hunting parties with his male entourage. He seems not to have noticed that Eulenburg and possibly others in his circle were not much interested in women so that it came as a tremendous shock to him when there was a public scandal.

The Kaiser, as the Eulenburg case so clearly demonstrated, was not perceptive when it came to character. Nor was he good at understanding the points of view of others. Eulenburg himself, possibly the Kaiser's closest friend and one who loved him for himself, wrote in 1903: 'H.M. sees and judges *all* things and *all* men purely from his personal standpoint. Objectivity is lost completely and subjectivity rides on a biting and stamping stallion.'[42] He was always quick to feel affronted but frequently insulted others. Germany was in theory a federation of princely states with Wilhelm as first among equals, but he so condescended to and browbeat his fellow rulers that most tried to avoid seeing him if they possibly could.

Wilhelm much preferred talking to listening. In the first twelve years of his reign he gave over 400 official speeches as well as many unofficial ones.[43] The whole court used to worry, said Lerchenfeld, when the Kaiser was about to make a speech because they never knew what he was going to say.[44] Often he said very silly or tendentious things indeed. He was fond of saying that he would 'smash', 'destroy', 'annihilate' those who stood in his or Germany's way. Unveiling a military monument in Frankfurt in the first year of his reign, he declared that he would not give up any of the territory his ancestors had gained: 'We would rather leave our 18 army corps and 42 million inhabitants on the battlefield than to yield even a single stone ...'[45] Perhaps his single most notorious speech is the one he gave in 1900 to send off the German expedition to put down the Boxer Rebellion. They would be facing a savage foe and they must not be soft. *'Anyone who falls into your hands falls to your sword!'* In a sentence that lived on to haunt the Germans, he told the soldiers to be like the Huns of old: 'You should give the name of Germany such cause to be remembered in China for a thousand years that no Chinaman, no matter whether his eyes be slit or not, will dare look a German in the face.'[46]

Although he admired toughness in others and sought it for himself, Wilhelm was emotionally fragile. He was torn 'with doubts and self-condemnation', said Wilhelm Schoen, one of his diplomats. His entourage worried endlessly about his nerves, his tendency to get agitated, and his bursts of violent temper.[47] When he ran up against situations, often of his own making, which he could not handle, he would often collapse and talk of abdicating, even of committing suicide. 'At such times', Schoen said, 'it needed all the Empress' powers of persuasion to revive his courage and induce him to carry on his office, promising to do better.'[48] Did he have, wondered an Austrian military attaché in Berlin, 'as one says, a screw loose'? It was a fear shared by many of those who worked with him. In 1903 Eulenburg went on the Kaiser's usual North Sea cruise. It was a time when Wilhelm was normally at ease, relaxing and playing cards with his faithful entourage but he had become increasingly moody. 'He is difficult to handle and complicated in *all* things', Eulenburg wrote despairingly to Bülow. Wilhelm changed his opinions from moment to moment, yet always insisted that he was right. 'Pale, ranting wildly', Eulenburg went on, 'looking restlessly about him and piling lie upon lie he made such a terrible impression on me that I still cannot get over it.'[49]

To understand Wilhelm, and his contemporaries and posterity have spent quite a bit of time doing just that, it is necessary to go back to his childhood, indeed perhaps to his birth itself. His mother, Vicky, was only eighteen when she had him and the delivery was extremely drawn out and difficult. It is possible that the infant suffered a temporary lack of oxygen and perhaps brain damage. Once they realised Wilhelm was alive, the doctors were preoccupied with the young mother, who was in a pitiable state. It was only some hours later that it was noticed that the baby's left arm had been pulled out of its socket.[50] The arm never grew properly in spite of a range of treatments from electric shocks to strapping it inside the carcass of a hare. Wilhelm's suits and uniforms were carefully cut to disguise the handicap but it was an awkward one for someone who was expected and certainly expected of himself to cut a dashing military figure on horseback.

His mother, who admitted to Queen Victoria that she did not at first pay much attention to her children (there were to be eight in all), then overcompensated by overseeing every detail of his education. Her mother warned her: 'I often think too great care, too much constant watching, leads to the very dangers hereafter which one wishes to avoid.'[51] The old queen was right. Wilhelm disliked his rigid and humourless tutor and the attempts to make him into a good liberal. His parents, the crown prince and princess, had dreams of turning Germany into a properly constitutional monarchy and an inclusive modern state. Vicky did not help matters by making it quite clear she felt in most things that Germany was inferior to Britain. This put them at odds with the stuffy and conservative Prussian court and more importantly with Wilhelm I and his exceedingly powerful minister, Bismarck. Although the young Wilhelm had an intense and often loving relationship with his mother, he came increasingly to resent her. The same was to be true of his relationship with Britain.

To his mother's dismay, he gravitated towards precisely the elements in Prussian society which she most disliked: the landed Junker class with its reactionary outlook and suspicion of the modern world, the military with their narrow, hierarchical values, and Wilhelm I's deeply conservative court. The young prince admired his grandfather greatly as the monarch who had brought glory to the Hohenzollerns by uniting Germany under their rule. He also took advantage of the feud between Wilhelm I and his parents. As a young man, when he did not want to go on a trip with his father, he prevailed on his grandfather to intervene. While the crown prince was cut out of all involvement in government affairs at Bismarck's instigation, Wilhelm was allowed to go on diplomatic missions and 1886 was posted to the Foreign Office for experience, something that had never been permitted his father. In a rare moment of reflection, Wilhelm told Bismarck's son that his good relationship with his grandfather, the king, was 'unpleasant' for his father: 'He was not under his father's authority, he received not a penny from his father; since everything derived from the head of the family, he was independent of his father.'[52]

When he was eighteen, Wilhelm joined an elite regiment where, he later claimed, he felt instantly at home. 'I had lived through such fearful years of unappreciation of my nature, of ridicule of that which was to me highest and most holy: Prussia, the army and all the fulfilling duties that I first encountered in this officer corps and have provided me with joy and happiness and contentment on earth.'[53] He loved the army, loved the company of his fellow officers (and filled his household with them), and particularly loved that it was all going to be his one day. That day came much sooner than anyone thought.

The old King Wilhelm died in March 1888. His son, who was already seriously ill with cancer of the throat, followed him three months later. The timing is one of the great What Ifs of modern history. What would have happened if Frederick, with the support of his wife Vicky, had ruled Germany, say for the next two decades? Would they have moved it firmly away from absolutist rule towards a proper constitutional monarchy? Would they have brought the military under firm civilian control? Would Germany have followed a different path in international affairs, perhaps moving towards greater friendship, even an alliance, with Britain? With Wilhelm II Germany got a different sort of ruler and a different fate.

Wilhelm's accession to the throne would not have mattered so much, though, if he had been, like his grandmother, uncle, and cousin, the hereditary ruler of Britain. While they had influence, often considerable, they did not have Wilhelm's power. He could, for example, appoint the ministers he wanted, direct the military and shape Germany's foreign policy. Where the British rulers had to deal with a Prime Minister and Cabinet who were responsible to a powerful Parliament, Wilhelm appointed and sacked his Chancellors and ministers as he wished. While he was obliged to go to the Reichstag for funding, he, or in practice his ministers, were usually successful in obtaining what they needed. It is true that they learned how to manage him (Eulenburg before his disgrace was particularly adept) and that they did not always keep him fully informed about sensitive issues. Nevertheless he could and did interfere to determine policies and appointments.

It also would not have mattered if Wilhelm had been, like his distant relation Prince Wilhelm of Wied, the king of Albania. But he was ruler of one of the most powerful countries in the world. As Zedlitz said after one of Wilhelm's nervous collapses: 'He is a child and will always remain one – but a child that has power to make everything difficult if not impossible.' And he went on to quote from the book of Ecclesiastes, 'Woe to the country that has a child for King!'[54] And Germany was both powerful and complicated, a dangerous thing to put into the hands of someone such as Wilhelm. It was rather like giving a powerful motor car to Toad in the children's classic, *Wind in the Willows*. (Interestingly, Wilhelm hated cars when they first appeared on the grounds that they frightened the horses; as soon as he had one he became, according to Bülow, 'a fanatical motorist'.[55])

With the unification of the German states into the Reich in 1871, Germany became the most populous country in Europe west of Russia, which meant that it also had an advantage in potential recruits for its armed forces. Moreover, the German army was widely regarded as the best trained, with the best officers, in the world. By 1911 there were nearly 65 million German citizens compared to 39 million in France and 40 million in Great Britain. (Russia had 160 million, one of the reasons France valued it so highly as an ally.) Germany was rapidly becoming Europe's most dynamic economy. In 1880 Britain was the world's leading exporter with 23 per cent of the world's trade while Germany had 10 per cent. By 1913 Germany was looking to overtake Britain: it now had 13 per cent of the world's trade while Britain had slipped to 17 per cent. In some of the sectors in which economic power was measured in that period Germany was already ahead. It overtook Britain in steel production in 1893 and by 1913 was the world's largest exporter of machinery.

With industrialisation came unions and, even in Germany where social benefits were ahead of most other countries, labour unrest and strikes. In 1896–7 there was a major strike in the great port of Hamburg and from that point on periodic strikes in different parts of the country right up to the war. In most cases the aims were economic but increasingly they were political as well, to bring about changes in German society. Membership of unions grew significantly, from under 2 million in 1900 to 3 million by 1914. Even more worrying for Germany's ruling classes was the appearance of a powerful socialist party. By 1912 the Social Democratic Party (the SPD) was the largest party in the Reichstag with almost a third of the seats as well as a third of the popular vote.

Germany was not alone in feeling the strains brought by rapid change but it had a political system particularly ill equipped to deal with them. Bismarck, great statesman though he was, had created a gimcrack system and constitution which worked only when he was in charge and not always then. In theory, according to the constitution, Germany was a federation comprising eighteen different states. It had a federal parliament, the Reichstag, elected by universal male suffrage, with responsibility for approving federal budgets. It had a federal council, the Bundesrat, made up of representatives from the states, with the right to oversee such crucial areas as foreign affairs and the army and navy. Theory was one thing, reality another. The council never became important; Bismarck never had the slightest intention of sharing his power or that of Prussia. He combined the offices of German Chancellor and Prussian Minister-President and the practice continued until the end of the Great War. He was also Foreign Minister and ran foreign affairs largely out of the Prussian Foreign Ministry. With overlapping jurisdictions it was never clear where responsibility really lay.

Yet Bismarck and his successors could not run Germany entirely to suit themselves; as the years went by they had to deal with a Reichstag that could claim, with reason, to represent the will of the German people and which could mount a formidable challenge to government policies by threatening to withhold approval of the Budget. The decades between 1871 and 1914 were marked by a series of political crises and at times deadlock and both Bismarck and Wilhelm II and his advisers contemplated abolishing the constitution and going back to absolute rule. 'Blockheads', 'idiots', 'dogs': these were the ways Wilhelm talked about members of the Reichstag, and he was fond of saying that it would do them good to be taught who was really the master in Germany.[56]

Apart from the political uproar that would have caused, it is highly doubtful that such a move would have given Germany a more coherent and unified government. Bismarck and his successors did not believe in cabinets where policies were hammered out and agreed upon or, even, apparently, in basic co-ordination between the different branches of government. So, for example, the Foreign Office would not know what the military were planning and vice versa. Indeed, matters got worse rather than better when Wilhelm II came to the throne because he tried to exert direct control over the army and navy through his own cabinets of advisers and insisted that German ministers report directly to him. The result was even less co-ordination and sharing of information than before.

The new federation was also like a weak rider trying to control a strong horse. Prussia which contained 65 per cent of the country's territory and 62 per cent of its population, overshadowed and dominated all the other members from the kingdom of Bavaria in the south to the city-state of Hamburg in the north. And Prussia, with a state legislature dominated, thanks to a restricted franchise and carefully managed voting system, by conservatives, remained a strongly right-wing counter force within a Germany in which moderate conservative, liberal and socialist forces were growing, including in Prussia itself. Moreover, the Prussian Junker families held a privileged position in Prussian society and dominated Germany's institutions, especially its army and its Foreign Office. Their values – loyalty, piety, duty, devotion to family, a reverence for tradition and the established order, an acute sense of honour – were in some ways admirable but they were also conservative, if not reactionary, and increasingly out of step with the modern Germany.[57]

Wilhelm's closest companions came from that world and he shared many of their values. In the early years of his reign, however, he did have a concern, which came perhaps from his mother, with improving the lot of the poorer classes in society. This put him on a collision course with his Chancellor, Bismarck. Where Wilhelm wanted to improve working conditions, Bismarck wanted to smash the burgeoning socialist movement. In 1890 the Chancellor lost control of the Reichstag and did his best to stir up a political crisis so that he would have an excuse to destroy it and tear up the constitution. Wilhelm I might have gone along with such a plan but his grandson was not prepared to do so. The new Kaiser was increasingly alarmed by Bismarck's intransigence and was not in any case prepared to submit to his guidance (or to that of any one else for that matter). The final showdown came in March 1890 when the Kaiser criticised Bismarck for not keeping him properly informed, about foreign as well as domestic issues, and made it clear that he would be the final authority in Germany. Bismarck resigned and left Berlin for his country estate, where he lived out an embittered retirement.

Wilhelm was now his own master and that of Germany. His concept of what it meant to be the German monarch was, as might be expected, a grandiose one. As he said in a speech in Königsberg shortly after his accession: 'We Hohenzollerns receive our crown only from Heaven and in the duties connected to it we are responsible only to Heaven.'[58] He did not intend, as the dispute with Bismarck showed, to delegate his responsibilities to his Chancellor or a Cabinet. Indeed, he increased the number of officials who reported directly to him and established a royal headquarters to supervise the military. The trouble, though, was that he wanted the power and the glory and the applause without the hard work. 'You see', says Rat of Toad in *Wind in the Willows*, 'he will insist on driving himself, and he's hopelessly incapable. If he'd only employ a decent, steady, well-trained animal, pay him good wages, and leave everything to him, he'd get on all right. But no; he's convinced he's a heaven-born driver, and nobody can teach him anything; and all the rest follows.'

Wilhelm was both lazy and incapable of concentrating on anything for long. Bismarck compared him to a balloon: 'If you don't keep fast hold of the string, you never know where he'll be off to.'[59] Although he complained about how overworked he was, Wilhelm cut back significantly on the regular schedule of interviews with military chiefs, Chancellor and ministers which his grandfather had faithfully maintained. Some ministers saw him only once or twice a year. Many grumbled even so that the Kaiser was inattentive and complained if their reports were too long.[60] He refused to read newspapers and tossed long documents aside in irritation. Although he insisted he would be responsible for the annual fleet manoeuvres of his new navy, he lost his temper when he found he was expected to consult with his officers and work out the details: 'To hell with it! I am the Supreme War Lord. I do not decide. I command.'[61]

He also spent more than half his time during his reign away from Berlin or his palace in nearby Potsdam. William the Fidgety, as his cousin King George V of Britain described him, loved travelling, perhaps in part, as one courtier suspected, to get away from his wife's stifling domesticity.[62] He visited his other palaces (dozens of them), went to his friends' hunting lodges, and took long cruises on one of his several yachts. His ministers had to commute to wherever he was and even then did not always get to see him because 'Wilhelm the Sudden' was notorious for changing his plans at the last minute. His subjects joked that Germans no longer sang 'Hail to the Conqueror' but 'Hail to you in the special train'.[63]

Germans made quite a few jokes about their ruler. When the satirical weekly *Simplicissimus* had an unflattering cartoon of him on its cover, Wilhelm's rage against the editor and cartoonist only increased its circulation. When he laid out an Avenue of Victory in Berlin in 1901 and lined it with giant kitschy statues, Berliners promptly called it Puppet Alley. But if the Kaiser was a joke it was not always a very good one. In 1894 a young classical scholar, Ludwig Quidde, published a pamphlet on Caligula in which he describes the Roman emperor's rushing from one task to another, 'caught in nervous haste', his 'hunger for military triumphs', and his 'fantastic idea' of conquering the sea. 'Theatricality', it said, 'is an ingredient in imperial insanity.'[64] The pamphlet sold 250,000 copies in the years before 1914.

Of all his responsibilities, Wilhelm took particular pride in his relationship to the armed forces. Under the German constitution (which he proudly said he had never read)[65] he was supreme commander of the German armed forces; officers took an oath of loyalty to him, not to Germany. 'We belong to each other,' said Wilhelm to the armed forces in one of his first acts after he became Kaiser, 'we were born for each other and will cleave indissolubly to each other, whether it be the will of God to send us calm or storm.'[66] He and his ministers successfully resisted most attempts by the Reichstag to examine military matters and indeed tended to treat elected politicians and much of the general public with suspicion. They must remember, Wilhelm told recruits on one occasion, that he might call on them one day to maintain order in the country: 'With those recent socialist turnovers, it is totally possible that I will order you to shoot your own relatives, brothers, even parents ...'[67]

Wilhelm adored 'My Army' and much preferred soldiers to civilians. Where he could he appointed them to government and diplomatic posts. He almost always appeared in military dress and loved riding at the head of marches and taking the salute. He insisted on taking part in army games which meant that their value as a training exercise was minimal because he always had to win. It was not unknown for him to stop everything so that he could take forces from one side and add them to the other (usually his own).[68] He fussed over the army's uniforms (he made thirty-seven changes to their design between 1888 and 1904). He also tried to keep his beloved military safe from the corrupting influences of the modern world; 'The Gentlemen of the Army and the Navy', read one of his orders, 'are hereby requested to dance neither Tango nor One-Step nor Two-Step in uniform, and to avoid families in which these dances are performed.'[69]

Wilhelm had considerable powers under the constitution in foreign affairs as well; he could appoint and dismiss diplomats and conclude treaties. He did not regard his Foreign Office on Wilhelmstrasse or the diplomatic service with the same affection as his military. Diplomats were lazy 'swine' who were always seeing difficulties. 'I will tell you something,' he once said to a senior official. 'You diplomats are full of shit and the whole Wilhelmstrasse stinks.'[70] Wilhelm thought of himself, though, as a master of diplomacy and insisted on dealing directly with his fellow monarchs, often with unfortunate results. Sadly, he had no clear policies beyond a vague desire to make Germany, and himself, important and, if possible, avoid war. 'He was peaceful,' said Lerchenfeld, the Bavarian envoy in Berlin, 'wanted to be on good terms with all powers and he has tried in the course of the years to ally with the Russians, the English, the Italians, the Americans and even with the French.'[71]

When Wilhelm dismissed Bismarck, the English satirical magazine *Punch* carried a cartoon called 'Dropping the Pilot'. Wilhelm himself said in a triumphant telegram to the Grand Duke of Saxe-Weimar: 'The position of Officer of the Watch of the Ship of State has come to me … Full steam ahead.'[72] Unfortunately, that is just what he was going to do, and with a real navy.

CHAPTER 4

Weltpolitik:
Germany's Place on
the World Stage

In the summer of 1897 the Kaiser was a happy man. 'What a joy,' he wrote to his friend Eulenburg, 'to have to deal with someone who is devoted to you body and soul, and also can understand and wants to understand!'[1] The object of this enthusiasm was Bernhard von Bülow, his new Foreign Secretary, who would, so Wilhelm hoped, be his Bismarck, putting the Kaiser and his country at the centre of world affairs where they belonged (and perhaps sorting out Germany's tumultuous internal politics as well). For the years since Bismarck's dismissal had not gone all that well for Wilhelm. Ministers had combined against him and disagreed with his policies, his fellow German princes had chafed under his and Prussia's rule, and the Reichstag had impudently demanded a share in Germany's government.

Wilhelm and his ministers had fought back, urging Germans to bury their differences and work for a greater Germany with, of course, Prussia at its heart. In 1890, the Prussian Ministry of Education decreed that the history taught in schools show the greatness of the Prussian state and its rulers: 'One of the most essential purposes of the *Volksschule* [elementary schools] is to point out to the children the blessings which come to them through the regained national unity, independence, and culture which were restored by the hard and self-sacrificing struggle of the glorious Hohenzollern rulers.' Wilhelm thoroughly approved. 'We must', he told a conference of headmasters, 'bring up nationalistic young Germans, and not young Greeks or Romans.'[2]

Triumphs abroad were meant to play their part in building the different German states into a strong Reich. Wilhelm was both public and exuberant about his ambitions for Germany and for himself. There would be a New Course in his reign, he told his mother: 'For ever and ever there will be only one true Emperor in the world and that is the German Kaiser ...'[3] And both he and Germany should have commensurate influence around the world. As he said to Eulenburg in 1893: 'Without being a world figure one was nothing but a poor appearance.'[4] Germany must have a say in the division of the remaining parts of the world which seemed to be up for the taking. 'In distant areas', he said in 1900 as he launched a new battleship, 'no important decision should be taken without Germany and the German Kaiser.'[5] He took to describing himself as 'the *arbiter mundi*' – and, of course, of Europe. On his visit to his dying grandmother he assured the new British Foreign Minister, Lord Lansdowne, that 'I am the balance of power in Europe since the German constitution leaves decisions about foreign policy to me'.[6]

The reality, galling to Wilhelm in the first years of his reign, was that Germany's foreign relations had not been well managed since 1890. Where Bismarck had tried, usually successfully, to keep on good terms with all the other powers, his successors had allowed Germany to drift into one camp, that of the Triple Alliance with Austria-Hungary and Italy. The first costly mistake had been the failure to renew the Reinsurance Treaty with Russia under which each country bound itself to remain neutral if attacked by a third. That it was partly a mistake says something about the indifferent quality of those in charge of Germany's foreign policy after 1890. The new Chancellor, Leo von Caprivi, was a soldier, and, while intelligent and sensible, he had little background in foreign affairs. He allowed himself to be talked out of renewal by the Foreign Office, in particular by its leading figure, Friedrich von Holstein, who had come to oppose a close friendship with Russia. The result was to encourage the Russians to look elsewhere, in particular to France, with whom Russia signed a secret military agreement in 1894.

4. Heavily influenced by the American naval theorist Alfred Mahan who believed that sea power was the key to world power, Wilhelm II of Germany set out to build his own big navy. He thus set off a costly naval race with Great Britain which in turn helped to persuade the British that they needed to look for allies against Germany.

Moreover what Holstein and his colleagues had hoped for, a rapprochement with Britain, which was on bad terms with both Russia and France, and its closer adherence to the Triple Alliance did not happen. The British already had an understanding with Austria-Hungary and Italy to guarantee the security of the Mediterranean (which largely meant opposing Russian attempts to force the Ottoman Empire to give up control of the crucial passage from the Black Sea to the Mediterranean or French moves to expand their empire). As a result of the lapsing of the Reinsurance Treaty Russia had more to worry about on its frontiers and was less of a threat to British interests in the Mediterranean. Germany also found that its partners in the Triple Alliance grew more assertive as Germany's position weakened.

It did not help that German policy oscillated in those years between

1890 and 1897 between attempts to win over either Russia or Britain or that German leaders veered back and forth from blandishments and threats. On particular issues, moreover, German policies were too often incoherent. In 1894 Caprivi told the German ambassador in London that the Solomon Islands were of crucial importance to Germany; two months later, Berlin had lost interest.[7] The British were not the only Europeans to find German policies a mystery. It also did not help that the Kaiser, who fancied himself a master diplomat, intervened with increasing frequency and often with disastrous effects. While there is still some dispute about the origins of the Kruger telegram, which he dispatched in 1896 to show support for the Transvaal in the Boer republic's struggle against Britain, it seems to have been the result of an attempt on the part of his government to prevent him from doing anything worse. (Wilhelm had initially suggested, among other things, establishing a German protectorate over the Transvaal and sending German troops to Africa, which would have a challenging task, given the dominance of British sea power at the time.)[8]

In 1897 German policy and governance took a decisive turn which was to push Germany further along the path towards confrontation with Britain. Wilhelm, with the support of Eulenburg and other leading conservatives, decided that the time had come to put his own men into key positions in the German government. Among other changes, he brought back Alfred von Tirpitz, an admiral from the German China squadron, to be his Minister of the Navy and so, as we shall see, set in motion the Anglo-German naval race. And Bernhard von Bülow, the German ambassador in Rome, was summoned to be Foreign Secretary. His impact on German policy was perhaps less dramatic than that of Tirpitz, but he also played a part in the steps that led from peace to war.

Bülow, the man who was supposed to solve Germany's international problems, was an amusing, charming, cultivated, and clever career diplomat. He was also intensely ambitious and, like his new master, Wilhelm, lazy. 'He would be quite a fellow', Bülow's brother once said, 'if his character could only attain the height of his personality.'[9] Although the family came originally from Denmark, his father had become the new Germany's Foreign Secretary in 1873, working loyally as the great Bismarck's subordinate. Bismarck took a fancy to the son and Bernhard moved steadily upwards in the diplomatic service, cutting a swathe through Europe's capitals and making along the way a name for himself as an inveterate ladies' man. He met his match in his wife, who was the daughter of a leading family in Rome. Although she was married at the time, she divorced her husband, also a German diplomat, and married Bülow, devoting herself to furthering his career.

Over the years, Bülow had gained a deserved reputation among his colleagues for being devious, untrustworthy and slippery as an eel, said Holstein, who initially considered him a friend. 'Bernhard von Bülow', wrote Holstein in his diary, 'is clean-shaven and pasty, with a shifty look and an almost perpetual smile. Intellectually plausible rather than penetrating. He has no ideas in reserve with which to meet all contingencies, but appropriates other people's ideas and skilfully retails them without acknowledging the source.'[10] Bülow was both adept at making people feel they had said something clever and at giving the impression that he was sharing important information with them. 'Bernhard makes a secret of everything', his mother-in-law said. 'He takes you by the arm, leads you to the window and says: Don't say anything, but there's a little dog down there who's pissing.'[11] He was like a cat, said a woman who knew him, who caught mice by putting out their favourite cheese.[12]

From 1897 onwards he turned all his attention to catching his new master. Wilhelm, Bülow assured him repeatedly, was 'brilliant', 'splendid', 'completely accurate', and always said the right thing. It is very difficult to handle the British and requires infinite skill, he told the Kaiser in 1900: 'But just as the Hohenzollern eagle wiped the two-headed Austrian eagle off the field and clipped the wings of the Gallic cock, so with God's help and Your Majesty's strength and wisdom, it will also deal with the English leopard.'[13] Just to reinforce the message, he repeatedly sent fulsome praise of the Kaiser to Eulenburg, no doubt in the knowledge that it would be shown to Wilhelm. 'Of all the great kings', Bülow wrote shortly after his appointment, 'he is by far the most significant Hohenzollern who has ever lived.'[14] He would, he assured the Kaiser himself, be his 'tool' and enable him to assert his personal rule over Germany. In 1900 a grateful Wilhelm made him Chancellor.

In the first years, Bülow managed the Kaiser with considerable success. He sent short memoranda spiced up with bits of gossip, avoided formal meetings, where Wilhelm would get bored, and made a habit of going for a walk with him every morning. The von Bülows had Wilhelm to lunch and dinner and kept him entertained. Nevertheless, Bernhard the Obliging, as one of his critics called him, was prepared to disregard or modify the Kaiser's wilder policies where he could, especially since the Kaiser often forgot what he had said in the heat of the moment. Nor did Bülow really want to carry out the coup d'état against the German parliamentary institutions which the Kaiser so wished for. What he wanted to do was manage the German people as well as their ruler and, as much as possible, bridge their differences. His policy, then and when he later became Chancellor, was one strongly promoted by Wilhelm and his conservative advisers of bringing together German nationalist and conservative forces in support of the crown and at the same time undermining the growing socialist movement and the strong regional feelings, in the south for example, which had never really accepted Prussian rule.

Sammlungspolitik, as it was known, needed a core organising principle and this was to be pride in Germany. The government, Bülow believed, must adopt 'a courageous and generous policy that knows how to uphold the joy in the present character of [our] national life, a policy that mobilizes national energies, a policy attracting the numerous and ever-growing *Mittelstand* [middle class]'.[15] An active foreign policy was clearly crucial in doing this. The fuss over Samoa, Bülow said revealingly, 'has absolutely no material, but an ideal and patriotic interest for us'. And he gave orders that German newspapers were to treat the issue in such a way as 'strengthens the trust in our foreign policy internally'.[16] His key strategy in foreign affairs was to manoeuvre to ensure that Germany continued to rise up the table of world powers. That might well mean stirring up conflict among the other nations. In 1895 he had told Eulenburg: 'I consider an Anglo-Russian collision not as a tragedy but as "an aim most fervently to be desired".'[17] Let the two of them exhaust themselves while Germany quietly grew stronger.

As far as specific policies went, Bülow believed in maintaining the Triple Alliance with Austria-Hungary and Italy and was privately cool on the idea of an agreement with Britain. Much better for Germany, he felt, to remain neutral between Britain and Russia in their continuing conflict. 'We must hold ourselves independent between the two', he wrote, 'and be the tongue on the balance, not the pendulum oscillating to and fro.'[18] If he inclined to either side, it was probably towards Russia, which he felt in the longer run was likely to be the stronger of the two powers. As for Britain, he held that sooner or later it would realise that it had to be on friendly terms with Germany because of British enmity with both Russia and France. It never seems to have occurred to him that the British might come up with other solutions to their isolation.

In directing Germany's foreign policy he had the support, at least initially, of one of the Foreign Ministry's cleverest, most powerful, and strangest figures, Friedrich von Holstein of the Political Division. Eulenburg called Holstein 'the Monster of the Labyrinth' and the name has stuck. The epithet was unfair because Holstein was no monster but a highly intelligent and dedicated servant of the German state who did his best to further its interests internationally. Like all nicknames, though, it had an element of truth. He was secretive and saw conspiracies everywhere. Bismarck's son Herbert described him as having 'an almost pathological delusion of persecution'.[19] While Holstein could be cruel and cutting to others, he was himself highly sensitive. He lived extremely simply in three small and unpretentious rooms and, apart from target shooting, seemed to have had no other interests beyond his work. He rarely went out in society and did his best to avoid meeting the Kaiser, of whom he increasingly disapproved. When the Kaiser tried to drop by the Wilhelmstrasse to meet Holstein, the latter disappeared on a long walk.[20] When the two men finally met in 1904 at a large dinner, it is said that they talked about duck hunting.[21]

Holstein always refused the highest offices within the Wilhelmstrasse, preferring to be the power behind the scenes, keeping track of the reports coming in and out, spinning his intrigues and rewarding friends and punishing his enemies. His office adjoined that of the Foreign Secretary and he developed the habit of wandering in through the door whenever he pleased. Although he had been close to Bismarck, who relied heavily upon him, he fell out with the old Chancellor, his son, and his supporters primarily over the issue of Russia. Holstein opposed the Reinsurance Treaty and the very idea that Germany and Russia could build a friendship. Perhaps because he had thoroughly disliked his time as a young diplomat in St Petersburg, then the capital of Russia, his hatred and fear of Russia was one of the few consistent strands in his foreign policy.[22] In time he and Bülow would part company over the same issue.

In his first speech to the Reichstag, in December 1897, Bülow laid out his vision for Germany's foreign policy with particular reference to what looked like the coming partition of China. His speech was calculated to appeal to a wide swathe of German opinion. 'We must demand that the German missionary and the German entrepreneur, German goods, the German flag and German ships in China are just as respected as those of other powers.' Germany was willing to respect the interests of other powers in Asia as long as its own were respected in turn. 'In a word: we don't want to put anyone in the shadow, but we too demand our place in the sun.' The world must recognise, he went on, that the old order had changed: 'The times when the German left the earth to one of his neighbours, the sea to the other, and reserved for himself the heavens where pure doctrine reigns – these times are over.'[23] (Bülow's speech was very well received; its phrases, said the Württemburg representative in Berlin, 'have already become almost proverbial and are on everyone's lips'.[24]) Two years later, again in a speech to the Reichstag, Bülow used the term *Weltpolitik* for the first time. Although today, curiously enough, it often translates as 'environmental policy', in those days it meant a global or world policy, and one, moreover, which many outside Germany looked at with the deepest suspicion. Allied to it was the equally slippery notion of *Weltmachtstellung*, or 'world power'.

The terms reflected the widespread notion among patriotic Germans that the country's remarkable economic progress, the rapid spread of German investment and trade around the world, and Germany's advances in such areas as science ought to be matched by an increase in its standing in the world. Other nations must recognise Germany's achievements and its changed position. For liberals this meant Germany providing moral leadership. As one of them wrote wistfully from the vantage point of the 1940s: 'My thoughts always wander back to the time when [we] co-operated in that fine effort: work for Greater Germany, peaceful expansion and cultural activities in the Near East ... A peaceful Germany, great, honoured and respected.'[25] For right-wing nationalists, though, and that included the Kaiser and his closest advisers as well as the numerous members of patriotic societies, it meant rather political and military power and, if necessary, a struggle against other powers.

In those years while the new Kaiser and Germany were feeling their strength, an elderly history professor was attracting packed audiences at his lectures at the University of Berlin. Heinrich von Treitschke was one of the intellectual fathers of the new German nationalism with its longing for a place in the sun. Through his lectures and writings, which included a very popular multi-volume history of Germany, he influenced a whole generation of Germany's leaders to take pride in the great German past and in the extraordinary achievements of Prussia and the Prussian army in building the German state. For Treitschke patriotism was the highest of all values and war was not only a necessary part of human history but a noble and elevating one. If only Germany seized its opportunities, it would rise, as it deserved, to world dominance.[26] He was, said Bülow, whose favourite writer he was, the 'prophet of the national idea'.[27] When Helmuth von Moltke, the future chief of the German general staff, read Treitschke's history as a young man he was 'captivated' and wrote later to his wife that 'a spirit of patriotism and love of the German Fatherland drifts through the whole work, without violating historical truth; it is superb'.[28] The Kaiser was surprisingly lukewarm; although he liked the general drift of Treitschke's writings, the historian did not praise the Hohenzollerns highly enough.[29]

What *Weltpolitik* actually meant in terms of concrete policies was another matter. As Field Marshal Count von Waldersee, who commanded the European forces suppressing the Boxer Rebellion, wrote in his diary when the idea first started to circulate widely: 'We are supposed to pursue *Weltpolitik*. If I only knew what that is supposed to be; for the time being it is nothing but a slogan.'[30] It did seem, though, to imply that Germany acquire its fair share of colonies. Treitschke certainly argued so. 'All nations in history', he said in his lectures, 'felt the urge to impress the stamp of their authority on barbaric countries while they felt strong enough to do so.' And Germany was now strong enough; its high birth rate was evidence of German vitality. Yet Germany was cutting a poor figure by comparison with Britain and other empires: 'It is therefore a vital question for the nation to show colonial drive.'[31]

Germans such as Treitschke were by no means alone in thinking that colonies were a good thing. An assumption widely held at the time in Europe was that colonies brought tangible wealth and the intangible benefits of prestige to their owners. And the depression in agricultural prices and the cycle of business slumps which lasted from 1873 to 1895 made German political and business leaders, like their counterparts elsewhere, acutely aware of the need to export and to secure foreign markets. Critics of empire could point, and did, to the awkward fact that colonies often cost much more to manage and defend than they ever brought in or that investment, trade and emigration tended to flow to parts of the world such as the United States, Russia, and Latin American which were not colonies. Caprivi, for one, thought that Germany's natural markets were in central Europe. Belief, as so often, was not to be shaken by inconvenient evidence. There was something so exciting in looking at a map and seeing all the coloured pieces that belonged to one's nation. Surely territory and population, no matter how poor or how scattered, added up to power in the world. And, as the then British Foreign Secretary, Lord Rosebery, put it in 1893, acquiring new colonies was 'pegging out claims for the future'.[32]

In Germany the question of colonies was a sensitive one. Here was a powerful country, one of the most powerful in the world, yet it did not have its India or its Algeria. True, Germany had scooped up some odds and ends in Africa and the Pacific, but its empire was insignificant beside those of France and Britain. Even little bourgeois Belgium had the immense Congo. The need to catch up and look like a proper great power increasingly preoccupied Germans. In both the Wilhelmstrasse and the military imperial ambitions found strong support. As the head of the Colonial Division in the Foreign Ministry was noting as early as 1890, 'No government, no *Reichstag*, would be in the position of giving up colonies without humiliating itself before Germany and Europe. Nowadays a colonial policy has supporters in all parts of the nation …'[33] Among the general public, the Pan-German League and the Colonial Society may not have had all that many members but they made up for it with the noise and vehemence of their demands.

There were sceptics too, of course, on both the left and the right, who pointed to the expense of colonies and the limited returns they so frequently produced. The great Bismarck himself had never been much interested in colonies (or in a big navy to protect them). As he said in 1888 to an explorer who was trying to interest him in Africa: "'My map of Africa lies here in Europe. Here lies Russia, and" – pointing to the left – "here lies France, and we are right in the middle; this is my map of Africa.'"[34] His successor, Caprivi, took much the same attitude: 'The less Africa the better for us!'[35]

While Bülow had not initially been an enthusiast for colonies, he rapidly came round to include them as part of his vision. In his speech to the Reichstag in December 1899, he threw out a challenge: 'We cannot permit any foreign power, any foreign Jupiter, to tell us: "What is to be done? The world is already partitioned."' He added an ominous prophecy: 'In the coming century, Germany will either be the hammer or the anvil.'[36] A tricky question was where these colonies were to come from since so much of the world was already divided up among other powers. The decaying Ottoman Empire was one possibility and so Germany started to look into building railways and lending money to the Ottoman government. In 1898 the Kaiser made an extended visit to the Middle East and, carried away by the moment, gave a dramatic speech in Damascus: 'May the Sultan and his 300 million Muslim subjects scattered across the earth, who venerate him as their Caliph, be assured that the German Kaiser will be their friend for all time.'[37] China, another declining empire, also looked promising and the seizure of the port of Tsingtao (Qingdao) at Kiachow (Jiaozhou) Bay and other concessions in the Shantung peninsula appeared a good first step. There was also a bizarre attempt by German colonial enthusiasts, acting with the approval of Tirpitz, to secretly buy up land in one of the Danish Virgin Islands in the Caribbean until Germans held a majority share. At this point the German government was to step in and buy the whole island from Denmark for a naval base. Wilhelm fortunately opposed the plan, which would have embroiled Germany in a completely unnecessary dispute with the United States and quite probably Britain as well.[38]

There was enough German activity and German rhetoric, however, to alarm a British government and a British public already inclined to look at Germany with suspicion. Moreover, in Germany, both in government circles and among the general public there was a growing propensity to identify Britain, often openly, as the main obstacle to Germany's *Weltpolitik*. Student notes taken at Treitschke's lectures show him attacking Britain repeatedly. Why, he asked in the 1890s, did Germany 'have to throw itself at Grandma's head in such an undignified way, since in England even every little baby is determined to deceive us'. (Not surprisingly, a visit Treitschke made to England only served to confirm his views: London, he said, was 'like the dream of a drunken devil'.[39]) In 1900 the ambassador of Austria-Hungary in Berlin sent a long and perceptive memorandum to Vienna in which he noted that the leading German statesmen were looking ahead to the time, no doubt many years hence, when their country would succeed Britain as the world's leading power and remarked on the 'universally dominant anglophobia' in Germany.[40] Wilhelm also expected the future to see the rise of Germany and the decline of Britain. As he said in a speech in Hamburg in 1899, 'Old empires pass away and new ones are in the process of being formed.'

His attitude to Britain, though, like his relations with the British half of his family, was much more ambivalent than that of many of his subjects. His mother had unwisely held up everything British as a model and he understandably reacted badly. She wanted him to be an English gentleman; he became a Prussian officer. She was liberal; he was conservative. He had come to hate his mother – and indeed treated her badly after his father died – but some of his happiest childhood memories were of visiting Britain with his parents. He had played with his cousins at Osborne on the Isle of Wight and had visited British naval shipyards. He had often climbed aboard Nelson's flagship the *Victory* and once helped to fire the guns on the *St Vincent*, named after Nelson's great contemporary. When Queen Victoria made him an honorary admiral of the British navy shortly after his accession, Wilhelm was overjoyed. 'Fancy wearing the same uniform as St Vincent and Nelson. It is enough to make me quite giddy.'[41] He sent his grandmother a portrait of himself in his new uniform which he then wore on all possible occasions, including, it is said, to a performance of *The Flying Dutchman*.[42] (He also took his honorary rank as an invitation to give the British much unwanted advice about their navy.)

As an adult he complained repeatedly about 'the damned family' in Britain but he nevertheless deeply loved his grandmother Queen Victoria. Indeed, she was one of the few people in the world he would listen to. He resented what he saw as British arrogance and condescension but could still say to Theodore Roosevelt in 1911: 'I ADORE England.'[43] Daisy Cornwallis-West, who had become the Princess of Pless, thought that his love and admiration for Britain were genuine and that his frequent criticisms were like those of a family member who felt he was misunderstood:

That was the real grievance. The Emperor felt that he was never properly understood or appreciated by either Queen Victoria, King Edward, King George or the British people. Feeling his own sincerity and believing in himself, he sought to force his personality on us. As an actor of ability in a favorite part will sometimes endeavor to win by charm or subtlety, so the Emperor too often tried to dominate British public opinion by acts which antagonized us – or worse still – merely bored or amused us.[44]

That was certainly the case when Wilhelm took up yacht racing at Cowes with his usual enthusiasm. The British were at first inclined to be flattered when the Kaiser became a member of the Royal Yacht Club (proposed by his uncle Edward), bought a yacht and appeared each summer in the early 1890s for the annual regatta. Queen Victoria, who had to put him up with his entourage at Osborne, remarked to no avail that 'these annual visits are not quite desirable'.[45] Wilhelm was unfortunately a poor sport; he complained frequently about the rules and suggested that the handicapping was unfair to his yacht, the *Meteor*. His uncle complained that Wilhelm thought he was the 'Boss of Cowes' and apparently said to friends in 1895: 'The regatta at Cowes was once a pleasant holiday for me, but now that the Kaiser has taken command there, it is nothing but a nuisance.'[46] And there were other incidents to spoil the summer days: Salisbury apparently not getting a message to come to Wilhelm's gold-plated steam yacht, the *Hohenzollern*, for an important discussion, or Wilhelm insisting that he and Prince Edward continue their race even though it made them late for dinner with the queen.

The Kaiser's relations with his uncle were particularly difficult. Wilhelm may have resented the fact that Edward, 'fat old Wales', was charming, confident and widely liked. Wilhelm's natural prudishness, no doubt fanned by his wife, Dona, was also offended by his uncle's predilection for beautiful women and raffish friends and he cannot have endeared himself by sending the prince an admonishing letter while the older man was involved in a particularly tricky scandal. In his wilder moments, he took to referring to his uncle as a Satan, 'an old peacock', 'the arch-intriguer and mischief-maker in Europe'.[47] On Edward's side, there was the failure of the older, more assured man to understand the complicated younger one whose bluster hid a sense of insecurity. Edward and his Danish wife Alexandra, who had never forgiven Prussia for seizing Schleswig-Holstein from Denmark, saw Wilhelm as the epitome of Prussian militarism. 'Willy is a bully,' he once said, 'and most bullies, when tackled, are cowards.'[48] At his last meeting with Wilhelm in 1909, Edward, now king, wrote, not entirely accurately: 'I know the German Emperor hates me and never loses an opportunity of saying so behind my back, while I have always been so kind and nice to him.'[49] Theodore Roosevelt felt that Wilhelm's emotions were more complicated, that he had 'a real affection and respect for King Edward and also a very active and jealous dislike for him, first one feeling and then the other coming uppermost in his mind and therefore in his conversation'.[50]

Trouble between the two probably started when Wilhelm's father was dying and Edward arrived to support his beloved sister, Crown Princess Victoria. Edward's remarks such as 'William the Great needs to learn that he is living at the end of the nineteenth century and not in the Middle Ages' may well have gotten back to the Kaiser. Two months after his accession, Wilhelm made it clear that he would not meet his uncle in Vienna although they had separately planned to be there at the same time. Edward was obliged to leave before his nephew's arrival. Bismarck tried to explain away the incident to the British by blaming Edward's attitude to Wilhelm: 'The prince treated him as an uncle treats a nephew, instead of recognizing that he was an Emperor who, though young, had still been of age for some time.' Salisbury thought the Kaiser must be a 'little off his head'. Queen Victoria was furious when she wrote to her Prime Minister: 'this is really too *vulgar* and too absurd as well as untrue almost *to be believed*. We have always been very intimate with our grandson and nephew and to pretend that he is to be treated *in private as well* as in public as "His Imperial Majesty" is *perfect madness!*'[51] She hoped, she told Salisbury, that the relations between Germany and Britain would not be damaged: 'The Queen quite agrees that that should not be affected (if possible) by these miserable personal quarrels; but the Queen very much fears that with such a hot-headed, conceited, and wrong-headed young man, devoid of all feeling, this may at ANY moment become impossible.'[52]

If both countries had been constitutional monarchies, family quarrels would have ruffled the waters for a moment and produced much gossip but caused no lasting damage. The problem in this case was that the German ruler did have considerable powers and was prepared to use them to achieve his ends of making Germany a world power. And that meant, in the mind of Wilhelm himself, and many of those around him, having a blue-water navy, capable of projecting German power on the high seas, to protect German trade and investment and, importantly, German colonies, both the existing ones and the ones to come. In 1896 Wilhelm, in a speech which received considerable publicity, had asked the German people 'to help me bind fast this greater German empire to our own empire at home'.[53] Such a view was not particular to Germany; it was coming to be widely accepted in this period that naval power was a key component of world power. How otherwise had Britain – or the Netherlands or France, for that matter – built and maintained their great empires?

Sometimes it takes one person to put into words what is intuitively already suspected; the role of the sea found its great theorist in the little-known commander of the Naval College in the United States, not yet itself a great naval power. In 1890 Captain Alfred Mahan published his classic work, *The Influence of Sea Power upon History*. He was fifty at the time, a trim, lanky man who had never much liked going to sea. In many ways, he was the opposite of the rip-roaring sailor. He was taciturn, unsociable, reserved, and prudish. (He refused to let his daughters read Zola's novels.) He was also exceptionally high-minded; he would not let his children use government pencils.[54]

He first got the idea which would make him famous when he was reading Roman history and realised how different things might have been if Hannibal had invaded by sea rather than by land over the Alps, and, crucially, had been able to get support from Carthage by water. 'Control of the sea', Mahan believed, 'was an historic factor which had never been systematically appreciated or expounded.'[55] And expound it, he did. In his books, he went back into history to argue that whether it was the Anglo-Dutch wars of the seventeenth century or the Seven Years War between Britain and France in the eighteenth, sea power was almost always the deciding factor. And it ensured prosperity in peace as well as victory in war. 'In these three things', Mahan wrote, 'production, with the necessity of exchanging products, shipping, whereby the exchange is carried on, and colonies, which facilitate and enlarge the operations of shipping and tend to protect it by multiplying points of safety is to be found the key to much of the history, as well as of the policy, of nations bordering upon the sea.'[56] A strong navy protected the key highways for trade and communication across the oceans, and, equally importantly, enabled the seizing and holding of colonies. Its battle fleets could serve as a deterrent, especially if they were situated in key strategic locations. 'The fleet in being', as Mahan and others called it, did not necessarily have to fight; it could be used to put pressure on a hostile power in peacetime and make that power think twice before risking its own fleet, even if it were bigger.[57] In war, though, it was the duty of the battle fleet or fleets to destroy the enemy in a decisive battle.

Mahan and what came to be called in English the navalists did not have it all their own way. There was another school of thought about naval strategy, which initially had the support of Wilhelm's own Naval Cabinet, which argued that the way to weaken the enemy and win wars was to attack his commerce. In the increasingly interdependent world of the late nineteenth century, few countries could survive long, much less wage war, without seaborne trade. So, instead of investing in large and expensive battleships, it made much more sense to build fast cruisers and torpedo boats and the new submarines to attack enemy merchant shipping. Indeed, the big battleships with their heavy armour plating and armaments also made nice targets for smaller, faster boats, mines, and submarines. The *guerre de course*, as the French called it, was what the British had used to considerable effect in the Elizabethan age when the government licensed what were essentially pirates to seize the Spanish galleons with their gold and silver from the New World. And when the Great War finally came, that indeed proved to be one of the most effective weapons that Germany used against the Allies: submarine warfare, carried out by an arm of the German navy that had been despised and neglected in peacetime came close to choking off the supplies which Britain needed to carry on the war.

Mahan's theories, though, had the great advantages of apparently being proved by history and appealing to national pride. A torpedo boat simply did not compare with a great battleship and commerce-raiding was not the high drama of war in the way in which the clash of mighty ships was. His writings were hugely influential in the United States, where they spurred on the ambition of Roosevelt and others for American colonies and navies, in Britain, where they seemed to explain British world dominance, and in Germany. The Kaiser fell on *The Influence of Sea Power upon History*; 'I am just now not reading but devouring Captain Mahan's book and am trying to learn it by heart,' he wrote to a friend in 1894. With government support, the book was translated into German and serialised in magazines, and copies were placed on every German naval vessel. Up to that point, Germany's main military strength had been its army while its navy had been small and mainly performing as a coast guard. Wilhelm now became fixated on the idea that Germany needed a strong navy for the high seas, with big battleships. In a crisis between Greece and the Ottoman Empire over Crete in 1897, the British with their naval power were able to end the dispute while Germany sat on the sidelines. 'Here again', Wilhelm complained, 'one can see how much Germany suffers for lack of a *strong fleet*.'[58] Since he already had supreme command of the navy under the German constitution and had made several changes to its organisation to bring its different departments increasingly under his direct control, the Kaiser was in a position to do something about remedying that, provided, of course, that he could get the necessary funds from the Reichstag.

Mahan provided the intellectual underpinning but there was something else at work in Wilhelm's longing for a big navy. He had seen and admired the British navy close up, from the time he was a child. The effect on him had been much like the first sight of a motor car on Toad in *Wind in the Willows*: 'Glorious, stirring sight!' As a young man he had gone to represent his family at Queen Victoria's Golden Jubilee in 1887 and the sight of the great naval review had further fuelled his passion for navies. In 1904, when his uncle, now Edward VII, paid a visit to the German naval base at Kiel, the Kaiser toasted him at a dinner of the Kiel Yacht Club (modelled on the one at Cowes): 'When as a little boy, I was allowed to visit Portsmouth and Plymouth hand in hand with kind aunts and friendly admirals, I admired the proud English ships in those two superb harbours. Then there awoke in me the wish to build ships like these someday, and when I was grown up to possess as fine a navy as the English.' Wilhelm, almost in tears at his own eloquence, moved three cheers for the king. Edward's reply was restrained; 'My dear Willy, you have always been so very nice and friendly with me that I find it difficult to express my gratitude for all your kindness in a way that would really do you justice.' Bülow forbade the representative of a prominent news agency to wire the Kaiser's effusions to Berlin: 'I composed, as often before on such occasions, another – equally friendly, but more sober – Imperial address …' His master was rather hurt – 'You've left out the best bits' – but Bülow was firm: 'If you describe our fleet, constructed with such heavy cost, sometimes with danger, as the outcome of your own personal inclinations and juvenile memories, it will not be easy to obtain further millions for naval construction from the Reichstag.' The Kaiser got his point: '*Ach*, that damned Reichstag.'[59]

The 'damned Reichstag' was indeed a problem. It was not showing much enthusiasm for a much bigger navy. The socialists, whose number was growing, liberals and moderates of various stripes, and even some conservatives, were not ready to approve the necessary funding, especially when Wilhelm and his Naval Cabinet could not enunciate a clear case for why such an expense was needed. In 1895 when the Kaiser asked for thirty-six cruisers, the Reichstag gave him four; in 1896 it rejected all his demands. At the beginning of 1897, the Reichstag again challenged the Kaiser's naval estimates. At that point he turned to the man who, he hoped, would get him his navy.

Alfred Tirpitz was on the other side of the world, commanding Germany's East Asian Squadron and, among other things, scouting for a promising harbour on the north China coast. (He chose Kiachow Bay, which Germany duly seized that autumn.) Although he was initially reluctant to give up his command and come back to Germany, Tirpitz bowed to the Kaiser's wishes and became the Secretary of State for the Navy. (He was to hold the office for eighteen years.) It was another crucial step towards 1914: it gave the Kaiser the navy he wanted and altered Germany's naval strategy. In so doing, it set Germany on a collision course with Britain.

In 1897, Tirpitz was forty-eight years old, a decade older than Wilhelm. Unlike many of those in the Kaiser's immediate circle, he was not noble but came from the educated professional classes. His father was a mildly liberal lawyer who became a judge and his mother, a doctor's daughter. Tirpitz grew up in the east of Prussia in what is now a part of Poland and absorbed the love of Prussia and the strong sense of duty to king and country that was typical of the time and the milieu.

His idol then and for the rest of his life was Frederick the Great and he read and re-read Thomas Carlyle's biography. In his early life, however, the future admiral did not exhibit much promise. He was an indifferent student, showing an aptitude mainly for fighting in the streets. Without the right connections he was unlikely to fare well in the army so, perhaps by default, he chose the navy, which was more open to talent, as a career.

The Prussian navy he joined in 1865 was small and many of its ships were antiquated. It had to rely on foreign shipyards for repairs. The army had the glorious past, the glamour and the bulk of the resources for Prussia's defence. As Prussia drew the other German states into its orbit to create Germany, the navy played an insignificant role. Yet it gradually expanded and modernised and Tirpitz steadily ascended the ranks of officers, making his mark as someone who could both master the technical details and think about the wider strategic issues. In 1888 he was appointed captain in command of an armoured cruiser, an impressive promotion for one still so young. By 1892 he was chief of staff for the Naval Command in Berlin. He came to have the nickname 'The Master' as well as 'The Eternal' (for surviving where others did not).

Tirpitz always found time to read widely, although history was his favourite subject. He attended Treitschke's lectures in Berlin and absorbed his ideas about the inevitable rise of Germany – and the equally inevitable hostility of Britain. He also read Mahan and took firmly on board the notions about the importance of sea power and the need for countries to possess battle fleets.[60] 'It is characteristic of battle on the open sea', he told his superior officer in 1877, 'that its sole goal is the annihilation of the enemy. Land battle offers other tactical possibilities, such as taking terrain, which do not exist in war at sea. Only annihilation can be accounted a success at sea.'[61] In 1894 he wrote a major memorandum, one section of which, 'The Natural Purpose of a Fleet is the Strategic Offensive', became famous. In it he dismissed the claims of those who argued for a defensive role for navies, including the building of costal defences, and asserted that the command of the sea 'will be decided in the main by battle as in all ages'. Furthermore he became convinced that Germany was engaged in a life-or-death struggle for its place in the sun. The race was on for the remaining unclaimed pieces of the globe, and those nations which did not get their share would enter the twentieth century under a crippling handicap.[62]

Tirpitz was an imposing figure with his sharp eyes, broad forehead, large nose and a massive beard which ended in two sharp prongs. 'Of all the advisers of William II', said Beyens, 'there was no one who gave such an impression of strength and authority.'[63] Curiously, Tirpitz had no particular love for the sea and preferred to spend his long summer holidays working out his plans in his house in the Black Forest. He was also more emotional than he appeared. While he could be ruthless and determined in his battles with his colleagues and the politicians, occasionally the pressures proved too much: his secretary would sometimes find him weeping at his desk at the end of the day.[64] His memoirs and other writings are full of self-justification and complaints about anyone who ever opposed him.

Tirpitz was, said someone who knew him well, 'a very energetic character. He has too big a head of steam not to be a leader. He is ambitious, not choosy about his means, of a sanguine disposition. High as the heavens in his own joys but never relaxing in his creative activity, no matter how crushed he may appear ...'[65] His son later said of him that his motto was: 'If man does not have the courage to do something he must *want* to have it.'[66] He could have been equally successful in business, for he understood about organisation, management and team building. A senior officer gave a more ambivalent assessment as Tirpitz was about to become the Naval Secretary. 'His otherwise successful performance in responsible posts has shown a tendency to look at matters one-sidedly, and devote his whole energies to the achievement of some particular end without paying enough attention to the general requirements of the service, with the result that his success has been achieved at the expense of other objectives.'[67] The same might be said of Germany's international policy in the years before 1914.

When Tirpitz took office under the Kaiser, the two men had already met on several occasions. The first seems to have been in 1887, when Tirpitz was part of the entourage accompanying the young Prince Wilhelm to Queen Victoria's Golden Jubilee. The two apparently had long talks. The key early meeting, though, was in Kiel on the Baltic in 1891, when, after an inconclusive general discussion about the future of the navy, the Kaiser asked Tirpitz for his opinion. 'So', said Tirpitz in his memoirs, 'I described how I conceived the development of the navy, and as I had been continually jotting down my ideas on the subject, I was able to give a complete picture without any difficulty.'[68]

Tirpitz arrived in Berlin in June 1897 and almost immediately had a long audience with the Kaiser. The new Secretary of the Navy was scathing about the existing ideas on the German navy (including the Kaiser's own). What was needed was a strategy of attack and not the commerce-raiding or defensive measures that his predecessor and others had advocated, and that meant more big armoured battleships and armoured cruisers and far fewer of the fast and lightly armoured cruisers and torpedo boats that had been favoured up to this point. Such a navy would stir pride among Germans and – this was music to both the Kaiser's ears and Bülow's – help to create a new national unity. And, as Tirpitz made clear, Germany's chief enemy at sea could only be Britain.

Unlike his compatriots such as Treitschke, Tirpitz did not hate Britain. Indeed, he sent his daughters there to a well-known private school, Cheltenham Ladies College. The whole family spoke excellent English and were devoted to their English governess. He was quite simply a Social Darwinist with a deterministic view of history as a series of struggles for survival. Germany needed to expand; Britain as the dominant power was bound to want to stop that. So struggle there would be; economic, certainly, but most probably military as well until Britain conceded that it could not carry on in opposition to Germany.

The central aim of a new naval bill, he told the Kaiser in that first meeting, must be 'the strengthening of our political might [and] importance against England'. Germany could not take on Britain everywhere around the world but what it could do was pose a serious threat to the home islands from German bases in the North Sea. Providentially, under the Anglo-German Agreement of 1890 Germany had traded its rights in Zanzibar for the rocky island of Heligoland, which could provide useful in guarding the approaches to the German ports on the North Sea. So if Britain, as Tirpitz thought likely, tried to attack the German coast or the German navy itself in wartime, its battle fleet would suffer significant losses. His strategy remained fixed over the years: to destroy the British fleet a hundred miles west of Heligoland. And Germany had the further advantage of being able to concentrate its fleet while Britain had to disperse its own around the world. 'Since even English naval officers, admiralty etc. fully know this,' he told the

Kaiser, 'then even politically it comes to a battleship war between Heligoland and the Thames.'[69] He does not seem to have considered seriously the possibility that the British navy would choose to avoid a full-scale battle; that instead it would blockade Germany from a distance to prevent supplies from coming in by sea; or that it would bottle up the German navy by closing the Straits of Dover and the passages between Norway and Scotland rather than attempt an attack on the coast or the German navy, all of which happened in the Great War.[70] Even more importantly, Tirpitz was also wrong about how Britain would react to his naval building programme.

In the next few years, Tirpitz laid out his notorious risk theory to the Kaiser and Bülow and their closest colleagues. It was both simple and audacious. His aim was to put Britain in a position where the cost of attacking Germany at sea would be too high. Britain had the biggest navy in the world and aimed to keep it superior in strength to any two other navies: the two-power standard, as it was known. Germany would not try to match that; rather it would build a navy strong enough that Britain would not dare to take it on because in so doing it would run the risk of suffering such damage that it would be left seriously weakened in the face of its other enemies.

If Britain did decide to wage a naval war with Germany, according to Tirpitz, it would be setting itself up for its own decline because, whether it won or lost, it would suffer losses. That would embolden its other enemies, most likely France and Russia, which also had strong navies, to attack the now weakened Britain. As the preamble to Tirpitz's second naval bill of 1899 put it: 'It is not necessary that the battle fleet at home is equal to that of the greatest naval power. In general this naval power would not be in a position to concentrate its entire naval forces against us. Even if it succeeds in encountering us with a superior force, the destruction of the German fleet would so much damage the enemy that his own position as a world power would be brought into question.'[71]

It says something about Tirpitz's narrow focus that he seems to have expected that the British would not notice this very clear hint that they were in Germany's sights.

And he was not alone. His colleagues, such as Bülow, and the Kaiser counted on time to build up their navy to the point that it was strong enough to carry out the strategy. Germany would have to be careful in this 'danger zone' while it was still much weaker than Britain not to alarm its rival. As Bülow put it, 'in view of our naval inferiority, we must operate so carefully, like the caterpillar before it has grown into a butterfly'. In twenty years, when his navy was finally ready, the Kaiser said to the French ambassador, 'I shall speak another language.'[72] If they were not careful, however, the British might be tempted to do something pre-emptive. What particularly weighed on the minds of the German decision-makers was the fear of another Copenhagen – the pre-emptive attack in 1807 when the British navy bombarded the Danish capital and seized much of the Danish fleet in order to prevent it from being used to support Napoleon.[73]

In their more optimistic moments, though, Tirpitz, the Kaiser and their colleagues hoped that they might get the upper hand over Britain without war. The risk strategy was not unlike nuclear deterrence during the Cold War, mutually assured destruction as it was known. What prevented the Soviet Union and the United States from attacking the other with their long-range nuclear weapons was the knowledge that enough of the enemy's nuclear arsenal would survive, whether in reinforced silos on land, long-range bombers or submarines, for it to inflict unacceptable damage in retaliation. Indeed, Tirpitz sometimes behaved and spoke as though he never really intended Germany's battle fleet to be used; during the several European crises before 1914 when there was talk of war which might involve Britain and Germany, he invariably said that the navy was not yet ready. Rather he seems to have hoped it could achieve the goal of forcing Britain to come to terms simply by being in existence.

Once Germany had achieved that position of strength where its navy could pose the unpalatable prospect of future decline to Britain, the British would surely realise that they had no alternative but to accept the inevitable and come to a firm understanding with Germany, perhaps even joining the Triple Alliance. For that reason both Tirpitz and Bülow were cool on the alliance offered by Chamberlain at the end of the 1890s. It was too soon. Writing after the Great War (in an attempt to show that Germany had not been responsible for its outbreak), Tirpitz declared: 'Regarding the way of thinking of the English people as it prevailed at the turn of the century, I did not believe in the *fata morgana* of a benevolent understanding by which Joseph Chamberlain may have lured perhaps himself but certainly some Germans in bound-less dreams. A treaty that was concluded according to the English desire to rule would never have been in accordance with the German necessi-ties. For this, equality would have been the precondition.'[74]

Within weeks of his arrival back in Berlin in the summer of 1897, Tirpitz had drafted a completely new naval bill which focussed on what were often called ships of the line or capital ships – those battleships and heavy cruisers that would take the crucial part in an all-out sea battle. Eleven battleships were to be built in the next seven years and the German navy was to increase in the long run to sixty ships of the line. Significantly, the law both fixed the strength of the navy and stipu-lated that classes of ships should automatically be replaced when they became obsolete, a timetable also defined in the bill. This provided what Tirpitz called the 'Iron Budget'. As he promised the Kaiser, he intended to remove 'the disturbing influence of the Reichstag upon your Maj-esty's intentions concerning the development of the Navy'.[75] In this and subsequent naval bills, as Tirpitz said in his memoirs, 'The *Reichstag* surrendered the possibility of refusing money for the new types of vessels, which were increasing in size and cost, unless it was prepared to bring upon itself the reproach of building inferior ships.'[76]

Tirpitz's first naval bill was a terrific gamble because, while he had the enthusiastic support of the Kaiser and of Bülow, it was not at all clear that the Reichstag would fall in line. He was, as it turned out, a master of lobbying and public relations. One of his first acts as Secretary of the Navy was to set up a 'Section for News and General Parliamen-tary Affairs' which became a highly effective tool for mobilising public opinion. In those months while he was preparing the naval bill, and over the next decades, his office poured out a flood of memoranda, statements, books, photographs and films. It staged special events, for example sending a hundred torpedo boats along the Rhine in 1900, and the launches of battleships were to become increasingly elaborate. In the run-up to the voting on the naval bill in March 1898, Naval Office representatives fanned out across Germany to speak to key opinion makers whether in business or universities. The Office organised 173 lectures, printed 140,000 pamphlets and distributed copies of Mahan's classic work on sea power. Journalists were given special tours of naval ships and particular attention was paid to propaganda in the schools.

Public bodies such as the Colonial League with its 20,000 members or the Pan-German League were asked to help the cause and did so with enthusiasm, distributing thousands of pamphlets.[77] This was not simply a case of manipulation from above; the idea of the navy touched a chord with German nationalists of all classes. It had perhaps a particular appeal to the growing middle classes, where it was seen as more liberal and more open as a career for their children than the army. And although the Navy League was founded in 1898 as an elite organisation by a group of industrialists, by 1914 it was going to have over a million members associated with it.

Tirpitz threw himself into the work. He arranged for a group of leading industrialists and businessmen to issue a resolution in support of the naval bill and even managed to obtain a grudging promise of support from Bismarck. He visited Germany's other rulers; the Grand Duke of Baden for one was completely charmed: 'such an excellent personality', he wrote to the German Chancellor, Caprivi, 'a man whose character and experience are equally splendid'.[78] In Berlin, Tirpitz spent hours chatting genially with selected Reichstag members in his office.

When the Reichstag was in session again in the autumn, the Kaiser, Tirpitz, and Bülow all addressed it, cooing like turtle doves. The bill was merely a defensive measure, said Wilhelm. 'A policy of adventure is far from our minds,' added Bülow (although it was in this speech he also mentioned Germany's place in the sun). 'Our fleet has the character of a protective fleet,' Tirpitz claimed. 'It changes its character not one bit as a result of this law.' His bill was going to make the Reichstag's work much easier over the next years by getting rid of the 'limitless fleet-plans' of the past.[79] On 26 March 1898, the First Navy Law passed easily by 212 votes to 139. The Kaiser was ecstatic: 'Truly a powerful man!' Among other things, Wilhelm revelled in being free of the need to get approval from the Reichstag – and took the credit for himself. As he boasted to the controller of his household in 1907, when yet another Navy Law was passed: 'He absolutely fooled the members of the Reichstag. They had not the smallest idea, he added, when they passed it, what its consequences would be, for the law really meant that anything he wanted would have to be granted.' It was, he went on, 'like a cork-screw with which I can open the bottle any moment I like. Even if the froth spurts to the ceiling, the dogs will have to pay until they are black in the face. I have now got them in the hollow of my hand, and no power in the world will stop me from drinking the bottle dry.'[80]

Tirpitz immediately started work on his next steps. As early as November 1898 he proposed increasing the tempo for building capital ships from the present three per year. A year later, at an audience in September 1899, he told the Kaiser that more ships were an 'absolute necessity for Germany, without which she will encounter ruin'. Of the four great powers in the world – which he counted as Russia, Germany, the United States and Britain – the last two could be reached only by sea. Therefore sea power was essential. And he reminded the Kaiser about the eternal struggle for power. 'Salisbury's speech: the great states become greater and stronger, the small smaller and weaker is also my view.' Germany must catch up. 'Naval power is essential if Germany doesn't want to go under.' He wanted a new naval bill, before the expiry of the first in 1903, to double the fleet. Germany would then have forty-five ships of the line. True, Britain would have more. 'But', he went on, 'also against England we undoubtedly have good chances through geographical position, military system, torpedo boats, tactical training, planned organizational development, and leadership united by the monarch. Apart from our by no means hopeless conditions of fighting, England will have lost [any] inclination to attack us and will as a result concede to your Majesty sufficient naval presence … for the conduct of a grand policy overseas.'[81]

The Kaiser not only agreed completely, he rushed off and announced that there would be a second naval bill at a speech in Hamburg. Tirpitz had to present the bill earlier than he had planned but in fact the timing turned out to be good. The outbreak of the Boer War in October 1899 and the British seizure of steamers off southern Africa at the end of the year inflamed German opinion. The Second Navy Law passed in June 1900 and duly doubled the size of the German navy. Later that year the grateful Kaiser promoted Tirpitz to the rank of vice admiral and expunged his middle-class background by ennobling him and his family. The future looked clear for Germany to continue through the 'danger zone' towards its rightful position in the world.

Yet to achieve this triumph, the German government was going to pay a high price. It had bought the support of the important agrarian interests in the German Conservative Party, the DKP, by promising a tariff to keep out cheap Russian grain and in 1902, it duly brought in a protective measure. The loss of an important market further antagonised the Russians, already annoyed by Germany's seizure of Kiachow Bay in China and by German moves into the Ottoman Empire. German public opinion against Britain and in favour of a big navy had been useful but once stirred up it was not easy to calm it down again. Most importantly of all the British, both decision-makers and the public, had started to take notice. 'If they could just sit still in Germany', Hatzfeldt, the German ambassador in London, complained, 'then the time would come soon when fried pigeons would fly into our mouths. But these continuous hysterical up- and down-turns of Wilhelm II and the adventurous navy policy of Mr von Tirpitz will lure us on to destruction.'[82]

Tirpitz made three crucial assumptions: that the British would not notice that Germany was developing a big navy; that Britain would not and could not respond by outbuilding Germany (among other things, Tirpitz assumed that the British could not afford a big increase in their naval budget); and that, while being pressured into making friends with Germany, Britain would not decide to look for friends elsewhere. He was wrong about all three.

CHAPTER 5

Dreadnought:
The Anglo-German
Naval Rivalry

In August 1902 another great naval review took place at Spithead in the sheltered waters between Britain's great south coast port of Portsmouth and the Isle of Wight, this time to celebrate the coronation of Edward VII. Because he had suddenly come down with appendicitis earlier in the summer, the coronation itself and all festivities surrounding it had been postponed. As a result most of the ships from foreign navies (except those of Britain's new ally Japan) as well as those from the overseas squadrons of the British navy had been obliged to leave. The resulting smaller review was, nevertheless, *The Times* said proudly, a potent display of Britain's naval might. The ships displayed at Spithead were all in active service and all from the fleets already in place to guard Britain's home waters. 'The display may be less magnificent than the wonderful manifestation of our sea-power witnessed in the same waters five years ago. But it will demonstrate no less plainly what that power is, to those who remember that we have a larger number of ships in commission on foreign stations now than we had then, and that we have not moved a single ship from Reserve.' 'Some of our rivals', *The Times* warned, 'have worked with feverish activity in the interval, and they are steadily increasing their efforts.' They should know that Britain

5. In the years before 1914 European countries engaged in an increasingly intense and expensive arms race on land and at sea. New and improved technologies brought faster and stronger battleships including the mighty dreadnoughts. Here Wilhelm II, his uncle Edward VII and President Emile Loubet play their high stakes power while the rising powers of Japan and the United States start to join in.

remained vigilant and on guard, and prepared to spend whatever funds were necessary to maintain its sovereignty of the seas.[1]

Although *The Times* did not name Britain's rivals, there can have been little doubt in its readers' minds that Germany was rapidly coming to take the foremost place among them. While the British still counted France and Russia as potential enemies, opinion, among both the ruling elites and the general public, was increasingly worried about their neighbour on the North Sea. In 1896 a best-selling pamphlet, 'Made in Germany', by the journalist E. E. Williams painted an ominous picture: 'A gigantic commercial State is arising to menace our prosperity, and contend with us for the trade of the world.'[2] Look around your own houses, he urged his readers. 'The toys, and the dolls, and the fairy books which your children maltreat in the nursery are made in Germany: nay, the material of your favourite (patriotic) newspaper had the same birth-place as like as not.' From the china ornaments to the poker for the fire, most of the furnishings were probably made in Germany. And it got worse still: 'At midnight your wife comes home from an opera which was made in Germany, has been here enacted by singers and conductor and players made in Germany, with the aid of instruments and sheets of music made in Germany.'[3]

A new factor was making itself felt in Europe's politics and its inter-national relations: public opinion, which was to put unprecedented pressures on Europe's leaders and limit their freedom of action. As a result of the spread of democracy and the new mass communications as well as greatly increased literacy, publics were not only better informed but also felt more connected to each other and to their nations. (We face our own revolution in the way we gain information and relate to the world with the internet and the growth of social media.) In the world before 1914, railways, telegraph lines and then telephones and radios transmitted domestic and international news at unprecedented speed. The foreign correspondent became a respectable professional and, increasingly, newspapers preferred to use their own nationals rather than rely on locals. Russians, Americans, Germans or Britons could read about their nation's most recent disasters or triumphs at their breakfast tables – and develop their own views which they could make known to their governments. Some, especially in the old ruling elites, deplored the change. 'Small, closed circles of courtly and diplomatic individuals' no longer managed international relations, said the head of the German Foreign Office's press section. 'The public opinion of the nations has acquired a degree of influence on political decisions previ-ously unimaginable.'[4] The fact that there was a German press bureau showed how governments understood that, for their part, they needed to manipulate and use public opinion at home and abroad by control-ling the information they fed journalists, placing pressure on newspaper proprietors to take a favourable line or by outright bribery. The German government tried to buy support in the British press but since it could only afford to subsidise a small and unimportant paper its efforts served to do little but make the British even more suspicious of Germany.[5]

In 1897 Lord Northcliffe's mass circulation *Daily Mail* ran a series which urged its readers 'for the next ten years fix your eyes very hard on Germany'. The German menace, pride in Britain, appeals to patriotism, demands for a stronger navy, these were all to be common themes with the Northcliffe papers (which by 1908 included the *Daily Mirror* and the more elite *Observer* and *Times*)[6] and indeed with others such as the *Daily Express* and the left-wing *Clarion*. Their editors were not so much creating public opinion as telling the public what it wanted to hear but the effect of the press campaigns and the alarmist writings of men such as Williams was to stir up public emotions and elevate patriotism into jingoistic nationalism.[7] Salisbury complained that it was like having 'a huge lunatic asylum at one's back'.[8]

At the start of the twentieth century, relations between Britain and Germany were worse than they had been at any time since Germany appeared on the map of Europe. The failure of the talks between Chamberlain and the German ambassador in London, the public and private outbursts of the Kaiser, the well-reported anti-British and pro-Boer sentiment among the German public, even the silly controversy over whether Chamberlain had insulted the Prussian army, all left their residue of mistrust and resentments in Britain as well as in Germany. Valentine Chirol, who had been *The Times*' correspondent in Berlin until 1896, wrote to a friend at the start of 1900: 'Germany is, in my opinion, more fundamentally hostile than either France or Russia, but she is not ready yet … She looks upon us as upon an artichoke to be pulled to pieces leaf by leaf.'[9] Moreover, British statesmen suspected, with some reason, that Berlin would be happy to see Britain drawn into conflict with France and Russia – and might even do what it could to hurry matters along. In 1898, when France and Britain came close to a war over their competing African claims, Wilhelm claimed that he was like a bystander with a bucket of water at a fire, doing his best to calm things down. Thomas Sanderson, the Permanent Undersecretary at the Foreign Office, commented that the Kaiser was more like someone 'running about with a lucifer match and scratching it against powder barrels'.[10]

While some in Britain had worried as early as the 1890s about what a new powerful Germany meant for the balance of power at sea,[11] it was Tirpitz's Navy Laws of 1898 and 1900 that significantly increased British unease about Germany. Even though their underlying purpose was not yet clear, Lord Selborne, Tirpitz's British counterpart as First Lord of the Admiralty, was telling his colleagues in the Cabinet by the autumn of 1902: 'the German navy is very carefully built up from the point of view of a new war with us'.[12] In 1903, Erskine Childers, a respectable civil servant, wrote his only novel, a gripping story of espionage and adventure, to warn his fellow countrymen of the dangers of a German invasion. *The Riddle of the Sands* was an instant success and is still in print. (Childers joined the Irish rebels after the Great War and was shot by a military firing squad; his son became the President of Ireland in 1973.) Articles started to appear in the British press suggesting a preventive attack on the German fleet.

Thanks to its geography Britain had generally been able to regard the growth of powerful land forces on the Continent with equanimity. It could never do the same on the seas. The British navy was at once its shield, its means of projecting its strength and its lifeline to the wider world. Every schoolchild was taught how the navy had seen off the Spanish Armada (with some help from the weather and Spanish incompetence) in the sixteenth century and had helped to bring Napoleon down at the beginning of the nineteenth. With the navy, Britain had defeated the French in the worldwide struggle of the Seven Years War and gained control of an empire that stretched from India to Quebec. And it needed the navy to protect that empire and its huge informal network of trade and investment around the world.

It was a policy supported not just by the ruling elites but by much of the British public. The British across the political and social spectrum took great pride in their navy and in the two-power standard. At the 1902 coronation review, the sightseeing ships, more than a hundred of them, were chartered by groups that ranged from the travel agent Thomas Cook and Sons to the establishment Oxford and Cambridge Club to the Civil Service Co-Operative Society. When the navy put on a week-long show in London in 1909, complete with mock fights, fireworks and special children's programmes, it was estimated that there were nearly 4 million spectators.[13] Tirpitz, Wilhelm and their fellow enthusiasts for a big German navy which could challenge Britain's never understood how vitally important the Royal Navy was for the British and that failure of imagination was to cost them, and Europe, dearly.

'The Empire floats on the Royal Navy,' said Admiral Jacky Fisher,

and for once he was not exaggerating.[14] Britain's continuing prosperity
and the stability of British society, so many assumed, floated on it as
well. Britain's very success as the first industrialised power of the nineteenth century was also its Achilles heel. The continuing health of the
British economy depended on Britain's ability to obtain raw materials
from overseas and send its exports out. If Britain did not control the
seas, would it not always be at the mercy of those who did? Moreover,
by 1900 Britain relied on imports to feed its growing population; some
58 per cent of the calories the British consumed came from overseas and
there was simply no way, as the experience of the Second World War
was going to show, of making those up by increasing home
production.[15]

In 1890, long before Kaiser Wilhelm and Tirpitz set the new
German naval building programme underway, the United Services
Institute in London initiated a debate which highlighted another worry.
Was the Royal Navy up to the job of protecting British trade? Did it
have enough fast cruisers, for example, to patrol the world's most
important trading routes, or to scout out the enemy's fleets in wartime
and raid his commerce? By the mid 1890s a newly formed Navy League
was noisily demanding more spending on the navy.[16] In 1902 the *Daily
Mail*, the most successful of the new mass-circulation newspapers,
found cause for concern even in the great coronation naval review:

> To the casual eye this great fleet, as it lies peacefully at anchor in the
> historic harbour, makes the bravest of shows. But true wisdom
> demands that we must look beneath the surface and consider how
> far it is fit for the purpose for which it was designed. What cannot
> but strike the observer is that it is much weaker than the fleet
> assembled in 1897 for the late Queen's Jubilee. No doubt our squad-
> rons are stronger than they were at that date ... but there is also the
> fact that in the meantime a powerful navy has grown up in the
> North Sea which has to be considered in the balance of power.[17]

As Selborne, one of the more competent First Lords of the Admiralty in the period before the war, said: 'Our stakes are out of all
proportion to those of any other Power. To us defeat in a maritime war
would mean a disaster of almost unparalleled magnitude in history. It

might mean the destruction of our mercantile marine, the stoppage of our manufactures, scarcity of food, invasion, disruption of Empire.'[18]

And what would happen to society if the food supplies flowing in by ship were choked off? Shortages, perhaps even starvation, would, it was assumed, hit the poor first. In the two decades before 1914, many in the ruling classes, whether military or civilian, foresaw a grim picture of an embattled Britain with widespread riots, perhaps even revolution. Did they really think that the upper classes would be safe in wartime, an army general asked a meeting at the United Services Institute in the late 1890s? 'From the East End of London the masses would march to the West End, would sack our houses, would snatch the bread out of our children's mouths, and say, "If we are to starve, justice declares we should starve together."'[19] It would rapidly become impossible to wage war, so the Director of Naval Intelligence, Prince Louis of Battenberg (and grandfather of the Duke of Edinburgh) wrote in 1902: 'The panic of the inhabitants of the United Kingdom produced by the dislocation of seaborne trade in the early phases of the war may be sufficient to sweep away any Government bent on seeing the war out.'[20]

Famine, or the fear of it, increasingly cast its shadow over the navy's war plans and it seeped into the public consciousness as well.[21] By the end of the nineteenth century, influential groups and individuals were agitating for government action to protect and stockpile food supplies. In 1902 a cast which sounded like the Twelve Days of Christmas – with its 5 marquises, 7 generals, 9 dukes, 28 earls, 46 admirals and 106 Members of Parliament – came together to form the Association to Promote an Official Enquiry into our Food Supply in Time of War. (They succeeded in getting a Royal Commission which agreed that there was a problem but did not make any dramatic recommendations.)

Interestingly, the Association's members also included trade union leaders, perhaps in an attempt to co-opt an increasingly important, and problematic, set of organisations. Nobody questioned the steadfastness of the working classes, 'their patriotism, their courage, or their endurance', the Association's manifesto said; 'but with a population in constant hunger a position of great danger would arise, and if it were continued, a disaster to the country could neither be escaped nor long postponed'.[22] Of course, doubting the loyalty and reliability of the working classes was precisely what many of the British upper and middle classes were doing before 1914. Studies by the great Victorian social reformers such as Charles Booth had uncovered the appalling conditions in which many of the poor lived, and the consequences for their health, and, it was feared, for their attachment to their own society. Would the men of the lower classes fight to defend Britain? And could they? Although Britain did not have a conscript army, revelations about the number of volunteers who had been unable to meet the army's physical standards during the Boer War further raised worries in official circles about the manpower available to defend Britain in a major conflict.

There were other worrying signs that Britain was becoming a more divided society as time went on. The Irish question had flared up again and Irish nationalists were pushing for self-government, even independence. Trade unions were growing; by 1900 their membership was 2 million (and was to double again by 1914) and concentrated in areas that were crucial to the British economy such as mining or the docks. Strikes were longer and frequently violent. And with the broadening of the franchise, political power now seemed within the reach of the workers and their middle-class supporters. By the time the 1906 election was over, there was an official Labour Party with twenty-nine seats in the House of Commons. The popular novelist William Le Queux published a highly successful novel, *The Invasion of 1910*, which had Germany invading Britain while the socialists agitated for peace and mobs in the streets of London shouted 'stop the war'. The *Daily Mail* serialised the book and sent men out through London dressed in spiked helmets and Prussian-blue uniforms to carry placards with advertising. (At Northcliffe's insistence, Le Queux also obligingly changed the putative German invasion route to reach the maximum interested readership.)[23]

The government, both the Conservative and the Liberal one which took its place in late 1905, found itself in the awkward but familiar situation of balancing security needs with fiscal ones. Germany, it was generally agreed, was a growing threat and the navy must be strong enough to deal with this as well as the longer-standing threats from France and Russia. (The British army received about half of what the navy did from the defence budget.) Yet the advances in technology – stronger armour plating, better engines, bigger guns, for example – also were expensive. In the fifteen years between 1889 and 1904, the cost of battleships, the heavyweights among naval vessels, had doubled and that of the lighter, faster cruisers had gone up five times. In addition, its far-flung empire meant that Britain had to have forces stationed around the world. In the two decades before 1914, overall defence spending took up approximately 40 per cent of the British government expenditure, a higher proportion than in any other of the great powers, and British taxes per head were also significantly higher.[24]

At the same time government spending on social programmes was going up. Like their continental counterparts, the British government worried about domestic unrest and saw measures such as unemployment insurance or old-age pensions as a way of heading it off. And the new Liberal cabinet formed in 1906 contained radicals such as David Lloyd George for whom spending on social welfare was not just a wise precaution but a moral obligation. Could Britain's economy afford both new warships and pensions? Successive Chancellors of the Exchequer feared that it could not. If the government tried to raise taxes it might well provoke unrest, especially among the poorer classes. As C. T. Ritchie, Conservative Chancellor in 1903, put it: 'One of the greatest dangers that I am afraid of is that, with one shilling income tax [in the pound; i.e. 5 per cent], and with bad times entailing want of employment, and perhaps an appreciably increased price of bread, there will be a violent reaction …'[25]

In an attempt to find a middle way between higher taxes and cuts to defence spending, successive governments before 1914 tried to find both savings and efficiencies. A new Committee of Imperial Defence came into being in 1904 to co-ordinate defence planning and, so it was hoped, budgets; much-needed reforms were made in the army after the end of the Boer War; and the navy was brought into the modern age. Its minister, Selborne, may not have been the cleverest of men; his Cecil sister-in-law (he was married to one of Lord Salisbury's daughters) said of him, 'Willy has what one might call an early English sense of humour … simple, hearty and unwearied by repetition.'[26] Nevertheless he was energetic, committed to improving the navy, and, most importantly, prepared to back reformers, in particular Admiral John Fisher.

Jacky Fisher, as he was always known, shoots through the history of the British navy and of the prewar years like a runaway Catherine wheel, showering sparks in all directions and making some onlookers scatter in alarm and others gasp with admiration. He shook the British navy from top to bottom in the years before the Great War, bombarding his civilian superiors with demands until they usually gave way and steamrollering over his opponents in the navy. He spoke his mind freely in his own inimitable language. His enemies were 'skunks', 'pimps', 'fossils' or 'frightened rabbits'. Fisher was tough, dogged and largely immune to criticism, not surprising perhaps in someone from a relatively modest background who had made his own way in the navy since he was a boy. He was also supremely self-confident. Edward VII once complained that Fisher did not look at different aspects of an issue. 'Why should I waste my time,' the admiral replied, 'looking at all sides when I know my side is the right side?'[27]

Fisher could be charming; he made Queen Victoria laugh, not an easy matter, and was invited frequently to stay with her at Osborne on the Isle of Wight. 'I believe, dear Admiral, that I would walk to England to have another waltz with you,' the young Grand Duchess Olga of Russia wrote to him.[28] He was also dangerous to cross and could be vindictive. 'He laughs,' said Alfred Gardiner, a prominent journalist, 'he cracks jokes, he talks with voluminous geniality, but behind all these breezy externals of the seaman are his "three R's of War" – "Ruthless, Relentless, Remorseless" – and his "three H's of gunnery" – "Hit first, hit hard, keep on hitting".'[29] Fisher did not seek battles, whether against his political opponents or enemy nations, but if they came he believed in waging all out war. His great hero was, as for so many in the British navy, Horatio Nelson, the victor in the naval war against Napoleon. Indeed Fisher delayed taking up his appointment in 1904 as the First Sea Lord (the operational head of the navy) until 21 October, the anniversary of Nelson's death at the Battle of Trafalgar. He frequently quoted Nelson's saying 'He would be a ——— fool who fought an enemy ten to one when he could fight him a hundred to one.'[30]

Nelson's successor was born in 1841 in Ceylon, where his father was first an army captain and then an unsuccessful tea planter. According to Fisher, his parents, whom he scarcely knew, were both very handsome: 'Why I am ugly is one of those puzzles of physiology which are beyond finding out.'[31] And it is true that there was something strange, inscrutable, even savage about his face. 'The full eye', said Gardiner, 'with its curiously small pupil, the wide, full-lipped mouth, dropping mercilessly at the corners, the jaw jutting out a good-humoured challenge to the world, all proclaim a man who neither asks nor gives quarter.' There were rumours for years that Fisher was part-Malay, which might, thought a German naval attaché, explain why he was so cunning and unscrupulous.[32]

God and country were Fisher's key articles of faith. He believed that it was right and fitting that Britain should rule the world. God had protected his country as he had the fabled Lost Tribes of Israel who would one day return in triumph. 'Do you know', he once said, 'that there are five keys to the world? The Straits of Dover, the Straits of Gibraltar, the Suez Canal, the Straits of Malacca, the Cape of Good Hope. *And every one of those keys we hold.* Aren't we the lost tribes?'[33] The Bible, the Old Testament in particular with its many battles, was his favourite reading and he went whenever he could to hear sermons. A visitor once called at his town house on a Sunday morning to be told, 'The Captain has gone to Berkeley Chapel.' 'Will he be in this after-noon?' the caller asked. 'No, he said he was going to hear Canon Liddon at St. Paul's.' 'Well, this evening?' 'In the evening he is going to Spur-geon's Tabernacle.'[34] Fisher also loved dancing and his wife and family, but the navy was his passion.

On its behalf, he waged war on inefficiency, laziness, and obstruc-tiveness. He was known to sack incompetent subordinates on the spot. 'None of us on his staff could be certain we would still have the job the next day,' said one.[35] When he became First Sea Lord, he was given a huge file on a dispute with the War Office over who should pay for some Highlanders' spats which had got ruined by saltwater when the navy landed them on a beach. He threw the whole lot of paper on the fire in his office.[36] He decided that he wanted a wireless telegraph on top of the Admiralty in Whitehall; the Post Office raised difficulties so one day six sailors simply appeared and swarmed up into a cupola and installed the necessary equipment.[37]

Fisher was, inevitably, a divisive figure within the navy and among its supporters. He was accused of playing favourites and of going too fast and too far in his reforms. Yet change was certainly needed. If Churchill did not actually mock the traditions of the Royal Navy as 'rum, sodomy, and the lash', the jibe was not far off. The navy had become complacent and hidebound over the long decades of peace. It clung to old ways, because that is how things were done in Nelson's day. Discipline was harsh; the cat-o'-nine tails, as it was known, could lay a man's back bare in a few strokes. On his first day in the navy in 1854 the thirteen-year-old Fisher fainted when he saw eight men flogged.[38] (The practice was finally abolished in 1879.) Ordinary sailors continued to sleep in hammocks and eat their staples of hardtack biscuits (often complete with weevils) and unidentifiable meat (and with their fingers). Training badly needed to be overhauled and updated; it did not make much sense after all to spend so much time on sailing when the ships were virtually all steam powered. Education, even for officers, was regarded as a necessary evil and merely to impart basic knowledge. Young officers were not properly educated or indeed encouraged to take an interest in such mundane matters as firing practice much less tactics and strategy. 'Polo and pony-racing and amusements', remembered an admiral of his early days in the service, 'were more important than gun drill ...' Many senior officers actively disliked firing the guns because the smoke made the paintwork on the ships dirty.[39] The navy had no war college to teach the arts of war, much less international relations or politics. Its senior commanders generally did not bother their heads with war plans although they were good at marshalling their ships for naval reviews or for carrying out elaborate manoeuvres (although in one of the great Victorian scandals Admiral Sir George Tryon sent his flagship the *Victoria* straight into the side of the *Camperdown*, sinking the *Victoria* along with 358 men).

Fisher's reforms to the navy started before he became First Sea Lord. As commander-in-chief in the Mediterranean and then Second Sea Lord, he had done much to improve naval education including laying the foundations for a proper war college; he had insisted on sustained gunnery practice; and he had promoted and encouraged a band of bright young officers. 'The increasing average age of our Admirals is appalling!' he had told his superiors. 'In a few years you'll see them all going about with gouty shoes and hot-water bottles!'[40] After 1904, when he held the highest command post in the navy, he set in motion even more sweeping changes. 'We must have no tinkering!' he wrote to a fellow reformer. 'No pandering to sentiment! No regard for susceptibilities! No pity for anyone!'[41] In spite of protests from their officers, he ruthlessly scrapped over 150 obsolete ships. He trimmed and reorganised shipyards to make them more efficient (and cheaper). He ensured that the neglected Naval Reserve Fleet have nucleus crews on board so that they could rapidly take their place on the seas in a crisis. His boldest piece of reorganisation was to bring much of the navy home from far-off posts and concentrate its ships, especially the most up-to-date, close to the British Isles. He amalgamated scattered squadrons so that there was one great Eastern Fleet based on Singapore, another at the Cape of Good Hope, one in the Mediterranean and two more, the Atlantic and the Channel, near at hand. Fisher's redistribution of the navy meant that three-quarters of its force could be used if necessary against Germany. And following Nelson's principle that 'the battleground should be the drill ground', the Atlantic and the Channel fleets made a practice of carrying out extensive manoeuvres in the North Sea.

As soon as he took over as First Sea Lord, Fisher set up a group to work on what was going to be his greatest innovation of all, a new super battleship. (It also drew up designs for a new heavy battlecruiser, the *Invincible*.) The idea of having a battleship which combined speed, heavy armour, and heavy, long-range guns was already in the air, partly because technology was now advanced enough to make it possible. New turbine engines, for example, could move heavier weights through the waters at high speeds. (In 1904 Cunard decided to put turbines into its new *Lusitania* and *Mauretania*, the largest passenger ships of their day.) In 1903 an Italian ship designer published an article outlining a possible design, which he described as 'an ideal battleship for the Royal Navy', and the Japanese, German, American and Russian navies were also known to be considering the possibilities for a new super battleship.[42] The stunning Japanese victory over the Russian navy in the Tsushima Strait in May 1905 seemed to prove that the future of naval warfare lay with fast battleships, the new high-explosive shells and the big guns to deliver them. (The Japanese fleet used 12-inch (30.5cm) guns; the measurement refers to the muzzle diameter, which meant that they were firing very big shells indeed.)[43] While Fisher has sometimes been criticised for taking the naval arms race to a new level by building ships which made every other type obsolete, it is difficult to see how the jump ahead could have been avoided.

The Fisher committee did its work with great dispatch and on 2

October 1905 the keel was laid for what was going to be HMS *Dreadnought*. It was formally launched by the king in February 1906 in the presence of huge and enthusiastic crowds. By the end of the year the ship was ready for service. *Dreadnought*, the first of a whole new class of battleships, was the Muhammad Ali of the seas – big, fast and deadly. The largest battleships to date had been some 14,000 tons; *Dreadnought* was 18,000. Where top steaming speed had been eighteen knots, *Dreadnought* could do twenty-one and more with its turbine engine (made by Charles Parsons, who had so scandalised the navy by showing off his *Turbinia* at the Diamond Jubilee naval review). Fisher considered speed even more important a protection than armour but *Dreadnought* had plenty of that as well, some 5,000 tons above and below its waterline. And like Muhammad Ali it could sting like a bee. It carried ten 12-inch guns as well as batteries of smaller guns and, since the guns were mounted on turrets, *Dreadnought* and her successors could virtually fire on the whole area around them. As *Jane's Fighting Ships* said in 1905: 'It is hardly too much to say that, given her speed, gun power, range and the smashing effect of the concentrated force of heavy projectiles, the *Dreadnought* should easily be equal in battle-worthiness to any two, probably to three, of most of the ships now afloat.'[44]

Although the immediate impetus behind the move to dreadnoughts and heavy cruisers seems to have been fear of the combined power of the French and Russian navies, the British naval planners increasingly saw the German navy as their main enemy of the future.[45] Relations were starting to improve with France and Russia but they continued to worsen with Germany. British planners assumed that, whatever the official German line, the German fleet was designed for action in the North Sea; it had a restricted cruising radius, for example, and cramped crew quarters which made long voyages difficult. It did not help either that the Kaiser carelessly signed a letter to his second cousin the tsar as the Admiral of the Atlantic.[46] Fisher certainly felt no doubts: as he said in 1906 as the naval race with Germany was heating up, 'Our only probable enemy is Germany. Germany keeps her *whole* Fleet always concentrated within a few hours of England. We must therefore keep a Fleet twice as powerful concentrated within a few hours of Germany.'[47] From 1907 the Admiralty's war plans focussed almost entirely on the possibility of a naval war with Germany in the seas around Britain. The

Committee of Imperial Defence, set up to co-ordinate British strategy and advise the Prime Minister, concurred: as it said in 1910, 'In order to avoid exposing our fleets to the risk of suffering defeat in detail, naval action in remote waters might therefore have to be postponed until by the clearing of the situation on home waters adequate naval force could be brought to bear.'[48]

To ease the financial burden of the navy the British government looked to the empire. New ships were launched with 'colonial wine' and frequently given names such as the *Hindustan* or the *Good Hope*.[49] The self-governing 'White' dominions of Canada, Australia, New Zealand and later South Africa, proved curiously unmoved.[50] In 1902 they collectively contributed some £150,000 and, even after considerable pressure from the British government, that only climbed to £328,000 in the following years.[51] Canada, the senior dominion, did not want to contribute anything at all, arguing that it had no immediate enemies. 'They are an unpatriotic, grasping people', said Fisher, 'who only stick by us for the good they can get out of us.'[52] It was to take the intensifying of the naval race with Germany to change minds in the empire. In 1909, both New Zealand and Australia started their own dreadnoughts and in 1910 Canada moved cautiously towards establishing its own navy and bought two cruisers from the British.

In Britain itself, another key part of government, the Foreign Office, was also coming to share the navy's view that Germany was a menace. Where the older generation which had grown up in the days of splendid isolation still hoped to keep Britain on civil if not friendly terms with all the other powers, the younger one was increasingly anti-German. Sanderson, the Permanent Undersecretary between 1894 and 1906, wrote in 1902 to Sir Frank Lascelles, the British ambassador in Berlin, that there was a worrying tendency among his colleagues to think badly of the Germans: 'There is a settled dislike of them – and an impression that they are ready and anxious to play us a shabby trick. It is an inconvenient state of things for there are a good many questions in which it is important for both countries that we should work cordially together.'[53] Rising stars such as Francis Bertie, to be ambassador in Paris from 1905 to 1918, Charles Hardinge, Permanent Undersecretary from 1906 to 1910, or Arthur Nicolson, ambassador in Russia during the same period and then Permanent Undersecretary (and also father of Harold Nicolson), were all deeply suspicious of Germany.[54] Those who did not share the prevailing anti-German view in the decade before 1914 tended to be marginalised or retired. In 1908, in what was a key change, Sir Frank Lascelles, who had been British ambassador in Berlin since 1895 and who strongly supported friendship with Germany, was replaced by Sir Edward Goschen who was convinced that Germany was hostile to Britain.

Oddly enough, the man who articulated the Foreign Office concerns about Germany most forcefully was himself partly German and married to a German. In his admiration for the great German historians, his love of music – he played the piano extremely well and was a gifted amateur composer – his slight German accent, and, some would say, his enormous capacity for work, Eyre Crowe was always something of an oddity in a Foreign Office still staffed largely by the British upper classes. The son of a British consul and a German mother, he had grown up in Germany, in a cultivated upper-middle-class world which resembled that which had produced Tirpitz. His parents had known the doomed emperor Friedrich Wilhelm and his English wife Princess Victoria and shared their liberal hopes for Germany. Crowe had deep affection for Germany and German culture but he deplored what he saw as the triumph of Prussianism with its authoritarianism and stress on military values. He was also highly critical of what he saw as 'the erratic, domineering, and often frankly aggressive spirit', which, in his opinion, animated German public life. Germany was looking for a place in the world commensurate with its new power; that much Crowe understood and indeed sympathised with. But he objected strongly to the way in which Germany's leaders had gone about it, demanding colonies, for example, from other powers and using its military power as a threat. As he said in a letter to his mother in 1896, Germany had got used to thinking that it could treat Britain badly 'like kicking a dead ass. The animal coming alive and displaying the features of a lion instead, has somewhat bewildered those sportsmen.'[55] He made it his mission in the Foreign Office to urge his superiors to stand up to what he described as German blackmail.

On New Year's Day 1907 Crowe, who had recently been put in charge of the part of the Foreign Office which looked after Germany and the other western European states, submitted what became his most famous memorandum to Sir Edward Grey, the Foreign Secretary. In its forceful arguments, its grasp of history, and its attempt to understand Germany's motivations, it can be compared to George Kennan's 'Long Telegram' to Washington at the start of the Cold War which laid out the sources of Soviet conduct and the policy of containment. Crowe argued, as Kennan did later, that his country was facing an opponent which would continuously try to seize the advantage unless it was checked. 'To give way to the blackmailer's menaces enriches him, but it has long been proved by uniform experience that, although this may secure for the victim temporary peace, it is certain to lead to renewed molestation and higher demands after ever-shortening periods of amicable forbearance. The blackmailer's trade is generally ruined by the first resolute stand made against his exactions and the determination rather to face all risks of a possibly disagreeable situation than to continue in the path of endless concessions. But, failing such determination, it is more than probable that the relations between the two parties will grow steadily worse.'[56]

Britain's foreign and defence policy, Crowe argued, was determined by geography, both its position on the periphery of Europe and its possession of a huge overseas empire. It was almost 'a law of nature' that the British would favour a balance of power to prevent a single country gaining control of the Continent.[57] Nor could Britain concede control of the seas to another power without endangering its very existence. Germany's policy of building up its navy might be part of an overall strategy to challenge Britain's position in the world or it might be the result of 'a vague, confused, and unpractical statesmanship, not fully realizing its own drift'.[58] From Britain's point of view it did not really matter. In either case, Britain must meet the German naval challenge, yet do so firmly and calmly. (Kennan was to give similar advice about the Soviet Union forty years later.) 'Nothing', Crowe wrote, 'is more likely to produce in Germany the impression of the practical hopelessness of a never-ending succession of costly naval programmes than the conviction, based on ocular demonstration, that for every German ship England will inevitably lay down two, so maintaining the present, relative British preponderance.'[59]

Once the British had made their move to build the first dreadnought, Tirpitz and the Kaiser and their supporters were indeed faced with a clear choice: to give up the race and try to mend fences with Britain or respond by trying to keep up in the race and build their equivalent of the dreadnoughts. If they chose the latter Germany would face considerable increased costs: new materials and technologies, higher maintenance and repair, and bigger crews all added up to a sum double that of the existing battleships. In addition, docks would have to be rebuilt to handle the bigger ships and the Kiel Canal, which allowed them to be built in the secure shipyards on the Baltic coast and then be brought through in safety to German ports on the North Sea, would have to be widened and deepened.[60] Moreover, money absorbed by the navy would not be available to the army, which was facing a growing threat from Russia. The decision as to which path to take could not be postponed for long lest Britain get too far ahead.

In the early part of 1905, months before the keel for *Dreadnought* was laid, the German naval attaché in London reported back to Berlin that the British were planning a new type of battleship, more powerful than any in existence.[61] In March 1905 Selborne presented the estimates for the navy for the coming year to Parliament. They included one new battleship but he did not provide any details, and while he mentioned Fisher's committee, he said that no public good would be served by making its report public. That summer Tirpitz retreated, as he liked to do, to his house in the Black Forest. There, amidst the pines and firs, he consulted with some of his most trusted advisers. By the autumn, he had made his decision; Germany would build battleships as well as battlecruisers to match the new British ones. As Holger Herwig, a leading historian of the German naval race, has observed: 'It speaks volumes for the nature of the decision-making process in Wilhelmian Germany that the British challenge was accepted without input from the chancery, the foreign office, the treasury, or the two agencies directly responsible for naval strategic planning, the admiralty staff and the High Seas Fleet!'[62] Tirpitz presented a new naval bill which provided for increased spending – some 35 per cent over the naval bill of 1900 – to cover the costs of dreadnoughts as well as six new cruisers. Germany would build two dreadnoughts and one heavy cruiser per year.

Not all Germans by any means shared the fears or accepted the need for a large and expensive navy. Even in the navy itself, there was grumbling that Tirpitz's focus on more and more ships meant that there was

not enough money for personnel or training.[63] In the Reichstag, deputies from the centre and left but also from the right attacked the growing
deficits, which were caused in part by the naval budget. The Chancellor,
Bülow, was already struggling to plug the holes in the German budget
and deal with a Reichstag which was reluctant to raise taxes, but fortu-
itously there was a major crisis and war scare over Morocco as the new
navy bill, the Novelle, reached the Reichstag and it was passed by a large
margin in May 1906.[64] Bülow nevertheless became increasingly worried
about the financial crisis looming for Germany and his own difficulties
in dealing with the Reichstag. And there seemed to be no end in sight
to the naval spending: 'When will you be sufficiently advanced with
your fleet', he asked Tirpitz pointedly in 1907, 'so that the ... unbearable
political situation will be relieved?'[65] Tirpitz's timetable for getting out
of the danger zone (as Germany quietly tried to get to the point where
it had a navy strong enough to pressure Britain) kept being extended
further into the future.

As far as the Kaiser and Tirpitz were concerned the responsibility for
taking the naval race to a new level rested with what Wilhelm called the
'entirely *crazy Dreadnought policy* of Sir J. Fisher and His Majesty'. The
Germans were prone to see Edward VII as bent on a policy of encircling
Germany. The British had made a mistake in building dreadnoughts and
heavy cruisers, in Tirpitz's view, and they were angry about it: 'This
annoyance will increase as they see that we follow them immediately.'[66]
That did not stop the German leadership from being anxious about the
immediate future. Tirpitz's danger zone had just got longer and, so far,
the British showed no signs of wanting to make an agreement with
Germany. 'No allies in sight,' said Holstein sardonically to Bülow.[67]
Who could tell what the British might do? Did their history not show
them to be hypocritical, devious and ruthless? Fears of a 'Kopenhagen',
a sudden British attack just like the one in 1807 when the British navy
had bombarded Copenhagen and seized the Danish fleet, were never far
from the thoughts of the German leadership once the naval race had
started. On Christmas Eve in 1904, when the war between Russia and
Japan was causing international tensions, Bülow told Ambassador Lascelles that the German government had seriously feared that Britain,
which was allied to Japan, might attack Germany, which had been offering considerable support to Russia. Fortunately the German ambassador

in London who had been summoned back to Berlin had managed to persuade his superiors, including a very worried Kaiser, that the British had no intention of starting a war.[68] Such fears spread out into German society and caused bursts of panic. At the start of 1907, parents in the Baltic port of Kiel kept their children home from school because they had heard that Fisher was about to invade. That spring, too, Lascelles wrote to Sir Edward Grey, the British Foreign Secretary: 'The day before yesterday, Berlin went stark raving mad. There was a fall of six points in German securities on the Bourse and a general impression that war was about to break out between England and Germany.'[69] Taking out the German fleet in a sudden action did occur to some in Britain, notably Fisher, who suggested it on a couple of occasions. 'My God, Fisher, you must be mad!' the king said, and the idea went nowhere.[70]

In the military and civilian circles around the Kaiser, however, the possibility of war with Britain was increasingly discussed as a realistic prospect. And if war was coming then it was important to step up Germany's preparations and deal as well with the 'unpatriotic' Germans such as the Social Democrats who resisted higher defence spending and who advocated a policy of friendship towards other European powers. The German Navy League became increasingly strident in its warnings of impending danger and its demands for more and more naval spending, even turning on its patron Tirpitz for not acting quickly enough. Indeed, so some leading figures on the right thought, it might be possible to kill two birds with one stone: the government should challenge the left and the liberal moderates by presenting a greatly increased budget for the navy, more than Tirpitz wanted, to the Reichstag. If the deputies rejected it, that would be an excellent opportunity for the Kaiser to dissolve the Reichstag and try for a more favourable nationalist majority or perhaps even carry out the coup he had talked about in the past and get rid of such inconveniences as a free press, universal male suffrage, elections, or the Reichstag itself. In late 1905, as Tirpitz was preparing his Novelle, he grew concerned that his beloved navy was going to be used as a 'battering ram' to force through political and constitutional change in Germany. He had no objections to crushing the left but he worried about whether the attempt would succeed without serious internal upheavals and that it might make the British finally notice that Germany's navy was expanding fast.[71]

By 1908, as the tensions in Europe rose again over the Bosnian crisis, Bülow was increasingly sceptical about the value of Tirpitz's navy and Germany's isolation in Europe. Could Germany, he demanded of Tirpitz, 'calmly and with confidence envisage an English attack?'[72] Tirpitz, who later said he felt deserted, replied that Britain was unlikely to attack at present and that therefore the best policy for Germany was to continue to build up the navy. 'Every new ship added to our battle-fleet means an increase in risk for England if she attacks us.' He dismissed the warnings from Count Paul Metternich, the German ambassador in London, that it was the German naval programme that was alienating Britain. The main reason for British hostility was economic rivalry with Germany, and that was not going to vanish.[73] Backing down would cause serious political troubles at home. 'If we undermine the Navy Law which is already in great danger due to the whole situation', he wrote to one of his loyal aides in 1909, 'we do not know where the journey is going to take us to.'[74] Tirpitz's final argument for keeping up the naval race was one that has been used repeatedly to justify continuing programmes or wars: Germany had already poured in so many resources that backing down would nullify the sacrifices that had been made. 'If the British fleet can be made permanently so strong', he wrote in 1910, 'that it would incur no risk in attacking Germany, then German naval development will have been a mistake from the historical point of view.'[75]

In March 1908 Tirpitz got through the Reichstag a new supplementary naval bill, the Second Novelle, which shortened the lives of the existing ships in the German navy and therefore speeded up the rate of replacements (and small ships could be replaced by larger ones). Instead of three new battleships per year, the rate increased to four for the next four years, after which it would drop to three per year for, as Tirpitz hoped, eternity. The Reichstag would yet again approve a naval programme over which it would have no further control. By 1914 Germany would have had the equivalent of twenty-one dreadnoughts, which would have significantly narrowed the gap between Britain and Germany if Britain had chosen not to respond.[76] Tirpitz assured the Kaiser that Germany would get away with the increase: 'I have framed the *Novelle* as your Highness wished it, so that internationally and domestically it looks as small and harmless as possible.'[77] Wilhelm sent a long personal letter intended to be reassuring to Lord Tweedmouth, now the First Lord of the Admiralty: 'The German Naval Bill is not aimed at England and is not a "Challenge to British Supremacy of the Sea", which will remain unchallenged to generations to come.'[78] Edward VII was not pleased at what he saw as extraordinary interference by his nephew in writing to a British minister and many in Britain shared that view.[79]

Bülow, who had the unenviable role of trying to find money to carry out Tirpitz's new building programme, was coming round to the opinion that Germany could not afford the strongest army and the second largest navy in Europe. 'We cannot weaken the army', he wrote in 1908, 'for our destiny will be decided on land.'[80] His government faced a serious financial crisis. Germany's national debt had nearly doubled since 1900 and it was proving difficult to increase revenue. Some 90 per cent of all central government spending went on the army and navy and in the twelve years between 1896 and 1908, thanks in large part to naval spending, the total expenditure on the military had doubled and was going up for the foreseeable future. When Bülow tried to raise the issue of reining in naval spending, one of Wilhelm's entourage begged him not to because it only made the Kaiser 'very unhappy'.[81] Bülow struggled on throughout 1908 trying to put together a plan for tax reforms which could get through the Reichstag but his proposals for expanding inheritance taxes infuriated the right and new consumption taxes had a similar impact on the left. He finally submitted his resignation to Wilhelm in July 1909, having failed to solve the problem. Tirpitz prevailed because in the end he had the Kaiser behind him.

In the meantime, the British had started to take notice of the increased tempo of German naval building. Initially, as he had hoped would be the case, they had not reacted to Tirpitz's first Novelle of 1906. In December 1907 the Admiralty had in fact proposed slowing down the rate of building for battleships so that in 1908–9 it would construct only one dreadnought and one heavy cruiser. This was also in line with what the Liberal government, which had promised both to make savings and spend on social programmes, wanted. Over the summer of 1908, however, concern, both among the public and in government circles, began to mount. The German fleet cruised in the Atlantic. What did that mean? An anonymous article, 'The German Peril', published in the respected *Quarterly Review* in July, warned that if Germany and Britain got into a conflict, the Germans were likely to invade. 'Her naval officers have sounded and sketched our harbours and studied every detail of our coasts.' According to the author (who was J. L. Garvin, the editor of the Sunday paper the *Observer*) some 50,000 Germans, disguised as waiters, were already in place in Britain ready to spring into action when the signal was given. Shortly after the article appeared, the famous German aviator Count Zeppelin flew to Switzerland in his new dirigible. That sent Garvin, now writing under his own name in the *Observer*, into fresh predictions of the menaces gathering around Britain.[82]

In August that year, Edward VII paid a visit to his nephew Wilhelm in the pretty little town of Kronberg. Although the king had been armed with a paper by the British government outlining its concerns about German naval spending, he thought it wiser not to raise the issue with Wilhelm. It might, Edward thought, 'possibly have spoilt the happy effect of the conversation which had taken place between them'. After lunch, the Kaiser, still in a cheerful mood, asked Sir Charles Hardinge, the permanent head of the Foreign Office, to smoke a cigar with him. The two men sat side by side on a billiard table. He thought, said Wilhelm, that relations between Britain and Germany were quite good. Hardinge, as he wrote in his memorandum of their discussion, had to disagree: 'There could be no concealment of the fact that a genuine apprehension was felt in England as to the reasons and intention underlying the construction of a large German fleet.' He warned that, if the German programme went ahead, the British government would be obliged to ask Parliament to approve an extensive shipbuilding programme and he had no doubt that Parliament would agree. That would be, in Hardinge's opinion, a most unfortunate development: 'There could be no doubt that this naval rivalry between the two countries would embitter their relations to each other, and might in a few years' time lead to a very critical situation in the event of a serious, or even a trivial, dispute arising between the two countries.'

Wilhelm replied sharply, and inaccurately, that there was no reason for British apprehensions, that the German building programme was not a new one, and that the relative proportion of the German and British fleets remained the same. (According to the melodramatic account he sent Bülow, he told Hardinge, 'That is sheer idiocy. Who has been pulling your leg?') Furthermore, Wilhelm said, it had become a point of national honour for Germany that its naval building programme should be completed. 'No discussion with a foreign Government could be tolerated; such a proposal would be contrary to the national dignity, and would give rise to internal troubles if the Government were to accept it. He would rather go to war than submit to such dictation.' Hardinge stood his ground and said that he was merely suggesting that their two governments should have a friendly discussion and that there was no question of dictation.

He also challenged the Kaiser's assertion that Britain would have three times as many battleships as Germany in 1909. 'I said that I was at a loss to understand how His Majesty arrived at the figures of the relative strength of the two navies in battle-ships in 1909, and could only assume that the sixty-two first-class battle-ships of the British fleet comprised every obsolete vessel that could be found floating in British harbours and that had not been sold as scrap iron.' Wilhelm claimed in his version of the conversation that he put Hardinge in his place: 'I too am admiral of the British Fleet and know it well – far better than you, since you are only a civilian and know nothing at all about it.' At this point the Kaiser sent an aide for a summary of naval strength published annually by the German admiralty which would show that the German figures were right. Hardinge said dryly that the Kaiser gave him a copy 'for my own edification and conviction' and that he had told Wilhelm that he only wished he could accept the figures as correct.

Wilhelm's version is characteristically quite different: Hardinge had a look of 'speechless astonishment' and Lascelles, who, Wilhelm claimed, completely accepted the German figures, 'had difficulty in restraining his laughter'. The conversation ended, so the Kaiser told Bülow, with Hardinge plaintively asking, 'Can't you stop building? Or build less ships?' to which Wilhelm responded, 'Then we shall fight, for it is a question of national honour and dignity.' He looked Hardinge squarely in the face and the latter had flushed, bowed deeply, and asked to be forgiven for his 'ill-considered expressions'. The Kaiser was delighted with himself. 'Didn't I give it properly to Sir Charles?' Bülow had trouble believing this account and his suspicions were confirmed by his colleagues who had been present at the conversation which, they said, was quite amicable. Hardinge had been frank but respectful and the Kaiser had remained in good temper.

It is unfortunate but not surprising that the conversation failed to produce a greater understanding between Britain and Germany. Hardinge's warning that, if Germany continued to up the tempo of its naval building, his government would be forced by public opinion to undertake 'a large counter-programme of naval construction' was ignored. Indeed, according to Bülow, Wilhelm came away from the Kronberg meetings convinced that he had persuaded his British visitors of the rightness of Germany's position. What is more Moltke, his army chief of staff, had assured him that Germany was fully prepared militarily. Therefore there was no reason for Germany to be cautious or to slow down the rate of its naval building. 'With Englishmen', Wilhelm assured Bülow, 'the only thing that worked was frankness; ruthless, even brutal frankness, – that was the best method to use with them!'[83]

In reality British suspicions were growing stronger, aided that same summer by what was in fact an innocent move by the German navy to support German shipyards. Schichau, a large shipbuilder in Danzig, asked in the summer of 1908 for an early contract to build one of the large battleships scheduled for the following year. Otherwise, so its management feared, it might have to lay off its skilled workers and the whole economy of Danzig would suffer. (When Danzig, as Gdansk, became part of Poland after 1945, the Schichau works were made part of the Lenin shipyard and later still were the site of the Solidarity movement of the 1980s.) The German navy agreed but, although the completion date for the battleship remained unchanged, the decision inadvertently set off alarms in Britain. That autumn the British naval attaché in Berlin informed his government that an extra battleship was being built and the British drew the conclusion, correct in fact but based on the wrong evidence, that the Germans had speeded up the tempo of their naval building.[84]

At this stage there occurred one of those unfortunate incidents which seemed to mark relations between Britain and Germany in the years before 1914. On 28 October the *Daily Telegraph* published what was described as an interview with the Kaiser. In fact it was a journalist's version of conversations which had taken place the previous year between Wilhelm and an English landowner, Colonel Edward Stuart-Wortley, who had lent his house to the Kaiser for a private stay. The two men chatted on several occasions, or rather, it seems, Wilhelm held forth about how he had always wanted good relations between Germany and Britain and how the British did not appreciate all he had done for them. He criticised Britain's new friendship with France. The British alliance with Japan was also a great mistake and he made dark reference to the Yellow Peril: 'But much as I may be misunderstood, I have built my fleet to support you.' Stuart-Wortley, who listened credulously to all this, decided that if only the British could read Wilhelm's real views instead of being misled by a malicious anti-German press, relations between their two countries would somehow mend overnight. In September 1908, Stuart-Wortley handed over his notes of the conversations to a journalist from the *Daily Telegraph* who wrote them up as an interview and the result was sent on to Wilhelm for his approval.

Wilhelm, rather unusually, behaved correctly and sent the 'interview' to his Chancellor. Perhaps because Bülow was busy, as he later claimed, or, as his enemies charged, too much the courtier to challenge his master, he merely glanced at the document and sent it on to the Foreign Ministry for its views. Again the 'interview' slipped through without proper scrutiny, in yet another example of the chaotic manner in which the German government worked. Someone along the way should have taken proper care because the Kaiser was known for his indiscretions. On more than one occasion the German authorities had been obliged to use their influence, even pay handsomely to suppress his potentially embarrassing effusions.[85] As it was, the document made its way into the pages of the *Daily Telegraph* accompanied by Wilhelm's fond hopes that he could win the British over.[86]

For someone who liked to tell his officials frequently that he understood the British much better than they did, Wilhelm got it wrong both in tone, which was self-pitying and accusatory, and in substance. The British, he complained, 'are mad, mad, mad as March hares'. How could they fail to see that Wilhelm was their friend and that all he wanted was to live on good and peaceful terms with them? 'My actions ought to speak for themselves, but you listen not to them but to those who misinterpret and distort them. That is a personal insult which I feel and resent.'[87] After more in this vein, Wilhelm then turned to the vitally important help he had given Britain during the Boer War. He had, he pointed out with some truth, prevented the other European powers from intervening against Britain during the Boer War. What is more, with his own hands, he had drawn up a plan of campaign for the British forces; his own general staff had reviewed it before he sent it on to the British government. He was amazed, he went on, that the British seemed to think the German navy was directed against them when it was quite clear that Germany needed its navy for its growing empire and trade. Britain would be glad of Germany's navy one day when it realised that Japan was not its friend and that he and his country were.

At any other time the British might not have paid much attention to Wilhelm's words but they were published when the naval race was entering an ominous new stage and after a summer of public apprehension about a German invasion. In addition there was a serious crisis in the Balkans over Bosnia and tensions between France and Germany over Morocco which some feared might lead to war. While many simply took the interview as further evidence that the Kaiser was unbalanced, Crowe prepared an immediate analysis for the Foreign Office in which he concluded that it was part of a concerted attempt by Germany to lull British public opinion, and supporters of a big navy called for more spending. Sir Edward Grey, the Foreign Secretary, did his best to calm emotions in London and wrote privately to a friend, 'The German Kaiser is ageing me; he is like a battleship with steam up and screws going, but with no rudder, and he will run into something some day and cause a catastrophe.'[88]

There nearly was a catastrophe this time but it was in Germany and came close to finishing the Kaiser. 'A mood first of bewilderment', wrote one of the inner circle, 'and later of despair and indignation took hold of all circles of the people.'[89] Germans were appalled and enraged that their ruler would make such a fool of himself, and not for the first time. Conservatives and nationalists disliked his professions of friendship for the British and the liberals and the left wing felt that it was high time that the Kaiser and his regime were brought under parliamentary control. Ominously, the Prussian War Minister was one of the few of his officials to offer strong support; General Karl von Einem told the Kaiser that the army was loyal and could deal with the Reichstag if necessary. Bülow made a very half-hearted defence of his master in the Reichstag and Wilhelm, who carried on with his usual round of autumn visits and shooting, suddenly collapsed into a profound depression. It must have been unnerving for his fellow guests on the beat as he alternated between fits of weeping and moments of fury.[90] As one said: 'I had the feeling that in William the Second I had before me a man who was looking with astonishment for the first time in his life on the world as it really is.'[91] Von Einem for one felt that something had broken in his master and that Wilhelm was never the same confident ruler again.[92] Although the storm blew over and Wilhelm kept his throne, both he and the monarchy were seriously weakened. He never forgave Bülow for what he saw as a betrayal and the affair became another reason to dismiss his Chancellor.

In Britain the *Daily Telegraph* affair became part of the context for a passionate debate within the governing Liberal Party. The Liberals had been elected with pledges to carry out both economies and social reforms, in particular to provide old-age pensions, yet they found themselves, thanks to the naval race, facing increased expenditure rather than less. They could not, however, ignore what seemed to be a serious threat from Germany and rising public concern. The Admiralty had abandoned its modest programme of 1907 and had rather come to the conclusion that it needed a minimum of six new dreadnoughts. In December 1908, the First Lord, Reginald McKenna, brought the proposal to Cabinet. The new Prime Minister, Herbert Asquith, was sympathetic but had to deal with a deeply divided Cabinet.

The main opposition to the sharp increase in the naval budget came from 'the economists' led by two of the most interesting and controversial politicians in modern British politics. David Lloyd George, the radical from a modest Welsh background, made common cause with that maverick member of the British aristocracy, Winston Churchill, to resist what both men saw as unnecessary spending which would threaten the social reforms they wanted. As Chancellor of the Exchequer, Lloyd George would have to find the £38 million for the dreadnoughts if they were approved. He told Asquith that the Liberals were losing support in the country by failing to tackle 'the gigantic expenditure on armaments built up by the recklessness of our predecessors'. Lloyd George warned his leader of the possible consequences: 'When the £38 million navy estimates are announced the disaffection of these good Liberals will break into open sedition and the usefulness of this Parliament will be at an end.'[93]

The Conservative opposition, much of the press, and bodies such as

the Navy League and the Defence Committee of the London Chamber
of Commerce weighed in. So did armaments manufacturers who had
been hit by the depression of 1908; shipyards, for example, had been
laying off engineers and workers. A Conservative leaflet said: 'Our Navy
and our unemployed may both be starved together; and soon will be if
you don't turn this Government out.'[94] The king let it be known that he
wanted eight dreadnoughts. And he was in tune with much of public
opinion. 'We want eight and we won't wait' was the popular slogan
coined by a Conservative MP.

In February 1909, Asquith managed to broker a compromise that
the Cabinet accepted: Britain would start four dreadnoughts in the
coming financial year and four more by the spring of 1910 if it became
apparent they were needed. (In the end the four extra dreadnoughts
were built after Germany's allies Austria-Hungary and Italy started
their own programmes.) The Liberals fell in line and the government
easily defeated a motion of censure brought by the Conservatives to the
effect that its policy was not securing the safety of the empire. The press
campaign gradually died down and public attention focussed on the
Budget Lloyd George proposed at the end of April 1909. In his speech
Lloyd George was still very much a radical but one who had become
concerned over Britain's position in the world. The Budget was designed
to raise money to change the lives of Britain's poor, to wage war 'against
poverty and squalidness'. He had, though, no intention of neglecting
the country's defences. 'Such a stupendous act of folly would, in the
present temper of nations, not be Liberalism but lunacy. We don't
intend to put in jeopardy the naval supremacy which is so essential not
only to our national existence, but, in our judgement, to the vital interests of Western civilisation.' To pay for both the social reforms and
defence, he proposed to raise old taxes, from ones on alcohol to death
duties, and institute new ones, on land. The rich, including the landed
aristocracy, complained bitterly. The People's Budget, as it was coming
to be known, was bringing a revolution in British society. The landed
classes threatened to lay off estate workers and the Duke of Buccleuch
announced that he would have to cancel his annual subscription of one
guinea to the local football club. Lloyd George, who loved a good fight,
was unrepentant. The rich had wanted the dreadnoughts, he said, and
now they did not want to pay. And of what value, after all, were the

aristocracy? 'A fully-equipped duke costs as much to keep up as two Dreadnoughts – and they are just as great a terror – and they last longer.'[95]

The House of Lords, perhaps as Lloyd George had intended, rejected his Budget in November 1909 even though it was unprecedented for the upper chamber to reject a Finance Bill. Asquith dissolved Parliament and fought an election in January 1910 on that issue. His government won, although with a reduced majority, and the following April the Lords wisely let the Budget pass. The next year, after a prolonged political storm, the House of Lords accepted the Parliament Bill which ended its dominance for ever. Unlike Germany, Britain was able both to surmount its financial crisis and keep firm parliamentary control over its affairs. It also won the naval race: when the time the Great War broke out Britain had twenty dreadnoughts to Germany's thirteen and a decisive advantage in all the other categories of ships.

The naval race is the key factor in understanding the growing hostility between Britain and Germany. Trade rivalry, competition for colonies, nationalist public opinion, all played their part but those factors also existed in whole or in part in the relationships between Britain and each of France, Russia and the United States. Yet in none of those cases did they lead to the deepening suspicions and fears that came to mark the relations between Britain and Germany in the years before 1914. And it so easily could have been different. Germany and Britain were each other's largest trading partners before 1914 (an inconvenient example for those who argue that the more nations trade with each other, the less likely they are to fight). Their strategic interests could have meshed so neatly, with Germany the biggest land power in Europe and Britain the biggest at sea.

Yet once Germany started to build a strong fleet, it was bound to make Britain uneasy. The Germans may have wanted a blue-water fleet, as they so frequently said, to protect their overseas trade and their colonies, and because big navies were a sign of being a major power just as nuclear weapons are today. The British could have lived with that as they lived with growing Russian or American or Japanese naval power. What they could not accept were the consequences of geography. Whether the German fleet was in the Baltic or in its ports on the German North Sea coast, it was concentrated close to the British Isles.

And by 1914 with the widening of the Kiel Canal (completed in June that year), the German ships could avoid the riskier passages leading past Denmark, Sweden and Norway into the North Sea.

Far from forcing Britain into friendship, as Tirpitz planned, the naval race created a deep gulf between Germany and Britain and brought the hardening of both elite and public opinion in both countries against the other. Equally important, it persuaded Britain that it needed to find new allies to counterbalance the German threat. Bülow was right when he wrote to Tirpitz after the Great War, that even if Germany had been dragged into the war through 'our clumsy handling of a Balkan problem ... there is the question of whether France and particularly Russia would have let it come to war had public opinion in England not been so greatly enraged precisely at the construction of our great ships'.[96]

And what if some of the funds poured into the navy had gone to the army? If it had been able to add men and weapons, so that German land forces had been stronger in 1914, would its attack on France have succeeded that summer, as it so nearly did? What would that have meant for the Great War and for Europe? The naval race also raises the issue of how important individuals are in history. There could not have been a naval race without the economic, manufacturing and technological capacity in each country to sustain it. Nor could it have gone on without public support. It would not have started in the first place, however, without the determination and drive of Tirpitz and the Kaiser's willingness – and ability, allowed him under the imperfect German constitution – to back him to the hilt. When Tirpitz became Secretary for the Navy, there was not a strong lobby within the governing elites for a big navy and not yet strong public support. Both were to come later, as the navy grew.

Thanks to the naval race, the options for maintaining Europe's long peace were narrowing and the path towards war was becoming more pronounced. Britain's first major foreign policy initiative as a result of the naval race – its move towards mending relations with France – was a defensive one but in retrospect it is easy to see how that too tilted the odds in favour of war. What is noticeable, too, in that decade before 1914 is how frequently and easily the possibility of war, even a general war, was part of ordinary discussion throughout Europe.

CHAPTER 6

Unlikely Friends:
The Entente Cordiale
between France and Britain

I n 1898 a tiny mud-brick village on the Upper Nile with a ruined fort and a handful of inhabitants barely getting by on subsistence farming nearly caused a war between France and Britain. Fashoda, now Kodok in the new state of South Sudan, was where French and British imperial ambitions in the north half of Africa came up against each other. France, with its ambitions to build a great empire stretching from its possessions on the west coast of Africa across to the Nile, was moving eastwards across Africa. Britain, which controlled Egypt and assumed Egypt's interests in the Sudan, was moving southwards towards its existing colonies in East Africa. In their chess match played out on the map of Africa, one imperial power was bound to check the other. What also complicated their game is that other players – Italy and Germany – were looking to join in so that the time to make moves was getting shorter.

The French had never forgiven the British for seizing control of Egypt when there were widespread disturbances there in 1882, even though it was through the ineptitude and indecision of the French government that Britain had acted alone. Although the British had expected their occupation to be temporary they had found it easier to get in than out. As the years went by the expanding British administration added to

6. After 1900, a new and unexpected friendship – the Entente Cordiale –
grew between France and Great Britain as a common fear of growing
German power encouraged them to overcome their ancient hatreds. In a
highly successful visit to Paris in 1903 Edward VII helped to win over French
public opinion. Here Edward and President Loubet wear each other's
national dress under a caption saying England and France forever! Along the
sides plaques bearing the names of their great past battles of Waterloo and
Crecy, are decorated with olive branches while the banner at the top reads
Peace, Honour, Victory.

French chagrin. For Germany, Egypt was a handy wedge to keep France
and Britain apart. Within France an active colonial lobby reminded
French politicians and the French public of France's historic ties to
Egypt – had Napoleon not conquered it and had the Suez Canal not
been built by the great French engineer Ferdinand de Lesseps? – and
demanded that France acquire colonies elsewhere in compensation.
Morocco, next to the French colony of Algeria, was one attractive possibility and Sudan, lost to Egypt since an Anglo-Egyptian force under
General Charles Gordon was defeated by the Mahdi in 1885, another. A

UNLIKELY FRIENDS | 133

French engineer also caught the interest of the French government in 1893 by pointing out that dams on the Upper Nile could cause all sorts of problems downstream in Egypt. The decision was taken in Paris to send an expedition to claim Fashoda and the surrounding territory.

The plan was for a small force led by Major Jean-Baptiste Marchand to march stealthily eastward from the French colony of Gabon on the west coast of Africa, with the French leaders of the expedition posing where necessary as travellers merely interested in exploring the possibilities for trade, and stake claim to Fashoda before the British got wind of what was happening. The French seemed to have thought that they might find local allies, perhaps even the victorious Mahdi and his army in Sudan. That in turn might trigger an international conference to settle boundaries along the Upper Nile and reopen the question of control over Egypt. Unfortunately, from the French perspective, things went badly wrong. To begin with the expedition was delayed for various reasons and did not finally set out until March 1897. Second, the French colonial lobby and sympathetic newspapers had been quite openly discussing its prospects and obligingly providing maps well before it started so that the British had plenty of time to respond. Even before Marchand set out from Brazzaville, the British government warned that a French move towards the Nile would be seen as an unfriendly act.[1] Third, Emperor Menelik of the independent African state of Ethiopia, who had agreed that the French could send expeditions westwards through his country to reinforce Marchand at Fashoda, avoided keeping his promise and instead sent the unwitting French off on huge detours.[2]

For a year and a half Marchand and seven other French officers, along with 120 Senegalese soldiers, struggled across Africa. Accompanied by porters, often pressed into service along the way, the expedition carried an enormous quantity of supplies including 10 tons of rice, 5 tons of corned beef, 1 ton of coffee, and 1,300 litres of red wine as well as champagne to celebrate its anticipated success. It also brought along quantities of ammunition, a small river steamer (which the porters had to carry in pieces, at one point through 120 miles of bush), as well as presents for the locals – who generally fled at the approach of the strangers – such as 16 tons of coloured beads and 70,000 metres of coloured cloth. In addition there was a mechanical piano, a French flag and vegetable seeds.[3]

By the time the Marchand expedition drew near to Fashoda and the Nile in the late summer of 1898, the British had a clear idea of where it was headed and what its purpose was. While the French were establishing themselves in Fashoda, Britain already had an army moving south from Egypt under the command of General Horatio Herbert Kitchener, who was under orders to retake the Sudan. (The young Winston Churchill came along as a war correspondent.) On 2 September the British and Egyptian forces overwhelmingly defeated the Mahdi's army at Omdurman outside Khartoum. Kitchener then opened sealed orders which he had been sent from London to discover that he was to move north up the Nile to Fashoda and persuade the French to withdraw. On 18 September he arrived at Fashoda with five gunboats and a large enough force to outnumber the French comfortably.

At Fashoda itself, relations were perfectly amicable. The British were impressed by the way the French had made themselves comfortable with their flower gardens and their vegetables, especially the haricots verts. The French were delighted to get recent newspapers from home although horrified to learn about the Dreyfus affair which was now dividing France: 'An hour after we opened the French newspapers [we] were trembling and weeping,' said one of the expedition. Kitchener gave Marchand a whisky and soda. ('One of the greatest sacrifices I ever made for my country', the Frenchman later said, 'was to drink that horrible smoky alcohol.') The French provided warm champagne in return. Both parties politely but firmly claimed the surrounding territory and both refused to withdraw.[4]

Word of the stand-off sped northwards by steamship and telegraph. The reactions in Paris and London were much less temperate than on the ground. For Britain and France, of course, their confrontation at Fashoda was weighted down with memories of a long and turbulent shared history. Hastings, Agincourt, Crécy, Trafalgar, Waterloo, William the Conqueror, Joan of Arc, Louis XIV, Napoleon, all ran together into a picture on the east side of the Channel of perfidious Albion and on the other of treacherous France. And Fashoda was also about the long struggle for world dominance since the sixteenth century. From the St Lawrence River to the fields of Bengal, British and French forces had fought for empire. The old rivalry had been freshened by much more recent competition: over Egypt, of course, but also elsewhere in the decaying Ottoman Empire. The two countries clashed too in Asia – where the French Empire in Indochina and the British one in India were bumping up against each other in the still independent nation of Siam – in West Africa, and in the Indian Ocean island of Madagascar, which the French had seized over British protests in 1896. In the autumn of 1898 during the Fashoda crisis, French newspapers had headlines 'No Surrender to England', while their British counterparts warned that they would stand for no more tricks from the French. 'Yielding now', said the *Daily Mail*, 'we should only have to face more preposterous demands tomorrow.'[5]

Behind the scenes in both countries there was much coming and going in government offices, and war plans were drawn up just in case they were needed. The British weighed the merits of an attack on the French naval base of Brest and put their Mediterranean Fleet on alert. From Paris, Thomas Barclay, a prominent British journalist and businessman, heard rumours that mayors in ports along the Channel had been ordered to requisition local churches for hospitals. He also wrote an article for the local English-language paper on what might happen to British nationals in France if war broke out. The British ambassador warned that there might be a military coup against the French government, which was already tottering; if the soldiers took over they might well welcome a war with Britain to unite the country.

Queen Victoria told Salisbury 'a war for so miserable and small an object is what I could hardly bring myself to consent to' and urged him to find a way to compromise with the French. Salisbury calculated that the French did not want a war and he was right.[6] At the start of November the French agreed to withdraw Marchand and his force from Fashoda (the official reason given was for the sake of their health). Marchand refused the offer of a passage on a British steamer and the expedition marched on eastwards, reaching Djibouti on the Indian Ocean six months later. (Fashoda is still poor but today its population is much bigger thanks to the refugees created by the Sudan's civil wars and by famine.)

When the Boer War broke out the following year French public opinion cheered the South African republics on. The 1900 graduating class at the military academy at St Cyr called itself the Transvaal year.[7] The British ambassador in Paris reported gloomily to Salisbury that

French public opinion was taking great pleasure in Britain's troubles. 'Your Lordship will, I am sure, enter into the feelings which the painful situation cannot but cause to the Representative of the Queen in a country which appears to have gone mad with jealousy, spite, and resentment.'[8] Félix Faure, the French President, told a Russian diplomat that Britain not Germany was his country's chief enemy, and again there was talk on both sides of the Channel about the possibility of war.[9]

The Fashoda crisis and its aftermath left behind bitterness on both sides, but it also had a salutary effect. Like the Cuban missile crisis of 1962, the prospect of outright war frightened the protagonists and cooler heads began to think of ways to avoid such dangerous confrontations in the future. In Britain, those such as Chamberlain and Balfour who wanted to move away from isolation had no strong preferences as to possible allies. Like their great predecessor Lord Palmerston, they believed that Britain had no permanent allies or enemies but only permanent interests. As Chamberlain said, 'If his idea of a natural alliance with Germany must be renounced, it would be no impossibility for England to arrive at an understanding with Russia or with France.'[10] Baron Eckardstein, the German diplomat whose memoirs are entertaining but unreliable, may have been telling the truth when he claimed to have overheard a conversation at the start of 1902 between Chamberlain and the new French ambassador in London, Paul Cambon. 'While we were smoking and drinking coffee, after dinner, I suddenly saw Chamberlain and Cambon go off into the billiard room. I watched them there and noted that they talked together for exactly 28 minutes in the most animated manner. I could not of course catch what they said and only heard two words "Morocco" and "Egypt".'[11]

The difficulties in contemplating a friendship between two enemies of such long standing as Britain and France were considerably greater on the French side. If the British were feeling uneasy about their position in the world, the French were acutely aware of their own decline and their present vulnerability. That tended to make them more rather than less resentful and heightened their suspicions of Britain. Memories of past glories and past humiliations can also be a heavy burden; for the French they included the glorious long reign of Louis XIV when France dominated Europe and when French civilisation from philosophy to fashion was the model for the entire continent. More recently, as the monuments, the paintings, the books, the Rues Napoleons in virtually every French city and town reminded the French, Napoleon and his armies had conquered almost the whole of Europe. While Waterloo had brought an end to his empire, France had continued to be a great power with the capacity to influence the world's affairs. Another Napoleon, nephew of the first, and another battle had brought a dramatic change.

In 1870 Emperor Napoleon III had led France to a devastating defeat at Sedan at the hands of Prussia and its allied German states. And, as the French noted bitterly, not a single other nation had come to France's aid, yet another black mark against Britain. In the aftermath of the Franco-Prussian War, as France struggled to create a new workable regime, and French fought French, Bismarck had imposed a heavy peace: France had to accept an occupation until it paid a large indemnity (larger, it has been argued, than the one Germany eventually paid France after the Great War) and it lost the two provinces of Alsace and Lorraine on its eastern borders. In a final humiliating touch, the Prussian king was made emperor of the Germans in Louis XIV's Hall of Mirrors at Versailles. 'Europe', as one British journalist famously said, 'had lost a mistress and gained a master.' In Brussels, a Russian diplomat took a longer-term view: 'It seems to me that on 2 September [when the French army surrendered at Sedan] the first stone was laid for a future Franco-Russian alliance.'[12]

In the succeeding years, until his downfall in 1890, Bismarck did his best to ensure that France was incapable of taking revenge. He played the game of diplomacy as only he could, making this alliance then that, tilting towards one power or another, promising, cajoling or threatening, but all to keep Germany at the centre of international relations and France isolated and friendless. Russia, which was also threatened by the rise of a powerful Germany at the heart of Europe, and which like France had a long border with the new country, could have been an ally for France but Bismarck cleverly appealed to the conservatism of Russia's rulers to draw Russia into a tripartite alliance, the Dreikaiserbund, with the third conservative power of Austria-Hungary. And when rivalries between Russia and Austria-Hungary threatened to disrupt that alliance, he negotiated a secret Reinsurance Treaty with Russia in 1887, the one that Germany was carelessly going to fail to renew in 1890.

Bismarck also held out promises to France, of increased commercial links with Germany for example. French and German banks worked together to lend money to Latin America or to the Ottoman Empire. Trade between the two countries increased to the point where there was even talk of a customs union. (That was going to have to wait a few more decades.) Bismarck also gave German support for France's acquisition of colonies in West Africa or the Far East in what became French Indochina. He backed French moves into what had been Ottoman territory in North Africa. Germany supported France as well when it established a protectorate, as one of the more veiled forms of imperialism was known, over Tunisia in 1881 and watched benignly while the French extended their influence into Morocco. With any luck, so Bismarck calculated, French empire building might well bring France into conflict with Britain and Italy; at the least it would stop France from making friends with either. And if the French were looking abroad, they were less likely to brood resentfully about their defeat by Germany and the loss of their two provinces.

In Paris, in the Place de la Concorde, the statue for Strasbourg, the capital of Alsace, was draped in black mourning as a reminder of that loss. It was commemorated in songs, novels, paintings and, on the battlefields themselves, with annual ceremonies. French textbooks told students that the Treaty of Frankfurt which ended the Franco-Prussian War was 'a truce, not a peace; which is why since 1871, all Europe lives permanently under arms'.[13] To call someone or something 'Prussian' in France was a deadly insult. It was horrible for French patriots that Alsace and the southern part of Lorraine – of particular significance as the birthplace of Joan of Arc – were now Elsass and Lothringen and the new border was marked by sentry posts and fortresses. Each year the graduating class of the French army's cavalry school visited the border where it ran through the Vosges mountains so that they could examine the slope down which they would charge when war broke out again between France and Germany.[14] Twenty-six years after France's defeat Paul Cambon walked around Versailles with his brother Jules, also a diplomat, and was acutely reminded of France's disgrace at the hands of Germany, 'like a burn that doesn't heal'.[15]

Yet, with the passage of time, there was healing. While few French were prepared to give up for ever the hope of regaining Alsace and

Lorraine, they accepted that France could not for the foreseeable future afford another war. As the future socialist leader Jean Jaurès put it in 1887, 'neither war nor renunciation'. With some notable exceptions, the younger generation which was coming of age in the 1890s and 1900s no longer felt as strongly about the loss of Alsace and Lorraine or longed passionately for revenge on Germany. A noisy nationalist minority such as General Georges Boulanger – 'Général Revanche' – demanded that the government do something, but generally stopped short of advocating war. Boulanger served to discredit his own cause when he made a half-hearted stab at a coup in 1889 and then fled to Belgium, where he committed suicide a year later on the grave of his mistress. As Adolphe Thiers, France's first provisional President after the catastrophe of 1870–71, had remarked: 'Those who speak of vengeance and of revenge are thoughtless, the imposters of patriotism, whose statements have no echo. Honest people, the real patriots, want peace while leaving to the far off future the responsibility to determine all of our fates. As for me, I want peace.' The sentiment appears to have been widely shared among France's subsequent leaders, even if it was not something they cared to articulate too frequently for fear of being attacked by the nationalist right. The public too, at least until the nationalist revival in the years immediately before 1914, seems to have been largely unenthusiastic, indeed apprehensive, about the prospect of another war even for Alsace and Lorraine.[16] Intellectuals made fun of the dreams of military adventure. 'Personally, I would not give the little finger of my right hand for these forgotten lands,' wrote the prominent intellectual Remy de Gourmont in 1891. 'I need it to shake the ash off my cigarette.'[17] In left-wing and liberal circles in particular, pacifist and anti-militarist sentiments were growing. In 1910 another politician, like Thiers on the right, carefully laid out the French position at a ceremony to commemorate the fortieth anniversary of one of the other key French defeats in the Franco-Prussian War. Raymond Poincaré, who was to be President of France when the Great War broke out, and who himself came from the part of Lorraine that remained French, said: 'France sincerely desires peace. She will never do anything to disturb it. To maintain it, she will always do everything that is compatible with her dignity. But peace condemns us neither to forgetfulness nor to disloyalty.'[18]

The French also had much to preoccupy them at home in the

decades after 1871. The antipathies dating back to the Revolution and the Napoleonic period – the religious against the anti-clerical, royalists against republicans, left against right, revolutionaries against conservatives and reactionaries – remained to divide French society and undermine the legitimacy of one form of government after another. Indeed, even in 1989 when France commemorated the bicentennial of the Revolution there were deep disagreements about what it meant and how it should be remembered. The Third Republic which was born in defeat and civil war added another layer of divisions. The new Provisional Government not only had to make peace with a triumphant Germany but it also had to deal with the Paris Commune which had seized power in the name of revolution. In the end, and it was to be a scar that the Third Republic carried, the government turned its guns on the Communards; after a week of savage fighting their barricades were dismantled, the Commune dissolved, and the last rebels executed in the Père Lachaise cemetery.

The new republic looked as though it would last even less time than the First Republic of 1792, which had been overthrown by Napoleon twelve years later, or the Second which met the same fate at the hands of his nephew in 1851 after only three years. The Third Republic had many enemies, from the Communards on the left to royalists on the right, and few friends. As Gustave Flaubert said, 'I defend the poor Republic but I don't believe in it.'[19] Indeed, at times even republican politicians seemed not to believe in it as they jockeyed for office – between 1871 and 1914 France had fifty different ministries – and, far too often, appeared to be interested only in what they could make from what the public took to calling the Whore or the Republic of Cronies. In 1887, the son-in-law of the President was discovered to be selling honours, even the Légion d'Honneur; for a time, '*vieux décoré*' was an insult. In 1891–2 the Panama Canal Company collapsed, carrying away with it millions of francs and the reputations of the great de Lesseps and Gustave Eiffel, builder of the famous tower, as well as those of scores of deputies, senators, and ministers. When President Faure died in the arms of his mistress it was at least a different sort of scandal. Not surprisingly there were those in France who looked for a hero, a man on horseback, to gallop up and turn the whole sordid lot out of government. Yet even those men were failures, from Marshal MacMahon, who as President tried to bring back the monarchy (at least, said a cartoon, 'the horse looks intelligent') to the unfortunate Boulanger.

By far the most damaging scandal of all for the Third Republic was the Dreyfus affair, which was at once very simple in its central issue – had Captain Alfred Dreyfus, of the army's general staff, been rightly or wrongly convicted of passing French military secrets to the Germans? – and very complicated in its details with forgeries, lies, honest and dishonest army officers, and alternative suspects. Dreyfus, who was wrongly convicted with trumped-up evidence, showed extraordinary stoicism and fortitude in the face of public disgrace and a savage punishment while the military authorities, particularly those in the general staff, and the government showed, to put it mildly, a marked unwillingness to investigate the increasingly threadbare case against him. Indeed, certain members of the general staff took steps to create new materials which could be used against Dreyfus only to find, as in the Watergate scandal many years later in the United States, that an attempt to conceal the initial crimes led them deeper and deeper into the morass of criminal conspiracy.

The affair had been simmering on for some time before it burst into the open in 1898. Dreyfus had been hastily convicted at a court martial, and dispatched to the French penal colony on Devil's Island in the Atlantic off the coast of South America in 1894. His family and the handful of supporters who were convinced of his innocence agitated to have the verdict reopened. They were aided by the fact that the passing of French secrets to the Germans continued, and encouraged to hope when Colonel Georges Picquart, who was put in charge of investigating this second traitor, concluded that the espionage had been the work all along of the dissolute Commandant Ferdinand Esterhazy and that the army's proceedings against Dreyfus were a miscarriage of justice. Faced with this unwelcome result, the military authorities and their supporters in the government took the view that, whatever the rights and wrongs of the Dreyfus conviction, the army could not afford to have its prestige and reputation undermined. So Picquart's reward for his work was to be sent off to Tunisia, where the army may well have hoped that he would rot, and, when he refused to recant, to be dismissed, arrested and charged on grounds which turned out to be as flimsy as those in the Dreyfus case.

In January 1898, as the affair was already stirring public interest, Esterhazy was tried before a court martial and acquitted. Two days later the great writer Emile Zola published his famous letter, 'J'Accuse', addressed to the President of the Republic, Faure of amorous fame, in which he laid out the facts of the case and accused the military and the government of a shameful cover-up. He also accused Dreyfus's opponents of using the fact that Dreyfus was a Jew to stir up anti-Semitism, and of undermining the republic and its liberties. And this, he said, at a time when France was preparing for the great Paris Exposition, which would crown a century of truth and freedom. As he defiantly pointed out in his letter, Zola expected to be charged with libel and the government, with some misgivings, obliged. He was tried and sentenced for insulting the army but fled to England before he could be incarcerated.

By this point the affair had developed into a major political crisis and French society was dividing into Dreyfus supporters, the Dreyfusards, and opponents, the Anti-Dreyfusards. Radicals, liberals, republicans, anti-clericals (often overlapping categories) tended to fall into the first camp with royalists, conservatives, anti-Semites, supporters of the Church and the army, into the second. But it was never as clear-cut as that: families, friends, professions, all were divided by the affair. 'This five years' war was fought out in the newspapers', wrote Thomas Barclay, the British journalist and businessman, 'in the law courts, in the music-halls, in the churches, and even in the public thoroughfares.'[20] One family dinner ended in court when a son-in-law, who was an Anti-Dreyfusard, slapped his mother-in-law who was for Dreyfus. His wife sued for divorce. Among artists, Pissarro and Monet were Dreyfusard, Degas and Cézanne Anti. The editorial board of a cycling journal split and the Anti-Dreyfusards left to set up their own journal, devoted to the car. In February 1899 Paul Déroulède, a right-wing firebrand and notorious Anti-Dreyfusard, tried to carry out a coup against the Dreyfusard Emile Loubet, who had just been elected as President to succeed Faure. Déroulède was a much better agitator than leader and the attempt fell flat. That summer, though, Loubet had his hat smashed in by the cane of an Anti-Dreyfusard at the horse races at Auteuil.[21]

Although moderates on both sides were increasingly concerned about the future of the republic, it proved difficult to wind the affair down. In 1899 Picquart was released from jail and Dreyfus was brought back from Devil's Island to face a second court martial. It was a measure of the passions surrounding the affair that when Dreyfus's lawyer was shot in the back by an attacker (who was never caught) passers-by in the conservative town of Rennes refused to help him. Dreyfusards for their part spoke darkly of a right-wing plot. Although this time the judges split, Dreyfus was again found guilty with extenuating circumstances. The verdict and the resulting pardon by Loubet were too much for his opponents and not enough for his supporters. Dreyfus demanded a retrial, which he finally obtained in 1906. The Court of Appeal annulled the verdict and Dreyfus was reinstated in the army, as was Picquart. While the latter died in a hunting accident in January 1914, Dreyfus, who had retired from the army, re-enlisted and fought in the Great War. He died in 1935.

The Third Republic, perhaps to everyone's surprise, survived the affair. It was more stable than it sometimes appeared and it also benefited from an unwillingness on the part of most French, no matter how deeply divided they were, to risk another civil conflict. And there was more continuity than it might at first seem. Although governments came and went with great frequency the same names popped up again and again. When Georges Clemenceau, the ferocious radical politician and journalist who himself held office several times before and during the war, was accused of making a profession of bringing down governments, he replied: 'I have overthrown only one. They are all the same.'[22] The civil servants also provided continuity. Indeed, they gained considerable autonomy and influence as governments came and went.

At the Quai d'Orsay, the home of the Foreign Ministry, and among French diplomats stationed abroad, the prevailing attitude was one of contempt for the politicians and a reluctance to take direction from them. With some exceptions, Foreign Ministers were not interested in foreign affairs or in office long enough to acquire an understanding of them. The French parliament, preoccupied as its members were by the search for office or by political combat, provided little sustained oversight.[23] The commission responsible for foreign and colonial affairs was ineffectual and lackadaisical. It could ask for documents from the Quai d'Orsay or to see the minister but could do nothing when, as often happened, it was refused. The politician (and leading Dreyfusard) Joseph Reinach complained to the British ambassador: 'Its forty-four members gossip a lot; they recount confidential information to their wives, to their mistresses, to their intimate friends, who, themselves, also gossip.'[24] The French press generally had more information and influence than the French parliament. Since almost half the Foreign Ministers under the Third Republic had been journalists themselves at one time or another they understood well how useful or dangerous the press could be.

The Dreyfus affair did nevertheless leave lasting damage. The old divisions in French society were reinforced and fed by new grievances. If many on the right were confirmed in their contempt for republican and liberal values, on the left the hostility to tradition, to religion and to the military was likewise strengthened. Radicals used the affair to bring the army, which they viewed unfairly as nothing more than a repository of conservatism and a home for unreconstructed aristocrats, under control. Officers suspected of not having the correct republican outlook were purged and promotions, particularly at the highest levels, increasingly came to depend on the right sort of political credentials and connections. The consequence was to damage morale and further lower the prestige of the army. Respectable families by and large did not want their sons going into the army. In the decade before the Great War the number and the quality of applicants for the officer corps went down sharply. In 1907 Adolphe Messimy, a future Minister of War who was at that time a leading radical critic of the army, said in parliament that all officers seemed to need was a good primary education. Certainly the army did little to improve on this. Its curriculum for its officers, even at the elite staff level, was patchy, out of date, and incoherent. Too often, moreover, conformity was rewarded and talent passed over. On the eve of the Great War, the French army was poorly led, overly bureaucratic and unwelcoming to new ideas and techniques. 'Democracies are uneasy,' wrote General Emile Zurlinden, among the more principled of those who had tried and failed to resolve the Dreyfus affair. 'They have a tendency to suspect men to whom talent and circumstances draw attention, not because they do not recognize their qualities and services but because they tremble for the republic.'[25]

The Dreyfus affair also had international ramifications. Both sides had supporters who believed that the affair was part of a larger international conspiracy. One prominent nationalist reflected the suspicions on the right when he said that 'a gang of free-masons, Jews and foreigners are trying, by discrediting the army, to hand over our country to the English and the Germans'.[26] Anti-clerical Dreyfusards, by contrast, saw the hand of the Pope at work, particularly through the Jesuits. Outside France the affair had a particularly unfortunate effect on British opinion at a time when relations between France and Britain were already very tense thanks to the Fashoda incident and then the Boer War which started in 1899, shortly after the unsatisfactory result of Dreyfus's new trial. The British were generally Dreyfusards and by and large saw the affair as fresh evidence, if any were needed, for the unreliability and moral turpitude of the French. In Hyde Park, 50,000 people attended a rally to show their support for Dreyfus. Queen Victoria sent her Lord Chief Justice to Rennes to observe the court proceedings and complained to Salisbury about the 'monstrous, horrible sentence against the poor martyr Dreyfus'. She cancelled her annual holiday to France in protest and many of her subjects followed suit. Businesses seriously considered boycotting the Paris Exposition of 1900.[27] 'At least one can say for the Germans', the head of the Paris Municipal Council told Barclay, 'they are *des ennemis francs*. They don't conceal that they want to swallow us up as soon as they dare. With them we know where we are. But with the English, nobody knows where he is. They are not even unconsciously hypocritical and perfidious. They deliberately lead you on with promises and sweet words, and after they have shoved you over the precipice turn their eyes to Heaven, thank God they are a moral people and pray for your soul!'[28]

As the new century started France was in a vulnerable state both at home and abroad. Its relations with Britain were abysmal, correct but cool with Germany, and strained with Spain, Italy and Austria-Hungary, all of which were rivals in the Mediterranean. Yet France had managed to break out of the quarantine in which Bismarck had placed it and make one, very important, alliance, with Russia. It was an unlikely friendship between the republic with its revolutionary past and the autocratic power in the east. It was also an important stage on the road which led Europe to the Great War. Although it was conceived by both France and Russia as a defensive alliance, it looked, as such alliances often do, quite different from another perspective. Since Poland had not yet been reconstituted on the map of Europe, Germans could, and often did, see their country as encircled with a hostile power on each of its eastern and western borders. From the Franco-Russian alliance much would follow, not least Germany's drawing closer to Austria-Hungary as the one sure ally it could count on to keep it from being further encircled.

Even Bismarck might not have been able to keep France isolated indefinitely but the failure in 1890 of his successors to keep Germany's Reinsurance Treaty with Russia opened a door which the French were quick to go through. Russia offered an exit from isolation and its geography meant that in any future conflict with France, Germany would have to look eastwards over its shoulder. More, Russia held what France lacked – huge manpower. The demographic nightmare that the French faced, and were to face again in the 1920s and 1930s, was that their population was static while Germany's was growing. By 1914, there were 60 million Germans to 39 million French. In an age when armies relied more on quantity than quality, that meant more potential soldiers for Germany.

What helped to make Russia receptive to the idea of an alliance was that France could provide what it badly needed: capital. The Russian economy was expanding rapidly and it needed more funds than the government could raise within Russia. While German banks had once been the chief source of foreign loans for Russia, they were now increasingly lending within Germany itself, where demand was also growing. London was another possibility for raising loans but the poor state of Russian–British relations meant the British government and British banks were reluctant to lend to a country which might at any moment become an enemy. That left France among the major European powers. Thanks to the thrift of its people, it was awash with capital looking for good investments. In 1888, two years, before the Reinsurance Treaty lapsed, French banks made the first of what were going to be many loans to the Russian government. By 1900 France was by far the biggest foreign investor in Russia (bigger than Britain and Germany combined), fuelling the rapid expansion of Russian industries and infrastructure. In 1914 the railway lines along which Russian armies moved to their frontiers had been largely built with French money.

French investors, as they were to discover to their cost when the Bolsheviks took over and cancelled all foreign debts, had a quarter of all their foreign investments in Russia.[29]

Both sides had to overcome the past: Napoleon burning Moscow in 1812, Tsar Alexander I and his troops marching in triumph through Paris two years later, or the Crimean War. Both had to swallow their suspicions whether Russia's of French republicanism and anti-clericalism or France's of tsarist autocracy and orthodoxy. Yet the Russian upper classes admired French styles and often spoke French more easily than they did Russian, and in the last quarter of the nineteenth century the French discovered a taste for the great Russian novels and Russian music. More importantly, the Russian Foreign Ministry and its military leaders had grown alarmed by the end of 1880s at the possibility that Britain, considered an unfriendly power, might join the Triple Alliance of Germany, Austria-Hungary and Italy. Russia would in that case be as isolated as France. Crucially, for he had the last word, the tsar at the time, Alexander III, was coming around to the idea of a French alliance. He was influenced by his wife, who, as a member of the Danish royal family, loathed Prussia for defeating her country and taking the duchies of Schleswig-Holstein. He also seems to have been deeply affronted by the German decision not to renew the Reinsurance Treaty in 1890. A month after the treaty lapsed, Russian generals talked about a possible military agreement to a French general who was attending their annual army manoeuvres.[30]

The following year France and Russia worked out a secret military agreement in which they agreed to come to each other's defence if either was attacked by a member of the Triple Alliance. It was an indication of the boldness of the step for both parties that it took another year and a half to get the agreement ratified. And over the next decade there were going to be moments when the Franco-Russian alliance nearly fell to pieces when the interests of the two parties diverged or clashed. In 1898, for example, the French were deeply disappointed when the Russians refused to support them over Fashoda. The alliance in itself did not bring war in 1914 but its existence added to the tensions in Europe.

Although the agreement was a secret one, it was evident to onlookers that there had been a significant shift in Europe's international relations. In 1891 the tsar gave Russia's most important decoration to the French President. That summer the French fleet paid a courtesy visit to the Russian naval base at Kronstadt, just west of St Petersburg, and the world saw the extraordinary sight of the tsar standing to attention while the Marseillaise was played, although, as a revolutionary song, it was banned in Russia. Two years later, a Russian fleet called in at Toulon for a return visit. The French crowds shouted 'Vive la Russie! Vive le Tsar!' and the visitors were entertained with dinners, receptions, luncheons, toasts, and speeches. 'There was scarcely a woman in Paris', reported one journalist, 'who would not have been ready to forget her duties to satisfy the desire of any of the Russian sailors.'[31] The British ambassador was amused at the enthusiasm shown by good republicans for the tsar and his regime but felt that the outpouring of French emotion was understandable: 'The people of France, like all Celtic nations, are sensitive and morbidly hungry for sympathy and admiration. The German war and its results wounded their vanity to the quick, and though they have borne their humiliation with patience and dignity they do not the less resent it.'[32]

In 1898, shortly before the Fashoda crisis, the man who would steer France into another improbable alliance, this time with its old enemy Britain, became Foreign Minister. Unusually, for the Third Republic, Théophile Delcassé, was going to stay in office for seven years until another crisis, this time over Morocco, forced him to resign. From a modest background, he came from the south near the Pyrenees. His mother had died in 1857 when he was five and, when his father – a minor court official – remarried, the new wife was cool towards the boy, who was often sent away to stay with his grandmother. He obtained a university degree in French and classical literature and tried, with little success, to be a playwright. To support himself he took up first teaching and then journalism, which, like many ambitious young men in France, he saw as a vehicle to enter politics. In 1887 he married a rich widow who was prepared to devote her fortune to his career and two years later he was elected to the French parliament as a moderate radical. He chose to make his first speech on foreign policy and it was, by his own account, a great success.[33]

Plain featured, dark-complexioned and small (he wore shoes with elevated heels), Delcassé was an unprepossessing Foreign Minister. His enemies called him 'The Gnome' or 'The Hallucinated Lilliputian'. Nor did he have marked intellectual abilities. Nevertheless he was very effective through a combination of determination, persuasiveness, and hard work. He claimed that he frequently got to his office before dawn and left after midnight. He was also fortunate that Loubet, who was President of France for much of his tenure, left him alone to do as he pleased. (Loubet's presidency, said Paul Cambon, one of France's most important diplomats, was 'no longer anything but a decoration which is useful for nothing'.)[34] Delcassé's failings were his contempt for most politicians and much of the Quai d'Orsay and his love for secrecy, which meant that those who should have known key French policies and initiatives were often kept in the dark. 'How many times', said Maurice Paléologue, French ambassador for many years in Russia, 'have I heard an anxious voice behind me as I was leaving the room: "Don't put anything on paper!" or "Forget everything I've just told you," or "Burn it."'[35]

Although he had learned self-control, Delcassé was a man of strong passions and the greatest of these was France itself. He was fond of quoting the words of his nationalist hero Léon Gambetta that France was 'the greatest moral personality in the world'. As a journalist he had written articles urging that French schoolchildren be taught that they were superior to little Germans and British children.[36] Like others of his generation, he had been heartbroken at France's defeat in 1870–71; his daughter noticed that he could never bring himself to talk of Alsace and Lorraine. Unusually, though, he did not hate Germans or German culture; he was a great admirer of Wagner.[37] He nevertheless took it as given that France could not have a rapprochement with Germany and was therefore an early and enthusiastic supporter of the alliance with Russia.

Delcassé saw France's national revival lying in part in the acquisition of colonies and from an early stage in his political career worked closely with the powerful colonial lobby. He also shared the increasingly popular view that France had a Mediterranean destiny which was one of the reasons that he found it so hard to forgive the British for seizing Egypt. Like other French nationalists of the period, he dreamed of French influence extending itself into the Arab territories of the creaking Ottoman Empire. And, like many of his compatriots, including those on the left, he believed that French rule would confer the benefits of civilisation. As Jaurès, the great socialist leader, said of Morocco, 'France's right to do so is all the greater since there is no question of surprise attack and military violence and because the civilization which she represents to the natives of Africa is certainly superior to the present state of the Moroccan regime.'[38] In pursuit of empire, Delcassé, the strong anti-clerical, discovered an enthusiasm for protecting the Christian minorities under Ottoman rule in such areas as Syria and Palestine. And he looked southwards to North Africa, where France already had the large colony of Algeria, at Morocco, which was increasingly falling into anarchy. In pursuit of French goals, he was prepared to work with France's neighbours, Italy and Spain, with Germany possibly, but more importantly, with Britain.

As early as the mid 1880s, Delcassé had wanted a better understanding with Britain. More, he had an even grander scheme: to bring about what eventually became the Triple Entente between France, Russia and Britain. The conclusion of the Franco-Russian Agreement in 1894 was for him an important first step and when he took up the post of Foreign Minister in 1898, he told the British ambassador that he thought it 'eminently desirable' that there should be a cordial understanding between Britain, France, and Russia. 'I really do believe that the little man is honest in saying this,' the ambassador told Salisbury. The British Prime Minister, however, was not prepared to abandon his policy of isolation and at the end of the decade Fashoda and the Boer War sent France's relations with Britain into an even deeper freeze.[39]

After Fashoda, Delcassé started to work quietly towards acquiring Morocco. With the flimsy excuse that they needed to protect a geological expedition, French forces moved in from the Algerian border and occupied key oases in the south of Morocco. In 1900 Delcassé worked out a deal with the Italians where Italy would have a free hand in Libya while France would have one in Morocco. He also negotiated with Spain in, said Cambon, 'a state of nervous over-excitement such as I have never seen him in, and that is saying a good deal'.[40] That attempt failed because of changes of government in Spain but the failure may have helped to persuade Delcassé that the time had come to consider seriously some form of arrangement with Britain. He was also under considerable pressure from his old friends in the colonial lobby who had come to the conclusion that the way forward for France was to give up its claims in Egypt in return for British recognition of French dominance in Morocco.

French public opinion, always a factor to be taken into account, was also starting to shift. The end of the Boer War, and the British treaty with the Boers in May 1902, removed one source of animosity to Britain. Shortly afterwards a sudden crisis in Latin America brought home to the French the welcome realisation of how much the British public hated and feared Germany. Venezuela, which owed money to British and German interests, was refusing to pay up and Germany suggested the two countries mount a joint naval expedition, to which Britain, with some reluctance, agreed. The British were right to be cautious; the United States, seeing a violation of the sacred Monroe Doctrine and always inclined to be suspicious of Britain, was infuriated. In Britain there was a public outcry and consternation in the Cabinet about risking relations with the United States, which had only recently improved and, more vehemently still, about working with Germany. Kipling published a poem in *The Times* just before the Christmas of 1902 which asked 'Was there no other fleet to find/ That you strike bands with these?' and went on to a rousing last verse:

> *In sight of peace – from the Narrow Seas*
> *O'er half the world to run –*
> *With a cheated crew, to league anew*
> *With the Goth and the shameless Hun!*

Prince Metternich, the German ambassador in London, who was a strong supporter of better Anglo-German relations, said he had never seen such hostility in Britain towards another nation.[41]

Early in 1903, Delcassé took the decision that France should attempt to settle its differences with Britain and he instructed Paul Cambon, his trusted ambassador in London, to open discussions with the new British Foreign Secretary, Lord Lansdowne.[42] Cambon was well ahead of his Foreign Minister on this. He had floated several proposals to Lansdowne over the previous two years: that France give up its old treaty rights in the British colony of Newfoundland or possibly accept British control of Egypt in return for a free hand in Morocco or that France and Britain divide Morocco up. The British had listened with interest but not committed themselves. They suspected, rightly, that Cambon was acting on his own authority, as he so often did.

Small, dignified, impeccably dressed, and walking with a slight limp, Paul Cambon had a strong sense of his own importance. His career had been distinguished: France's representative in Tunisia, then ambassador to Spain and the Ottoman Empire, he had gained a reputation for being highly effective and honest, as well as stubborn and resistant to orders from those he felt were incompetent, which included most of his superiors. He believed, as he told his son, 'Diplomatic history is only a long recital of attempts by agents to achieve something and of resistance from Paris.'[43] While he agreed with Delcassé's policies and shared his ambitions to make France a great power again, he saw diplomats as active partners in the making of foreign policy. His time in Constantinople as ambassador had given him a dislike for Russia and a profound mistrust of its ambitions at the eastern end of the Mediterranean but he was a realist who saw the advantages for France in having Russia as a friend. He did not, however, think Russia – 'moins utile qu'embarrassante' – could be relied upon. One of his great fears was that Russia and Germany would recreate their old friendship which would leave France isolated in Europe again.[44] Early on in his career, Cambon had come to the conclusion that France should look to Britain. As the Moroccan issue heated up, he also worried that Britain was getting too involved there and that France would lose Morocco unless it did a deal over Egypt while it still could.

Although he spent much of his career in Britain, from 1898 to 1920, Cambon had no particular enthusiasm for the British or British culture. He went to London only out of a sense of duty. When he was invited to dine with Queen Victoria at Windsor Castle shortly after his arrival he found the old queen lively but the meal appalling. 'I would not tolerate such a dinner in my home.'[45] Nothing ever changed his mind about British food. He opposed the opening of British schools in France and felt French raised in Britain were mentally deficient.[46] When Oxford gave him an honorary degree in 1904 to celebrate the new friendship between Britain and France, Cambon wrote a funny and highly critical account to his brother Jules of the heat and the interminable ceremonies. 'The Latin and Greek verses pronounced with an English accent were simply frightful.' Of the final oration praising the university, he said, 'I did not make the least effort to pay attention; I was exhausted.'[47] Although he was in London for over two decades, he never learned to speak English properly. At his meetings with the monolingual Grey, the Foreign Secretary from 1905, he spoke slowly and distinctly in French while Grey did the same in English.[48] He did, though, develop a grudging admiration for the British. Queen Victoria's funeral was chaotic: 'But the superiority of the British is that it is a matter of complete indifference to them if they appear to be stupid.'[49]

Cambon's task in London was complicated by the fact that the British did not yet have a clear policy towards an entente with France. They were also, and the French had some inkling of this, playing their own game in Morocco. Although Britain did not have a fixed policy on Morocco, there were certainly those in the government, like Chamberlain, who seriously considered the idea of turning it into a protectorate or, until relations worsened at the start of the century, perhaps dividing it with Germany.[50] In the Admiralty there was talk of establishing naval bases or ports along Morocco's Atlantic and Mediterranean coasts, or at the very least, preventing other nations such as Germany, Spain or France from doing so.

Where today the international community sees failed or failing states as a problem, in the age of imperialism the powers saw them as an opportunity. China, the Ottoman Empire, Persia, all were weak, divided, and apparently ready to be carved up. So was Morocco, which was becoming increasingly anarchic by 1900. The death of the strong and capable Sultan Hassan I in 1894 had left it in the hands of a teenager, Abdelaziz. 'He is not bad looking, but podgy and puffy; good features and good clear eyes,' said Arthur Nicolson, stationed there as a British diplomat. 'He didn't look unhealthy, but like a boy who ate too much.'[51] Abdelaziz proved unable to keep control of his subjects. While his administration grew increasingly corrupt, powerful regional leaders asserted their independence, pirates attacked merchants along the coasts and bandits raided caravans in the interior and kidnapped the rich for ransom. Late in 1902 a rebellion threatened to topple the whole rickety regime.

The young sultan played in his palaces and, as the French noticed, surrounded himself with British servants from grooms to the man who fixed his bicycles. (He did, to be fair, also have a Frenchman to make his soda water.) Abdelaziz's most trusted adviser and commander-in-chief of the Moroccan army, and this particularly alarmed the French, was Kaid Maclean, a former British soldier. 'He was small and round, with a clean white beard, and the gayest eyes that ever shone above a bagpipe,' said Nicolson, who thought him a kindly, honest man. 'Arrayed in a turban and a white bernous he would stride along the garden paths blowing into the bagpipes. "The Banks of Loch Lomond" would squeal out into the African sunshine.'[52] When Maclean visited Britain in 1902 and was invited to stay at Balmoral and given a knighthood by Edward VII, most French diplomats concluded that their suspicions of the British were well founded. Delcassé's representative in Morocco reported gloomily that the British would use every means from persuasion to bribery in Morocco and when those failed the wives of British diplomats knew what they had to do to further Britain's interests.[53]

Cambon nevertheless continued to press Lansdowne. The two men had held several talks in the course of 1902 in which the various colonial issues, from Siam to Newfoundland, which still divided their two countries were explored. Lansdowne was interested but cautious since he still hoped for a better understanding with Germany and it is possible that, if Germany had not started the naval race and if German diplomacy had been better, he might have got what he wanted. As it was, he came to share the exasperation of much of the Foreign Office with German methods and rhetoric. 'I have been struck', he wrote to a colleague at the end of 1901, 'by the comparative friendliness of the French. At this moment if I am to have a tiresome minor affair with one of the Embassies, I would sooner have it with the French Embassy than with any other. Their manners are better and in substance they are easier to deal with than the rest.'[54]

Like his mentor Salisbury, Lansdowne was an aristocrat from an ancient family who entered public service out of a sense of duty. A thin, neat man, he had started out a Liberal, like all his family, and served in Gladstone's Cabinet and then as governor-general of Canada, which he loved, not least for its salmon fishing. He had parted ways with his fellow Liberals over Home Rule for Ireland and joined the Conservatives who opposed it. In 1900, when an ailing Salisbury was persuaded to give up the Foreign Office, he appointed Lansdowne, to some surprise, as his successor. If Lansdowne was not a great or a flamboyant

Foreign Minister, he was a solid and sensible one. Like Salisbury he would have preferred Britain to remain free of all entanglements but he had come round reluctantly to the idea that Britain needed friends and so supported the alliance with Japan and made overtures to both Russia and Germany, neither of which had so far produced results.

By 1902 newspapers in both France and Britain as well as chambers of commerce were advocating a greater understanding between their two countries, and in Egypt the effective ruler of the country, the forceful British representative Lord Cromer, was also coming to the view that a settlement that allowed France Morocco would improve the situation in Egypt for the British administration. (As members of the Caisse de la Dette which protected foreign holders of Egypt's debt, the French had been able to block any reforms in Egypt's finances.)[55] In the early part of 1903, Lansdowne took a small step in the direction of a larger agreement when he and Cambon agreed that British, French and Spanish banks could make a joint loan to Morocco. Then in March 1903 King Edward decided, with the approval of his ministers, to pay a visit to Paris.

Although the French, as good republicans, had a greatly exaggerated sense of the powers of the British monarchy and tended to see the subsequent Entente Cordiale as Edward's personal policy, his visit was important as a gesture of goodwill and in warming up French public opinion towards the possibility of an entente with Britain. And it signalled a new attitude and a new beginning, much as President Nixon's trip to Beijing did in 1972. Most importantly of all, it was a success. When Edward arrived in Paris his reception by the crowds was cool, even hostile, at times and the occasional shout could be heard of '*Vivent les Boers!*' and '*Vive Fashoda!*' Delcassé, who was accompanying the guests, kept saying loudly, '*Quel enthousiasme!*' The French government went all out to entertain the king (and French merchants joined the festivities with special souvenirs from postcards to walking sticks with the king's head, even a new coat called 'Le King Edward'). There was a grand banquet at the Elysée Palace with *crème Windsor, oeufs à la Richmond, selle de mouton à l'anglaise* and *pudding à la Windsor* while the Quai d'Orsay served *jambon d'York truffée champenoise* at its lunch. Edward behaved impeccably throughout and replied to the toasts in excellent French. At the Elysée banquet, he talked of his many happy memories of Paris, a city where one meets 'all that is intelligent and beautiful'. At the theatre one evening he saw a famous French actress in the lobby and said, 'Mademoiselle, I remember applauding you in London where you represented all the grace and spirit of France.' Word spread through the audience and he was cheered as he entered his box. Even the horse races he attended provided a good omen when a horse named John Bull won. When he left Paris, the crowds were shouting *Vive Edouard! Vive notre bon Teddy!* and, understandably, *Vive la République!*[56]

Delcassé was delighted with the visit and convinced that the British government was now ready for a sweeping agreement, in part because Edward in private conversations seems to have gone well beyond what a constitutional monarch should do. The king had expressed full support for France's sway over Morocco and warned Delcassé against the 'mad and malicious' Kaiser.[57] Two months later, President Loubet and Delcassé paid a return visit to London. There was a minor contretemps beforehand when the king made it clear that he expected French officials to wear the official court dress which included knee breeches, *culottes* in French. This, for a nation which remembered the *sans-culottes*, the lower-class republicans who led the Revolution of 1789, would have caused an uproar in France. Edward gave way and the visit went off splendidly. That autumn delegations from the French and British parliaments exchanged visits, something that was both unprecedented and a sign that the entente went deeper than the top levels of government.

In the course of Loubet's visit, Delcassé told Lansdowne that he was in favour 'of a comprehensive settlement' and the two men agreed that Morocco, Egypt, and Newfoundland were the outstanding problems. For the next nine months negotiations, difficult at times, took place in London between Cambon and Lansdowne. Siam was divided into spheres of influence and competing claims and grievances in Madagascar and the New Hebrides (now Vanuatu) were sorted out relatively easily. Newfoundland nearly wrecked the whole agreement, as the smallest issues so often do. What was ostensibly at stake were the fishing rights that French fishermen had enjoyed alone off the coast of the island since the Treaty of Utrecht in 1713. Whether a lobster was a fish or not also caused considerable debate. If they were to give up their rights, the French demanded compensation elsewhere, preferably the British colony of Gambia in West Africa. The French were stubborn partly because they were under pressure from their own fishermen and chambers of commerce in French ports, partly because the rights in Newfoundland were one of the last remnants of the French Empire in North America.[58] In the end both sides gave way; the British offered territory to the north of Nigeria, a small slice of Gambia, and some islands off the coast of the West African French colony of Guinea and the French settled for less than they had wanted. The centrepiece of the agreement was the deal over Egypt and Morocco: France accepted British suzerainty in Egypt while Britain effectively gave Morocco over to France's influence. Although the French promised not to change the political status quo there, France was conveniently to be responsible for maintaining order. In order to ensure that Britain's sea route into the Mediterranean remained secure, there were to be no fortifications on the nearby part of the Moroccan coast which at its closest was fourteen miles to the south of the British naval base at Gibraltar. Secret clauses made it clear that both sides did not expect Morocco to remain independent for long.[59]

On 8 April 1904, less than six years after the Fashoda crisis, Cambon came to Lansdowne's room in the Foreign Office to sign the agreements. Delcassé was waiting anxiously in Paris and Cambon rushed to the French embassy to use the new and unfamiliar telephone which had just been installed. '*It's Signed!*' he shouted at the top of his lungs.[60] Although there was some criticism in France that Delcassé had given away too much, the agreement was approved in the French parliament. In Britain, the news was received with enthusiasm. France would be much more useful as an ally against Germany than Japan. Imperialists were also pleased because Britain was confirmed in its control of Egypt while opponents of empire welcomed an end to imperialist rivalries. The *Manchester Guardian* spoke for liberals and the left when it said: 'The value of the new friendship lies not in the avoidance of disputes, but in the chance that it affords a genuine alliance between the democracies in both countries for the furtherance of the democratic cause.'[61]

In Germany, where the leadership had never taken the possibility of a friendship between Britain and France seriously, the reaction was one of shock and dismay. The Kaiser told Bülow that the new situation was troubling; with England and France no longer at odds, 'the need to take account of our position becomes ever less pressing'.[62] The well-connected

Baroness Spitzemberg wrote in her diary: 'There is profound gloom at the Foreign Ministry over the Franco-British agreement on Morocco, one of the worst defeats of German policy since the Dual Alliance.' The rabidly nationalist Pan-German League passed a resolution to say that the agreement on Morocco showed a 'humiliating disregard' of Germany, which had been treated like a third-rate power. The National Liberals, a conservative party which usually supported the government, demanded a statement from the Chancellor while the Kaiser made speeches saying that the new world situation might oblige Germany to intervene and pointed out that the German armed forces were ready and strong.[63]

Britain and Germany had already drifted apart and public opinion in both countries was speeding the process but the Entente Cordiale, as it came to be known, helped to solidify the gulf between them. And while British statesmen such as Lansdowne may have believed that they were only settling colonial disputes, in reality the new friendship between two European powers had significance for the balance of power in Europe. France, with its existing Russian alliance, was now in a stronger position as regards Germany, although how much stronger remained to be seen. Britain would soon face choices over whether to back France in moments of crisis or risk losing its friendship. As Sir Francis Bertie said in 1907 when he was ambassador in Paris: 'The danger for us to avoid will be to make the French lose confidence in our support and drive them into some arrangement with Germany, detrimental to us while not being harmful to the French. At the same time we must not encourage the French to rely on our material support to the extent of encouraging them to beard the Germans.'[64] Like it or not, Britain was likely to become involved with France's disputes in Europe, in particular ones arising because of Morocco. Germany also had interests there and, with justification, felt that these had been ignored and it was not going to be long before Germany made its displeasure known.

Lloyd George recalled in his war memoirs that he went visit to the Liberal elder statesman, Lord Rosebery, on the day the entente was announced. 'His first greeting to me was: "Well, I suppose you are just as pleased as the rest of them with this French agreement?" I assured him that I was delighted that our snarling and scratching relations with France had come to an end at last. He replied: "You are all wrong. It means war with Germany in the end!"'[65]

CHAPTER 7

The Bear and
the Whale:
Russia and
Great Britain

In the North Sea on the night of Friday 21 October 1904 the moon was nearly full but there were patches of mist. Some fifty British trawlers from Hull were spread out over seven or eight miles on the fishing ground of Dogger Bank midway between the north of England and the coast of Germany as the Russian Baltic Fleet sailed past. It was heading for the Channel and then onwards on a doomed voyage to the Far East. The trawlers had their nets out and on deck, under acetylene lights, their crews were gutting the catch. For the fishermen it was a welcome change from routine: they joked and laughed as they saw the lights marking out the battleships and their searchlights playing on the water. It was light enough that they could see the faces of the Russian sailors. 'I called all hands on deck', said Captain Whelpton, a trawler skipper, 'to witness what I thought was going to be a brilliant spectacle.' Suddenly a bugle sounded and there was a rattle of artillery and machine guns. 'Good god!' exclaimed Whelpton. 'This is not blank, lie down lads and look after yourself.'[1] The trawlers did not have time to haul in their heavy nets and so they sat there immobilised on the sea while the firing went on for perhaps twenty minutes. The Russian fleet then steamed on, leaving two men dead, others wounded and a trawler on its way to the bottom of the ocean. Shortly afterwards one of the Russian ships mistook another in the fleet for a Japanese warship and fired on it as well. The whole episode was indicative of the confusion and muddle that marked the Russian war effort.

British public opinion was enraged at the Russian fleet – 'Drunk as Usual' said the *Daily Mail* – and so was the government. It demanded a full apology from the Russian government and complete reparations for the damage. The Russians refused at first to admit that their fleet had done anything wrong, arguing that they had good reason to suspect that Japanese torpedo boats had made their way to European waters to attack the Russian Baltic Fleet. Lansdowne rejected this and demanded on 26 October that the Russian fleet put in at Vigo, on the Atlantic coast of Spain, until the matter was sorted out. 'If it were allowed to continue its journey without calling at Vigo,' he told the Russian ambassador, 'we might find ourselves at war before the week was over.' The Russians responded the following day with belligerence; they had 'indisputable proof' that the Japanese were planning to attack the fleet. In any case it was the fault of the trawlers that they got attacked, added Admiral Rozhdestvensky, commander of the Baltic Fleet, for they had got in his way. That evening, Lansdowne felt 'as if the betting was about even as between peace & war'.[2] Although war was averted on this occasion, the Dogger Bank episode was yet another of what were becoming frequent war scares in Europe. It also worsened, if that were possible, relations between Britain and Russia. And for Russia it was part of the unfolding catastrophe of its war with Japan.

Russia had stumbled into war with Japan in the Far East through a mixture of incompetence, unfounded optimism about its own abilities, and contempt, much of it racialist, for the Japanese. Russian ambitions to build its influence in Manchuria and Korea, and perhaps eventually to absorb them into the growing Russian Empire, had led it into conflict with other European powers, especially the British, and most dangerously of all with Japan, which was rapidly modernising and becoming a significant player in Asia. In 1894–5 Japan had fought a war with the moribund Chinese Empire, partly over who was to control Korea, and had won a decisive victory. In the peace, China recognised the independence of Korea, thus paving the way for Japan to move in.

7. The wounded Russian bear turns on its own ruler. The country nearly had a revolution in 1905 when it suffered a crushing military defeat in the Far East at the hands of Japan. Although Tsar Nicholas' regime survived, and even made some reforms, another war and a second revolution were to sweep the old order away for good in 1917.

(Korea was to become part of the Japanese Empire in 1910.) Japan also got possession of Taiwan and some nearby islands as well concessions to build railways and ports in the Chinese territory of Manchuria. That last was too much for Russia, which led the other European powers in a concerted action to force Japan to back away from Manchuria. The Japanese had reason to feel aggrieved when Russia promptly extracted its own concessions there, including the right to build a southern spur of the Trans-Siberian Railway across the north of Manchuria as well as a north–south railway, and a lease on territory at its southern tip including the ports of Port Arthur (today Lushun) and Dairen (Dalian). China was too weak to do anything about this move into its territory but the other powers were alarmed at Russia's aggressive policies. The Boxer Rebellion brought further tensions when Russia used it as an excuse to send its troops to occupy key points along the course of the north–south railway line which it was building through Manchuria from Harbin (Heilongjiang) in the north to the leased territories in the south. By the time the Russo-Japanese War broke out in 1904, Russia had found itself dangerously isolated. Even its ally France made it quite clear that their alliance only covered Europe.

On the night of 8 February 1904 Japanese torpedo boats attacked Russian ships lying at anchor at Port Arthur without warning. One Japanese force landed north of Port Arthur to cut the railway line and attack the port and another landed in nearby Korea at Inchon (famous almost half a century later as the site of the American landing in the Korean War) to move northwards to the Yalu River, the border with Russia. The folly of provoking a war with Japan when Russian supplies and reinforcements had to come from thousands of miles away along the single-track and still unfinished line of the Trans-Siberian Railway rapidly became apparent. Russia suffered a string of defeats over the next eighteen months. Port Arthur was besieged and the Russian Far Eastern Fleet was bottled up. Attempts to break the siege by land or sea only led to heavy Russian losses. Port Arthur surrendered at the start of January 1905 and by then most of the Russian Pacific Fleet lay at the bottom of the sea.

The news reached the Baltic Fleet at Madagascar as it was making its way around the world to relieve the siege. (The fleet had been obliged to go around the tip of Africa because the British would not allow it to pass through the Suez Canal.) The admiral in command decided to make a run for the Russian Pacific port of Vladivostok. On 27 May 1905, as the fleet went into the Tsushima Strait between Korea and Japan, the Japanese fleet was waiting for it. The subsequent battle was one of the most stunning naval victories in history. The Russian Baltic Fleet was annihilated and over 4,000 men drowned and even more captured. Japanese losses amounted to 116 men and a few torpedo boats.

Russia was forced to accept President Theodore Roosevelt's offer to mediate and the Japanese, who were reaching the limit of their resources, were prepared to talk as well. That August Russian and Japanese representatives met in a navy yard at Portsmouth, New Hampshire. Roosevelt's motives were mixed: he genuinely felt that the United States had a moral obligation as one of the world's civilised nations to foster peace but he also loved the opportunity for the United States, and himself, to be in the centre of great events. As far as the belligerents were concerned, he disapproved, as did many Americans, of Russian autocracy and he had initially been sympathetic to Japan, a 'desirable addition' to the international order, even going so far as to admire the way the Japanese had started hostilities with a surprise attack on Russia without bothering with formality of declaring war. As Japan crushed Russia, though, he became concerned for the American position in Asia and worried that the Japanese might turn their attentions to China. Having brought the two sides together, Roosevelt did not himself take part in the discussions but watched at a distance from his estate on Long Island, trying to contain himself as both sides dragged out the negotiations. 'What I really want to do', he complained, 'is give utterance to whoops of rage and jump up and knock their heads together.'[3] In September Russia and Japan finally signed the Treaty of Portsmouth. Japan got half of the Russian island of Sakhalin and the Russian concessions at the southern tip of Manchuria. The following year Roosevelt won the newly instituted Nobel Peace Prize.

The war cost Russia more than territory: it had 400,000 casualties, a large part of its navy was destroyed, and it spent 2.5 million roubles it could ill afford. 'A war with Japan would be extremely unpopular', General Aleksei Kuropatkin, the Minister of War, had warned the tsar in November 1903 shortly before hostilities broke out, 'and would increase the feeling of dissatisfaction with the ruling authorities.' The governor-general of the Caucasus went even further. 'War must not be allowed,' he told Kuropatkin. 'The question of a war could become "dynastic".'[4] Both men were right. There had been little enthusiasm among the public for the war, right from the start, and by 1904 there already existed considerable dissatisfaction with the government among the intellectuals, the growing middle classes, and the more enlightened landowners who were active in the new local governments.

Periods of extraordinarily rapid development such as Russia had been experiencing especially since the 1890s are not easy to accommodate. Russia's boom brought promise of a better future but it had also unsettled an already divided society. The magnates in Moscow and St Petersburg lived in magnificent mansions and assembled great collections of art and furniture while their workers lived in squalor and laboured long hours in appalling conditions. While in the poorer villages, peasants rarely ate meat and lived close to starvation, especially in the long winter months, the great landowners lived in the same style as their counterparts in richer European countries. Even the extravagant Prince Yusupov (later to be the assassin of Rasputin) could not run through his fortune which included well over half a million acres of land as well as mines and factories, not to mention the silver vases which he liked to fill with uncut gems and pearls. In 1914 Countess Kleinmichel, one of the leaders of society in St Petersburg, gave what she thought of as a small fancy-dress ball for her nieces: 'I sent over three hundred invitations, for my house could not hold a greater number, and as the Russian custom is to give a supper at little tables, it was also as much as my kitchen could undertake.'[5]

In spite of censorship and repression, demands for an end to autocracy and for representative government and civil liberties were coming from all sides. Balts, Poles, Finns, Ukrainians, among Russia's many subject peoples, were also pushing for greater autonomy. A small but fanatical minority had long since given up hope of reform and were instead committed to overthrowing the old order violently through acts of terrorism or armed insurrection. Between 1905 and 1909 nearly 1,500 provincial governors and officials were assassinated. Industrial workers, their numbers growing too as Russia's industrialisation charged ahead, showed an increasing militancy. In 1894, the year that Nicholas II became tsar, there were sixty-eight strikes; ten years later there were over five hundred.[6] Although the radical socialist parties on the left were still banned and their leaders in exile, they were beginning to assume leadership in the emerging workers' organisations. By 1914 the best-organised party, the Bolsheviks, dominated most of the unions and held the majority of the seats for workers in the Duma, the new Russian parliament.

In the years before 1914 Russia was a giant organism moving in several directions at once and it was not clear what its final shape might be. Parts especially out in the remoter countryside looked much as they had done for centuries while the big cities with their electric lights, trams, and modern shops, looked like Paris or Berlin or London. Yet the impression of an eternal unchanging rural Russia – as the tsar and many conservatives as well as later observers thought – was highly misleading.

The end of serfdom in 1861, the spread of communications, the growth of literacy, the movement of peasants into the cities to work (and their return to see their families), were shaking village life and undermining its institutions. Elders, priests, traditions, and the once all-powerful village commune no longer had the power over village life that they once had.

Modernity was challenging the old certainties in both the urban and rural areas. The religious still venerated icons and believed in miracles and ghosts; the new industrialists were busy buying up the work of Matisse, Picasso or Braque to build some of the world's great collections of modern art. Russian traditional folk art coexisted with experimental writers and artists: Stanislavsky and Diaghilev were revolutionising theatre and dance. Daring writers were challenging accepted morality while at the same time there was a spiritual revival and a search for deeper meaning in life. Reactionaries wanted to go back to the time before Peter the Great opened up Russia to European influences; extreme revolutionaries, many of them in exile such as Lenin or Trotsky, wanted to smash Russian society.

Economic and social changes that had taken a century or more in western Europe were compressed into a generation in Russia. And Russia did not have strongly developed and deeply rooted institutions that might have helped to absorb and manage the changes. The most stable country in Europe, Britain, had had centuries to build its parliament, local councils, laws, and law courts (and had weathered crises including a civil war along the way). More, British society had grown incrementally and slowly, taking generations to develop attitudes and institutions, from universities to chambers of commerce, clubs and associations, a free press, the whole complex web of civil society which sustains a workable political system. Closer to home, Russia's neighbour Germany may have been a new country but it possessed old institutions in its cities and states and had a confident and large middle class capable of sustaining a strong society. Austria-Hungary was more fragile and was also struggling with burgeoning nationalisms but it too had a society whose institutions were more fully realised than Russia's.

There are two contemporary parallels for what Russia faced in the decade or two before 1914. One is the Gulf States which have gone in a single lifetime from a modest and manageable way of life where change came slowly, to an international world where their sudden wealth made them players, from one-storey mud-brick buildings to the glitter of Las Vegas and skyscrapers going higher and faster. But the Gulf States have the great advantage of being small both geographically and in terms of population, and are therefore, for better or worse, capable of being manipulated by strong forces or individuals, whether from outside or within. Their rulers were, with some external support, skilful enough to manage the rapid changes, or, if they were not, briskly replaced. For the tsar the challenge was infinitely greater: to somehow keep control of a Russia, so huge and so diverse, where everything, whether population or the distance from its European borders to the Pacific, was so vast.

The second contemporary parallel to the Russia before the Great War is therefore China. It too had faced the challenges of change with a regime that was sadly unprepared and it too lacked the robust institutions that might have eased the transition from one form of society to another. It took China nearly half a century and appalling human costs, from the collapse of the old dynastic system to the emergence of Communist rule, to get a stable government – and it could be argued that China is still struggling to build the lasting institutions it needs if it is not to regress to an increasingly ineffective and corrupt regime. It is not surprising that Russian society, caught as it was in a transition from the old to the new, creaked and started to buckle under the strains. Things might have worked out if there had been time and if Russia had managed to avoid costly wars. Instead it fought two, the second even more disastrous than the first, within a decade. Many of Russia's leaders, including by 1914 the tsar himself, knew well the dangers of war but for some of them there was also the seductive temptation of rallying society around a noble cause and healing its divisions. In 1904 the Minister of the Interior, Vyacheslav Plehve, is reported to have said that Russia needed 'a small victorious war' which would take the minds of the Russian masses off 'political questions'.[7]

The Russo-Japanese War showed the folly of that idea. In its early months Plehve himself was blown apart by a bomb; towards its end the newly formed Bolsheviks tried to seize Moscow. The war served to deepen and bring into sharp focus the existing unhappiness of many Russians with their own society and its rulers. As the many deficiencies, from command to supplies, of the Russian war effort became apparent, criticism grew, both of the government and, since the regime was a highly personalised one, of the tsar himself. In St Petersburg a cartoon showed the tsar with his breeches down being beaten while he says, 'Leave me alone. I am the autocrat!'[8] Like the French Revolution, with which it had many similarities, the Russian Revolution of 1905 broke old taboos, including the reverence surrounding the country's ruler. It seemed to officials in St Petersburg a bad omen that the empress had hung a portrait of Marie Antoinette, a gift from the French government, in her rooms.[9]

On 22 January 1905, a giant procession of workers and their families, dressed in their best clothes and singing hymns, wended its way towards the Winter Palace to present a petition to the tsar demanding sweeping political and economic reforms. Many of them still regarded the tsar as their 'Little Father' and believed that he only needed to know what was wrong in order to make changes. The authorities, already jumpy, called out the army which cracked down brutally, firing point blank into the crowd. By the end of the day some hundreds were dead or wounded. Bloody Sunday helped to set off what was a dress rehearsal for the revolution of 1917 and which very nearly became the real thing. Throughout 1905 – 'the year of nightmares', the dowager empress called it – and into the summer of 1906 – Russia was hit by strikes and protests. Some of the many nationalities within the Russian Empire saw a chance for freedom and there were mass popular demonstrations against Russian rule from the Baltic provinces and Poland down to the Caucasus. Peasants refused to pay rent to their landlords and in some parts of the countryside seized the land and animals and plundered the big houses. Some 15 per cent of Russia's manor houses were burned in this period.[10] Ominously, in the summer of 1905 sailors in the Black Sea Fleet on board the battleship *Potemkin* mutinied.

By the autumn the tsar was isolated in his country estate at Tsarskoye Selo outside St Petersburg as the railways and telegraphs stopped working. Shops ran out of supplies, electricity went off, and people were afraid to go out. For six weeks in the city itself a Soviet of Workers Deputies was an alternative authority to the government. A young radical, Leon Trotsky, was one of its leading members as he was to be again with another Soviet in the 1917 revolution. In Moscow the new revolutionary Bolshevik Party was planning its armed uprising. Under huge pressure from his own supporters, the tsar reluctantly issued a manifesto in October promising a responsible legislature, the Duma, as well as civil rights.

As so often happens in revolutionary moments, the concessions only encouraged the opponents of the regime. It appeared to be close to collapsing with its officials confused and ineffective in the face of such widespread disorder. That winter a battalion from Nicholas's own regiment, the Preobrazhensky Guards, which had been founded by Peter the Great, mutinied. A member of the tsar's court wrote in his diary: 'This is it.'[11] Fortunately for the regime, its most determined enemies were disunited and not yet ready to take power while moderate reformers were prepared to support it in the light of the tsar's promises. Using the army and police freely, the government managed to restore order. By the summer of 1906 the worst was over – for the time being. The regime still faced the dilemma, though, of how far it could let reforms go without fatally undermining its authority. It was a dilemma faced by the French government in 1789 or the Shah's government in Iran in 1979. Refusing demands for reform and relying on repression creates enemies; giving way encourages them and brings more demands.

The Russo-Japanese War and its aftermath left Russia seriously weakened at home and dangerously vulnerable abroad. Its navy was shattered and what was left of its army largely deployed against the Russian people themselves. Colonel Yury Danilov, one of Russia's most efficient officers, said: 'As an infantry regiment commander I was able to be in touch with real military life and the army's needs during 1906–1908. And I cannot think of any better description for the period up to and including 1906–1910 and maybe even for a longer time than as one of total military helplessness.'[12] Russia needed to rebuild and overhaul its armed forces but it faced two difficult if not insurmountable challenges: first, a strongly entrenched resistance to change in both the military and the civilian establishments and, second, the costs of such a refurbishment. Russia had the ambitions of a first-rate power with the economy of a developing but still backward country. To make matters worse, in the first decade of the twentieth century, military expenditures were climbing throughout Europe as military technology became more expensive and armies and navies grew bigger. The Soviet Union faced a similar challenge after 1945; it managed to keep up with the United States in the military area but at the cost of much sacrifice for Soviet society and in the end the effort helped to bring down the regime.

In Russia in the years after 1905 much hinged on what the man at the top decided to do. Nicholas II was an absolute monarch who could appoint and dismiss ministers at will, determine policy, and, in wartime, command the armed forces. Before 1905, unlike his cousin Wilhelm in Germany, he did not have to worry about a constitution, an elected parliament, or the rights of his subjects. Even after the concessions of that year, he had greater power than either the Kaiser or the Austrian emperor, both of whom had to deal with greater control over their governments and over spending from their legislatures and who, in addition, had states inside their empires with strongly entrenched rights of their own. Nicholas's character and views are therefore of crucial importance in understanding Russia's road towards the Great War.

Nicholas was only twenty-six in 1894 when he became tsar of Russia. Queen Victoria had yet to celebrate her Diamond Jubilee and her grandson, the future George V, was a naval officer. In Germany Wilhelm had been on his throne for just six years. No one including Nicholas himself had expected him to become ruler so early on. His father, Alexander III, was massive and strong; it is said that he had once saved his family by holding up the roof of their carriage in a train crash. He fell ill, though, in his late forties with kidney disease and perhaps hastened his end by continuing to drink hard.[13] Nicholas, who had loved and admired his formidable father, was grief-stricken when he died. He was also in despair, said his sister, the Grand Duchess Olga: 'He kept saying that he did not know what would become of us all, that he was wholly unfit to reign.'[14]

He was probably right. Russia at the turn of the century, with all its problems, might have been too much for any ruler, but Nicholas was better fitted to be a country squire or the mayor of a small town. Perhaps because his father had been such an overwhelming personality, he lacked confidence. He compensated, being rigid and stubborn where a wiser and more self-assured person would have been prepared to make compromises or be flexible. He disliked opposition or confrontation. 'He grasps what he hears,' said a former tutor, 'but grasps only the meaning of the isolated fact, without relation to the rest, without connection to the totality of other factors, events, currents, phenomena ... For him there exists no broad, general view worked out through the exchange of ideas, arguments, debate.'[15] He was also notoriously indecisive. An observer reported that the common view was: 'He has no character, that he agrees with each of his ministers in spite of the fact that they report the opposite of one another.'[16] Under Nicholas, Russian policy at home and abroad was to be fitful, erratic and confused. He had an excellent memory and his courtiers claimed that he was intelligent but he sometimes showed a credulity which verged on the simple-minded. A foreign contractor, for example, once persuaded him that it was possible to build a bridge across the Bering Strait to join Siberia to North America. (The contractor was to get vast concessions of land along the proposed railway line leading to the bridge.)[17]

His upbringing had not equipped him with an understanding of Russia, much less of the wider world. Nicholas's childhood was, unlike that of Wilhelm, a happy one. The tsar and tsarina adored their children but perhaps tried too hard to protect them. Nicholas and his brothers and sisters were educated at home and rarely mixed with other children. As a result Nicholas did not have what other monarchs such as Wilhelm, Edward VII and George V had, and that was some experience of education with other young men of his age and much less the opportunity to meet people of different classes. Nor did he know his country. The Russia of Nicholas and his siblings was a deeply unreal bubble of privilege, of palaces, special trains, and yachts. Occasionally another Russia intruded, horrifyingly so when their grandfather, Alexander II, was assassinated by a bomb and Nicholas was taken to his deathbed. For Nicholas and his family the real Russia was peopled by happy loyal peasants like those who worked on the imperial estates. There was little in their education or their lives to challenge that simplistic view or make them aware of the tremendous changes that Russian society was undergoing.[18]

Nicholas followed a course of studies like that of a young Russian nobleman. He acquired languages – he spoke French, German, English and Russian fluently – studied history, which he liked, and learned some mathematics, chemistry and geography. When he was seventeen he was given special courses in such subjects as law and economics, although he does not appear to have shown much enthusiasm for them.

What he also learned were exquisite manners and strong self-control from an English tutor. 'I had rarely', said Count Sergei Witte, his Prime Minister, 'come across a better-mannered young man than Nicholas II. His good-breeding conceals all short comings.'[19] When he was nineteen, Nicholas was given a commission in the Preobrazhensky Guards. He loved being with the rich young aristocrats who were his fellow officers, loved the easy-going life in the mess with its many amusements and loved the uncomplicated ordered days in camp. He told his mother that he felt completely at home, 'one of the genuine consolations of my life now!'[20] Like Wilhelm, he kept a strong affection for the military for the rest of his life. (And he also loved to fuss about the details of uniforms.) As his cousin the Grand Duke Alexander Mikhailovich said of Nicholas: 'He developed an immense liking for military service. It appealed to his passive nature. One executed orders and did not have to worry over the vast problems handled by superiors.'[21] After his military service, Nicholas was sent off on a world tour, which he liked rather less. He conceived a particular dislike for Japan and the Japanese when a policeman, who had gone mad, tried to kill him.

Even in his mid twenties Nicholas remained curiously callow. Witte, who was concerned about the education of the future tsar, suggested to Alexander III that he give Nicholas some experience by making him chair of the Commission for the Construction of the Trans-Siberian Railway. 'Have you ever tried to discuss anything of real consequence with him?' Alexander asked. Witte said he had not. 'Well he's an absolute child,' said the tsar. 'His opinions are utterly childish. How could he preside over such a committee?'[22] Early in his reign Nicholas complained to his Minister of Foreign Affairs: 'I know nothing. The late emperor did not foresee his death and did not let me in on any government business.'[23]

A slight, handsome man with blue eyes, Nicholas took more after his mother, a Danish princess whose sister had married Edward VII of Britain. He and George V, his first cousin, looked strikingly similar, especially when they both grew small, neat, pointed beards. His contemporaries found Nicholas charming but somehow elusive. Each time he met the tsar, said one of his diplomats, 'I had carried away the impression of great kindness and extreme personal *politesse*, of a ready and subtle wit slightly tinged with sarcasm, and of a very quick though somewhat superficial mind'.[24] Outside his immediate family and trusted courtiers, who were usually military men, he was guarded. As tsar, he would manifest a pattern of at first placing confidence in a particular minister and then coming to resent that dependence, which in turn would lead to the man being dismissed. Shortly before the outbreak of the Russo-Japanese War, the War Minister General Kuropatkin tried to resign in protest against the tsar's undermining of his authority. The tsar, he felt, might trust him more when he was out of office. Nicholas agreed: 'It is strange, you know, but perhaps that is psychologically accurate.'[25]

Nicholas inherited one of Russia's most outstanding statesmen of the prewar period, Sergei Witte, from his father. Witte was, as a British diplomat said, 'a strong and energetic man, absolutely fearless, and of extraordinary initiative power'.[26] As Minister of Finance between 1892 and 1903, Witte built his ministry into the core of Russia's government with responsibility for the country's financial management and its economy. He tried to make Russia's agriculture and local government more efficient, partly so Russia could export grain in order to raise the necessary funds for development. He pushed Russia's rapid industrialisation and the exploitation of its newly acquired territories in the Far East. The Trans-Siberian Railway was very much Witte's project. As he accumulated power, however, he also attracted enemies and those came to include Nicholas. In 1903 Witte had a long and apparently amicable audience with the tsar: 'He shook my hand. He embraced me. He wished me all the luck in the world. I returned home beside myself with happiness and found a written order for my dismissal lying on my desk.'[27]

Nicholas brought to his reign three key beliefs: in the Romanovs, the Orthodox religion and Russia. And for him they were virtually interchangeable. In his mind, his family had been entrusted with Russia by God. 'If you find me so little troubled,' Nicholas said to one of his officials during the troubles of 1905, 'it is because I have the firm and absolute faith that the destiny of Russia, my own fate and that of my family are in the hands of Almighty God who has placed me where I am. Whatever may happen, I shall bow to His will, conscious that I have never had any other thought but that of serving the country he has entrusted me with.'[28] Reverence for his father and a determination to conserve the regime as it had been handed down by his ancestors made Nicholas deeply conservative and noticeably fatalistic. In the first year of his reign, he turned down a very moderate request from the representatives of the fledgling local governments, the *zemstvos*, for a greater say in running their own affairs. 'Let everyone know that, devoting all my strength to the good of my people, I will preserve the principles of autocracy as firmly and undeviatingly as did my late unforgettable father.'[29] To Nicholas as to his father, autocracy was the form of government that suited the Russian people, in all their diversity, best. He explained to his Minister of the Interior in October 1905 why he was resisting conceding a Duma and civil rights: 'You know, I don't hold to autocracy for my own pleasure. I act in this sense only because I am convinced that it is necessary for Russia. If it was simply a question of myself I would happily get rid of all this.'[30]

The problem was that Nicholas wanted to conserve the power bequeathed him but he had very little idea of what he wanted to do with it. Nor did he have an ability to pick good advisers or listen to them. He tended to rely on those who were close to him such as his mother or Romanov uncles and cousins who, with few exceptions, were venal and idle. He also had a series of pious advisers if not charlatans, one the Frenchman M. Philippe, a former butcher from Lyons, the most notorious of all the Russian holy man Rasputin, whose religious fervour did not make up for their many deficiencies. Already deeply religious, Nicholas also dabbled in the spiritualism which was so popular across Europe at the time. The tsar, said the British ambassador in 1906 'will not derive much useful counsel or assistance from planchette or spirit rapping'.[31] His officials worried about the influence of the court on the tsar but had limited means to counteract it. When he was forced to have a Council of Ministers after 1905, he did his best to ignore it. He saw his ministers only when he chose to and most usually separately. He was invariably courteous but detached and uninterested except for matters involving foreign affairs, the military or internal security. Most felt, correctly, that he did not have confidence in them. As one said to another early in Nicholas's reign: 'God preserve you from relying on the Emperor even for a second on any matter; he is incapable of supporting anyone over anything.'[32] His ministers and officials noticed that if they raised subjects that he did not want to discuss, he politely but firmly declined to take notice. As he gained in confidence over the years, Nicholas asserted himself more and became less likely to listen to unwanted advice.

The Russo-Japanese War came about largely because Nicholas had come to resent Witte's control of policy in the Far East and so listened to a group of ambitious reactionaries who wanted to get their hands on Far Eastern resources. They urged that Russia extend its influence into northern Korea and consolidate its hold in Manchuria, even at the risk of a confrontation with Japan. They played on both Nicholas's mistrust of his own officials and his contempt for Japan, strengthening his view that it was best to be firm with such 'a barbarous country'.[33] With their enthusiastic support, Nicholas dismissed Witte in 1903 and appointed a special Viceroy for the Far East who promptly made relations with Japan even worse. The Russian Foreign Office, which had been side-lined in the Far East, unsuccessfully tried to reassure international opinion, which was growing increasingly concerned about the incoherence of Russia's foreign policy and the possibility of war. Even Nicholas showed some concern. 'I do not wish war between Russia and Japan,' he ordered, 'and will not permit this war. Take all measures so that there is no war.'[34] Matters by this point were out of control: the Japanese, whose proposals for an understanding over Korea and Manchuria had been repeatedly rebuffed, decided on war. As Russia's Foreign Minister, Count Vladimir Lamsdorff, said in 1904, 'The complete disorganization of our political activity in the Far East, the occult intervention of a pack of irresponsible adventurers and intriguers, has led us to a catastrophe.'[35]

In the course of his reign, Nicholas's ministers found themselves in an almost impossible situation as servants of both Russia and the tsar. Even when they felt strongly that a particular policy should be adopted they could not bring themselves to disagree with the tsar. Vladimir Lenin, as yet a little-known revolutionary, perceptively called it the 'crisis of the heights'.[36] Yet because the regime was highly personalised when matters went wrong, as they did in the Russo-Japanese War and, on a much greater scale, in the Great War, Russian public opinion, an increasingly important force, tended to place the blame on the tsar himself.

What made matters worse and added to Nicholas's isolation was his marriage. Not that it was unhappy, quite the opposite, but it created a cocoon of cosy domesticity and an increasingly effective barrier against the world. Nicholas and Alexandra had loved each other since they were teenagers. She was German, from the small duchy of Hesse-Darmstadt, although as a granddaughter of Queen Victoria, Alexandra preferred to describe herself as English. Queen Victoria, who was strongly anti-Russian, fortunately took a liking to Nicholas and gave her approval. Alexandra herself was the main obstacle because she could not at first face giving up her Protestant faith and converting to Russian Orthodoxy. After a tremendous struggle with herself and much pressure from her family, who wanted such a glorious alliance, she gave way and, in floods of tears, accepted Nicholas. (It may be too, as some unkindly said, that she wanted to get away from her oldest brother's new wife.[37]) Like converts often do, she was to become more Orthodox and more Russian than the Russians. She also devoted herself heart and soul to Nicholas and to his interests, as she conceived them to be.

Their wedding was both magnificent and sombre. It had been planned before Alexander III's sudden decline and death and took place a week after his funeral. Was that a bad omen, as people later said? If so, the coronation which followed a year and a half later was much more so. The ceremony itself went off well but there was a disaster at the great public celebration on the outskirts of Moscow which followed, where beer and sausages and commemorative presents were going to be distributed. Russians had come from all over the country, many of them on the new railways, and by early morning some half a million people had assembled. The crowd panicked at rumours that there was not enough to go round and in the ensuing stampede thousands were trampled and over a thousand, perhaps more, crushed to death. That evening, the French embassy was holding a ball on which France had lavished millions of roubles. Reluctantly, under pressure from their ministers who wanted to celebrate the French alliance, the young tsar and tsarina attended. It was a bad mistake which helped to give the young couple a reputation for heartlessness.[38]

Alexandra was more intellectual than Nicholas and loved discussions, especially about religion. She had a strong sense of duty and believed that, as a good Christian, she had an obligation to help the less fortunate. As tsarina, she set an admirable example by working with charities from famine relief to care for the sick. She was unfortunately also highly emotional, neurotic, and painfully shy. Where her mother-in-law had entered easily into St Petersburg society and had presided with aplomb over the elaborate court balls and receptions, Alexandra was awkward and clearly unhappy in public. 'She never spoke a single pleasant word to anyone,' said a critical grande dame. 'She might have been a block of ice, freezing everyone round her.'[39] Like Wilhelm's wife, she was also prudish and unforgiving of the sins of others. She decided to invite only women with spotless reputations to court balls; the result was the elimination from the list of most of the leaders of society.[40] She was equally determined when it came to supporting her favourites for posts, even when they were manifestly unsuited. As one of the senior court officials said, she had 'a will of iron linked to not much brain and no knowledge'.[41]

Alexandra also brought another disadvantage to her new position, but it was one that did not become apparent for several years. Through Queen Victoria, she was a carrier of the gene for haemophilia, a disease which normally strikes only males. Haemophiliacs lack the substance which makes blood clot with the result that any cut, any bruise, virtually any accident, might cause their death. Alexandra's and Nicholas's only son Alexis had the disease and nearly died on several occasions during his childhood. His frantic mother scoured Russia and Europe for a cure, calling to the child's bedside doctors, charlatans, savants, reputed miracle workers, and, fatally for the reputation of the imperial family, the corrupt and degenerate Rasputin.

As Alexandra's health deteriorated, partly as a result of frequent pregnancies, she withdrew from much social life. Nicholas rarely visited his capital, especially after 1905. Even his mother, who rarely criticised him, said: 'The Emperor sees no one, he ought to see more people.'[42] By preference and for security reasons, the family lived outside St Petersburg on the imperial estate at Tsarskoye Selo, behind high spiked fences which, after 1905, were topped by ten feet of barbed wire. In the summers they migrated to the equally secluded estate at Peterhof beside the Baltic Sea. There were also trips on the imperial yacht, to imperial hunting lodges or the imperial palace in the Crimea.

The family at the heart of all this grandeur, surrounded by a rigid and complicated etiquette and served by thousands of servants, guards and courtiers, was a simple and happy one, its members intensely private and curiously unworldly. Alexandra prided herself on her thrift and the tsar proudly wore out his clothes. The court doctor's son later wrote of their world: 'The enchanted little fairyland of Tsarskoye Selo slumbered peacefully on the brink of an abyss, lulled by the sweet songs of bewhiskered sirens who gently hummed "God Save the Tsar".'[43] Both were devoted to their sick son and their four daughters, excessively so in the opinion of Charles Hardinge when he was British ambassador to Russia during the Russo-Japanese War. Nicholas seemed oddly unmoved, he reported, by the events of Bloody Sunday and the upheavals in his capital and rather than seeing advisers spent his time hunting, his great passion, and playing with the baby Alexis. 'I can only explain', Hardinge told London, 'by that mystic fatalism which is deeply imbued in his nature, together with the idea that a miracle will be performed & that all will come right in the end.'[44]

In 1905 it took the visible and mounting evidence that his regime was losing control over Russia as well as strong pressure from virtually everyone close to him including his mother to convince Nicholas that he had to make substantial concessions and that he had to bring back Witte to lead the government. At the beginning of October he reluctantly agreed to see his former Finance Minister, who set as his condition for taking up office the granting of a constitution and civil liberties. Nicholas tried to persuade his cousin Nicholas Nikolayevich to set up a military dictatorship instead but after a fearful scene in which the Grand Duke apparently threatened to shoot himself on the spot if Witte was not appointed gave way. 'My only consolation,' the unhappy tsar wrote to his mother, 'is that such is the will of God, and this grave decision will lead my dear Russia out of the intolerable chaos she has been in for nearly a year.'[45] After 1905 Nicholas continued to hope that miracles would happen and that he could go back on his promises. In the years before the war, he did his best to undermine the constitution and to limit civil liberties. He opened the first Duma in April 1906 and dissolved it that same July. In 1907, he issued a decree which changed the electoral laws so that conservative landowning forces had greater representation in the Duma and liberals and the left considerably less. Nicholas also did his best to ignore Witte (although he was duly grateful to him for getting a large loan from France which saved Russia from going bankrupt) and was successful in getting rid of him shortly before the Duma met for the first time.

Nevertheless it was impossible to reverse course completely. From

1905 onwards the government had to deal with the new factor of public opinion. The press, in spite of attempts by the authorities to censor it, was increasingly outspoken. Deputies in the Duma had the freedom to speak there without fear of prosecution. Political parties were still weak and without deep roots in Russian society but they were capable, if only given time, of developing into more formidable political forces. True, the new constitution described the tsar as the Supreme Autocratic Power and he still controlled foreign policy, the military and the Ortho- dox Church, and had the right to appoint and dismiss ministers, veto any piece of legislation, dissolve the Duma and declare martial law. Yet the fact that there *was* such a document implied that there were limits to his power. The Duma was largely a talking shop with ill-defined powers but it did have the right to ask government ministers to come before it for questioning and to appropriate money for the army and navy if it chose (although it could not refuse to approve the govern- ment's military budget).

Nicholas also had to accept a Council of Ministers which was intended to function like a Cabinet to co-ordinate and direct govern- ment policy and whose chair would be the link between all the ministers and the tsar. Witte, its first chair, found his position impossible because Nicholas continued to consult individual ministers as he pleased. His successor, Peter Stolypin, lasted until 1911, partly because the tsar, at first, trusted him, and partly because Nicholas withdrew from much day-to- day involvement with policy after 1905. Nicholas also admired him, as did many in the ruling circles, for his physical courage. In 1906 terrorists blew up his summer villa near St Petersburg; some dozens were killed or wounded and two of his own children seriously injured but Stolypin bore himself with great fortitude and self-control.[46]

Tall, erect, sombre, with correct and formal manners, Stolypin impressed almost everyone who came into contact with him. He was as talented and energetic as Witte and like him was dedicated to bringing about reform and progress in Russia. And like his predecessor he was naturally authoritarian and determined to crush the revolutionaries. He recognised, though, that the government would have to work with at least some of the new political forces emerging in Russia and he tried with some success to build a conservative coalition in the Duma. To undercut the appeal of the revolutionaries among the peasants, he promoted reforms to allow peasants to own the land they worked. In the long run, though, the old pattern asserted itself and Nicholas became envious and resentful of the power of his Prime Minister. By 1911, a British diplomat reported, Stolypin was depressed and felt his position to be insecure. In September his fate was settled, with dreadful finality, when a terrorist, who seems also to have been a police agent, walked up to him at the opera in Kiev and shot him point blank. Mortally wounded, Stolypin is reported to have said, 'I am done for,' or, more dramatically, 'I am happy to die for the Tsar.'[47] He died four days later. It is just possible that, if he had survived, he would have provided strong leadership for the next years, perhaps even acting as a force for caution and moderation when the great European crisis came in the summer of 1914.

There had always been an element of bluff in Russia's claim to be a European power. As Alexander II's Foreign Minister said in 1876: 'We are a great, powerless country. True. There is nothing more fortunate than knowing that truth. One can always dress up finely but one needs to know that one is dressing up.'[48] Sometimes Russia had dressed up to spectacular effect, when, for example, it had helped to defeat Napoleon and Tsar Alexander I marched his troops through Paris at the end of the Napoleonic Wars or when Russian troops had helped to save the Habsburg monarchy during the revolutions of 1848. It had also known defeat with the Crimean War in the middle of the nineteenth century and of course most recently the Russo-Japanese War. Stolypin was deeply aware of Russia's weakness both domestically and internationally after the war and how the two were linked. 'Our internal situation,' he commented shortly after he became Prime Minister, 'does not permit us to conduct an aggressive foreign policy.'[49] He was determined, unlike his successors, to avoid provocative international moves. Any more failures abroad were likely to set off fresh revolutions at home. On the other hand an appearance of weakness might encourage the other powers to take advantage of Russia.

The fundamental problem for Russia in its foreign relations stemmed from its geography. It had few natural defences against invaders. Throughout its history Russia had suffered repeated invasions whether Mongols (Tartars to the Russians), Swedes, Prussians, or French (and was to experience yet two more dreadful ones at the hands of Germany in the twentieth century). The Tartars ruled over the Russian heartland for 250 years yet, unlike the Moors in Spain, said Pushkin, 'having conquered Russia, they gave her neither algebra nor Aristotle'.[50] Its vulnerability had left Russia another legacy in the centralised and authoritarian government which finally emerged. In the early twelfth century in the first work of Russian history, the people of Rus in today's Ukraine are described as inviting a potential ruler: 'Our whole land is great and rich, but there is no order in it. Come to rule and reign over us.'[51] Putin has recently made the same justification for Stalin in Russian history – that he and his regime were necessary to hold Russia together in the face of the challenges from its enemies. A related consequence was Russia's unending search for security by pushing its frontiers outwards. By the end of the eighteenth century it had absorbed Finland and the Baltic states and its share of divided Poland. Although it increasingly turned eastwards, Russia still saw itself as a European power. Europe, after all, was seen as the centre not just of world power but of civilisation.

Russia had always been big by comparison with other European countries but in the nineteenth century it ballooned out to become the biggest country in the world as Russian explorers and soldiers, followed by Russian diplomats and officials, pushed its borders southwards and eastwards, down towards the Black Sea and the Caspian, to Central Asia and across the Ural mountains into Siberia and on to the Pacific for 5,000 miles. The whole of the United States as well as the other European countries could fit comfortably into Asiatic Russia and there would still be lots of territory to spare. The American traveller and writer George Kennan (a distant relation of his namesake the great American Soviet expert) tried to explain the immensity of Russia's new territories: 'If a geographer were preparing a general atlas of the world, and should use, in drawing Siberia, the same scale that is used in Stieler's "Hand Atlas" for England, he would have to make the Siberian page of his book nearly twenty feet in width to accommodate his map.'[52]

Empire brought prestige and the possibility, yet unrealised, of resources and wealth. It also brought more problems for Russia: its population was spread even more thinly and now included greater numbers of non-Russians, Muslims from Central Asia, Koreans, Mongols and Chinese in the East. New borders brought new and potentially unfriendly neighbours, in the Far East, China and Japan; in Central Asia, the British Empire; in the Caucasus, Persia (modern day Iran), which the British were also eyeing; and around the Black Sea, the Ottoman Empire, declining but propped up by other European powers. Moreover, in an age in which sea power was increasingly seen as the key to national power and wealth, Russia still possessed only a handful of ports which could be used all year round. Shipping from ports on the Black Sea and the Baltic had to go out through narrow straits which could be closed in time of war and the new Pacific port of Vladivostok lay thousands of miles away from the heart of Russia at the end of a fragile railway. As Russia became a major exporter, especially in food, the passage from the Black Sea to the Mediterranean via the Bosphorus, the Sea of Marmara and the Dardanelles – known collectively at the time as 'the Straits' – became particularly vital; 37 per cent of all its exports and 75 per cent of its crucial grain exports were flowing past Constantinople by 1914.[53] If that pipeline were closed, say by Germany, Sergei Sazonov, who was by then Foreign Minister, felt that it would be a 'death sentence for Russia'.[54] From Russia's point of view it made eminent sense to search for secure warm-water ports but, as Kuropatkin had warned Nicholas in 1900, it ran a great risk: 'However just our attempts to possess the exit to the Black Sea, to acquire an outlet to the Indian Ocean, and to obtain an outlet to the Pacific, these missions touch so deeply on the interests of almost the entire world that in pursuit of them we must be prepared for a struggle with a coalition of Great Britain, Germany, Austria-Hungary, Turkey, China, and Japan.'[55] Of all Russia's potential enemies, Britain, with its worldwide empire, seemed to be the most immediately threatening.

In Britain itself, public opinion was strongly anti-Russian. In popular literature, Russia was exotic and terrifying: the land of snow and golden domes, of wolves chasing sleighs through the dark forests, of Ivan the Terrible and Catherine the Great. Before he made Germany the enemy in his novels the prolific William Le Queux used Russia. In his 1894 *The Great War in England in 1897*, Britain was invaded by a combined French and Russian force but the Russians were by far the more brutal. British homes were burned, innocent civilians shot and babies bayoneted. 'The soldiers of the Tsar, savage and inhuman, showed no mercy to the weak and unprotected. They jeered and laughed at piteous appeal, and with fiendish brutality enjoyed the destruction which everywhere they wrought.'[56] Radical, liberals and socialists all had many reasons to hate the regime with its secret police, censorship, lack of basic human rights, its persecution of its opponents, its crushing of ethnic minorities and its appalling record of anti-Semitism.[57] Imperialists on the other hand hated Russia because it was a rival to the British Empire. Britain could never come to an agreement with Russia in Asia, said Curzon, who had been Salisbury's Undersecretary at the Foreign Office before he became Viceroy in India. Russia was bound to keep expanding as long as it could get away with it. In any case, the 'ingrained duplicity' of Russian diplomats made negotiations futile.[58] It was one of the rare occasions on which he agreed with the chief of the Indian general staff, Lord Kitchener, who was demanding more resources from London to deal with 'the menacing advance of Russia towards our frontiers'. What particularly worried the British were the new Russian railways, either built or planned, which stretched down to the borders of Afghanistan and Persia and which now made it possible for the Russians to bring force to bear. Although the term was not to be coined for another eighty years, the British were also becoming acutely aware of what Paul Kennedy called 'imperial overstretch'. As the War Office said in 1907, the expanded Russian railway system would make the military burden of defending India and the empire so great that 'short of recasting our whole military system, it will become a question of practical politics whether or not it is worth our while to retain India'.[59]

There were always those on both sides who would have preferred to lower the tensions, and the expense, by getting a settlement of the outstanding colonial issues. By the 1890s the British were prepared to recognise that they could no longer prevent Russia from using the Straits between the Black Sea and the Mediterranean for its warships and the Russians, in particular the military, were ready to adopt a less aggressive policy in Central Asia and Persia.[60] In 1898 Salisbury had proposed talks to Russia to sort out the differences of their two countries in China, but these unfortunately had gone nowhere and indeed relations worsened again as Russia took advantage of the Boxer Rebellion to move its troops into Manchuria. In 1903, the appointment of a new Russian ambassador to London offered the opportunity for fresh talks. Count Alexander Benckendorff was very well connected (he had been a page to Tsar Alexander III), rich and indiscreet. He was Anglo-phile, liberal in his sympathies and deeply pessimistic about the future of the tsarist regime. 'In Russia', he told the French ambassador when they were both posted to Copenhagen, 'on the surface, people are all sentiment; they have a tenderness for the Tsar etc. It is exactly as in France on the eve of the Revolution.'[61] In London, he and his wife became part of society and Benckendorff set himself to improve rela-tions between his country and Britain. Taking advantage of the considerable leeway that diplomats had in those prewar days, he encour-aged both sides to think that the other was more amenable to discussions than was actually the case. In 1903 Lansdowne, the British Foreign Sec-retary, and Benckendorff held talks on outstanding issues such as Tibet and Afghanistan but again these did not reach any conclusion. With the worsening relations between Russia and Britain's ally Japan, any talk of rapprochement was put on hold, not to be resumed until after the Russo-Japanese War.

The technological and industrial revolutions of the nineteenth century added to Russia's burdens as a great power. As one advance fol-lowed another, the arms race speeded up, and became more expensive. Railways and mass production made it possible to create, move and supply bigger armies. Once the other continental powers had gone down that road, Russia's rulers felt that it had to follow suit even though its resources were not a match for its neighbours Austria-Hungary and the new Germany. The alternative, difficult if not impossible to contem-plate, was to give up the attempt to be part of the club of great powers. Becoming a second-class power, worse 'an Asiatic state', said Alexander Izvolsky, Foreign Minister between 1906 and 1910, 'would be a major catastrophe for Russia'.[62]

It was a dilemma similar to the one faced by the Soviet Union during the Cold War: Russia's ambitions were fully developed but its economy and its taxation system were not. In the 1890s Russia was spending less than half the amount per soldier that France and Germany were.[63] Every rouble, moreover, spent on the military meant less for development. In 1900, according to one estimate, the Russian govern-ment was spending ten times more on its army than on education and the navy received more than the key ministries of Agriculture and Justice.[64] The Russo-Japanese War made the situation much worse. It nearly bankrupted Russia and left it with huge budget deficits. Although the armed forces badly needed re-equipping and retraining, the funds were simply not there. In 1906 the key military districts in the west around Warsaw, Kiev and St Petersburg did not receive sufficient resources even to carry out shooting practice.[65]

The war also reignited a debate over whether Russia's true interests lay in Asia or Europe. Kuropatkin and the Russian general staff had long been concerned about the drain of resources away from the European frontiers to the east. While Witte was building the Trans-Siberian Railway, construction of railways in the west of Russia virtually stopped, and this at a time Germany and Austria-Hungary as well as smaller powers such as Rumania were continuing to build. In 1900 the Russian general staff estimated that Germany could send 552 trains a day to their common frontier while Russia could send only 98. For financial reasons, the increase of Russian armed forces in the west was also frozen. 'To the delight of Germany', Kuropatkin wrote in 1900, 'in directing our attention to the Far East we are giving her and Austria a decisive preponderance in forces and materiel over us.'[66] During the Russo-Japanese War one of the nightmares for the Russian military was the fear that Germany and Austria-Hungary would use the opportunity to move against Russia, perhaps to pinch off Russian Poland, which jutted out dangerously westwards. Fortunately for Russia, Germany decided on a policy of friendly neutrality in the war in an attempt to wean it away from France and, as one of Russia's spies in Vienna confirmed, Austria-Hungary was more preoccupied with a possible attack on its ally Italy.[67]

As Russia faced the difficult years of recovery and rebuilding after the Russo-Japanese War ended, the fear remained, as did the need to make choices both in the allocation of resources and foreign policy. If Russia's interests lay in the east then it needed stability in the west. What that implied was an alliance or at least a détente with Germany and Austria-Hungary. There were ideological and historical arguments in favour of such a move: the three conservative monarchies had an interest in the status quo and in resisting radical change. There were strong historical arguments too in favour of an alliance between Russia and Germany. The links between Germans and Russians went back centuries; Peter the Great had imported Germans to work for him, in his new industries, for example, and over the years German farmers had helped to settle the new lands opening up as Russia expanded. Russia's upper classes had intermarried with their German counterparts and many old families bore German names such as Benckendorff, Lamsdorff, or Witte. Some, especially the Germans from Russia's Baltic possessions, still spoke German rather than Russian. The tsars – including Nicholas II himself, of course – commonly looked to the German princely states for wives. For Russia to move towards Germany, though, would mean abandoning the French alliance and, almost certainly, access to French financial markets. It was also certain to be opposed by the liberals who saw the alliance with France, and perhaps in the longer run with Britain, as encouraging progressive forces for change within Russia. And not all conservatives were pro-German; landowners were hurt by Germany's protective tariffs on agricultural products and food-stuffs. Germany's seizure of Kiachow Bay in northern China in 1897 challenged Russian ambitions for dominating China and Korea and in subsequent years increasing German investment and influence in the Ottoman Empire on Russia's doorstep caused further concern in official circles.[68]

If, on the other hand, Russia decided that its main threats and opportunities lay in Europe, then it needed to come to terms with its enemies in the east, both actual and potential. Peace with Japan needed to be accompanied by settlement of its outstanding issues with China and, much more importantly, with that other imperial power in the East, Great Britain. Few choices in foreign policy are irrevocable and in the decade before 1914 Russia's leaders tried to keep their options open, maintaining the alliance with France, but making overtures to all three of Britain, Germany, and Austria-Hungary to try to remove sources of tension.

Although the French alliance had caused difficulties initially, Russian opinion had largely come around to seeing it as a good thing, a neat matching of Russian manpower with French money and technology. Of course, there were strains over the years. France tried to use its financial leverage over Russia to shape Russian military planning to meet French needs or to insist that Russia place its orders for new weapons with French firms.[69] The Russians resented this 'blackmail', as they sometimes called it, which was demeaning to Russia as a great power. As Vladimir Kokovtsov, Russia's Minister of Finance for much of the decade before 1914, complained: 'Russia is not Turkey; our allies should not set us an ultimatum, we can get by without these direct demands'.[70] The Russo-Japanese War also brought strains, with the Russians thinking that France was not doing enough to support them and the French desperately trying to avoid getting dragged into a war on the side of Russia against Japan, the ally of their new friend Britain. On the other hand, France did prove helpful to Russia in negotiating the settlement of the damages arising from the Dogger Bank incident. Delcassé also allowed the Russian Baltic Fleet to use ports in France's colonies in the Far East as it made its way towards Manchuria.

Even Russian conservatives who still hoped for a closer relationship with Germany consoled themselves by arguing that the alliance with France actually made Russia stronger and therefore more impressive in German eyes. In the opinion of Lamsdorff, the Foreign Minister between 1900 and 1906: 'In order to have good relations with Germany and make her amenable, we need to *maintain an alliance* with France. An alliance with Germany would isolate us, most probably, and would become a disastrous slavery.'[71] A small, fussy man, Lamsdorff was a bureaucrat of the old school, utterly loyal to the tsar and deeply averse to change. Count Leopold von Berchtold, the Austrian diplomat who later became Foreign Minister, met him in 1900:

> Except for a short moustache, he was clean shaven and bare-headed, sat ramrod straight. He tried to impress at every opportunity, too polite, not unintelligent and also not without education, a wandering archive. Un rat de chancellerie. Through constant sniffing in dusty files he became a yellowed parchment himself. I could not help but get the impression of having an abnormality before me, an aged but inchoate nature, in whose circulation system ran watery jelly instead of red blood.[72]

Lamsdorff's colleagues would have agreed: as one said unkindly, Lamsdorff was at least honest and hard-working but 'brilliantly incapable and mediocre'.[73] Nevertheless Lamsdorff was probably right in thinking that Russia's long-term interests lay in balancing between the powers and he was open to discussions with any of the other powers including Britain. As he told a member of the Foreign Ministry, Baron Marcel Taube, in 1905: 'Believe me, there are times in the life of a great people when this absence of a too-pronounced orientation with regard to that power x or y is still the best policy. I call that, myself, the policy of independence. If it is abandoned, you will see one day when I am no longer here – that it will not bring happiness to Russia.'[74] His successors could enter into new combinations and engage in new wars, which, he warned, 'will end in a revolution'.[75] Keeping a free hand in foreign policy after 1905 was almost impossible for Russia, however, partly because its own weakness meant it needed allies and partly because Europe was well along the road to dividing itself into opposing alliances.

After 1904, with its Entente Cordiale with Britain in place, France put considerable pressure on Russia to come to a similar understanding with Britain. 'What horizons will open to us', said Delcassé, the Foreign Minister, in 1904, 'if we could lean simultaneously on Russia and England against Germany!'[76] Of course, what France hoped for in the longer term was a full-blown military alliance between the three powers. While Russian liberals would have welcomed a friendship with the leading liberal power in Europe, the Russian leadership was reluctant. The tsar disapproved of British society and, while he had admired Queen Victoria, did not like Edward VII, whom he found immoral and dangerously free with his friendships. When, as a young man, he had stayed with Edward, he had been shocked to find, for example, that the fellow guests included horse-dealers and, worse, Jews. As he wrote to his mother: 'The Cousins rather enjoyed the situation and kept teasing me about it; but I tried to keep away as much as I could, and not to talk.'[77] More importantly, perhaps, Nicholas saw Britain as Russia's chief rival around the world. He was also furious with the British for their hostility during the Russo-Japanese War, which he blamed, so he told Wilhelm II, on Edward VII, 'the greatest mischief maker and the most dangerous intriguer in the world'.[78]

Until 1906, when they were replaced, his chief advisers, Witte and Lamsdorff, were also lukewarm if not hostile to the idea of an understanding with Britain. Witte would have preferred to revive the old German friendship and perhaps to join the Triple Alliance of Germany, Austria-Hungary and Italy. Given the growing rivalries between Russia and Austria-Hungary in the Balkans, this last was highly unlikely. Even less probable was Witte's hope of creating a continental alliance with France, Russia and Germany to isolate Britain.[79] The French made it clear that they were not prepared either to bury their differences with Germany or abandon their entente with Britain.

Germany, not surprisingly, did its best to drive France and Russia apart. The German Foreign Office made clumsy attempts during the Russo-Japanese War to create suspicions between France and Russia. The Kaiser wrote in English, one of their shared languages, to his dear cousin Nicky with much advice about how to conduct the war and sympathy for Russia's mounting losses. Wilhelm, so he told the tsar at the beginning of June 1904, had expressed his amazement to the French military attaché in Berlin that France was not coming to the aid of its Russian ally against the rising Asian power.

> After many hints and allusions I found out – what I always feared – that the Anglo-French agreement had the one main effect, viz.: to stop the French from helping you! *Il va sans dire*, that if France had been under the obligation of helping you with her Fleet or Army I would of course not have budged a finger to harm her; for that would have been most illogical on the part of the Author of the Picture 'Yellow Peril'! [Wilhelm had given Nicholas this painting which was done to his instructions by his favourite artist.]

Wilhelm rather undercut these kind sentiments by ending his letter with a heavy-handed hint to his cousin that it was an opportune moment for Russia to sign a commercial treaty with Germany.[80] That autumn, as Russia's losses in the Far East mounted up, Wilhelm and Bülow secretly offered an alliance against an unspecified European power. Wilhelm wrote privately to Nicholas: 'Of course the alliance would be purely defensive, exclusively directed against European aggressor or aggressors, in the form of a mutual fire insurance company against incendiarism.' He was dismayed – 'my first personal defeat' – when Nicholas turned him down.[81]

Wilhelm liked to believe that he could manage Nicholas, who was some ten years younger and a less forceful personality. 'A charming, agreeable and dear boy,' Wilhelm wrote to Queen Victoria after one of their early meetings.[82] In fact Nicholas found Wilhelm exhausting in person and resented the stream of letters with their unsolicited advice. Witte discovered that a good way to get his master to agree to something was to tell him the Kaiser opposed it.[83] Wilhelm's gifts of what he described as his own paintings were typically tactless. The 'Yellow Peril' allegory, for example, showed a manly German warrior defending the swooning Russian beauty. Bülow had his own candidate for the most embarrassing: 'Kaiser William, in magnificent attitude and shining armour, was standing in front of the tsar, with a huge crucifix in his raised right hand, while the tsar looked up admiringly at him in humble, almost ridiculous position, clad in a Byzantine garment, rather like a dressing gown.'[84] As he did so often, the tsar retreated into polite disengagement. Wilhelm for his part was exasperated with what he saw as Nicholas's lack of spine. When during the Russo-Japanese War he urged the tsar to go all out, Bülow warned him not to encourage Russia too openly lest Germany get dragged in. 'From the point of view of the statesman you may be right,' replied Wilhelm. 'But I feel as a sovereign and as a sovereign I am sickened by the way Nicholas lets himself down through his flabby behavior. This sort of thing compromises all sovereigns.'[85]

In the summer of 1905, as Russia was suing for peace with Japan and the country was in turmoil, Wilhelm made another concerted effort to lure Nicholas away from the French alliance. The two rulers made a rendezvous with their yachts off the Finnish island of Björkö. Wilhelm sympathised with Nicholas over Russia's predicament and joined him in railing against the perfidy of France and Britain. On 23 July Bülow received a delighted telegram from Wilhelm to say that Russia and Germany had made a treaty on board the tsar's yacht. 'I have received many strange telegrams from the Kaiser,' Bülow later said, 'but never one so filled with enthusiasm as this one from Björkö.' Wilhelm described the scene at length. The tsar had said again how hurt he was by France's failing to support Russia; in response Wilhelm had said why did not the two of them there and then make a 'little agreement'. He pulled out a copy of the treaty Nicholas had turned down the previous winter. Nicholas read it through while Wilhelm stood silently by, making, he told, a short prayer and gazing out at his own yacht with its flags flying in the morning breeze. Suddenly he heard Nicholas say: 'That is excellent. I quite agree.' Wilhelm forced himself to be casual and handed a pen to Nicholas. Wilhelm then signed in turn. A representative of the Foreign Office, who had been sent along to keep an eye on Wilhelm, countersigned for Germany and a Russian admiral, who was not allowed by Nicholas to read the text, obediently did the same for Russia. 'Tears of joy stood in my eyes', Wilhelm went on in his description for Bülow, ' – to be sure, drops of perspiration were trickling down my back – and I thought, Frederick William III, Queen Louisa, Grandpapa, and Nicholas I must surely be near at the moment. At any rate they must have been looking down full of joy.'[86] A month later he wrote to Nicholas to exult in their new alliance which would allow their two nations to be the centre of power and a force for peace in Europe. The other members of the Triple Alliance, Austria-Hungary and Italy, would of course support them and the smaller powers such as the Scandinavian countries would inevitably see that their interests lay in swimming into the orbit of the new power bloc. Japan might even join, which would serve to cool down 'English self-assertion and impertinence'. And, the Kaiser went on, Nicholas need not worry about his other chief European ally: '"Marianne" [France] must remember that she is wedded to you & that she is obliged to lie and bed with you, & eventually to give a hug or a kiss now & then to me, but not to sneak into the bedroom of the ever intriguing *touche-à-tout* on the Island.'[87] (This last was a dig at Edward VII, whose love affairs were notorious.)

When Bülow saw the treaty joy was the last thing he felt. He was annoyed that Wilhelm had acted without consulting him first, something the Kaiser had taken to doing rather too frequently, and dismayed when he saw that Wilhelm had made a change, limiting the scope of the treaty to Europe. One of Russia's great advantages as an ally was that it could threaten India and so keep Britain in check in Europe. After consulting his colleagues in the Foreign Office, who shared his views, Bülow submitted his resignation, perhaps less in earnest than to teach his master a lesson.[88] The Kaiser's dreams fell to pieces and so did he. 'To be treated like this by the best and most intimate friend I have had', he wrote in a highly emotional letter to Bülow, 'without any reasonable ground being given, has dealt me such a terrible blow that I have completely collapsed and fear that a serious nervous trouble may result from it.'[89] The reaction of the Russian Foreign Minister, Lamsdorff, was less dramatic but equally damning. He suggested politely to the tsar that the Kaiser had taken advantage of him and pointed out that the treaty was incompatible with Russia's obligations towards France. In October, Nicholas wrote to Wilhelm to say that the treaty would need France's approval. Since this was never going to happen, the Björkö agreement was effectively void.

When Wilhelm and Nicholas met on their yachts again in the summer of 1907 both Bülow – who had graciously given way to Wilhelm's plea to remain in office – and the new Russian Foreign Minister, Alexander Izvolsky, were in attendance. The visit went off with no difficulties beyond an unfortunate impromptu speech by the Kaiser in which he boasted of his mighty navy and hoped that the tsar would soon build a new one. 'Now the only thing missing', said a Russian aide sourly about the Kaiser to one of his German counterparts, 'is for him to slap him in the face.'[90] Björkö was the last significant episode of personal diplomacy between two monarchs, which would have seemed quite normal in the nineteenth century but was out of place in the twentieth when the increasing complexities of modern societies gave greater authority to officials even in absolute monarchies. An unfortunate consequence was to deepen suspicion of Germany and Wilhelm himself, both in Russian official circles and among the general public. The government found that it was increasingly handicapped when it tried to improve relations with its western neighbour. The British ambassador reported on a conversation with the tsar in 1908:

> The Emperor admitted that from the point of view of the relations of Russia to Germany, the liberty of the press had caused him and his government considerable embarrassment since every incident that occurred in any distant province of the empire, such as an earthquake or thunderstorm, was at once put down to Germany's account, and serious complaints had recently been made to him and the government of the unfriendly tone of the Russian press.[91]

At the start of 1906 Witte, who had inclined towards an alliance with Germany, had something of a change of heart, perhaps as a result of the Björkö affair, and told the British embassy in St Petersburg that what Russia needed at this critical juncture in its history was the sympathy and support of a great liberal power. It also helped that Britain was a great financial power capable of making the loans that Russia so desperately required. If Britain could give tangible proof of its friendship, Witte felt, an overall understanding would soon follow.[92] Loan negotiations were in fact going on between the Russian government and Barings Bank with the encouragement of the British Foreign Office, but because of political upheavals in both countries they were not concluded until the spring of 1906.[93] Under pressure from Witte, Lamsdorff agreed to opening discussions on Persia and Afghanistan. These moved slowly; Lamsdorff was unenthusiastic and both countries were preoccupied by a crisis over Morocco which threatened to bring a major European conflict.

In the spring of 1906 the situation suddenly became more favourable to an understanding. Witte was dismissed and Lamsdorff asked the tsar to accept his resignation because he could not face the prospect of dealing with the new Duma. 'You would have to wait a long time,' he told Taube, 'before I would deign to speak to those people there.'[94] The new Prime Minister, Stolypin, was much more open to the idea of a détente with Britain, partly because of Russia's weakness and partly because Britain had successfully hemmed Russia in along its eastern and southern frontiers by renewing its treaty with Japan in 1905, signing a convention with Tibet, and moving more aggressively into Persia. Izvolsky, Lamsdorff's successor, was even more convinced that Russia's interests lay in Europe and that the key to rebuilding its status as a power lay in maintaining the French alliance and coming to some sort of understanding with the British. Both men also agreed in the years after 1906 that, given the developments in Russia's internal politics, the Duma and public opinion had to be involved in foreign policy.

Izvolsky and Taube had a long discussion shortly before he took up office. His goals, the new Foreign Minister told Taube, were to put relations with Japan on a solid and friendly footing and 'liquidate the inheritance of Count Lamsdorff in Asia'. Then, he went on, 'Russia could turn afresh, after an interval of many years, towards Europe, where its traditional and historic interests have been practically abandoned for the sake of these ephemeral dreams about the Far East for which we have paid too dearly ...'[95] Izvolsky was one of those Russians who saw Europe as the club they wanted most in the world to join. As he said in 1911 after he had left office, the policy of closer relations with

France and Britain was 'perhaps less secure but worthier of Russia's past and of her greatness'.[96] He was more of a gambler than Stolypin but, unfortunately for Russian foreign policy, he also tended to lose his nerve at inopportune moments.

Izvolsky, almost everyone agreed, was charming, ambitious and intelligent as well as vain and easily flattered. He was also highly sensitive to criticism. He had Lamsdorff's capacity for hard work and attention to detail but unlike his predecessor he was a liberal and had considerably more experience of the world outside Russia. In appearance, in the words of the future Austrian Foreign Secretary Leopold von Berchtold, he was of 'middle height, blond hair parted and with a ruddy face, broad forehead, cloudy eyes, compressed nose, protruding brow, a monocle, and a faultless suit'.[97] Although he was generally considered to be ugly, Izvolsky took great pride in his appearance, wearing well-cut suits from Savile Row in London and cramming his feet into shoes that were too small with the result, said one observer, that he walked like a pigeon.[98]

His family were minor nobility of modest means but they had managed to send Izvolsky to the best school in St Petersburg, the Imperiale Alexandre Lycée, where he had mixed with much grander and much richer young men. It had made him, Taube felt, snobbish, egotistical and materialistic. As a young man Izvolsky was desperate to marry well. One well-connected widow who turned him down was later asked if she regretted having missed the chance to marry someone who had done so well. 'I have regretted it every day', she replied, 'but congratulated myself every night.'[99] He eventually married the daughter of another Russian diplomat but there was never enough money for him to live in the grand style to which he aspired and there was always gossip in St Petersburg about the way in which rich men got their promotions under him.[100] Taube, who worked with him closely over the years, always felt that there were two men with quite different values warring inside Izvolsky: the statesman and the greedy courtier.[101]

The British were initially apprehensive about Izvolsky's appointment. The British ambassador in Copenhagen reported to London on a conversation with his French counterpart, who knew Izvolsky well; the new Russian Foreign Minister, it appeared, was lukewarm about the French alliance and inclined to be pro-German.[102] This, fortunately for the future of Anglo-Russian relations, was misleading. Izvolsky was determined to negotiate an understanding with Britain and the tsar, although he made a face at the idea, was now ready to give his approval.[103] The situation in Russia was starting to improve and it looked as though a revolution had been averted so the British had a party with which to negotiate. On the British side, there was a new Liberal government and a new Foreign Secretary, Sir Edward Grey, who were determined to pursue the opportunity. One of Grey's first meetings after he took office in December 1905 was with Benckendorff to assure the Russian ambassador that he wanted an agreement with Russia. In May 1906 Sir Arthur Nicolson arrived as British ambassador in St Petersburg with authority from the Cabinet to sort out with Izvolsky the three main irritants in the relationship: Tibet, Persia and Afghanistan. The locals were not, of course, consulted while their fate was decided thousands of miles away.

The negotiations were long and tedious as might be expected between two parties, 'each of which thought the other was a liar and a thief', as one British diplomat put it.[104] And there were moments when the talks were nearly broken off, when, for example, Izvolsky got worried that Germany was going to object, or when the British Prime Minister, Henry Campbell-Bannerman, tactlessly made a speech saying 'Vive la Douma'. Tibet, where part of the Great Game had been played out between British and Russian agents, was the easiest to settle. Both sides agreed not to try to get concessions out of the weak Tibetan government or to establish political relations with the Dalai Lama and, in a clause that would cast a shadow over Tibet's future, Russia agreed to recognise China's suzerainty over the country.

Afghanistan took longer and was not finally settled until the late summer of 1907. The Russians made the greatest concessions, accepting that Afghanistan was in the British sphere of influence and that Russia was only to deal with the Emir through Britain. In return Britain promised only that it would not occupy or annex Afghanistan – as long as the Emir kept to his treaty agreements with them. The most difficult issue of all to settle was Persia, although news of a German railway loan to the Shah helped to keep both sides focussed. It also helped that Izvolsky was prepared to go to considerable lengths to get an agreement. In the summer of 1906, when there was discussion in St Petersburg of promoting a Russian–Persian bank in Teheran (which would have alarmed the British), he said firmly: 'We are trying to conclude an alliance with England and, as a result, our policy in Persia must conform to that fact.'[105] After much debate over demarcation lines, it was agreed that Persia would have a Russian zone of influence in the north, a British one in the south to protect the Gulf and the routes to India, and a neutral zone between them. The British ambassador in Teheran warned that the Persian government had heard rumours about the negotiations and would be seriously concerned and angry. With the insouciance towards the non-European world typical of the time, the British Foreign Office replied that the Persians should understand that the agreement was in fact respecting the integrity of their country.[106] The Straits between the Black Sea and the Mediterranean, which had caused so much trouble in the nineteenth century, were left out on the grounds that the convention only dealt with Asia but Grey gave Benckendorff to understand that the British would not make difficulties for the Russians in the future over their access to the Straits.[107] On 31 August 1907 the Anglo-Russian Convention 'containing arrangements on the subject of Persia, Afghanistan and Thibet [sic]' was signed in the Russian Foreign Office.

Everyone understood that more was involved than the 'arrangements'. Although Germany publicly welcomed the news on the grounds that it furthered peace, Bülow told the Kaiser that Germany was now the chief object of British anxieties and jealousy. Rumours of war went round Berlin and the German press carried stories about how the country was now encircled. The following summer Wilhelm made a belligerent speech at a military review: 'We must be guided by the example of Frederick the Great who, when hemmed in on all sides by foes, had beaten them one after another.'[108] He also gave an interview to an American journalist from the *New York Times* in which he talked bitterly about Britain's 'perfidy' and how war was now inevitable. In an attempt to win over American opinion, he accused the British of betraying the white race by allying with Japan and said that one day Germany and the United States would have to fight shoulder to shoulder against the Yellow Peril. German officials were appalled when they saw the finished article. Fortunately, so were President Theodore Roosevelt and the editors at the *New York Times* and the article was never published. Its contents, however, reached the British Foreign Office and eventually the French and the Japanese.[109] The British saw the interview as more evidence of the Kaiser's volatility and failed to take the underlying German concerns seriously. As so often happens in international relations, they could not understand that what looked like a defensive move on their part could look different from another perspective.

The British government, despite its many critics, remained pleased about the entente with Russia. Grey later wrote in his memoirs: 'The gain to us was great. We were freed from an anxiety that had often preoccupied British Governments; a frequent source of friction and a possible cause of war was removed; the prospect of peace was made more secure.'[110] Some friction remained, especially over Persia, where tensions continued to flare up until the Great War. The French were delighted and had hopes of building the Triple Entente into a strong military alliance. Both Britain and Russia were much more cautious and steered away even from using the term Triple Entente. Indeed, in 1912 Izvolsky's successor, Sergei Sazonov, said firmly that he would never use it.[111]

As soon as the Anglo-Russian Convention had been signed, Izvolsky reached out to the Triple Alliance, signing an agreement with Germany on the Baltic and proposing to Austria-Hungary that they work together in the Balkans. Britain, likewise, continued to hope for a winding down of the naval race with Germany. In the end, however, it proved to be beyond the capacity of Russia's leaders to bridge the growing chasm between Britain and France on the one hand and Germany and Austria-Hungary on the other, or to keep Russia out of the mounting arms race. By 1914, in spite of periodic struggles to escape, Russia was firmly on one side. Bismarck had warned of this many years earlier: in 1885 he had written to Wilhelm's grandfather that an alliance of Russia, Britain and France 'would provide the basis for a coalition against us more dangerous for Germany than any other she might have to face'.[112]

CHAPTER 8

The Loyalty of the Nibelungs: The Dual Alliance of Austria-Hungary and Germany

n March 1909 as a crisis over Bosnia between Russia and Austria-Hungary threatened to start a war, Bülow, the German Chancellor, assured the Reichstag that Germany would stand behind its ally down the Danube with 'Nibelungen loyalty'. It was a curious metaphor to use. If he was referring to the Wagner operas the Ring Cycle (and he knew the composer's family), then the Nibelungs stand for greed and treachery. If he meant the historic Nibelungs (as the Germans called the Burgundian kings of the Middle Ages) then indeed there was loyalty, but it led to destruction. According to myth, the Burgundian court, surrounded by its enemies, refuses to surrender Hagen who has betrayed and murdered Siegfried, and in his defence the Burgundians die to the last man.

For all the professions of loyalty, the German leadership had mixed feelings about Austria-Hungary. They were aware of its many weaknesses and they found that Austrian charm did not make up for what they saw as the Austrian slapdash ways of doing things. Germany's problem was that it had few possibilities of finding allies elsewhere. It

8. German leaders liked to claim that Germany stood by its ally Austria-Hungary with loyalty worthy of the Nibelungs. It was a curious choice of metaphor which shows something of the ambiguities and strains in the Dual Alliance. According to the myth portrayed here the noble Burgundian warriors of the Middle Ages die to the last man as the result of intrigues between two women.

had alienated Great Britain by the naval race and as long as Tirpitz and the Kaiser refused to back down, the British were not going to be friendly. Partly in response to Germany's challenge, Britain had moved closer to both France and Russia and, although the British said and perhaps even believed that the Triple Entente was defensive and non-binding, nevertheless the three countries had got into the habit of consulting each other and making shared plans. Their officials, whether civilian or military, had built links and made friendships.

If Germany was looking for friends, France, with its military alliance with Russia and its Entente Cordiale with Britain, could no longer be intimidated, as it had been in Bismarck's day, and it was not going to choose freely to align itself with its eastern neighbour. Russia was a more likely prospect for Germany for any number of reasons but for the time being its need for French money and its relief at settling its outstanding issues with Britain in the east made it resistant to German attempts to woo it. Among the great powers that left only Italy, which was indeed part of the Triple Alliance but since it was both weak militarily and deeply at odds with the other member of the Alliance, Austria-Hungary, it could not be depended upon. In southern Europe, if Germany wanted support against Russia or for itself and Austria-Hungary, the prospects were slim: the Ottoman Empire was in rapid decline and the smaller states in southern Europe – Rumania, Bulgaria, Serbia, Montenegro, Greece – were sensibly watching and waiting to see which way events would fall out.

That left Austria-Hungary. As Heinrich von Tschirschky, Germany's ambassador to Vienna since 1907, was to say pensively in 1914: 'How often do I ask myself whether it is really worth it to attach ourselves so firmly to this state which is almost falling apart and to continue the exhausting work of pulling it along with us. But I cannot see any other constellation that could replace the still existing advantages that lie in an alliance with the Central European power.'[1] In the years before 1914, Germany, rightly or wrongly, increasingly saw itself as encircled. (Of course, its neighbours saw it quite differently as a great economic and military power dominating the centre of Europe.) With a friendly Austria-Hungary to the south, it still had one frontier which it did not have to worry about. Count Alfred von Schlieffen, the chief of Germany's general staff who gave his name to one of the most famous military plans of the twentieth century, wrote in 1909, after he had left office: 'The iron ring forged around Germany and Austria only remains open towards the Balkans now.' The enemies of Germany and Austria-Hungary – France, Britain, and Russia – were bent on their destruction but biding their time until internal divisions, in Austria's case among its many nationalities and in Germany's among its political parties, did their malign work. At a given moment, he warned, 'the doors are to be opened, the drawbridges let down, and the million-strong armies let loose, ravaging and destroying …'[2]

What also worried Germany was that Austria-Hungary might itself decide to drift away from the Triple Alliance. There were those on both sides in Russia and Austria-Hungary, including the monarchs themselves, who still hankered after a conservative alliance with or without Germany. And in Austria-Hungary there were plenty who hated Italy and would have much preferred to wage war on it rather than on Russia. Many Austrian patriots found it hard to forgive and forget that the unification of Germany had come at the expense of their empire's traditional role as one of the leading German states. It also did not help that the Germans tended to patronise their ally, the Kaiser saying, for example, what a loyal second Austria-Hungary was in a conflict. German officials often treated their Austrian counterparts in a high-handed way. 'I had never been in any doubt', said Bülow in his memoirs, 'that, if we accept the comparison which that experienced diplomatist, Talleyrand, made between States in alliance and a horse and rider, we must play the part of rider in our alliance with the Danubian monarchy.'[3]

It was never going to be as simple as that and Germany was to find that its horse headed where it wanted, particularly down into the Balkans. In taking on Austria-Hungary as an ally, Germany also took on its ambitions and its quarrels in a volatile part of the world where the rapid decline of the Ottoman Empire in Europe was not only drawing in both Russia and Austria-Hungary but stimulating the appetites of the small independent Balkan states. The challenge for Germany was to reassure Austria-Hungary that it was firmly in support but to keep it from acting recklessly. As Bülow said, with the advantage of hindsight:

> There was a danger that the Dual Monarchy, if tried too far, would lose its nerve and fall into the clutches of Russia as the terrified dove falls to the snake. Our policy would have to put forth every effort to keep Austria faithful to ourselves and, in case of war – which, if we were skilful, was avoidable, but which naturally remained a possibility – to be assured of the co-operation of the Imperial and Royal army, still formidable and efficient enough in spite of the inner weakness of the Monarchy. On the other hand, we must avoid letting Austria drag us, against our will, into a world war.[4]

On paper and on the map, Austria-Hungary looked an impressive ally. In today's terms, it stretched from southern Poland down to the north of Serbia and included the Czech Republic, Slovakia, Austria, Hungary, the south-western corner of Ukraine, Slovenia, Croatia, and Bosnia and a large piece – Transylvania – of Rumania. It had a population of more than 50 million, a strong agricultural sector, resources from iron to timber, growing industries, a rapidly expanding railway network, a peacetime army of nearly 400,000 as well as a modern navy. Its great capital cities of Vienna and Budapest and the smaller cities too, Prague for example, or Zagreb, had been modernised and beautified with proper drains, tramways, electricity, and massive and heavily decorated public buildings and solid bourgeois apartment blocks. The Dual Monarchy's universities ranged from the Jagiellonian in Cracow (one of the oldest in Europe) to the Vienna Medical Schools and its schools and colleges were expanding fast. By 1914 80 per cent of the empire's population could read and write.

While there were parts of the Dual Monarchy which seemed not to have changed at all – peasant life in Galicia or Transylvania, for example, or, at the other end of the social scale, the intricate ritual of the court in the great imperial palaces – the modern world was shaking up Austria-Hungary, producing new communications, enterprises, and technologies as well as new values and attitudes. The old restrictions which kept Jews out of certain professions had gone, for example, although a new and virulent anti-Semitism, sad to say, was to make its appearance in the years before 1914. While the Dual Monarchy's economic growth could not match that of Russia's, it was at an average of 1.7 per cent per year in the two decades before 1914. The empire's development followed a pattern familiar from western Europe, with the growth of industries and a corresponding move of peasants from the countryside into the cities and towns and, in spite of booms and busts, a gradual spread of prosperity throughout a wider section of the population. The Czech lands, which were already advanced technologically and commercially, had the highest concentration of modern industry such as the great Skoda works which produced some of the best guns in Europe. Vienna also had modern industry on its outskirts including the Daimler works. By 1900, Budapest was catching up as well as becoming a banking centre for much of eastern Europe. Although Hungary's economy remained predominantly agricultural, it was industrialising fast in the years after 1900.

Government spending on such things as infrastructure and social programmes, which was also increasing, helped what looked set to be a steady march towards modernisation and greater prosperity. The picture was not entirely rosy, however. Austria-Hungary's imports greatly exceeded its exports and government debt was climbing. Its military expenditure remained the lowest of all the big four powers; in 1911 it was spending just over a third of what Russia was.[5] Any increase in international tension was bound to be bad for Austria-Hungary's fiscal health. Moreover, progress inevitably brought its own problems and strains. Small peasant farmers and the minor landholding nobility, for example, saw the prices for such products as wheat going down in the face of competition from Russia. The decades before 1914 saw increased peasant strikes and protests and the break-up of some of the old estates. In the towns and cities, craftsmen who could no longer compete with the output of modern factories and industrial workers whose conditions were often appalling were becoming organised and militant.

In some ways politics in the Dual Monarchy were similar to those elsewhere in Europe: the old landed classes hoped to hang on to power and influence, radicals were anti-clerical, middle-class liberals wanted greater freedoms, at least for themselves, and the new socialist movements wanted reform or in some cases revolution. And like Europe itself, Austria-Hungary included a range of ways of governing from autocracy to parliamentary democracy. The Austrian half had a parliament elected, after 1907, by universal male suffrage; in Hungary by contrast the franchise was restricted to about 6 per cent of the population. While Franz Joseph, the emperor from 1848 to 1916, was not as powerful as the tsar, nor was he as constrained as the king of Great Britain. The Austrian emperor determined foreign policy and was the supreme commander of the armed forces but his powers were laid out in constitutional laws. He appointed and dismissed ministers and had emergency powers, which his government used frequently, to govern without parliament yet he could not modify the constitution. The business of government nevertheless went on, taxes were collected and bills were paid. The emperor himself was popular with most of his people and the prospect of revolution seemed much more remote than in Russia.

What made German statesmen ask themselves in the decades before 1914 whether they had made the right choice in allying with

Austria-Hungary was the question mark over its long-term survival. In an age of growing national consciousness, it, like the Ottoman Empire, was increasingly at the mercy of its nationalities. Lord Durham said of Canada in 1838 that it consisted of two nations warring within the bosom of a single state and the conflict between French and English is still working itself out there over a century and a half later. How much greater the challenge was for Austria-Hungary, which recognised ten or eleven main languages. This had not mattered for centuries, when people defined themselves by religion or ruler or village and not by nationality. By the late nineteenth century, however, nationalism – the identifying of oneself as a member of a group distinguished by language as well as religion, history, culture or race – was a force for change all over Europe. Just as a growing sense of belonging to something called the German or the Italian nation had helped lead to the creation of a German and an Italian state, Polish, Hungarian, Ruthenian, Czech and still more nationalisms were pushing inside Austria-Hungary towards greater autonomy if not full independence.

Austria-Hungary had no strong countervailing identity around which its citizens could rally since it was not so much a country as a collection of properties acquired by the Habsburgs over the previous millennium through skilful manoeuvring, marriage and war. Franz Joseph had so many titles, ranging from emperor to count, that they were often written with many an etc. etc. There were, of course, those who believed in a multinational empire: perhaps of mixed nationalities themselves, or the great aristocratic families whose connections and interests spanned the empire and indeed often Europe itself, or Habsburg loyalists who put duty to the dynasty above all else. The army too was a genuinely multinational organisation and it dealt with the language issue in a sensible way. Soldiers had to know the basic technical and command words in German but otherwise they would usually be placed in regiments where their fellow soldiers spoke the same language. Officers were expected to learn the language of the soldiers under their command. It is said that during the war one regiment found that English was the most common language and so used that.[6]

The only other truly imperial institution was the monarchy itself. It had lasted for centuries and had seen out invasions, conquerors from Suleiman the Magnificent of the Ottomans to Napoleon, civil wars and revolutions while the empire had grown, contracted, grown again, and, in the second half of the nineteenth century, contracted yet again. The Habsburgs traced their descent back to Charlemagne but they first made their mark on the history of Europe when one of their number was elected Holy Roman Emperor. Over the succeeding centuries the family virtually made the title its own until it was finally abolished by Napoleon in 1806. The Habsburgs endured, however, and Emperor Franz of Austria, as he now was, lived to see the defeat of Napoleon and reigned until 1835, when he was succeeded by his gentle and simple-minded son, Ferdinand. His grandson, Franz Joseph, became emperor in 1848, a year of revolutions all over Europe, when the dynasty tottered and the Austrian Empire itself nearly fell to pieces. His uncle Ferdinand was persuaded to abdicate and Franz Joseph's own father, who was only slightly more competent than his brother (he had been nicknamed 'the Good' because no one could think of anything else), agreed to step aside as well. (The Habsburgs dealt ruthlessly and briskly with the frequent consequences of inbreeding.) The new emperor, who had just turned eighteen, reportedly remarked 'Goodbye, youth.'[7]

He was a handsome and dignified man and remained slim with an erect military bearing until the end of his days. His tutors had set up a programme for him of history, philosophy and theology as well as languages including, in addition to the German which was his first tongue, Italian, Hungarian, French, Czech, Polish, Croatian, and Latin. His memory, fortunately, was excellent and so was his capacity for work. He had applied himself to his studies with determination. 'My birthday', he wrote in his diary in 1845, 'and more important still my fifteenth. Fifteen years old – and only a little more time to go to get educated! I must really pull my socks up, really mend my ways!'[8] That strong sense of duty stayed with him all his life. So, after the events of 1848, did a hatred of revolution and a determination to preserve the dynasty and his empire. He was not a reactionary, however; he accepted with a degree of fatalism that change had occurred and might have to occur in the future. Changes there would be: the gradual loss of most of his Italian territories and then, after defeat in 1866 by Prussia, the exclusion of Austria from the German Confederation.

His empire was slowly shrinking, but Franz Joseph kept up the state of his great ancestors. In Vienna alone he had two palaces: the gigantic

Hofburg and the Schönbrunn, his favourite, built by Maria Theresa as a summer place (with 1,400 rooms and a huge park). Count Albert von Margutti, who served as the emperor's aide-de-camp for nearly two decades, remembered his first meeting: 'With beating heart I ascended what is known in the Hofburg as the "Chancery Staircase", an enormous flight of steps leading to the ante-room of the audience chamber.' Guards in magnificent uniforms stood at the top of the stairs while the door into the emperor's presence was flanked by two officers with drawn swords. 'Everything went off like clockwork and quite noiselessly; notwithstanding all the people present, there was a silence which greatly intensified the impressiveness of the occasion.'[9]

At the heart of the grandeur was a man who liked plain food, predictable routines, and, for relaxation, hunting and shooting. He was a good Catholic without thinking much about it. Like his fellow sovereigns Nicholas II and Wilhelm II, Franz Joseph loved the military life and almost always appeared in uniform. Like them too he was sent into a rage when the details of army uniforms were wrong. Apart from that, he was invariably courteous to everyone although always conscious of rank. He only shook Margutti's hand once, to recognise that he had been promoted. (Margutti regretted ever after that no one else at court had seen this momentous gesture.)[10] Franz Joseph found modern art puzzling but his sense of duty took him to public art exhibitions and the opening of important new buildings, especially if they were under royal patronage.[11] His taste in music ran to military marches or Strauss waltzes and, while he liked the theatre and from time to time the prettier actresses, he preferred the old favourites. He did not like unpunctuality, loud laughter or people who talked too much.[12] He had a sense of humour, of a rather basic sort. He had climbed the Great Pyramid in Egypt, he wrote to his wife, Empress Elisabeth, with the help of Bedouin guides. 'As they mostly only wear a shirt, when they are climbing they leave a lot exposed, and that must be the reason why English women so happily and frequently like to scale the pyramids.'[13]

In his later days, Franz Joseph slept on an army camp cot in a bedroom of the utmost simplicity, or, as Margutti said, 'downright penury'. He followed a strict and spartan routine, waking just after four in the morning and having himself rubbed down with cold water. He drank a glass of milk and then worked alone until seven or seven thirty, when he started conferences with his advisers. From ten until five or six in the afternoon he saw his ministers and dignitaries such as ambassadors, stopping only for a half-hour to eat a light lunch alone. In the evening he dined alone or with guests. He hated wasting time and insisted on meals being served at a rapid pace with the result that the younger members of the family often did not have time to eat before the meal ended. Unless there was a court ball or reception he was in bed by half past eight. For all the studied simplicity of his life, he had a strong sense of his own dignity and the respect owed him.[14]

Franz Joseph had adored his strong-willed mother. 'Is there anything dearer on earth than one's mother?' he asked when he heard that Wilhelm's mother had died. 'Whatever differences may separate us the mother is always the mother, and when we lose her we bury a good part of ourselves in her grave.'[15] His personal life was complicated and often sad. His brother, Maximilian, had been executed in Mexico after a failed attempt to establish a kingdom there, and the widow had gone mad. His only son, Rudolf, a troubled and unhappy young man, had committed suicide with his teenage mistress at his hunting lodge of Mayerling. The authorities covered up the scandal but that did not stop rumours, many of them wild conspiracy theories, floating about. Franz Joseph carried on, as he always did, but wrote to the actress Katharina Schratt, who was perhaps his closest friend in the world, that 'things can never be the same'.[16] To add to his burdens, the heir was likely to be his nephew, Franz Ferdinand, whom he did not particularly care for.

Franz Joseph's marriage had long since ceased to provide him with any comfort. He had adored Elisabeth, his cousin, whom he had married when she was only seventeen, but things had not turned out well. Elisabeth was charming, vivacious and lovely, and, as a girl, delightfully wayward and impulsive. She never, unfortunately, grew up. She hated the court, ceremonials, and obligations, and did her best to avoid them. Yet she could, when she wanted, be helpful to her husband. She so charmed the Hungarians by learning their language and wearing their national dress that they gave the royal couple a summer palace outside Budapest. She loved riding, travelling, and herself. Although she was widely agreed to be a beauty, she always worried about her looks. She made an album of the most beautiful women in Europe, but that only reduced her to tears.[17] Throughout her life, she exercised fanatically and ate as little as possible. 'Her waist', wrote Queen Victoria in her diary, 'is smaller than anything one can imagine.'[18] In 1898, when her anarchist assassin stabbed Elisabeth in the heart, she did not die immediately because her corsets were so tight that she bled only very slowly.

Franz Joseph soldiered on, working methodically through his piles of papers as though, somehow, through sheer hard work and attention to detail, he could stave off chaos and hold his empire together. 'God help us', he was fond of saying, 'if we ever fall into the ways of the Latin races.'[19] As the years of his long reign went by, he was nevertheless increasingly in the position of someone riding two ill-matched horses. Hungary, with its long past as an independent kingdom, had always fitted awkwardly under the Habsburg crown. The Hungarian aristocracy and minor nobles who dominated society and politics were highly conscious of their own language (different from almost any other in the world), history, and culture, and deeply proud of their own constitution and laws. In the revolutionary year of 1848–9 they tried, but failed, to make Hungary independent. In 1867 they took advantage of the Austrian Empire's crushing defeat at the hands of Prussia to negotiate a new arrangement with the emperor, the famous Compromise.

It created a new entity whose name said it all: Austria-Hungary or the Dual Monarchy. It was a partnership between Hungary, which still included Transylvania, Slovakia and Croatia, and the remaining Habsburg territories in the west, which came to be called for convenience Austria and which swept up from the Adriatic and the Alps towards the vanished kingdom of Poland and then eastwards to the Russian border. Each part ran its own affairs with its own parliament, ministers, bureaucracy, law courts, and armed forces. The sole remaining shared activities were foreign affairs and defence as well as the finances to pay for them, each with its own minister who met together as the three common ministers, and the only other remaining link was the emperor himself, or as he was known in Hungary, the king. Otherwise the Dual Monarchy was not so much a compromise as a never-ending negotiation. Delegations nominated by each parliament met once a year to work out any necessary agreements on common tariffs, for example on railways, but, at the insistence of the Hungarians, only communicated in writing to avoid any notion that there was a shared government.

Financial and commercial matters came up for renegotiation every ten years and usually caused difficulties.

Of all the major European powers, Austria-Hungary had the poorest mechanisms for sharing information among ministries and co-ordinating policies. True, the three common ministers met from time to time along with the Prime Ministers from both Hungary and Austria, but while they discussed foreign and defence issues they did not act as an executive. Between the autumn of 1913 and the start of the July crisis in 1914, the Common Ministerial Council, as it was known, met just three times, and then only to talk about relatively trivial matters. Nor did the emperor take charge of overall policy or encourage anyone else to do so; Franz Joseph would speak to his ministers only separately and only concerning their own areas of responsibility. And although he continued his dogged routine of work, he was ageing. He turned eighty in 1910 and his health, robust for so long, was beginning to fail. By the time the war came he was increasingly isolated from the public gaze inside the Schönbrunn palace and reluctant to intervene in disputes among his ministers. The vacuum of leadership meant, among other things, that strong individuals or departments often made policy and in areas outside their own purview.[20]

The Hungarians were initially delighted with the Compromise and commissioned a new parliament building for Budapest. 'There must be no place for caution, calculation and thrift,' said their Prime Minister, and the Hungarian architect took him at his word. The Hungarian parliament buildings, which drew on every architectural style and form of ornamentation from Gothic to Renaissance to baroque, and used up eighty-four pounds of gold in their decoration, were the biggest in the world when they were finished. What went on inside was outsized in another way. Politics was a national sport and the Hungarians played to win, against each other with biting rhetoric, even challenges to duels, and, when that palled, against Vienna.[21] Some of the worst scenes came during a prolonged and bitter crisis between Budapest and Vienna over the joint army.

Successive Hungarian political leaders and their followers demanded a series of measures to make a large part of the Dual Monarchy's army more Hungarian, with exclusively Hungarian regiments commanded by Hungarian-speaking officers and flying the Hungarian flag. This threatened the efficiency and unity of the army and, as the French military attaché pointed out, there were not in any case enough Hungarian-speaking officers to go round. When Franz Joseph tried to calm the situation in 1903 by issuing an anodyne statement that his armed forces were animated by a spirit of unity and harmony and treated all ethnic groups with respect, he simply threw more fuel the way of the Hungarian nationalists in Budapest. 'Ethnic' came out as 'tribal' in Hungarian, which was seized upon as a deadly insult.[22] The Hungarian parliament was paralysed by filibustering and negotiations between Budapest and Vienna came to a halt. At the end of 1904, when the Hungarian Prime Minister, István Tisza (who was to be in office again in the summer of 1914), tried to move matters forward, the opposition swarmed into the chamber armed with coshes, knuckle dusters and revolvers, smashing the furniture and beating up the parliamentary guards. Although the opposition won the subsequent election it refused to take office until Franz Joseph conceded their demands on the army, which he refused to do. The stand-off ended in 1906 when the emperor threatened to introduce universal suffrage in Hungary and the opposition fell to pieces.

The Hungarians, after all, had their own nationalities problem, one which they had managed to ignore successfully up to this point. Hungarians, or Magyars, as they liked to be called, were only a bare majority within Hungary's borders but the restricted franchise gave them almost all the seats in parliament. By 1900 national movements – Serb, Rumanian, Croat – were igniting around Hungary, fuelled by this lack of power as well as resentment at government promotion of Hungarian in schools and offices. They were also mirrored by growing nationalist movements elsewhere, both inside Austria-Hungary and around its borders. In 1895 a Congress of Nationalities met in Budapest to demand that Hungary become a multinational state. The Hungarians reacted with alarm and anger. Even the relatively liberal Tisza simply could not accept that there were other nations with legitimate national aspirations within Hungary. In his view Rumanians, except for extremists, were like the peasants on his estate and knew that they needed to work with Hungarians: 'I know that they are gentle, peaceful, respectful of gentlemen, and grateful for every good word.'[23]

Throughout the Dual Monarchy, the rising tide of nationalism brought with it endless and insoluble fights about schools, jobs, even street signs. The question on the census asking people to put down their mother tongues became a vital marker of national strength and national groups took out advertisements urging the 'right' answers. Nationalist movements often overlapped with economic and class issues: Rumanian and Ruthenian peasants, for example, challenged their Hungarian and Polish landlords. Yet such was the force of nationalism that classes which in other countries formed socialist or liberal or conservative parties here split apart on national lines.

Because Austria-Hungary's population had been so mixed by centuries of history almost every locality had its own nationalist struggles: in Slovenia, Italians against Slovenes, in Galicia, Poles against Ruthenians, and Germans, it seemed, against everyone, whether Italians in the Tyrol or Czechs in Bohemia. In 1895 the Austrian government fell because German speakers objected to parallel Slovene classes in a secondary school; two years later conflict between Czechs and Germans over the use of Czech in government business in Bohemia and Moravia led to violence in the streets and the fall of another Prime Minister; and in 1904 there were violent demonstrations by Germans when an Italian law faculty was established in Innsbruck. New railway stations remained nameless because no one could agree on which language to use. Perhaps it was no accident that it was a Viennese, Sigmund Freud, who was to come up with the notion of the narcissism of small differences. As he wrote in *Civilization and Its Discontents*, 'it is precisely communities with adjoining territories, and related to each other in other ways as well, who are engaged in constant feuds and in ridiculing each other …'[24]

'An air of unreality pervaded everything,' said Henry Wickham Steed, a British journalist assigned to Vienna. 'Public attention was fixed on trifles – a squabble at the Opera between a Czech and a German singer, a row in Parliament over the appointment of some obscure official in Bohemia, the attractions of the latest comic opera or the sale of tickets for a charity ball.'[25] The younger generation either became bored and cynical about politics or joined new political movements which promised to clean up the mess, by violent means if necessary. Austria-Hungary was being weakened and its international position damaged by the 'defective solution of the nationality question', the future Foreign Minister of Austria-Hungary, Alois von Aehrenthal, wrote to his cousin in 1899. 'The hereditary defect of the Austrian – pessimism – is already seizing the youth and threatens to stifle every idealistic impulse.'[26]

National differences led not only to a breakdown of civility in the streets but to increasing stalemate inside the Dual Monarchy's parliaments. Political parties, divided as they mostly were on linguistic and ethnic lines, were mainly interested in promoting the interests of their own group and in blocking the others. Deputies blew trumpets, rang cowbells, banged gongs, beat on drums and hurled inkpots and books around to silence their opponents. The filibusters became a normal tactic; in one of the most famous a German deputy spoke for twelve straight hours during the struggle to prevent Czech being given equal status with German in Bohemia and Moravia. 'In our country', a conservative aristocrat wrote to a friend, 'an optimist must commit suicide.'[27] The government somehow muddled through, increasingly by using its emergency powers. When war came in August 1914, the Austrian parliament had been suspended for several months and was not to meet again until the spring of 1917.

Nationalism also undermined the bureaucracy as appointments became a way for parties to reward their followers. As result the size and costs of the bureaucracy went up enormously. Between 1890 and 1911 there was a 200 per cent increase in the numbers of bureaucrats, most of them new appointments. In Austria alone there were 3 million civil servants for a total population of some 28 million. Even the simplest decisions were wound about with red tape or, in reality, coloured twine, black and yellow for imperial matters, red, white, and green for Hungary, or, when it was annexed, brown and yellow for Bosnia. A single tax payment in Vienna went through the hands of twenty-seven different officials. In the Adriatic province of Dalmatia, a commission set up to report on ways to improve the bureaucracy discovered that the collection of direct taxes cost twice as much as it raised. The commission painted a dispiriting picture of inefficiency and waste throughout the country: while civil servants were expected, for example, to work five to six hours a day, few did even that. In the Foreign Office, a new recruit said he rarely received more than three or four files a day to deal with and no one minded if he came in late and left early. In 1903 the British embassy had to wait for ten months to get an answer about the duty on

Canadian whisky. 'The dilatoriness of this country, if continued in progressive ratio, will soon rival that of Turkey,' a British diplomat complained to London.[28]

Not surprisingly, the public tended to describe the bureaucracy as a broken-down old nag but the consequences were far from a joke. The contempt for what the Viennese satirist Karl Kraus called *Bürokretinismus* served further to undermine public confidence in their government. And the costs of the bureaucracy meant, among other things, that there was less money for the armed forces which in any case remained caught up in the endless political struggles. Until 1912, the Hungarian parliament had refused to agree to increased funding or the number of men being conscripted annually unless it got concessions on such matters as the language issue in return. It took a crisis in the Balkans on the Dual Monarchy's doorstep to bring about a modest improvement. Even so, by 1914 Austria-Hungary was spending less on its army than was Britain (which had by far the smallest army of all the powers in Europe). The Dual Monarchy's total defence budget was well under half of that of Russia, its most formidable enemy.[29]

Austria-Hungary was by no means the corpse on the Danube, as some in its ally Germany had taken to calling it, but it clearly was sick. Various cures were considered and rejected or found to be unworkable. During the crisis with Hungary over the language issue and the army, the Dual Monarchy's military drew up plans to use force in Hungary but the emperor refused to contemplate it.[30] Hopes of making the bureaucracy truly national and above politics foundered in the face of inertia and entrenched nationalisms. Universal suffrage as a way of linking the masses closer to the crown was tried in Austria but it only produced more voters for the new populist national parties. Or there was Trialism, a new sort of compromise with the South Slavs, a term increasingly being used for the Serb, Slovene and Croat inhabitants of the southern part of the Dual Monarchy as well as those in the Balkans. A South Slav bloc would counterbalance Austria and Hungary and satisfy South Slav nationalist demands. It was rejected out of hand by the Hungarians. For many the last hope was the heir to the throne, Franz Ferdinand, who was relatively young and energetic and undoubtedly full of ideas, largely authoritarian and reactionary ones. Perhaps he could roll back change and make the Dual Monarchy a proper autocracy again with a strong central government. He certainly looked and acted the part of a decisive ruler.

Franz Ferdinand was a tall, handsome man with large expressive eyes and a loud and domineering voice. If his moustache was not quite a match for Wilhelm's it nevertheless twirled smartly into sharp points. His private life, after the usual youthful indiscretions, was impeccable. He had married for love and was a devoted husband and father. He had an eye for beautiful things and did much to save Austria-Hungary's architectural heritage. He was intellectually curious and, unlike his uncle the emperor, read the newspapers thoroughly. He was also greedy, demanding, and intolerant. He was known for beating dealers down to get the paintings and furniture he wanted. He was unforgiving with subordinates for even the smallest of mistakes. Among others, he hated Jews, Freemasons and anyone who criticised or challenged the Catholic Church to which he was passionately devoted. He also loathed Hungarians ('traitors') and Serbs ('pigs'). They should, he said frequently, be crushed. There was something excessive about both his pleasures and hatreds. When he hunted he preferred to have the game, great quantities of it, driven towards him as he shot until his guns turned red hot. It was said that he once suddenly demanded that a herd of deer be rounded up and shot all 200 of them as well as one of the beaters by mistake.[31]

It had not been expected that he would be the heir to the throne but the execution of his uncle Maximilian in Mexico, the suicide of his cousin Rudolf, and his own father's death from typhoid which he got from drinking the water of the River Jordan in the Holy Land, left him in 1896 at the age of thirty-three as the next acceptable male heir. (Franz Joseph's youngest brother Ludwig Victor was still alive but surrounded by far too much scandal.) Franz Ferdinand himself had been seriously ill with tuberculosis shortly before father's death; he was dismayed to see people paying court to his younger brother. He had recovered after a sea voyage and was to remain in good health until 1914.

The emperor did not much care for his new heir and their relations took a marked turn for the worse in 1900 when Franz Ferdinand insisted on marrying Countess Sophie Chotek. She was pretty, with a good reputation, and came from an old aristocratic family in Bohemia, but she was not of the right rank for a Habsburg. Although the emperor eventually gave way he imposed conditions: Sophie would not get the rank or privileges of a Habsburg duchess and their children would not be eligible for the throne. This slight, which her husband resented bitterly, and the indifference which his uncle displayed towards his heir's views added to Franz Ferdinand's highly developed sense of insecurity. 'The archduke has the feeling', said one of his loyal aides, 'he is undervalued [and] from this feeling there results an understandable jealousy of high functionaries, who in the army or public life enjoy great prestige.'[32] Perhaps as a result, his temper, always ferocious, became close to uncontrollable. There were rumours of him shooting his revolver wildly, attendants who were really male nurses, and a story, reported by the British ambassador in Vienna, that the emperor was thinking of passing him over for the succession because of doubts about his sanity.[33]

Whether this was true or not, and there were always many rumours about the Habsburgs, Franz Joseph gradually began to give Franz Ferdinand greater responsibilities. He provided him with a lovely baroque palace, the Belvedere, and allowed him to set up his own military office and in 1913 made him Inspector General of the Armed Forces, which gave him considerable latitude to deal with the military, although Franz Joseph himself remained the commander-in-chief. The Belvedere became almost a second court as Franz Ferdinand built his own network with politicians, bureaucrats, officers, and journalists. Here he developed his ideas for saving the Dual Monarchy: by centralising power and the armed forces, getting rid of the Compromise with Hungary, and creating a new federated state to include Hungarians, Germans, Czechs, Poles, and South Slavs. He had no particular fondness for parliamentary institutions and would have governed without them if he had had the opportunity. Count Ottokar Czernin, who was to become Foreign Minister during the war, doubted whether he could have succeeded: 'The structure of the Monarchy which he was so anxious to strengthen and support was already so rotten that it could not have stood any great innovations, and if not the war, then probably the Revolution, would have shattered it.'[34]

In foreign policy Franz Ferdinand's preference was for maintaining the German alliance and getting a closer understanding with Russia, the other great conservative monarchy. He would have happily ended the alliance with Italy, which he hated for any number of reasons from its treatment of the Pope to its absorption of the Kingdom of the Two Sicilies which had been ruled by his grandfather.[35] Although he was said to be a warmonger, he was in fact more cautious than he frequently sounded because he knew that Austria-Hungary was too weak and divided to risk an aggressive foreign policy. As he said presciently to the Foreign Minister in 1913 during the last Balkan crisis before the Great War:

> Without giving up everything, we should do anything to uphold peace! If we enter a great war with Russia, it would be a catastrophe, and who knows whether our right and left flanks will function; Germany has to deal with France and Rumania makes excuses due to the Bulgarian threat. Therefore now is a very disadvantageous moment. If we wage a war specifically with Serbia, we will quickly overcome that hurdle, but what then? And what would we have? First all of Europe would fall on us and see us as disturber of the peace and God help us, if we annex Serbia.[36]

It is one of the smaller tragedies of the summer of 1914 that in assassinating Franz Ferdinand the Serb nationalists removed the one man in Austria-Hungary who might have prevented it going to war. We can never know what might have happened and it may be, in an age of increasingly intransigent nationalisms, that the multinational empire was doomed even without war.

For Austria-Hungary its internal and external policies were intimately linked and shaped by the nationalist forces which it confronted. Where it had once reached out to bring Germans or Italians or South Slavs under its rule, by the second half of the nineteenth century it was on the defensive, trying to prevent national groups around its borders from taking away its territory. Italian unification had, step by step, stripped away most of Austria-Hungary's Italian-speaking areas and Italian irredentists still eyed the South Tyrol. Serbian ambitions now threatened to do the same for South Slav territories including Croatia and Slovenia in the south of the Dual Monarchy; Rumanian nationalists longed for the Rumanian-speaking parts of Transylvania; and Russian agitators were working on the population of Ruthenia in the eastern part of Galicia to persuade them that they really belonged inside Russia. And the problem was only going to get worse as national groups outside Austria-Hungary increasingly strengthened their links to their compatriots inside what some were coming to call 'the prison of nations'.

Pessimists – or perhaps they were simply realists – within Austria-Hungary believed in trying to maintain the status quo and preventing further divisions at home and decline abroad. The emperor certainly fell within that camp. So did the Foreign Minister until 1906, Count Agenor Gołuchowski. He was handsome, charming, rather lazy (his nickname was Gołuchschlafski – *schlaf* means sleep – for his general air of somnolence), and pragmatic. He was well aware of Austria-Hungary's weakness and believed in a quiet foreign policy without sudden or exciting initiatives. His policies were based on the views that Austria-Hungary needed to maintain the Triple Alliance with Germany and Italy, keep on good terms with Russia and avoid falling out in the Balkans or over the Ottoman Empire, and, if possible, continue the agreements with Great Britain and Italy over the Mediterranean.

Optimists believed that the Dual Monarchy needed to and indeed could show that it was still a great power and in so doing build national unity. They resented Austria-Hungary's weakness at home and in its own neighbourhood, and its inability to join in the scramble for colonies around the world. The Austrian ambassador in Washington, an experienced diplomat, wrote to one of his colleagues in 1899:

> The way the great power politics have been developing through extra-European issues, is leading us to sink further into the background as a power factor. Within our lifetimes the problems which the politics of the eighties revolved around have become obsolete, such as our dominance in Italy in the fifties and our rivalry with Prussia in the sixties. No one is happy; unlike the previous period, we only want to hold on to the status quo and our only ambition is existence.

And, he concluded glumly, 'Our prestige has sunk about as far as the level of Switzerland.'[37] On Austria-Hungary's own doorstep though, there were temptations for gains in the Balkans and perhaps further afield along the coast of Asia Minor as the Ottoman Empire faded away.[38]

Seven years later, by which time Austria-Hungary's position had deteriorated still further, Conrad von Hötzendorf, the new chief of staff and one of the most influential men in the Dual Monarchy, laid out his views on foreign policy. Austria-Hungary needed to be forceful and positive both to show the world that it must be taken seriously but, equally important, to inspire its own citizens with pride in their country and overcome its enervating domestic disputes. Success abroad, and that included military success, would lead to more support for the government at home, which in turn would generate support for a more aggressive foreign policy. That result, which was the only possible one if Austria-Hungary were to survive, depended on strong armed forces. As Conrad put it a few years later: 'It must always be kept in mind that the destinies of nations and dynasties are settled on the battlefield rather than at the conference table.'[39]

He was not alone by any means in holding such views: they were shared by many senior military men across Europe. What made his situation different was that he was able through a combination of his own personality and the incoherence in government in Austria-Hungary to exert great influence over both domestic and foreign policies. Apart from a year's interlude in 1912, he was chief of staff from 1906 to 1917, during the prewar years with their growing crises, the arms race, and the tightening of the alliances, then in those crucial weeks of 1914 when the world went to war, and finally during the war itself as Austria-Hungary lurched from one disaster to another.

He was fifty-four years old when he became the most important military leader in the Dual Monarchy next to Franz Joseph himself. He was a devoted servant of the empire and the emperor. Born in Vienna into a German-speaking family, like many in the old empire Conrad learned several languages along the way including French, Italian, Russian, Serbian, Polish, and Czech. He felt that speaking many languages was part of what it meant to be Austrian. (When he became chief of staff he went to the Berlitz school to add Hungarian; Franz Ferdinand said he would be better off learning Chinese.[40])

Conrad was intense, self-confident, and vain (he never wore his glasses if he could help it). He had great energy and stamina and sat well on a horse, always important for officers in the European armies of the day. He could be charming; he was also very good at getting his own way. His subordinates tended to love him but he quarrelled frequently with colleagues and superiors including Franz Ferdinand, who had initially wanted him in the post. Conrad's background was relatively modest, certainly in comparison to other high-ranking officers (his father's family were minor nobility and his mother's father was a painter) and he had risen through the army through his own intelligence and hard work. This last quality had perhaps been instilled by his mother, who had always made him finish his homework before he could have supper. She remained a great influence on him and she and his sister came to live with him when Conrad's father died. Conrad liked and respected women and had been happily married. When his wife died in 1904 at the relatively young age of forty-four, about a year before he became chief of staff, he was desolate. He had the first of what were to be recurring attacks of depression. He had never had much faith in religion and he now became cynical about its promises and increasingly doubtful about whether life had much meaning. That pessimism was to cast its shadow for the rest of his life and sit strangely with his repeated calls for positive action.[41]

By the standards of the time Conrad was a mildly unconventional officer. He was bored by hunting and impatient of formality. He also read widely – history, philosophy, politics, fiction – and formed strong views. One of his core beliefs, shared by so many at the time, was that existence was about struggle and that nations rose and fell depending on their ability to adapt. He hoped that Austria-Hungary would; he often doubted that it could. In politics he was conservative and, like his patron Franz Ferdinand, anti-Hungarian; in foreign policy, however, he was adventurous, even reckless. He saw Italy as a major, perhaps the major, threat to the empire, luring the country's Italian citizens away and challenging Austria-Hungary in the Adriatic and the Balkans. When Russia was temporarily laid low in the aftermath of the Russo-Japanese War, he urged his government to carry out a preventive war to crush Italy. After he became chief of staff he continued to press for war. 'Austria never has started a war,' Franz Joseph told him. Conrad replied, 'Unfortunately, your majesty.' Although both the emperor and Franz Ferdinand rejected the idea of war on Italy, they did allow Conrad to strengthen Austria-Hungary's fortifications in the South Tyrol along the border with Italy, thus diverting scarce resources from modernising

and equipping the empire's armed forces. Conrad also undertook osten-
tatious staff exercises along the border, in one case practising an Austrian
defence against Italy along the Isonzo River, later to be one of the
bloodiest battlefields on that front in the Great War.[42]

Conrad saw Serbia as another enemy. He had come to dislike the
South Slav inhabitants of the Balkans after serving in the force which
put down rebellions in Bosnia and Herzegovina at the end of the 1870s.
Their peoples in his view were primitives, driven by 'bloodlust and
cruelty'.[43] As Serbia grew in strength and moved into Russia's orbit
after 1900, Conrad called for a preventive war against it as well, but until
1914 the emperor resisted him. After the Great War Conrad argued that
Austria-Hungary's defeat had been the price paid for missing its opportunities by not going to war against Serbia and Italy when it could. 'The
army is not a fire extinguisher, one cannot let it rust until the flames are
coming out of the house. Instead it is an instrument to be used by goal-
conscious, clever politicians as the ultimate defence of their
interests.'[44]

Conrad's ambitions to do something dramatic and on a large scale
were fuelled by personal turmoil in his life. In 1907, he fell deeply in love
again. Gina von Reininghaus was beautiful, less than half his age, and
had a husband and six children. They sat together at a dinner and he
poured out his sorrow at the death of his wife and his loneliness.
According to Gina's later account, as Conrad was leaving the party, he
turned to his aide and said that he would have to leave Vienna immediately. 'This woman will become my destiny.' Far from leaving, Conrad
declared his love and urged her to divorce her husband and marry him.
This would have both been difficult (she would have lost custody of the
six children, among other considerations) and caused a damaging
scandal and she resisted. At some point, though, in the next few years
Conrad and Gina became lovers with the acquiescence of her husband,
who took the opportunity to start his own affair. Conrad wrote her
letter after passionate letter, most of which he never sent, and he never
stopped longing to make her his wife. During the Bosnian crisis in 1908
he wrote that it looked like war. Perhaps, he dared dream, he would
return victorious. 'Then, Gina, I would break all the chains, in order to
win you, the greatest happiness of my life, as my dear wife. But what if
things don't happen this way and this rotten peace continues to drag on,

what then Gina? In your hands lies my destiny, completely in your hands.' She saw the letter for the first time in 1925, after his death. He had finally got the war he wanted and had married Gina in 1915, after strings had been pulled in high places to get her an annulment.[45]

Fortunately for the peace of Europe in the short run, Conrad did not get his wish for war in 1908 or in the next set of crises in the Balkans between 1911 and 1913. The archduke was also becoming disillusioned with his protégé and perhaps somewhat jealous of Conrad's reputation as the Dual Monarchy's leading military thinker and strategist. Conrad did not show the necessary deference and took orders badly. The two men disagreed over the training of the army and its use. Franz Ferdinand would have willingly used it against domestic opposition, in Hungary and elsewhere, while Conrad insisted that it be kept for external wars. The final break came over Italy: in 1911 it went to war with the Ottoman Empire over Libya and Conrad saw this as the perfect moment to invade while Italian forces were occupied in North Africa. Both the emperor and his heir rejected his advice, as did the Foreign Minister, Aehrenthal. When an anonymous article appeared in a Vienna newspaper reflecting Conrad's views and attacking Aehrenthal, the old emperor felt that he had no choice but to replace his chief of staff. Conrad was not dismissed altogether, however, but given a prestigious post in the army. He was reinstated a year later as chief of staff but Franz Ferdinand continued to regard him with mistrust and wrote to the new Foreign Minister, Leopold Berchtold, in 1913 warning him not to be influenced by Conrad. 'For naturally, Conrad will again be for all kinds of wars and a great Hurrah-Policy, to conquer the Serbs and God knows what.'[46]

Franz Joseph and Franz Ferdinand were concerned to protect Austria-Hungary's great power status but they were essentially conservative, as were most of the empire's statesmen, in their approach to foreign affairs and preferred peace to war. Since the wars of the 1860s, which it had lost, Austria-Hungary had concentrated on building defensive alliances and trying to eliminate sources of conflict with the other powers. For several decades it remained on good terms with both of its two largest neighbours, Germany to the west and Russia to the east. It helped that all three were conservative monarchies opposed to revolution, as they had been during the wars of the French Revolution, at the

Congress of Vienna in 1815, in 1830 and again in 1848. In 1873 Bismarck had formed the League of the Three Emperors but it lasted only until 1887, although the idea came up again from time to time until as late as 1907.

In 1879 Austria-Hungary showed which way its loyalties were likely to lie in the long run by signing an alliance with Germany whose main aim was to contain Russia. Both signatories promised to come to each other's aid if Russia attacked one or the other; they would remain neutral, 'benevolently' so, if a third party attacked either one unless that third party was supported by Russia, in which case they would also intervene. The treaty, which was renewed at intervals, lasted until the end of the Great War. Austria-Hungary's other main pact was the Triple Alliance with Germany and Italy, first signed in 1882, and which survived until the outbreak of war in 1914. The signatories promised to help Germany and Italy if either was attacked by France, and to come to each other's aid if attacked by two or more powers.

Although the preamble described the Triple Alliance as 'essentially conservative and defensive', it contributed to the division of Europe as much as the Triple Entente of later years did. Alliances, like weapons, may be categorised as defensive but in practice their use may well be offensive. The Triple Alliance, like the Triple Entente, had the effect of encouraging its members to work together in the international arena and during the increasing number of crises; it established links of co-operation and friendship and created expectations of support in the future; and it led to shared planning and strategies particularly between Germany and Austria-Hungary. Arrangements meant to provide security were in 1914 to put pressure on their members to remain true to their alliance partners and so turn a local conflict into a more general one. Italy, the weakest of the European powers, in the end proved to be the only one willing to stand aside in 1914.

Italy had joined the Triple Alliance partly because its monarch, King Umberto, liked the idea of conservative support at a time when his country was experiencing social and political upheavals which looked far too much like revolutions and partly for protection against France. The Italians could not forgive the French for seizing the port of Tunis, which had long been an object of Italian interest, or for extracting territory from Italy in return for France's support in the Italian wars of unification. Moreover, being part of an alliance with Germany, the dominant power on the Continent, satisfied Italy's longing to be considered among the great powers.

The Triple Alliance, however, also brought Italy and Austria-Hungary together which was never going to go smoothly. Both sides were well aware that there was the potential for conflict along their common frontiers. Austria-Hungary, which had already lost the rich provinces of Lombardy and Venetia to Italy, had the deepest suspicions of Italian designs on its own territory including the Italian-speaking areas in South Tyrol and the Adriatic port of Trieste, what had once been Venetian territories at the top of the Adriatic and down Austria-Hungary's Dalmatian coast as well as what Italian patriots called Italy's 'natural boundaries' up to the highest points along the Alps. The crumbling of the Ottoman Empire opened up new vistas for Italian expansion just across the Adriatic. Ottoman Albania and the independent state of Montenegro offered what Italy as a naval power badly needed – ports. Nature, as the Italians were fond of complaining, had made the western side of the Adriatic flat and muddy with only a few harbours and no natural defences while the eastern side had deep, clear seas, and good natural harbours. The Austrians were not pleased when Italy allowed an Albanian National Congress to be held in Naples in 1903 or when King Umberto's heir married one of the many daughters of the king of Montenegro or when the Italian inventor Guglielmo Marconi opened the first telegraph station there.[47] Italians for their part saw Austria-Hungary as the enemy which had blocked unification and continued to stand in the way of the completion of the Italian national project and was hostile to Italian ambitions in the Balkans. Some Italian politicians argued, though, that the Triple Alliance could be useful in putting pressure on Austria-Hungary to concede territory. As one said in 1910: 'All efforts must unite to preserve the Austrian alliance until the day when we are ready for war. That day is still far off.'[48] It was closer than he realised.

For Austria-Hungary, its key relationship was with Germany. Memories of defeat by Prussia in the 1860s had faded with time, especially since Bismarck had wisely offered generous peace terms. On both sides public opinion shifted significantly towards friendly feelings, and, as Russia's power grew again after 1905, a feeling that Teutons needed to stick together against Slavs. At the highest levels of society, the bureaucracy, and the officer corps were dominated by German speakers who tended to feel an affinity with Germany rather than with Russia. Franz Joseph and Franz Ferdinand both got on well with Wilhelm II and Franz Ferdinand was particularly grateful to him for treating his wife, Sophie, with full honours. The old emperor liked Wilhelm from the first because he had dismissed the hated Bismarck, but he also came to regard him as a friend, something that was increasingly rare in his life. Wilhelm made a point of visiting Franz Joseph frequently, every year in the period immediately before the Great War, and the younger man was deferential and charming. Wilhelm made repeated declarations of his friendship for Austria-Hungary. 'For whatever reason you mobilize,' he assured Franz Joseph and his chief of staff in 1889, 'the day of your mobilization is also the day of mobilization for my army, and the Chancellors can say what they want.' The Austrians were delighted, especially since the Germans were to repeat their promise in the crises which lay ahead. Franz Joseph sometimes worried that Wilhelm was too impulsive but, as he told his daughter after a visit in 1906, he trusted in his peaceful intentions. 'It has done me good to shake hands once more with the emperor: in the present times, peaceful on the surface but stormy below, we cannot meet too often to assure each other, eye to eye, how sincerely we both desire peace and peace alone. In this endeavour we can indeed rely on mutual loyalty. He would no more think of leaving me in the lurch than I him.'[49]

There were, inevitably, strains in the relationship over the years. Although Germany was Austria-Hungary's biggest trading partner, German tariffs, for example to protect its own farmers, hurt producers in the empire. And Germany's economy was simply more expansive and dynamic; in the Balkans, where Austria-Hungary had been used to being the dominant economic power, German competition was increasingly sharp. When newspapers in Germany attacked Czechs or when the Prussian government treated its Polish minority badly, that caused repercussions across the border in Austria-Hungary. Germany's handling of its foreign policy also worried its ally. Gołuchowski expressed a common view in 1902 when he wrote to Austria-Hungary's ambassador in Berlin:

Altogether, the ways that German policy has been going of late give indeed great cause for concern. The ever-increasing arrogance, the desire to play the schoolmaster everywhere, the lack of consideration with which Berlin often proceeds, are things which create a highly uncomfortable atmosphere in the field of foreign affairs, and cannot but have harmful repercussions on our own relationship with Germany in the long run.[50]

Yet in the long run the relationship remained strong because each needed the other and, increasingly, as the divisions in Europe deepened, their leaders felt that they had no alternatives.

While Austria-Hungary continued to reach out to one member, Russia, of the Triple Entente, it allowed its relations with France and Great Britain to attenuate, like, said a young diplomat, a good wife who is so loyal that she will not go out to see old friends if her husband does not approve. And, to be fair, the old friends were not always welcoming. France and Austria-Hungary had moved in different directions politically since the Third Republic was established in 1871. The Establishment in Vienna, monarchical, aristocratic, and Catholic, disliked what it saw as a France dominated by anti-clericals, Freemasons, and radicals. In foreign relations France was tied to Russia and would not do anything that would upset its crucial alliance. French money markets were therefore closed to Austria-Hungary. In the Balkans French diplomats tried to win over Serbia and Rumania to the Triple Entente while French investment and businesses were cutting into Austria-Hungary's markets. The French armaments firm of Schneider, for example, was winning new orders in the Balkans by the first decade of the twentieth century while firms from Austria-Hungary were losing out. From time to time French statesmen such as Delcassé worried about the future collapse of Austria-Hungary and the emergence of a massive German state in the centre of Europe, but they took no steps to improve relations.[51]

Austria-Hungary's relations with Britain over the years had been closer and more cordial than with France. Although Britain had its own radical traditions, it was seen from Vienna as a more stable and conservative society than France and one where the aristocracy, quite properly, still dominated politics and the civil service. The appointment of Count Albert Mensdorff in 1904 as Austria-Hungary's ambassador was seen as a clever move since he was closely related to the British royal family and welcome in British aristocratic circles. And there were no colonial rivalries as there were between Britain and Russia, for example, to drive Austria-Hungary and Britain apart. Even in the Mediterranean where the two were both naval powers, they shared an interest in keeping things calm, especially at its eastern end. For both the other was a convenient counterweight against Russia. During the Boer War, Austria-Hungary was one of the few powers that supported Britain. '*Dans cette guerre je suis complètement Anglais*,' said Franz Joseph in 1900 to the British ambassador in the hearing of the French and Russian ambassadors.[52]

Nevertheless relations gradually cooled. The agreements on maintaining the status quo in the Mediterranean, which was partly about blocking Russian control over the Straits between the Black Sea and the Mediterranean, were effectively dead by 1903 as each country moved to make its own accommodation with Russia. From London, Austria-Hungary was increasingly seen as being under the dominance of Germany. As the naval race heated up, for example, the British feared that every new ship built by Austria-Hungary would simply add to German naval strength. And once Britain came to an understanding with Russia in 1907, it did its best to avoid anything, such as supporting Austria-Hungary in the Balkans or the Mediterranean, that would disrupt an important relationship. As Austria-Hungary's own relationship with Russia frayed, its relations with Britain grew even cooler.[53]

Austria-Hungary found it increasingly difficult to remain on good terms with both Germany and Russia as those latter two drifted further apart. Although Franz Joseph and his Foreign Ministers regretted the trend, Austria-Hungary found its relations with Russia more difficult than those with Germany. The awakening of Slav nationalism in Austria-Hungary stirred Russian interest and sympathy but for the empire that only added a layer of complication to its internal troubles. Even if Russia did not appoint itself protector for Europe's Slavs, its existence was enough to make its neighbour wary of its intentions.

The changes in the Balkans brought Austria-Hungary fresh worries. As the Ottoman Empire receded, not willingly, from Europe, the new states – Greece, Serbia, Montenegro, Bulgaria and Rumania – that appeared were potential friends for Russia. They had predominantly

Slav populations (although Rumanians and Greeks would insist that they were different) who largely shared the Orthodox religion with Russia. And what about the remaining European territories of the Ottoman Empire such as Albania, Macedonia, and Thrace? Would they become the object of intrigues, rivalry and war? In 1877, the Dual Monarchy's Foreign Minister, Julius Andrassy, observed that Austria and Russia 'are immediate neighbours and must live with one another, either on terms of peace or of war. A war between the two Empires ... would probably only end with the destruction or collapse of one of the belligerents.'[54]

By the end of the nineteenth century Russia also saw the dangers posed by the disintegration of the Ottoman Empire. Since it could no longer count on German friendship after the lapse of the Reinsurance Treaty and was in any case turning its attention to the Far East, its rulers were amenable to a détente with Austria-Hungary in the Balkans. In April 1897 Franz Joseph and his Foreign Minister Gołuchowski received a warm welcome in St Petersburg. While military bands played the Austrian anthem and Austria's yellow and black flag and Hungary's red, white, and green one flew alongside the Russian one in the spring breeze, the tsar and his guests rode in open carriages along Nevsky Prospekt. That night the two emperors exchanged warm toasts at a state banquet and expressed their hopes for peace. In subsequent conversations, the two sides agreed to work together to keep the Ottoman Empire intact and to make it clear to the independent Balkan nations that they could no longer play off one of them against the other. Since the Ottomans might well lose their grip in their remaining Balkan territories, Russia and Austria-Hungary would work together on a division of the Balkans and then present a united front to the other powers. Russia got a promise that, whatever happened, the Straits would remain closed to foreign warships coming into the Black Sea and Austria-Hungary got, or thought it did, an understanding that it could annex the territories of Bosnia and Herzegovina, which had been occupied by its forces since 1878, at some future date. The Russians, however, later sent a note saying the annexation 'would raise a more extensive question, which would require special scrutiny at the proper times and places'.[55] In 1908 that question would indeed be raised in a particularly damaging way.

For the next few years, however, Russia and Austria-Hungary remained on relatively good terms. In the autumn of 1903 the tsar visited Franz Joseph at one of his hunting lodges and the two discussed the deteriorating situation in Macedonia, where the Christian population was in open rebellion against its Ottoman rulers (and also busy killing each other for being the wrong kind of Christian). They agreed they would present a common front on required reforms to the Ottoman government in Constantinople. The following year Austria-Hungary and Russia signed a Neutrality Treaty and there was even talk, which went nowhere, of reviving the Three Emperors League with Germany.

Nevertheless, all was not well in the relationship. Neither side entirely trusted the other, especially where the Balkans were concerned. If the Ottoman Empire was going to disappear, and that looked increasingly likely, each country wanted to be sure that its interests were protected. Austria-Hungary wanted a strong Albania to emerge to block South Slav access to the Adriatic (Albanians were, providentially, not Slavs); Russia did not. Quietly, and sometimes quite openly, the two vied for influence in Serbia, Montenegro, and Bulgaria. Even over Macedonia, the two disagreed over the details of the reforms. After its defeat in the Russo-Japanese War, when Russia turned its attention back to the west, the chances of a confrontation in the Balkans grew markedly. Moreover, once Russia had mended its relations with Great Britain in 1907, it no longer needed to rely as much on Austria-Hungary to help it in the Mediterranean and in dealing with the Ottoman Empire. And there had been a crucial change in the leadership in Austria-Hungary in 1906; Conrad became chief of staff and Aehrenthal, who wanted a more active foreign policy than Goluchowski, had become Foreign Minister. As Europe entered into a series of crises, the two great conservative powers were moving further apart, dangerously so in the troubled Balkans which lay between them.

CHAPTER 9

What Were
They Thinking?
Hopes, Fears, Ideas,
and Unspoken Assumptions

———

W riting at the start of the 1930s Count Harry Kessler, the son of an Anglo-Irish beauty and a rich German banker who was given a hereditary title by Wilhelm I, looked back across the Great War at the Europe of his youth:

> Something very great, the old, cosmopolitan, still predominantly agrarian and feudal Europe, the world of beautiful women, gallant kings, and dynastic combinations, the Europe of the eighteenth century and the Holy Alliance was growing old and weak, dying out; and something new, young, energetic, and still unimaginable was in the offing. We felt it like a frost, like a spring in our limbs, the one with muffled pain, the other with a keen joy.[1]

Kessler was uniquely well placed to witness the hopes and fears, and to record the thinking of Europeans in those years before 1914. He was born in 1868, came of age in the last part of the century, and was still in the prime of life when the Great War broke out. (He died in 1937 as war was marching again towards Europe.) Educated at a British private

9. The Zabern incident of 1913 started when a German officer in a small town in Alsace referred to local civilians in a disparaging way which set off popular protests. The military authorities over-reacted, raiding newspaper officers and arresting civilians on flimsy charges. While the German civil authorities were concerned to bring the military under control, the military closed ranks and refused to back down. It was for many in Germany and elsewhere a chilling example of the way in which the German army saw itself as outside civilian control.

school and a German Gymnasium, with family in Britain, Germany and France, a German grandee and snob who also longed to be an intellectual and an artist, and a homosexual who loved beautiful women as well as men, he moved easily across social, political, sexual, and national lines. His diaries, which he kept throughout his life, are filled with lunches, teas, dinners, cocktails, outings with Auguste Rodin, Pierre Bonnard, Hugo Hofmannsthal, Vaslav Nijinsky, Sergei Diaghilev, Isadora Duncan, George Bernard Shaw, Friedrich Nietzsche, Rainer Maria Rilke, or Gustave Mahler. And when he is not in artists' studios or at the ballet or the theatre, he is at court balls in Berlin or gentlemen's clubs in London. He helps to draft the plot and libretto for Richard Strauss's *Der Rosenkavalier*; he also discusses Germany's relations with Britain with Theobald von Bethmann Hollweg, the Chancellor who succeeded Bülow.

Kessler moved in very special circles and what he saw and heard there was not necessarily representative of Europeans as a whole. (Since there were not public opinion polls in those days there are limitations on how full a picture we can ever get.) On the other hand, people who make it their business to think about society or try to portray it often have antennae out which sense undercurrents before they manifest themselves on the surface. In the period before 1914 artists, intellectuals, and scientists increasingly challenged older assumptions about rationality and reality. It was a time of intense experimentation in circles which were then avant garde but whose ideas were to enter the mainstream in succeeding decades. The cubism of Picasso and Braque, the attempts of the Italian constructivists such as Balla to capture movement, the free-flowing dance of Isadora Duncan, the deeply erotic ballets staged by Diaghilev and danced by Nijinsky, or the novels of Marcel Proust, all in their own ways were acts of rebellion. Art, so many in the new generation of artists held, should not be about upholding the values of society; it should be shocking and liberating. Gustav Klimt and the younger painters he led out of the establishment Association of Austrian Artists challenged the accepted wisdom that art should be realistic. One of the goals of the Viennese Secession was *not* to show the world as it actually was but to probe beneath the surface into the life of instinct and emotion.[2] The Viennese composer Arnold Schoenberg freed himself from the accepted forms of European music with its rules about harmony and order to create works that were dissonant and disturbing. 'Inside, where the man of instinct begins, there, fortunately, all theory breaks down.'[3]

Old institutions and values were under attack and new ways and new attitudes were emerging. Their world was changing, perhaps too fast, and they had to attempt to make sense of it. 'What were they *thinking*?' is a question often asked about the Europeans who went to war in 1914. The ideas that influenced their view of the world, what they took for granted without discussion (what the historian James Joll called 'unspoken assumptions'), what was changing and what was not, all are important parts of the context within which war, even a general

European war, became a possible option in 1914. Of course, not all Europeans thought and felt the same; there were huge differences by class, country and region. And many people, just as today, were like the writer Stefan Zweig's parents, living life as it came and not reflecting much about where the world was going. When we look back at the years before 1914 we can see the birth of our modern world, but we should also recognise the persistence and force of older ways of thinking and being. Millions of Europeans, for example, still lived in the same rural communities and in the same manner as their ancestors. Hierarchy and knowing one's place in it, respect for authority, belief in God, still shaped the way in which Europeans moved through their lives. Indeed, without the persistence of such values, it is hard to imagine how so many Europeans can have gone off willingly to war in 1914.

In the end the decisions that took Europe into that war – or failed to prevent it – were made by a surprisingly small number, and those men – few women played a role – came largely but not entirely from the upper classes, whether the landed aristocracy or the urban plutocracy. Even those, such as Cambon brothers, who came from the middle classes, tended to absorb their values and share their outlook. The class of the ruling elites, whether civilian or military, as well as their hopes and fears is one key to understanding them. Another is their upbringing and education, and yet a third the wider world around them. Their ideas and attitudes had been laid down in their youth twenty or thirty years earlier, but they were aware of how their own societies were evolving and of new ideas that were in the air. They were capable of changing their views just as democratic leaders of today are on such matters as same-sex marriage.

What Kessler also picked up on in his diaries was a sense among artists, intellectuals and political elites that Europe was changing rapidly and not always in ways they liked. Europe's leaders were frequently uneasy about their own societies. Industrialisation, the scientific and technological revolutions, the play of new ideas and attitudes, were shaking societies across Europe and calling old, long-established practices and values into question. Europe was both a mighty continent and a troubled one. Each of the major powers had prolonged and serious political crises before the war, whether over the Irish question in Britain, the Dreyfus affair in France, the stand-off between crown and parliament in Germany, the conflicts among nationalities in Austria-Hungary or the near revolution in Russia. War was sometimes seen as a way of getting beyond the divisions and the antipathies and perhaps it was. In 1914 in all the belligerent nations there was talk of the nation in arms, the Union Sacrée, the holy union where divisions, whether of class, region, ethnicity or religion, were forgotten and the nation came together in a spirit of unity and sacrifice.

Kessler was part of a generation that lived during one of the greatest and most fast-moving periods of change in the history of human society. By the time he was in his early thirties and went to the Paris Exposition of 1900 (which he thought a 'disconnected, wild mishmash'),[4] Europe was already markedly different from the world of his youth. Population, trade, cities, all were bigger. Science was unlocking one puzzle after another. And there were more factories, more miles of railway tracks, more telegraph lines, more schools. There was more money to spend and more to spend it on: the new cinema, cars, telephones, electricity, bicycles, mass-produced clothing and furniture. Ships were faster and in the summer of 1900 the first Zeppelin was climbing into the sky. In 1906 the first aeroplane flight in Europe took place. The motto for the new Olympics could have stood for Europe: 'Faster, Higher, Stronger'.

Only in part, however. Too often when we look back at the Europe of that last decade of peace, we see the prolonged golden summer of another, more innocent age. In reality European pre-eminence and the claims of European civilisation to be the most advanced in human history were being challenged from without and undermined from within. New York was competing with London and Paris as a centre of finance and the United States and Japan were cutting into European markets and European power around the world. In China and throughout the great Western empires, new nationalist forces were gathering strength.

And change of the sort that Europe was experiencing comes with a price. Europe's economic transformation brought terrific strains and repeated cycles of boom and bust raised doubts about the stability and future of capitalism itself. (It was not just in Vienna that Jews were identified with capitalism; economic instability also provided additional fuel for anti-Semitism across Europe.)[5] All over Europe, in the last two decades of the nineteenth century agricultural prices were depressed (partly because of competition from the New World) and the effects of that depression rippled through farming communities, driving small landowners to bankruptcy and peasant farmers to penury. Although urban populations benefited from cheaper food, each European country also experienced downturns in its business cycle or stagnation and contraction in particular industries. In Austria-Hungary, for example, a Black Friday in 1873 ended a frenzy of speculation and thousands of enterprises, both big and small, including banks, insurance companies and factories, went bankrupt. And unlike our times, most countries did not have safety nets to catch the unemployed, the uninsured, and the unfortunate who tended to come mainly, but not entirely, from the lower classes.

Although working conditions had improved dramatically in the western European countries over the course of the nineteenth century, they were often dreadful further east, where the industrial revolution was newer. Even in developed countries such as Britain and Germany, pay was still low and hours long by comparison with today. After 1900, when prices started to rise, the working classes found themselves increasingly squeezed. Perhaps as important, they felt themselves to be excluded from power and undervalued as human beings.[6] The huge migration out of Europe may be an indication of dissatisfaction with the prevailing social and political structures as much as a search for better opportunities. Some 5 per cent of Britain's population emigrated between 1900 and 1914 and unskilled labourers made up the single largest group by occupation.[7] Others chose to stay and fight and throughout Europe in the years before 1914 there was a marked upswing in union membership and strikes. This rise in social tension and labour unrest caused deep concern among military and political elites. Even if revolution were averted, would an alienated working class make good citizens or, perhaps as important, good soldiers? Indeed, would they come to the defence of their country at all? On the other hand, that fear could make war seem desirable, to appeal to patriotism or as an excuse to crack down on the rebellious elements in society.

The old upper classes, whose wealth largely came from landowning, distrusted much of the New World and feared with reason that their hold on power was weakening and their way of life was doomed. In France revolution had already destroyed much of the status and power of the old landed aristocracy, but everywhere across Europe the aristocracy and gentry were under threat from falling agricultural and land prices, their values under challenge from a new urbanised world. Franz Ferdinand, and he spoke for many Austrian conservatives, blamed the Jews for the end of the old hierarchical society which had been based on sound Christian principles.[8] In both the Austrian and German officer corps the mood seems to have been one of pessimism about the future of their way of life.[9] That may well have affected the willingness of the leading generals to go to war in 1914. As the Prussian Minister of War, General Erich von Falkenhayn, said on 4 August as the war became a general one: 'Even if we will perish, it was nice.'[10]

During Europe's last decades of peace, the upper classes fought a determined rearguard action. Although social mobility was on the increase thanks to economic and social change, birth still counted for much. Even in London, where society had always been more open to talent and wealth, the distinguished American mining engineer and future President Herbert Hoover found the stratified nature of British society 'a constant marvel – and grief'.[11] Nevertheless, across Europe the newly rich industrialists and financiers were making their way into upper-class circles, often by acquiring titles, or by marrying their children into the aristocracy, a transaction where wealth was exchanged for birth and social status. Yet members of the old upper classes still dominated the higher levels of politics, bureaucracy, the military, and the Church in most European powers in 1914. Moreover, their old values proved surprisingly resilient and indeed seeped out into the rising middle classes, who themselves aspired to become gentlemen by adhering to the same standards of honourable behaviour.

Intangible yet very precious, honour was, so the upper classes believed, something that came with birth; gentlemen had their honour and the lower classes did not. As Europe went through its rapid social changes in the last part of the nineteenth century, honour became both an attribute that the old landowning classes could cling to with increasing determination as something that distinguished them from the newly prosperous middle classes and, for the socially ambitious, a mark of a higher and better social status. Honour could be lost by unworthy behaviour, although what that meant was never entirely clear-cut, or by failing to defend it, with one's life if necessary by committing suicide or by fighting a duel which often amounted to the same thing. When Colonel Alfred Redl, a high-ranking intelligence officer in Austria-Hungary, was discovered to be selling his country's top-secret military plans to the Russians, Conrad's first reaction was that Redl must be given a revolver to do the right thing. He was left alone with a pistol and duly blew his own brains out.

Duels, which were fought over matters of honour, not only persisted in nineteenth-century Europe but indeed increased, among students, for example, in universities in Germany and Austria-Hungary. The duel by this point had become so surrounded with rules and rituals that guides had to be drawn up to deal with such technical questions as choice of weapons – usually swords or pistols – and place, and, even more complicated, who was entitled to give a challenge (honour was compromised if the challenger was not worthy of being an opponent) and on what grounds (cheating at cards or making insulting remarks, for example; according to one Austrian guide, staring at someone while toying with a dog whip was quite enough).[12] The closest equivalent we have today are the street gangs where the slightest signs of disrespect can lead to death.

Although duelling was outlawed in most European countries, the authorities generally looked the other way and the courts were slow to convict. Indeed, those in positions of authority, including the Hungarian Prime Minister István Tisza, sometimes resorted to duels themselves. In Budapest there were special fencing schools for those whose skills needed a quick tuning up.[13] Georges Clemenceau, the radical French politician who was Prime Minister between 1906 and 1909 and again in the latter days of the Great War, fought a dozen duels against political opponents. Even as an old man he practised fencing every morning.

The Dreyfus affair produced its own crop of duels. Duelling was accepted in artistic circles as well with the young Marcel Proust challenging a critic of his work while Claude Debussy drew a challenge from the Belgian writer Maurice Maeterlinck for not casting his mistress in Debussy's opera *Pelléas et Mélisande*, for which Maeterlinck had written the libretto.[14] In Germany Kessler challenged a bureaucrat who blamed him for a scandal caused by a show of Rodin drawings of naked young men. The only European country where duelling was no longer accepted as something that gentlemen did was Great Britain. But then, as the Kaiser was fond of saying, the British were a nation of shopkeepers.

Honour and its bodyguard the duel were taken particularly seriously in the armies of continental Europe. As a handbook on the Austrian army said in 1889: 'The strict interpretation of military honor ennobles the officer corps in its entirety and endows it with the character of knighthood.' (The late nineteenth-century enthusiasm for the Middle Ages was yet another way of avoiding the modern world.) In the French army officers could be dismissed for refusing a challenge. Although there were anti-duelling campaigns across Europe, they made little headway against the military authorities. In 1913 Falkenhayn protested to the German Chancellor that 'the roots of the duel are embedded and grow in our code of honor. This code of honor is a valuable, and for the Officer Corps, an irreplaceable treasure.'[15] Indeed, as the high commands worried increasingly about the dilution of their officer corps by the sons of the bourgeoisie, duels and codes of honour became more important rather than less as ways of instilling the right values.[16]

Since many of the men in charge of Europe's international relations came from the same upper-class backgrounds (and often were related), it is not surprising that they too used the language of honour and shame. (We still use it from time to time today although we are more likely now to talk in terms of a nation's prestige or influence.) In 1909, when Russia gave way in the crisis over Bosnia-Herzegovina, a Russian general confided to his diary: 'Shame! Shame! It would be better to die!'[17] In 1911, in an interview with the newly appointed Russian ambassador to Bulgaria, the tsar stressed that Russia would not be ready for a war until 1917 at the earliest but then added: 'Though if the most vital interests and the honour of Russia were at stake, we might, if it were absolutely necessary, accept a challenge in 1915 …'[18] Unfortunately for Europe, what honour and insult consisted of was often determined as subjectively as it was for individuals. The cause might seem trifling, said General Friedrich von Bernhardi, a well-known writer on military matters, but defending the nation's honour was justification for war: 'Nations and States can achieve no loftier consummation than to stake their whole power on upholding their independence, their honour, and their reputation.'[19] The conservative historian Treitschke, who so influenced the generation that was in power by 1914, even used the language of the duel: 'If the flag of the State is insulted, it is the duty of the State to demand satisfaction, and if satisfaction is not forthcoming, to declare war, however trivial the occasion may appear, for the State must strain every nerve to preserve for itself the respect which it enjoys in the state system.'[20]

There was something almost desperate in the stress on honour, whether for the individual or the state. It reflected fears that the material success of Europe, so evident in the new cities, the railways, or the great department stores, was leading to a coarser, more selfish and more vulgar society. Was there not a spiritual emptiness which organised religion seemed incapable of filling? That disgust with the modern world and what the eminent German poet Stefan George called 'the cowardly years of trash and triviality' led some intellectuals to welcome war as something that would cleanse society. The German Walther Rathenau, who was an unusual combination of a very successful industrialist and a leading intellectual, published *Zur Kritik der Zeit* in 1912 in which he expressed concerns about the effects of industrialisation and the loss of ideals and culture. As he wrote to a friend just before the Great War: 'Our era is one of the most difficult of the numerous transitional periods – ice age, catastrophes.'[21] Rathenau nevertheless was an optimist of sorts, believing that the world would eventually regain the spiritual, cultural and moral values which it was losing in the early stages of capitalism and industrialisation.[22] His older compatriot Friedrich Nietzsche had entertained no such hopes: 'For long now our entire European culture has been moving with a tormenting tension that grows greater from decade to decade, as if towards a catastrophe: restless, violent, precipitate, like a river that wants to reach its end.'[23]

Nietzsche, who became a professor in Basle at the remarkably young age of twenty-four, was brilliant, complicated, and sure that he was right. What he was being right about is difficult if not impossible to pin down since he wrote copiously and frequently contradicted himself. What drove him on was a conviction that Western civilisation had gone badly wrong, indeed had been going wrong for the past two millennia, and that most of the ideas and practices which dominated it were completely wrong. Humanity, in his view, was doomed unless it made a clean break and started to think clearly and allow itself to feel deeply.[24] His targets included positivism, bourgeois conventions, Christianity (his father was a Protestant minister) and indeed all organised religion, perhaps all organisation itself. He was against capitalism and modern industrial society, and 'the herd people' it produced. Humans, Nietzsche told his readers, had forgotten that life was not orderly and conventional, but vital and dangerous. To reach the heights of spiritual reawakening it was necessary to break out of the confines of conventional morality and religion. God, he famously said, is dead. (Surely one of the reasons that Nietzsche's thought was so appealing is that he had a gift for aphorisms and the telling phrase, like the philosopher Jacques Derrida in a later generation.) Those who embraced the challenge Nietzsche was throwing down would become the Supermen. In the coming century, there would be a 'new party of life' which would take humanity to a higher level, 'including the merciless destruction of everything that is degenerate and parasitical'. Life, he said, is 'appropriation, injury, conquest of the strange and weak, suppression, severity ...'[25] The young Serbian nationalists who carried out the assassination of Archduke Franz Ferdinand and so precipitated the Great War were deeply impressed by Nietzsche's views.

His work, for all its incoherence and complexity, was riveting to a younger generation who felt that they wanted to rebel but were not sure against what. Kessler, who was an ardent admirer and loyal friend, wrote in 1893: 'There is probably no twenty-to-thirty-year-old tolerably educated man in Germany today who does not owe to Nietzsche a part of his worldview, or has been more or less influenced by him.'[26] It is not surprising that a conservative newspaper in Germany called for his work to be banned. Part of Nietzsche's appeal was that it was easy to read a great deal into his work, and people including socialists, vegetarians, feminists, conservatives and, later, the Nazis did. Sadly, Nietzsche was not available to explain himself; he went mad in 1889 and died in 1900, the year of the Paris Exposition.

The Exposition celebrated reason and progress but Nietzsche and his admirers spoke for the other forces that were stirring in Europe: a fascination with the irrational, with emotions, with the supernatural. For those, an increasing number it seemed, who felt that life at the end of the nineteenth century lacked something, there were other ways of getting in touch with the spiritual world than attending churches. Séances where the furniture moved, tables echoed to taps from unseen and presumably astral hands, strange lights suddenly appeared and the dead communicated with the living through Ouija boards or mediums were wildly popular. Even Conan Doyle, the creator of the most famous of all scientific detectives, Sherlock Holmes, developed a deep interest in what was called spiritualism. While Doyle remained a Christian, others were drawn to the more ecumenical Theosophy. Its Russian founder, Madame Helena Blavatsky, who was a cousin of the infinitely more prosaic Sergei Witte, claimed to be in communication with ancient masters somewhere in Tibet, or perhaps they were in the ether. She and her disciples wove together bits and pieces of Western mysticism and Eastern religions, including reincarnation, to talk about an unseen spiritual world which was the true reality. Races and cultures rose and fell, according to her teachings, and nothing could be done to change that cycle. General Helmuth von Moltke, the chief of the German general staff after 1905, who contemplated the prospect of a general war with gloomy resignation, was a follower.

God may have been dead and attendance at church was falling off but Europeans were intensely interested in the spiritual. The lectures of Henri Bergson, the gentle philosopher, at the Collège de France in Paris were packed with students and members of fashionable society. He challenged the positivist view that everything can be measured and explained. The inner self, its emotions, its unique memories, its unconscious, in other words its spiritual essence, existed outside time and space – and beyond the reductionist reach of science. (In one of those coincidences that cannot be made up, Bergson married a cousin of Proust's mother.)[27] Bergson's influence showed itself in sometimes curious ways before the Great War. The French military took his ideas of an animating force in life – *l'élan vital* – to argue that spirit in soldiers was ultimately more important than weapons. Henri Massis, at the start of his career as a leading intellectual, said that Bergson delivered his generation 'from the systematic negation and doctrinaire scepticism of the past'.[28] In 1911 Massis and his friends led a campaign against the academic establishment, accusing them of promoting an 'empty science' and pedantry while neglecting the spiritual education of their students.[29]

In its Palais des Beaux-Arts, the Exposition of 1900 largely celebrated the arts of the past (only a small room was devoted to French contemporary artists and a single painting by Gustav Klimt hung in the exhibit devoted to art from Austria-Hungary), but outside in Paris,

Berlin, Moscow, or Vienna, young artists and intellectuals were challenging traditional forms, rules and values and the very idea that there was something called reality. In Proust's great and unfinished work *In Remembrance of Times Past*, memory itself is partial and fallible and what the narrator had thought to be certainties about himself and others repeatedly shift.

Modernism was both a revolt and an attempt to establish new ways of thinking and perceiving and it worried the older generation. In 1910, in an effort to hold back the tide, Pope Pius X was to make priests swear an oath against modernism. 'I entirely reject', said one part, 'the heretical misrepresentation that dogmas evolve and change from one meaning to another different from the one which the Church held previously.'

It is difficult to tell how many Europeans were affected by this plethora of new ideas. Certainly the more daring in the younger generation were increasingly contemptuous of and bored with the values and rules of their elders. Some among the young were fascinated by the pagan world which seemed freer and more in tune with nature than their own. Nudism, the cult of the sun, clothes that mimicked the smocks and clogs of peasants, free love, vegetarianism, communes, even the garden suburbs were all part of the revolt against modern industrial civilisation. In Germany thousands of young men and women became, if only briefly, *Wandervogel* (the wandering birds), setting off hiking or bicycling into the countryside.[30] While many in the older generation, especially among the traditional elites, also had doubts about the modern world, the young made them uneasy, as did the working classes and often for the same reason. Would they fight if called upon? Or, worse still, would they revolt against their own rulers? Although such fears haunted military planners across Europe, this particular one turned out to be groundless; when the Great War came the young like the working classes flocked to join up.

It is striking just how many fears rippled through European society in the period before 1914. In an unsettling parallel with our own times, there was considerable anxiety about terrorists who were implacable enemies of Western society yet who lived anonymously in its midst. As with Al Qaeda in 2001 after the September 11 atrocities, no one knew how many terrorists there were or how strong or widespread their networks. All that was known was that they seemed to strike at will and that the police had only limited success in catching them. The last part of the nineteenth century and the first of the twentieth saw an upsurge in terrorism across Europe, especially in France, Russia and Spain, and in the United States. Often inspired by anarchism which saw all forms of social and political organisation as tools of oppression, or simply by nihilism, terrorists set off explosions, hurled bombs, stabbed and shot, frequently with spectacular success. Between 1890 and 1914 they murdered, among others, Sadi Carnot, the President of France, two Prime Ministers of Spain, Antonio Cánovas in 1897 and José Canalejas in 1912, King Umberto of Italy, President McKinley in the United States (whose assassin was inspired by Umberto's murder), Empress Elisabeth of Austria, the Russian statesman Stolypin and the Grand Duke Sergei, an uncle of the tsar. Their victims were not only the powerful and the prominent: bombs dropped into audience at a performance of *William Tell* in Barcelona killed twenty-nine and a bomb thrown at King Alfonso of Spain on his wedding day missed him but killed thirty-six onlookers. Terrorist acts led to repression, often severe, by the authorities which for a time merely stirred up more violence.

Paris endured two years of terrorist attacks in the early 1890s. When anarchists were sentenced for their part in a demonstration which ended in a riot, bombs blew up the homes of the judge and prosecutor in the trial. The perpetrator was turned in by a suspicious waiter; another bomb then blew up the café where the latter worked. Six policemen were killed when they tried to defuse a bomb placed at the offices of a mining company involved in a bitter strike. An anarchist threw a bomb into the Café Terminus – to get, he said, at 'good little bourgeois' who were satisfied with things the way they were – and another threw a bomb onto the floor of the French parliament in protest against an unjust world which left his family starving. For a time people did not dare to go out to public places for fear of where the terrorists would strike next.[31]

What added to the fear was that the terrorists were so sweeping in their condemnation of society that there seemed no way to reach them. Often, when they were caught, they refused to give reasons. McKinley's assassin would say only 'I done my duty'.[32] Or their choice of target was frighteningly random. 'I am an anarchist by conviction,' said Luigi Lucheni, the unemployed Italian workman who killed Elisabeth of Austria. 'I came to Geneva to kill a sovereign, with the object of giving an example to those who suffer and those who do nothing to improve their social position; it did not matter to me who the sovereign was whom I should kill.'[33] The anarchist who finished his meal in a Paris café and then calmly murdered a fellow diner said merely, 'I shall not be striking an innocent if I strike the first bourgeois that I meet.'[34] Terrorism, again like Al Qaeda, lost much of its support before the war even in sympathetic left-wing and revolutionary circles as a result of increasing disgust with its methods. The fear, though, that European society was under attack, did not go away so easily.

There was a more insidious fear too, that perhaps the terrorists were right, that Western society was thoroughly corrupt and decadent and ought to be thrown into the dustbin of history. Or, and this led to a glorification of military virtues and of war itself, the time had come to reinvigorate the nation and make it ready to fight for its existence. François Coppée, an ardent French nationalist who was often known as the poet of the humble, complained to an Englishman in Paris that 'Frenchmen were degenerating, that they were becoming too materialist, too absorbed in the race for enjoyment and luxury, to retain that grand subordination of self to great causes which had been the historic glory of the French character'.[35] In Britain, where a classical education had always been stressed, the analogy with the fall of Rome – including the predilection of the ancient world for 'unmanly vices' – came easily. In 1905 a young Conservative published a highly successful pamphlet, *The Decline and Fall of the British Empire*, whose topics included 'The Prevalence of Town over Country Life, and its disastrous effect upon the faith and health of the British people', 'Excessive Taxation and Municipal Extravagance' and 'Inability of the British to defend themselves and their Empire'.[36] General Robert Baden-Powell, the founder of the Boy Scouts, made frequent reference in his manual *Scouting for Boys* to the need for the British to avoid the fate of that great earlier empire. 'One cause which contributed to the downfall of Rome', he told his young readers, 'was the fact that the soldiers fell away from the standard of their forefathers in bodily strength.'[37] The enthusiasm for sport of various kinds which was growing at the turn of the century was in part a reflection of greater leisure as working hours got less but its advocates often also saw it as a way of reversing national decline and preparing the young to fight. The *Almanach des sports* approved of soccer – *le football* – when the new sport made its way into France from Britain around 1900, describing it as 'a veritable little war, with its necessary discipline and its way of getting participants accustomed to danger and to blows'.[38]

Prosperity and progress were, it was feared, inflicting damage on the human species and making young men less fit for war. The speed of change – and more literally speed itself, whether cars, bicycles, trains or the new aeroplanes – was, so some medical experts thought, unsettling the human nervous system. 'Neurosis lies in wait for us,' wrote a French doctor in 1910. 'Never has the monster made more victims, either because ancestral defects accumulate or because the stimulants of our civilization, deadly for the majority, precipitate us into an idle and frightened debilitation.'[39] In 1892 Max Nordau, the doctor son of an Orthodox rabbi from Budapest, published a highly successful attack on degenerate modern art and on the modern world in general which voiced the same concerns. *Degeneration*, which was translated into several languages and sold widely across Europe, charged further that materialism, greed, a restless search for pleasure, and the loosening of the bonds of traditional morality which led in turn to 'unbridled lewdness' were destroying civilisation. European society, Nordau said, was 'marching to its certain ruin because it is too worn out and flaccid to perform great tasks'.[40] The sexual imagery is interesting and not at all unusual for a period when commentators often lamented the lack of virility of their own nation.

Men, or so it was feared, were getting weaker, even effeminate, in the modern world and masculine values and strength were no longer valued. It was a bad sign, according to Field Marshal Sir Garnet Wolseley, commander-in-chief in Britain from 1895 to 1900, that ballet dancers and opera singers now were valued so highly in British society.[41] The Germany military authority Wilhelm Balck, who wrote one of the leading handbooks on tactics, believed that modern man was losing his physical powers as well as his 'fanaticism and religious and national enthusiasm of a bygone age' and warned, 'The steadily improving standards of living tend to increase the instinct of self-preservation and to diminish the spirit of self-sacrifice.'[42] In both Germany and Britain there were concerns among the military about the poor physical condition of their recruits. An inquiry after the Boer War shocked the British public by finding that 60 per cent of the volunteers had been rejected as unfit.[43]

And homosexuality, it was suspected, was on the increase, particularly among the upper classes. That would surely undermine the family, one of the foundation stones of a strong state. Could homosexuals be loyal to the nation? Maximilian Harden, the journalist who destroyed the Kaiser's close friend Philip Eulenburg, talked about how homosexuals tended to find each other out and form cliques. Like anarchists or Freemasons, their loyalties appeared to transcend borders. Such fears may help to explain why scandals involving homosexuals such as Oscar Wilde caused such widespread outrage and concern. In his newspaper, Harden used terms such as 'unmanly', 'weak', 'sickly' to describe Eulenburg and his circle. A leading German psychiatrist, Dr Emil Kraepelin, whom Harden quoted as an authority, added suggestibility, unreliability, lying, boastfulness, and jealousy to the list of homosexual characteristics. 'There is not the slightest doubt', said Kraepelin, 'that contrary sexual tendencies develop from the foundation of a sickly, degenerate personality.'[44]

Women, on the other hand, appeared to be getting stronger and more assertive and were abandoning their traditional roles as wives and mothers. Surely Edvard Munch's painting of 1894, originally entitled *Love and Pain* but which has always been known as *Vampire*, can be read as a more general fear of women sucking life out of men? The militant suffragettes in Great Britain, a powerful minority of those who wanted votes for women, fed such fears when they declared war on men. 'What we are going to get', said one of their leaders in 1906, 'is a great revolt of women against their subjugation of body and mind to men.'[45] It was precisely for that reason that conservatives resisted more liberal divorce laws and freely available contraception. A doctor who wrote a successful book for mothers which included advice on birth control was found guilty of 'infamous conduct in a professional respect' by a council of his peers.[46]

Another worrying indicator that virility was flagging, at least in certain countries, was a decline in fertility. In France, the birth rate fell sharply from 25.3 live births per 1,000 of population in the 1870s to 19.9 by 1910.[47] Although its neighbour Germany's birth rate declined slightly in the same period, it still remained significantly higher which meant, in practical terms, that there were more German men available every year for military service. This gap was a matter of public discussion and concern in France before 1914.[48] It was too bad about French civilisation, Alfred Kerr, a leading German intellectual, told a journalist from *Le Figaro* just before the war, because it was over-ripe. 'A people whose men don't want to be soldiers, and whose women refuse to have children, is a people benumbed in their vitality; it is fated to be dominated by a younger and fresher race. Think of Greece and the Roman empire! It is a law of history that the elder societies shall cede their place to the younger, and this is the condition of the perpetual regeneration of humanity. Later our turn will come, and the ferocious rule will apply to us; then the reign of the Asiatics will begin, perhaps of the blacks, who can tell?'[49]

The decline in fertility also raised another concern about the future of European society: that the wrong sorts of people were reproducing. The upper and middle classes feared the working classes as a political force; they also suspected that the poor were more likely to harbour vices such as drunkenness and promiscuity or physical and mental defects which they would pass on to their children, thus weakening the race. For racialists there was another worry still: that people they deemed inferior such as Jews or the Irish were increasing in numbers while the right classes or ethnic groups were shrinking. In Great Britain moral crusades to reinforce the family and its values (does it sound familiar?) picked up momentum, perhaps not by coincidence as the naval race with Germany intensified. In 1911 the National Council on Public Morals issued a call to the British public to take seriously its responsibility to educate its young to believe in marriage and to produce healthy children. The signatories, who included eight peers, several bishops, leading theologians and intellectuals, as well as the heads of two Cambridge colleges, claimed that this was the way to 'cope with the demoralisation which is sapping the foundation of our national well-being'.[50] In the years before 1914 the eugenics movement, advocating the breeding and cultivation of human beings as if they were cattle or vegetables, also found considerable support among political and intellectual elites. In 1912, the First International Eugenics Conference took place in London; its honorary patrons included Winston Churchill, then First Lord of the Admiralty, Alexander Graham Bell, and the emeritus president of Harvard

University Charles W. Eliot.[51] With such attitudes, war often seemed desirable, both as the honourable way to struggle against fate and as a way of reinvigorating society. Dangerously for Europe, war also came to be accepted by many as unavoidable.

In 1914, on the eve of the war, Oswald Spengler finished his great work *The Decline of the West*, which argued that there were natural life cycles for civilisations and that the Western world had reached its winter. Underlying much of such concern about degeneration and decline were widely shared assumptions drawn from Darwin's theory of evolution. Although he was talking about the evolution of species over thousands of years and in the natural world, it struck many intellectuals in the nineteenth century that his ideas could be applied to human societies as well. Using Darwin in this way seemed to fit conveniently with nineteenth-century views of progress and science. Social Darwinists, as they came to be known, believed that they could explain both the rise and the disappearance of different societies with the help of such concepts as natural selection. (Herbert Spencer, one of Social Darwinism's key figures, preferred to call it the survival of the fittest.) And in a leap which had no scientific basis and which was to reinforce racialist theories, Social Darwinists generally assumed that human beings were not a single species but a variety which they confusingly and interchangeably called races or nations. Further confusion was added by the fact that it was not always clear whether a type of people was being described or a political unit such as a state. Another difficulty lay in determining which nations were moving up the evolutionary scale and which were doomed to extinction. And was there any way to alter the direction of travel? Social Darwinists suggested that there was, that nations could and ought to pull themselves together. If they failed in the attempt, perhaps they deserved their fate. After all, Darwin himself gave the subtitle of *The Preservation of Favoured Races in the Struggle for Life* to his *On the Origin of Species*.

Such ideas were very much in the air in the years before 1914 and even those who had never read Darwin or Spencer accepted without question that struggle was a fundamental part of the evolution of human society. Not surprisingly Social Darwinism resonated with military men, for it seemed to justify and indeed elevate the importance of their calling, but it also infused the thinking of civilians, whether writers such as Zola, political leaders like Salisbury, or businessmen like Rathenau. It could produce either pessimism that there was no way for a weaker society to avoid extinction, or a sort of grim optimism that as long as there was the possibility of struggle there was hope. As might be expected, in the prewar crises and in 1914 itself decision-makers generally favoured the latter view. As the Austrian general Conrad, whose writings reflect the strong influence of Social Darwinism, put it: 'A people that lays down its weapons seals its fate.'[52] As an indication of just how far such attitudes had permeated, a young British captain wrote from the trenches during the Great War: 'It has been rightly said that any living organism that ceases to fight for its existence is doomed to destruction.'[53]

What Social Darwinism did as well was to reinforce a much older view, expressed by Hobbes among others, that international relations were nothing more than an endless jockeying for advantage among nations. And in that struggle, war was to be expected, even welcomed. 'Is not war', asked an article in the *Journal of the Royal United Services Institution* in 1898, 'the grand scheme of nature by which degenerate, weak or otherwise harmful states are eliminated from the concerted action of civilized nations, and assimilated to those who are strong, vital, and beneficial in their influences? Undoubtedly this is so …'[54] And it was not just nature that benefited from war; it was the individual nations themselves. 'All petty and personal interests force their way to the front during a long period of peace,' said Bernhardi in a controversial and influential book, *Germany and the Next War*, which was published just before the Great War. 'Selfishness and intrigue run riot, and luxury obliterates idealism.'[55] In an analogy that was often used, war was compared to a tonic for a sick patient or a life-saving operation to cut out diseased flesh. 'War', said the Italian Futurist and future fascist Filippo Tommaso Marinetti, 'is the sole hygiene of the world.'[56] What comes out in Kessler's diaries, among much else, is an acceptance of war as a probability; time and again at moments of crisis Kessler's friends and acquaintances talk, often in a quite matter-of-fact way, about the prospect of hostilities breaking out.

Those in positions of power in European countries were inevitably affected by the intellectual currents of their time; they also found that they had to deal with something unknown to earlier statesmen such as

Metternich: the public. The nature of politics throughout Europe was changing as society changed and the broadening of the franchise brought new classes into political life and fuelled new political movements. The old liberal parties which stood for free markets, the rule of law, and human rights for all were losing ground to socialist parties on the left and to increasingly chauvinistic nationalist parties on the right. A new breed of politicians was going outside established parliamentary institutions to appeal to popular fears and prejudices and their populism, especially among the nationalist parties, frequently included anti-Semitism. The old hatred of Jews as the killers of Christ was now updated to portray Jews as aliens, whether by religion or blood, who did not belong with the French or the Austrian or the Russian people.[57] In Vienna, the rising politician Karl Lueger discovered that he could mobilise the lower classes by appealing to their fears of change and capitalism, their resentment of the prosperous middle classes, and their hatred of Jews, who came to stand in for the first two. He did so with such success that he became a mayor, over the opposition of Franz Joseph, in 1897 and remained, highly popular, in office until he died in 1910. His abilities as a political organiser impressed the young Adolf Hitler who had moved to Vienna in 1907.[58] Hatred and fear of others was projected onto other societies as well as within one's own and helped to create the atmosphere in which war became more appealing.

Thanks in part to the new media, the nation was now acquiring a vivid personality of its own – think of John Bull or Marianne or Uncle Sam. Although identifying with a nation rather than with a region or a village was relatively new for most Europeans, many of them were making up for lost time. For nationalists the nation was both greater and more important than the individual human beings who made it up. Unlike its members, the nation was eternal or close to it. One of the key assumptions of late nineteenth-century nationalism was that there had been something called a German or a French or an Italian nation for centuries, its members marked out from their neighbours by shared values and practices, usually better ones than those of their neighbours. 'From the time of their first appearance in history the Germans showed themselves a first-class civilized people,' said Bernhardi.[59] (In Europe only Austria-Hungary and the Ottoman Empire did not, for obvious reasons, develop strong nationalist sentiments; they had too many, separate and conflicting, already.) While the general pattern was the same – members of a nation were identified by such shared attributes as language or religion and linked together by their history – the content of nationalism inevitably varied. The British had a Waterloo railway station; the French had Austerlitz. In Russia, governments in the last part of the century followed a policy of Russifying the many national minorities, forcing Polish or Finnish students, for example, to learn in Russian and go to Orthodox services. And Russian nationalism encompassed not only Russia's own past but increasingly Panslavism with Russia itself as the natural leader of all Slavs. The new nationalism did not bode well for minorities, whether linguistic or religious. Could Polish-speakers ever be truly German? Could Jews?[60]

While not all nationalists by any means were racists, there were those who regarded nations as separate species as much as cats or dogs are. Much research went on by professors and enthusiastic amateurs to measure such things as skull or penis size, make lists of racial characteristics, or examine skeletons in an attempt to come up with scientific classifications in which the races were ranked. How they were ranked usually depended on the nationality of whoever was doing the ranking. In Germany Ludwig Woltmann, a doctor and social anthropologist, developed elaborate theories to prove that the Germans were essentially Teutons while the French were Celts, an inferior race. True, France had enjoyed great achievements in the past but those, Woltmann was convinced, were due to the French race's Teutonic roots, before the Celtic strain had come in to dilute it. He spent much time in France looking at statues of eminent French of the past to spot their Teuton characteristics.[61]

The ideas which underpinned the development of nationalism across Europe owed much to the work of historians, Treitschke, for example, who created the national histories which came to dominate the field. And they were promoted by patriotic leagues such as the veterans associations in Germany or the Ligue des Patriotes in France or the National Service League in Britain. Past national glories and present triumphs were celebrated all over Europe with festivals and commemorations. 'We learnt', said a distinguished British soldier, 'to believe the English were the salt of the earth and England the first and greatest country in the world. Our confidence in her powers and our utter disbelief in the possibility of any earthly Power vanquishing her, became a fixed idea which nothing could eradicate and no gloom dispel.'[62] While the British celebrated the 100th anniversary of Trafalgar in 1905, the Russians had their great victory over Napoleon at Borodino in 1812 to celebrate in 1912. The following year Germans outdid them both with a huge celebration of the 1813 Battle of Leipzig which included a display put on by some 275,000 gymnasts. And nationalism was fostered as well by eager volunteers, whether political leaders, teachers, bureaucrats or writers. In Germany, it has been estimated, most of the novels written for adolescents before the Great War dealt with the nation's great military past, from the defeat of a Roman army by Germanic tribes to the wars of unification.[63] The popular British novelist G. A. Henty who wrote over eighty books about stirring adventures (whether his heroes were with Clive in India or Wolfe in Quebec the plots were always identical and invariably showed the triumph of the plucky British boy) was clear about his purpose: 'To inculcate patriotism in my books has been one of my main objects, and so far as it is possible to know, I have not been unsuccessful in that respect.'[64]

Education was seen as particularly important in giving the young the right ideas, perhaps because it was feared that they might so easily get the wrong ones. A manual for French schools which was revised just before the Great War pointed to the beauty of France, the glories of French civilisation, and the ideas of justice and humanity which the French Revolution had showered on the world as reasons for French patriotism. 'War is not probable', French children were to be taught, 'but it is possible. It is for that reason that France remains armed and always ready to defend itself.'[65] In 1897 80 per cent of the candidates taking the higher French secondary-school qualification, the *baccalauréat*, stated that the purpose of history was primarily patriotic. This was not particular to France; the history taught in countries across Europe was increasingly focussed on the nation, showing its deep roots, its longevity and its glorious accomplishments. In Great Britain in 1905, the new Board of Education published 'Suggestions' for teachers which recommended using patriotic poems to teach the right sort of British history. (To be fair, they also suggested that the history included the achievements of peace as well as those of war.)[66] In Germany, where the teaching of history tended to mean Prussian history, a leading educator told teachers that their purpose should be to develop 'a patriotic and monarchical spirit' and make the young aware that they must be prepared to defend Germany against its many enemies. 'To defend honor, liberty, and right; to offer up life, health and property on the altar of the Fatherland, these have always been the joy of German youths.'[67]

Nations in such a view needed the enthusiastic support of their members if they were to endure. They were, or so many nationalists held, like organisms in the natural world. They struggled for survival and to evolve. Like other organisms they needed nourishment and a secure and adequate habitat.[68] Bernhardi argued that, while there were universal laws governing the rise and fall of nations and their states: 'We must not forget that States are personalities endowed with very different human attributes, with a peculiar and often very marked character, and that these subjective qualities are distinct factors in the development of States as a whole.'[69] So even immutable laws could be bent by the right people. Moreover, nations such as Germany with 'the greatest physical, mental, moral, material, and political power' ought to prevail; that could only benefit humanity as a whole. What Germany needed, in his view, was more space and, if necessary, they must use force to acquire it. (The Nazis were later to make this idea of *Lebensraum* one of their key goals.) 'Without war', he went on, 'inferior or decaying races would easily choke the growth of healthy budding elements, and a universal decadence would follow.'[70] In the view of nationalists such as Bernhardi, and it is possible to find similar quotations from British or French writers, the needs of the nation were in themselves justification for aggression.

Moreover, imperialism came increasingly to be seen as a measure of a nation's power and vitality and as an investment for the future, not least as a way to get space for expansion. As Tirpitz said in 1895 as he was dreaming of a great German navy and empire: 'In my view Germany will quickly sink back from its great power position in the coming century if we do not promote our general maritime interests energetically, systematically and without delay – to no small extent also because the great new national task and the economic benefits to come will offer a strong palliative against educated and uneducated Social Democrats.'[71] (No matter that most of the new colonies did not pay for themselves or that few Europeans showed any desire to move to Africa or Asia when they could go to North or South America or Australia.) British schools celebrated Empire Day. 'We drew union jacks', a working-class Englishman remembered, 'hung classrooms with flags of the dominions, and gazed with pride as they pointed out those massed areas of red on the world map. "This, and this, and this", they said, "belong to us."'[72]

Although Salisbury complained in 1901 of the 'present passion for Imperialism as if it were a sort of zone of poisonous atmosphere we have got into',[73] he found, as other statesmen were discovering, that public opinion was both volatile and exigent when it came to colonies. Bülow, for example, found himself hemmed in during his quarrel with Britain over Samoa at the turn of the century; he was obliged to turn down a generous offer of compensation elsewhere from Chamberlain for fear of what the German public and, equally important, the Kaiser would say.[74] Although most of the colonial disputes in Africa and the Far East had been settled by the time of the Great War, there was still potential for conflict over China, where a revolution in 1911 had led to a shaky Republican government, and much closer to Europe in the Ottoman Empire. Moreover, the hostilities stirred up between Britain and Germany in Africa and the South Pacific or between France and Germany over Morocco remained to increase the antipathies of one European people to another. At the celebrations for the Kaiser's fifty-fifth birthday in January 1914, the German Chancellor Bethmann Hollweg told Jules Cambon, the French ambassador in Berlin:

> For forty years, France has pursued a grandiose policy. It has secured an immense empire for itself in the world. It is everywhere. During this time, an inactive Germany did not follow this example and today it needs its place in the sun ... Every day Germany sees its population growing by leaps and bounds; its navy, its trade and industry are making unparalleled developments ... it is forced to expand somehow or other; it has not yet found that 'place in the sun' which is its due.[75]

Such national rivalries were, in the minds of Social Darwinists, perfectly natural. As Kurt Riezler, a thoughtful German journalist who became a close adviser to Bethmann Hollweg, put it: 'Eternal and absolute enmity is fundamentally inherent in relations between peoples.'[76]In setting off the naval race, Tirpitz was convinced that conflict was bound to come between the declining power of Britain and the rising one of Germany. In 1904 August Niemann, a well-known German authority on war, wrote: 'Almost all wars have, for centuries past, been waged in the interests of England, and almost all have been incited by England.'[77] Nationalism was not just about pride in one's own nation; it required an opposite to define it and fed on fears of others. All across Europe, the relations between Germany and Russia, Hungary and Rumania, Austria and Serbia, or Britain and France, were coloured and often poisoned by national and racial fears of the other. When Count Zeppelin's airship was destroyed by a storm in 1908, the British suspected that much of the patriotic excitement in Germany and the rush by the German public to subscribe funds to replace the airship was directed against Britain.[78] It is easy to find examples of hostility on the British side too, in the Foreign Office, for example, which was increasingly dominated by those such as Eyre Crowe who were suspicious and apprehensive of Germany. In 1904 Francis Bertie, the British ambassador in Rome, wrote to a friend in the Foreign Office: 'Your letter of the 2nd breathes distrust of Germany and you are right. She has never done anything for us but bleed us. She is false and grasping and our real enemy politically and commercially.'[79] While there were always British and Germans, right up until the outbreak of war in 1914, who talked in terms of shared values, even a shared Teutonic heritage, their voices were drowned out by the increasing hostility which permeated all levels of society. That had the effect of limiting the options for the leaders in both countries who were swayed by their own views and the pressure from their publics. In 1912, for example, when there was a serious attempt made to wind down the naval race, the accumulated suspicions and the state of public opinion in both countries undercut it.

The mutual antipathy between Germany and France was even greater than that between Germany and Britain, and as complicated. Both found things to admire in the other: French civilisation for the Germans and German efficiency and modernity for the French.[80] Germans feared, though, and with reason, that the French had not forgotten their defeat in 1870–71 and, with less reason, that France would go to war to get back Alsace and Lorraine. German planners saw France as Germany's main enemy and German newspapers paid more attention to France than to any other European country before the Great War. On the other hand, Germans could and did console themselves with the thought that the Third Republic was corrupt and incompetent and France itself divided.[81] German commentators on France frequently stressed French frivolity and immorality (while obligingly telling their readers where to find both when they visited Paris).[82] The French for their part looked at a Germany which was outstripping France economically and in terms of population but told themselves that Germans were unimaginative and rigid in their thinking. In an 1877 novel, *Les Cinq cents millions de la Bégum*, the popular writer Jules Verne has a French doctor (who has devoted his life to doing good) and a German scientist splitting a large fortune from a common Indian ancestress. (The German is writing a paper entitled 'Why Do All French People Suffer, to One Degree or Another, from Hereditary Degeneration?' when he gets the news.) Each decides to build a new city in the United States. The Frenchman chooses a site by the sea in Oregon to build a city Prince Charles would approve of; it is based on 'freedom from inequality, peace with neighbours, good administration, wisdom among its inhabitants, and bountiful prosperity'. The German chooses to build his Steel City in Wyoming, close to a mine. From his Tower of the Bull he drives his workers on ruthlessly to mine, smelt and make armaments. The only food is 'withered vegetables, mounds of plain cheese, quarters of smoked sausage meat, and canned foods'.[83]

French intellectuals were fascinated by Prussia and Prussianism in particular. Perhaps, it was suggested, the dreary flat Prussian landscape and the grey weather had made Prussians a dour, grasping people. A French sociologist argued that the fact that they had moved across the face of northern Europe over the centuries made them rootless and therefore more easily manipulated by their rulers.[84] Georges Bourdon, a journalist from *Le Figaro*, who did a series of interviews in Germany in 1913 to, so he said, put an end to 'the senseless competition in armaments, and to the international distrust and nervousness', could not bring himself to like or trust the 'gratuitously arrogant and boastful' Prussians. 'It was a poor, unfortunate race, driven by necessity to a life of grinding toil; it has only comparatively recently arrived at any degree of prosperity, and this it has gained by force; thus it believes in force, and never relaxes its attitude of defiance.'[85]

In both countries highly unflattering and alarming stereotypes developed of the other, thanks in part to a variety of publications from school textbooks to popular novels. Interestingly, in both countries Germany was usually portrayed as a man in uniform (although for the French the image was a semi-comic, semi-alarming one of a brutal soldier with outsize moustaches) while France was a woman (in German depictions either helpless or over-sexed or both).[86] In France, perhaps as a mark of the Entente Cordiale, what had been *le vice anglais* now became *le vice allemand*; French academic studies purported to show that German men were more likely to be homosexual than the French. Almost all homosexuals, one such study offered as proof, loved Wagner.[87]

Many across Europe deplored the new nationalist fervour. Salisbury hated what he called 'jingoism' and J. A. Hobson, a leading liberal journalist and intellectual, attacked 'That inverted patriotism whereby love of one's own nation is transformed into the hatred of another nation, and the fierce craving to destroy the individual members of that other nation ...'[88] Concern about the impact of nationalism on war came from an unexpected quarter. In 1890 the elder Helmuth von Moltke, who planned and oversaw Germany's victories in its wars of unification, told the Reichstag that the age of 'Cabinet' wars, that is wars determined by rulers for limited ends, was over: 'All we have now is people's war, and any prudent government will hesitate to bring about a war of this nature, with all its incalculable consequences.' The great powers, he went on, will find it difficult to bring such wars to an end or admit defeat: 'Gentlemen, it may be a war of seven years' or of thirty years' duration – and woe to him who sets Europe alight, who puts the first fuse to the powder keg!'[89]

He died the following year before he could see the rise of nationalism and the increasing jitteriness in Europe, the heightened rhetoric, the expectations every time there was a crisis that war might break out, and the fears: of being attacked, of spies and, although the term had not yet been invented, of fifth columns waiting inside societies to make their move. He also did not live to see the ways in which the public came to accept and even welcome the prospect of war and the way in which the values of his world were embraced by civilians.

Militarism has two faces: the placing of the military on a pinnacle, largely above criticism, in society and that wider sense, of military values such as discipline, order, self-sacrifice and obedience permeating and influencing civilian society. After the Great War, militarism was held to be one of the key forces which pushed Europe towards the conflict and, on the winning side, German, or, as it was more often known, Prussian militarism was singled out for special opprobrium and with some reason. Both Wilhelm II and the Prussian army, which became the core of the German army after 1871, had always insisted that the military answered only to the Kaiser and were above criticism by mere civilians. Moreover, they firmly believed, and many German civilians agreed with them, the army was the noblest and highest expression of the German nation.

Yet militarism was a more general phenomenon across Europe and throughout societies. In Britain small children wore sailor suits and on the Continent schoolchildren frequently wore little uniforms; secondary schools and universities had cadet corps; and heads of state – except in republican France – normally dressed in military uniform. It is rare to see photographs of Franz Joseph, Nicholas II or Wilhelm II in civilian clothes. And their officials, many of whom had done military service in elite regiments, often followed suit. When he attended the Reichstag for the first time as Chancellor, Bethmann Hollweg was in a major's uniform.[90] A century later the only political leaders routinely appearing in uniform were military dictators such as Saddam Hussein and Muammar Gaddafi.

At the time, militarism was usually blamed by liberals and the left on capitalism, which, so it was argued, was engaged in an all-out competition for control of the world. 'Wars between capitalist states', said the resolution of the socialist Second International at its congress in Stuttgart in 1907, 'are as a rule the result of their rivalry for world markets, as every state is not only concerned in consolidating its own market, but also in conquering new markets, in which process the subjugation of foreign lands and peoples plays a part.'[91] The ruling classes stirred up nationalism to divert the workers away from their own interests. Capitalists fuelled the arms race and capitalists profited from it.

The idea that Europe's tensions were the product of economic rivalry persisted long after the Great War but the evidence is simply not there to support it. Trade and investment between many of the belligerents were increasing in the years before 1914. Britain and Germany indeed were each other's largest trading partner. While it is true that some manufacturers gained by the arms race, tension was often as good as outright war and sometimes better since they were often engaged in selling to several different sides at once. Before the Great War the German firm of Krupp upgraded the Belgian fortresses while it was also developing the heavy artillery for the German army to use against them. The British firm Vickers licensed German firms to make the Maxim machine gun and used a licence from Krupp to make fuses for explosives.[92] Bankers and businessmen involved in exports and imports generally looked at the prospect of a major war with dismay; it would bring high taxes, disrupt trade, and cause them severe losses, perhaps even bankruptcy.[93] The great German industrialist Hugo Stinnes warned his fellow countrymen against war, saying that Germany's real power was economic and not military. 'Just let another three or four years of calm development go by and Germany will be the uncontested economic master in Europe.' He himself bought into French enterprises and iron-ore fields and established a new mining company in the north of England in years immediately before war.[94]

Like imperialism or liberalism, how Europeans reacted to militarism and what they thought of the military depended on which country they lived in and where they were situated politically. Overall the two old empires of Austria-Hungary and Russia were probably the least militaristic of the European powers before the war. In Austria-Hungary, the army, with its largely German-speaking officer corps, was a symbol of the regime and therefore an object of suspicion for the increasingly militant national movements within the empire. What civilian organisations there were promoting military training and values tended to be nationalist; the Sokol gymnastic movement in Austria-Hungary, for example, was for Slavs only.[95] In Russia the newly emerging political class saw the army as an arm of the absolutist regime, its officers drawn from a narrow segment of society. Russian public opinion and Russian intellectuals did not take pride in colonial conquest or past military victories because such things seemed to have little to do with them. In 1905, while the Russo-Japanese War still went on, the novelist Aleksander Kuprin enjoyed great success with his novel *The Duel*, which showed army officers as, among other things, drunken, dissolute, venal, lazy, bored, and brutal. He does not seem to have been exaggerating.[96]

In the last few years before the Great War, the tsar and his government took measures to strengthen the martial spirit among young civilians by making physical exercises and military drill compulsory in schools and by encouraging youth groups. In 1911 Baden-Powell visited Russia to inspect them. While the public tended to view initiatives from the government with suspicion there was some popular support and a number of organisations formed, although they never reached more than a tiny number of young Russians.[97]

Militarism and the military also divided Europeans politically. The left tended to look on both with disapproval, conservatives with admiration. The upper classes in most countries sent their sons to be officers, while the working classes saw conscription as a burden. It was never completely clear-cut, though. While many in the middle classes, businessmen and shopkeepers for example, resented their taxes supporting an idle military and its expensive equipment, others aspired to the values and style of the officer class. In Germany being an officer in the reserves was a mark of social status even for professionals. Jews, left-wingers, members of the lower classes, even men who had married the wrong sort of wives had almost no chance of being chosen. Reserve officers who voted the wrong way in elections or took what were seen as radical stands were summarily dismissed.[98]

Growing nationalism too gave the military added importance as the defenders of the nation and, in the case of Germany, as its creator. As a German major told the French journalist, Bourdon, in 1913: 'Such and such a country may possess an army, but Germany is an army that possesses a country. That is why every event in public life at once affects military life, any wave of emotion, happy or the reverse, turns the people instinctively to its army.'[99] And much as socialists might deplore it, the working classes across Europe frequently showed an enthusiasm for the military, turning out for brass bands, marches, or celebrations of past victories. In Britain, cigarette manufacturers tapped into popular feeling by including cards depicting famous generals and admirals with their packages. The manufacturers of a famous meat extract had a highly successful advertisement during the Boer War in which the ride of the British commander-in-chief, Lord Roberts, across the Orange Free State spelled out Bovril.[100]

The schoolmasters, writers, generals, or politicians who told the young to take pride in the great military victories of the past, who urged them at speech days and in print to be obedient and patriotic and to hold themselves always at the ready to sacrifice themselves for their nation, and who encouraged the boys to emulate their country's soldiers and sailors and the girls to prepare to look after them, had no idea, of course, that they were helping to prepare a generation psychologically for the Great War. They saw the instilling of military values as part of the attempt to counteract the damaging effects of the modern world and arrest the decline of the nation. General Sir Ian Hamilton, who was a British observer at the Russo-Japanese War, came back to Britain deeply concerned about the rise of Japan and its martial spirit. Fortunately Japan was an ally and Britain therefore had time to foster a similar spirit in its children. 'From the nursery and its toys to the Sunday school and its cadet company, every influence of affection, loyalty, tradition and education should be brought to bear on the next generation of British boys and girls, so as deeply to impress upon their young minds a feeling of reverence and admiration for the patriotic spirit of their ancestors.'[101] Team sports, so loved in the boarding schools of Victorian England, were generally considered good because they fostered healthy habits and, perhaps more important, work and loyalty for the team. One of the most famous poems of its time, Henry Newbolt's 'Vitaï Lampada', starts with a cricket game where the batsman knows that the hopes of the team rest on his shoulders. 'Play, play up! Play up! And play the game!' his captain tells him. The next verse takes the reader to the desert sands in Sudan, 'sodden red', where a British force is facing annihilation. 'But the voice of a schoolboy rallies the ranks:/ "Play, play up! Play up! And play the game!"'

In Britain and Germany in particular the years before 1914 saw a proliferation of enthusiastic volunteer associations with a military character, such as the navy leagues, which suggests that militarism was coming from the grass roots as well as from above. In Germany, where, thanks to conscription, there was a large body of men with military experience, about 15 per cent of the adult male population belonged to veterans associations. These were largely social but they also provided funerals for their members with military honours and organised celebrations for such national events as the Kaiser's birthday or the anniversaries of famous battles.[102] British advocates of military preparedness pushed for expanding the army with recruits coming from volunteers or conscription. In 1904, the hero of the Boer War, Lord Roberts of Kandahar, known affectionately by the British public as Bobs, resigned as commander-in-chief to devote himself to the National Service League which advocated training all able-bodied men for, at the very least, defence of the British Isles if not service overseas. In 1906 he worked with Le Queux on his alarmist novel *The Invasion of 1910* and in 1907 he published his own best-seller, *A Nation in Arms*, which argued for national service on grounds both of defence of the nation and overcoming its social divisions. The League, which had 35,000 members by 1909, tended to draw its support from conservatives. Liberals and those on the left mistrusted the military and strongly disliked the idea of compulsory military service.

In both countries concerns about the young and their supposed decadence fed into militarism. What would set them on the right path, surely, was healthy living and a dose of discipline. In Britain such organisations as the Lads Drill Association and the Boys and Church Lads Brigade tried to reach out to urban and lower class young men. The most famous of all, the Boy Scouts, was founded in 1908 by another hero of the Boer War, Baden-Powell. Within two years it had 100,000 members and its own weekly magazine. He wanted, said Baden-Powell, to transform Britain's lost boys and young men from 'pale, narrow-chested, hunched up, miserable specimens, smoking endless cigarettes' into healthy and energetic patriots.[103] Initially he allowed girls to become Scouts as well but this produced a public outcry; a letter to the conservative weekly *The Spectator* complained that the young men and women came back from expeditions to the countryside in a 'state of very undesirable excitement'. Baden-Powell and his sister moved with dispatch to set up the Girl Guides, which had as one of its aims preparing young women 'to make themselves of practical use in case of invasion'.[104] Two German officers who had also had experience in Africa, in this case in the brutal German repression of the Hereros in German South West-Africa, set up the Pfadfinder, modelled on the Boy Scouts but with an emphasis on a 'German spirit'. Pfadfinder were exhorted to be loyal to the Kaiser and to his military, which stood armed and always ready to defend his Reich. Military men sat on the executive committee and often ran the local branches.[105]

In Germany the army establishment and conservatives had initially resisted spreading military training through society; it might give the population the dangerous radical idea that the army belonged to the people. Although there was conscription, not everyone eligible was called up so that it was possible to select reliable recruits, not socialist or liberal ones.[106] The success of youth groups organised by the Social Democratic Party in the years just before the war did much to change conservative minds. In 1911 the Kaiser issued a Youth Decree calling for a concerted effort to save the nation's young from, so it seemed, the modern world, and to educate them to be patriots. Colmar Freiherr von der Goltz, one of Wilhelm's favourite generals and a prominent conservative thinker and military theorist, had long been trying to overcome the army's resistance to military training for young boys; now the Kaiser gave him approval to set up a league for German youth, to get them physically fit, train them to be obedient and teach them about the glorious Prussian past, 'so that they will recognize that service to the Fatherland is the highest honor of the German man'. By 1914 the league claimed a membership of 750,000, partly by counting in members of other similar youth organisations, not, of course, the socialist ones.[107]

In France such organisations never had a mass appeal, partly because they were caught up in the political divisions within French society. On the one hand, a strong anti-militaristic tradition in France dated back to the French Revolution when the army had been seen initially as the tool of the old regime, and subsequent rulers, Napoleon or his nephew Napoleon III for example, had also used the army to maintain themselves in power. Yet the Revolution had also produced citizen militias fuelled by the idea of the nation-in-arms to defend against the forces of reaction, which the right and many middle-class liberals had come to regard with deep suspicion. The aftermath of the Franco-Prussian War had added fresh divisive memories: the more radical citizens of Paris had organised themselves into a Commune with a National Guard and the government of France had waged war on it with its own forces.

In the shock of the defeat of 1870–71, it is true, there was considerable discussion across the political spectrum about how to prepare the French to defend their country. In 1882 the government decreed that all schools should have drill organisations, the *bataillons scolaires*. While there was an initial burst of activity and a big parade in Paris, they never took root throughout France and the government quietly abandoned the programme. In 1889 the abortive coup by General Boulanger reminded good republicans that military training, especially of the wrong sort of people, could lead to trouble. At the grass roots as well, after 1871, a number of shooting and gymnastic societies sprang up with a clear military purpose. (As one sceptical conservative paper noted, it was not clear how doing arms drill and turning somersaults was going to safeguard France from its enemies.) Most of the societies dwindled into social clubs where members could show off their special tight-fitting uniforms. The societies also got caught up in French politics so that in villages there would be one run by the priest and another by the anti-clerical schoolteacher.[108]

In the Third Republic, the army itself never enjoyed the prestige of the German army or the British navy and the Dreyfus affair damaged it still further. In any case French society was deeply divided about what sort of army it wanted. The left talked in terms of a people's militia solely for self-defence while the right wanted a proper professional army. For republicans in general, the officer corps was a home for conservatives and aristocrats (often overlapping categories) with profoundly anti-republican views and the Dreyfus affair gave them the opening to carry out a purge, dismissing suspect officers and promoting those seen to be reliable. Frequently, being Catholic, especially educated by the Jesuits, seems to have been the main black mark; enterprising French officers hastened to join anti-Catholic Masonic lodges.[109] In 1904 a major scandal broke when it turned out that the radical Minister of War had persuaded certain Masons to draw up a secret blacklist of some 25,000 officers who were suspected of being Catholic and anti-republican. Army morale, not surprisingly, was left even lower than it had previously been. Nor did it do anything for the military's relations with the general public when the government increasingly used it to put down strikes and left-wing demonstrations.[110] In the years before 1914, even while French nationalism was reviving so too was anti-militarism. Every year when conscripts went off to do their service, railway stations would be the scene of protests while the new soldiers frequently joined in to sing revolutionary songs such as the Internationale. Army discipline suffered; officers had to deal with drunkenness, frequent acts of insubordination and even outright mutiny.[111] In the last years before

1914, the government, perhaps realising that matters had gone too far and that the French army was not up to the job of defending France, tried to reorganise and reform the army. It had left it very late, though.

From Germany, the Kaiser had watched the French troubles with delight. 'How can you ally with the French?' he asked Nicholas when the tsar visited Berlin in 1913. 'Don't you see that the Frenchman is no longer capable of becoming a soldier?'[112] Even in Germany, however, relations between the military, in particular the army, and society suffered strains from time to time. The spread of the franchise and the growth of the centrist parties and the SPD helped to bring the army's privileged position in German society into question. Much to the annoyance of the Kaiser and his court, the Reichstag insisted on examining military budgets and questioning military policies. In 1906 an enterprising swindler did something that was perhaps worse; he held the army up to ridicule. Wilhelm Voigt was an unprepossessing petty criminal who bought himself an eclectic selection of second-hand officers' clothes in Berlin. Dressed in what was by all accounts a shabby and unconvincing uniform, he took over command of a small unit of soldiers, who followed him obediently, and led them to the nearby town of Köpenick, where he proceeded to march into the city hall, arrest the senior officials and seize a considerable sum of money. Although he was eventually arrested and sent to jail, he became something of a folk hero. Plays were written and later a film made of his exploit and his wax image joined the famous and notorious figures at Madame Tussaud's in London. He himself made a small fortune by touring Europe and then North America telling the story of the Captain of Köpenick. While many in Germany itself and in hostile countries such as France deplored the episode as an example of the servility of the Germans at the sight of a uniform, others found it delightfully subversive of the German army.[113]

In 1913 a much more serious incident took place in Alsace which highlighted both the privileged position of the military within Germany and the ability of the Kaiser to protect it. A young lieutenant stationed in the pretty mediaeval town of Zabern (today Saverne in France) near Strasbourg started the trouble by using an insulting epithet to describe the locals and then, when there was a protest, his superior officer escalated matters by arresting civilians, sometimes at bayonet point, for such crimes as laughing out loud at soldiers. German soldiers also ransacked the offices of the local newspaper which had been reporting on the affair. The civilian authorities in the region were horrified at the breach of laws and the government in Berlin was concerned about the potential impact on relations with the locals and with France. Although much of the German press was now highly critical of the military's behaviour and there were questions in the Reichstag, the army high command and the Kaiser closed ranks and refused to admit that the military in Zabern had done anything wrong or that any disciplinary action needed to be taken. (In fact they did move the regiment which had perpetrated the offences out of Alsace and the officer responsible for the arrests was quietly court-martialled.) The crown prince, an inferior imitation of his father, sent a wild telegram complaining of the 'shamelessness' of the local population and hoping that they would be taught a lesson. ('I'd like to know', a Berlin cartoon had the Kaiser asking, 'where the boy picked up that damned habit of telegraphing.')[114] Bethmann, the Chancellor, who was convinced that the soldiers in Zabern had broken the law and who had urged the Kaiser to insist on disciplining the perpetrators, in the end chose loyalty to the crown and went before the Reichstag at the start of December 1913 to defend the army's authority to do as it pleased with its own. Although the Reichstag responded with a motion of no confidence in the government, which passed by a large majority, Bethmann, thanks to weakness of the German constitution, was able to continue in office as though nothing had happened.[115] There was clearly strong support in Germany for asserting civilian control over the army and it is possible that might have happened. Seven months later, however, the German leadership was making decisions in a serious European crisis with a military that saw itself as autonomous.

Militarism was a relatively new term – it first seems to have been used in the 1860s – and its impact on European society in the subsequent decades owed something to both nationalism and Social Darwinism. It reflected contemporary fears about degeneracy and it also showed the strong influence of older pre-modern ideas about honour. Europeans were preparing themselves psychologically for war before 1914; some also found the prospect exciting. Life was easier, especially for the middle and lower classes, but it was not necessarily more interesting. Far off colonial wars, while the publics followed them with interest, did not fully satisfy longings for glory and great deeds. The spread of literacy as well as the new mass newspapers, historical novels, thrillers, pulp fiction, or Westerns showed alternative, more enthralling worlds. To the dismay of anti-war liberals, war was glamorous. As one said in Britain, 'Long immunity from the realities of warfare has blunted our imaginations. We love excitement not a whit less than the Latin races; our lives are dull; a victory is a thing the meanest of us can understand.'[116] The younger generations wondered, as they sometimes do today, how they would match up in great conflicts. In Germany, young men who had done their military service felt inferior to their elders who had fought in the wars of unification and longed for a chance to prove themselves.[117]

The Futurist Marinetti was by no means the only artist who longed for the violent destruction of comfortable bourgeois society and an end to what one called the 'rotten, filthy peace'.[118] The poet Gabriele D'Annunzio, another Italian, had a huge impact on the young across Europe with his exaltation of power, heroism, and violence.[119] In 1912, during the Italian war with Turkey, he boasted to Kessler about the impact of his nationalist poems on 'this tempest of blood and fire that passes over the Italian people'.[120] In Britain Rupert Brooke, one of the promising poets of the younger generation, longed for 'some kind of upheaval' and the conservative Catholic writer Hilaire Belloc wrote: 'How I long for the Great War! It will sweep Europe like a broom, it will make kings jump like coffee beans on the roaster.'[121] The young French nationalist Ernest Psichari, who was a hero to much of his generation for his exploits in French colonial Africa, attacked pacifism and what he saw as France's decline in his *Call to Arms*, published in 1913. Drawing on religious imagery, as nationalists so often did in the period, he looked forward, he said, to 'the great harvest of Force, toward which a sort of inexpressible grace precipitates us and ravishes us'.[122] He was killed the following August.

CHAPTER 10

Dreaming of Peace

In 1875 Countess Bertha Kinsky, a forceful and lovely but impoverished young woman, was obliged to take a post as a governess with the Von Suttner family in Vienna. The story was not an unusual one for unmarried but well-educated women. Nor was it strange when one of the sons of the house fell in love with her and she with him. His parents, however, opposed the marriage: to begin with she was seven years older than their son. More importantly she was penniless, and although she carried the name of one of the most ancient of all the great Czech families, the circumstances of her birth had caused something of a scandal. Her mother was middle class, not noble, and was some fifty years younger than her husband, a general. The child was never really accepted by her grand relations, who sometimes referred to her as a bastard.[1] While she rejected much of her background during her adult life and became by the standards of her class a daring free thinker and radical, she kept much of its style including a certain insouciance towards money.

Once her romance was discovered, it was clearly impossible for her to go on living in the household in Vienna so impulsively she left for Paris to take up a post as private secretary to a rich Swedish manufacturer, Alfred Nobel. It was the start, although neither of them knew it at the time, of a partnership in the cause of peace. She stayed with him only for a few months and then, following her heart, returned to Vienna and eloped with Arthur von Suttner. The couple made their way to the Caucasus in Russia where they lived from hand to mouth until Bertha discovered that she had a talent for writing, both books and short pieces for German-language publications. (Arthur, who seems to have been a much less forceful and energetic character, gave French and riding lessons.) She also discovered, first hand, the horrors of war, when a conflict between Russia and Turkey, which involved fighting in the Caucasus as well as in the Balkans, broke out in 1877. By the time she and Arthur made their way back to Vienna in 1885, Bertha had become convinced that war must be made obsolete. In 1889 she published her most famous work, *Lay Down Your Arms!*, a heart-rending and melodramatic story of a young woman of noble birth whose tribulations include financial ruin, cholera, and the loss of her first husband in battle. She remarries only to see her new husband go off to war in the conflict between Austria-Hungary and Prussia. Defying her relatives, she goes in search of him and sees for herself the ghastly condition of the wounded after the Prussian victory. She is reunited with her husband but unfortunately they find themselves in Paris during the Franco-Prussian War and he is shot by the Commune. 'Deep convictions, but untalented' was Tolstoy's conclusion when he read the novel.[2] Nevertheless it enjoyed a great success and was translated into several languages including English. Its sales gave its author, at least temporarily, funds to support herself, her family, and her unending and indefatigable work for peace.

She was a great publicist and superb lobbyist. Among much else she founded the Austrian Peace Society in 1891 and edited its journal for many years; she was active in the Anglo-German Friendship Committee; she bombarded the powerful of the world with letters and petitions; she wrote articles, books and novels to educate the public about the dangers of militarism, the human costs of war and the means by which it could be avoided; and she spoke widely at conferences, peace congresses, and on lecture tours. In 1904 President Teddy Roosevelt gave her a reception at the White House. She persuaded the rich, among them the prince of Monaco and the American industrialist Andrew Carnegie, to support her work. Her most important patron of all was her old friend and employer, Nobel. His fortune was based on his patenting and production of the new and more powerful explosive of

10. Before 1914 a powerful international peace movement was committed to outlawing or at least limiting war. Although one of its goals was to end the arms race, it had little success. In this cartoon, at one end of the table Mars, the God of War, is chewing on a dreadnought while figures representing the world's powers, including France's Marianne, an Ottoman Turk, a British admiral and Uncle Sam, angrily demand their meal of weapons. The poor waitress Peace struggles with her heavy trays, her wings bedraggled and her head bowed; 'Every hour is lunch hour at the Dreadnought Club'.

dynamite which had immediate application for mining but which was, in the longer run, to add to the increasingly greater destructiveness of modern weapons. 'I wish', he once said to Suttner, 'I could produce a substance or machine of such frightful efficacy for wholesale devastation that wars should therefore become altogether impossible.'[3] When he died in 1896, he left part of his considerable fortune to endow a prize for peace. Suttner, who was yet again in financial difficulties, turned her lobbying talents to the prize and in 1905 was awarded it.

In her views, she was very much a product of the confident nineteenth century with its trust in science, rationality and progress. Surely, she thought, Europeans could be made to see how pointless and stupid war was. Once their eyes had been opened they would, so Suttner fervently believed, join her in working to outlaw war. While she shared the Social Darwinist concepts about evolution and natural selection, she – and it was typical of many in the peace movement – interpreted them differently from the militarists and generals such as her compatriot,

Conrad. Struggle was not inevitable; evolution towards a better more peaceful society was. 'Peace', she wrote, 'is a condition that the progress of civilization will bring about by necessity ... It is a mathematical certainty that in the course of centuries the warlike spirit will witness a progressive decline.' John Fiske, a leading American writer and lecturer in the last quarter of the nineteenth century, who helped to popularise the idea of the United States' manifest destiny to expand into the world, believed that it would happen peacefully through American economic power. 'The victory of the industrial over the military type of civilization will at last become complete.' War belonged to an earlier stage of evolution and indeed to Suttner was an anomaly. Eminent scientists on both sides of the Atlantic joined her in denouncing war as biologically counter-productive: it killed the best, the brightest, and the most noble in society. It led to the survival of the unfittest.[4]

The growing interest in peace also reflected a shift in thinking about international relations from the eighteenth century: they were no longer a zero-sum game; by the nineteenth century there was talk of an international order in which all could benefit from peace. And the history of the century appeared to demonstrate that a new and better order was emerging. Since the end of the Napoleonic Wars in 1815 Europe had, with minor interruptions, enjoyed a long period of peace and its progress had been extraordinary. Surely the two things were linked. Moreover, there appeared to be growing agreement on and acceptance of universal standards of behaviour for nations. In time, no doubt, a body of international law and new international institutions would emerge, just as laws and institutions had grown within nations. The increasing use of arbitration to settle disputes among nations or the frequent occasions during the century when the great powers in Europe worked together to deal with, for example, crises in the decaying Ottoman Empire, all seemed to show that, step by step, the foundations were being laid for a new and more efficient way of managing the world's affairs. War was an inefficient and too costly way of settling disputes.

Further proof that war was becoming obsolete in the civilised world was the nature of Europe itself. Its countries were now tightly intertwined economically and trade and investment cut across the alliance groupings. Britain's trade with Germany was increasing year by year before the Great War; between 1890 and 1913 British imports from

Germany tripled while its exports to Germany doubled.[5] And France took almost as many imports from Germany as it did from Britain while Germany for its part depended on imports of French iron ore for its steel mills. (Half a century later, after two world wars, France and Germany would form the European Iron and Steel Community which became the basis of the European Union.) Britain was the world's financial centre and much investment in and out of Europe flowed through London.

As a result the experts generally assumed before 1914 that a war between the powers would lead to a collapse of international capital markets and a cessation of trade which would harm them all and indeed make it impossible for them to carry on a war for longer than a few weeks. Governments would not be able to get credit and their people would become restive as food supplies grew short. Even in peacetime, with an increasingly expensive arms race, governments were going to run into debt, raise taxes or both, and that in turn would lead to public unrest. Up-and-coming powers, notably Japan and the United States, which did not face the same burdens and enjoyed lower taxes, would be that much more competitive. There was a serious risk, leading experts on international relations warned, that Europe would lose ground and eventually its leadership of the world.[6]

In 1898, in a massive six-volume work published in St Petersburg, Ivan Bloch (also known by the French version of his name as Jean de Bloch) brought together the economic arguments against war with the dramatic developments in warfare itself to argue that war must become obsolete. Modern industrial societies could put vast armies into the field and equip them with deadly weapons which swung the advantage to the defence. Future wars, he believed, were likely to be on a huge scale, draining resources and manpower; they would turn into stalemates; and they would eventually destroy the societies engaged in them. 'There will be no war in the future', Bloch told William Thomas Stead, his British publisher, 'for it has become impossible, now that it is clear that war means suicide.'[7] What is more, societies could no longer afford the costs of keeping up in the arms race afflicting Europe: 'The present conditions cannot continue to exist forever. The peoples groan under the burdens of militarism.'[8] Where Bloch, prescient though he was, turned out to be wrong was in his assumption that even the stalemate could not last for long; in his view European societies simply did not have the material capacity to fight wars on such a massive scale for more than a few months. Apart from anything else, the absence of so many men at the front would mean that the factories or mines would fall idle and farms would go untended. What he did not foresee was the latent capacity of European societies to mobilise and direct vast resources into war – and to bring in underused sources of labour, notably from the women.

Described by Stead as a man of 'benevolent mien',[9] Bloch, who was born to a Jewish family in Russian Poland and later converted to Christianity, was the closest thing Russia had to a John D. Rockefeller or an Andrew Carnegie. He had played a key role in the development of Russia's railways and founded several companies and banks of his own. His passion, however, was the study of modern war. Using a wealth of research and a multitude of statistics, he argued that advances in technology, such as more accurate and rapidly firing guns or better explosives, were making it almost impossible for armies to attack well-defended positions. The combination of earth, shovels, and barbed wire allowed defenders to throw up strong defences from which they could lay out a devastating field of fire in the face of their attackers. 'There will be nothing', Bloch told Stead, 'along the whole line of the horizon to show from whence the death-dealing missiles have sped.'[10] It would, he estimated, require the attacker to have an advantage of at least eight to one to get across the firing zone.[11] Battles would bring massive casualties, 'on so terrible a scale as to render it impossible to get troops to push the battle to a decisive issue'.[12] (Bloch shared the pessimistic view that modern Europeans, especially those living in cities, were weaker and more nervous than their ancestors.) Indeed, in the wars of the future it was unlikely that there ever could be a clear victory. And while the battlefield was a killing ground, privation at home would lead to disorder and ultimately revolution. War, said Bloch, would be 'a catastrophe which would destroy all existing political institutions'.[13] Bloch did his best to reach decision-makers and the larger public, handing out copies of his books at the first Hague Peace Conference in 1899 and giving lectures, even in such unfriendly territory as the United Services Institute in London. In 1900 he paid for an exhibit at the Paris Exposition to show the great differences between wars of the past and the ones to come. Shortly before he died in 1902, he founded an International Museum of War and Peace in Lucerne.[14]

The view that war was simply not rational in economic terms reached the wider European public through the unlikely agency of a man who had left school at fourteen and knocked about the world as, among other things, a cowboy, pig farmer, and prospector for gold. Norman Angell was a small, frail man who was frequently ill but who nevertheless lived to be ninety-four. Those who met him over his long career agreed that he was good-natured, kind, enthusiastic, idealistic, and disorganised.[15] He eventually found his way into journalism and worked in Paris on the *Continental Daily Mail* before the Great War. (He also found time to set up the first English Boy Scout troop there.) In 1909 he published a pamphlet, *Europe's Optical Illusion*, which grew over many subsequent editions into the much longer *The Great Illusion*.

Angell threw down a challenge to the widely held view – the great illusion – that war paid. Perhaps conquest had made sense in the past when individual countries subsisted more on what they produced and needed each other less so that a victor could cart off the spoils of war and, for a time at least, enjoy them. Even then it weakened the nation, not least by killing off its best. France was still paying the price for its great triumphs under Louis XIV and Napoleon: 'As the result of a century of militarism, France is compelled every few years to reduce the standard of physical fitness in order to keep up her military strength so that now even three-feet dwarfs are impressed.'[16] In the modern age war was futile because the winning power would gain nothing by it. In the economically interdependent world of the twentieth century, even powerful nations needed trading partners and a stable and prosperous world in which to find markets, resources, and places for investment. To plunder defeated enemies and reduce them to penury would only hurt the winners. If, on the other hand, the victor decided to encourage the defeated to prosper and grow, what would have been the point of a war in the first place? Say, Angell offered by way of example, that Germany were to take over Europe. Would Germany then set out to ransack its conquests?

But that would be suicidal. Where would her big industrial population find their markets? If she set out to develop and enrich the component parts, these would become merely efficient competitors, and she need not have undertaken the costliest war of history to arrive at that result. This is the paradox, the futility of conquest – the great illusion which the history of our own Empire so well illustrates.[17]

The British, so he argued, had kept their empire together by allowing their separate colonies, notably the dominions, to flourish so that all had benefited together – and without wasteful conflict. Businessmen, Angell believed, had already realised this essential truth. In the past decades, whenever there had been international tensions which threatened war, business had suffered and as a result, financiers, whether in London, New York, Vienna or Paris, had got together to put an end to the crisis 'not as a matter of altruism, but as a matter of commercial self-protection'.[18]

Yet a majority of Europeans still believed, dangerously so Angell warned, that war was sometimes necessary. On the Continent states were building up their militaries and Britain and Germany were engaged in a naval race. Europeans might think that their strong military forces were only for defensive purposes but the overall effect of militarism and the arms race was to make war more likely. Europe's political leaders must see that and they too must abandon the great illusion. 'If the Statesmen of Europe could lay on one side, for a moment, the irrelevant considerations which cloud their minds, they would see that the direct cost of acquisition by force must in these circumstances necessarily exceed in value the property acquired.'[19] Given the jittery state of Europe at the time, Angell's timing was excellent and the reception to his ideas was encouraging to the advocates of peace. The king of Italy apparently read his book and so did the Kaiser 'with keen interest'. In Britain both the Foreign Secretary, Sir Edward Grey, and the Leader of the Opposition, Balfour, read it and were deeply impressed.[20] So was Jacky Fisher who described it as 'heavenly manna'.[21] (Fisher's view on war was quite simple: he did not want it but would fight all out if he had to.) Enthusiasts clubbed together to set up a foundation so that the ideas of what came to called Angellism could be studied at universities.[22]

In the last decades of the nineteenth century and the first one of the twentieth, organised movements for peace and against the arms race and militarism more generally, which drew support largely but not entirely from the middle classes, were developing as well across Europe and in North America. In 1891 an International Peace Bureau, which still exists today, was established in Berne to bring together national peace societies, specifically religious organisations such as the Quaker Friends for Peace, or international bodies to promote arbitration and disarmament. There were peace crusades, petitions to governments, and international peace conferences and congresses and new words such as 'pacifist' or 'pacifism' or even 'pacificism', which covered a range of opinion from hostility to war under all circumstances to attempts to limit or prevent it, were coined. In 1889, on the anniversary of the French Revolution, ninety-six members of parliaments in nine different countries met in Paris to found the Interparliamentary Union to work for the peaceful settlement of disputes among their nations. By 1912 it had 3,640 members from twenty-one different countries, mostly European but including the United States and Japan. In the same auspicious year of 1899, the first of what were to be twenty Universal Peace Congresses before 1914 met, with 300 delegates from Europe and the United States.[23] When the 1904 Congress met in Boston it was opened by John Hay, the Secretary of State. The cause of peace had become respectable enough that the old cynic Bülow welcomed a meeting of the Interparliamentary Union in Berlin in 1908. While he was well aware, he said in his memoirs, that 'the dreams and illusions' of most pacifists were foolish, the meeting nevertheless provided a good opportunity 'for destroying certain anti-German prejudices'.[24]

Bülow did not have to worry much about home-grown pacifists. The German peace movement never had more than about 10,000 members, who were drawn mainly from the lower middle classes. Unlike Britain, for example, it did not attract eminent professors, leading businessmen or members of the aristocracy. Where senior clergy supported the British or American movements, in Germany the churches generally denounced it on the grounds that war was part of God's plan for mankind.[25] Nor did liberals take the lead in supporting peace in Germany as they did in other countries such as Britain and France. In the heady excitement of the great victory over France and the unification of Germany in 1871, German liberals had by and large forgotten their previous reservations about Bismarck and his authoritarian and anti-liberal regime and thrown their support to the new Reich. Even the left-liberal Progressive Party regularly voted funds for the army and the navy.[26] Peace was not an attractive cause in a country which had been created by war and where the military held such a place of honour.

In Austria-Hungary the peace movement was similarly small and lacking in influence. In addition it was increasingly caught in national-ist politics. German-speaking liberals, for example, moved from a position of opposition to war in the 1860s and 1870s to support for the Habsburgs and the empire. While they continued to advocate arbitra-tion they also supported conscription and a more active foreign policy.[27] Further east, in Russia, pacifism was confined mainly to fringe religious sects such as the Doukhobors, although it could be argued that Tolstoy was a peace movement in himself.

The strongest and most influential peace movement before 1914 was in the United States, followed closely by Britain and France. In each country, pacifists could point, and frequently did, to their own histories for examples of overcoming deep divisions and outright conflicts from civil wars to revolutions and their success in building stable and pros-perous societies with workable institutions. The mission to the world of such fortunate countries was to spread their superior and peaceful civil-isation for the benefit of all. 'We have become a great nation', Teddy Roosevelt said, 'and we must behave as beseems a people with such responsibilities.'[28]

American pacifism, which had deep roots in American history, was also fuelled at the turn of the century by the progressive movement which aimed to reform society at home and spread peace and justice abroad. Clergy, politicians and travelling lecturers carried the message across the country and citizens organised themselves to work for honest local government, slum clearance, temperance, public ownership of utilities, or international peace. Some forty-five new peace societies appeared between 1900 and 1914 with support from a cross-section of society from university presidents to businessmen, and powerful organ-isations such as the Women's Christian Temperance Union had their own subsections on peace.[29] From 1895, the Quaker businessman Albert Smiley sponsored an annual conference on international arbitration at Lake Mohonk in New York State and in 1910 Andrew Carnegie endowed the Carnegie Endowment for International Peace. When peace had been achieved, he stipulated, the funds could be used to cure other social ills.[30]

The great orator and politician William Jennings Bryan, who ran three times for President on a progressive platform, was famous for his lecture 'The Prince of Peace' at the Chautauqua adult education fairs which spread from their original home in New York State to hundreds of American cities and towns. 'All the world is in search of peace,' he told his rapt audiences, 'every heart that ever beat has sought for peace, and many have been the methods employed to secure it.' In 1912 Bryan became President Woodrow Wilson's Secretary of State and he set himself to negotiate 'cooling off' treaties where parties would promise not to declare war, sometimes for at least a year, and instead refer their disputes to arbitration. Despite loud criticism from Teddy Roosevelt, who thought Bryan – 'that human trombone' – a fool and his plans futile, Bryan had signed thirty of the treaties by 1914. (Germany, however, refused.)

In both the United States and Britain the Quakers, small in numbers but influential, played an important part in the leadership of the movement while in France pacifists were strongly anti-clerical. In France, it has been estimated, there were some 300,000 people involved in various ways in the peace movement before 1914.[31] In all three countries, the peace movement was able to draw on strong liberal and radical traditions of hostility to war on moral and social grounds to appeal to significant sections of public opinion. War was wrong but it was also wasteful, diverting much-needed resources from righting the ills of society. Militarism, the arms race, an aggressive foreign policy, and imperialism were all seen as interrelated evils which needed to be tackled if there were to be a lasting peace. In each country, a strong liberal press and organisations devoted to wider social causes as well as leading politicians such as Bryan or Keir Hardie, leader of the British parliamentary Labour Party, helped to disseminate the message. The French Ligue des Droits de l'Homme with its 200,000 members regularly passed motions in favour of peace while teachers' conferences talked about building a history curriculum that was not nationalist and militaristic.[32] In Britain, powerful radical newspapers and journals such as the *Manchester Guardian* and *The Economist* put their support behind such issues as disarmament and free trade as a way of making the world a better place. When the new Liberal government took office in 1905 it faced pressure to do more about peace from the increased numbers on its radical wing and from the new and growing Labour Party.[33]

Individuals and bodies such as church groups also did their bit towards peace by attempting to bring the peoples of potentially hostile nations together. In 1905 the British set up an Anglo-German Friendship Committee headed by two radical peers. Church delegations and a Labour group led by the future Prime Minister Ramsay MacDonald visited Germany and George Cadbury, the Quaker chocolate tycoon, invited a party of German municipal officials to visit his model town of Bournville.[34] The ubiquitous Harry Kessler helped to organise an exchange of public letters between German and British artists to express admiration for each other's culture as well as a series of banquets to promote friendship which culminated in one at the Savoy Hotel in 1906 where Kessler himself spoke along with George Bernard Shaw and Lord Haldane, a leading Liberal politician, in favour of better British relations with Germany. (Kessler found time to note the beautiful nearly naked back and the pearls of Alice Keppel, the mistress of Edward VII, who was among the many leaders of society present.)[35] In France, Romain Rolland wrote his great series of Jean Christophe novels, whose central figure is a tormented but brilliant German composer who eventually finds recognition and peace in Paris, to show his love of music but also, so he told Stefan Zweig, in the hopes of furthering the cause of European unity and making Europe's governments stop and think about the dangers of what they were doing.[36]

For all the growth in pacifist sentiments there was also wide and often bitter disagreement about how to achieve a peaceful world. Just as some argue today that the spread of democracy is the key – on the debatable grounds that democracies do not fight each other – so in the years before 1914 there were those, often French thinkers citing the great ideals of the French Revolution, who held that establishing republics and, where necessary, freeing national minorities to govern themselves, would ensure peace. An Italian peace activist said in 1891: 'From the premises of liberty follow those of equality, which by progressive evolution lead to the solidarity of interests, the fraternity of truly civilized ... peoples. War, therefore, among civilized peoples is a crime.'[37] The lowering of trade barriers and taking other steps to encourage further integration of the world's economy were seen as yet other ways of promoting peace. Such actions had considerable support, not surprisingly, in Britain, where free trade had brought great benefits in the nineteenth century, as well as in the United States. Or, as forerunners of the Wikileaks activists of today argued, the key goal should be to get rid of secret diplomacy and secret treaties. A small minority, mainly in the English-speaking world, followed Tolstoy in holding that violence should always be met by non-violence and passive resistance while at the other pole were those who argued that wars could be divided into just and unjust and that in certain circumstances, defence against tyrants or unprovoked attacks for example, war was justified.

One issue on which most of the peace movement could agree before 1914 and which showed more progress than disarmament was the arbitration of international disputes. Arbitration by independent commissions had been used during the nineteenth century with occasional high-profile successes such as the 1871 settlement of American claims against Britain arising out of the activities of the Confederacy's ship *Alabama*, which had been built in a British port. In spite of protests from the Union, the British had let the ship sail out into the high seas, where it sank or captured more than sixty Union ships. The victorious American government demanded compensation from Britain – Canada, it was suggested, would do nicely – but in the end the United States settled for an apology and a cash payment of some $15 million. Year after year the Universal Peace Congresses passed resolutions calling on the governments of the world to build a workable system for arbitration. Partly as a result of such public pressure and partly because they too wished to avoid war, governments increasingly turned to arbitration in the last part of the century. Over half the 300 settlements between 1794 and 1914 took place after 1890. Moreover, an increasing number of states signed bilateral arbitration agreements. Optimists hoped that one day there would be a multilateral arbitration agreement, a court with teeth, and a body of international law, and perhaps, so the most idealistic thought, a world government.[38] As an American said: 'It is the resistless logic of modern humane progress which is bringing arbitration into such esteem.'[39]

Other activists preferred to concentrate on disarmament or at least limiting arms. Then as now it could be argued that the existence of weapons and a military and the almost inevitable concomitant of an arms race made war more likely. Arms manufacturers themselves were a frequent target of peace advocates who saw them as deliberately stirring up tension, even conflicts, in order to peddle their wares. So when the young tsar unexpectedly issued a public invitation in 1898 to the world's powers to meet to discuss the 'grave problem' as a result of the unprecedented increase in armaments and to work together solve it, peace activists such as Suttner were delighted. Indeed, the invitation, with its references to 'terrible engines of destruction' and the horrors a future war would bring, could have been written by one of them. The tsar seems to have been motivated partly by idealism and also by the practical consideration that Russia was having trouble in keeping up with the spending of other European powers.[40] A second Russian note suggested topics that might be discussed including a freeze on increases in each country's military, limits on some of the new and more deadly weapons that were appearing, and regulations on the conduct of war.[41]

The governments of the other European powers were lukewarm or, in the case of Germany, hostile to the idea but they had to deal with the enthusiastic response from the public. Petitions and letters urging the delegates to work for peace poured in from around the world. In Germany a campaign to endorse a declaration of support for disarmament got over a million signatures. The document, which was sent to The Hague, also gave a taste of the way in which nationalism was going to undermine the attempts at disarmament before 1914. 'We do not want Germany to disarm', it said, 'as long as the world around us bristles with bayonets. We do not want to diminish our position in the world or refrain from any advantage which we can get from a peaceful contest of nations.'[42]

'I'll go along with the conference comedy,' said the Kaiser, 'but I'll keep my dagger at my side during the waltz.'[43] For once his uncle in Britain agreed with him. 'It is the greatest nonsense and rubbish I ever heard of,' said Edward.[44] Germany went to the conference intending to wreck it if it could do so without taking all the blame. Its delegation was headed by Georg zu Münster, the German ambassador to Paris, who strongly disliked the whole idea of the conference, and included Karl von Stengel, a professor from Munich, who published a pamphlet shortly before the proceedings started in which he condemned disarmament, arbitration and the whole peace movement.[45] The directions that Holstein in the German Foreign Office gave the delegates said: 'For the state there is no aim superior to the protection of its interests … In the case of great powers these will not necessarily be identical with the maintenance of peace, but rather with the violation of the enemy and competitor by an appropriately combined group of stronger states.'[46]

Among the other powers, Austria-Hungary was as unenthusiastic. The instructions of its Foreign Minister, Gołuchowski, to its delegates said: 'Existing relationships do not permit any essential results to be achieved. On the other hand, however, we ourselves would scarcely wish that anything could be achieved, at least in so far as military and political questions are concerned.'[47] France, where there was a strong peace movement, was more inclined to support the conference but its Foreign Minister, Delcassé, was concerned that the assembled delegates might pass resolutions which would imply that France must give up hopes of peacefully regaining Alsace-Lorraine: 'For my part, even if I am Foreign Minister, I am a Frenchman first and cannot prevent myself from sharing the feelings of other Frenchmen.'[48] Great Britain, which sent Admiral Jacky Fisher as one of its delegates, was willing to discuss arbitration but had little interest in disarmament. The Admiralty told the government that a freeze on naval forces was 'quite impracticable', and that any restriction on new and improved weapons 'would favour the interests of savage nations, and be against those of the more highly civilised'. As for trying to regulate war, 'their Lordships are averse to binding the country in this manner, as such an arrangement would be almost certain to lead to mutual recriminations'. The War Office was equally blunt: none of the measures proposed by the Russians were desirable.[49] The United States sent a delegation headed by Andrew White, its ambassador to Berlin, and which included Alfred Mahan, the proponent of naval power. 'He has had very little, if any sympathy', wrote White in his diary, 'with the main purposes of the conference.'[50] The American position was one of general support for peace but to resist discussion of arms limitations on the grounds that American forces, both naval and military, were so small that the Europeans should leave them alone.[51] In the course of the conference White made an eloquent statement to this effect. The British military attaché reported to London: 'The French Admiral remarked to me at the close of the speech that the Americans had destroyed the Spanish navy and commerce, and now wanted no one to destroy theirs.'[52]

Delegations from some twenty-six nations including most of the European powers as well as the United States, China, and Japan, along with peace activists led by Suttner and Bloch, assembled in The Hague in May 1899. (Suttner's hotel flew a white flag in honour of her presence and her cause.) The Dutch, who because of their geography had much to fear from a war between France and Germany, gave a lavish opening reception and were to provide generous hospitality throughout the conference. 'Probably since the world began', said White, 'never has so large a body come together in a spirit of more hopeless skepticism as to any good result.'[53] The Dutch royal family put one of its palaces at the disposal of the conference, which met in the great entrance hall, decorated appropriately enough with a large painting of Peace in the style of Rubens. Delegates speculated about the motives of the Russians, who, many suspected, only wanted to buy time to strengthen their military.[54] One member of the German delegation, a military officer, made an unfortunate impression when he gave an exceedingly belligerent speech in which he boasted that his country could easily afford its defence expenditure and that furthermore every German saw military service 'as a sacred and patriotic duty, to the performance of which he owes his existence, his prosperity, his future'.[55]

The Belgian head of the commission looking into armaments correctly told his own government that no one was serious about disarmament.[56] The conference did, however, produce agreements on relatively minor arms issues: to have a moratorium on the development of asphyxiating gas, to ban the dum-dum bullet which caused terrible wounds, and to forbid the throwing of projectiles out of balloons. It also approved what became the first of a series of international agreements on rules for the conduct of war such as the humane treatment of prisoners of war or civilians. Finally, and this was a significant step forward in international arbitration, the conference agreed on a Convention for the Pacific Settlement of International Disputes with a number of provisions including commissions of inquiry in the case of disputes between states. In 1905 Russia and Britain were to use one such commission successfully to resolve the Dogger Bank incident when the Russian navy had fired on British fishing vessels.

The Convention also provided for the establishment of a Permanent Court of Arbitration. (A few years later the American philanthropist

Andrew Carnegie donated the funds for the neo-Gothic Peace Palace in The Hague which still houses it today.) While the German government, with the full support of the Kaiser, initially intended to oppose the establishment of the Court, it eventually decided that Germany should not be alone in opposition. 'Lest the Tsar make a fool of himself in front of Europe,' the Kaiser said, 'I shall go along with this nonsense. But in practice I shall continue to rely on and appeal to only God and my sharp sword. And shit on all their decisions!' The German delegates managed to add so many exceptions to the final document that it looked, as Münster said, like 'a net with many holes'.[57] Although it was to settle a dozen cases before the Great War, the Court depended, as it does today, on the willingness of governments to bring issues before it. The German government expressed its public satisfaction at the 'happy conclusion' to the conference while its delegate Stengel chose to denounce it loudly.[58] Yet again German diplomacy had been unnecessarily clumsy and had left behind an impression of a belligerent power which was not prepared to co-operate with the others.

In 1904 Roosevelt called for a second Hague Conference but the outbreak of the Russo-Japanese War effectively postponed it until May 1907. By this point the international outlook was darker. The Anglo-German naval race was in full swing and the Triple Entente was forming. Sir Henry Campbell-Bannerman, the new British Liberal Prime Minister, suggested that arms limitation be put on the agenda. Since he also claimed that British sea power had always been a benevolent force for peace and progress, it is perhaps not surprising that the reaction from the Continent was one of cynicism and hostility.

The widespread public sentiment in favour of peace further alarmed many of those in positions of authority, statesmen or the military for example, who felt that war was a necessary part of international relations and that pacifism would undercut their ability to use force. And conservatives saw in pacificism a challenge to the old order. As Alois von Aehrenthal, Foreign Minister of Austria-Hungary between 1906 and 1912, wrote to a friend, 'The monarchies are against the international peace movement because the peace movement is against the idea of heroism – an idea essential to the monarchical order.'[59]

In Russia, where the government wanted a free hand to rebuild its forces after the devastating losses of the recent war, the new Foreign

Minister, Izvolsky, said that 'disarmament was an idea just of Jews, socialists, and hysterical women'.[60] When Bülow told the Reichstag shortly before the conference opened that Germany had no intention of discussing limitations on armaments at The Hague, he was greeted with laughter and cheers.[61] Austria-Hungary followed its ally. 'A platonic declaration' should dispose of the issue nicely, said Aehrenthal.[62] The French found themselves in an awkward position, torn between supporting their old ally Russia or their new friend Britain, and privately hoped that the whole matter could be given a decent burial. The United States, which had initially supported the idea of arms limitations, was now backing down; Roosevelt had become increasingly concerned about the growth of Japan's naval power in the Pacific and was thinking of building dreadnoughts.[63]

This time representatives from forty-four countries assembled in The Hague and as before there were large numbers of peace activists including Bertha von Suttner and Thomas Stead, the radical English journalist, who organised an international Peace Crusade to put pressure on the powers. (The latter was soon afterwards to do a complete about turn; by the time he went down on the *Titanic* in 1912 he had become a fervent advocate for more dreadnoughts.)[64] This time several Latin American countries were represented; they put on, said a Russian diplomat, banquets of 'peculiar interest and attractiveness'. The Dutch again went all out to be hospitable; they faced competition from the Belgians who put on a mediaeval tournament for the delegates.[65]

The British realised that disarmament was a lost cause and graciously gave way; in a session of the conference which lasted for a mere twenty-five minutes, the senior British delegate put forward a resolution to the effect that 'it was highly desirable that the Governments should resume serious study of this question'.[66] It passed unanimously and the arms race, which by now was affecting the land forces as well, went on. While the Germans were more diplomatic than at the first Hague Conference, they still managed to derail an attempt to get an international arbitration treaty. Their senior delegate, Adolf Marschall von Bieberstein, the ambassador to the Ottoman Empire, gave a speech in which he simultaneously praised arbitration and said that the time had not yet come to introduce it. He later said that he was not sure himself whether he had been for or against. A Belgian delegate wished that he could die as painlessly as Marschall had killed the idea.[67] Eyre Crowe, a leading opponent of Germany at the Foreign Office, who was in The Hague as a British delegate, wrote to a colleague in London: 'The dominating influence has clearly been fear of Germany. The latter has followed her traditional course: cajoling and bullying in turn, always actively intriguing.'[68] As before there were some minor improvements to the rules of war but the overall reaction among the public was that the conference had been a failure. 'A nice peace conference!' said Suttner. 'You hear only about wounded and sick persons and belligerents.'[69] A third Hague Conference was planned for 1915 and by the summer of 1914 a number of states had already set up groups to prepare for it.

If governments did little to advance the cause of peace in the prewar years, for the peace movement one other great hope remained – the Second International, which was an organisation founded in 1889 to bring together the world's workers and their socialist parties. (The First International founded by Marx himself in 1864 had fallen to pieces a dozen years later over doctrinal differences.) The Second International was truly international with member parties across Europe, and from Argentina, India and the United States, and it could surely only grow as industrialisation spread. It was united by a shared enemy in capitalism and by an ideology strongly influenced by Karl Marx, whose old collaborator Friedrich Engels had been present at its first congress and whose surviving daughter and two sons-in-law remained much involved in its development. Most importantly the Second International had the numbers; by the eve of the Great War, some twenty-five different parties were affiliated with it including the British Labour Party with forty-two Members of Parliament and the French Socialists with 103 seats and a fifth of all the votes cast in France. The most important party of all was the German SPD with its million and more members, a quarter of German votes, and, after the election of 1912, its 110 seats which made it the biggest single party in the Reichstag. If the workers of the world could unite – and they had no nation, Marx had famously said, but only the interests of their class – they had within their power the means to make war impossible. Capitalism exploited workers but it also needed them to keep the factories going, the railways running, and the ports working – and to fill up the ranks in their armies when they were mobilised. 'Your dry powder? Your excellency!' a militant French socialist apostrophised the Kaiser. 'Can't you see that four million German workers have pissed in it!'[70] (One of the reasons that the German War Ministry resisted increasing the size of the army for so long was its fear that recruits from the working classes would not fight loyally.) And when socialism had finally triumphed, there could be no more war at all. As Karl Liebknecht, one of the leading figures on the left of the German Social Democratic Party, said contemptuously to Suttner: 'What you are trying to achieve, peace on earth, *we* will attain – I mean social democracy, which in truth is a great international peace league.'[71]

Suttner did not much care for socialists. Workers in her view needed the patronage of their betters if they were to become a useful part of society. 'They must first', she said, 'overcome their coarseness.'[72] In general relations between the largely middle-class peace movement and the socialists were difficult in the decades before 1914. The upper and middle classes were scared off by the revolutionary rhetoric and the socialists tended to regard liberals as the kindly face of capitalism, helping to mask its true nature from the workers. When it came to issues of peace, the socialists had little patience for issues dear to anti-war liberals such as arbitration and disarmament; what was more important was to overthrow capitalism, which was seen as the cause of war. Engels in 1887 had painted a grim picture of a future great war in Europe which would bring famine, death, sickness, and the collapse of economies and societies and finally of states. 'Crowns will roll by dozens in the gutter and no one will be found to pick them up.' It was impossible to predict where it would all end. 'Only *one* result is absolutely certain: general exhaustion and the establishment of the conditions for the final victory of the working class.'[73]

Yet did European socialists really want victory at that price? Would it not be better both to work against war and use peaceful means to acquire power? The spread of the franchise and the improvement in the conditions of the working classes, especially in western Europe, seemed to promise another route using the ballot box, the law, and co-operation with other political parties where their interests overlapped rather than that of bloody revolution. The attempt to revise the Marxist orthodoxy which held that change occurred through the violent clash between one class and another caused painful and divisive debates within the European socialist parties, notably the German Social Democratic Party, and was to shake the Second International as well. After many debates in which the works of the great socialist fathers Marx and Engels were ransacked for support by both sides, the German socialists voted to uphold revolutionary orthodoxy. The irony was that they were in practice becoming reformist, even respectable. The trade unions, whose membership was growing, were perfectly prepared to work with business to get benefits for their members and, at the local level, socialist members of such bodies as town councils co-operated with middle-class parties. At the national level, however, the socialists kept to the old stance of hostility, voting against the government on all occasions, and their deputies ostentatiously remained seated when the Reichstag gave its cheer for the Kaiser.[74]

The German socialist leadership feared, with good reason, that there were many in the government who would have liked any excuse to revive Bismarck's anti-socialist laws. Nor did the Kaiser help matters by publicly reminding his soldiers that they might have to shoot their own brothers. The election of 1907, which was fought in an upsurge of nationalist feeling in the aftermath of Germany's brutal repression of an uprising in its colony of Southwest Africa, shook the socialists. They were accused by the nationalist right of being unpatriotic and lost forty of their eighty-three seats in the Reichstag. This in turn strengthened the moderate wing of the party: a new SPD deputy, Gustav Noske, promised in his maiden speech in the Reichstag that he would repel foreign aggression 'as implacably as any member of the bourgeoisie'.[75] The party leadership also did its best to keep its own left wing under control, resisting all suggestions for general strikes or revolutionary activities.[76] If the German government had been wiser and picked up on the many signals that the SPD was no longer a serious threat to the established order, it might well have brought the socialists into mainstream politics. Instead the government continued to treat the socialists with suspicion, doubting their loyalty. As a result the socialist leadership had little reason to abandon their lip service to Marxist orthodoxy, whatever they and their members were doing in practice.

The key person responsible for this mix of ideological conformity and timidity was a small, slim man, August Bebel. He was the SPD's chief organiser, its main parliamentary spokesman and the man largely responsible for maintaining the adherence to Marxism. His parents

were working class, his father a non-commissioned officer in the old
Prussian army and his mother a domestic servant. By the time he was
thirteen he was an orphan and his remaining relatives apprenticed him
to a carpenter. In the 1860s he was converted to Marxism and devoted
the rest of his life to politics. He opposed both Germany's war of unification against Austria in 1866 and its war against France in 1870 and
was consequently convicted of treason. Although he used his time in
prison to read widely and to write a tract on women's rights, he always
remained more comfortable with organising – at which he was a master
– than theorising. He helped to found the Social Democratic Party in
1875 and built it into a large and well-disciplined organisation.

Bebel was part of the German delegation at the founding of the
Second International and over the years the SPD became its most
important member thanks to its size and discipline. The German pre-
scription for the constituent members of the International was simple
and rigid: they must keep the class struggle in mind at all times and
there must be no compromise, no deals with bourgeois parties, no taking
part in bourgeois governments or supporting bourgeois causes. At the
1904 congress in Amsterdam, Bebel condemned the French socialist
leader Jean Jaurès for supporting the French republic during the Dreyfus
affair: 'Monarchy or republic – both are class states, both are a form of
state to maintain the rule of the bourgeoisie, both are designed to protect
the capitalist order of society.' The Germans and their allies, who
included the more doctrinaire French socialists, pushed through a resolution condemning any attempts to move away from the class struggle
'in such a way that instead of conquering political power by defeating
our opponents, a policy of coming to terms with the existing order is
followed'. Jaurès, who believed passionately in socialist solidarity,
accepted the resolution. Where others might have despaired or been
bitter he simply set himself to work to bring together the different fac-
tions in both the French and the international socialist movement.[77]

It was typical of Jaurès that the cause was more important than
himself and that he did not bear grudges. In his own life his friendships
crossed ideological lines and in politics he was always ready to reach out
to his opponents. 'His human sympathy was so universal', said Romain
Rolland, 'that he could be neither nihilistic or fanatical. Every act of
intolerance repelled him.'[78] Among the socialist leaders before 1914

Jaurès stands out for his common sense, his grasp of political realities, his willingness to work for compromises and his optimism. With an unshakeable trust in reason and the essential goodness of human nature, he believed until the day he died that the purpose of politics was to build a better world. Although he had studied Marx and the rest of the socialist canon thoroughly, his socialism was never doctrinaire. Unlike Marx he did not see history unfolding itself in an inevitable pattern through class struggle; for Jaurès there was always room for human initiative and idealism, always the possibility of different and more peaceful paths to the future. The world he wanted was one based on justice and freedom for all, and one that brought happiness. A goal of socialism, he once said, should be to allow the common people 'to savor all the joys of life which are now reserved for the privileged'.[79]

Solid and broad-shouldered with an open, friendly face and beautiful deep-set blue eyes, Jaurès barrelled through his life with enormous energy. He was both a consummate politician and a thoughtful intellectual who could have been a great classical scholar. He was a clever, even brilliant man, but this did not make him arrogant or unkind. He married a dull woman who did not share his interests but he remained loyal to her. Although he had lost his own faith in God as a young man, he raised no objections when she gave their children a religious upbringing. He loved good food and wine but would frequently forget to eat when he was engaged in his other enthusiasm of good conversation. He did not care about wealth or status. His apartment in Paris was comfortable but shabby and his desk was made of boards set on trestles. He himself dressed in clothes which, said Ramsay MacDonald, who saw him at a socialist congress in 1907, looked as though they had been thrown on with a pitchfork. With a battered straw hat on his head, Jaurès strolled along completely unselfconsciously, said MacDonald, 'like a youth upon a new world, or a strolling player who had mastered fate and discovered how to fill the moments with happy unconcern'.[80]

Jaurès was born in 1859 in Tarn, in the southern part of France, to a middle-class family but experienced what it was like to be close to poverty as his father moved restlessly from one unsuccessful pursuit to another. His mother, who seems to have been the strong one in the family, managed to send him to a local boarding school where he won more prizes than any other student ever had. His talent and accomplishments took him to Paris for further schooling and ultimately to the Ecole Normale Supérieure, then as now the hothouse in which much of the elite of France is formed. Even at a relatively young age, Jaurès showed a strong concern for social issues and it was not surprising that he chose to go into politics. First elected to parliament in 1885, he was defeated in 1889 and spent the next four years teaching in Toulouse and serving on the municipal council, practical experience which was to give him a lasting appreciation of the importance of bread-and-butter issues to voters. He served as a member of the French parliament for thirty-five years and was head of the French Socialist Party for ten of those. He was a great speaker. Mopping his brow from the effort, he spoke with deep conviction, eloquence and emotion whether in parliament, socialist congresses, or the towns and villages of France as he criss-crossed the country. He found time as well to write copiously and he edited the new socialist paper *L'Humanité* from 1904 and wrote over 2,000 articles for it during the next ten years.

After his defeat in 1904 at the congress of the Second International Jaurès became increasingly concerned about the deterioration in the international situation and devoted much of his energies to the cause of peace. He had long supported arbitration and disarmament but he now studied war itself. Being Jaurès, he undertook a serious study, reading military theory and the history of war and working with a young French army captain, Henry Gérard. One night as the two men sat in a café in Paris, Jaurès described what a future war would be like: 'the cannon-fire and the bombs; entire nations decimated; millions of soldiers strewn in mud and blood; millions of corpses …' During a battle on the Western Front some years later, a friend asked Gérard why he was staring into space. 'I feel as though all this is familiar to me,' Gérard replied. 'Jaurès prophesied this hell, this total annihilation.'[81] Within France, Jaurès proposed transforming the French military from a professional force focussing on the offensive into a citizens' militia such as the Swiss had where soldiers did six months of service and then came back for short spells of training. This new army would be used only to defend the country. That, he argued, was how the French Revolution had defeated the armies sent against it by its enemies – by arming the nation. Not surprisingly, his ideas were rejected by the political and military establishment although in retrospect his stress on the defensive made a lot of sense.[82]

He did not have much more success with stirring up the Second International to action even though the issue of what it should do to prevent war or in the face of a general European war was on the agenda at every one of its congresses from 1904 onwards. Unfortunately it was clear from early on that profound and potentially damaging divisions of opinion existed. Jaurès and those who thought like him, such as the British Labour MP Keir Hardie, believed that socialists should use all weapons possible against war, whether agitation in parliament, mass demonstrations, strikes or, if necessary, an uprising. The German socialists, however, for all their revolutionary talk, showed the same caution in practice as they did at home. The key issue over which the different sides fell out was whether there should be agreement on concrete steps to be taken should war come. The Germans were simply not prepared to commit themselves or the Second International in advance to such measures as calling a general strike even though most socialists (and indeed Europe's political and military leaders as well) believed that this would make it impossible for nations to wage war. Jaurès, for his part, was not prepared to split the socialist movement by insisting on it. The differences were concealed behind fine-sounding resolutions which condemned war, asserted the determination of the working classes of the world to prevent it, and were deliberately vague about how this would be done. As the Stuttgart congress resolution said in 1907: 'The International is not able to lay down the exact form of working class action against militarism at the right place and time, as this naturally differs in different countries.'[83] Seven years later the International was going to be faced with the biggest challenge of its existence.

In the remaining years before the Great War, the Second International remained confident that it could work effectively for peace. Despite its rhetoric, it was losing some of its old tendency to see capitalism in black and white terms as the enemy. With the spread of investment and trade, capitalism was knitting the world together and surely this made the chances of war less. Even the old hardliner Bebel said in 1911: 'I openly admit that perhaps the greatest guarantee of world peace lies in this international export of capital.' And when the powers successfully managed the crises in the Balkans in 1912 and 1913, these seemed more evidence that capitalism was now on the side of peace. At its Basle congress in 1912 the Second International went so far as to state that it would now work with middle-class pacifists.[84]

There was also encouraging evidence of socialist solidarity in the face of international tensions. In January 1910, the socialist parties from the different Balkan countries met in Belgrade to find common ground. 'We must break down the frontiers', their statement said, 'that separate these peoples whose cultures are identical, these countries whose economic and political fortunes are closely linked, and thus shake off the yoke of foreign domination which robs nations of the right to determine their own fate.'[85] In the spring of 1911, as relations were particularly strained between Austria-Hungary and Italy, socialists from both countries campaigned against higher military expenditures and the threat of war.[86] The moment of greatest hope came in the autumn of 1912 when the First Balkan War broke out. Socialists across Europe, 200,000 of them in Berlin, another 100,000 outside Paris, held massive demonstrations for peace, and the Second International held an emergency congress. Over 500 delegates from twenty-three different socialist parties (only the Serbs had chosen not to come) met in the Swiss city of Basle. Children dressed in white led them through the streets to the great red sandstone Gothic cathedral. Luminaries of the socialist movement climbed up into the pulpit to condemn the war, indeed war in general, and to assert the power of the working classes. Jaurès, who spoke last, made one of his greatest speeches. 'We will leave this hall', he concluded, 'committed to the salvation of peace and civilization'. The congregation, for that is what it seemed, sang one last song and the organ played Bach. 'I am still dizzy with all I have lived through,' the Russian revolutionary Alexandra Kollontai wrote ecstatically to a friend.[87] Three months later, the two largest parties in the Second International, the French and the German, issued a joint manifesto condemning the arms race and promising to work together for peace.[88] That summer, however, while the French socialists were opposing a proposal that would make the French army bigger, the German Social Democrats in the Reichstag voted for an increased budget for the German army.

The fundamental weakness of the Second International was not merely national differences on strategy and tactics; it was nationalism itself. This too was masked by language; at every congress before 1914 speakers from all countries uttered noble sentiments about the international brotherhood of the working classes and no doubt most meant what they said. As early as 1891, however, a Dutch delegate to the Second International's second congress had uttered the awkward but prophetic words: 'The international sentiments presupposed by socialism do not exist among our German brothers.'[89] He could have said the same of the other socialist parties and of the unions. Nationalism, it turned out, was not merely something whipped up and imposed on the rest of the nation by the ruling classes; it had deep roots in the different European societies. It manifested in the nationalistic songs of French workers or the pride which German workers took in their military service.[90] It is easier perhaps to see the impact of nationalism on the Second International in retrospect, the inability, for example, of the different socialist parties to agree on how May Day should be celebrated, the polemics in 1905–6 between the leaders of German and French unions during the first crisis over Morocco, or the criticisms of the German and French socialist parties of the other's way of doing business.[91] The attempt in 1910 by socialists in the Balkans to build a united front foundered the following year as the Bulgarian socialists who were already busy fighting among themselves turned on the Serbs.[92]

In 1908 the Austrian Socialist Party criticised its own government's annexation of Bosnia-Herzegovina but showed little sympathy for Serbian resentment at the action. Indeed, Austrian socialists tended to assume that their own country had a civilising mission in the Balkans.[93] Nor were they alone. Although it was a given in socialist theory that imperialism was bad, in the years before 1914 there was an increasing tendency for European socialists to defend the possession of colonies on the grounds that the superior civilisation was bringing benefits to the inferior one. Some German socialists went further still and argued that Germany needed more colonies for the economic benefits they brought the German working classes.[94] In 1911, when Italy launched an openly imperialist war on the Ottoman Empire in order to seize territory in North Africa, the right wing of the Italian Socialist Party voted with the government. Although the party later expelled the deputies its secretary made it clear that he resented the pressure from the Second International: 'All criticism must cease and all requests for more energetic manifestations – from whatever quarter they emanate – must in justice be described as exaggerated and irrational.'[95]

The following year the Belgian Camille Huysmans, who ran the Second International's bureau, had to give up temporarily the idea of holding its next congress in Vienna because of tensions among the socialists of different nationalities. 'The situation in Austria and Bohemia', he wrote, 'is *quite deplorable*. Our comrades there devour each other. Discord has reached a peak. Feelings are running high and if we assemble in Vienna we shall have a congress of strife which will make the worst possible impression on the world. Not only the Austrians and Czechs are in this situation; the same is true of Poland, the Ukraine, Russia, and Bulgaria.'[96] The relationship between German and French socialists was the cornerstone of the Second International (just as that between Germany and France is the key one for the European Union today) and both sides repeatedly stressed how important it was. Yet in 1912 Charles Andler, a professor of German at the Sorbonne, known for his sympathies towards both socialism and Germany, brought into the open an uncomfortable truth. German workers, he wrote in a series of articles, were more German than they were internationalists and they would, if war came, for whatever reason, support Germany.[97]

The middle-class peace movement proved no more immune to nationalism than the Second International. Italian pacifists were bitterly disappointed when their Austrian counterparts refused to demonstrate in favour of the rights of minorities (who included, of course, Italians within Austria-Hungary).[98] Alsace-Lorraine had long caused trouble between German and French pacifists with the former arguing that the inhabitants of the two provinces were happy and prosperous under German rule while the French pointed to evidence of their oppression, for example the numbers of French-speakers who were emigrating.[99] Both sides found it difficult to trust each other. 'Were we to disarm,' said a German pacifist in 1913, 'the chances are a hundred to one that the French ... would attack.'[100] There was no more trust between British and the German pacifists. When there was a crisis over Morocco in 1911 which threatened to bring war between Britain and Germany, Ramsay MacDonald said in the House of Commons that he hoped 'no European nation will assume for a single moment that party divisions in this country will weaken the national spirit or national unity'. The following year a leading German pacifist criticised his colleagues for defending Britain, which, he said, 'is threatening the vital security of our national growth'.[101] Pacifists across Europe tried to reconcile their convictions with their nationalism by making a distinction between wars of aggression and defensive ones. And surely it was right to defend liberal institutions, even imperfect ones, against autocratic regimes. French pacifists, for example, were always clear that the republic had to be defended just as their forebears had defended the French Revolution against its foreign enemies.[102] In 1914 one of the goals of Europe's leaders as the crisis deepened was to persuade their own populations that a decision to go to war would be entirely for defensive reasons.

War itself was the final element that undermined the attempts to maintain peace in Europe. Bloch had hoped that as the technology changed to make war both more deadly and more industrial, the glamour surrounding it would dissipate. In fact the contrary happened; the spread of militarism and the sheer excitement of war made it enormously appealing to many Europeans. Even Angell, who tried so hard to persuade his readers that war was irrational, was obliged to admit: 'There is something in warfare, in its story and in its paraphernalia, which profoundly stirs the emotions and sends the blood tingling through the veins of the most peaceable of us, and appeals to I know not what remote instincts, to say nothing of our natural admiration for courage, our love of adventure, of intense movement and action.'[103]

CHAPTER II

Thinking about War

———

Helmuth von Moltke, the architect of Prussia's victories in the German Wars of Unification, was a handsome man, who with his iron cross and his well-fitting uniforms, looked like what he was, an officer from Prussia's landowning Junker class. The picture is at once true and misleading. Moltke the Elder – as he is now known to distinguish him from his nephew, the chief of Germany's general staff in 1914 – was indeed a Junker, from that class which over the centuries had farmed their estates in the north and north-east of Prussia, had lived simply and honourably, and had sent their sons to be officers in the Prussian army. Generation on generation, as Prussia had expanded, they had fought and died in its service, as they were expected to. (Names that were there in the Seven Years War appear again in Hitler's war.) Junkers, both men and women, were brought up to be physically tough, uncomplaining, brave, loyal, and honourable. Von Moltke shared his class's conservative values, its uncomplicated piety, and its sense of duty. In personal terms, though, he was far removed from the 'brainless virility and punctilious brutality' that, according to the satirical weekly *Simplicissimus*, characterised the Junker officer. Moltke loved art, poetry, music, and theatre. He read widely, from Goethe to Shakespeare to Dickens and in several languages. He translated several volumes of Gibbons's *Decline and Fall of the Roman Empire* and wrote a romantic novel as well as a history of Poland. More importantly for the evolution of Germany and its army, he was in certain crucial ways a very modern man who understood that large organisations need such things as systems, information, training, and a shared vision and ethos if they are to succeed. If he had been born in another time and place, he could have been Germany's Henry Ford or Bill Gates. As it was, he dealt as well as anyone could with the challenge faced by the officer corps of armies all over Europe: how to combine the values of a warrior caste with the demands of industrial warfare. The tensions that brought, however, were going to carry on into the Great War itself.

Moltke, who was born in 1800 during the Napoleonic Wars and died in 1891, lived through the transformation of European society, of European armies, and of the ways in which wars were fought. He was six when Napoleon's armies marched or rode into Prussia and crushed its army at the Battle of Jena. In 1870, as chief of the Prussian general staff, he was responsible for the successful campaign against France. This time the armies were carried to the battlefield by trains. Twenty years later, shortly before he died, the network of railway lines covering Europe had tripled and the first vehicles powered by internal combustion engines had appeared. Armies had once been constrained in size by how many supplies they could either carry with them or forage as they moved along and limited in their reach by how far and how fast the soldiers could march. By the end of the nineteenth century, trains could take Europe's much bigger armies over great distances and resupply them from the factories behind the lines which kept pumping out the materials, from weapons to boots, that they needed.

The industrial revolution made it possible to have bigger armies and Europe's population growth had enlarged the pool of manpower. Prussia was the first to tap the pool successfully; it used conscription to take recruits out of civilian society and give them several years of military training. It then returned its trained soldiers to civilian life but kept their skills sharp by putting them in reserves where they did periodic training. In 1897 Germany had 545,000 soldiers in uniform but another 3.4 million who could be called back to the army.[1] The other continental powers had little choice but to follow suit. Only Britain, thanks to the protection of the seas and its navy, was able to stay with a small volunteer army. On the Continent, by the end of the nineteenth century, all the powers had standing armies – in other words soldiers actually in

11. Before 1914 the European powers came to expect that a general war was likely. They engaged in an arms race and planned to fight on the offensive. Here five of the powers, Britain, France, Germany, the Ottoman Empire or Turkey and Russia confront each other, all armed to the teeth. Uncle Sam looks on from a distance in dismay saying 'Them fellers over there want to disarm but none of 'em dast do it first!'

their units with their weapons – and much bigger potential armies dispersed throughout society, ready to come into existence as soon as the mobilisation orders were given. When Moltke was twelve years old and Napoleon started his march towards Moscow, the French army and its allies numbered some 600,000 men, the largest force Europe had ever seen. In 1870 Moltke presided over the mobilisation of 1.2 million men of Prussia and its allies. In 1914, two decades after his death, the Central Powers put over 3 million men into the field.

Moving such huge numbers was like moving whole towns and cities. The men had to be formed into their units, got to the right railway stations, and put on the right trains. Equally important, they had to have the right equipment, from food to weapons and ammunition to the horses and mules they needed for cavalry and transportation once they left the trains. The floods of men and animals with their mounds of equipment moving towards the designated battlefields would coalesce into larger units, the division, in most armies around 20,000 men strong, and then corps of two or more divisions. Each division and corps had to have its own specialised units, from artillery to engineers, if it was to move and fight effectively. When Germany called up over 2 million men, with their tons of materials and some 118,000 horses, in the summer of 1914, it took 20,800 trains just to get them ready to be moved towards the frontiers. Trains fifty-four cars long transported troops and their equipment towards France on the crucial Hohenzollern bridge across the Rhine at Cologne every ten minutes in the first two weeks of August.[2] If things went wrong – as they did with the Trans-Siberian Railway in the Russo-Japanese War – it could be catastrophic for the war effort. Supplies could go in opposite directions from the men who needed them or sit for weeks or months on railway sidings while men or whole units could wander about trying to find where they were meant to be. In 1859 Napoleon III sent a large force by train to Italy to fight Austria: the men arrived without blankets, food or ammunition. 'We have sent an army of 120,000 men into Italy', he said, 'before having stocked up any supplies there.' It was, he admitted, 'the opposite of what we should have done'.[3]

Moltke was one of the first men to grasp that the new age demanded new and much more elaborate ways of organising. Armies had to draw up their plans, make maps, and collect as much information as possible beforehand because the time between mobilisation for war and combat had shrunk dramatically. Before the nineteenth century, armies had moved slowly on foot. As Frederick the Great, George Washington or the Duke of Wellington sent out cavalry scouts to get the lie of the land and try to locate the enemy, they also did their planning. By the time he had confronted the enemy on the eve of battle, Napoleon had the disposition of his own troops and those of his opponent clearly in his mind; he could draw up his battle plans and give out his orders for the morning. That was no longer possible; the army that failed to do its planning well ahead of time was an army which would be useless. When Moltke joined the Prussian army in 1819 it already possessed in embryonic form what was going to become in his hands the most important institutional innovation for armies of the modern world. The general staff became the brains which gave ideas, organisation and ultimately leadership to the behemoths which were coming into existence. Staff officers collected information about other armies, made sure that maps were ready and up to date, and drew up and tested war plans. Austria-Hungary, for example, had plans for wars against Russia, Italy, or Serbia.

Underpinning the war plans, and one of the most important parts of the work of the general staffs, were hundreds of pages of detailed mobilisation and railway plans. These included everything from the size and speed of the trains and their timetables to stopping times to take on water and fuel.[4] Germany, in this again the model for other European armies, had long since made sure that the building, running and co-ordination of railways met military needs. By 1914 the lines running west to the French and Belgian borders, for example, had a greater capacity than ordinary civilian traffic required.[5] When the elder Moltke told the Reichstag that mobilisation timetables needed a single standard time to be implemented throughout Germany, it immediately agreed. Within the German general staff, the Railway Section before 1914 was staffed by some eighty officers, chosen for their brains rather than their family backgrounds. (A majority came from the middle classes and today they would probably be computer nerds. In his early days with the section General William Groener, its head in 1914, spent his weekends working out railway timetables with his wife.)[6] Among the other powers, Britain was again the anomaly when it came to railways; until 1911 there was little liaison or consultation between the British army and British railway companies.[7]

When Moltke became head of the Prussian general staff in 1857 it had a handful of officers and was scarcely known and little heeded by the rest of the officer corps. In 1866 in the war with Austria when Moltke sent orders directly to the field commanders, one said: 'This is all very well but who is General Moltke?'[8] By 1871, with two great victories to its credit, the German general staff, as it now was called, was seen as one of Germany's national treasures and its influence and power had grown correspondingly. By the 1880s, with the elder Moltke still in charge, it had several hundred officers and several different sections. It also became the model for the general staffs of the other continental powers, although none of the others held the same unique and privileged position as the German general staff.[9] In 1883 it won the right of direct access to the monarch and increasingly saw itself as free to concentrate on preparing for and waging war, leaving such matters as international relations and diplomacy to the civilians.[10] 'The highest art of diplomacy is from my point of view', said Moltke the Younger, 'not to keep peace by all means but to shape the political situation of a state permanently in such a way that it is in a position to enter a war under advantageous conditions.'[11] Such attitudes were dangerous because the two spheres, military and civil, and the two activities, peace and war, could not be so neatly divided; the general staff was to make decisions on military grounds – famously the decision to invade Belgium in 1914 – which were to have serious political implications.

As war planning necessarily became more detailed and complicated another danger arose. The size of the plans, the work involved in creating them, and the work necessary to change them became arguments for not altering them. In 1914 when Austria-Hungary made a last minute change in its troop movements, it meant hastily revising eighty-four boxes of instructions.[12] Officers who had spent much of their working lives making the plans as foolproof as possible had, whether or not they realised it, a vested interest and pride in their handiwork. The thought of throwing out years of work and improvising was something the military in all the European powers instinctively recoiled from.[13] Moreover, the military planners tended to get locked into focussing on a single scenario for war rather than a range. A staff officer in the railway planning office of Austria-Hungary's army saw the danger that the military might concentrate on perfecting the plans for only one eventuality and not be prepared for a sudden change in foreign policy and strategic objectives. In his view the military never successfully reconciled the two demands: 'on the one hand, to make plans as thoroughgoing as possible to obtain a maximum of speed to enable the high commands a basis for their first efforts; on the other hand, to be ready to fulfil the fundamental duty of the field railways, namely "to satisfy all demands of the leaders at any time"'. Did the systems, he asked, which had been created over so many years leave enough freedom of decision to the leaders? The great crisis of 1914 provided an answer. When the Kaiser asked Moltke the Younger in 1914 whether Germany's war plan could be changed to allow it to fight on one front only – against Russia – rather than as planned against France and Russia at the same time,

Moltke flatly said it was not possible and, while the Kaiser was displeased, neither he nor his government questioned the assertion. Over the decades, and not just in Germany, both military and civilian leaders had come to accept that military planning was the business of the experts and that civilians had neither the knowledge nor the authority to ask searching questions or dispute their decisions.

The charge that the rigidity of the prewar plans created doomsday machines that once set in motion could not be stopped has had considerable currency as one of the causes, if not the main cause of the Great War. Yet, complex as they were, railway and mobilisation schedules could be and indeed were altered in their details every year by the military as more information came in, new lines were opened, or strategic objectives were modified. And their overall goals could have been changed or alternative plans drawn up. After the war, General Groener of the German general staff's Railway Section claimed that he and his men could have produced new plans in July 1914 to mobilise only against Russia and not France – and done so without a delay that would have been dangerous to Germany. During the Great War itself, the military found that they could put together plans quickly to move large numbers of men by rail from one part of the battlefront to another.[14] The first striking example of this capacity came in the first month of the war, when the German command on the Eastern Front switched an army corps of some 40,000 men a hundred miles to the south. The mobilisation plans were not the trigger for war themselves; rather Europe's civilian leaders failed, first by not informing themselves as to what their war plans entailed and secondly by not insisting on a range of plans rather than a single encompassing one.

What the plans did do to bring about the Great War was put additional pressure on the decision-makers by shortening the time in which decisions had to be taken. Whereas in the eighteenth century and even the first part of the nineteenth, governments usually had months to think about whether or not they wanted or needed to go to war, they now had days. Thanks to the industrial revolution, once mobilisation started armies could be at their frontiers and be ready to fight within a week, in the case of Germany, or in the case of Russia with its greater distances, just over two weeks. The European powers had a pretty good idea of how long each of them would take to mobilise and be ready to fight. It was critical not to get too far behind in the process. A partially completed mobilisation when the enemy was on the frontiers and already fully mobilised was the nightmare of Europe's military and one which many civilians came to share.

What is striking about the decision-making in 1914 is how it was accepted that even the briefest of delays meant danger. Conrad argued in Austria-Hungary that every day mattered in getting the Austrian troops assembled in Galicia facing the frontier with Russia; any delay might leave them half-ready in the face of a massive Russian attack. General Joseph Joffre and Moltke, the chiefs of staff in France and Germany respectively, warned their governments that even a day, perhaps even a few hours, would exact a terrible cost in blood spilt and territory lost to the enemy. And the civilians, overwhelmed by their responsibility and trusting the professionals, did not question them, asking for example whether it might not be better to prepare defensive positions and wait for the enemy to attack.[15] So once a neighbouring power started mobilising or even showing signs of preparations it was hard for its neighbours to resist mobilising as well. Not to do anything could be suicide but mobilising too late was seen as not much better. In 1914 those were the arguments that the military made to their civilian leaders to urge them to give the orders. Similar arguments were made, and with a much shorter time scale of minutes rather than days, to President Kennedy during the Cuban missile crisis: that if he waited to launch his missiles at the Soviet Union it would be too late because Soviet ones might already be in the air. He chose to ignore the military advice; in 1914 not all civilian leaders would show such independence.

It is also easy to see in retrospect that the military planners worked in too much of a vacuum. While it varied from power to power, the general staff planners saw themselves as technicians, working out the best ways to defend the nation, and leaving diplomatic and political considerations to the civilians. The difficulty, and it is always present in the relations between the civil and the military leadership, is that matters and issues cannot always be divided neatly into military and non-military. The German general staff decided that it needed to move into Belgium for sound strategic reasons if it were to attack France successfully, yet that invasion in 1914 was going to cause severe damage to

Germany's reputation among neutral powers, tellingly so in the United States, and bring Britain into a war it might otherwise not have entered. Too often, the civilians did not know, or did not care to inform themselves, about what the military were planning; the extent of the discussions over a number of years between the British and the French general staffs came as a surprise to most in the British Cabinet in 1914. It also worked the other way round. The French military stationed two divisions, which it could well have used elsewhere, along the common border between France and Italy only to find out, seven years after the fact, that the French and Italian governments had signed a secret agreement to remove tensions there.[16]

Even different branches of the military in a single country did not always share information or co-ordinate their efforts. Under Jacky Fisher, the British navy refused to give the army its war plans for fear of leaks. In 1911 at a long and stormy meeting of the Committee of Imperial Defence, Fisher's successor, Sir Arthur Wilson, made it clear that the navy had no plans and little interest in transporting British troops to the Continent even though the army had been considering the possibility for some time. Although German military circles feared amphibious attacks on Germany's Baltic coast, the German army and navy made just one attempt, in 1904, to carry out joint manoeuvres there.[17] It was apparently only in 1912, two years before the Great War, that the German Chancellor was informed of what was in the German war plan.[18] In 1914, so Admiral Tirpitz claimed in his memoirs, he and the navy still had no idea what the German army was planning.[19]

The new stress in Europe's military on technical expertise did not always sit easily with the values of the classes from which so many officers came. When an officer from one of the particularly fashionable British cavalry regiments thought of applying to the Staff College which the British army had, with some reluctance, set up, a fellow officer was firm: 'Well, I will give one piece of advice, and that is to say nothing about it to your brother officers, or you will get yourself jolly well disliked.'[20] In the army of Austria-Hungary, cavalry officers called those in the artillery the 'powder Jews' and even among artillery officers themselves riding was considered to be more important than technical expertise.[21] While the increasing size of the continental armies obliged them to draw more officers from the urban middle classes, this shift did not lead to a greater enthusiasm and respect for technical or academic prowess; indeed the middle-class officers seem to have absorbed aristocratic values, in taking up duelling for example, not the other way round.

While this had disadvantages and served to deepen the gulf between armies and their own societies, it also reinforced cohesiveness in the officer corps and certain character traits that were valued among the aristocracy – a sense of duty, physical bravery, facing death without flinching – which were what the military required as well. The sort of war which they mostly envisaged, though, was one that was increasingly anachronistic as the nineteenth century wore on. The European military looked back to the great soldiers of the past for inspiration: Alexander the Great, Julius Caesar and, closer in time, such figures as Frederick the Great or Napoleon. And the modern-day soldiers longed to emulate the great attacks of the past with their infantry assaults, their hand-to-hand fighting and their cavalry charges.[22] Military histories, even of more recent wars, reinforced the romantic, heroic view of war and held up for admiration individual acts of prowess. European commentators on the Russo-Japanese War were full of admiration for the Japanese soldiers who fought and died like true warriors – and worried that Europeans were no longer capable of behaving in the same way.[23] But the war that Europeans were being asked to face by 1900 *was* different in significant ways from those of the past. The industrial revolution had produced weapons that were more powerful, more reliable and more accurate and their much greater range meant that soldiers often did not see the enemies they were killing. It was much easier to defend positions than to attack: as yet the technologies to overcome a strong defence, such as aircraft and armoured vehicles, did not exist. As a French general reportedly said after the long-drawn-out Battle of Verdun in the Great War, 'Three men and a machine gun can stop a battalion of heroes.'

With advances in metallurgy, guns, from the standard weapons of soldiers to artillery, were stronger and more durable; with new explosives, including those invented by Alfred Nobel, they fired much further; and with rifling they were much more accurate. Soldiers in Napoleon's time had muskets which, with good training, they could reload – standing up – and fire three times a minute, and which were only accurate up to forty-five metres. (That is why it had been both necessary and possible for soldiers to hold their fire until they could see the whites of the enemy's eyes.) By 1870 the soldiers had rifles which were accurate up to almost half a kilometre; what is more they could load and fire six times a minute, and from the breech as they lay down, which meant that they were not exposed to enemy fire. By 1900 rifles were accurate – and lethal – over a greater distance, sometimes even up to a kilometre, and the new machine guns could fire hundreds of rounds a minute. The numbers had climbed and were continuing to climb all round: field artillery, which had an average range of just over half a kilometre in 1800, had almost seven kilometres in 1900; heavier guns, often mounted on railway undercarriages, had a range of ten kilometres. So attackers had to survive several kilometres of shell fire then several hundred metres of intense rifle and machine-gun fire on their way towards the enemy.[24]

Bloch warned about this last, the zone of fire, and the growing advantage of the defence, and about the likelihood of stalemates on the battlefield that would last for months or years. Yet Europe's military planners dismissed his work. After all, as a Jew by birth, a banker, and a pacifist he was everything they tended to dislike. When he gave three lectures at the United Services Institute in the summer of 1900, the audience of largely military men listened politely but showed no signs of being persuaded by what he said. 'So-called non-jingoism, or non-militarism', was the view of one major-general; 'namby-pamby so-called humanitarianism'.[25] In Germany one of the leading military historians of the day, Hans Delbrück, said: 'From a scientific standpoint the work does not have much to recommend it. It is a rather uncritical and poorly arranged collection of material; and although it is embellished with illustrations, the treatment is amateurish with vast amounts of detail that have nothing to do with the actual problem.'[26] As Bloch himself complained, the military were like a priestly caste who did not like outsiders meddling: 'Military science has from time immemorial been a book with seven seals, which none but the duly initiated were deemed worthy to open.'[27]

Nevertheless the European military did have a sense of what the problem was and had devoted attention to it. How could they not? They tried out the new weapons themselves and studied the evidence from recent wars. European military observers had gone to the American

Civil War of 1861–5 or to that between Turkey and Russia in 1877 and seen for themselves how a combination of well-prepared defensive positions including trenches in combination with rapid firing had devastated the attackers and caused much larger losses among them than the defenders. At the Battle of Fredericksburg in 1862, to take only one of many examples, the Union threw waves of soldiers against well-defended Confederate positions. All the attacks failed and the Union lost over twice as many soldiers as the Confederacy. It is said that the Union wounded scattered across the battlefield begged their comrades not to continue their fruitless attacks. Closer to hand the European military had the evidence of the Franco-Prussian War, where, for example, 48,000 Germans had held a line of some thirty-five kilometres against 131,000 French.[28] The Boer and Russo-Japanese wars more recently still had added fresh evidence: Boer farmers well hidden in the ground had inflicted devastating losses on British frontal attacks and the same pattern had been true in the Far East.

While pacifists hoped that progress was making war obsolete and used wars such as the Russo-Japanese and the Boer as evidence of its folly, the military and indeed many of the civilian leaders in Europe could not envisage a world without war, a bias reinforced by Social Darwinist ideas that societies had natural, hereditary enemies and that conflict among them was inevitable. The French military in the years before the Great War developed, for example, a theory of an 'eternal' Germany which was a deadly and determined enemy to France. In dispatch after dispatch French military attachés in Berlin warned their superiors that Germany was a dark and malignant force which would stop at nothing to destroy France.[29] The German military had a corresponding view of a France motivated by centuries of hostility and envy as well, of course, as by a desire for revenge after its recent defeat. Europe's leaders also saw war in less apocalyptic ways, as a necessary tool of statecraft. Recent history, the unifications of Italy and Germany in particular, seemed to show that war produced results at relatively low cost. Before 1914 too there were those in positions of power in Europe who saw merit in preventive war, to cut an enemy down to size before it was too late. In each of the major crises between 1905 and 1914 preventive war was considered seriously as an option by men in positions of power and in more than one country. It was not only the publics in

Europe who were being prepared psychologically for the Great War; it was their leaders as well.

Europe's military planners did their best to explain away the problems of the offence and the growing cost in terms of life. Recent wars had not, for example, been fought properly as the most advanced, European armies would fight them. 'Those savage encounters do not deserve the name of war,' a European general said of the American Civil War to Bloch, 'and I have dissuaded my officers from reading the published accounts of them.'[30] The British military argued that their losses in South Africa were an aberration due to the terrain and space of South Africa so there were no useful lessons for Europe. And the Japanese had after all won in their war with Russia, in the generally accepted view, precisely because they were prepared to attack and take much bigger casualties than the Russians. So the lessons were not that the attack no longer worked but that it had to be pressed harder, with more men.[31] Military history, which was treated with reverence in the European military as the source of wisdom about war, was called in to support the arguments.[32] The battles with clear outcomes, Leipzig in 1813 or Sedan in 1870 for example, tended, however, to get more attention than inconclusive or defensive ones. Cannae in the Punic Wars, when Hannibal defeated a much larger Roman force by bringing his wings to encircle the Romans, was a particular favourite of military colleges and it inspired General Alfred von Schlieffen of the German general staff when he drew up his plans to defeat France with a giant pincer movement around its armies.[33]

The reluctance of Europe's military to come to terms with the new ways of war can be explained partly by bureaucratic inertia: changing such things as tactics, drills, or training methods is time-consuming and unsettling. The very cohesiveness armies demanded of their officers led to a collective mentality where originality and loyalty were prized less than being a good team player. Moreover, the military were trained and were expected, as they are today, to solve problems and achieve results. It is psychologically easier to think in terms of action; in a war that means to take the offensive and force a decision. Before 1912, when Russia was still thinking in terms of a defensive war against Germany or Austria-Hungary or both, its regional commanders complained about the difficulty of making clear plans.[34] To attack was also bolder and more glamorous; sitting in a well-defended position or fortress seemed, well, rather unimaginative, even cowardly. 'The defensive', said a British major general in 1914, 'is never an acceptable role to the Briton, and he makes little or no study of it.'[35]

Yet we should not assume that the military planners before 1914 were unique in their dogged insistence on the offensive; history and the present are littered with examples of the striking capacity of human beings to overlook, minimise, or explain away evidence that does not fit comfortably with deeply held assumptions and theories. What some historians have christened the cult of the offensive grew stronger if anything before 1914 in the thinking of Europe's military planners (and to be fair in that of the Americans and the Japanese as well), perhaps because the alternative – that war had evolved to a point where there would be huge losses and mutual attrition without a clear victory for either side – was so unpalatable and so difficult to comprehend.

The future Supreme Allied Commander in the Great War, Ferdinand Foch, then an instructor at the French Staff College, worked out an elaborate proof in 1903 to show that two battalions of attackers would fire 10,000 more bullets than one battalion of defenders and so gain the upper hand.[36] Technology and the power of the defence would be overcome by making sure that the attackers outnumbered the defence by a large margin. Far more important than numbers, though, was the psychological factor: soldiers must be motivated through their training and by appeals to their patriotism both to attack and to die. They, and their generals, must accept large losses without losing heart. So, for example, bayonet drill was seen as important because it imbued the soldiers with the desire to attack.[37] And so were dashing uniforms: '*Le pantalon rouge, c'est la France!*' exclaimed a former War Minister when his successor proposed to take away the traditional red trousers and put the French soldiers into camouflage dress.[38]

Character, motivation, morale, these were widely seen before 1914 as the key ingredients for the success of the offensive. In stressing the importance of the psychological factor, the military drew on thinking current in the wider European society of the times. The work of Nietzsche or Bergson, for example, had awakened interest in the power of the human will. In his classic 1906 work on infantry training, Colonel Louis de Grandmaison, one of the leading French military theorists of the prewar period, said: 'We are rightly told that psychological factors are paramount in combat. But this is not all: properly speaking, there are no other factors, for all others – weaponry, maneuverability – influence only indirectly by provoking moral reactions ... the human heart is the starting point in all questions of war.'[39]

The offensive was also a way of papering over the fissures in societies and their armies by inspiring them to look to the common good and fight for a common cause. For the French army, which had been badly mauled in the aftermath of the Dreyfus affair and where morale among both officers and men was low, the offensive promised a way forward. When Joseph Joffre took over its command in 1911, he argued that thinking defensively had left the army with no clear sense of purpose: 'To create a coherent doctrine, to impose it on officers and men alike, to create an instrument to apply what I considered the right doctrine – that I held to be my urgent duty.'[40] In the armed forces as well as in the militaristic organisations of civilian society such as youth movements, the emphasis on inculcating such values as self-sacrifice went beyond giving fresh advantage to the offensive in war. It was also as much about overcoming the deficiencies of modern society and reversing what many, especially in the old ruling classes, felt to be the degeneration of the race and the deterioration of society. For those officers from those classes, a decreasing number but still an influential group, the attempt offered a way back to what they felt was a better society and one in which their values were paramount. That distinguished Victorian soldier Sir Garnet Wolseley, from the Anglo-Irish gentry, a class which shared many of the values of the German Junkers, advocated conscription for Britain on the grounds that it was an 'invigorating antidote' against the weakening effects of modern society: 'National training keeps healthy and robust the manhood of a state, and in saving it from degeneration nobly serves the cause of civilisation.'[41] When German civilians laughed at the military's discomfiture over the fraudulent Captain of Köpenick, Hugo von Freytag-Loringhoven, a leading military theorist and educator, wrote in disgust that such mockery was the product of 'pure egoism and a dependence on comfort and easy living'. Death in battle, he said, was 'life's ultimate reward'; in his many writings about war he painted pictures of German soldiers of the past marching willingly into the face of enemy fire.[42]

When they envisaged the wars of the future, Europe's military thought in terms of decisive battles to annihilate the enemy forces and they found comfort in past victories. 'The officer corps had formed its ideas through the study of the wars of Napoleon and Moltke', said Groener of his fellow staff officers in the German army, 'a rapid flowing of the army over enemy territory; the war's decision in a few, mighty strokes; a peace in which a defenceless enemy is forced to accept the conditions of the victor without demur.'[43] In Germany, too, the memories of the great victory at Sedan in 1870 were still fresh and they came to haunt the officer corps just as memories of the victory at the Tsushima Strait cast its shadow over Japanese naval thinking before and during the Second World War. Victories should not be partial ones which led to negotiation; they should be so decisive that the enemy was finished and accepted whatever peace terms were offered. At the level of tactics, the military planners continued to see cavalry in the same critical role that it had played for Napoleon when he threw it into the attack as the enemy infantry lines were wavering. The war in South Africa had underscored another use, as mounted firepower to manoeuvre round the enemy flanks, but the cavalry in European armies themselves resisted being used, as it was said, like American roughriders. 'It must be accepted as a principle', said the 1907 British cavalry manual, 'that the rifle, effective as it is, cannot replace the effect produced by the speed of the horse, the magnetism of the charge, and the terror of cold steel.'[44] There was talk too of breeding stronger and faster horses to gallop quicker across the fire zone.

Attack, battles, a war itself, all were to be fast and, crucially, short. 'The first great battle', an officer told the French parliament in 1912, 'will decide the whole war, and wars will be short. The idea of offense must penetrate the spirit of our nation.'[45] Talk such as this was whistling in the dark; European leaders, both civilian and military, knew that future wars could be long. It was now possible to keep their armies in the field for much longer than in the past when the impossibility of bringing up sufficient supplies indefinitely and the ravages of disease when large numbers of men were in camp had set natural limits to the length of campaigns. The European planners of the late nineteenth century feared long wars of attrition and they doubted the abilities of their own societies to endure them.

Some also suspected that war was escaping from their control and that it was increasingly difficult to bring it to a conclusion. Armies could win clear victories as Prussia and its allies had done at Sedan but the peoples might not accept the verdict. After Sedan the French people had mobilised themselves and fought on. In 1883, the great German military theorist Colmar von der Goltz published his influential work *The Nation in Arms* in which he analysed the new phenomenon of war between whole peoples and warned that it might take a long time and unacceptably high costs for one side to defeat the other. 'Only when, after the greatest of exertions on both sides, a crisis supervenes, followed on one side by inevitable exhaustion, [do] events begin to move more rapidly.'[46] A few years later, the elder Moltke gave his famous warning in the Reichstag about the age of Cabinet wars being over and the new age of the wars of peoples starting. Conservatives had particular reason to fear the results of war, whether economic bankruptcy, social unrest, or revolution. Shortly before the outbreak of the Great War, a leading Russian conservative, P. N. Durnovo, in a famous memorandum warned that war for Russia would almost certainly lead to its defeat and, inevitably, revolution.

In Austria-Hungary, two years earlier, Blasius Schemua, who was briefly chief of the general staff, had made similar arguments to his own government: people did not properly understand what war would bring.[47] Yet Schemua, unlike Durnovo, did not go on to urge his government to avoid war if at all possible. Rather, like his predecessor (and successor) Conrad, he argued for a more aggressive foreign policy and accepted with a mix of resignation and hope that war might come as a result. Perhaps the people of Austria-Hungary would recognise that crass materialism did not fulfil their spiritual needs; with the right leadership a new, more heroic age could dawn.[48] In Germany, many, perhaps a majority, of Germany's military leaders before 1914 doubted that a short decisive war was possible yet they continued to plan for such a war because they could see no alternative. In a war of stalemate and attrition Germany might well lose and they, as a group, fall from their pedestal within German society.[49] The striking absence of serious planning before 1914 for a long war, whether stockpiling materials or drawing up measures to manage the economy, is clear evidence that civilian and military leaders in Europe simply did not want to confront that nightmare of defeat and social upheaval.[50] At best they hoped that even a stalemated war of attrition would not last that long; on this the military across Europe agreed with Bloch, that the resources would run out and the war effort collapse. Like losing gamblers who saw no way out except to put everything on a throw of the dice or a spin of the roulette wheel, too many of Europe's military planners, like the Germans, suppressed their own doubts and put their faith in a short decisive war which would settle things one way or the other. Victory might produce a better, more united society; if they lost, they had been doomed already.[51] In 1909 a diplomat from Austria-Hungary fell into conversation with a Russian general at the St Petersburg Yacht Club. The Russian was looking forward to a good war between their two countries. 'We need prestige', he told the Austrian, 'to strengthen tsarism, which deserves a great victory like every regime.' When the two encountered each other again in the 1920s it was in the newly independent state of Hungary and the Russian was a refugee.[52]

If there were few such as Conrad among Europe's leaders before 1914 who wished for war, the great majority accepted that it was a tool that could be used and hoped it was one that could be controlled. As Europe suffered a series of crises in the decade before 1914 and as the alliances grew tighter, its leaders, and their publics, got used to the idea that war might break out. The members of the Triple Entente – France, Russia, and Great Britain – and Germany, Austria-Hungary and Italy in the Triple Alliance, came to expect that any conflict between two powers would probably bring in their partners. Within the alliance systems, promises were made, visits were exchanged, and plans were drawn up which created expectations, hard to disappoint in a moment of crisis. A general war, fought at the heart of Europe, was becoming thinkable. The impact of crises helped as much as militarism or nationalism to prepare Europeans psychologically for the Great War.

For the most part, they believed that they were justifiably defending themselves against forces that would destroy them, whether in Germany against encirclement, Austria-Hungary against Slav nationalism, France against Germany, Russia against its neighbours Germany and Austria-Hungary, or Britain against Germany. The alliance systems and the different alliances within each pledged support only in response to an attack on the partner. And in an age when public opinion and the public's willingness to support a war mattered, it was the concern of the civilian and military leaders to make sure that their countries were seen as the innocent parties in any outbreak of hostilities.

Once war came, however, the European powers were prepared to attack in their own defence. Almost every military plan drawn up by European general staffs before 1914 was an offensive one, carrying the war into the enemy's territory and seeking to achieve a quick and overwhelming victory. That in turn put pressure on the decision-makers during the increasingly frequent international crises to go to war quickly to seize the advantage. Under Germany's war plan in 1914, it needed to get troops into Luxembourg and Belgium before any declaration of war, and that indeed is what happened.[53] And the plans themselves contributed to the international tensions by bringing armed forces closer to war readiness and encouraging an arms race. What may seem like a reasonable way of protecting oneself can look very different from the other side of the border.

CHAPTER 12

Making the Plans

———

ermany's war plan, the most controversial to this day, was locked in an iron safe to which the chief of staff held the key, and only a small circle knew its strategic goals. After the Great War, as its contents gradually became known, the plan was the subject of much debate and has remained so ever since. Does it show that Germany wanted the Great War? That Germany's leaders were determined to dominate Europe? Is it the evidence needed to support the infamous clause in the Treaty of Versailles of 1919 which made Germany take responsibility for the war? Or does the Schlieffen Plan merely demonstrate that Germany, like all the other powers, was making military plans for eventualities that might never arise? That it was a plan made out of weakness and not strength, defensive in its intent against the aggressive encirclement of the Triple Entente? Such questions cannot be fully answered without knowing what the German general staff were thinking before 1914 but that will remain forever a matter of debate and speculation since the military archive in Potsdam was first partially looted by the Russians (some of those records have been returned since the end of the Cold War) and then destroyed by Allied bombing in 1945.

The answer to the questions about the Schlieffen Plan probably lies somewhere in between the different poles. Germany did feel itself to be outnumbered by its potential enemies, with the odds getting worse as time went by, yet its leaders too often thought in terms of a military

12. Fears of each other played a big part in the calculations of the European powers before 1914. Germany, despite its economic success, its strong army and its commanding position in the centre of Europe, felt itself to be surrounded by enemies which were waiting to tear it apart, along with its ally Austria-Hungary. Here the Russian bear advances from the east, while France strikes through Alsace and Lorraine while Britain – Perfidious Albion – steps across the Channel.

solution instead of exploring the alternatives to war. By 1912 the British had effectively won the naval race and there was an opportunity, indeed one which would be explored by both sides, to re-establish relations between Britain and Germany on a more friendly footing. Russia did not want a war if it could avoid one and was taking steps to lower tensions with Austria-Hungary. Hugo Stinnes was right when he said before the Great War that in a few years Germany would be the economic master of Europe. And with that economic dominance would come German cultural and political power. That has happened in the twenty-first century but only after the terrible detours of two world wars.

The German war plan was the work of many hands over many years and laid out in detail the mobilisation and movements of German forces in the event of war, and it was updated and revised yearly. To this day, however, it bears the name of General Alfred von Schlieffen, chief of the German general staff between 1891 and 1905, even though it was much modified by his successor the younger Moltke. The Schlieffen Plan, as we will call it for convenience, has produced polemical arguments worthy of the forum in Rome and hair splitting of an order to delight mediaeval scholars, which continue to engage academics today. Between the two world wars, Schlieffen's defenders argued that his plan was a work of genius finely tuned like a Swiss clock, which would have worked if Moltke, an inferior version of his famous uncle, had not meddled with the works. Had it been allowed to run as it had been designed in the first instance, it would have brought Germany victory in the first months of the war and so averted both the long-drawn-out agony of the Great War and Germany's humiliating defeat at its end. Yet, as others have rightly pointed out, the plan was a gamble based on unrealistic assumptions, among them that German forces were sufficient to the tasks it imposed and that the command structure and logistics for huge armies on the move were adequate. And perhaps its greatest flaw was that it did not allow for what the great German theorist of war, Clausewitz, called friction and the Americans call Murphy's Law; no plans on paper ever work as they are meant to once they encounter real conditions, and what can go wrong, will go wrong.

The man who tried to take such uncertainty out of war and who left his mark on both Germany's war plan and its general staff, was, like so many of the country's senior officers, from the Prussian Junker class. Schlieffen's parents came from two of its very grandest families, with huge estates and a web of family connections which gave them access to the highest political and military circles in Germany. For all their wealth and power, families such as those of Schlieffen lived surprisingly simple lives on clear, straightforward principles. They believed in hierarchy, hard work, frugality and a firm purpose in life, whether as the mother of children or an army officer. His parents and Schlieffen himself were also part of an early nineteenth-century reawakening of Lutheran Protestantism which wedded deep religious faith to a belief that Christ would save human beings if only they would open themselves to his message. Pietists such as the Schlieffens valued duty, comradeship, and a life of faith and good works. They were also deeply conservative, rejecting the scepticism of the Enlightenment and what they saw as the levelling ideas of the French Revolution.[1]

Shy and reserved, Schlieffen was an indifferent student and his early military career was undistinguished, although he gained a reputation for being conscientious and hard-working. Although he was in both the 1866 war between Prussia and Austria and the war with France in 1870–71 he saw little active service. One of his younger brothers died in action in 1870 and in 1872 he suffered a further loss when his wife, a first cousin, died shortly after giving birth to their second daughter. In 1875 his professional fortunes improved significantly when he was put in command of his own regiment. He also caught the attention of the elder Moltke who thought him a promising officer who might one day be his successor at the general staff. Since all appointments at the upper levels of the military were made by the Kaiser, it helped that Schlieffen managed to make a favourable impression on the future Wilhelm II and the members of his entourage.[2] In 1884 Schlieffen moved to the general staff and in 1891 Wilhelm, who was now Kaiser, appointed him as its head. Schlieffen was always careful to manage that relationship, ensuring, for example, that Wilhelm's side always won the annual autumn army manoeuvres and that his sudden interventions did not reduce them to a complete shambles.

When he received news of his appointment, Schlieffen wrote to his sister: 'A difficult task has been given to me, yet I am imbued with the firm conviction that the Lord … will not forsake me in a situation into which he has placed me without my effort or desire.'[3] Like his close friend Holstein in the Foreign Office, he drove himself and his subordinates hard. An aide once received a military problem to work out on Christmas Eve which had to be returned the next day.[4] Schlieffen was often at his desk by six in the morning and, after a ride in the great Berlin park, the Tiergarten, worked through the day until his dinner at seven. He would then continue work until ten or eleven in the evening and round out his day at home with an hour of reading military history to his daughters.[5] His staff and colleagues found him unfathomable and difficult. He would sit through presentations and discussions in silence but suddenly lob in a question from an unexpected angle. He gave out little praise but was frequently cutting and critical. He would have slept better, he told a young major who had nervously inquired after his well-being, if he had not read the major's report just before going to bed.[6]

Unlike the two Moltkes who preceded and succeeded him, Schlieffen had few interests outside his work. During a staff ride when one of his aides called his attention to the beautiful sight of a river in the distance, Schlieffen merely said 'an insignificant obstacle'.[7] His reading was largely focussed on military history, which he used as a means of discovering the formulas for victory and the ways to minimise, as much as possible, uncertainty in war. His favourite battle was Cannae, when Hannibal defeated the Romans, and a close second, Sedan, where the German confederation encircled the French and forced their surrender in 1870. From his study of history, he drew the conclusion that smaller forces can defeat larger ones if they outmanoeuvre them. 'Flank attacks are the essence of military history,' he laid down as infallible dogma.[8] He also concluded that only offensive plans could bring victory. 'The armament of the army has changed', he wrote in 1893, 'but the fundamental laws of combat remain the same, and one of those laws is that one cannot defeat the enemy without attacking.'[9]

What haunted him was the possibility of Germany finding itself in a war of attrition which left both sides exhausted and neither the victor. In an article he wrote after his retirement, he painted a grim picture of the country's economy collapsing, its industries unable to carry on and its banks failing, and its population reeling under privations. Then, he warned, 'the red ghost that lurks in the background' would destroy Germany's existing order. Although, as the years went by, Schlieffen grew increasingly pessimistic about Germany's chances in the next war, he set himself doggedly to working out a plan that could bring a quick and decisive victory. From his perspective there was no alternative. To rule out war was not only cowardly; the Germany he knew and wanted to protect was already under threat and a prolonged period of peace where its enemies, socialists and liberals, grew in power would destroy it as much as a war of attrition. Schlieffen went forward towards war because he could see no alternative.[10]

The problem confronting him was that the alliance between France and Russia which was developing throughout the 1890s presented Germany with the nightmare possibility of a war on two fronts. Germany could not afford to divide its forces to fight all-out wars on both of those fronts so it would have to engage in a holding action on one side while it struck hard on the other to gain a quick victory. 'Germany must strive, therefore', he wrote, 'first, to strike down one of these allies while the other is kept occupied; but then when the one antagonist is conquered, it must, by exploiting its railroads, bring a superiority of numbers to the other theatre of war, which will also destroy the other enemy.'[11] While he initially thought of striking first at Russia, Schlieffen had changed his mind by the turn of the century: Russia was strengthening its forts to give it a strong defensive line running north to south through its Polish territories and building railways which would make it easier to bring up reinforcements. Any German attack ran the risk of getting bogged down in sieges and then a long-drawn-out campaign as the Russians retreated into their vast interior. It made sense, therefore, for Germany to stay on the defensive in the east and deal with Russia's ally France first.

Schlieffen's plan was complicated in its details, involving as it did millions of men, but simple and bold in its concept. He would pour armies into France and defeat the French in under two months. The traditional invasion route into France (or route out, in the case of French troops) was in that part of France between the borders of Belgium and Luxembourg in the north and Switzerland in the south. The French loss of its two eastern provinces of Alsace and Lorraine had not changed that; indeed, it had given France a slightly shorter and straighter border to defend. Schlieffen ruled out that route. The disposition of the French armies and their war games showed that they would be expecting an attack in that direction. France, which had a long tradition of fortress building, had also reinforced its new border with two lines of 166 forts and put another ring of forts around Paris as well.[12] In 1905 the French parliament voted a further large sum to strengthen its frontier forts. That left Germany, if it chose to fight an offensive war, the option of coming at France on its flanks, either in the south through Switzerland – which had the disadvantage of being mountainous and prepared to defend its passes – or the Low Countries of Belgium, the Netherlands and Luxembourg with their flat terrain, good roads and excellent railway networks. The choice of the northern route was easy. Schlieffen determined on a giant flanking movement down into France to catch the French armies in a trap, just like Sedan.

In the event of war, some four-fifths of Germany's army would move west while the remaining fifth fought a defensive action against Russia in the east. In the west the attacking German armies on the great right wing, facing westwards out from Germany, would sweep through the Low Countries, with, as the saying had it, the sleeve of the German soldier furthest on the right brushing the Channel, and down into France towards Paris. The much smaller German left wing to the south of the great fortress at Metz below Luxembourg would confront the French armies in their expected attack. As the plan developed it became more elaborate and more rigid; by 1914 the German armies were expected to be in Paris forty days after the start of hostilities. If the French did as expected and attacked across their shared border into Germany, they would be moving further away from the main battle-fields. When they realised that the main German attack was approaching in the west behind their forces, the French, it was hoped, would be demoralised and caught in confusion as they tried to switch troops from their thrust into Germany to meet the challenge in the west (itself a dangerous move because they would still have the German left wing to their east). If all unfolded as it should in the Schlieffen Plan, the main French armies would be caught between the two wings of the German forces and surrender. In the meantime, the much smaller German force in the east would stand on the defensive waiting for the slow Russian mobilisation and expected attack westwards. By the time the Russians could approach the Germans in any numbers, the war would be over in the west and German troops could be sent eastwards to deal with them.

Schlieffen simply ignored or brushed away the broader implications. Under his plan, a conflict with Russia would automatically trigger a German offensive against France. (And the likelihood of such a conflict was growing in the first decade of the new century as Germany's ally Austria-Hungary was increasingly at loggerheads with Russia in the Balkans.) Schlieffen did not allow for the possibility of France choosing to stay neutral, whatever its treaty with Russia said (and France was only bound to come to Russia's aid if Russia were the innocent party). Furthermore, German troops would invade three small countries with which they had no quarrel. In the case of Belgium Germany would also be breaking an international undertaking which it had inherited from Prussia to respect Belgium's neutrality. Since Britain was one of the other signatories to the original treaty, it might well feel that it had an obligation to enter the war against Germany, a prospect which became more real as its relations with Germany worsened and Britain drew closer first to France and then to Russia. The Schlieffen Plan, and in this it remained the same until 1914, virtually ensured that Germany would fight on two fronts, thus risking a more general war.

In 1913 Moltke narrowed Germany's options still further by putting an end to the general staff's only alternative to the Schlieffen Plan, the Eastern Deployment Plan, which provided for a conflict with Russia alone, with France remaining neutral. And even if France had chosen to come to the aid of its ally, the Germans could have fought defensively in the west. The general staff, however, seems to have thought that too much time and effort was going into drawing up plans for a war which did not promise quick results. In 1912 a German war game confirmed this view: Germany's main offence against Russia ended inconclusively when the players taking the Russian role retreated into the interior of Russia.[13] So in the crisis of 1914, Germany had just one plan; whatever France chose to do Germany was going to attack it if threatened by a Russian mobilisation. A war which started in the east would almost inevitably spread to the west with whatever consequences that might follow.

There was a further risk built into German war plans which increased the likelihood of war. Of all the European mobilisation plans, the German was the only one that flowed seamlessly through from the first notices calling the armies up to war itself. By 1914 Schlieffen's heritage had produced a highly complex mobilisation process with eight clear stages. The first two warned the military in confidence that a state of tension existed so that they could take appropriate measures in preparation for mobilisation, such as cancelling leave. The third stage, the 'imminent threat of war', was to be announced publicly and the third and lowest category of reserves, the Landsturm, called up so that the higher level of reserves were ready to join the regular armies. Stages four and five were the actual mobilisation of Germany's forces as troops assembled in their units and were sent by trains to their designated places on the frontiers. The last three stages moved the troops from their trains into the 'attack march' across the borders and then to the final stage of the attack on the enemy.[14] The plans worked superbly in the summer of 1914 to that last stage of the attack. Although the troops could in theory be halted at the borders, the plans had such momentum built in that it was highly unlikely. And so the German government was deprived of the ability to use mobilisation as a deterrent or to have a cooling-off period, before the first blood was shed, when negotiations could take place.

As Schlieffen saw it, his duty was to devise the best military plan for Germany; he left diplomacy, which like most of the general staff he saw as useful merely for preparing the ground for war, to the civilians. Yet he did not see it as his responsibility to inform them in detail of what he was planning. Nor did he or his successor Moltke co-ordinate with the navy, the Kaiser's Military Cabinet, the commanding officers of the army corps who would be responsible for carrying out the plan or with the Prussian Ministry of War and the smaller ministries of war in the component states of Germany, which were responsible for the size of the army, its armaments and some parts of the mobilisation.[15] And although both Schlieffen and Moltke felt that they did not have enough troops to carry out the plan successfully, they nevertheless stuck to it without making a strong case to the Ministry of War for expanding the armed forces or challenging the increasing sums going into Tirpitz's navy.

The direction of Germany's overall strategy and the co-ordination of the key parts, both civil and military, of the government needed a Bismarck but there was no one of his stature before 1914. Bismarck himself was in part to blame for leaving behind a system where the lines of control were not clearly drawn and where there was little will to draw them. The only institution capable of providing co-ordination and overall direction was the monarchy but Wilhelm was not the man to do it. He was too lazy, too erratic and too easily distracted yet he guarded his position as the supreme authority jealously. When an admiral in the Ministry of the Navy suggested in 1904 that there should be a council including the senior army and navy leaders, the Chancellor, and the Kaiser to consider what Germany should do in case of a war simultaneously with Britain and France, he got nowhere.[16]

The civilian leaders, for their part, accepted the artificial distinction insisted upon by the military leadership that they had exclusive jurisdiction in all matters military, from war planning to the conduct of war itself. (This did not stop the military from intervening in areas which were not clearly military; the activities of the military attachés in Europe's capitals who reported directly back to their superiors in Berlin had long been a problem for the German diplomatic service.) Even when the decisions being made by the military had political or international impact, the German civilian leaders chose to stand aside. In 1900 Holstein, still the key figure in the Foreign Office, was told that Schlieffen intended in his plans to ignore international agreements such as the one guaranteeing Belgium's neutrality. After some thought, he replied: 'If the Chief of the General Staff, particularly such a pre-eminent strategical authority as Schlieffen, considers such a measure imperative, then it is the duty of diplomacy to concur in it and to facilitate it in every possible manner.'[17] The political leadership not only abdicated responsibility; it had little idea of what the military were thinking or planning. Bethmann, the Chancellor from 1909 to 1917, said after the Great War: 'During my entire tenure no type of war council was ever held, at which politics might have intervened in the military crosscurrents.'[18] The civilians would not have been supported in any case by the Kaiser had they challenged his military. In 1919, as he contemplated Germany's defeat, Bethmann said: 'No reasonably serious observer could have failed to appreciate with the utmost clarity the enormous perils of a two-front war. For the civilian side to have tried to foil a thoroughly thought-out military plan described as absolutely essential would have entailed an intolerable responsibility.'[19]

In 1905 Schlieffen was kicked by a friend's horse and laid up for several months. 'I am nearly 75 years old', he wrote, 'almost blind, half deaf and now have a broken leg too. It is high time I take my leave and I have good reason to believe that my repeated requests for retirement will be granted this year.'[20] He may have been making the best of the situation; the Kaiser, as he did so often, was losing faith in him and preparing to replace him.[21] Schlieffen left office on New Year's Day 1906. Even after his retirement, though, he continued to exert influence over the general staff whose members by and large revered him as one of Germany's greatest generals. As German troops moved towards France in 1914, General Groener wrote: 'The spirit of the blessed Schlieffen accompanies us.'[22] Perhaps inevitably, any successor would have seemed second best and the younger Helmuth von Moltke suffered from the comparison in his lifetime and after his death.

One morning in the autumn of 1905 Chancellor Bülow was taking his morning ride in Berlin when he ran into his old friend the younger Moltke. 'I was struck by the anxiety in his face.' The two men rode side by side and Moltke revealed that the cause of his concern was Schlieffen's retirement: 'His Majesty insists on making me his successor and everything in me dislikes the thought of this appointment.' Moltke felt, he told Bülow, that he did not possess the right qualities for such a demanding post: 'I lack the power of rapid decision; I am too reflective, too scrupulous, or if you like, conscientious for such a post. I lack the capacity for risking all on a single throw.'[23] He was probably right but he had the burden of a great name which he felt he ought to live up to and a sense of duty. Conrad claims that Moltke told him that he warned the Kaiser not to appoint him, asking: 'Does your Majesty really think that you can twice win first prize in the lottery?'[24] Moltke nevertheless accepted the post and held it until the autumn of 1914, when he was dismissed in the wake of the failure of the German plan, which had become as much his as Schlieffen's, to deliver victory. General Erich von Falkenhayn, the War Minister and Moltke's successor, said cruelly: 'Our General Staff has completely lost its head. Schlieffen's notes do not help any further, and so Moltke's wits come to an end.'[25]

Moltke was a big, heavy-set man who looked the picture of a bold Prussian general but in reality, as his conversation with Bülow shows, he was introspective and insecure. In some ways nicer, with broader interests, than his immediate predecessor – Moltke read widely, for example, played the cello, and kept a studio where he painted – he was also lazier and less forceful. He started well enough with a step that won approval from his fellow officers: he managed to stop the Kaiser from coming to the autumn manoeuvres and causing his usual chaos. (Wilhelm was amazed when Moltke told him that his side had always been allowed to win.)[26] Nevertheless Schlieffen himself and many of the senior officers saw him as an unsatisfactory choice for what was widely considered the key position in Germany. Moltke never mastered the work of the general staff in the detail Schlieffen had done and tended to let its various departments run in their accustomed fashion while he spent more time on managing the Kaiser and his Military Cabinet.[27] In the opinion of both the Russian and Austrian-Hungarian military attachés in Berlin, Moltke was not up to the responsibilities of his great office. 'His military character and technical expertise', the Austrian told Vienna, 'are not greater than an average officer.'[28]

The new chief of staff also had a fatalism, sometimes verging on outright pessimism, about the world which was fed by his fascination with one of the new occult religions that were sweeping through Europe at the time. His wife, a woman of strong character, stronger many said than Moltke himself, was a follower of Theosophy, that jumble of Eastern religion and spiritualism founded by Madame Blavatsky. In 1907 both Moltkes became disciples of the guru Rudolf Steiner, who talked about a new spiritual age dawning on the earth. (His Waldorf schools which stress developing the imagination and creativity still flourish today, much favoured by the middle classes.) While Moltke's wife welcomed the prospect of a new age, Moltke himself was gloomy: 'Mankind must first go through much blood and suffering before it reaches that far.'[29]

As chief of the general staff, Moltke contented himself with continuing much of his predecessor's work. The general staff, which was a large part of Schlieffen's legacy, continued to function smoothly. It had increased significantly during Schlieffen's tenure in its professionalism, cohesiveness and size, from fewer than 300 officers to over 800. There was a still larger number of officers out in the field who had circulated in and out on tours of duty and as a result shared the ethos of what was said in a contemporary joke to be one of five perfect institutions in Europe. (The others were the Curia of the Catholic Church, the British Parliament, the Russian ballet and the French opera.) Staff officers, said Harry Kessler, were 'reserved, cool, clear, hard, polite: all as if manufactured according to a model'. Dedicated, competent, hard-driving, they knew themselves to be part of an elite machine whose purpose was to ensure that Germany was prepared for war. The other key part of Schlieffen's legacy was not a final plan but an overall strategic direction and method of planning. Year by year in the two decades before 1914, the general staff tested its plans in field manoeuvres – some with thousands of men and their equipment – war games, or on paper. All were analysed for issues, gaps, or shortcomings, and the results cycled back into the planning process. On 1 April every year, each unit of the German army had its updated plans and orders. 'They have turned war', Kessler rightly said of the general staff, 'into a great bureaucratic business enterprise.'[30] And, as with other great enterprises, there was a danger that process was becoming more important than broader strategic thinking and that fundamental assumptions including the need for a two-front war went unexamined and unchallenged.

'If you believe the doctors', Salisbury once remarked, 'nothing is wholesome; if you believe the theologians, nothing is innocent; if you believe the soldiers, nothing is safe.'[31] With the formation of the Triple Entente, the German general staff saw a world where an offensive war was the only way for Germany to break its encirclement. Increasingly its military leaders also came to accept the possibility, indeed the desirability, of a preventive war. 'I consider it the duty of a responsible politician and general', wrote Groener unapologetically in his memoirs, 'that when he sees a war inevitably coming to trigger it at a moment that offers the most advantageous prospect.' In 1905, during the first Morocco crisis which came at a time when Russia was temporarily disabled, no one could guess for how long, by defeat and revolution, Germany's top leadership, Groener and Schlieffen included, seriously considered war on Britain and France.[32] The Saxon military representative in Berlin reported back to Dresden: 'A war against the allies France and Britain continues to be regarded as a possibility at the highest level here. His Majesty the Emperor has therefore ordered the chief of the general staff of the army and the chief of the navy staff to prepare a joint plan of campaign. His Excellency Count Schlieffen is of the opinion that all available forces of the land army should be marshalled against France and that the protection of the coast should be left largely to the navy ... The war will be decided in France, not at sea.'[33] In subsequent crises, over the Austrian annexation of Bosnia-Herzegovina in 1908, the second Morocco crisis in 1911, and the Balkan wars of 1912 and 1913 the German military leadership again considered preventive war but the Kaiser, who genuinely seems to have hoped to maintain the peace, refused to approve it. Ominously, the military grew increasingly impatient with what they saw as his weakness. War was on its way, Falkenhayn said, and neither the 'great "peace" emperor', nor the pacifists could stop it.[34]

Germany had the option, of course, of fighting defensively but its military never seriously considered it. A defensive war did not fit well with the existing strong bias towards the offensive or Germany's desire to break out of what it saw as its encirclement. In his last war game,

Schlieffen explored the possibility but, unsurprisingly, concluded that it was better to stick with an offensive plan.[35] Moltke simply followed the master. While he did not change the direction of Schlieffen's plan, however, he updated and modified it as such factors as technology and the international situation changed. Although he was later blamed for tinkering with a perfect plan and so causing Germany's defeat, he correctly saw that, as it stood, Schlieffen's last iteration of the plan, in a memorandum written in 1905 shortly before he retired, made certain assumptions that had not lasted: for example that Russia was not a threat because of its defeat and internal problems or that France was unlikely to mount a strong attack into the south of Germany. In the five years after Schlieffen's retirement, Russia recovered quicker than expected and continued its rapid programme of railway building and the French appeared to be thinking of an offensive into Alsace and Lorraine. Consequently Moltke left more of a force in the east and increased the size of the German left wing so that there would now be twenty-three divisions south of Metz and fifty-five on the right wing to its north. Although his critics later said that he had stripped the right wing of forces and so destroyed the Schlieffen Plan, he left the right wing as it was and found additional forces through using his reserves in the front lines.[36] He continued to expect, like Schlieffen, that Germany would fight a holding action against Russia and he too gambled on a massive and quick victory in the west. In a memorandum in 1911 Moltke wrote that once France's armies had been defeated in a few great battles the country would not be able to continue fighting.[37]

Like Schlieffen before him he assumed that the French government would recognise its hopeless situation and sit down with the German one and make a peace. Yet both men had lived through the Franco-Prussian War when the French nation had fought on after the defeat at Sedan. As a sceptical German general reportedly said in Schlieffen's time: 'You cannot carry away the armed strength of a great Power like a cat in a bag.'[38] In September 1914, when their armies had won a series of victories, the German generals discovered that they had no plans for an extended war if France refused to capitulate.[39]

Moltke made two further changes to Schlieffen's plans. Where Schlieffen had German forces cutting across the little piece of the Netherlands – the 'appendix' – that jutted down between Germany and

Belgium, Moltke decided to respect the neutrality of the Netherlands. Revealing the pessimism which existed side by side with his hopes for a quick offensive, he wrote in 1911 that if the war turned out to be longer than expected, the Netherlands would be a very useful 'windpipe' that would allow Germany to get supplies by ship from other neutral countries. That decision meant that the German armies heading towards France now had to squeeze through a much narrower space. The German First Army on the western end of the right wing, for example, had to manoeuvre 320,000 men with all their animals and equipment in an area six miles wide between the strongly fortified Belgian city of Liège and the Netherlands border. And the German Second Army, with 260,000 men, was in an area of the same size just to the south of Liège and in fact part of the German forces had to go through the city itself. If the Belgians decided to resist, Liège had the potential to delay, perhaps by weeks, the German advance. What is more, four railway lines which the Germans intended to use to move southwards met there and it was vital that they be seized undamaged. A United States army study commissioned after the Great War concluded that the destruction of one bridge, two tunnels and a steep part of the tracks would have prevented the Germans from sending any trains across northern Belgium towards France until 7 September, over a month after the start of the war. (In the event, demolition charges were laid but the orders of the Belgian commander to blow them were not carried out.)[40] Moltke therefore made a second change to Schlieffen's plan: German advance forces, moving even before any formal declarations of war, would take sudden swift action to seize Liège. So yet another pressure to set things in motion would confront the German decision-makers in 1914.

Bülow, according to his memoirs, raised the question of invading Belgium with both Schlieffen and Moltke but in neither case did the Chancellor push the matter. Nor, as far as he could ascertain, did the military and the Foreign Office ever discuss such an invasion.[41] In 1913, Gottlieb von Jagow, the new Foreign Secretary, learned about the planned violation of Belgian neutrality and raised a mild protest; when Moltke told him in spring 1914 that it would be impossible to change plans, Jagow apparently raised no further objections.[42] The Kaiser, perhaps feeling some apprehension about violating a treaty signed by his ancestors, tried to persuade the Belgian king, Leopold II, of the need for his country to be friendly towards Germany. Unfortunately he did so with his usual lack of tact, boasting to his guest, who was on a state visit to Berlin, about Germany's strength. 'Whoever, in the case of a war, was not for me', he told his shaken guest, 'was against me.' Leopold left in such a state of shock that he put his officer's helmet on back to front.[43] In the autumn of 1913 Wilhelm tried again, with Leopold's successor, his nephew Albert I (and also a relative of Wilhelm through his mother, a Hohenzollern princess), when the young king was on a visit to Berlin. Wilhelm assured Albert that a war with France was getting close and that it was all the fault of the French. At the state banquet at Potsdam, Moltke assured Albert that the Germans would 'overrun everything' and asked the Belgian military attaché what Belgium intended to do when the war started. The Belgian ambassador in Berlin was in no doubt as to the purpose behind Wilhelm's and Moltke's behaviour: 'They were an invitation to our country, face to face with the danger that threatened western Europe, to throw herself into the arms of the stronger, arms ready to open, to clasp Belgium – yes, and to crush her.'[44] The Belgians promptly informed the French and stepped up their own preparations for war. Although the German military professed contempt to their Belgian counterparts – 'chocolate soldiers' – German forces were now likely to face a Belgian army of some 200,000 as well as the obstacles of Belgium's great network of fortresses, including Liège.

Although the British firmly refused to commit themselves in advance, the German invasion of Belgium ran a high risk of bringing Britain into the war. Moltke took this seriously enough that he placed three and a half divisions in the north of Germany to guard against a possible amphibious attack.[45] He claimed, however, that he was not concerned about a British force arriving to support the French and the Belgians. 'We shall manage', he reportedly said to Jagow, 'the 150,000 British.'[46] Indeed, there was a long-standing and deeply held view among both the army and the navy leadership that, while the German navy was not yet ready to take on the British navy, Germany could use France to lure the British onto the Continent and defeat them on land.[47] The German military as a whole did not take the British army seriously, especially after its defeats in the Boer War. German observers noted that drill and field manoeuvres, something the German army took very seriously, were sloppy and disorganised in the British army.[48] After the Great War, an officer remembered: 'Every one of us was dying not only to defeat the English, but also to take every last one prisoner. How often was there talk about this in peacetime.'[49] If war came, the British navy, undoubtedly, would use the old British tactic of a blockade of Germany's ports but, as the German high command calculated, that would take time to bite into Germany's imports and, if all worked on land as it should, the war would be over before the blockade made a difference.

Germany's main concern, as it had been since its victory in 1871, was France. Thanks to the work of spies – one of whom, of course, was eventually uncovered in the Dreyfus affair – the reports of their attachés in Paris, and careful reading of the French press and parliamentary debates, the German military before 1914 had a pretty accurate portrait of French military strength. They also had worked out that the main French armies would be concentrated on the common border between their two countries – between a spot south of the western part of the Belgian border down to the Swiss border – and expected that the French would probably take the offensive in a war in the northern part of Lorraine.

What the Germans never settled in their own minds was how strong the French really were and, as important, how well they would fight. It was certainly evident that the French military had suffered considerable damage as a result of the Dreyfus affair. Political interference and the divisions within French society had left a demoralised officer corps and unruly troops and the Germans noted with satisfaction the frequent episodes of ill-discipline and even open mutiny in the years before 1914.[50] Moreover, the French, both officers and men, treated drill and military exercises in a casual off-hand manner. 'It makes a very peculiar impression', the German military attaché in Paris noted in 1906, 'when one occasionally sees a squad in the afternoon at Vincennes playing football instead of training.' In mock battles, troops who were supposed to be in a simulated firing line made themselves comfortable, sometimes reading the newspapers which they bought from the enterprising sellers who wandered about the designated battlefield.[51] On the other hand, the French did come from the same nation as the great Napoleon and his soldiers and they had a tradition of fighting well, with great courage. Even their lack of discipline perhaps gave them an advantage over the Germans. The same German military attaché shocked by the football at Vincennes also told Berlin: 'Perhaps the Frenchman can only be treated in this manner, and certainly in his case temperament, especially in the face of the enemy, replaces much that can only be cultivated by routine and discipline in people with more slowly flowing blood.'[52]

When it came to the Russians, the Germans formed a more coherent view and one which was more generally shared in Europe. Russia was a great power in name only and its armed forces were backward, poorly organised and badly led. The ordinary Russian soldier was tough and dogged in defence but such qualities were not suited for the modern war of the offensive. The officers, said a German counterpart who was an observer at the Russo-Japanese War, 'were devoid of morality, of any sense of duty or responsibility'. Russia's defeat at the hands of Japan had shown the Russian deficiencies in the starkest terms and it was clearly going to take the Russian military years to recover and rebuild.[53] Even when it became clear a few years after the Russo-Japanese War that Russia was recovering and re-equipping its armed forces, the German general staff still planned to leave an army of about thirteen divisions on its eastern frontiers with Russia and leave the bulk of the fighting in the east to its ally Austria-Hungary until the expected German victory over France allowed Germany to move more of its forces eastwards. The size of Russia and its underdeveloped railway network meant in any case that Russian armies would be slow to reach their own borders. As Moltke told Conrad in 1909: 'Our foremost intention must be to achieve a speedy decision. This will hardly be possible against Russia.'[54]

The German high command did not have a particularly high opinion of Austria-Hungary's fighting ability but they assumed that their ally was at least a match for Russia. In 1913 the German general staff made a damning evaluation of the armed forces of Austria-Hungary. The army was weakened by its ethnic divisions and the prolonged financial and political crisis with Hungary meant that it had not been able to train and equip sufficient soldiers. Over the preceding decades, little had been done to bring the armed forces up to date and although reforms had been started, these would not be complete until 1916. The railway network was entirely inadequate for the necessary movements of troops. The officers, a further German assessment noted in 1914, were dedicated and loyal to the crown but the general standard of the army was low.[55] The Germans nevertheless counted on Austria-Hungary to keep Russia occupied for the forty days or so that would elapse before France was defeated and German troops could head east to wrap up the war. As Schlieffen said in 1912 shortly before he died, 'Austria's fate will not be decided along the Bug but along the Seine!'[56]

Germany had an even lower opinion of the army of its other ally, Italy. 'The order of march defies description', said the German military attaché in Rome; 'every man does as he likes, and I saw stragglers in masses, troops who broke ranks without permission in order to buy things for themselves.'[57] Even more than the armies of Austria-Hungary, the Italian army suffered from a shortage of funds and manpower, outdated equipment, and inadequate training. Its senior officers were, with few exceptions, unimpressive and its junior officers resentful of their superiors, their conditions and their poor prospects for promotion. Not surprisingly morale was bad throughout the army.

It was not clear in any case that Italy would remain in the Triple Alliance. By 1902 its relations with France had improved markedly and Italy had secretly promised not to join any German attack on France. As a naval power itself in the Mediterranean, Italy had always preferred to be on good terms with the world's leading naval power Britain. At the same time Italy's relationship with Austria-Hungary, never good, was worsening. The two countries were rivals in the western part of the Balkans and in both there was talk and planning for war against the other. While Conrad in Austria-Hungary thought in terms of attack, the Italian general staff, aware of its own weakness, planned for a defensive war. Italy's promises of military support to Germany sat awkwardly with its growing concern about Austria-Hungary. In 1888, shortly after the Triple Alliance was formed, Italy had promised to send troops through Austria to support Germany along the Rhine against any French attack. Although Alberto Pollio, the chief of the Italian general staff between 1908 and 1914, was initially reluctant to keep the commitment, in February 1914 the Italian government confirmed that, should a war break out, it would send three army corps and two cavalry divisions to the upper Rhine to join the left wing of the German army. In the crisis that July the German military leadership continued to hope for the Italian troops, although with considerable reservations about Italy's reliability or usefulness.[58]

Germany could manage without Italy, and in the event did, but in the last decade before the Great War it badly needed to hang on to Austria-Hungary. In spite of periodic attempts to reach out to Russia or to Britain, it had few other possibilities for allies. The Ottoman Empire was too weak, and the smaller powers such as Rumania or Greece rightly tried to stay out of conflicts if they could. As the years went by and Germany faced a strengthening Triple Entente, its Dual Alliance with Austria-Hungary assumed greater and greater importance. That meant in turn that Germany had to back Austria-Hungary up when it got into confrontations in the Balkans or, more seriously still, with Russia.

Bismarck had always intended the alliance to be a defensive one and had resisted any attempts, such as binding military agreements, to make it something more. He had, though, allowed staff talks which gave Austria-Hungary to understand that Germany would send a substantial number of troops to the east for combined operations against Russia in the event of a Russian attack on Austria-Hungary. When Wilhelm II assumed the throne, he repeatedly signalled, at least rhetorically, enthusiasm for a closer relationship. After Schlieffen became the German chief of staff in 1891, however, the allies' strategic goals diverged as the Germans increasingly saw France as their main enemy while the Austrians continued to focus on Russia. At their first meeting, General Friedrich von Beck, the Austrian chief of staff, found Schlieffen 'taciturn and not very obliging'. Schlieffen for his part did not put much trust in the Austrians: 'Those characters will only desert or run over to the enemy.' In 1895 he cut back sharply on Germany's commitments in the eastern theatre of war and made it clear that Germany would only carry out a small attack on to Russian soil. Beck was furious, not least because the German decision nullified years of Austrian staff work.[59] From that point on, relations between the two general staffs were correct but cool and there was no detailed joint military planning.

It was in not until 1908–9, at a moment when it looked as though Austria-Hungary might go to war with Serbia over Bosnia, that the Dual Alliance shifted away from Bismarck's limited and defensive conception and became something closer, more offensive, and more dangerous for the stability of Europe. Wilhelm II again took a hand, telling Austria-Hungary: 'Emperor Francis Joseph is a Prussian field marshal and hence he has only to command and the entire Prussian Army will follow his command.'[60] More importantly, the militaries from Austria-Hungary and Germany started to talk again and from that point on until the summer of 1914 they exchanged letters and visits which served to build up an expectation that they would consult and act together to support each other in moments of crisis.[61] Schlieffen and Beck had by this time passed from the scene and their successors, Moltke and Conrad, established a warmer relationship. Conrad revered the elder Moltke and was to wear a medallion with the great German general's image around his neck during the Great War.[62] On New Year's Day in 1909 Conrad initiated an exchange of letters with Moltke to clarify what Germany would do if Austria-Hungary went to war with Serbia and Russia came in to support the little Balkan country. Austria-Hungary expected and Germany accepted that such a Russian move would bring the Dual Alliance between them into play and that Germany would be bound to come to Austria-Hungary's defence. (And of course if Russia attacked Germany the same would hold true.) Both sides wanted a commitment from the other to go on the offensive against Russia at the start of a war without undertaking to do the same itself. As a result the letters are full of expressions of respect and friendship and short on concrete promises. Since Conrad intended to destroy Serbia first even if Russia came into the war, he needed Germany to promise significant support in the north against Russia, in particular to undertake to attack southwards from East Prussia into Russian Poland while Austria-Hungary attacked northwards from Galicia. Moltke, of course, wanted to keep German forces in the east small so that he could concentrate on defeating France. In the end the two allies made promises they probably knew they could not keep: when war broke out, Austria-Hungary promised to attack Russia as soon as possible and Germany for its part promised to join in from the north even before the war against France was finished.[63]

Its geography meant that Austria-Hungary had to think of more possible scenarios for war than did Germany – against any of Russia, Serbia, Montenegro, Italy, or, after 1913, Rumania. And there was always the possibility that the enemies could combine: Serbia and Montenegro, with or without Russian support, or Serbia and Italy. Conrad himself was initially fixated on Italy but increasingly Serbia obsessed him as well.[64] He talked frequently of destroying 'the nest of vipers' in war and incorporating its territory into Austria-Hungary. To cope with the challenges facing Austria-Hungary, Conrad drew up several different war plans to cover the possible combinations of enemies and fronts, and to give himself maximum flexibility, he placed a force in each of the Balkans (Minimalgruppe Balkan) and Galicia (A-Staffel) up by the border with Russia, and set up a third force (B-Staffel) which could swing to support either of the others as needed. This was optimistic, given the state of Austria-Hungary's railways. Its railway lines down to its borders with Serbia were inadequate at best. In the north Russian railway building was outstripping Austria-Hungary's so that by 1912 it could run 250 trains a day to the border with Austrian Galicia where Austria-Hungary could manage only 152.[65] In addition, the Hungarians had insisted for nationalistic reasons on building a self-contained railway system within their state so that very few lines connected the Hungarian and Austrian railway networks. Although Conrad begged for an accelerated programme of railway building, objections from both the Hungarian and Austrian parliaments to spending the necessary money, especially if it would benefit the other half of the empire, meant that little had been done by 1914.[66]

Although Conrad and his general staff continued to work on their plans for a war against Italy and, in 1913, drew up plans for a war on Rumania, by 1914 they assumed that the most likely prospect was a war against Serbia which might well then bring in Russia. Like the other European military, the Austrian-Hungarian military also placed their faith in the power of the offensive and did not think in terms of a war of defence.[67] Yet Austria-Hungary's army when mobilised was under a third of Russia's; its spending was the lowest of all the powers, less even than that of Britain which had a much smaller army.[68] Conrad's plans were optimistic, indeed blindly so, given the state of the armed forces and the worsening international situation for Austria-Hungary as Italy and then Rumania drifted away from the Dual Alliance in the last years of the peace.

The military in Germany and Austria-Hungary continued to talk, perhaps to reassure themselves as much as anything, about their expected successful offensives in the east. Moltke quoted Schlieffen to Conrad to say that the German attack on France would really settle everything and that Austria's fate would be decided there and not in the east. Nevertheless, Moltke went on, the war in the east mattered greatly, representing as it did a showdown between the Teutonic races and the Slavs: 'To prepare for this is the duty of all states which carry the banners of Germanic *Kultur*.' Conrad in his reply noted that a crusade of this sort would not go down well in Austria-Hungary: 'We can hardly rely upon our Slavs, who form 47% of the population, to be enthusiastic about a struggle against their allies.'[69] Very little was done, however, by way of co-ordination or sharing information. On 4 August 1914, the day the Germans invaded Belgium, the German military attaché in Vienna said: 'It is high time that the two general staffs consult now with absolute frankness with respect to mobilization, jump-off time, areas of assembly and precise troop strength ...'[70] It was much too late for that, but the understanding between Austria-Hungary and Germany had served to turn a war in the Balkans into a general European one.

Russia, the object of Austria-Hungary's and Germany's attentions in the east, had a pretty good idea of what the war plans of the Dual Alliance were. By 1910 the Russians had seen enough of German army manoeuvres, railway building and military dispositions to come to the conclusion that the main German attack would go against France. While the Russians continued to overestimate, by about 100 per cent, how many troops Germany would leave in the east, they still felt confident that they would outnumber the Germans and that German strategy would favour Russia. If the Germans attacked, as expected, from East Prussia, they were likely to do so only as a quick thrust to keep the Russians off guard. Germany was then likely to withdraw its forces westwards behind the fortifications of the Masurian Lakes and wait to see what the outcome of the fighting in France was. That would give the Russians time to complete their slower mobilisation.[71]

The Russians had an even more accurate picture of the war plans of the other partner in the Dual Alliance. All the powers had spies as well as military attachés in each other's countries but Russia probably had the most successful one of all in Colonel Alfred Redl, an officer with the general staff of Austria-Hungary. He was recruited around 1901 by the Russians, who offered him the money he badly wanted and threatened to expose his homosexuality which in those days would have led

1. The Paris Exposition of 1900 celebrated peace and prosperity as well as Europe's dominance in the world. Its exhibits, though, hinted at some of the tensions which were going to bring an end to one of the longest periods of calm in Europe's turbulent history.

2. A family wedding in Coburg in 1894 shows the many connections that linked the European royal families. Most of those present were related to Queen Victoria, seated in the front dressed in her customary black. Her grandson, Wilhelm II, the ruler of Germany, is on the left and behind him, his cousin Nicholas, about to become the Tsar of Russia. Victoria's son, the future Edward VII, is just behind the latter while the future Tsarina, Alexandra, stands between Wilhelm and Victoria.

3. Although Wilhelm (right) was devoted to his grandmother Queen Victoria, he had an uneasy relationship with her son and successor Edward VII (left) whom he suspected of plotting to create a coalition against Germany. Edward reciprocated the mistrust and found his nephew tiresome.

4. Otto von Bismarck was the greatest statesman of his time. He not only created the new state of Germany in 1871 but he dominated the international relations of Europe.

5. The Emperor Franz Joseph of Austria-Hungary ruled over a diminishing and troubled empire at the heart of Europe (1848–1916). With a strong sense of duty, he lived a life marked by rigid routine and unceasing work.

6. For many, Robert Cecil represented the calm self-assurance of the British upper classes and of Great Britain itself. Rich, clever and well-connected, he was a Conservative prime minister three times between 1885 and 1902.

7. Jan (or Ivan) de Bloch was a Russian financier who understood that the new general war could lead to stalemate and costs which Europe's societies would not be able to bear.

9. Forceful and opinionated, Admiral John Fisher revitalised and reorganised the British navy to meet the growing challenge from Germany. He brought back much of the fleet into home waters and initiated the building of the huge dreadnoughts.

8. Alfred von Tirpitz was convinced that Germany needed a big navy in order to become a world power. Wilhelm II who shared his aspirations made him Secretary for the Navy in 1897 and Tirpitz set in train a massive naval building programme.

10. Dedicated to re-establishing French power and prestige after its humiliation at the hands of Bismarck and Germany, Théophile Delcassé was one of the longer serving and more competent foreign ministers of the Third Republic.

11. Nicholas II, Tsar of Russia, and his German wife Alexandra (centre), lived in seclusion with their children outside St Petersburg and continued to believe, in the face of growing unrest in the country, that the Russian people were still loyal to them. From left to right the daughters are Marie, Olga, Tatiana and Anastasia. The little boy is Alexei, heir to the throne, and suffering from the life-threatening condition of haemophilia. All were murdered by the Bolsheviks in 1918.

12. Bloody Sunday, as it became known, took place in January 1905 during the unrest in Russia which had been set off by military defeat in the war with Japan. As a peaceful procession including many workers marched towards the Winter Palace in St Petersburg to present a petition to the Tsar asking for reforms, troops fired on them.

13. Jean Jaurès, a leading French socialist, was one of Europe's most vociferous pacifists. He hoped to build the Second International of left-wing parties and unions into a strong and united force opposed to war. In the final crisis of 1914 he struggled until the very end for peace. A French right-wing nationalist shot him shortly before the outbreak of war.

14. Bertha von Suttner, an author and activist, was one of the most prominent figures in the growing international peace movement before the Great War. She worked tirelessly for disarmament and peaceful methods of settling disputes and persuaded the explosives magnate, Alfred Nobel, to leave a considerable fortune to endow the peace prize in his name.

15. All across Europe civilians were urged to emulate the military and demonstrate such qualities as discipline, sacrifice and patriotism. Scouts and cadets were a manifestation of militarism. These boys in the Balkans also show the growing readiness for war in that troubled part of the world.

16. Commemorating great figures and events of the past helped to fuel the intense nationalism which marked so many European societies before 1914. While it was often promoted by leaders anxious to overcome divisions in the nation, nationalism also came from the grass roots. Here locals in a small French town celebrate Joan of Arc despite the fact that she fought against France's new friend Britain.

17. General Joseph Joffre (left) became chief of the French general staff in 1911. Efficient and phlegmatic, he inspired confidence in the politicians. Like many, he was wedded to the idea of the offensive. His civilian companion at these army manoeuvres was President Raymond Poincaré (centre), an ardent nationalist.

18. Helmut von Moltke, chief of the German General Staff, was a pessimist and depressive who felt himself inadequate for the duties of his office. In the crisis of 1914 he suffered a breakdown.

19. Clever and competent, Vladimir Sukhomlinov was also vain and corrupt. While he helped to prepare the armed forces for war, he was over-optimistic about their capacity to take the offensive. In 1916 he was tried on charges of abuse of power and treason.

20. Alfred von Schlieffen gave his name to the Schlieffen Plan which assumed that Germany would have to fight a two front war against Russia and France. By violating Belgian neutrality, which Germany had promised to uphold, the plan significantly increased the chances of Britain entering the war.

21. Bernhard von Bulow was Germany's chancellor and in charge of its foreign policy from 1900–09. He managed, for the most part, to keep his difficult ruler Wilhelm under control but was unable to prevent the developing naval race with Britain.

22. In 1905, Kaiser Wilhelm rode through the narrow streets in Tangier which were lined with cheering crowds who may have hoped that he would save Morocco from French domination. His government, which hoped to break apart the very recent friendship between France and Britain, insisted on the visit against Wilhelm's better judgement.

23. Herbert Asquith was Liberal prime minister from 1908 to 1916. An adept politician who kept a divided party together and had to deal with an increasingly turbulent Britain and a rebellious Ireland, he left foreign affairs largely to Grey.

24. Like most leading statesmen in Austria-Hungary, foreign minister Alois Aehrenthal came from the aristocracy. Deeply conservative, he was dedicated to serving the emperor and maintaining Austria-Hungary as a great power.

25. Sir Edward Grey, British foreign secretary between 1905 and 1916, was a Liberal who believed in the Empire, a statesman who disliked foreign countries, and a prig who suspected everyone else of low motives.

26. Known as 'Apis' or the Bull on account of his formidable physique and character, Colonel Dragutin Dimitrijević was head of Serbian military intelligence in 1914. Deeply involved in secret Serb nationalist societies, he encouraged the plot to assassinate the Austrian Archduke Franz Ferdinand in Sarajevo.

27. The Bulgarian troops on their way to fight the Ottoman Empire in the First Balkan War of 1912 have little idea of what lies in store. Although the Ottomans were defeated by an alliance of Balkan states, the Bulgarian army was badly mauled.

28. Franz Ferdinand, the heir to the throne of Austria-Hungary, and his wife Sophie set out on a summer morning in Sarajevo on their last trip. The timing could not have been worse since it coincided with the Serbians' national day. In spite of warnings of terrorist plots security was lax. His death removed the one man close to the emperor who might have counselled against war. Gavrilo Princip (inset), a passionate Serbian nationalist, himself fired the shots that killed the royal couple. Because he was underage at the time he could not be executed. Sentenced to prison, he died of tuberculosis in 1918, unrepentant about the European catastrophe which he had helped to set off.

29. On 31 July 1914 Germany took the first step towards general mobilisation and so to making war on France and Russia. Standing outside the old arsenal in Berlin, a lieutenant announces the state of 'imminent threat of war' in the traditional way.

30. Count Franz Conrad von Hötzendorf saw his nation as surrounded by enemies, from Italy and Serbia in the south to Russia in the east. His recommendation in the several crises before 1914 was invariably for war.

31. Handsome, cultivated and exceedingly rich, Count Leopold Berchtold was Austria-Hungary's foreign minister from 1912–15. Although he preferred peace, he became increasingly convinced that Serbia had to be destroyed.

32. István Tisza was an Hungarian aristocrat who twice headed the government. Clever, proud and headstrong he was committed to maintaining Hungarian dominance over the large national minorities within Hungary's borders. Initially reluctant to support a war on Serbia he eventually swung round.

33. Like many other civilian leaders, Theobald von Bethmann-Hollweg, Germany's chancellor between 1909 and 1917 frequently chose to appear in military uniform. While he hoped for improved relations with Great Britain, he was not strong enough to overcome Wilhelm and Tirpitz and bring an end to the naval race.

34. In a scene that was repeated across Europe, families in Berlin wave goodbye to the men who have been called back into uniform. These troops from the reserves may well have been heading for the front lines, something the French had not counted on. As a result, French armies and the tiny British Expeditionary Force faced a stronger German attack than they had expected.

35. French nationalists had never accepted the loss of the provinces Alsace and Lorraine to Germany in 1871 and in Paris, the statue representing Strasbourg, the capital of Alsace, had been draped with mourning. As France and Germany go to war in August 1914, crowds rushed to the Place de la Concorde and tore off the black crepe.

36. Although much worse destruction was to follow, the burning of the great library at Louvain by German troops as they passed through Belgium was a symbol of what the Great War did to European civilisation. The act also helped to turn opinion in neutral countries, most importantly in the United States, against Germany.

to his disgrace. Redl spent the next years passing on to his Russian paymaster such top-secret information as Austria-Hungary's mobilisation plans and crucial details about its fortresses along the shared border between the Dual Monarchy and Russia in Galicia. He also betrayed Austria-Hungary's agents in Russia, who were sent to jail or executed.[72] Like other spies, the flamboyant Guy Burgess in Britain in the 1950s, for example, the surprising thing is that Redl was not caught sooner. Although he came from a modest middle-class background and ostensibly had to live on his army salary, he always had lots of money to throw around, on expensive cars, flats, clothes (after his unmasking he was discovered to own 195 dress shirts) or his young male lovers. In 1913 German intelligence tipped off their colleagues in Austria-Hungary to the existence of a traitor and provided the information that two envelopes full of banknotes were waiting for collection by someone called Nikon Nizetas at the main post office in Vienna. Redl duly turned up in disguise to claim them but even then he almost escaped discovery because the detectives who were staking out the post office lost his trail. They only picked it up again by accident but by the evening Conrad, the chief of staff, had enough evidence to send a party of officers to confront Redl and force his confession and subsequent suicide.[73] Although the high command in Austria-Hungary scrambled to change its secret codes and its railway timetables, it could not change its overall strategy before 1914. As a result of Redl's treachery, the Russians had an accurate picture of how and where Austria-Hungary would attack and of its plans against Serbia as well.

In making their own plans the Russians nevertheless faced a number of problems. To begin with Russia's size meant that its mobilisation took much longer than that of its neighbours to the west. When the call came, the average Russian soldier had to travel over twice as far as his German or Austrian counterpart. The Russian railway system was developing fast, thanks in part to French loans, and much of it was concentrated in the west, in the Polish territories and the European part of Russia, but it was still underdeveloped in comparison to those of Germany and Austria-Hungary. Most of the Russian lines, for example, were still single-tracked, which meant that running trains along them was slower. Only 27 per cent of its lines were double-tracked compared to 38 per cent for Germany. Nevertheless the German military estimated that by 1912 new railway building had helped to halve the Russian concentration time on the German border.[74] (If the Russians chose to attack into Germany they would face a problem, however, which also affected Germany coming east: Russian railway lines were of a wider gauge than in the rest of Europe so that everything, men and their equipment included, would have to be trans-shipped.) In 1914, even after the improvement in the railways, it still took twenty-six days fully to mobilise the armies in the European part of Russia while it took Austria-Hungary sixteen days and Germany twelve.[75] That discrepancy was going to put additional pressure on the tsar to order Russian mobilisation early in the crisis that summer.

Geography also gave Russia a rich choice of potential enemies. In the east, Russian territories remained under threat from Japan while in Europe Russia had a particular vulnerability in its Polish lands. While the dismemberment of Poland at the end of the eighteenth century had brought Russia a rich prize with good natural resources including coal and, by the twentieth century, with strong industries and a population of some 16 million Poles, it also created an exposed salient 200 miles from north to south which stretched 230 miles westward with German territory in the north and west and Austrian-Hungarian territory to the south. 'Our sore spot', a Russian military report called it.[76] Moreover, Russia had more potential enemies than even Austria-Hungary and its vast size created particular challenges when it came to situating its forces or moving them about. In Europe Sweden had been a threat on and off since the seventeenth century and the Russian general staff continued to count it as an enemy right up to 1914. Rumania, with its German king and its continuing resentment that Russia had taken part of Bessarabia in 1878, was potentially hostile. Russia had fought two wars with the Ottoman Empire in the nineteenth century and the two powers remained rivals in the Caucasus and the Black Sea.

Lecturers at the Russian War Academy had been stressing since 1891 that it was impossible to avoid a conflict with the Dual Alliance of Austria-Hungary and Germany and the Russian military increasingly focussed on this as their main challenge in the west. As a consequence they tended to interpret developments in those other countries in the most pessimistic fashion. When the military in Austria-Hungary failed to get the budget increases it wanted from parliament in 1912, the

Russians immediately assumed this was mere window-dressing designed to conceal a real increase in spending. The Russian military also believed, quite wrongly, that Franz Ferdinand was the leader of the war party in Austria-Hungary. The views of Russian diplomats who understood other countries better frequently did not reach the military and the tsar made little attempt to co-ordinate the different branches of his government.[77] What was generally accepted among the Russian leadership, however, was that any conflict in the Balkans could turn into general war.[78]

The Russian general staff, which tended to take the gloomiest possible view, saw as its worst case the Dual Alliance along with Sweden and Rumania attacking in the west while Japan and, improbably, China attacked in the east.[79] Then, so the military feared, the Ottoman Empire would probably join in as well and the Poles would take the opportunity to rise up. Even if the worst did not happen, its geography presented Russia, as it had done for centuries, with a strategic choice of whether to focus on Europe or the south and east. Although both Izvolsky, the Foreign Minister after the Russo-Japanese War, and Stolypin, Prime Minister until 1911, looked westwards, there were still influential voices among the Russian leadership arguing that Russia had a mission in the east and that Japan remained its chief enemy. In 1909 one of their number, Vladimir Sukhomlinov, became Minister of War.

Sukhomlinov remains, not without reason, a highly controversial figure but he did undertake a series of much-needed reforms in Russia's armed forces and thanks to him, Russia entered the Great War relatively well prepared. He improved training and equipment, updating armaments and creating dedicated units for such things as field artillery. In the five years before the Great War Russia also increased the number of men it was recruiting and training by 10 per cent so that in time of war it would be able to mobilise over 3 million men. Sukhomlinov reorganised the army's structure and command system and set up a new and more efficient system for mobilisation. In addition he pulled troops back from the western part of Poland to the interior of Russia, where they would be both safer from attack and more readily available to be sent eastwards if Russia's relations with Japan deteriorated again.[80] He tried as well to get rid of Russia's line of forts in the western part of Poland, which, as he pointed out, sucked up money and resources which could be better used elsewhere. This last caused a huge outcry. The tsar's cousin, the Grand Duke Nicholas Nikolayevich, who had conceived a passionate hatred for Sukhomlinov, opposed any destruction of the forts and he had many supporters in the military. The War Minister was obliged to back down.[81]

He had many enemies by this point and was going to accumulate more, partly because he was upsetting established traditions and vested interests, partly because of his own personality. He was devious, ruthless, and charming. Although he was short and bald, many women found him irresistible. His many detractors at the time and since accused him of everything from senility to corruption to high treason and a Russian diplomat described him as the evil genius of Russia. His own colleagues complained that he was lazy and incapable of sustained application to the many challenges facing him. General Aleksei Brusilov, one of Russia's most competent generals, said: 'Undoubtedly a man of intelligence, a man who could grasp a situation and decide upon his course very rapidly, but of a superficial and flippant mentality. His chief fault was that he would not probe things to the bottom and was content if his orders and arrangements made a show of success.'[82] Sukhomlinov was, however, as even his enemies recognised, a master of Russia's bureaucratic politics. He built networks of supporters throughout the army and the Ministry of War through the clever use of patronage and, as important, flattered the tsar on whom his continuation in office depended.[83]

Sukhomlinov, who was born in 1848 to a minor gentry family, had enjoyed an outstanding career as a soldier. He graduated near the top of his class from the Staff College and gained a reputation for bravery in the Russo-Turkish War of 1877-8. By 1904 he was a lieutenant general and in command of the important Kiev military district. When disturbances broke out in Kiev in the aftermath of the Russo-Japanese War Sukhomlinov was made governor-general of a larger area which includes much of today's Ukraine. He restored law and order and put an end to the disgraceful and brutal treatment of the local Jews, something for which many conservatives never forgave him. He also fell in love with a much younger and beautiful married woman who was going to become his third wife. Their affair and her subsequent divorce caused a considerable scandal, and her insatiable demands for luxuries were going to lead to the whiff of corruption that always surrounded Suk-homlinov. 'There is something about General Sukhomlinov that makes one uneasy,' said Maurice Paléologue, the French ambassador in St Petersburg. 'Sixty-two years of age, the slave of a rather pretty wife thirty-two years younger than himself, intelligent, clever and cunning, obsequious towards the tsar and a friend of Rasputin, surrounded by a rabble who serve as intermediaries in his intrigues and duplicities, he is a man who has lost the habit of work and keeps all his strength for conjugal joys. With his sly look, his eyes always gleaming watchfully under the heavy folds of his eyelids, I know few men who inspire more distrust at first sight.'[84]

Sukhomlinov survived in his position until 1915 because he had the tsar's support, but that was a mixed blessing. Nicholas was not an easy master and in his anxiety to guard his own power he played his minis-ters off against each other. Although he was an amateur in military affairs, he felt obliged as the supreme authority to intervene. In 1912 he ended a debate over tactics and strategy by saying, 'Military doctrine consists of doing everything which I order.'[85] Although Sukhomlinov tried to co-ordinate the advice the tsar received even he failed to reform the chaotic and incoherent nature of Russian decision-making and the military continued to keep crucial information from the civilian leaders. In 1912, for example, the Russian and French military agreed they would not pass on the details of their military understandings to the Russian Prime Minister.[86]

In the years immediately before the Great War Sukhomlinov was rethinking his earlier assumption that Russia needed to count Japan as its main enemy. Moreover, turbulence in the Balkans was turning Russian attention westwards and the French, not surprisingly, were encouraging this. What France needed if a general war broke out was an early Russian attack on Germany in the east to take the pressure off French forces in the west. Over the years the French used their financial hold over Russia, which badly needed foreign loans, to persuade their ally to make a commitment to such an attack. The French also did their best to ensure that their loans to Russia for railways produced lines that would take Russian forces swiftly to the German frontier. While the Russian leadership frequently resented French demands, by 1911 the Russian chief of staff had given way and promised France that Russia would attack Germany in East Prussia fifteen days after the start of a war. The promise was reiterated right up to the outbreak of war even though there were those in the Russian leadership who felt that it was a mistake and that Russia's interests lay in avoiding a war with Germany if at all possible and, in any case, concentrating on its chief enemy, Austria-Hungary.[87]

Russia had several strategic options on its western frontiers: to fight a defensive war until such time as it was ready to counter-attack, to focus its main attack on one of Austria-Hungary or Germany, or to take them both on at once. In retrospect a strong defence and retreat into Russia's vast spaces as a first stage, with a counter-attack in strength against one enemy at a time, made the most sense for Russia. By 1912 the military, though, had ruled out an entirely defensive war and had accepted the general European enthusiasm for offensive war. Russia's own most recent war, against Japan, seemed to show that the Russian forces had lost because they had sat waiting for the Japanese to attack. Russian military instruction, regulations and orders now stressed the power of the offence and paid little attention to the defence.[88] In the Black Sea too Russia was planning amphibious attacks on the upper part of the Bosphorus to gain control of the all-important Straits out of the Black Sea, this in spite of the fact that Russia's Black Sea Fleet was weak and it did not possess adequate troop transports.[89]

Between 1910 and 1912 there was an intense high-level debate within the Russian military about strategy. One group felt that it had a moral obligation to France to strike first and in strength against Germany. Sukhomlinov himself increasingly saw Germany as Russia's main enemy.[90] Their opponents wanted to concentrate on Austria-Hungary partly because it was Russia's main rival in the Balkans and partly because the Russian military felt confident that they could defeat its armies, something they did not consider possible with Germany. The Russian military had a healthy, perhaps obsessive, respect for German military strength and efficiency. They tended to compare themselves unfavourably in all respects against the Germans, something the Russian ruling classes had done for centuries.[91] A French officer was struck by how little hatred of Germany there was among his Russian colleagues.[92] Furthermore, in spite of Redl's spying, the Russians under-estimated how many forces Austria-Hungary would put on the border in Galicia and assumed that Russia would have a significant advantage. The Russians also expected that Austria-Hungary's nationalities problem would finally become too much for it and that the Slavs and Hungarians within the empire would rebel when war broke out.[93] Finally, and this weighed heavily with the Russians, if the Austrians, who were expected to attack fifteen days after the start of a war, had initial successes, Russia's unhappy Polish subjects might well take heart and rise up themselves. As the Russian chief of staff said to his French counterpart in 1912: 'Russia cannot expose herself to defeat at the hands of Austria. The moral effect would be disastrous.'[94]

At a meeting in February 1912, presided over by Sukhomlinov, the military hammered out a compromise 'to direct the main forces against Austria, while not generally rejecting an offensive into East Prussia'.[95] As a Russian general later said, it was 'the worst decision of all'.[96] Russia's new military plan, 19A, provided for mobilisation and an early attack against both Austria-Hungary and Germany and divided up Russian forces so that in neither theatre would Russia have a decisive advantage. In addition, while its enemies would be fully ready by the sixteenth day after the start of war, Russia would have only 50 per cent of its forces in place. By attacking in the north, Russia created a further and, as it turned out, dangerous problem for itself since its two northernmost armies would have to go on either side of the fortified German positions at the Masurian Lakes in East Prussia.[97] Although there was meant to be a variant, Plan 19G, where Russia remained on the defensive against Germany and sent most of its forces to attack Austria-Hungary, that plan was never worked out in detail. Nor did the military have plans for mobilising against just one enemy. In the crisis of 1914 Russia's leaders were to find that they were committed to an attack on both Germany and Austria-Hungary.

Among Russia's military before 1914 there was widespread concern about the new plan. Although he said publicly that Russia was ready for war, in private Sukhomlinov himself was pessimistic about Russia's preparations.[98] Officers in the different military districts pointed out problems with logistics and supplies and raised concerns about the difficulties of communications and control over what was going to be a very extended Russian front. In the only war game to test even a part of Plan 19A, held at Kiev in April 1914, participants noticed that the stress on speed meant that Russia would have to attack both Austria-Hungary and Germany long before it was ready, and that there were no detailed plans worked out for the war or for co-ordinating actions among Russia's several armies.[99] It is hard to explain the mix of fatalism and optimism with which Russia's leadership approached the likelihood of war. Perhaps the only explanation is that they dared not stay still; the memories of the near revolution of 1905–6 were too near. If the regime faltered it might die anyway. The war which so many thought was inevitable might offer a way out: victory could bring its salvation. And perhaps defeat was better than dishonour and the betrayal of the promises which Russia had made to its ally in the west.

For France the Russian alliance was essential to its survival. Without the threat in the east, Germany would be able to turn all its force on France. Yet the French never quite freed themselves from doubts about Russia. Would Russia resume its old relationship with Germany? When the tsar met the Kaiser at Potsdam in 1910, for example, many in France worried that the two were going to make some form of alliance. And even if Russia were a secure ally, would the Russian forces be able to take on the most professional army in Europe? In the years immediately after the Russo-Japanese War, the French were all too aware that Russia's armed forces were shattered and incapable of engaging in a war. The Russians, understandably from their point of view, were also not anxious to make binding military commitments to the French. From the first convention of 1892, the French had pressed for details of troop numbers and dispositions while the Russians had stalled. The French worried about the slowness of Russia's mobilisation despite its new railways and found the Russian military lackadaisical and vague. As a French staff report said: 'As a result of her endless winters and interminable communications, Russia attaches no importance to time.'[100] The Russians for their part were irritated by the French insistence on precision and detail, even by what they saw as over-punctilious French manners.[101]

What the French wanted most of all and finally got was a promise from the Russians to attack Germany early while France was doing the same but both sides were cagey about both numbers of troops committed and timing. While the general staffs of each country held regular talks and there were frequent exchanges of visits by both military and civilian leaders, neither side ever entirely trusted the other. The Russians only told the French about their war plan, 19A, in 1913, a year after it had been approved, and implied that more Russian forces were being committed to the front against Germany than was the case.[102] In the last peacetime meeting in the late summer of 1913 between the French chief of staff, Joffre, and General Iakov Zhilinski, his Russian counterpart, the two men, said a Russian observer, were like card players: 'Zhilinski, not having enough trumps, was keeping them out of play and Joffre tried in one way or another to extract them from his partner.'[103]

While Russia, like the other powers, had to think of at least two potential enemies, France was focussed, as it had been since 1871, on Germany. It is true that Italy was potentially hostile but relations had improved to the point that the French assumed from 1902 onwards that Italy would remain neutral in any war. That meant that France could move the bulk of its forces northwards to face Germany. For much of the period before 1914, the French military had thought primarily in terms of a defensive war: of letting the German attack wear itself out on France's fortifications along the border with Alsace and Lorraine until the French saw the opportunity for a counter-attack. From 1892, as well, the French also took into account the possibility that Germany might violate Belgian neutrality and send its right wing down through the western part of Belgium and little Luxembourg. So France strengthened its great fortress at Verdun, some sixty kilometres from each of the German, Luxembourg, and Belgian frontiers, and in successive plans moved more forces northwards.

When it came to the details of French strategy and the management and direction of the army, matters were much more complicated. Republicans had a long-standing suspicion of the military but in their attempts to get firm civilian control had set up a system which was incoherent. Leadership of the army was divided between the Ministry of War and the general staff and mechanisms to co-ordinate the two simply did not work. The frequent changes of government in the Third Republic did not help: in 1911 alone France had three different Ministers of War, one who was not there long enough to meet his own senior officials, and the third, Adolphe Messimy, who survived for over six months and actually managed to set in train some reforms which brought about a more unified military command. The Radicals who had dominated the government since the Dreyfus affair had carried out their purges of officers suspected of right-wing views and had left army morale, already low, even lower.

Politics also affected decisions about such matters as length of service and training. Those on the left, with the revolutionary national guards in mind, wanted a citizens' army where men received a certain amount of training but remained civilian in their outlook. The right wanted a professional army where the men became good soldiers, loyal to their officers and their unit. The left wanted a greater use of reserves on the grounds that this involved all of society in its own defence; the right, and that included many of the senior army officers, despised reserves who, they felt, had been so contaminated by their time in civilian society as to be useless as soldiers. Even uniforms got caught up in the political struggles over what sort of army France should have. Messimy wanted to follow the example of the other European armies and put the men into uniforms that would make them difficult to see on the battlefield. The right seized on this as a threat to France's glorious military traditions. The new uniforms, said the right-wing press, were appalling and against French taste. The caps looked like something jockeys would wear and the officers were to be dressed like stable boys. It was an attempt, said the conservative *Echo de Paris*, to destroy the authority of the officers over their men and the Masonic lodges that had plotted it would no doubt be pleased. (It was on this occasion that a former Minister of War exclaimed that red trousers were France.) In any case, said one member of parliament, the army should use up all its old uniforms before wasting money on new ones. Funding for new uniforms was approved shortly before the war started, too late to help the French soldiers who went off to fight in their bright uniforms.[104]

Weak leadership and political interference exacerbated other problems in the army. Training was out of date and ineffectual; the quality of staff officers was low; and key tactics, such as how to manoeuvre men on the battlefield, had not been agreed upon or taught.[105] It was in these circumstances that a group of young reformers started to push the doctrine of the offensive as a way to reinvigorate the army. As in other parts of Europe, they also reflected the concerns of their own wider society, that its members were becoming decadent and were no longer prepared to die for the nation. In the case of France, memories of the past cast a shadow too, whether the *furia francese* of the French troops that had so terrified the Italians in the fifteenth century, the furious charges of French revolutionaries at the Battle of Valmy in 1792 which had scattered the appalled forces of the conservative powers, or the troops who had fought and died under Napoleon to conquer Europe. In the general staff, the head of the Planning Bureau, Colonel Louis de Grandmaison, inspired his young colleagues with his prescriptions for saving France. Defensive war was cowardly; only the offensive was worthy of a virile nation. Battles were in their essence moral contests where will and energy were the deciding factors. French soldiers must be so inspired by patriotism that they would do as their ancestors had done and pour across the battlefields to overwhelm the enemy. A sudden rapid attack, said Grandmaison in the course of two famous lectures that he gave at the French war college in 1911, paralyses the enemy. 'He can no longer maneuver and very quickly becomes incapable of all offensive action.'[106] In 1913 the authors of new tactical regulations for the French army accepted the Grandmaison view, saying firmly, 'Only the offensive yields positive results.' The bayonet, said the regulations, was still the key weapon for infantry; drums and bugles would sound; and officers would lead the charge.[107] 'Success will come', the regulations promised, 'not to the one who has suffered the least losses, but to the one whose will is the steadiest and whose morale is the most highly tempered.'[108] And, as in the other powers, the French military assumed that the next war would also be short. Neither they nor the government made preparations to stockpile supplies, mobilise industry or defend natural resources, many of which were in the north near the German border.[109]

In 1911, in the midst of a crisis with Germany, Messimy was given authority by the government to reorganise the Ministry of War and the army command structure to give the chief of staff greatly increased powers both in peace and in war. At the same time he appointed a new chief of staff and, among the several possibilities, he chose the one most firmly wedded to the doctrine of the offensive. General Joseph Joffre was both bourgeois – his father was an artisan who made barrels – and a solid republican. His nickname was the 'crab', both because of his size and because he did not move to the right. Politicians liked him and he knew how to manage them well. In character he was calm, even in moments of great crisis, stubborn, and determined to get his way. His career, like him, had been solid rather than dazzling. He had made a name for himself as an efficient and dependable officer in a couple of France's colonial wars and as the director of the army's Engineers. He was good at routine and paperwork and he understood logistics and communications. His supporters, and they were many, admired him for his capacity to make decisions and for his confidence, even in dark moments, that France would win out. In 1912 he was asked whether he thought about the possibility of a war. 'Yes, I think about it,' he replied, 'I think about it all the time. We shall have it, I will make it, I will win it.'[110] His opponents found him rather inflexible and unimaginative. As one of France's most distinguished generals said: 'He submits to events. He does not create them ... Joffre knows nothing of strategy. To organize transportation, resupply, to direct armories – that's his business.'[111]

By the time that Joffre took over the French had a pretty good idea that the Germans were planning to come through Luxembourg and at least part of Belgium. The French Foreign Ministry at the Quai d'Orsay and the French national police had both managed to break German codes (although rivalry between the two meant that often they did not share information).[112] In 1903 a spy who called himself the Avenger and who may have been a German staff officer, handed over early versions of Schlieffen's plans. He appeared in heavy disguise with bandages wrapped around his head so that only his moustaches stuck out. This seemed theatrical to some and there were concerns about whether his information was really a German plant to deceive the French.[113] French agents also got copies of a later plan in 1907 and German war games for 1912 and 1913 and they got the last German plans before the Great War, which came into effect in April 1914. The Russians sent the French a warning a month later that their sources indicated that Germany would try to crush France first and then turn to Russia.[114] There was plenty of other evidence over the years of German intentions: Germany strengthened its fortresses in the northern part of its border with France: it enhanced its railway network in the Rhineland on the borders with Belgium and Luxembourg; in small German towns it built new railway platforms, so long that they could only be useful for the military to detrain with all their men, horses and equipment; and they improved the bridges across the Rhine at Düsseldorf which would make it easier for them to move into the north of Belgium.[115]

The French military took the prospect of an invasion of Belgium seriously. With each revision of their military plans they increased their forces north and north-west of Verdun.[116] In the years just before the war, French staff officers made regular tours of Belgium and in 1913 a question in the final exam at the military college at St Cyr asked how French and Belgian forces could block a German invasion.[117] (Belgium itself in a doomed attempt to stay out of a major conflict stepped up its defence preparations and made it clear that it would defend itself against any power that violated its neutrality.) Joffre did ask his own government whether he could move troops into Belgium before Germany did but was turned down. He would only be allowed to move into Belgium once the Germans had made the first breach of its neutrality. The French government did not want to alienate the British whose help, particularly at sea, they saw as essential in a war with Germany and important too in reassuring French public opinion that France would eventually triumph.[118]

In considering German plans for Belgium, however, the French made one assumption that was to prove nearly fatal for them in 1914. They did not think that the Germans would be able to send a large force west of Liège, between the west bank of the Meuse River, which ran north and south, and the sea. Here the French military were caught by their own biases against reserve soldiers; they assumed that, like them, the German officers would consider reserves too close to civilian life to make effective soldiers and would use them for less important tasks such as guarding communications lines, besieging fortresses, or running facilities such as hospitals behind the lines but not in the front lines.[119] The French knew accurately how many soldiers Germany had under arms and that was enough for Germany to defend against a French attack along the Alsace-Lorraine border and to carry out an invasion of Belgium east of Liège and the Meuse but not enough for a large sweep further into western Belgium. In fact the German military, with some reluctance, had come round to the idea of putting reserves in the front lines. Evidence that they were in fact planning to move west of the Meuse mounted up immediately before 1914. By 1910 the French noticed that the German army was buying lots of cars, particularly useful for western Belgium, which was flat with good roads.[120] In 1912 French military representatives in Brussels were warning that Germany appeared to have the capacity to go directly against Liège or swing west.[121]

Here Joffre's stubbornness proved to be a handicap: he simply refused to accept evidence which went against what he had decided. And when counter-evidence turned up – a document, for example, apparently written by the German general Erich Ludendorff saying that Germany would not use its reserves in the front lines – he chose to believe it.[122] Nor was he alone. Many in the French military, swept away as they were by the glamour of the offensive, continued to focus on attacking Germany in the hopes that they could settle the war early and quickly before the Germans could mount a serious offensive of their own. Early in 1914 when several senior French generals gave their opinion that a German invasion of Belgium would go west of the Meuse, Joffre again refused to listen.[123] He went into the start of the Great War believing that he would have to fight the Germans in Lorraine and further north, in eastern Belgium and Luxembourg, and that his forces were roughly equal to Germany's for the opening battles. If the British forces arrived in time, he thought, they and the French together would outnumber the Germans.[124] He left some 190 kilometres, stretching westwards to the Channel from the French town of Hirson just south of the Belgian border, unprotected. If the British sent their forces – which was not at all a sure thing – they would cover the gap. In August 1914, four British divisions were to find themselves in the path of two German armies.[125]

Joffre's plan, the infamous XVII, was approved by the government at the start of May 1913 and the details were worked out and distributed to the army a year later. He moved still more of the French forces northwards to the Belgian border and positioned them so that they could deal with a German attack coming from eastern Belgium, Luxembourg or northern Lorraine. The plan, he said firmly in his memoirs, was to get the troops into their concentration positions, not a plan for making war. He gave each army commander alternatives for their operations against the Germans but otherwise gave no indication about what he was thinking beyond saying that he intended to attack somewhere in the north-east once all the French forces were in their assigned places. In August 1913, at a meeting with the Russians, he promised that France would start its offensive operations against Germany on the morning of the eleventh day after mobilisation.[126] If he ever contemplated a defensive strategy on France's frontiers, he did not share those thoughts at any point before 1914.

Army manoeuvres in 1912 and 1913 showed significant problems in co-ordination and command. As Joffre said in his postwar memoirs: 'Many of our generals proved themselves incapable of adapting to the conditions of modern war.'[127] The French army also was seriously behind the other European powers, and in particular Germany, in heavy field artillery. This was the consequence of years of poor planning, lack of resources and disagreements among the soldiers themselves over how the big field guns should be used, whether to soften up the enemy before the attack or in support of the waves of attacking soldiers. Perhaps making the best of a bad job, the French army inclined towards the latter. The advocates of the offensive also argued that the battles of the future were going to be so fast moving that heavy artillery, which was cumbersome to move, would not be able to keep up and that therefore it was better to rely on light field artillery, where France was strong, and use the heavier artillery where possible to support the troops as they attacked.[128] Joffre allowed nothing to shake his conviction that French forces must attack.

In the last years of the peace, France experienced a surge of confidence and, at least in Paris, a marked display of nationalism. Its army under Joffre had been given a new sense of purpose. Over in the east its great ally Russia appeared to have recovered from its setbacks in the war with Japan and the subsequent near revolution and was modernising fast. 'Belief in the power', said Messimy, 'and above all the wealth of soldiers in the numberless Russian army was well established in 1914 in our opinion, whether the army headquarters or the general public.'[129]

The war plans of all the major continental powers reflected a deeply rooted faith in the offensive and an unwillingness to contemplate the alternative of a defensive strategy. Joffre's plan, for all its vagueness, at least had the merit of flexibility. In the case of both Germany and Russia, their plans determined that they would open fronts against two enemies at once and their military had not provided the option of fighting one or the other. Nor had their politicians seen fit either to inform themselves of the contents of their military plans or to insist on providing direction. The war plans of the continental powers by 1914 were dangerously like hair triggers which only a slight disturbance could set off. While the military and their plans did not by themselves cause the Great War, their infatuation with the offensive and their acceptance of war as both necessary and inevitable made them put pressure on those making the decisions in moments of crisis. The military advice almost invariably tended towards war. Moreover, the lack of communication between the different sets of leaders meant that the military drew up plans which turned out to limit, sometimes in dangerous ways, the choices before the decision-makers.

The series of crises which occurred between 1905 and 1913 not only fuelled the arms race and the preparation of military plans and arrangements; they served to tighten the ties that bound each of the two loose alliances together and to deepen the gulf between them. By the summer of 1914, more promises had been made and obligations and expectations were heavier. In the minds of decision-makers and, often, their publics, the memories and apparent lessons left by the crises also became part of their thinking in that fatal summer and their weapons were to hand to deal with those who had wronged them in the past.

CHAPTER 13

The Crises Start:
Germany, France
and Morocco

I n the early spring of 1905, Kaiser Wilhelm was on one of his frequent cruises, this time southwards down the Atlantic coast on a German steamer, the *Hamburg*. He had contemplated visiting Morocco's Atlantic port of Tangier before he steamed on into the Mediterranean through the Straits of Gibraltar so that his guests could get a taste of the Muslim world but had thought better of it. The *Hamburg* was too big to go into the harbour and, if the seas were rough, it would be difficult to get into smaller boats for the trip to shore. Tangier itself was said to be full of anarchist refugees from Europe. Furthermore, at a time when the status of Morocco was becoming an international issue, he did not want to do anything of a political nature. His government, however, had other ideas. Bülow, the Chancellor, and his close adviser in the Foreign Office, Holstein, felt that the time had come for Germany to show that France could not have Morocco all to itself. The representative of the Foreign Office on board was under strict instructions to get the Kaiser on shore. Bülow sent a flurry of encouraging telegrams from Berlin and planted stories of the planned visit in the German papers to make it difficult for the Kaiser to back down.[1]

When the *Hamburg* anchored off Tangier on the morning of 31

March, a stiff wind was blowing from the east. A local German representative clambered aboard in full cavalry uniform, including spurs, as did the commanding officer of the French cruisers which were anchored nearby. The wind dropped slightly and the Kaiser sent the chief of his bodyguard ashore to assess the situation. When he heard that the landing was not too difficult and that there was a huge and excited crowd waiting, Wilhelm finally agreed to make his visit. As he landed he was received by the sultan's uncle and representatives of the small German colony in Tangier and a white Arabian was led up for his ride through the town's narrow streets to the German legation. The horse shied at the sight of Wilhelm's helmet and he had trouble mounting and staying on. As the Kaiser and his party rode between ranks of Moroccan soldiers, hundreds of flags waved in the breeze, women ululated and showered them with flowers from the rooftops while wildly excited tribesmen fired guns in all directions.[2]

At the German legation the small diplomatic corps and local dignitaries, including, the Germans were later dismayed to learn, the great bandit El Raisuli, waited to greet the Kaiser. Although Bülow had repeatedly advised to him to stick to polite formalities, Wilhelm got carried away in the excitement of the moment. To Kaid Maclean, the former British soldier who was the sultan's trusted adviser, he said, 'I do not acknowledge any agreement that has been come to. I come here as one Sovereign [sic] paying a visit to another perfectly independent sovereign. You can tell [the] Sultan this.'[3] Bülow had also advised his master not to say anything at all to the French representative in Tangier, but Wilhelm was unable to resist reiterating to the Frenchman that Morocco was an independent country and that, furthermore, he expected France to recognise Germany's legitimate interests there. 'When the Minister tried to argue with me', the Kaiser told Bülow, 'I said "Good morning" and left him standing.' Wilhelm did not stay for the lavish banquet which the Moroccans had prepared for him but before he set off on his return ride to the shore, he found time to advise the sultan's uncle that Morocco should make sure that its reforms were in accordance with the Koran. (The Kaiser, ever since his trip to the Middle East in 1898, had seen himself as the protector of all Muslims.) The *Hamburg* sailed on to Gibraltar, where one of its escort ships accidentally managed to ram a British cruiser.[4]

13. The powers appear to be sitting peacefully around a hubble-bubble pipe which represents the conference at Algeciras to settle the first crisis over Morocco in 1905–06. In fact, they have guns to hand and bowls of explosives. The rivals France and Germany are beside each other while Britain represented by John Bull looks warily at Germany which it suspected, with reason, of trying to destroy the new British friendship with France. Spain and Italy who both want their own colonies in North Africa are waiting and Uncle Sam looks disapproving.

Back in Berlin, Holstein collapsed under the strain of waiting to see if the visit would go off. A few days later he wrote to a cousin: 'There will be moments of tension before the business is over.'[5] That was an understatement. In the first place the Kaiser's visit to Tangier represented a German challenge to France's ambitions in Morocco. At the very least, Germany wanted an Open Door policy in Morocco or, if it could not get equal access there for its businesses, compensation in the form of colonies elsewhere, perhaps in Africa. The Kaiser's visit was about much more than the fate of Morocco, though: Germany was trying to regain the position it had enjoyed under Bismarck as the power at the centre of

Europe's international affairs. Bülow and Holstein wanted to ensure that no major international agreement, whether a colonial one or one affecting Europe itself, could take place without Germany's involvement and approval. They saw a chance as well to destroy the Entente Cordiale between Britain and France and perhaps even the alliance between France and Russia and so break out of what they saw as Germany's encirclement in Europe. The Tangier visit therefore set off a major international crisis with talk of war between Germany and France, joined, quite possibly, by Britain. Public opinion became inflamed in all three countries which in turn limited the leeway of the decision-makers for manoeuvring. Although the Moroccan issue was eventually settled in 1906 by an international conference at Algeciras, it left in its wake a dangerous residue of mistrust and resentment among both the publics of the nations involved as well as their leaders. 'A generation ago', reported Britain's representative in Munich in 1907, 'the German public took but little interest in general foreign affairs … Things have changed since then.'[6]

From the point of view of the Germans, the spring of 1905 was as good a time as any to seize the initiative internationally. The Entente between Britain and France was very new – it had only been signed the previous April – and had not yet been tested. Russia had been embroiled in the war with Japan since the start of 1904 and was in no position to come to the aid of its ally France. Moreover, the Dogger Bank incident of the previous October had shown how easily Russia and Britain might find themselves at war. The United States might be friendly and surely would support the same sort of Open Door policy in Morocco as it had proposed in China. The Kaiser had temporarily forgotten about the Yellow Peril and was now envisaging a future German–Japanese–American alliance straddling the world. Roosevelt, however, made it amply clear that China was one thing, Morocco another; he was not prepared to explain to his citizens why an Open Door policy in Morocco, which most of them had never heard of, was an American interest.[7] Shortly after the Kaiser's visit to Tangier he told the German ambassador in Washington: 'I dislike taking a position on any matter like this unless I fully intend to back it up; and our interests in Morocco are not sufficiently great to make me feel justified in entangling our Government in this matter.'[8] This was not the only instance of the German leadership getting things wrong during the first Morocco crisis.

Holstein, who took a harder line than either Bülow or the Kaiser, was convinced that he could use the crisis to put relations between France and Germany on a footing satisfactory to his country. The British had obligingly demonstrated at Fashoda that the French would respond to firmness; France had backed down and later come looking to its old enemy for friendship. He hoped to show the French, however, that they could not count on the British. 'The French will only come closer to the idea of rapprochement with Germany', he wrote during the later stages of the Morocco crisis, 'when they have seen that English friendship ... is not enough to gain Germany's agreement to the French seizure of Morocco, but rather that Germany wishes to be loved on its own account.'[9] France could be then made to renounce publicly all hopes of regaining Alsace and Lorraine and recognise that the Treaty of Frankfurt, which had ended the Franco-Prussian War, was permanent. Bringing France to heel would have a salutary effect on Italy as well; it had been showing disturbing signs of friendship with France.[10]

A test of strength with Britain was also overdue. The year before Germany had given Britain notice that it wanted to negotiate on all outstanding colonial issues but the British would only agree to discuss Egypt where Germany had some rights as one of Egypt's many international lenders. If the Entente between Britain and France were broken, Holstein believed that an isolated Britain would be more amenable. Moreover, Holstein noted in the summer of 1904, Germany could not afford to appear weak: 'If we submit to this brusque rejection of our *legitimate* demands on the part of England, then we can be certain that every demand made by Germany, or at least by the present German government, no matter where or to whom, will be rejected with similar nonchalance in the foreseeable future. The significance of the German–English negotiations goes far beyond the present case.' He made the same argument over Morocco: 'Not only for material reasons, but even more to preserve her prestige, Germany must oppose the intended annexation of Morocco.'[11]

In his more optimistic moments, Holstein dreamed of a complete reshuffling of the key players on the international scene. Those in both France and Britain who thought the Entente Cordiale a mistake would attack it at the first sign of trouble. France, Holstein confidently hoped, would cave in and leave Britain and become Germany's ally. Russia would then have little alternative but to follow suit; Germany had offered it a treaty, unsuccessfully, in 1904, but the time would come again. In the meantime the Kaiser appeared to have a good relationship with his cousin, the tsar, to whom he was sending helpful letters on how to conduct the war with Japan. In the long run, Europe might see a Triple Alliance of Germany, France and Russia which would isolate Britain much as France had been isolated after the Franco-Prussian War.

The situation in Morocco itself cried out for international involvement. The young sultan still did not have control of large parts of the country and foreign nationals, including Germans, repeatedly called out for reforms to bring law and order. In May 1904 El Raisuli had brazenly kidnapped a rich American businessman, Ion Perdicaris, and his stepson from their luxurious villa just outside Tangier and carried them off on horseback into the interior. Roosevelt promptly dispatched a part of the American navy which happened to be cruising in the South Atlantic to Morocco's Atlantic coast and demanded the release of the two men, a position he kept to even as evidence emerged that Perdicaris might no longer be an American citizen. The Republican Party convention in Chicago that summer gave Roosevelt a rousing cheer for his message to the sultan: 'We want either Perdicaris alive or Raisuli dead.'[12] A thinner and sunburned Perdicaris appeared, along with his stepson, after a large ransom had been paid. In December that year the sultan, concerned that international interest was putting his country's independence in jeopardy, suddenly ordered all foreign military missions to leave. Although the French forced him to cancel the order and agree to receive a French mission in his capital, Fez, the state and future of Morocco were now a matter of international discussion. In any case, as people now recalled, under an agreement signed at Madrid in 1880 by all the major European countries as well as the United States, the powers had equal rights in such areas as trade in Morocco.

The French had not helped their own case by ignoring this in a high-handed manner, especially where Germany was concerned. In June 1904, for example, they had made a loan to Morocco and arranged special preference for themselves on future ones. That autumn France signed an agreement with Spain to divide Morocco into spheres of influence without informing or consulting Germany. Delcassé, the powerful French Foreign Minister, who was worried that part of the motive behind the German naval build-up was to challenge France for power in the Mediterranean and North Africa, was adamant about not negotiating with Germany over Morocco. One adviser, who had urged him in vain to talk to the Germans, complained that Delcassé simply called the Germans 'swindlers': 'But, in heaven's name, I'm not asking him for an exchange of romantic words or lovers' rings but for a business discussion!'[13] The French ambassador in Berlin sent repeated warnings back to Paris that France was playing with fire in Morocco and that Germany was becoming seriously annoyed. When the French mission arrived in Fez in January 1905 to press the sultan for concessions that would give France much greater power in his country, the Germans encouraged him to resist.[14]

In order to further what he saw as Germany's interests, Holstein was prepared to risk war although his preference was to avoid it. (Apart from anything else, at the outbreak of hostilities Wilhelm would assume military command which, said Holstein, 'since he is entirely incapable militarily, must lead to horrible catastrophes'.[15]) Again the timing was good from Germany's point of view: the French army was still badly demoralised after the Dreyfus affair; Russia was at war in the east; and the British army was recovering from the Boer War and in any case small. As for the British navy, as the German joke went, it had no wheels and so could not help in a quick land war.

Neither the Kaiser nor Bülow was as sanguine. The Kaiser, perhaps realising that his instincts were correct that the visit to Tangier would be trouble, was firm that he did not want a war. He blamed Bülow for forcing him to go, writing angrily that summer: 'I landed because you wanted me to, in the interests of the Fatherland, mounted a strange horse in spite of the impediment that my crippled left arm caused to my riding, and the horse was within an inch of costing me my life, which was your stake in the game! I had to ride between Spanish anarchists because you wished it, and your policy was to profit by it!'[16] The Chancellor himself had no regrets about trying to force France and Britain apart but he tended to think that a softer approach to France, offering to recognise its position in Morocco in exchange for compensation for Germany elsewhere, perhaps, might work as well as a bludgeon to break the Entente. And, as he pointed out to Holstein as the crisis was reaching its culmination in February 1905: 'Neither public opinion, Parliament, Princes, or even the army will have anything to do with a war over Morocco.'[17] In a speech to his generals in January on the occasion of Schlieffen's retirement, the Kaiser had made a similar point: 'I tell you here, however, that I will never fight a war for the sake of Morocco. In saying this I am relying on your discretion, and it must not leave this room.'[18] For the outside world, the divisions within the top German leadership were not apparent and the disagreements over tactics among them which led to Germany veering between bullying and reasonableness only deepened foreign mistrust of Germany's intentions.

The British did not behave as Holstein had hoped. 'The Tangier incident', said Edward VII, 'was the most mischievous and uncalled-for event which the German Emperor has ever been engaged in since he came to the Throne. It was also a political theatrical fiasco, and if he thinks he has done himself good in the eyes of the world he is very much mistaken.'[19] *The Times* called the visit 'a great political demonstration' and its correspondent in Vienna suggested that Bülow had seriously underestimated British determination to stand by France.[20] The strong anti-German faction in the Foreign Office had no doubt that the sudden German interest in Morocco was an attempt by Germany to destroy the Entente and urged that Britain must stand firm. From the Admiralty, Fisher warned that Germany was probably after a port on Morocco's Atlantic coast, something that would be 'vitally detrimental' to Britain. 'This seems', Fisher told Lansdowne, the Foreign Secretary, 'a golden opportunity for fighting the Germans in alliance with the French ...'[21] He was not going to be the only one over the next few months to talk about the possibility of war.

Lansdowne was more restrained: he would contemplate war, but only if vital British interests were threatened.[22] He shared, however, the general suspicion in London of Germany's motives. Even before the crisis started he had been concerned by reports that Germany was looking for closer relations with both Britain's ally Japan and the United States and he saw German diplomacy as generally motivated by a desire to obstruct Britain wherever possible. 'We shall, I have little doubt', he wrote to the British ambassador in Berlin that April, 'find that the Emperor avails himself of every opportunity which he can make in order to put spokes in our wheels.'[23] Lansdowne's policy as the crisis deepened was simultaneously to back the French but keep them from reckless moves. On 23 April he and his Prime Minister, Balfour, sent a strong message to Delcassé offering 'all the support we can'.[24] In May, Lansdowne agreed with Paul Cambon, the French ambassador in London, that the governments of Britain and France should be prepared to work together if the situation got worse, adding later that there should be 'full and confidential discussion'.[25] In spite of French pressure for a clearer commitment, even a defensive alliance, the Conservative government never went further than that.

Others did, however. From Paris, the strongly anti-German and headstrong British ambassador, Bertie, told a colleague in the Foreign Office, 'Let Morocco be an open sore between France and Germany as Egypt was between France and ourselves,' and went on to assure Delcassé that Britain would give France all the support in its power. There is evidence too that Fisher shared his views on the time being ripe to have a go at Germany with Delcassé.[26] That April, Edward VII cruised the Mediterranean on his yacht, making a point of visiting only French ports and extended his stay at the North African port of Algiers by several days. On his way back to Britain, he spent a week in Paris, where he met Delcassé twice.[27] Later that summer, when Edward visited the Continent to go to one of his favourite spas in Austria-Hungary, he pointedly avoided calling on the Kaiser. A Berlin paper had the British king saying: 'How can I get to Marienbad without meeting my dear nephew? Flushing, Antwerp, Calais, Rouen, Madrid, Lisbon, Nice, Monaco – all extremely unsafe! Ha! I simply go via Berlin: then I am sure not to meet him!'[28] In retaliation, the Kaiser refused to let his son the crown prince accept an invitation to visit Windsor in the autumn.[29]

After the Tangier visit the Germans kept the pressure up. They sent a mission to Fez to discuss a German loan and to encourage the sultan to resist French demands for reforms or greater control of his country; they put pressure on Spain to repudiate its earlier agreement with France to divide Morocco into spheres of influence; and they told the other powers including the United States that they wanted an international conference on the future of Morocco.[30] Through secret contacts with the French Prime Minister, Maurice Rouvier, the Germans also let it be known that they wanted Delcassé dismissed.

The Germans had always seen Delcassé as their main enemy in the French government and by the spring of 1905 they were becoming worried that he was about to make his position even stronger by offering to mediate in the continuing conflict between Russia and Japan. On 27 May the Japanese fleet had destroyed the Russian fleet at Tsushima and both sides were looking for a way to make peace. Delcassé, with his experience and the advantage of coming from a country with good relations with each of the combatants, would be an obvious choice and was himself eager to take the task on. Rouvier had naively let the Germans know this and they were appalled at the prospect. If Delcassé pulled it off, it would be a triumph for him and for France; it would tighten still further France's relationship with Russia; and it might well lead to another triple alliance, of France, Russia and Britain, or perhaps, with Japan, a quadruple one.[31] As Delcassé himself later said, his position in the French government would have been unshakeable if he had acted to settle the Russo-Japanese War.[32] Bülow wrote to his ambassador in Washington asking him to persuade President Roosevelt to offer his services as a mediator and so forestall a French or a British initiative. The Morocco question, Holstein said, was 'infinitesimal' by comparison with this prospect of success on the international scene for France or Britain.[33]

At the end of May the German government sent a series of increasingly forceful messages to the French government: Delcassé must go or they could not answer for the consequences.[34] Rouvier was panicky and crumbling fast. He had been worrying all year about a possible German surprise attack which, in his view, would lead to defeat and revolution in France just as it had in 1870–71. That February he had met with leading members of the French parliament's army and finance committees and asked for their assessment on the country's state of military preparedness. 'There is nothing,' they told him, 'no ammunition, no equipment, no stocks of provisions, and morale in the army and in the country is in an even worse state.' Rouvier had burst into tears.[35] Delcassé had not helped his own position by refusing to negotiate directly with the Germans or consult his colleagues. On 19 April his Morocco policy was attacked in parliament; speaker after speaker, from the right to the left, urged him to negotiate. Jaurès pointed out that Delcassé had started the crisis by demanding concessions from the government of

Morocco long before the Kaiser's Tangier visit: 'You ought also have taken the initiative in offering explanations and beginning negotiations.' Delcassé now suggested direct talks to the Germans but Bülow, scenting victory, insisted on an international conference. Delcassé resisted and insisted that Germany was bluffing and that Britain was ready to offer its support if war came.[36]

His colleagues did not agree and by the first week of June Rouvier had caved in to German demands for his dismissal. At a Cabinet meeting on 6 June Rouvier, with unanimous support, told Delcassé that he was dismissed. In a forgivable act of revenge, Delcassé handed the Prime Minister a file of cables deciphered in the Quai d'Orsay which showed Rouvier's secret dealings with the Germans.[37] When the news of Delcassé's dismissal came out, rumours of war ran through the French parliament and the salons in Paris and lots of men went out to buy heavy woollen socks and boots in preparation for mobilisation.[38] In London there was consternation and shock. Lansdowne wondered whether the Entente Cordiale would survive; the French, he told Bertie, appeared to be on the run.[39] In Berlin, by contrast, there was jubilation. 'Delcassé was the instrument chosen by our enemies to destroy us,' Bülow exclaimed and the Kaiser gave him the title of prince on the day of the dismissal, although Bülow himself always denied there was a connection.[40] 'Our cleverest and most dangerous enemy', said Holstein, 'has fallen', and 'our friend' Roosevelt was now mediating the end to the Russo-Japanese War so that neither France nor Britain would be able to gain any international prestige from that affair.[41]

In their triumph over the French, the Germans then overplayed their hand. Rouvier, who had decided to be his own Foreign Minister, offered direct negotiations and promised that Germany would have compensation in the form of colonies elsewhere. Bülow, with Holstein urging him on in the background, continued to insist on an international conference, to show France that it was alone among the powers without support from either Russia or Britain when it came to Morocco. 'If', said the Kaiser later, 'I had been told about this, I would have gone into it thoroughly and that idiotic Conference would never have taken place.'[42] Although the French reluctantly agreed to the conference at the start of July, German pressure had put Rouvier's back up; later that year he said to a close associate: 'If Berlin thinks it can intimidate me, it has made a mistake.'[43] French public opinion was also swinging towards greater firmness with Germany and an appreciation of the value of the Entente Cordiale. The future ambassador to Russia in 1914, Maurice Paléologue, then at the Quai d'Orsay, wrote at the end of July: 'There has been a recovery: no more fear, no more cowardice, no more bending to the German will; the idea of war is accepted.'[44]

The new mood in France reassured the British and Lansdowne let Paul Cambon, the French ambassador in London, know that the British would support the French on Morocco 'by the means which France considered best'.[45] While France and Germany quarrelled for the rest of the summer over the agenda for the conference, the British set out to demonstrate their friendship towards France to the world. Ships from the British navy paid a visit to the French Atlantic port of Brest during Bastille week in July. A month later French ships received a lavish welcome at Portsmouth and there was a huge banquet in Parliament's Westminster Hall.[46] The British and French navies may have started confidential talks about strategic co-operation that summer as well.[47]

At the end of 1905, the British government fell and a new Liberal government under Henry Campbell-Bannerman took office. Holstein, who continued to press for a hard line against France, took this to be good news since he believed that the Liberals wanted friendship with Germany.[48] Yet again, he was wrong in his assumption. Campbell-Bannerman, who was already a sick man, largely left Britain's foreign affairs to Sir Edward Grey, the new Foreign Secretary, who had no intention of making a sudden break with Lansdowne's policies. Like Lansdowne, Grey believed that maintaining the Entente was of crucial importance for Britain; if it were broken, France, Germany, and Russia might well come to terms, leaving Britain isolated once again. Like his predecessor as well, Grey wanted to support France against Germany without encouraging the French to behave rashly. He promised Cambon 'benevolent neutrality' but also noted that British public opinion, which was strongly in support of France, would not support a war with Germany over Morocco.[49] (Grey found the appeal to public opinion convenient as much when he did not want to do something as when he did.) As far as Germany was concerned, he would not make any sort of deal with it before the conference opened in spite of conciliatory messages from

Berlin. Bülow's fine words, he remarked, 'butter no parsnips, and if the parsnips are to be buttered, it must be done at the Conference. If that ends in conclusions not averse to the Anglo-French Entente there will be a real clearing of the sky …'[50]

The man who now was responsible for Britain's foreign policy and would remain so until his resignation in 1916 was, in the view of the Kaiser, 'a capable sort of country gentleman' and for once he was not far wrong. Sir Edward Grey came from one of those old, well-connected, landowning families which for so long had played a leading role in British society. As a young man, he inherited a baronetcy and a comfortable estate, Fallodon, in the north-east of England, as well as his Liberal politics. He was conservative in instinct but a moderate reformer, who accepted that new classes and new leaders were bound to change the face of politics. He feared, like many of his contemporaries across Europe, that a major war would bring revolution but hoped for a peaceful evolution. 'There are unpleasant years before us,' he remarked in 1911, adding that 'we shall work through to something better, though we who have been used to more than £500 a year may not think it better'.[51]

Although his contemporaries at the famous old English school of Winchester considered him endowed with great talent, he showed much more interest in fly-fishing on the nearby River Itchen than in his studies. His time at Winchester left its mark, though: Grey was always proud to call himself a Wykehamist and he kept something of the decent and clever schoolboy who was shocked at dishonesty in his adult life. 'German policy', he once commented, 'seems to have been based upon a deliberate belief that moral scruples and altruistic motives do not count in international affairs.'[52] Like other high-minded people, he failed to recognise when he himself was being ruthless or devious, perhaps because he took for granted that his motives were pure. Naturally reserved, he also learned to hide his emotions; his colleagues were invariably impressed by his calmness during crises. It helped too that Grey looked like a Roman senator and spoke firmly but with restraint. Lloyd George, the Welsh radical from a humble background, felt that Grey went a long way on his appearance: 'His striking physiognomy with the thin lips, the firmly closed mouth, and the chiselled features give the impression of cold hammered steel.'[53]

From Winchester, Grey went to Balliol College at Oxford, another forcing house for future leaders, but again he did a minimum of work. He was sent away for a period to see if he would be less lazy but came back unrepentant and managed to scrape a third in his degree, something of an achievement in itself.[54] He found his chief happiness at Fallodon, and, later on, at his small cottage on the Itchen as well, passing his days bird watching, fishing, walking, and reading. At the relatively young age of twenty-three, he married a woman who shared his passionate love of the English countryside. Dorothy would have been happy to spend the rest of her life there, avoiding London which she saw as a modern Sodom and Gomorrah, spewing out depravity and disease. She despised social life, perhaps because she was awkward and shy or perhaps because she felt herself superior to most others. 'I believe', she wrote complacently at the age of twenty-three, 'we have arrived at the state when we have got all the good out of people that we shall ever get.' She loved and admired her husband but when they returned from their honeymoon she made it clear to him that she abhorred sex. Grey, ever the gentleman, agreed that they should live together as brother and sister.[55]

Yet somewhere underneath Grey's lackadaisical exterior was ambition, or at the very least a strong sense of duty. His family connections brought him an appointment as private secretary to a Cabinet minister and then, in 1885, he ran successfully for Parliament, so starting a political career which lasted until his resignation in 1916. He showed an unexpected capacity for hard work but he refused to take part in what he saw as time-wasting social activities. He and his wife escaped London as often as they could for their cottage, where they lived simply, with a single servant, and saw few visitors. 'It was something special and sacred', said Grey, 'outside the normal stream of life.'[56]

In 1892 he was made the Parliamentary Undersecretary to the Liberal Foreign Secretary, Lord Rosebery. Grey was not an obvious choice for foreign affairs, then or later. Unlike his contemporary George Curzon, he had no interest in travel, unless it was to go shooting or fishing in Scotland, and never developed any. He scarcely knew the Continent and as Foreign Secretary would visit it only once, in 1914 as part of a royal visit to Paris. Nevertheless, when he took up his new post in 1905, he had developed a few firmly held ideas about the world. Within the Liberal Party he counted as an imperialist and supported a large navy. On the other hand, he felt that the time of dividing up the world had passed and it was now Britain's responsibility to rule what it already possessed wisely.[57] He approved of Lansdowne's move away from isolation and before the election made it clear that he intended to carry on his policies, including the Entente with France which he saw as the cornerstone of British policy in Europe. In September 1906 he wrote to his great friend Richard Haldane, a fellow Liberal imperialist, 'I want to preserve the entente with France, but it isn't easy, and if it is broken up I must go.'[58] Germany, Grey held with equal firmness, was Britain's chief enemy and posed the greatest threat and, in his view, there was little that could be done to change that. 'I do not doubt', he said in 1903, 'that there are many Germans well disposed to us, but they are a minority; and the majority dislike us so intensely that the friendship of their Emperor or Government cannot be really useful to us.'[59] As he saw it, Britain in the past had been too close to Germany and as a consequence was on bad terms with France and Russia. 'We were sometimes on the brink of war with one or the other; & Germany took toll of us when it suited her.'[60]

Grey's directions to Sir Arthur Nicolson, the British delegate to the international conference on Morocco, were straightforward:

> The Morocco Conference is going to be difficult if not critical. As far as I can discover the Germans will refuse altogether to concede to France the special position in Morocco, which we have promised France not only to concede to her but to help her by diplomatic methods to obtain. If she can succeed in getting this with our help it will be a great success for the Anglo-French *Entente*; if she fails the prestige of the *Entente* will suffer and its vitality will be diminished. Our main object therefore must be to help France to carry her point at the Conference.[61]

The conference opened on 16 January 1906 in the Spanish city of Algeciras, just to the north-east of Gibraltar. Shortly afterwards, Grey suffered a tragedy; his wife was thrown from her pony cart at Fallodon and died of her injuries. 'Thought was arrested', he remarked in his memoirs, 'and work was crippled.'[62] Grey offered to resign but Campbell-Bannerman encouraged him to carry on.

The conference provided distraction of a sort. By the time it started, the Germans had managed to persuade most international opinion that Germany was intent on picking a quarrel with France.[63] A quarrel there was, and by February the conference was deadlocked, apparently, over the issue of which foreign nations would train and command the Moroccan police (the French insisted on themselves and the Spanish and the Germans wanted an international condominium) and who would manage the State Bank. In reality the question was the ultimate control of the country itself. 'Morocco', Bülow said, 'has become a question of honour for us and especially the Kaiser.'[64] Germany, however, was increasingly isolated. Its only dependable ally, Austria-Hungary, was pressuring it to give way on the police issue.[65] Italy was lukewarm and its representative did its best to avoid controversy. From the United States, Roosevelt was also urging a compromise.[66] Nicolson followed his instructions to maintain Britain's support behind France. On 28 February a large British fleet arrived off nearby Gibraltar, just to underscore what that support might one day involve. Russia, which the Germans still hoped could be enticed into its camp, remained firmly behind its French ally. The Russians had little choice. Their finances were a wreck thanks to the Russo-Japanese War and the continuing revolution at home. Russia badly needed a major foreign loan if it were not to go bankrupt and France was the most likely source. The French made it a condition of any loans to Russia that they get co-operation at Algeciras.

By the end of March, Bülow was prepared to cut Germany's losses in spite of Holstein's advice to stand firm. An agreement was reached on 27 March that made France the senior partner in the organisation of the police and the dominant voice in the new State Bank. The Moroccans themselves were stunned; 'they had thought that the Conference would be like a court where France was reprimanded and powers would give some gentle advice on reforms'.[67] While the Germans put a good face on it, they knew that they had suffered a defeat. Although Germany had had a good case for insisting on international management of Morocco, and although international events had been running in its favour in the previous months, inept German diplomacy had thrown those advantages away. Bülow and Holstein had tried to do what Bismarck would have done, keeping potential enemies apart and building relationships with all, but they did not have his skill. Holstein threatened to resign again and this time Bülow manoeuvred to have his resignation accepted. So ended fifty years of Holstein's service for Germany. In his remaining years he was lonely, embittered, and poor (he had lost his money in a speculation) but did his best to keep pulling strings from behind the scenes. He stirred up Germany's best-known journalist, Maximilian Harden, to attack the Kaiser's favourite, Eulenburg, whom Holstein had long suspected of being soft on Madrid and had at least the satisfaction of seeing Eulenburg accused of homosexuality, dragged into the courts, and exiled from the Kaiser's inner circle. Bülow's own position with the Kaiser was shaken because of Morocco and rumours went round that he was about to be dismissed. During a Reichstag debate on the Algeciras Conference in April, the Chancellor collapsed and was obliged to leave Berlin for a long convalescence.[68]

The Kaiser himself was depressed. He had always been against making Morocco a cause for war, in part because he felt that conditions in Germany were too dangerous. The Socialists were planning big demonstrations for January 1906 to protest against the highly restricted franchise for the Prussian parliament. On New Year's Eve, he wrote a panicky letter to Bülow: 'First cow the Socialists, behead them and make them harmless, with a blood bath if necessary and then make war abroad. But not before and not both together.'[69] Germany, facing a hostile coalition of the Latin powers of France, Spain and Italy under Britain's dominance, temporarily replaced the Yellow Peril in the Kaiser's thinking. In one of his marginal notes on the minutes, he mourned: 'We have no friends any longer whereas these unsexed relics of the ethnic chaos left behind by Rome hate us cordially.'[70]

What is frightening in retrospect is how readily the countries involved in the Morocco crisis anticipated war. Grey, for example, told his friend Haldane that he was getting many reports that Germany intended to attack France in the spring of 1906 while in Berlin Bülow was expecting the same from France and Britain.[71] And there were some in the ruling circles in Germany who seriously contemplated a preventive war. After all, the recent success of Japan in its war with Russia seemed to show that striking first worked. Schlieffen, who was working on his last words on his plan before his retirement, may well have advocated a preventive war on France and it is certain that other senior military leaders were in favour.[72] The head of the Press Bureau in the Foreign Office received a memorandum from his superiors in December 1905 to alert him to the possibility that the Algeciras Conference might well put Germany in the position of either losing prestige in the eyes of the world or going to war: 'such a conflict in the spring is expected by many here, and desired by many'.[73]

In spite of German hopes, Russia had remained true to the alliance with France. As soon as the conference ended, Raymond Poincaré, then the Minister of Finance, told the Russian ambassador in Paris that the talks about a loan could resume. On 16 April a representative of the Russian government signed an agreement for a huge loan with a consortium of banks, led by French ones who provided half the funds. 'He talked about the services rendered at Algeciras', said Poincaré, 'in a tone which was almost embarrassing for me. He complained of the demands of the French banks which are, it is true, rather avaricious.'[74] In a short-sighted move, the German government forbade German banks to participate in any Russian loans in retaliation for Algeciras; '… they won't get a penny from us!' said the Kaiser.[75]

The new friendship between Britain and France had passed its first test and was considerably stronger as a result. In 1908 a Franco-British Exhibition opened in London to celebrate the Entente Cordiale. 'That adroit and charming phrase,' said an English guide, 'the general adoption of which among us is a delicate compliment to the French language, suggests more than it expresses. It stands for mutual appreciation and good-will, for common aims and interests; it covers sentiment, understanding and material relations …'[76] Delcassé and Paul Cambon certainly thought it covered more, that the British had offered them a defensive alliance at one point.[77] The British felt they had avoided making a firm commitment but recognised that the Entente was now closer. Grey wrote at the height of the deadlock at Algeciras:

> If there is war between France and Germany it will be very difficult for us to keep out of it. The Entente and still more the constant and emphatic demonstrations of affection (official, naval, political, commercial, Municipal and in the Press), have created in France a belief that we should support her in war. The last report from our naval attaché at Toulon said that all the French officers took this for granted, if the war was between France and Germany about

Morocco. If this expectation is disappointed the French will never forgive us.

And he hinted that his position, as a supporter of the Entente, would become impossible if Britain failed to back France. 'On the other hand', he added, 'the prospect of a European War and of our being involved in it is horrible.'[78] He continued to balance in the years before 1914, between working with France yet refusing to commit to a more formal alliance or make binding promises.

His balancing act was undermined by the official approval which he gave in the middle of January to talks, which had already taken place informally, between the Director of British Military Operations and the French military attaché in London. These were, as Grey described them to the handful of colleagues he informed, merely to find out what sort of help the two countries could offer each other. 'The whole matter', he insisted, 'was being studied academically.'[79] From this small beginning, however, grew a series of talks between the French and the British armies over the next years where information was exchanged and plans drawn up. French intelligence on Germany, France's war plans, the possible numbers of British troops and horses to be sent to France, port facilities, railway transportation, many of the sorts of details and arrangements which would be necessary if Britain were to send troops to support France against a German attack, were discussed and worked out before 1914. Their two navies also held discussions from time to time but formal conversations were not authorised by the British Cabinet until the summer of 1912.

It is the military conversations that have remained the most controversial over the years. Did Grey, that upright Wykehamist, deliberately deceive the Cabinet and the British people by keeping the talks and the arrangements that were being made secret? More importantly, did the conversations commit Britain to come to France's support in the event of a German attack on France? Grey himself repeatedly answered No to both questions before and after 1914 but the reality is less clear-cut. When the conversations started in 1906, Grey informed the Prime Minister, Campbell-Bannerman, but he did not tell the full Cabinet, perhaps because he feared opposition from the radical wing of the Liberal Party. The Cabinet was not officially informed of the conversations until 1911, during another serious crisis over Morocco. (The House of Commons and the public did not learn about them until Britain was about to go to war in 1914.) According to Lloyd George, most of the Cabinet were shocked: 'Hostility barely represents the strength of the sentiment which the revelation aroused: it was more akin to consternation.' Grey reassured his colleagues by saying that Great Britain was still quite free to do what it pleased.[80] Again this is debatable.

It is true that Grey, his colleagues and subordinates generally talked to the French in the conditional. Britain might, quite probably, come to France's aid but, so the British insisted, nothing in the talks could be taken as constituting a firm promise. Britain in this view kept its freedom to decide what it would do in the event of a war. In 1911 the Cabinet went so far as to pass a formal resolution to underline that Britain was not committed, directly or indirectly, to military or naval intervention.[81] Nevertheless, the repeated support that Britain gave to France diplomatically, over Morocco for example, was an indication of how strongly Grey felt about maintaining the Entente. For Grey and those, many of them senior officials in the Foreign Office, who felt like him, France's friendship was essential, and so increasingly was Russia's, if Britain were not to find itself isolated again as it had been during the Boer War.[82] And diplomatic support without the threat of force behind it in the end would not work, either with France's enemies or France itself. If the French did not feel that they could rely on Britain, to the point of military support, they might well make the best of a bad job and come to terms with Germany.

British strategic thinking was shifting in a way that made intervention on the side of France more likely. Up until 1907 the main concern of the British army had been the empire. The improvement of relations with the United States at the turn of the century, in part because of British recognition of American dominance in the New World, meant that Britain no longer had to worry about its North American colonies. The Anglo-Russian Convention of 1907 removed much British apprehension about the Russian threat to the jewel in the crown, India. The army had been reorganised and reformed after the Boer War and was now in a position to assess its role. It was responsible, as it had always been, for the defence of the British Isles in case of invasion but increasingly its leaders thought in terms of an expeditionary force to the Continent.[83] The growth of German power brought out the old British fear of a single nation dominating the coasts of the Netherlands, Belgium and perhaps even France, across which so much of Britain's trade flowed. Germany's control of the coasts would also put it in a position to invade Britain if it chose.[84]

The British military tended to assume that France would inevitably be defeated without support from Britain.[85] In 1912, Maurice Hankey, the Secretary to the Committee of Imperial Defence, the body responsible for British strategy, expressed a fairly common view of the French: 'They don't strike me as a really sound people.' They had, said Hankey, bad sanitation, poor water, and slow railways. 'I suspect', he went on, 'that the Germans could "beat them to a frazzle" any day.'[86] By the summer of 1911, the British military were thinking in terms of sending six infantry divisions and two brigades of cavalry to France, a total of 150,000 men and 67,000 horses. If the French assumptions about the number of men that Germany would use on the Western Front were correct, a British expeditionary force would tip the balance in favour of the Entente there.[87]

While the army was making plans, the British navy was not, or if it was, Fisher and his successor, Sir Arthur Wilson, were not sharing their thinking with anyone, especially with the army which they saw as a competitor for funds. They strenuously opposed the idea of a British expeditionary force as expensive and useless. The navy was the key service, responsible, as it had always been, for defending the home islands, protecting British commerce on the high seas, and carrying war to the enemy through blockading its ports and possibly making amphibious landings. The army could play a role here, Fisher allowed in words he borrowed from Grey, 'as a projectile to be fired by the Navy'.[88] Fisher in 1909 seems to have been thinking of series of small attacks on Germany's coasts; 'a mere fleabite! but a collection of these fleabites would make Wilhelm scratch himself with fury!'[89] Although Fisher was open-minded when it came to new technology – he leaned increasingly to fast cruisers rather than dreadnoughts and advocated using torpedoes and submarines to keep the German fleet penned up – he was not good at making strategic plans. When he was in office the first time, the navy did almost no planning; he was fond of saying that its chief war plan was locked away in his brain where it would stay for greater security.[90] 'The vaguest amateur stuff I have ever seen,' said a young captain of the Admiralty's war plans during Fisher's first period of tenure. He blamed Fisher himself, who generalised about war – 'the enemy is to be hit hard & often, and many other aphorisms' – but who never got down to solid detail.[91]

For much of the prewar period the two British services went their own way, making their own plans, and eyeing each other as dogs would fighting over a bone. In 1911, however, the second crisis over Morocco, which brought in its train the now seemingly inevitable war scare, forced a meeting of the Committee of Imperial Defence on 23 August 1911 to review the whole of British strategy. (This was the only time before 1914 that such a review took place.)[92] Asquith, the Prime Minister, took the chair and among the other politicians were Richard Haldane, the Secretary of State for War, Grey, and two new and rising young men, Lloyd George and Winston Churchill. Henry Wilson, the new Director of Military Operations represented the army, and Fisher's successor, Arthur Wilson, the navy. The army's Wilson gave a brilliant exposition of the situation on the Continent and outlined the purpose and plans for the expeditionary force. His naval namesake did an appalling job: he objected to the very idea of the army sending a force to the Continent and outlined instead a vague scheme for blockading Germany's North Sea coast as well as swooping in from to time to time to carry out amphibious raids. It also became clear that the navy had little interest in transporting the expeditionary force to France or protecting its communications.[93] Asquith thought the whole performance 'puerile'.[94] Shortly afterwards he brought in as First Lord of the Admiralty Winston Churchill, who promptly got rid of Arthur Wilson and also set up a naval staff to draw up war plans. Churchill threw his support behind a British expeditionary force too, and the navy started to work with the army.[95]

In 1912 Alexandre Millerand, a former socialist who had moved sufficiently to the right to become Minister of War, said of the British army: 'The machine is ready to go: will it be unleashed? Complete uncertainty.'[96] The French remained unsure of British intervention until the Great War started, though some of its leaders, both military and civilian, were more sanguine than Millerand. Paul Cambon, the influential ambassador in London, took away from Grey's repeated assurances of friendship, and the fact that he had authorised the military conversations, the conviction that the British saw the Entente as an alliance (although he was never to be quite sure what that implied).[97] In 1919 Joffre said: 'Personally, I was convinced that they would come, but in the end there was no formal commitment on their part. There were only studies on embarking and debarking and on the positions that would be reserved for their troops.'[98] The French viewed the growing hostility between Britain and Germany with relief and argued that the traditional British policy of keeping a balance of power in Europe (which had operated against France in the Napoleonic Wars) would now come to its aid. The French leaders also grasped that the British, as Grey had also said repeatedly, would be affected when it came to making a decision about war by who was to blame.[99] It was in part for this reason that the French were so careful to respond to events in the summer of 1914 and not take any steps that could be construed as aggressive.

The French military were encouraged by the presence of Henry Wilson as Director of Military Operations after 1910. He was an imposing figure, well over six feet tall, with a face which resembled, said a fellow officer, a gargoyle.[100] (Someone once addressed a postcard 'To the Ugliest Man in the British Army' and it reached him without difficulty.)[101] Wilson was 'selfish and cunning', as another colleague put it, skilled at political intrigue and good at finding influential patrons. He came from a moderately well-to-do Anglo-Irish family (and the cause of the Protestants in Ireland was always important to him) but had been obliged to make his own way in the world. As his presentation to the Committee of Imperial Defence demonstrated, he was clever and persuasive. He was also energetic and strong willed and had very clear views on strategy. In a paper he wrote in 1911 which was endorsed by the general staff, he took the view: 'we <u>must</u> join France'. Russia, he argued, was not going to be much help if Germany attacked France; what would save Europe from a French defeat and dominance by Germany was the rapid mobilisation and dispatch of a British expeditionary force.[102] When he took up his office, Wilson was determined to make sure this happened. 'I am very dissatisfied with the state of affairs in every respect,' he wrote in his diary. There were no proper plans for deploying the British expeditionary force or the reserves: 'A lot of time spent writing beautiful minutes. I'll break all this if I can.'[103]

. He rapidly established very good relations with the French military, helped by the fact that he loved France and spoke fluent French. He and the commandant of the French Staff College, the deeply Catholic Colonel Ferdinand Foch (as the future Field Marshal then was), became firm friends. 'What would you say,' Wilson once asked Foch, 'was the smallest British military force that would be of any practical assistance to you in the event of a contest such as the one we have been considering?' Foch did not pause to reflect: 'One single private soldier,' he replied, 'and we would take good care that he was killed.'[104] The French would do whatever it took to get Britain to commit itself. In 1909 they produced a carefully faked document, said to have been discovered when a French commercial traveller picked up the wrong bag on a train, which purported to show Germany's invasion plans for Britain.[105]

Wilson made frequent visits to France to exchange information about war plans and work out arrangements for co-operation. He bicycled many miles along France's frontiers, studying fortifications and likely battle sites. In 1910, shortly after his appointment, he visited one of the bloodier battlefields from the Franco-Prussian War in the part of Lorraine that remained to France: 'We paid my usual visit to the statue of "France", looking as beautiful as ever, so I laid at her feet a small bit of map I have been carrying, showing the areas of concentration of the British forces on her territory.'[106] Like his French hosts, Wilson assumed that the German right wing would not be strong enough to move nearer the sea, west of the Meuse in Belgium; the British expeditionary force would take its place on the French left wing to anticipate what was expected to be the weaker part of the German attack. There was some talk that the British might go to Antwerp but Wilson and his colleagues agreed that they could afford to be flexible and decide once the British forces had landed.

The British may have kept flexibility in their military plans but in political terms they were increasingly hemmed in. The first Morocco crisis of 1905–6 brought much greater co-operation and understanding between Britain and France but it also brought greater obligations. The crisis served as well to draw the lines more sharply between the powers in Europe. With the signing of the Anglo-Russian Convention in 1907, yet another line was drawn and another strand of obligations and expectations woven, this time between two former enemies. It was more difficult, too, to ignore public opinion. In both France and Germany, for example, important business interests as well as key figures such as the French ambassador in Germany, Jules Cambon, were in favour of better relations. In 1909 France and Germany reached an amicable agreement over Morocco. Nationalists in both countries made it impossible for their governments to move further and discuss improved economic relations.[107] Europe was not doomed to divide itself into two antipathetic power blocs, each with its war plans to the ready, but as yet more crises succeeded the first Moroccan one, it became more difficult to change the pattern.

CHAPTER 14

The Bosnian Crisis:
Confrontation between Russia and Austria-Hungary in the Balkans

I n 1898, Kaiser Wilhelm II sailed on his yacht the *Hohenzollern* up the Dardanelles and into the Sea of Marmara to pay his second state visit to Abdul Hamid, the Ottoman sultan. Wilhelm liked to think of himself as the friend and protector of the Ottoman Empire. (He also had every intention of getting as many concessions as possible for Germany such as the right to build railways on Ottoman territory.) He was drawn too by the glamour of Constantinople itself. One of the greatest and most ancient cities in the world, Constantinople had seen many great rulers from Alexander the Great, to Emperor Constantine, and much more recently Suleiman the Magnificent. The scraps of Greek, Roman, and Byzantine columns and ornamentation which were embedded in its walls and foundations as much as its magnificent palaces, mosques and churches were reminders of the great empires which had come and gone.

The German royal couple were rowed ashore in a state caique and while the Kaiser rode around the great city walls on an Arab horse, the empress made an excursion to the Asian coast of the sea. That night the sultan gave his guests a lavish banquet in a new wing of his palace

14. Although Africa and much of the Pacific had been divided up by 1900, the declining Ottoman Empire on Europe's doorstep offered increasing temptations. Here the weak Ottoman ruler, Abdul Hamid II, watches helplessly while Austria-Hungary in the shape of its emperor Franz Joseph seizes the Ottoman provinces of Bosnia and Herzegovina in 1908 and Ferdinand I of Bulgaria takes the opportunity to proclaim the independence of his kingdom, which was still nominally part of the Ottoman Empire. The resulting crisis heightened the tensions in Europe.

which had been built expressly for the occasion. It was followed by a magnificent display of fireworks. Below in the harbour electric lights picked out the silhouettes of the German warships which had accompanied the Kaiser's yacht. To mark his visit, the Kaiser presented the city with a large gazebo containing seven fountains, all made in Germany. With columns of porphyry, marble arches, a bronze dome decorated on the inside with gold mosaics and Wilhelm's and Abdul Hamid's initials carved into the stone, it still stands today at one end of the ancient Hippodrome where the Romans once raced their horses and chariots. For the sultan Wilhelm II had brought the latest German rifle, but when he tried to present it Abdul Hamid at first shrank away in terror thinking he was about to be assassinated. The heir to Suleiman the Magnificent who had made Europe tremble nearly four centuries earlier was a miserable despot so fearful of plots that he kept a eunuch near him whose sole duty was to take the first puff on each of his cigarettes.

The Ottoman Empire was, so most observers thought, doomed. It was nearly bankrupt with foreign interests holding most of its debt; its subjects were restive; and its administration was incompetent and corrupt. It was a sad ending to an empire which had been one of the greatest the world had ever seen. The Ottoman Turks had come out of Central Asia in the thirteenth century and had advanced inexorably westward across Turkey. In 1453 their armies took Constantinople. The last Byzantine emperor had sought death in battle – and found it – and so what had been the heart of Orthodox Christianity became a Muslim city. The Ottomans had kept moving, north into the Balkans in the south-eastern corner of Europe, into the Middle East and along the southern coast of the Mediterranean into Egypt and beyond. Rulers who tried to stand in their way were swept aside and their peoples subjugated. By the end of the fifteenth century the Ottoman Empire controlled most of the Balkans and by 1529 Ottoman armies had reached Vienna, which managed, only just, to withstand their siege. A decade later Budapest fell and most of Hungary became part of the Ottoman Empire. By the middle of the seventeenth century, at its greatest extent the Ottoman Empire in Europe included all or parts of the present-day countries of Hungary, Bulgaria, Rumania, Croatia, Serbia, Montenegro, Albania, Macedonia and Greece. The Ottomans also took over a big piece of what is today Ukraine and the southern Caucasus (where later the countries of Georgia, Armenia, and Azerbaijan would emerge). In addition the empire included Turkey, the Arab Middle East as far as the border with Persia down to the southern tip of the Arabian peninsula, and much of North Africa as far west as Morocco.

As empires went, Ottoman rule had been relatively mild. The Ottomans, who were largely Sunni Muslims, had allowed their subjects, which included many varieties of Christians and Jews, as well as Shia Muslims, to follow their own religious practices and within limits its many ethnicities, which ranged from Kurds to Serbs to Hungarians, were allowed to keep their languages and culture. Over the centuries, though, the empire had started to decline. Its fleets were defeated on the Mediterranean and on land its great rival, the Austrian Empire gradually pushed it back southwards, taking the prize of Hungary in 1699. In the course of the next century both Austria and Russia stripped yet more territory from the Ottoman Empire and in the nineteenth century France and Britain joined in the scavenging with the French taking Algeria and Tunis and the British Egypt and Cyprus. What was also destroying the Ottoman Empire was not just the passage of time and the resurgence of its enemies but the growth of nationalism throughout its territories, first in the European part. Greece won its independence in 1832 while Serbia, Rumania and Bulgaria moved from autonomy within the Ottoman Empire towards full independence.

When the long-expected final disintegration of the Ottoman Empire occurred, its remaining territories, huge in the Middle East and still considerable in the Balkans, would be up for grabs. While the competing ambitions between Germany, France, Russia, and Britain in the Middle East and North Africa fed tensions back into Europe, it was the rivalry between Austria-Hungary and Russia that in the end posed the greatest threat to Europe's long peace. The two powers had vital and incompatible interests at stake. While Austria-Hungary had little interest in the Ottomans' Asian territories, it was bound to care about what happened on its southern doorstep in the Balkans. It could not calmly contemplate an enlarged Serbia or Bulgaria, both of which were likely to seize any chance to enlarge their territory, which would in turn block Austria-Hungary's trading routes southwards to Constantinople and the Aegean ports, or, in the case of Serbia, threaten its Adriatic possessions along the Dalmatian coast. One or more large South Slav states, moreover, would act as a solvent on Austria-Hungary itself, arousing the national hopes of its own South Slavs in Croatia, Slovenia, and southern Hungary. And if the Balkan states gravitated, as they well might, towards Russia, Austria-Hungary would face a formidable coalition.

Russia for its part could not stand by while control of the Ottoman Straits fell into the hands of another power. So much of Russia's trade, some 40 per cent of its exports alone by 1912, went through those narrow waterways that any blockage could fatally weaken Russia's economy. For historical and religious reasons, too, Constantinople had once been the capital of the Byzantine Empire, to which Russia claimed to be the heir. The prospect of Austria-Hungary, a Catholic power, occupying it was almost as bad, at least to the devout Orthodox, as Muslims. Nor could the Russian Panslavs, an increasingly vociferous group, tolerate their fellow Slavs in the Balkans, the majority of whom were Orthodox like the Russians themselves, falling under the sway of Austria-Hungary.

In the nineteenth century, the great powers, led by Britain, had propped up the 'Sick Man of Europe' partly to prevent just such a dangerous scramble for territory. Russia's attempt, after its victory over the Ottoman Empire in 1878, to strip away a good deal of the Ottomans' European territory and create a big Bulgaria including the Macedonian territories, was stopped by the other powers, who handed Macedonia back to the Ottomans, leaving a smaller Bulgaria, nominally under Ottoman suzerainty. Macedonia, which had a large Christian population, was rapidly reduced to even greater misery than before through a combination of Ottoman incompetence and the activities of the different Balkan Christians outside the Ottoman Empire who did little but quarrel among themselves and fund different terrorist groups to stir up trouble among the Macedonians.

In the settlement of 1878 Austria-Hungary was compensated in the west by being allowed to occupy and administer Bosnia-Herzegovina, again under nominal Ottoman suzerainty. It was also allowed to keep troops in a small appendix, the Sanjak of Novi Bazar, which ran southwards from Bosnia-Herzegovina. This prevented Serbia from joining up with Montenegro to the west and allowed Austria-Hungary a narrow corridor through which it could run communications down into Macedonia, still Ottoman territory, and on southwards to the Aegean. The new territories were troublesome from the start; Austria-Hungary had to send a substantial force of troops in to put down an uprising by Bosnian Muslims who did not want to come under Christian rule.

By the end of the century, both Russia and Austria-Hungary had recognised the dangerous potential for conflict between them over the remains of the Ottoman Empire and, in 1897, came to an agreement to respect the territorial status quo in the Balkans. They also agreed that they would not interfere in the internal affairs of the existing Balkan states. Russia promised that it would respect Austria-Hungary's rights in Bosnia-Herzegovina. Finally, the two powers would together oppose any agitation against the principles they had just agreed. In 1900, Alois von Aehrenthal, an Austrian diplomat in St Petersburg, wrote optimistically to Gołuchowski, the Foreign Minister in Vienna, that Russia and Austria-Hungary were learning to trust each other: 'Without trust, diplomatic developments in the Balkans are impossible. The important matter will be to intensify the process of trust.'[1] It might be possible, he hoped, to come eventually to an agreement on spheres of influence in the Balkans with Austria-Hungary dominating the western part and Russia the eastern as well as the waters between the Black Sea and the Mediterranean, and Constantinople itself. The developments of the next few years appeared to bear out his hopes. 'Gone are the days,' said Lamsdorff, the Russian Foreign Minister in 1902, 'when Russia and Austria-Hungary came to loggerheads only out of love for the Balkan peoples.' In 1903, as the situation in Macedonia went from bad to worse, the two powers signed a further agreement to work together to put pressure on the Ottoman authorities to make much-needed reforms there. The following year, as Russia became embroiled in the war with Japan, it signed a neutrality agreement with Austria-Hungary which allowed Russia to move troops from their common border to the east.[2]

In 1906, however, under pressure from his nephew and heir, Franz Ferdinand, Franz Joseph made two important appointments which inaugurated new, more active policies for Austria-Hungary. Conrad took over as chief of the general staff and Aehrenthal became Foreign Minister. Many, especially in the younger generation of officers and officials, hoped that now the Dual Monarchy would stop its slow suicide and show that it was still vital and powerful, that successes domestically and in foreign affairs would feed each other to create a stronger state as achievements at home and abroad rallied the empire's inhabitants to their multinational state and the dynasty itself. A revitalised Austria-Hungary could also shake itself free of its growing and humiliating dependency on Germany and show that it was an independent actor in the world. While the two men agreed on the overall goals, the Foreign Minister preferred to use diplomacy rather than war. Conrad, who urged war relentlessly, later characterised Aehrenthal as 'a vain, self-indulgent ninny, who carried out his ambitions only in petty diplomatic ambiguities and things that were superficially successful' and claimed that he saw the army as an umbrella to be left in the cupboard until it rained.[3]

This, like much of what Conrad said about his colleagues, was unfair. Aehrenthal was prepared to use war, but only if absolutely necessary.

The new Foreign Minister was tall and slightly stooped, with fine, regular features and hooded eyes from which he peered out short-sightedly. Aehrenthal always looked weary, said Bülow, who found him 'reserved, indolent, almost apathetic'.[4] Aehrenthal was in fact very hard-working and had devoted his life to furthering the foreign policy of Austria-Hungary, serving, among other things, as a successful and respected ambassador to Russia. Like most of his colleagues he came from the aristocracy. 'Our diplomatic corps', said a staff officer, 'is like a Chinese wall. There is no entrance for people on the outside, people who don't belong.'[5] Aehrenthal's family were Czech nobility who had risen socially as a result of their service to the state. (His enemies liked to point out that he had bourgeois ancestors, perhaps even a Jew some-where.) He was far from being Czech in his loyalties, however; like many of his class, Aehrenthal was cosmopolitan and gave his primary allegiance to the dynasty and Austria-Hungary. In their service, he was dedicated, devious, duplicitous and ruthless. His weakness was that he tended to over-complicate matters. Nor was he good at taking advice. Count Leopold Berchtold, his colleague and later his successor, com-plained of his 'frightful characteristic of overlooking facts that do not fit into his complicated house of cards'.[6]

Although Aehrenthal was deeply conservative and shared the antip-athy of much of his class to liberalism and socialism, he believed that Austria-Hungary had to make reforms if it were to survive. Like his mentor, Franz Ferdinand, he hoped to create a South Slav bloc within the empire that would somehow blunt the endless tensions between the Austrian and the Hungarian halves. More, a new South Slav compo-nent of the empire would act as a magnet to the South Slavs in the Balkans, in Serbia, Montenegro or Bulgaria, and draw them into Aus-tria-Hungary's orbit, perhaps even bringing them inside the empire.[7] In foreign affairs, he shared the firm assumption of his predecessors that the German alliance was crucial for the survival of Austria-Hungary yet he also hoped to reach across the growing dividing line in Europe and build a stronger relationship with Russia. He longed to see the Three Emperors League of Austria-Hungary, Germany and Russia reborn to promote the causes, which he saw as interrelated, of conservatism and stability in Europe.[8] His years in St Petersburg had gained him the reputation of being pro-Russian (aided, so Bülow claimed, by an affair he had with a beautiful leader of society[9]) and he preferred, wherever possible, to work with the Russians.

Under Aehrenthal, however, Austria-Hungary and Russia were going to fall out badly and perhaps irredeemably over the fate of the small and poor Ottoman province of Bosnia-Herzegovina in the western part of the Balkans. The policy of moderation and co-operation in the Balkans which had existed between the two powers lay in shreds, to the ultimate ruin of both. What they had long feared, armed confrontation in the Balkans, nearly happened in 1908, again in 1912 and 1913, and finally broke out in 1914 and brought most of Europe down with it.

The downward spiral of the Ottoman Empire had made the temptations of picking up the spoils hard to resist for both powers. Austria-Hungary, too, which had never been a colonial power, had finally caught the prevailing infection of imperialism and some, including Conrad, were starting to think in terms of acquiring colonies, whether in the Balkans themselves or further afield in Ottoman Asia. Russia, for its part, was turning westward after its defeat at the hands of Japan in 1905 and Europe as well as real and potential allies in the Balkans were more important than they had once been. Influence there was a way of demonstrating that Russia was still a great power. By 1907, the understanding with Austria-Hungary to maintain the status quo in the Balkans was starting to fray as the two powers disagreed, for example over the reforms needed in the Ottoman territory of Macedonia.[10]

The Balkan nations, which had emerged from the Ottoman Empire in the course of the nineteenth century, were themselves now playing a part in international affairs as well. They had to manoeuvre between the two great powers of Russia and Austria-Hungary while keeping an uneasy eye on each other. Through the work of poets and historians, with the spread of modern communications, and with the spread of the idea from western Europe that human beings were properly divided into races or nations, what had been separate religious or ethnic identities were solidifying into Bulgarian, Greek, Serbian, Rumanian or Montenegrin nationalisms. Unfortunately for the peace of the Balkans the vagaries of history and the mix of peoples throughout the Balkans meant that each of these emerging nations could lay claim to another's territory, and in the case, of Bulgaria, Montenegro, Greece and Serbia to what was left of the Ottoman Empire's European territories. Increasingly the Balkan nations added to the complexity and instability of the international relations of their region as their governments, dominated more often than not by radical nationalists, called on ethnic or religious ties or rummaged through the past to find arguments for acquiring more territory, from each other, from the Ottoman Empire, or, in the case of Serbia and Rumania, from Austria-Hungary.

Rumania under Carol I, a determined and strong ruler who came from the Catholic branch of the Hohenzollerns, had successfully freed itself from the Ottoman Empire by 1880 but for Rumanian nationalists the Rumanian state was not yet complete. Some 3 million Rumanian speakers lived, not always happily, under Hungarian rule in Transylvania. (The total population of Rumania itself was just under 7 million.) On the other hand, Rumania was on bad terms with Bulgaria and its great neighbour Russia, both of which had taken territory Rumania thought was rightfully its. As Aehrenthal once said, Austria-Hungary's policy towards Rumania must 'prevent artificially fostered hate of Hungary from becoming stronger than the very fundamental fear of Russia'.[11]

In 1883, under pressure from Bismarck, King Carol signed a secret defensive alliance with Austria-Hungary but since only he and a couple of his minsters knew about it, Vienna could never be entirely comfortable that Rumania would be an ally in a general war. When he considered Austria-Hungary's strategic position, Conrad hoped at best that Rumania could put some sixteen divisions into the field against Russia; second best was Rumania's neutrality, which would at least tie down some Russian forces; worst of all would be for Rumania to switch sides. The German Kaiser, who placed an exaggerated faith in family ties, believed that, as the senior member of the Hohenzollern dynasty, he could keep Carol loyal to the Triple Alliance.[12] In the years before the Great War, Archduke Franz Ferdinand contemplated handing over Transylvania to Rumania and so weakening the Hungarians, whom he hated, and cementing the friendship with Rumania.[13] The archduke also liked Carol, who made sure that his duchess, Sophie, was received with full royal honours in Bucharest, something Franz Joseph had refused her.[14] Such hopes were illusory: the Hungarians would never have agreed to losing what many of them regarded as the cradle of the Hungarian nation. Unfortunately for the future of the secret alliance the Hungarians continued to deny the Rumanians within their borders political rights. Before 1914, the 3 million Rumanians in Hungary had five deputies in the Hungarian parliament while 10 million Hungarian-speakers had almost 400.[15]

Rumania's neighbour to the south, Bulgaria, was closer to Russia in the early stages of its independence. The Bulgarians, unlike the Rumanians who spoke a Latin language and who liked to think of themselves as the descendants of Roman settlers, spoke a Slavic language close to Russian and had looked to Russia for support and encouragement in their struggle in the 1870s to free themselves from Ottoman rule. Although Bulgarian dreams of a large and independent Bulgaria were blocked in 1878, unfortunately for the future stability of the Balkans, the Bulgarians themselves clung to the belief that the only just borders for their country where the ones they had briefly enjoyed. In the 1880s, in spite of objections from Russia which had set itself up as Bulgaria's patron, the Bulgarian government went ahead and brought the Ottoman province of Eastern Rumelia under its administration. Tsar Alexander III, the father of Nicholas, was enraged. Not only did he strip Prince Alexander, who had been summoned from Germany to rule Bulgaria, of his rank in the Russian army, but he did his best to drive him from Bulgaria's throne. In 1886 the tsar was successful and the following year Bulgaria elected another German prince, who became widely known to his subjects and throughout Europe as Foxy Ferdinand. Relations between Bulgaria and Russia remained cool. From Russia's point of view it had wasted resources and spilt good Russian blood in the war with the Ottomans to free the Bulgarians who had behaved with appalling ingratitude. By the start of the twentieth century the Russians, for all the talk of Panslavist brotherhood, increasingly saw Bulgaria, with its clear interest in detaching Macedonia from the Ottoman Empire, as a threat to stability in the Balkans, to Russia's status quo agreement of 1897 with Austria-Hungary, and to the safety of the Straits.

With Russia's rival chief rival for influence in the Balkans, Austria-Hungary, Bulgaria's relations were somewhat warmer. Austria-Hungary sold weapons to Bulgaria and dominated its international trade. From the point of view of the Dual Monarchy, Bulgaria had one further point in its favour. It was not Serbia; there were no Bulgarians living in Austria-Hungary to be lured away by nationalist siren songs from their co-nationals outside the empire's borders.[16] In 1891, a few years after Ferdinand became prince of Bulgaria, Franz Joseph invited him to Vienna. When the Russians complained, the Dual Monarchy's Foreign Minister expressed surprise: 'little Ferdinand' had known Franz Joseph since he was a boy. So when, in 1904 Bulgaria and Serbia signed an arrangement on customs, it set off alarm bells in Vienna which suspected the two Balkan powers were moving towards a union.[17]

Relations between Austria-Hungary and Serbia, which gradually freed itself from the Ottoman Empire in the nineteenth century to become an independent state in 1878, had initially been good. In the 1880s and 1890s the Serbian economy became closely intertwined with that of its great neighbour to the north and the first Serbian king, Milan, had even suggested to Austria-Hungary in 1885 that it might want to annex his country in return for a nice pension so that he could abdicate and enjoy the fleshpots of Europe. Vienna turned down the offer for fear of what Russia might say or do and the Minister of Foreign Affairs told the unhappy Milan that he had an obligation to stay in his country and be a good ruler.[18] In the next few years Milan managed to alienate Serbian nationalists by his subservience to Austria-Hungary and shock even his supporters by quarrelling openly with his Russian-born wife in various Belgrade cafés. In 1889, by now divorced from her, Milan finally managed to abdicate in favour of his thirteen-year-old son, Alexander. Unfortunately for the family and for Serbia, the boy grew up to be a chip off the parental block. In 1900 he married an older woman with a very shady reputation. In 1903 both were murdered, along with the Prime Minister and the Minister of War, in a particularly brutal fashion by nationalist officers. Peter Karageorgević, from a rival dynasty, became king and, after some political turbulence, the intensely nationalist Radicals under the cagey and cunning Nikola Pašić took over the government which they were to dominate until the end of the Great War.

The assassination not only set Serbia on a new path of confrontation with Austria-Hungary, it helped to build the chain of events which led to the summer of 1914. In 1906, in a clear indication that the new regime in Belgrade was determined to free itself from Austria-Hungary, the Serbian government, which had previously bought most of its armaments from the Dual Monarchy, awarded a substantial contract to the French firm of Schneider.[19] In retaliation, Austria-Hungary suspended its trade treaty with Serbia and closed its borders to Serbian exports (mainly livestock) on the spurious grounds that the animals had diseases. The 'Pig War' lasted until 1911 but it did not bring Serbia to heel. Although their economy suffered, the Serbians were able to look elsewhere, to France, for example, which had money to lend and arms to sell, but above all to Russia.

The new regime in Belgrade was not only hostile from the start to its great neighbour to the north but it was strongly Russophile. Russia, for its part, moved partly by emotion and partly by calculation, came to see its role as defending its little Balkan brother. And the little brother was motivated not just by hatred and fear of Austria-Hungary but by grand ambitions. Serb nationalists relied on history to claim what in the fourteenth century had been the kingdom of Tsar Dušan, and that included lands to the south of Serbia occupied mainly by Albanians, Bulgars, and Turks. Montenegro was more indisputably Serb but its ruling family was frequently at loggerheads with the Serbian dynasty so that might have to wait. In addition, the Montenegrin king, the artful Nicholas I, had married his numerous children well, two to Russian grand dukes, one to the heir to the Italian throne, and one to King Peter of Serbia himself. As well as history, the Serbian nationalists used linguistic and ethnic evidence to argue that other South Slavs, the largely Catholic Croats and the Muslims of Bosnia-Herzegovina, were really renegade Serbs who should be Orthodox in religion; so Bosnia, Herzegovina, Dalmatia, Istria, Croatia, and Slavonia, all inside Austria-Hungary, might also become part of a Greater Serbia. By the twentieth century, the growth of a transnational Yugoslav movement, which took its name from the Serbo-Croatian for South Slav, was causing considerable concern to the Habsburg authorities as its own South Slavs went to Belgrade for congresses and meetings and there was heady talk of an eventual union of Serbs, Croats, Slovenes and Bulgars.[20]

For Serb nationalists, Bosnia-Herzegovina was both a sore point and a temptation. The provinces' population was some 44 per cent Serb or Orthodox (the two were seen as virtually synonymous), 33 per cent Muslim, and about 22 per cent Croat or Catholic.[21] From the Serb nationalist point of view, the last two could be seen as part of the Serb nation even if they did not yet realise it. The provinces were under the control of what Serb nationalists increasingly saw as their enemy, Austria-Hungary, but, and this was important, they were still nominally part of the Ottoman Empire. If that empire finally disappeared, perhaps with a little help from its neighbours in the Balkans, Bosnia and Herzegovina might well become part of a Greater Serbia. That in turn would give Serbia a border with Montenegro, better still union, and access to the Adriatic, something which landlocked Serbia badly needed for trade. Agitators from Serbia were already busy in Macedonia and, after 1900, they increasingly moved into Bosnia-Herzegovina. The Serb-language press in both Belgrade and Sarajevo denounced Austria-Hungary's tyranny and called on the peoples of the provinces to rise up. In 1907, Serbs in Bosnia-Herzegovina ran their own elections for a national assembly which met in Sarajevo to demand an independent state within the Ottoman Empire.[22]

Austria-Hungary, which had administered the provinces efficiently if autocratically, had few supporters within Bosnia-Herzegovina. Since the Hungarians had insisted that no common funds be spent there, or even railways built that did not benefit Hungary in some way, Bosnia-Herzegovina remained a largely rural backwater. In an unsuccessful attempt to win over the landlords, who were largely Muslim, the provinces' governors had left the archaic landholding system alone with the result that they had alienated the tenants who were mostly Serb. While the Muslims still tended to look to Constantinople, the Serbs increasingly looked to Belgrade. Only the Croats showed some loyalty to Austria-Hungary.[23] 'When I was here, for the first time, in 1892', wrote a leading liberal from Vienna, 'the atmosphere was one of energetic progress, well-considered and full of eager hopefulness in the future; today, inactivity, doubt, apprehensiveness are the notes.'[24] On the credit side, the Dual Monarchy had provided greater security than its Ottoman predecessors and some progress had been made in communications and education but, as so frequently happened in other colonial empires, those developments also served to produce an educated class of nationalists.

By the time Aehrenthal took up his post as Foreign Minister, Serbia had become for Austria-Hungary's leaders both its most dangerous neighbour in the Balkans and an existential threat, undermining the empire in Bosnia-Herzegovina and stirring up nationalist longings among its own South Slavs. The conclusion that many in Austria-Hungary drew was that such troubles would disappear if Serbia did. Conrad and his fellow military argued for dealing with the problem by waging war on Serbia and annexing it to the empire. Although Aehrenthal initially told Izvolsky, his opposite number in Russia, that his aim was to preserve peace in the Balkans and improve conditions for the Christians still under Turkish rule (and, of course, remain on the best of terms with Russia), by 1907 he had given up hoping to win Serbia over by peaceful means.[25] In a memorandum the following year, he painted the prospect, a promising one for Austria-Hungary, of the growing antagonism between Serbia and Bulgaria over Macedonia leading to war. Then, so Aehrenthal hoped, Austria-Hungary could scoop up whatever was left of Serbia. In the longer run, an independent Albania bordering on the Adriatic and under Austrian-Hungarian protection might emerge. (The Albanians, who were possibly the oldest peoples in the Balkans and who spoke a language different from that of their Slavic neighbours, were conveniently starting to develop their own separate nationalism.) As for Bulgaria, in the ideal scenario for Vienna, it would be heavily in debt after its war with Serbia and therefore forced to lean on Austria-Hungary.[26]

'It is necessary', Aehrenthal wrote in a memorandum in February 1907, 'to end our passivity.' While it was dealing with Serbia, Austria-Hungary should also go ahead and annex Bosnia-Herzegovina. This would help to make up for the lands which the Dual Monarchy had lost in the unification of Italy. The emperor could then give the new provinces a constitution and join them with the other South Slav parts of Austria-Hungary to add a third element to the Dual Monarchy.[27] A strong revitalised empire could again play an independent part in Europe's affairs instead of being 'subservient sheep' to Germany. Having the empire called 'a brilliant second' by the Kaiser after the Algeciras Conference the year before still rankled in Vienna. 'I consider,' Aehrenthal told Berchtold, who had succeeded him as ambassador to St Petersburg, 'the *strong* emphasis of the German–Austrian–Hungarian alliance, under the present circumstances, not very clever and also not working towards a goal – at least from our standpoint.'[28]

Aehrenthal believed that the international scene was currently favourable for Austria-Hungary to assert itself in the Balkans, economically and politically, by building railways or, and this was a key element, by regularising the position of Bosnia-Herzegovina by incorporating it formally in the empire. Germany, which was afraid of isolation after its reverse in the Morocco crisis of 1905–6, would have little choice but to back its ally. France was well disposed and in any case busy with its new role in Morocco. Great Britain, which had traditionally been friendly to Austria-Hungary, was more of a problem. It was drawing closer to Russia and by demanding international intervention to bring about reforms in Macedonia was trying to undermine Austria-Hungary's position in the Balkans.[29] Edward VII had visited the kings of Spain and Italy; did this mean a fresh attempt to encircle Austria-Hungary and Germany?[30] Nevertheless Britain was unlikely to intervene in the Balkans unless the Straits were threatened. Italy was a problem but relations could surely be improved. Russia, whatever it felt, was weak after the war with Japan and its tentative overtures to the British had not yet developed into friendship. 'Yes, yes', Aehrenthal said to a junior colleague who tried to persuade him of the need to work with Izvolsky, the Russian Foreign Minister, 'but obviously (!!) if he doesn't go through thick and thin with us in the Balkans, then I shall be the one who will go FIRST to the English!'[31]

Aehrenthal recognised that there were risks in stirring up the Balkans. The international scene, he told Austria-Hungary's Common Ministerial Council in the autumn of 1907, was generally good but there were trouble spots, such as the Balkans themselves or Morocco, and there were turbulent forces at large in the world. 'The stage is set, the actors are ready, only the costumes are lacking for the play to begin. *The second decade of the 20th century may well witness very grave events*. In view of the combustible material about, they may come sooner.'[32] In 1908 Aehrenthal came close to setting that material alight but luck was with him and the world for the time being.

At the start of the year he announced to the assembled delegates from Austria and Hungary that he intended to build a railway southwards through the Sanjak of Novi Bazar to run into Macedonia and link up with the Ottoman railways running down to the ports on the Aegean or to Constantinople. Although Aehrenthal blandly said that the proposed railway was merely economic and did not therefore contravene any of the existing agreements on the Balkans, nobody outside Austria-Hungary, including much of the foreign press, believed him. The Serbians rightly saw the railway as Austria-Hungary's way of cementing its hold over the Sanjak and therefore preventing a union between Serbia and Montenegro as well as extending the Dual Monarchy's influence into the Ottoman Empire. The British were convinced that Austria-Hungary was working behind the scenes to block the reforms they were proposing in partnership with the Russians for Macedonia in return for approval for the railway from the sultan.[33] The British were also uneasy about Austria-Hungary's partner in the Dual Alliance. The naval race was continuing and the Reichstag was going to pass another of Tirpitz's naval bills in March. The proposed railway also undercut a project the Serbians and the Russians had to build a railway from the Danube across Macedonia to the Adriatic. The Russians, who had not been properly forewarned, were furious with Aehrenthal; a railway, which in that era was a sure way of spreading political influence, was going against their 1897 agreement with Austria-Hungary to respect the status quo in the Balkans.[34] Izvolsky, the vain and self-important Russian Foreign Minister, took the Sanjak railway as a personal insult and complained of Aehrenthal to the German ambassador: 'he has thrown a bomb between my legs'.[35] The Austrian-Hungarian Foreign Minister was unrepentant and in any case he had little use for Izvolsky, whom he thought a dangerous liberal and too much influenced by Russia's new friend, Great Britain.[36]

Nevertheless, Izvolsky, who was realistic about Russia's weak position after the war with Japan, was prepared to continue discussions with Aehrenthal on the other of his counterpart's schemes – for Austria-Hungary to annex Bosnia-Herzegovina outright – because he saw that Russia might be able to bargain for what it had always wanted and that was some form of control of the Straits. The two Foreign Ministers had started their discussions in person in the autumn of 1907 when Izvolsky visited Vienna, and these continued by letter, in spite of the uproar over the Sanjak railway, into the summer of 1908. Although he did not indicate a timetable, Aehrenthal made it clear that he intended to carry out the annexation. In return he was prepared to give up the empire's rights in the Sanjak and withdraw its garrisons. Izvolsky, who had, as he later pointed out, little to bargain with, suggested that Russia would accept the annexation if it got Austria-Hungary's support for changing the international agreements which governed the Straits to allow Russian warships, and only Russian warships, to move freely back and forth between the Black Sea and the Mediterranean.

In June Izvolsky also got, or so he believed, assurance of support from another quarter. To cement the entente between their two countries, Edward VII and Nicholas II met that month on each other's yachts off the Russian Baltic port of Reval (today Tallinn in Estonia). The two monarchs and their advisers, a formidable array which included Charles Hardinge, the head of the Foreign Office in London, Admiral Jacky Fisher, Stolypin and Izvolsky, discussed the matters of common interest such as the dangers of the naval race between Britain and Germany, the troubled state of Macedonia, and a project to share the building of a railway from the south coast of Persia up to the Russian border on Persia's north (which would conveniently challenge the planned German railway from Constantinople through to Baghdad).[37] While Hardinge later denied that the British had given any promises to the Russians on the matter of the Straits, Izvolsky returned to St Petersburg firmly convinced that the British would stand by Russia in revising the international agreements over them in Russia's favour.[38]

The Reval meeting had other far-reaching consequences; the Kaiser saw in it yet more evidence that his uncle and the other 'rascals' were plotting how to encircle Germany.[39] That again underscored the importance of the alliance with Austria-Hungary. 'We, allied to Austria,' Wilhelm boasted at the time of the Reval meeting to one of his favourite naval officers, 'don't need to fear an alliance of France, Russia and England. For that we are strong enough. Our army is second to none and our navy isn't made from cardboard, even if it can't match the English still for a while.'[40] Far to the south, in the Ottoman Empire, the reformist officers in the Committee of Union and Progress concluded that the Reval meeting meant that Britain and Russia were making plans to partition Macedonia.[41] In late July, the 'Young Turks' mutinied against the sultan and forced him to accept a constitution. That in turn put pressure on Aehrenthal to bring forward his timetable for annexing Bosnia-Herzegovina. If the Young Turks succeeded in establishing a strong government, they would be a much more formidable opponent than the old sultan. European newspapers carried reports that the new regime in Constantinople intended to reverse the disintegration of the Ottoman Empire in the Balkans and elsewhere. The Young Turks pointedly invited the inhabitants of the two provinces to send representatives to the new parliament in Constantinople. On the other hand, if the Ottoman Empire collapsed into chaos and civil war, which seemed equally likely, there would be a general scramble among the powers to grab its territory and Austria-Hungary needed to get in first.

By the end of the summer, Aehrenthal had approval from his own government to carry out the annexation. He also sent a memorandum to Izvolsky on 27 August in which he expressed the hope that Russia would be 'benevolent and friendly' if circumstances forced Austria-Hungary to annex Bosnia-Herzegovina. In recompense, he repeated, Austria-Hungary would withdraw its troops from the Sanjak. He did not promise more beyond saying that he hoped Russia and Austria-Hungary could work together to maintain the status quo elsewhere in the Balkans. To Schoen, the amiable and ineffective German Foreign Secretary, he downplayed the possibility of Russia's being concerned about the annexation: 'The Bear will growl and snarl, but won't bite or strike out with its claws.' Izvolsky was not at all inclined to snarl; he was prepared to accept the annexation but merely wanted to see what, if anything, Russia could get in return for not opposing it.[42]

On 16 September Aehrenthal and Izvolsky met quietly at the mediaeval castle of Buchlau in Moravia which belonged to Berchtold, the ambassador of Austria-Hungary in St Petersburg. Their purpose was to negotiate an agreement satisfactory to both on the annexation and opening up of the Straits issue. By this point the two Foreign Ministers did not like or trust each other; when Berchtold came into the room where they were meeting to tell them that lunch was ready, he found them both in an angry mood. Aehrenthal later said that he spent most of the morning listening to Izvolsky complaining about the Sanjak railway. Izvolsky, for his part, claimed that he was completely exhausted after hours of 'very stormy negotiations'. By the end of the day, nevertheless, the two men apparently had an agreement; Russia would be suitably benevolent if Austria-Hungary had to annex Bosnia and Herzegovina, and Austria-Hungary at the same time would leave the

Sanjak; Austria-Hungary would support Russia's proposals for changing the agreements on the Straits; and Montenegro and Serbia would be allowed to divide the Sanjak if the Ottoman Empire collapsed. Finally, and this was to become important, both would recognise Bulgaria if, as was likely, it declared its full independence sometime soon. When Izvolsky cabled the news to Nicholas, the tsar was 'extraordinarily pleased'.[43] Berchtold was so delighted that his castle had witnessed such a momentous meeting that he immediately arranged for a plaque to be put up.[44] Aehrenthal went back to Vienna and Izvolsky spent the evening playing bridge with his host.[45] The Russian perhaps had better luck with cards than with international negotiations.

No records were kept of the meeting and when the whole issue of Bosnia-Herzegovina blew up and became a serious international crisis, both men gave their own versions of what had taken place which, not surprisingly, varied on some key details. Did Izvolsky get a firm quid pro quo from Aehrenthal: Russian support for the annexation and Austrian-Hungarian support for Russia's getting what it wanted at the Straits? Aehrenthal denied it. In an attempt to exonerate himself, Izvolsky was to claim that Aehrenthal had double-crossed him by carrying out the annexation too soon: Russia, he argued, had not had time to prepare international opinion for a discussion of the Straits. This is not entirely true; when Izvolsky left Buchlau he understood that the annexation was coming soon, probably right after the delegations from the Austrian and Hungarian parliaments had been together for their annual meeting at the beginning of October.[46] And Izvolsky may have been planning some double-crossing himself by planning to call for an international conference of the powers to authorise the annexation. As Izvolsky wrote to St Petersburg shortly before the Buchlau meeting: 'Austria will appear in the character of the accused, while we will appear in the role of the defenders of the Balkan Slavs and even Turkey.' (Aehrenthal later insisted that the most that Austria-Hungary had ever agreed to or would was a conference to ratify the annexation after the fact.)[47] The most that can be said is that at Buchlau the two men made a cynical deal to get what they could out of the Ottoman Empire and neither expected the huge international uproar which followed.

After the Buchlau meeting, Izvolsky went off on a long-planned tour of Europe's capitals while Aehrenthal let his allies, Germany and

Russia, know of his intentions towards Bosnia-Herzegovina, without giving them a specific date. The annexation, however, was not the only move in the Balkans that had been speeded up by the Young Turk seizure of power. Bulgaria, which had long chafed at its status as part of the Ottoman Empire, was preparing to take the opportunity to declare its independence. Izvolsky had done his best to discourage the Bulgarians; he did not want it to look as though there was a widespread plot to destroy the Ottoman Empire. Moreover, the Ottomans still had enough force left to attack Bulgaria.[48] Aehrenthal had no such concerns. When Prince Ferdinand paid a visit to Budapest in late September, Aehrenthal dropped broad hints that things might be changing soon in the Balkans and suggested that Bulgaria look out for itself. He did not tell Ferdinand that Austria-Hungary was planning to annex Bosnia-Herzegovina on 6 October and Ferdinand, who was not known as Foxy for nothing, did not tell him that Bulgaria was going to announce its independence the day before.[49] Bulgaria duly went ahead and Ferdinand, who now took the title tsar, appeared in robes modelled on those of a Byzantine emperor which had been made for him by a supplier of theatrical costumes.[50] The Austrian-Hungarian announcement about Bosnia-Herzegovina duly came the following day and claimed that the annexation had the full support of Russia. Since the Russians never got what they had expected in return – the opening of the Straits to their warships – they felt they had been cheated. Austria-Hungary for its part felt no need to compensate them or Serbia, which also claimed Bosnia-Herzegovina. Together the Bulgarian declaration of independence and the annexation stirred up turmoil in the Balkans, pitted Austria-Hungary against Russia, and dragged the allies of each into a major international crisis with talk of war which lasted until the following spring.

The news of the annexation did not come as a complete surprise to Europe. The ambassador of Austria-Hungary in Paris had handed over the confidential letter from Franz Joseph to the French President three days early because the latter was going away for the weekend and rumours of the move had inevitably leaked out. The ambassador himself was unrepentant, writing to Aehrenthal: 'That I am by nature impulsive, I know only too well, but at my age it is difficult to change a basic characteristic.'[51] Berchtold who carried a similar letter to the tsar, had to chase the imperial yacht around the Gulf of Finland. The Russians were annoyed both at the speed with which the annexation had taken place and that they had not been officially told until the day it occurred. (Berchtold in fact wanted to resign his post as Austria-Hungary's ambassador there because he felt Aehrenthal had been less than completely honest with Izvolsky.[52]) In the Duma and the press, there was a storm of protest over the two provinces inhabited by fellow Slavs going to Austria-Hungary, and Izvolsky came under increasing attack for not safeguarding Russia's interests in the Balkans. Within the government, his fellow ministers were already angered as well by the fact that neither Nicholas nor Izvolsky had bothered to tell them about the discussions with Austria-Hungary until after the Buchlau meeting. Stolypin, the Prime Minister, in fact threatened to resign and he and Vladimir Kokovtsov, the Finance Minister, led the attack on Izvolsky after news of the annexation reached Russia. Nicholas began to back away from his Foreign Minister, who found his position weakening as the months went by.[53]

Germany was also offended by the manner of the announcement: the Kaiser felt that Aehrenthal had not played fair with Russia and complained that he learned the news from the newspapers. Austria-Hungary's long-serving ambassador, Count Ladislaus Szögyény, was obliged to visit Wilhelm at his hunting lodge in East Prussia to try to smooth things over. After a train trip of many hours, the unfortunate Szögyény was taken off in what he described as a 'splendid imperial motor car' which promptly turned over.[54] Wilhelm was concerned, with reason, that Germany risked losing its influence in Constantinople which it had carefully built up over the preceding years. He also felt that Aehrenthal unnecessarily alienated Russia when the Dual Alliance still had hopes of detaching it from the entente.[55] In the end, however, the Germans felt they had little choice but to support their chief ally. It was a dilemma they would face again in 1914.

In Austria-Hungary itself reactions were mixed. While the Hungarian government welcomed the increase of territory, it made it clear that it would not accept a third, South Slav, partner in the Dual Monarchy. As a result the status of Bosnia-Herzegovina was to remain, as one Hungarian politician said, 'floating like Mahomet's coffin in the air' under the administration of the joint Minister of Finance in Vienna.[56]

The empire's own South Slavs, who were becoming increasingly politically active, were lukewarm about the annexation. The emerging Croat–Serb coalition within the Croatian parliament openly opposed it. The governor of Croatia arrested some fifty deputies and charged them with treason. The subsequent trial was a travesty, with biased judges and flimsy or forged evidence, and the guilty verdict had to be overturned. 'This trial was an early fruit of the annexation policy,' wrote the leading Hungarian newspaper. 'All and everything it in it was politics.'[57] Forgery also played a part in another sensational trial in the same period. Dr Heinrich Friedjung, a leading nationalist historian and political figure, published articles claiming to have evidence that key South Slav political leaders within Austria-Hungary were in the pay of Serbia. The documents turned out to have been conveniently supplied (and forged) by the Dual Monarchy's Foreign Ministry. Both trials shamed the government and Aehrenthal in particular and served to alienate further the empire's South Slavs.

Among Austria-Hungary's ruling classes, however, there was jubilation at the news of the annexation. 'We have showed Europe once more that we are still a great power!' Franz Ferdinand wrote to Aehrenthal, 'Very good!' He advised Aehrenthal to treat the new provinces with an iron fist and to meet any attempts by Serbia to send in agitators with bullets or a salutary hanging or two. And any hostile reactions from the other powers could, the archduke was confident, be managed. 'The anger of England is costly but the fatty Eddy will already have consoled himself with a few bottles of champagne and the company of a few so-called ladies.'[58]

It was not going to be as easy as that. The Foreign Office by this point was dominated by suspicion of Germany and the Dual Alliance. The British were annoyed too at Austria-Hungary's by-passing of the international agreements on the Balkans and worried about the impact on the Ottoman Empire. The Liberal government approved of the Young Turks and did not wish to see them undermined. And if the Ottoman Empire was driven to the point of collapse British interests at the eastern end of the Mediterranean would be threatened. British policy in the crisis was a balancing act between supporting the Ottoman Empire, counteracting German and Austrian-Hungarian influence there, and keeping on good terms as much as possible with Russia while not supporting the changes to the agreements on the Straits which the Russians wanted. (The British eventually suggested opening the Straits to warships of all nations, which, of course, was the last thing the Russians wanted.)[59]

From the British point of view, the crisis came at a bad time. The naval scare, with its fears of German invasion, was in full swing (he knew for a fact, said a backbench Member of Parliament, that German agents had concealed 50,000 Mauser rifles and 7 million rounds of ammunition in the heart of London)[60] and the government was facing demands to increase its spending on the British navy. At the end of October the *Daily Telegraph* published its famous interview with the Kaiser, where Wilhelm blamed the British government for the bad relations between Britain and Germany, which further aroused British opinion against Germany. As Grey remarked to the British ambassador in Berlin: 'this is not a time when any nation can safely strike sparks'.[61] To add to the tensions, there was a serious crisis between France and Germany which had started over three German deserters from the French Foreign Legion in North Africa. On 25 September, the French had recaptured the deserters, who were being helped by the German consul in Casablanca. The German government promptly demanded an apology. As happened increasingly easily in those years, there was talk of war. By that November the British government was seriously considering what it would do if hostilities broke out between France and Germany.[62] Fortunately the issue was settled when the two sides agreed to refer it to arbitration.

In addition to the Casablanca incident, the French were largely preoccupied by domestic issues, with a rise in working-class militancy and the growth on the right of a new aggressive nationalism. The last thing France wanted was to be drawn into a quarrel in the Balkans in which it had little interest. Like Britain, it also wished to see a stable Ottoman Empire and a peaceful Balkans. French investors held as much as 70–80 per cent of the combined debt of the Ottoman Empire, Serbia and Bulgaria.[63] Nevertheless, although the Foreign Minister at the time, Stephen Pichon, disliked Russia and the Russian alliance, he recognised that France had little choice but to support its ally. So France denounced the annexation and supported Russia's call for an international conference. Privately, the French let the Russians know that France expected to co-operate with Britain over the Straits and, as the crisis worsened, urged the Russians to be reasonable and find a peaceful solution.[64]

In Constantinople, locals attacked Austrian-Hungarian businesses and set upon the Dual Monarchy's citizens in the streets while the Ottoman government supported a boycott of trade with Austria-Hungary. The most furious reactions of all came, understandably, in Serbia. Huge demonstrations marched through the streets of Belgrade and a mob tried to smash the windows of the Austrian-Hungarian embassy. The crown prince said he, like all Serbs, was ready to die for a Greater Serbia. (He never got the chance; he was removed from the succession the following year when he kicked a servant to death in a fit of rage and died of old age in Tito's Yugoslavia in 1972.) A new paramilitary group, Narodna Odbrana (National Defence), formed, which was to play an important part in politics in the next few years, and Serbian volunteers, with the connivance of the government, slipped over the borders into Bosnia-Herzegovina to stir up opposition to Austria-Hungary.[65]

The Serbian government sent representatives around Europe to win over public opinion. It also demanded compensation although it had no good legal grounds for doing so. 'Give us a pasture or mill', the Serbian ambassador in London begged his counterpart from Austria-Hungary, 'anything to mollify our country.'[66] In fact Serbia asked for much more – the Sanjak of Novi Bazar – which would link it to Montenegro, or even the reversal of the annexation. Montenegro also asked for compensation, specifically the end to the conditions imposed on it by the settlement of 1878 which prevented it from such things as having a navy. Both Serbia and Montenegro also took steps to mobilise their armies and ordered new weapons from abroad.[67] In an ominous foreshadowing of what was to come, Serbian officials talked about going to war if necessary. In late October, Nikola Pašić, who was to be Prime Minister in 1914, urged Russian leaders including the tsar himself and his ministers as well as prominent Panslavists to stand firm against Austria-Hungary, come what may. In a conversation with Izvolsky, he implied that Serbia might have to act alone, 'if it is a question of the existence, the honour, and the dignity of the people'.[68]

Izvolsky, who only a few weeks before had been preening himself on his successful negotiations with Austria-Hungary, was dismayed at the international reaction and, so he said, furious with Aehrenthal for a premature annexation before Russia could get its own demands in order. The Russian went, said Berchtold unkindly, from being a flamboyant peacock to a rampaging turkey.[69] Aehrenthal, who had got what he wanted and who was assured of German support, was unconcerned. When Izvolsky blustered about betrayal, Aehrenthal simply threatened to release their previous secret communications and his own version of the deal at Buchlau which would undermine Izvolsky's claims to be surprised. He adamantly refused to hold the international conference Izvolsky now insisted upon or to give compensation to the Ottoman Empire, much less to Serbia or Montenegro, whatever the two Balkan states said or did.

Conrad, who had strongly supported the annexation, urged his government to take the opportunity to wage a preventive war on Serbia and Montenegro; Italy too if it showed signs of intervening. He promised that he could defeat all three handily. Austria-Hungary could put over 700,000 men in the field along its southern borders while Serbia had at most 160,000 men, Montenegro a mere 43,000, and Italy, which was highly unlikely to fight, 417,000. What is more, Austria-Hungary's equipment and training was much superior to that of its enemies.[70] Once Serbia had been defeated, it should be incorporated into the empire. That last was too much for Aehrenthal, who understood the political difficulties; the most he would do to Serbia would be force it into a customs union. While he preferred the cheaper route of diplomacy to settle the crisis, he certainly did not rule out war.[71] 'Perhaps', he wrote to Franz Ferdinand near the start of the crisis, 'conflict between us and Serbia in the course of the next few months is unavoidable, and as soon as this is clear, I favour demonizing Serbia with all energy possible.'[72]

All that winter of 1908–9, said a member of the Foreign Ministry in Vienna, it felt as though they were on the brink of war.[73] Conrad prevailed upon the government to step up war preparations: he ordered new armaments, moved forces into Bosnia-Herzegovina, and delayed demobilising conscripts whose terms were up. He also increased his forces on Austria-Hungary's frontier with Serbia and made preparations to mobilise forces in Galicia near the border with Russia.[74] Franz Ferdinand, for all his hatred of the 'Balkan curs', acted as a brake on

Conrad's headlong dash towards war. Austria-Hungary, he argued to Aehrenthal, had much to lose by going to war. 'Please restrain Conrad', the archduke wrote to Conrad's adjutant, 'he must stop this warmongering. It would be tempting to strike down the Serbians ... but what use are such cheap laurels when we might risk the impossible war on three fronts? Then it would be the end of the song.'[75] Unfortunately, when another crisis broke out in the Balkans in 1914, Franz Ferdinand was no longer there to advocate restraint.

While Aehrenthal was enjoying the success of his annexation, Izvolsky, who was in Paris when the news broke, continued his increasingly desperate trip around Europe's capital cities to try to gain support at the very least for an international conference. (Bülow said maliciously that he really delayed his return to St Petersburg because the pretty and extravagant Madame Izvolsky wanted to do her Christmas shopping.)[76] Russia's own allies would do little but offer to help broker an end to the crisis. When the Russians asked Grey point blank that November what Great Britain would do if Russia went to war with Austria-Hungary over the Balkans, he temporised: 'so much depended upon how the quarrel arose, and who was the aggressor'. Privately, however, Grey told his close colleagues 'it would be very difficult for England to keep out of it'.[77] In Berlin Bülow was sympathetic (he had not completely given up hope of winning Russia back) but told Izvolsky Germany could do nothing. The Germans knew that Russia's financial situation was bad and calculated, rightly, that Russia was in no position to fight. The Kaiser happily wrote 'Bluff' on the memorandums that came across his desk saying that Izvolsky was threatening war.[78] When Izvolsky arrived back in St Petersburg at the start of November, Berchtold found him a broken man. 'He lay limp on his armchair. His eyes were dull, his voice raw, his speech like that of a dying man.'[79] Izvolsky had good reason to feel depressed; Russia had been made to look weak and isolated abroad and his own position had been seriously damaged. Izvolsky's own colleagues led by Stolypin made it clear that he could no longer have a free hand in foreign policy but must consult the Council of Ministers. To make matters worse, it turned out that neither he nor anyone in the Russian Foreign Office knew, as Aehrenthal was delighted to point out, that Russia had agreed a couple times in the 1870s and 1880s not to oppose the annexation of Bosnia-Herzegovina. 'You will understand', the tsar wrote to his mother, 'what an unpleasant surprise this is, and what an embarrassing position we are in.'[80]

The onset of winter in the Balkans made war unlikely until the following March but intense diplomatic activity continued. While Britain, France and Russia still insisted publicly on a conference, Britain was in fact prepared to see bilateral agreements. It took the lead in brokering a settlement between Bulgaria and the Ottoman Empire where the Ottomans would recognise Bulgaria's independence in return for compensation to cover such things as railways which had been built with Ottoman funds. Although Tsar Ferdinand (as he now was) had promised to be as meek as a lamb, he refused to pay the amount the Ottomans demanded and threatened war on the Ottoman Empire. The British persuaded the Russians to provide the necessary funds. An agreement was reached in principle in December 1908 but haggling over details went on until the following April.[81]

By the start of 1909, Austria-Hungary and the Ottoman Empire had also worked out a settlement whereby the former paid the latter an indemnity in return for recognition of the annexation. Here Britain intervened on the side of the Ottoman Empire, to get a substantial settlement for it. This served to persuade opinion in Austria-Hungary that Britain was its determined enemy, even, so Aehrenthal believed, to the point of using the Balkan troubles to have a general European war so that Britain could deal with the German navy. 'If England hopes to break us', he exclaimed to Friedjung, 'then they will find in me a spirited opponent, who won't make victory easy for them.'[82] In both countries the press joined in enthusiastically to attack the other. What had been a friendship of long standing throughout the nineteenth century between Britain and Austria-Hungary slid into the past as the dividing lines in Europe became more clearly drawn.

The most difficult issue to settle in the aftermath of the annexation was the question of compensation for Serbia, complicated by the fact that Russia was backing Serbia's demands and Germany was supporting Austria-Hungary. The most Aehrenthal was prepared to offer Serbia was some economic concessions such as access to a port on the Adriatic, but only if Serbia recognised the annexation and agreed to live on peaceful terms with Austria-Hungary. The Serbian government remained intransigent and, as spring melted the snows in the Balkans, the talk of war mounted again around Europe's capitals. The German government, mindful of its own defeat in the earlier Morocco crisis, was standing firmly behind its ally. 'This time', said Kiderlen, the acting Foreign Secretary, 'the others are about to cave in.'[83] What was not known publicly at the time was that Germany gave Austria-Hungary an assurance that, if a war between it and Serbia led to Russian intervention, the terms of the Dual Alliance would come into force and Germany would come into the war on Austria-Hungary's side. Germany was to make a similar promise in the crisis of 1914.

In St Petersburg, Stolypin, who remained opposed to war, told the British ambassador at the start of March that Russian public opinion was so firmly in favour of support of Serbia that the government would not be able to resist coming to its defence: 'Russia would have, in that case, to mobilise, and a general conflagration would then be imminent.'[84] In Berlin, where the *Daily Telegraph* affair was creating its own crisis, the war party, which included high-ranking members of the military, saw a war as a chance for Germany to escape from its troubles, both those at home and abroad.[85] The Kaiser, who was still recovering from his breakdown over the affair, was not enthusiastic about war but does not seem to have opposed it actively. He was much occupied, said a courtier, 'with momentous questions as those of new kinds of chin straps, new fastenings for helmet chains, double seams on soldiers' trousers, and frequent inspections of the Wardrobe.'[86] In Vienna Aehrenthal talked matter-of-factly about war. 'The Serbian scallywag wanted to steal apples from our garden and we have apprehended him and will only let him go if he promises lasting improvement.'[87]

In the middle of March the Serbian government rejected Austria-Hungary's offer in a note which the British found unnecessarily provocative. While Aehrenthal was drafting a reply, the German government decided to act. It sent what amounted to an ultimatum to St Petersburg to say that the Russian government must recognise the annexation. If Germany received 'any evasive, conditional, or unclear response', it would take that as a refusal on Russia's part: 'We would then withdraw and let events take their course.'[88] On 23 March the Russian government which had already been told by the War Minister that its military could not hope to fight Austria-Hungary, capitulated.[89] Serbia caved in a week later and sent a note to Vienna in which it promised to give up protesting the annexation, to step down its military preparations and disband the volunteer militias which had sprung up, and to live with Austria-Hungary 'on terms of friendly and neighbourly relations'.[90] In St Petersburg, Berchtold invited Izvolsky and Nicolson, the British ambassador, and their wives to a 'fin-de-crisis' dinner.[91] The Kaiser sent the tsar an Easter egg with thanks for helping to preserve the peace.[92] Some time later he told an audience in Vienna that he himself had kept the peace by standing should to shoulder with Franz Joseph like a knight in shining armour.[93]

For all Germany's firm stand, the crisis did cause concerns within the leadership over the country's preparedness for a war. Bülow, who had initially been a strong supporter of Tirpitz and his naval programme, was already having trouble getting the Reichstag to approve the funds. And, as he said to Holstein shortly before the annexation: 'We cannot weaken the army, for our destiny will be decided on land.' During the crisis itself, he sceptically asked Tirpitz point blank whether the navy was capable of withstanding a British attack. The admiral fell back on his standard answer: 'In a few years our fleet would be so strong that an attack on it even by Britain would mean a great military risk.'[94] Before he was eased out of office in the summer of 1909, Bülow started to explore the possibilities of ending the naval race with Great Britain. His successor, Bethmann Hollweg, was very much of the same opinion and he found a receptive audience in Britain, where radicals in the Cabinet and Parliament, led by Lloyd George, the Chancellor of the Exchequer, were determined both to cut spending and lower tensions with Germany. Talks started in the autumn of 1909 and continued through to the summer of 1911, when a fresh crisis over Morocco put them on hold. How much chance they had of succeeding then or later is debatable. Tirpitz and the Kaiser, whose word in the end was final, were prepared to offer a slowdown in the rate of German building but only one which would still have left Germany with two big ships to every three of Britain's, which was too close a margin to be acceptable to the British. And in return for slowing down its naval building, Germany would have expected a political settlement as well, with Britain promising to remain neutral if Germany got into a war with another European power. For the British, where suspicion of Germany was now deeply entrenched in the Foreign Office and in the minds of key members of the Cabinet, notably Grey himself, such a promise, which would have undermined if not destroyed the Triple Entente, was highly unlikely. What the British really wanted was an arms agreement which would let them cut naval expenditure significantly. Only after that were they prepared to talk about a political settlement. Although talks between the two sides started in the autumn of 1909, the German and British governments remained far apart and little progress had been made when another crisis in 1911, this one over Morocco again, put them on hold.

Like the past Morocco crisis and the one to come, the Bosnian affair left its share of memories, often bitter ones, and seemed as well to offer lessons. Conrad was in despair at seeing the opportunity for a preventive war slip by. He wrote to a friend 'with this resolution of the Balkan crisis a thousand hopes ... are buried for me. I have also lost the joy in my profession, and thus lost that which has sustained me in all circumstances since the age of eleven.'[95] He later wrote a long memorandum arguing that it would have been better to have dealt with Serbia militarily during the crisis and not to have postponed the inevitable conflict. In the future Austria-Hungary was going to face the choice of a war on several fronts or make 'far-reaching concessions' which might destroy it in any case. Conrad did find encouragement, however, in concluding that mobilisation together with the German ultimatum had worked to make Russia and Serbia back down. Aehrenthal concurred: 'a text-book example of how success is only certain if the *strength* is there to get one's own way ...'[96] Unwisely, he made little attempt to be magnanimous towards Russia, saying of Izvolsky: 'These controversies with this blackhearted ape bore me and I have decided not to reach out to him.'[97] Although Aehrenthal died of leukaemia in 1912, his anti-Serbian and anti-Russian views and his belief that Austria-Hungary must have an active foreign policy and, in particular, assert itself in the Balkans had a strong influence on a younger generation of diplomats, some of whom were going to play a key role in the events of 1914.[98]

The Russians, for their part, had little desire to mend fences with Austria-Hungary or with Germany. Izvolsky, who was going to be eased out of office after a decent interval and sent to Paris as the Russian ambassador, blamed Aehrenthal for destroying the accord in the Balkans between their two countries and warned the German ambassador that their rivalry was now bound to end in conflict.[99] After he received the German ultimatum, the tsar wrote to his mother: 'It is quite true that the form and method of Germany's action – I mean towards us – has simply been brutal and we won't forget it.' Germany, he went on, was trying again to separate Russia from its allies, France and Great Britain: 'Such methods tend to bring about the opposite result.'[100] The denouement of the Bosnian crisis was, said one deputy in the Duma, a 'diplomatic Tsushima' as bad in its own way as that appalling defeat in the Russo-Japanese War. The Duma promptly approved another increase in defence spending. Among the military there was increasing talk of getting ready for the next round with Austria-Hungary, which was sure to come in the next few years.[101] Russians of all classes, wrote Nicolson to Grey, felt bitterly ashamed that they had abandoned their Slavic brothers: 'Russia has suffered a deep humiliation and has renounced the traditional part which she had hitherto played in South-East Europe, and in the prosecution of which she had made so great sacrifices in the past.'[102] Such memories had not faded six years later.[103] 'Are we going to unleash a world war', Jaurès cried out to French journalists on the eve of the Great War, 'because Izvolsky is still furious over Aehrenthal's deception on the Bosnian affair?'[104] The answer must surely be yes, in part, although there are many other links in the chain of events leading towards 1914.

The Bosnian crisis strengthened the Dual Alliance between Germany and Austria-Hungary. It worsened, however, the relations between Austria-Hungary and Italy, the third partner in the Triple Alliance which had been all too well aware of the Dual Monarchy's preparations for war against it. In the autumn of 1909 the Italian king, Victor Emmanuel III, received the tsar and Izvolsky at Racconigi, his royal hunting lodge in the north-eastern corner of Italy. The Russian party ostentatiously took a roundabout route through Germany to avoid setting foot on the soil of Austria-Hungary. Italy also upped its defence spending, setting off a dreadnought race in the Adriatic with Austria-Hungary and strengthening its fortifications and forces along their common land borders. For its part Austria-Hungary, which had other enemies to worry about besides Italy, also increased its spending sharply – by more than 70 per cent between 1907 and 1912 – during and after the crisis.[105]

While the crisis also caused strains in the Triple Entente, it did not seriously damage it. Indeed, France, Britain and Russia became further accustomed to consulting each other on international issues. The French Foreign Minister, Stephen Pichon, issued instructions to his ambassadors to work with France's two partners as a matter of general principle.[106] Although Britain continued to insist on its freedom of action, it had shown during this crisis that it would stand by Russia just as it had shown France, and the world, in the Morocco one. Only Italy kept a certain distance from its partners in the Triple Alliance and maintained good relations with the Triple Entente. Increasingly the other powers felt that they had little choice but to stay where they were, whether it was Austria-Hungary and Germany needing each other or Russia and France. And as the earlier crisis over Morocco had led the British to start serious military talks with the French, this one set the Conrad–Moltke discussions in train.

In the Balkans themselves, the ending of the crisis did not bring either stability or peace. Ottoman Turkey was left, if possible, even more resentful of outside meddling in its affairs. Bulgaria was only temporarily appeased by its independence; it still dreamed of the greater Bulgaria that had been set up briefly in 1878 and looked longingly at the Macedonian territories. And the Sanjak, which Aehrenthal had abandoned in a gesture of goodwill towards the Ottoman Empire, remained a temptation for both Serbia and Montenegro to seize if the Ottomans, as was more than likely, weakened still further. Serbia had been obliged to submit to Austria-Hungary but it had no intention of keeping its promises. It surreptitiously funnelled support to a Greater Serbia movement and set about improving its army. Thanks to generous French loans, it was able to set up its own armaments factories and also buy weapons from France (the British were largely cut out of the market by their entente partner).[107] Serbia's relations with Austria-Hungary continued on their downward path. Both countries were obsessed, dangerously so, with the other.

Russia, driven in part by its own public opinion and with a desire for revenge on Austria-Hungary, continued to meddle in the Balkans. Its diplomats worked to promote an alliance of Balkan states under Russian tutelage which would act as a barrier against further inroads into the Balkans and the Ottoman Empire by the Dual Alliance and which might in time, so it was hoped, become Russia's ally there against Austria-Hungary. Russian ties with Serbia, in particular, grew stronger. In 1909 Nicholas Hartwig, an outspoken advocate of an active Russian policy in the Balkans, became Russia's ambassador in Belgrade. 'A sedate, bearded Muscovite of deceptive bonhomie', in Berchtold's words, he was a passionate Russian nationalist and Panslavist who hated Austria-Hungary passionately (although, curiously, Vienna was his favourite city in the world and he went there at every opportunity). Hartwig, who was still there in 1914, was both forceful and energetic and rapidly won for himself a position of considerable influence in Serbia which he used to encourage Serbian nationalists in their aspirations to a Greater Serbia.[108]

A year after the Bosnian crisis blew up, Hardinge, the head of the British Foreign Office, wrote to the British ambassador in Vienna: 'I entirely share your views as to the absolute necessity of an understanding of some kind between Austria and Russia as to the policy in the Balkans, otherwise it is unlikely that unbroken peace will obtain in those regions for many years ... Any other policy would inevitably end in a European war.'[109] Unfortunately, such an understanding never came again. Europe was to enjoy a short three years of peace before the next crisis came and then the next. And with each crisis, the two groupings of Europe's powers became more like full-blown alliances whose partners would support each other through thick and thin.

CHAPTER 15

1911:
The Year of Discords –
Morocco Again

O n 1 July 1911 the *Panther*, a small German gunboat with, as the Kaiser said dismissively, 'two or three little pop guns on board' anchored off the port of Agadir on Morocco's Atlantic coast.[1] Small, dusty and quiet, Agadir, which was closed to foreign traders, had so far escaped the interest of Western imperialists. There were rumours of minerals in the inland Atlas mountains but only a handful of firms, among them Germans, had started to prospect. There was some fishing – the local sardines were said to be delicious – and a few crops here and there where there was sufficient water. The local sheep and goats looked thin and unhealthy, reported a local German representative. 'It was certainly not an area that would attract or support German farmers. To top it all, the climate was unbearable.'[2]

The German government claimed that it had sent the *Panther* and the rather larger and more imposing light cruiser the *Berlin*, which arrived a few days later, to Agadir to protect German nationals in the south of Morocco. With a lack of attention to detail and a propensity to put itself in the wrong which was going to mark the whole affair, the German Foreign Ministry only informed the other powers with an interest in Morocco after the fact, which had the effect of making them even more annoyed than they might otherwise have been. The Germans also did not do a good job of explaining why they needed to send ships to Agadir. The Foreign Ministry only got round to getting support for its claim that German interests and German subjects were in danger in the south of Morocco a couple of weeks before the *Panther* arrived off Agadir, when it asked a dozen German firms to sign a petition (which most of them did not bother to read) requesting German intervention. When the German Chancellor, Bethmann, produced this story in the Reichstag he was met with laughter. Nor were there any German nationals in Agadir itself. The local representative of the Warburg interests who was some seventy miles to the north started southwards on the evening of 1 July. After a hard journey by horse along a rocky track, he arrived at Agadir on 4 July and waved his arms to no effect from the beach to attract the attention of the *Panther* and the *Berlin*. The sole representative of the Germans under threat in southern Morocco was finally spotted and picked up the following day.[3]

In Germany, especially on the right, reaction to the news of what came to be called the spring of the *Panther* was one of approval, with relief at an end to 'humiliation', and jubilation that Germany was taking action at last. After its setbacks earlier on in Morocco and in the race for colonies in general, with the fears of encirclement in Europe by the Entente powers, Germany was showing that it mattered. 'The German dreamer awakes after sleeping for twenty years like the sleeping beauty,' said one newspaper.[4] The other powers, France in particular, but also Britain, saw it differently, as yet another colonial conflict to trouble the peace of Europe and yet another threat to the stability of the international order. The crisis also came at a time when Europe's governments were already grappling with domestic problems. Across the Continent in 1911, economies were sliding into recession. Prices had been going up while wages had been falling behind, something that had hit the poorer classes hard. Working-class militancy was on the increase: in 1910, for example, Great Britain had 531 strikes involving some 385,000 workers; for 1911 there were almost twice as many strikes with 831,000 workers. In Spain and Portugal, rural strikes and violence were bringing large parts of the countryside close to civil war.[5]

Germany's sudden move was, as everyone recognised at the time, about much more than the fate of one German in southern Morocco or

AU COURS D'UN COMBAT SOUS LES MURS DE TRIPOLI
UN SOLDAT ITALIEN S'EMPARE D'UN ÉTENDARD VERT DU PROPHÈTE

15. Italy, the least of the Great Powers, shared the general ambition for colonies. When the Ottoman Empire appeared near to collapse in 1911, the Italian government decided to seize the two Ottoman provinces of Tripoli and Cyrenaica on the south shore of the Mediterranean. Although the cartoon shows the Ottoman soldiers defeated and a triumphant Italian officer seizing a green standard, symbolic of the Prophet Mohammad, in reality the Italians had to fight a strong resistance for years to come. The Italian move encouraged the Balkan nations to attack the Ottoman Empire the following year.

prospective mineral rights. It represented a challenge to France's dominance in Morocco and to the stability of the Triple Entente. The French government had to decide how much it dared concede to Germany and whether it was in a position to resist, especially militarily. The British and the Russians, on the Entente side, and the Austrian-Hungarians and the Italians in the Triple Alliance, had to weigh their need to support their alliance partners against getting dragged into a far-off colonial struggle in which they had no real interests. And yet again, as there had been with the first crisis over Morocco in 1904–5 and the

Bosnian crisis of 1908–9, talk of war ran round Europe's capitals. William Taft, who had succeeded Roosevelt as President, became so alarmed that he offered the services of the United States as a mediator.

In fact Germany had a very good case against France in Morocco and if it had managed things better could have gained considerable sympathy and even support from the other powers which had signed the Treaty of Algeciras in 1906 setting up the international regime for Morocco. Since that time successive French governments and officials in the Quai d'Orsay had flouted both the treaty's spirit and its provisions by trying to establish political and economic dominance over the country and its feckless sultan. Germany had initially been willing to accept that France had the equivalent of a protectorate over most of Morocco as long as German businesses had equal rights with French to exploit Morocco economically. In February 1909, at the height of the crisis over Bosnia, Germany and France had indeed signed an agreement to that effect. In Berlin, the French ambassador, Paul Cambon's younger brother Jules, worked assiduously to promote better economic and political relations between the two countries which, he argued presciently but in the end in vain, was best for both and for Europe.

That brief promise, sadly for the future, was not to be fulfilled at the time. France and Germany tried, and failed, to get an agreement on the borders between the French Congo, on the north side of the Congo River, and the West African German colony of Cameroon, and proposed joint ventures in the Ottoman Empire never got off the ground. In Morocco the local French officials increasingly threw their weight around. In 1908, when the weak Sultan Abdelaziz was deposed by his brother Abdelhafid, the French moved quickly to tie up the new ruler in knots with loans and agreements. While experienced hands like Jules Cambon warned that this was bound to lead to trouble with Germany, the Quai d'Orsay went blithely ahead. It was increasingly dominated by clever, self-confident young men, many of them products of the new School of Political Science, who were strongly anti-German and ambitious for France to play a more important role in Europe and build an even greater empire than it already had. The Ottoman Empire, they argued, was on its way out just as Austria-Hungary was and France must get in quickly to snap up its share of the remnants. With a new

French colony in Morocco added to the existing one in Algeria, France would have its equivalent to British India, its own jewel in the crown. The new men in the Quai d'Orsay were supported by the nationalist press in France, to which they frequently leaked confidential information, and by strong lobbies, in particular the colonial one. A succession of weak and ill-prepared ministers meant that the officials in the Quai d'Orsay went their own way with little interference.[6]

In March 1911, in one of the frequent changes of cabinets in the Third Republic, Jean Cruppi, yet another who knew almost nothing about his new responsibilities, took up the office of Foreign Minister for, as it turned out, four months. In that short period he managed, following the advice of his officials, to do considerable damage to Franco-German relations. One of his first acts was to break an agreement with Germany to build railways in Morocco. He then moved on to block economic co-operation in other areas as well as forcing Abdelhafid to sign away his rights as an independent ruler and place himself under French protection (as imperialistic doublespeak put it). Using the pretext of disorder in the country, Cruppi then gave the orders for French troops to occupy the capital, Fez. (The French persuaded the sultan to request their help three weeks after they had arrived.) The Spanish, who had become increasingly concerned about what they correctly saw as French aims to take over the whole country, promptly moved troops into their existing area of influence, along the Mediterranean coast of Morocco. The Moroccans, as much as they could, complained, and so did the other powers. The French promised to withdraw from Fez and the surrounding countryside but discovered one reason after another as to why they should remain.

In Germany, public opinion, which had been largely indifferent to colonies ten years earlier, now was seized with their importance.[7] The German government, which was already under considerable pressure from its own colonial lobby and from those German businesses with interests in Morocco, felt that it had much to gain by taking a firm stand. Germany's international position had deteriorated with the emergence of the Triple Entente and both its neighbours, France and Russia, were strengthening their armed forces. Although the naval talks with Britain continued, they were as far from producing concrete agreement as they had been when they first started in 1908 after the Bosnian crisis. Inside Germany opposition from both sides of the political spectrum to spending on the Kaiser's navy was growing and it was becoming even more difficult for governments to find the funds that were needed. Political divisions between the right and the left had deepened and the monarchy itself, as the *Daily Telegraph* affair had shown all too clearly, was growing in unpopularity. The temptation for Germany's new Chancellor, Theobald von Bethmann Hollweg, and his colleagues to have a good international crisis to bring all Germans together in support of their government was considerable.[8] According to Bülow, his successor longed for a dramatic success such as the one that Germany and Austria-Hungary enjoyed over the Bosnian annexation. Bülow, who came to resent and despise Bethmann as a weakling, also claimed that Bethmann said rather pathetically during the handover: 'I shall soon get the hang of foreign policy.'[9]

Bethmann's whole career had been in the Prussian and then the German civil service and he had almost no direct experience of foreign affairs. He had moved steadily upwards, helped by his own intelligence and industry, and by strong family connections including with the Kaiser himself. When Wilhelm was still an insecure eighteen-year-old, he had shot his first deer on the Bethmann Hollweg estate at Hohenfinow just east of Berlin and he visited it frequently thereafter. By 1905 Bethmann was a strikingly young Prussian Minister of the Interior; in 1907 he became Minister of the Interior for Germany as a whole; and then in 1909 Chancellor. Albert Ballin, a leading Hamburg businessman and a friend of the outgoing Chancellor, called him 'Bülow's revenge' and said that he had 'all the qualities which honour a man but ruin a statesman'.[10] It was unkind but not entirely untrue.

In appearance, Bethmann, who was tall and imposing, looked very much the strong Prussian statesman. Although as a child his own grandmother had exclaimed of him, 'What will become of Theobald? He is so ugly!' he made a distinguished adult, with his long face and his grey beard and moustaches.[11] Beneath that facade, however, was a more fragile being who had endured dreadful headaches as a child and who always worried about his health. He was deeply pessimistic by nature and tormented by doubts, about himself, and about the future of his class and his country. It is believed that he did not plant trees at Hohenfinow when he inherited it because he expected that Russia would overrun it before they ever grew to maturity. At each promotion, he wondered whether the gods would punish him for reaching beyond his capacity. When he became Prussian Minister of the Interior, he claimed that he was 'painfully experiencing the disparity between my ability and my duty every day'.[12] His tendency, pronounced as a young man, to be melancholy and introspective, shy of intimacy with others, never entirely left him. Although he was a clever and educated man with strong moral standards, he also had difficulty in making up his mind. 'I have good resolutions', he wrote while still a student to a close friend, 'and I intend to put them into practice.'[13] Good resolutions were not enough and both friends and enemies commented on his tendency to procrastinate. Bülow's wife reported that Madame Bethmann confided that she wished Theobald had not taken on the position of Chancellor. 'He's always so undecided, so hesitating, so given to worrying over trifles, till, really at times, he doesn't know what he is doing. Why it's become quite a family joke.'[14]

Even a more decisive man than Bethmann would have had trouble with the position of Chancellor. The problems inherent in the German governmental system were, if anything, worse than before. The Kaiser, his various entourages, and his favoured ministers, were independent actors and frequently worked at counter-purposes to the Chancellor. The Reichstag was increasingly polarised and the Social Democrats were winning more seats almost every time there was an election. The taxation system badly needed reforming to produce the tax revenue the government needed for the armed forces and its social programmes. In the wider German society the old conservative classes fought a deter-mined rearguard action to defend their powers and position while the middle and working classes pushed for a greater share. Bethmann tried to cope with the demands coming at him from all directions, from the Kaiser, his own colleagues and the Reichstag. It did not help that, with the growth of the Social Democratic Party, especially after 1912, he had more trouble than Bülow with the Reichstag and nor did he enjoy a close relationship with his difficult master. He found it harder than his predecessor had to manage the impetuous Kaiser, which led to repeated difficulties and tensions.[15]

Bethmann filled his position, said Bülow maliciously, 'neither as a thoroughbred nor a jumper, but as a good plow-horse, plodding along slowly and steadily, because there are no hurdles in sight'.[16] The remark contained a dig at Bethmann's background, which was not as noble as that of Germany's previous Chancellors although he had married well, to the daughter of a neighbouring, old aristocratic family. The Beth-mann Hollwegs had started out in the eighteenth century as prosperous Frankfurt bankers and moved, generation by generation, into the landed upper classes. Bethmann's grandfather was a distinguished jurist and scholar who was ennobled by Wilhelm I, and his own father used his considerable fortune to buy Hohenfinow and so become, by style if not by birth, a Prussian Junker. Under the elder Bethmann's management, Hohenfinow became a prosperous estate with some 1,500 inhabitants. The future Chancellor grew up in a large seventeenth-century manor house and was educated by private tutors until he was sent off to a boarding school which saw its mission as preparing the children of the nobility for government service either as soldiers or civil servants. Beth-mann absorbed many of the prejudices of his class, its distaste for commerce or for Jews, for example. 'You know that I am not of noble blood,' he explained to a fellow student, 'but when all external life func-tions move in a privileged circle it is imprudent and false to step out of line with even one foot.'[17]

Although Bethmann, like his father, frequently found the diehard Prussian reactionaries of his own world absurd, he remained firmly con-servative in his views. He disliked much about the modern world, such as its materialism, but attempted to find ways of bridging traditional and new values. A teenager when Germany was united, he became then and remained a passionate nationalist. In 1877, when a fanatic tried to assassinate Kaiser Wilhelm I, Bethmann wrote to a close friend of his shock: 'I cannot believe that our beloved German people is incapable of being one *Volk* and one state.' He regretted the divisions in German politics and deplored 'despicable socialists and unclear doctrinaire liber-als'.[18] As a civil servant and statesman he worked for unity and social peace, hoping that by making modest reforms and improving the lot of the poorer classes he could win their allegiance to the state.

On foreign policy, Bethmann's underlying views were straightfor-ward: that peace was preferable to war but that Germany must be prepared to fight, if diplomacy failed, to defend its interests and its honour. Germany, he told the Kaiser, in the summer of 1911 as the second Morocco crisis worsened, could not afford to back down because 'our credit in the world will suffer unbearably, not only for the present, but for all future diplomatic actions'.[19] That winter, before the *Panther* made its spring to Agadir, Harry Kessler had a long conversation with Bethmann at a dinner party in Berlin. The Chancellor was moderately optimistic about the international scene: he felt that Germany's relations with Russia were improving. There was indeed some evidence for this: Nicholas had visited Wilhelm in Potsdam the previous year and their two countries had come to an agreement over railways in the Ottoman Empire, thus removing a cause of tension, and the Germans had also promised that Germany would not join any more aggressive moves on the part of Austria-Hungary in the Balkans.[20] And, Bethmann told Kessler, Britain might well come round to a more reasonable frame of mind about Germany. Russia still posed a threat to the British in India and elsewhere, and that fact in the long run could only benefit Germany: 'They *must* feel quite uncomfortable, then they will approach us. That is what I am counting on.'[21] Bethmann, unlike many of his compatriots, did not hate Britain (indeed, he sent his son to Oxford) but he saw its entente with France and Russia as a threat to Germany and hoped to break it apart. During the Morocco crisis, Rathenau, the distinguished and thoughtful German businessman, had dinner with Bethmann at his Hohenfinow estate. The Chancellor was sure that Germany had been right to confront France: 'the Morocco Question welds England and France together and must therefore be "liquidated"'. He was depressed, though, and worried about the prospect of a war. 'I tell you this confidentially,' he said to Rathenau as he walked him to his car. 'It is somewhat *for show*. We cannot yield too much.'[22]

Bethmann had in fact had misgivings about sending the *Panther* on its mission but had allowed himself to be persuaded by the Foreign Office and its forceful secretary, Alfred von Kiderlen-Wächter.[23] Bethmann usually left foreign affairs to him and Kiderlen was more than happy to take charge. Big, blond, and brutally blunt, his face marked by duelling scares, Kiderlen was afraid of no one, not even the Kaiser, and nothing, including war. He was known equally for his wit, his sarcasm, his indiscretions and his rudeness. When there was talk of sending him to London as ambassador, Grey reportedly exclaimed: 'More dreadnoughts and the bad manners of Kiderlen – that would be too much!'[24]

Initially he had been a favourite of the Kaiser, who liked his risqué jokes and stories, but, typically, he had gone too far and his rude comments about his master had got back to him. As punishment Kiderlen had been sent off to languish as Germany's ambassador in Rumania. The empress, among his other enemies, also disapproved of his way of life; he lived openly for years with a widow who kept house for him. When Bülow raised this with him, Kiderlen replied ungallantly: 'Excellency, if I were to produce the *corpus delicti* for your inspection I think you would find it rather hard to believe in any illicit relationship between me and a fat old woman like that.'[25]

The Kaiser had initially resisted Bethmann's wish to bring Kiderlen back to Berlin as Foreign Secretary but gave way, saying only that his Chancellor would find he had a louse in his fur. Kiderlen showed little gratitude or respect for Bethmann whom he called the Earthworm (*Regenwurm*) and Bethmann for his part discovered he had been dealing with a stubborn and secretive man whom he nicknamed the Mule (*Dickkopf*).[26] Part of the reason German foreign policy frequently appeared to be erratic and incoherent during Kiderlen's tenure of office was that he refused to communicate with either his ambassadors abroad, his subordinates or his colleagues. At one point, Bethmann told friends, he had to get his Foreign Secretary drunk to find out what he was up to.[27] Kiderlen may not have known himself. As a senior general in the War Ministry complained at the height of the Morocco crisis, the dispatch of the *Panther* was all too typical of the incoherent nature of German foreign policy.

> There was no understanding whatsoever of what might arise from it and of how all these possibilities were to be dealt with; the order is said to have taken shape in a few hours one afternoon, without precise knowledge of local conditions, the anchorage and the like. It is hardly surprising that we now find ourselves more or less at a loss in the face of the resulting political difficulties.[28]

In creating the crisis, Kiderlen seems to have intended to force the French to negotiate in earnest over Morocco and, like Bethmann, he hoped that Britain could be detached from the Triple Entente. Kiderlen did not make clear from the first either to his own colleagues or to the

French what he had in mind as compensation for Germany, either in Morocco or elsewhere, perhaps as a deliberate tactic.[29] He assumed, with some reason, that the French were not prepared to fight and so he was prepared to engage in brinkmanship and bluff.[30]

Jules Cambon, who had worked so hard for a better understanding between his country and Germany, found Kiderlen exceedingly difficult to negotiate with. The two men were talking in Berlin about the Morocco issue in June when Kiderlen suddenly took six weeks off to go to a spa. Cambon visited him there towards the end of the month to suggest that France might be prepared to offer some form of compensation. Kiderlen, who had already dispatched the *Panther*, said only, 'Bring us something from Paris.'[31] His talks with Cambon started up again on 8 July, after the news of the *Panther*'s arrival had become public, with discussion of Germany's position in Morocco and the possibility of compensation somewhere in Africa. A week later Cambon demanded point blank what exactly Germany wanted; Kiderlen called for a map of Africa and pointed to the whole of French Congo. Cambon, so Kiderlen later claimed, 'nearly fell over backwards'. The demand, which leaked out, gave rise to much worried speculation in France and Britain, that Germany intended to build a vast empire across Africa, eventually taking in the huge Belgian Congo and the Portuguese colonies of Angola and Mozambique.[32] In fact neither Kiderlen nor Bethmann had any interest in Africa but they wanted to show that Germany could not be ignored.[33]

What could also not be ignored, and this made it more difficult in the end to settle the crisis, was public opinion in Germany itself. Kiderlen, who encouraged the colonial lobby and the nationalistic Pan-German League to take a hard line in order to scare the French, found that he had stirred up something that was difficult to contain. Jules Cambon observed after the crisis had ended: 'It is false that in Germany the nation is peaceful and the government is bellicose – the exact opposite is true.'[34] Bebel, the leader of the Social Democrats, was so concerned about the heated state of German public opinion that he asked the British consul in Zurich to warn London: 'A horrible ending seems inevitable.'[35] Across Europe in those last years of peace, from Russia where the Duma was increasingly active in foreign and military affairs, to Britain which had a long tradition of an informed public opinion, governments were finding that their ability to manoeuvre was increasingly circumscribed by their publics' emotions and expectations.

In France, where the reaction to the German moves was one of shock and anger, the crisis came at a bad time. At the end of May, an accident at an air show had killed the Minister of War and seriously wounded the Prime Minister. The government had struggled on only to collapse a month later. A new Cabinet was sworn in on 27 June, four days before the news that the *Panther* was at Agadir reached it. The new Foreign Minister had absolutely no experience in foreign affairs. The Prime Minister, Joseph Caillaux, a rich man with a shady reputation and a scandalous marriage to a divorced woman, intended to manage them himself. Caillaux had one great virtue and that was realism. When the crisis broke, he consulted Joffre, who had just become chief of staff, about France's chances in a war. The odds, Joffre told him, were not good so Caillaux decided that France had no option but to negotiate and instructed Jules Cambon, who had been wanting to settle the Morocco issue for months, to work with Kiderlen.[36] Like the Germans, the French were to find that their own press and public opinion added constraints to their negotiations.[37] The Foreign Ministry officials at the Quai d'Orsay also put up furious objections and did their best to undermine Cambon. 'They do not know what they want', he complained to a trusted colleague, 'they are constantly putting spokes in my wheels, getting the press excited and playing with fire.'[38] Cambon was reduced that summer to using the French military attaché in Berlin to send his reports to Caillaux through the Ministry of War.[39] As a result of such difficulties Caillaux himself undertook secret negotiations through the German embassy in Paris, something which later earned him accusations of treason.[40]

To complicate France's response to Germany, its ally, Russia, made it clear that it was not interested in being dragged into a war over Morocco. Izvolsky, who had now become Russia's ambassador in Paris, reminded the French that they had been lukewarm in supporting his country over the Bosnian crisis three years earlier. 'Russia of course', he said, 'remains faithful to its alliance, but it would have difficulty making its public opinion accept a war over Morocco.' And the Russians were not particularly clear about whether they would come to France's aid if it were attacked. Russia's army, Izvolsky claimed, would need at least two years before it was ready to fight. The tsar gave a mixed message to the French ambassador in St Petersburg: he would honour his word to France if necessary but it would be sensible of the French to come to terms with Germany.[41]

Britain, France's other key ally, initially took the position that France and Germany could sort matters out between them without its involvement. Apart from labour unrest, other domestic issues were preoccupying the government: the coronation of George V that June, renewed trouble over Irish Home Rule, increasingly large and sometimes violent demonstrations by suffragettes demanding votes for women, and the culmination of the struggle between the House of Commons and the House of Lords over parliamentary reform. On the international scene, Britain was having problems with both its entente partners. 'How difficult it is to work with the French,' said a member of the Foreign Office, 'who never seem to act in a straightforward manner.'[42] And Britain's relations with Russia were taking a downturn again, especially in Persia where the two continued to vie for influence.[43]

By contrast, relations with Germany had been improving somewhat in spite of the stalemate over the naval race. That May, before the crisis started, the Kaiser came to London for the unveiling of a memorial to his grandmother and the visit seemed to go off well (although as he was leaving he complained loudly about Britain to Louis Battenberg, a German prince who happened to be a senior British admiral).[44] In the Ottoman Empire German and British financial enterprises were co-operating in projects such as railways.[45] Radical and moderate members of the Cabinet and their supporters in Parliament were attacking the high expenditure on the navy and were putting pressure on Grey to improve relations with Germany, demanding among other things that a Cabinet committee be set up to oversee foreign policy, especially where Germany was concerned.[46]

Grey himself liked the idea of Britain acting as it had in the past as an arbiter among the powers and was not concerned at the prospect of Germany expanding its colonies in Africa. He urged the French to be moderate while hinting to the Germans that Britain might have to support France. What was important, he told both sides, was that British interests were respected in any new settlement on Morocco. The Foreign Office, which was now under the direction of Sir Arthur Nicolson, who was strongly anti-German, and the pro-French ambassador in Paris took a darker view from the start: the crisis was a rerun of the first Morocco affair and Grey must support the French strongly and visibly or the Entente was finished. Grey and his Prime Minister Asquith resisted the pressure until word reached London in the middle of July that Germany was demanding the whole of the French Congo.[47] 'We begin to see light,' Eyre Crowe, known for his deep suspicions of German foreign policy, wrote on a Foreign Office memorandum:

> Germany is playing for the highest stakes. If her demands are acceded to either on the Congo or in Morocco, or – what she will, I believe, try for – in both regions, it will mean definitely the subjection of France. The conditions demanded are not such as a country having an independent foreign policy can possibly accept. The details of the terms are not so very important now. This is a trial of strength, if anything. Concession means not loss of interests or loss of prestige. It means defeat, with all its inevitable consequences.

Nicolson agreed: 'If Germany saw the slightest weakening on our part her pressure on France would become intolerable to that country who would have to fight or surrender. In the latter case German hegemony would be solidly established, with all its consequences immediate and prospective.'[48] The Cabinet approved a message from Grey to the Germans that, as a result of the arrival of the *Panther*, the British were now more deeply concerned about the crisis and that they were obliged to stand by France. The Germans, and it may have been an indication of their clumsy handling of the whole affair, did not bother to reply for over two weeks, which only further deepened British suspicions.

It was an uncomfortable summer for Grey. He had suffered another personal tragedy earlier that year when his beloved brother George was killed by a lion in Africa and the Morocco crisis was keeping him in London, far from the respite of his estate at Fallodon. The Cabinet was divided over how firm to be with Germany and how much support to offer France. In the country, the wave of strikes went on and the heatwave was breaking records. (In the evenings Churchill would collect Grey and take him for a swim at his club.) On 21 July, after considerable discussion, the Cabinet decided to tell Germany that Britain would not accept any settlement over Morocco in which it did not participate. That evening Lloyd George spoke at a formal dinner at the official residence of the Lord Mayor of London. Britain, he claimed, had traditionally used its influence to support liberty and peace,

> But if a situation were to be forced upon us in which peace could only be preserved by the surrender of the great and beneficent position Britain has won by centuries of heroism and achievement, by allowing Britain to be treated where her interests were vitally affected as if she were of no account in the Cabinet of nations, then I say emphatically that peace at that price would be a humiliation intolerable for a great country like ours to endure. National honour is no party question.[49]

The Mansion House speech caused a sensation in part because it came from a man who had been known for his moderate views towards Germany. The German ambassador protested against the belligerent tone.

In Germany, the hardening of the British position shook Kiderlen, who was already encountering difficulties. Germany's ally Austria-Hungary was mildly disapproving. 'We stand loyally with Germany in the east', Aehrenthal told a confidant, 'and will always be faithful to our alliance duties, but I can't follow Kiderlen to Agadir ... We can't practise any politics of prestige.'[50] The Kaiser, who for all the ferocity of his comments and marginalia, invariably shrank from the prospect of war, was threatening to come back from his summer cruise of Norway. 'For I cannot let my Government act like this without me being on the spot and to oversee the consequences and to take a hand. Otherwise it would be inexcusable and make me look like a mere parliamentary ruler! Le roi s'amuse! And in the meantime we head for mobilisation! This must not happen with me away!'[51] On 17 July word came from the Kaiser's yacht that he did not want a war and by the end of the month he was back in Germany.

It is disconcerting in light of what was to come how jittery Europe was and how readily the possibility of war was accepted in what was after all a colonial dispute capable of being settled relatively easily by international agreement. By the start of August, the British army was considering whether it could get an expeditionary force quickly to the Continent and there was consternation when the Admiralty lost track of the German navy for twenty-four hours.[52] The British military authorities took some defensive measures, for example sending soldiers to guard weapons depots.[53] Later that month, in response to the continuing crisis, a special meeting of the Committee of Imperial Defence was called to examine Britain's strategic position and war plans and Grey came clean to his colleagues in Cabinet about the continuing staff talks between the British and the French armies. Rumours circulated that the German military was looking into landing troops at Agadir, even that Wilhelm had given the preparatory orders for mobilisation.[54] On 4 September, Henry Wilson, Director of War Operations, was so spooked by reports coming in from British military attachés in Germany and by a story that Germany was buying stocks of wheat, that he phoned the Café Royal in Piccadilly to warn Churchill and Grey, who were dining there. The three men sat up late into the night at Wilson's house discussing the situation.[55] In Germany there was serious discussion of a preventive war and even Bethmann seems to have felt that it might do the German people good.[56] 'The wretched Morocco story is beginning to get on my nerves,' Moltke wrote to his wife, adding:

> If we once again emerge from this affair with our tail between our legs, if we cannot bring ourselves to make energetic demands which we would be ready to force through with the sword, then I despair of the future of the German Reich. In that case I will leave. But before that I will make a request to get rid of the army, and to have us placed under a Japanese protectorate; then we can make money without being disturbed and we can turn completely simple-minded.[57]

On 1 August, after a meeting with the Kaiser at the Baltic port of Swinemunde (which was going to be badly damaged by Allied bombing in 1945), Kiderlen indicated that he was ready to drop his demands for the whole of the French Congo and seek a compromise with the French. The nationalist press in Germany moaned about 'humiliation', 'shame', and 'ignominy'.[58] 'If only we could have been spared this moment of unspeakable shame, of national dishonor,' said a leading conservative paper. 'Has the old Prussian spirit vanished, have we become a race of women, ruled by the interests of a few racially alien merchants?' Foreigners, the paper claimed, were calling the emperor '*Guillaume le timide, le valeureux poltroon!*'[59] Eminent businessmen led by Ballin, on the other hand, were calling for a settlement before Germany's economic situation got worse. At the start of September, fears of war led to a collapse of the stock market in Berlin.

Kiderlen and Jules Cambon rapidly reached an agreement in principle: part of French Africa for Germany in return for German recognition of France's dominance in Morocco. As so often happens with negotiations, they then spent three months haggling over the details, such as the banks of rivers or tiny villages in the interior of Africa which no one, apart from the locals whose wishes, of course, were not consulted, knew anything about. A little strip of territory nicknamed the Duck's Beak in the north Cameroons caused particular trouble. Kiderlen also caused a stir when he chose to take a brief holiday in the French resort of Chamonix with his mistress, who was rumoured to be a French agent. Although he intended to travel incognito, they were greeted at the station by the local prefect and a guard of honour. The nationalist French press was furious, not at the mistress but at what it felt to be a tactless choice of place. Kiderlen left her there for a few weeks and his letters to her, which he might well have assumed would be seen by the French, warned that Germany might have to fight if it did not receive satisfaction in the negotiations.[60]

The treaty which was finally signed on 4 November gave France the right to establish a protectorate over Morocco with a commitment to respect German economic interests. In return Germany got some 100,000 square miles of central Africa. Kiderlen and Cambon exchanged photographs. 'To my terrible adversary and charming friend', said Kiderlen's inscription, while Cambon put 'To my charming adversary and terrible friend'.[61] At the French railway station of Lyons, a porter recognised Cambon. 'Aren't you the ambassador at Berlin?' Cambon replied that he was. 'You and your brother in London have done us a great service. Without you we would have been in a fine mess.'[62]

As Grey said later, though: 'The consequences of such a foreign crisis do not end with it. They seem to end, but they go underground and reappear later on.'[63] The powers had fresh reasons to mistrust each other, and key decision-makers and their publics were closer to accepting the likelihood of war. Izvolsky, now Russian ambassador to France, wrote back to his successor in St Petersburg, that Europe's international order had been seriously weakened: 'There is no doubt that every local clash between the powers must undoubtedly result in a general European war in which Russia as well as every single other European power will have to participate. With God's help, the onset of this conflict can be delayed, but we have to take hourly into consideration that it can happen anytime, and we have to prepare ourselves every hour for this.'[64]

The Entente Cordiale between Britain and France had survived even though each side felt that the other had behaved badly. The French felt that the British could have backed them more firmly from the start while the British were annoyed with France for being difficult about the Congo and for trying to get hold of the Spanish area of Morocco.[65] The British Cabinet continued to be uneasy about the Anglo-French military talks. In November the Cabinet had two stormy meetings at which some of the moderates who opposed military commitments to France threatened to resign. Even Asquith was getting cold feet; as he wrote to Grey that September, the talks were 'rather dangerous' and 'the French ought not to be encouraged in the present circumstances to make their plans on any assumptions of this kind'.[66] While Grey argued hard for a free hand in foreign affairs he was forced for the first time to accept a degree of control by the Cabinet. It was agreed that there should be no exchanges between the British and French general staffs that amounted to a commitment on the part of Britain of military or naval intervention in a war, and if such communications did occur it should only be with previous Cabinet approval. The military talks continued nevertheless and Henry Wilson continued to travel to France and reassure his French counterparts that Britain would stand by them. And naval talks started which were to lead to an agreement in February 1913 for co-operation in the Mediterranean and in the waters between Britain and France, with the French concentrating on the former and the British on the latter. The British could tell themselves that they had not signed a military alliance with the French but the ties that bound their two countries had thickened and increased.

In France, the signing of the treaty with Germany was seen as a victory, as great, said some, as the taking of Algeria in 1830.[67] Caillaux's government fell, however, helped on its way by revelations that he had been in secret contact with the Germans, and a new government came in under the anti-German nationalist Raymond Poincaré. The crisis, which was seen as evidence that Germany was prepared to use war to get what it wanted, also had a profound impact on French opinion and stimulated France's own preparations for war.[68] The French military attaché in Berlin was later to warn that the German public was in a warlike mood and bitterly resented what it saw as a defeat over Morocco, and that it was not prepared to compromise or accept compensation in a future crisis. In his view a military confrontation between France and Germany was inevitable. Stephen Pichon, who had been Foreign Minister between 1906 and 1911 and who came back into office in 1913, Joffre, and a number of his leading generals, were strongly influenced by such reports.[69]

In Germany, the treaty was seen as another defeat, comparable to the one in the first Morocco crisis. When Bethmann had to defend the agreement in the Reichstag he got angry comments from the right: '*a defeat, whether we say so or not*'. The crown prince was seen in the gallery applauding demonstrably.[70] The empress, who normally did not interfere in politics, said reproachfully to Kiderlen: 'Are we always going to retreat before the French and put up with their insolence?'[71] The Kaiser himself received much of the blame. 'What has happened to the Hohenzollerns', asked a right-wing newspaper, 'from whom once a Great Elector, a Friedrich Wilhelm I, a Friedrich the Great, a Kaiser Wilhelm I have emerged?'[72] An American politician travelling in Germany heard army officers say that the Kaiser had made them look foolish in 1905 and 1911 and they would not let him do it again.[73]

The very real prospect of war in the summer of 1911 had brought home to Germans that Germany's strategic position was not good. The crisis further served to confirm the view in the minds of many Germans that their country was encircled by enemies.[74] It might well have to fight a three-front war, against France and Russia on land and Britain at sea, and it was not clear that its resources were adequate.[75] There were increasing doubts about whether the navy was ever going to be up to the task of taking on the British. And the widening of the Kiel Canal to allow the big battleships to go safely back and forth from the Baltic to the North Sea and make it possible for Germany to have a presence in both would not be finished until 1914. (The canal was opened on 24 June 1914, four days before the assassination at Sarajevo.) Tirpitz, as he had done before, took the opportunity of the crisis to demand a new naval bill. He wanted six more big ships over the next few years and to add a third active squadron to the navy. This, he argued, would rally the right wing and the middle classes against the left and 'take the wind out of the social-democratic and left-liberal parties'.[76] He met resistance from many of his own admirals who argued that to announce that Germany was building more dreadnoughts at a time of international tension might well lead to war with Britain. Bethmann too opposed Tirpitz, on grounds of both cost and the dangers. In the end he could not prevail against the Kaiser, who called him a coward and said he himself was not going to be intimidated by Britain. 'I told the Reich Chancellor', Wilhelm boasted to the chief of his Naval Cabinet, 'to remember that I was a successor to the Great Elector and Frederick the Great, who never hesitated to act when the time seemed to come. I also told the Chancellor that he should reckon with political Providence, which would see to it that a people with so much on their conscience as the English would one day be brought low.'[77]

The army, which over the years had watched quietly as increasing resources went to the navy, now made their own demands for enlargement. It was a question of 'self-preservation', Moltke said.[78] The Kaiser agreed to a compromise whereby both the army and navy got their new bills but with some cuts. German public opinion and the Reichstag, which had resisted increased expenditure, were now in a mood to approve them. The new Navy Law of 1912 provided for three new dreadnoughts and two light cruisers while, under the Military Law, the peacetime army was to expand over the next five years by some 30,000 men with changes in organisation such as a strengthened military transport system.[79] As a sop to Bethmann, he was allowed to reopen talks with Britain. Not surprisingly, the British approached these with some scepticism.

The Morocco crisis left another dangerous residue in the minds of Europe's leaders. It also led directly to a war between Italy and the Ottoman Empire in the autumn of 1911 which in turn paved the way for the Balkan wars of 1912 and 1913. Italy, which had watched the world-wide scramble for colonies with envy, now decided the time had come to add to its small collection of overseas territories. The Ottoman Empire was weak, torn as it was by internal divisions and fighting rebellions in Albania and Yemen, and the other powers were preoccupied by Morocco. Over the years Italy had obtained promises from Britain, France, Austria-Hungary, and Russia which recognised that Italy had special interests in two provinces of the Ottomans in North Africa: Cyrenaica and Tripoli. (Today we know them as Libya.) If the status in North Africa changed, as it clearly was about to with Morocco in 1911, then Italy could make a good argument for consolidating a hold, in some form or other, over Libya. Acquiring colonies also seemed a good deal easier than fulfilling that other dream of Italian nationalists – the seizing of Italian-speaking areas such as the great port of Trieste and the Trentino from Austria-Hungary – something which Italian weakness made a long way off in the future, if ever.[80] Austria-Hungary itself was more than happy to think of Italy directing its attention towards the southern shore of the Mediterranean and away from the Alps and the Adriatic.[81]

Italy's previous attempts at building an empire had, however, been spectacularly unsuccessful. Italian nationalists still resented France's seizure of Tunisia in 1881. History (after its defeat of Carthage, Rome had turned the region into its breadbasket), geography (the coast of Tunisia was directly across from Sicily), and emigration (there were some 130,00 Italians living in Tunisia by the time of the Great War) all made Tunisia Italian and not French. True, Italy had managed to establish two small and backward colonies in Eritrea and Somaliland on the Horn of Africa, but its attempt to take Ethiopia had resulted in a stunning defeat at the hands of the Ethiopians at Adowa in 1896. It was a deep humiliation for Italy, which had a strong desire to play a part on the European and world stage.

Italy was a great power largely by courtesy rather than in reality. In everything but poverty, it lagged behind the others. Its population was only 35 million; that of its neighbour and rival Austria-Hungary was 50 million. And it was losing large numbers, 873,000 in 1913 alone, through emigration.[82] Its railway network was undeveloped; it was less industrialised and more agricultural than the other Western powers; and it spent less on its military than all the others including Russia.[83] It was a new country, where the different regions and cities often inspired, as they do today, stronger loyalties than to Italy itself. There were deep divisions between the new working classes and their employers, between north and south and between the Catholic Church and the state. The dominant figure in politics in the years before 1914 was Giovanni Giolitti, a liberal reformer who tried to modernise Italy's economy, society and politics, but there was a feeling among the political classes and the public that it was all something of an improvisation and not terribly effective. At the highest levels of government, key officials such as the military and the civilian leaders simply did not communicate with each other. Italian chiefs of general staff, for example, did not know the terms of the Triple Alliance which they might one day have to go to war to uphold. In theory the king was in charge of foreign affairs and the military, but in practice Victor Emmanuel III, who succeeded his assassinated father in 1900, largely left his ministers alone. A small, fussy man he devoted his attentions to his beloved family, including his much larger Montenegrin wife, and his coin collection.

Foreigners came to Italy for its climate and its many beauties but they also laughed at it. Italians were seen as charming, chaotic, childlike but not a people to be taken seriously. In international affairs, the other powers, even its own allies in the Triple Alliance, tended to treat Italy as negligible. During the crisis over the Bosnian annexation, for example, Italy's suggestions for a settlement were brushed aside and there was no thought of giving it any compensation in the Balkans. (The dreadful earthquake at Messina made 1908 a particularly grim year for Italy.) Italian diplomats, who were increasingly drawn from old southern aristocratic families, were seen by their colleagues abroad as men of culture who were not always up to complicated negotiations, especially in matters involving trade or economics, and conservative in outlook, such as the Italian ambassador who hated motorcars and always had himself driven in a coach and four to meetings in Vienna with his Austrian-Hungarian counterparts. While Italy did in fact have capable diplomats, its poverty made their work difficult; embassies frequently did not have such modern basic equipment as typewriters.[84]

Italy's foreign relations were determined in part by its own weakness and its strategic position. It had potential enemies on either side, both on land and seaborne; its long coastline was impossible to defend properly and the navy admitted that it could not protect all the major ports.

Its armies were concentrated in the north to meet attacks from either France or Austria-Hungary, leading one deputy to remark that Italy's head was protected by a steel helmet but its body was naked.[85] Italian leaders tended, understandably, to be nervous, seeing malevolence everywhere and assuming, less reasonably, that Italy's enemies were irrational and likely to attack suddenly without good reason. After 1900 evidence of Austrian preparations along the common frontier heightened Italian fears; 1911 brought some relief when Conrad was removed – as it turned out only for a short time – from office.[86] As Europe divided itself into two power blocs, successive Italian Foreign Ministers tried desperately to manoeuvre between the two. As a deputy remarked in parliament in 1907: 'Unbreakable faithfulness to the Triple Alliance, sincere friendship for England and France, and cordial relations with the other powers always remain the bases of our foreign policy.'[87]

Italian foreign and military policy was cautious and defensive by necessity, but that did not stop Italian nationalists from dreaming that it might be different and that foreigners were wrong about Italy. They found some consolation in Social Darwinism: Italian soldiers because of the hardships of their lives were bound to be tougher than the decadent French or the soft Austrian-Hungarians.[88] More importantly, nationalists were determined to show that unification had produced a country that worked and that counted in the world. Italian governments insisted that Italy be represented in all major foreign developments; Italy even sent a handful of soldiers to China to be part of the international force putting down the Boxer Rebellion in 1900.[89] And since powers in the world of 1900 had empires, Italy should continue to build its own. Italian public opinion, which as in other countries was becoming more important with the spread of newspapers and the growth of special-interest lobbies, was generally in favour. Even the socialists, whose rhetoric was anti-imperialist, were not completely opposed.

During the summer of 1911, as the Morocco crisis intensified, there was increasing nationalist agitation in Italy. The press, colonial and nationalist societies, all talked about Libya. Since it also happened to be the fiftieth anniversary of the last stage – so far – of Italy's unification it seemed a good time to do something even more dramatic than building the gigantic Victor Emmanuel memorial in Rome. The Foreign Minister, Antonino di San Giuliano, found himself at the same hotel as the deputy chief of the naval staff and the two men discussed the logistics of the invasion. (The subtle and cynical San Giuliano, who came like so many of his colleagues from the Sicilian aristocracy, was there for his health; he blamed his many illnesses on his mother for leading too upright a life.)[90] When he returned to Rome, San Giuliano told Giolitti that the best time to move against the Ottomans in Libya was the autumn or the spring. The two men decided on September, only bothering to tell the army itself at the last moment.[91]

In what came to be nicknamed the 'policy of the stiletto', Italy delivered an impossible ultimatum to the Ottoman Empire on 28 September 1911 and announced that it would in any case have to go ahead and occupy the two provinces of Libya whatever the reply was. The Italian ships were already preparing to sail. Italy used the excuse of protecting Italian interests and Italian nationals with what can only be described as flimsy evidence. San Giuliano told the British ambassador in Rome, for example, that Italian flour mills in Tripoli were having trouble getting grain from local growers as a result of the machinations of the Ottoman authorities.[92] The left in Italy called for strikes in protest but as the British ambassador reported to London: 'even in the Socialist party opinions are divided and agitation is half-hearted'.[93]

An 'act of piracy', speakers in the German Reichstag said of the Italian invasion, and opinion outside Italy largely agreed, especially as the war dragged on and the Italians resorted to increasingly brutal methods to put down widespread local resistance.[94] The Second International condemned Italy but showed little sympathy for the Ottoman Empire, which it saw as backward and badly in need of civilisation.[95] The other great powers were unwilling to intervene for fear of driving Italy away and towards their opponents. Grey, who had hopes of detaching Italy from the Triple Alliance, told the Italian ambassador that he hoped 'Italy would so conduct affairs that the consequences might be as little far-reaching and embarrassing as possible'. When the Italian ambassador asked what Britain intended to do, Grey said he was speaking from 'the point of view of non-intervention'.[96] Even when the Italians seized Rhodes and the Dodecanese islands off the coast of Asia Minor the following spring, the powers did not react strongly. San Giuliano promised to give the islands up when the last Ottoman soldier left Libya but that day had not arrived before 1914.

The Italians paid a heavy price for their conquest, with a huge budget deficit and some 8,000 soldiers killed or wounded in the first year. So did the inhabitants of Libya, then and later. Their resistance continued until the 1920s, when Italy's new ruler, Benito Mussolini, ended it in the most brutal fashion at the cost of at least 50,000 Libyan deaths. Ottoman rule had been relatively mild and enlightened but under the Italians, Libya, which also came to include territories in the interior, went backwards. The different parts of the colony, which had their own histories and cultures, never truly came together as a country and Libya today is still paying the price for that in regional and tribal rivalries. Europe too paid a heavy price for Italy's aggression. The unspoken agreement among the great powers that the Ottoman Empire should be maintained was now in question. As the Rumanian Prime Minister said to the ambassador of Austria-Hungary that autumn: 'Two lead off the dance, but many are in it at the end.'[97] Kaiser Wilhelm, who was at his favourite hunting lodge at Rominten when the Italians made their move, predicted that more countries would now take advantage of the Ottoman Empire's weakness to reopen the issue of control over the Straits or in the Balkans to seek territory. It meant, he feared, 'the beginning of a world war with all its terrors'.[98] The first evidence that he was right came the following year as the Balkan nations joined forces against the Ottoman Empire.

Shortly before the Christmas of 1911 Sir Edward Goschen, the British ambassador in Berlin, reported to London that he had dined with Bethmann. The two men had talked in a friendly way about the events of the past year. The ambassador asked Bethmann whether he had found time lately to play his usual Beethoven sonatas, as was his custom before he went to bed. 'My dear friend,' replied Bethmann, 'you and I like classical music with its plain and straightforward harmonies; how can I play my beloved old music with the air full of modern discords?' Goschen demurred, saying that 'even the old composers used discords to lead to harmonies, and that the latter sounded all the sweeter for the discords which preceded them'. Bethmann agreed but added that 'in modern music as in the present political atmosphere the discords predominated'.[99] The New Year was to bring fresh discords to jangle Europe's nerves, this time in Europe itself, in the first of a series of Balkan wars.

CHAPTER 16

The First Balkan Wars

O n New Year's Day 1912 Paul Cambon, France's ambassador in London, wrote to his brother in Berlin: 'What does this year have in store for us? I hope that the big conflict will be avoided.'[1] Jules also dreaded the coming months:

> the failing health of the Emperor of Austria, the far-reaching plans attributed to the Heir-Apparent, the Tripoli war, the desire of the Italian government to extricate itself from the difficulties it had brought upon itself by mixing the disputes of others with its own, Bulgarian ambitions, the threat of trouble in Macedonia, the difficulties in Persia, the shock to the credit of China, all pointed to serious disorders in the near future and the only hope was that the gravity of the danger might lead to its being averted.[2]

He might have mentioned as well the rivalry between Great Britain and Germany or the mutual fear and hostility between Russia and Austria-Hungary. It was in the Balkans, however, that the greatest dangers were to arise: two wars among its nations, one in 1912 and a second in 1913, nearly pulled the great powers in. Diplomacy, bluff and brinkmanship in the end saved the peace but although Europeans could not know it, they had had a dress rehearsal for the summer of 1914. As they say in the theatre, if that last run-through goes well, the opening night will be a disaster.

The Balkan states, from Greece in the south to Serbia, Bulgaria, and Rumania in the north, were the poor relations of Europe, with few natural resources, underdeveloped infrastructures and only the beginnings of modern industry and commerce. In 1912, Serbia's capital, Belgrade, was a small provincial town, just starting to pave its main streets with wooden blocks, and with only one good hotel. In Rumania, where the national myth was that the inhabitants were a Latin people, descended from Roman legions, Bucharest aspired to be the Balkan Paris. The upper classes, who spoke French and wore the latest French fashions, particularly admired, said a sharp-eyed Russian journalist, 'Paris-by-night'. Leon Trotsky, in exile from Russia for his revolutionary activities, was there as a pseudonymous correspondent for a leading newspaper in Kiev. Elegant women and magnificently turned-out army officers glided along the boulevards of Bucharest, he went on, and at the crossroads, stood *pissoirs*, just like they had in Paris. Yet the differences were much greater than the similarities, from the eunuch cabmen (from a sect where the men were castrated after they had fathered two children) to the gypsies who played their violins in the nightclubs, or the barefoot children who begged on the streets.[3] In Montenegro, the capital was merely an overgrown village and the new royal palace looked like a German boarding house. (The old palace, the Biljarda, was named after the billiard table which had been carried up the mountains from the coast.) The king, Nicholas II, often sat under one of the few trees in his mountainous country to dispense his own version of justice to his subjects. He was linked to Italy and Russia through family ties – one daughter had married the king of Italy and two others were the wives of Russian grand dukes – but his foreign policy usually reflected whichever European power had just paid him a subvention. 'Your Majesty', said Conrad to Franz Joseph in 1912, 'King Nicholas reminds me of a candelabra.' The emperor was amused by Conrad's explanation: 'Look, he stands always with his arms stretched out there, always waiting for someone to give him something.'[4]

Rumania, then a much smaller country than the one of today, had a population of just under 7 million in 1910, Bulgaria some 4 million, and Serbia around 3 million. Montenegro had only 250,000 inhabitants. ('This isolated wrinkle of the world', said an unhappy Austrian-Hungarian diplomat who served in its capital, Cetinje, before the Great

16. The Balkans were the trouble spot of Europe where the ambitions of the great powers mixed with the rivalries among the Balkan nations themselves. In 1912 the Balkan powers briefly united to seize much of the remaining territory of the Ottoman Empire but they immediately fell out over the spoils. The great powers tried almost for the last time to impose a peace but as the caption says 'Unfortunately the united European fire brigade did not succeed in extinguishing the flames.'

War.)[5] Years of Ottoman rule had left societies that were still largely agricultural and deeply conservative although the landed upper classes and the tiny bourgeoisie increasingly aspired to be Western and modern. Political parties had emerged calling themselves Conservative, Liberal or Radical, even Socialist, but behind the labels lay a more old-fashioned network of family, regional and ethnic connections as well as simple autocracy. In Montenegro, whose mountains had saved it, alone among the Balkan states, from becoming part of the Ottoman Empire, Nicholas played with a constitution which he simply withdrew whenever he grew tired of politics; what opposition there was, and sometimes even his loyal supporters, went to jail or were executed as the mood took him. In Serbia, the Radicals and especially their leader Nikola Pašić, were fortunate enough to deal with a weak king, Peter, but in both Bulgaria and Rumania, stronger kings, German imports both, dominated politics.

To the rest of Europe the Balkan states were something of a joke, the setting for tales of romance such as *The Prisoner of Zenda* or operettas (Montenegro was the inspiration for *The Merry Widow*), but their politics were deadly serious – and frequently deadly with terrorist plots, violence and assassinations. In 1903 King Peter's unpopular predecessor as king of Serbia and his equally unpopular wife had been thrown from the windows of the palace and their corpses hacked to pieces. Nicholas of Montenegro hated Pašić and his fellow Radicals because he suspected, with good reason, that they had sent him assassins armed with bombs. The growth of national movements had welded peoples together but it had also divided Orthodox from Catholic or Muslim, Albanians from Slavs, and Croats, Serbs, Slovenes, Bulgarians or Macedonians from each other. While the peoples of the Balkans had coexisted and intermingled, often for long periods of peace through the centuries, the establishment of national states in the nineteenth century had too often been accompanied by burning of villages, massacres, expulsions of minorities and lasting vendettas.

Politicians who had ridden to power by playing on nationalism and with promises of national glory found they were in the grip of forces they could not always control. Secret societies, modelling themselves on an eclectic mix which included Freemasonry, the underground Carbonari, who had worked for Italian unity, the terrorists who more recently had frightened much of Europe, and old-style banditry, proliferated throughout the Balkans, weaving their way into civilian and military institutions of the states. The Internal Macedonian Revolutionary Organisation (IMRO) talked about Macedonia for the Macedonians but was widely suspected of working with Bulgarian nationalists for a greater Bulgaria which would include Macedonia. In Serbia, the government and the army were riddled with supporters of Narodna Odbrana (National Defence), which had been set up during the Bosnian crisis, and its even more extremist offshoot the Black Hand. In the First Balkan War, officers disobeyed their own government on several occasions, seizing, for example, the town of Monastir (which Serbia had promised to Bulgaria in a secret treaty) in the hopes that it would then be impossible to hand it over.[6] Although the Ottoman and Austrian-Hungarian authorities did their best to suppress all revolutionary and indeed most political activity among their own South Slav or Albanian subjects, they faced an uphill battle, especially since much of the home-grown conspiracies and terrorism were supported from outside. Bosnian students at the University of Vienna, for example, formed a secret society in reaction to the annexation of their homeland. 'If Austria-Hungary wants to swallow us', they declared, 'we shall gnaw its stomach,' and many of the students slipped over the border into Serbia for military training.[7]

The younger generation who were attracted to the secret societies were often more extreme than their elders and frequently at odds with them. 'Our fathers, our tyrants,' said a Bosnian radical nationalist, 'have created this world on their model and are now forcing us to live in it.'[8] The young members were in love with violence and prepared to destroy even their own traditional values and institutions in order to build the new Greater Serbia, Bulgaria or Greece. (Even if they had not read Nietzsche, which many of them had, they too had heard that God was dead and that European civilisation must be destroyed in order to free humankind.) In the last years before 1914, the authorities in the Balkan states either tolerated or were powerless to control the activities of their own young radicals who carried out assassinations and terrorist attacks on Ottoman or Austrian-Hungarian officials as oppressors of the Slavs, on their own leaders whom they judged to be insufficiently dedicated to the nationalist cause, or simply on ordinary citizens who happened to be the wrong religion or the wrong ethnicity in the wrong place. When Franz Joseph visited Bosnia in 1910, there was a plot to assassinate him; in Croatia, there were repeated attempts, some successful, on the lives of Habsburg officials.

In the early stages of their independence, the Balkan states had been content, or at least obliged, to pay attention to the great European powers. And the powers, especially Russia and Austria-Hungary before they fell out over the annexation of Bosnia, wanted to keep the status quo in the Balkans with the Ottoman Empire continuing to rule over its remaining European territories. Over the last decades of the nineteenth century, however, the obvious decline of the Ottomans had emboldened leaders across the Balkans to take matters into their own hands. In the name of protecting Christians still under Ottoman rule in Macedonia and elsewhere, Serbia, Bulgaria and Greece all sent money, weapons and agents to stir up resistance. The rise of the Young Turks and their policy of winning back control of Ottoman lands (and making them more Turkish) not surprisingly set off alarms throughout the Balkan states and among the Ottomans' own Christian subjects. By 1910, Albanians, Christian and Muslim alike, who were traditionally loyal to their Ottoman rulers, were in open revolt. The following year the Albanian revolutionaries joined forces with their Macedonian counterparts. The Ottoman authorities cracked down savagely, which only fuelled further unrest and violence. In the autumn of 1911 Italy's war on the Ottoman Empire set off renewed uprisings by Christians. In Macedonia that December a series of explosions destroyed police stations and mosques. In retaliation Muslim crowds attacked local Bulgarians. Throughout the independent Balkan states there were protest meetings and demonstrations against the Ottomans.[9]

Balkan leaders complained openly that they could no longer trust the great powers to protect the Christians under Ottoman rule and hinted that they might have to take action. Why maintain the status quo in the Balkans, a leading politician in Serbia asked Trotsky. 'Where was the status quo when Austria annexed Bosnia and Herzegovina? Why didn't the powers defend the status quo when Italy seized Tripoli?' And why should the Balkan states be treated as though they were somehow not European but like Morocco?[10] There was the chance, the Foreign Minister of Serbia admitted to the British ambassador in Belgrade, that Austria-Hungary would intervene if any of the Balkan nations moved to seize Ottoman territory but, as far as he, Milovan Milovanović, was concerned, it was better for Serbia to die fighting. If Austria-Hungary itself expanded further southwards into the Balkans, Serbia was finished anyway as an independent kingdom.[11]

Pride, nationalist ambitions, the temptations of a declining empire on their doorstep, the example of naked aggression set by Italy, and sheer recklessness, all brought the Balkan nations together – briefly, as it turned out – to drive the Ottoman Empire out of its remaining European possessions. From the autumn of 1911, emissaries were travelling secretly back and forth among the Balkan capitals or meeting as if by chance in one European city or another. Russia, and particularly the Russian ambassador in Constantinople, had long promoted the idea of a Balkan League to include the Ottoman Empire, which, so it was hoped, would both provide stability in the region and block the spread of German and Austrian-Hungarian influence south and eastwards. The Balkan states themselves, with visions of plundering the Ottoman Empire taking ever more solid shape, would have none of it. Sazonov, who succeeded Izvolsky in 1910 as Russian Foreign Minister, then tried to bring Bulgaria, Serbia, Montenegro, and Greece into an alliance to act as a barrier against Austria-Hungary's trying to move south if the Ottoman Empire collapsed.[12]

In the autumn of 1911, that collapse appeared imminent. Serbia and Bulgaria had been talking on and off since 1904 about some form of partnership, but the Bulgarians, led by Tsar Ferdinand, had always preferred to keep a free hand. Now the talks took on a new urgency. It helped too that a new government in Bulgaria's capital, Sofia, was pro-Russian and less inclined to worry about offending Austria-Hungary. Great Britain and France, which were warned by Russia that something was in the air, were not averse to a warmer relationship between the two Balkan powers. Its Triple Entente partners shared Russia's hopes of finding a cheap, local solution to containing German and Austrian-Hungarian expansion into the Ottoman Empire.[13] In Sofia and Belgrade, Anatol Neklyudov and Hartwig, the Russian ambassadors, worked hard to bring the Bulgarians and the Serbians together. Neklyudov at least foresaw the potential for trouble; 'The union of Bulgaria and Serbia contains one dangerous element – the temptation to use it for offensive purposes.'[14]

Hartwig had no such concerns. From the moment he had arrived in Belgrade in 1909 he had become a fervent supporter of the Serbian cause. He rapidly became an indispensable part of the political scene; everyone consulted him from the king down and each morning his study was filled with prominent members of Serbian society. He and Pašić were particularly close and with many a nod and a wink, Hartwig let the Serbian leader know that he need not take the warnings from Russia to tread carefully too seriously. When Sazonov sent a message to urge the Serbian government to be moderate in its foreign policy, Hartwig solemnly read it out. 'Have you finished, *mon cher ami*?' asked Pašić. 'All right! *C'est bien. Nous pouvons maintenant causer sérieusement!*' [We can now talk seriously.][15] Sazonov worried about Hartwig but did not have the strength to recall him, possibly because Hartwig's wife had good connections at court and among Panslavist circles in Russia.

At the end of September 1911 the Bulgarians let the Russians know that they were prepared to negotiate treaties first with Serbia and then with Montenegro and Greece. A leading member of Bulgarian government told Neklyudov that Bulgaria and Serbia needed to stand together not just to protect the Christians in the Ottoman Empire but to remain independent of the Central Powers.[16] Sazonov, who was recuperating from a serious illness in Davos, was delighted when Neklyudov brought him the news. 'Well,' Sazonov exclaimed, 'but this is perfect! If only it could come off! Bulgaria closely allied to Serbia in the political and economic sphere; five hundred thousand bayonets to guard the Balkans – but this would bar the road for ever to German penetration, Austrian invasion!'[17] It took another several months to hammer out the details of the agreement. In a warning of the troubles to come between the new allies, the main difficulty was the division of the Macedonian lands, right down to tiny villages, where Bulgarian and Serbian claims over-lapped.[18] The treaty which was finally signed in March 1912 contained secret clauses directed against the Ottoman Empire and made Russia the arbiter in any future disputes over the division of Macedonia. Bulgaria also promised to back Serbia if it got into a war with Austria-Hungary.

By this point foreign diplomats were picking up rumours about the new relationship and stories were starting to appear in the press. Sazonov blandly assured Russia's entente partners that the treaty was purely defensive and that Russia would use its influence to ensure that it remained so. Germany and Austria-Hungary initially showed little concern.[19] That spring of 1912, however, as details of the secret clauses leaked, the great powers started to suspect that more was at stake than a defensive arrangement. 'It is evident', wrote Nicolson, by now Permanent Undersecretary at the Foreign Office, to a British diplomat in St Petersburg, 'that the distribution of the spoils in Macedonia has been decided upon.' Sazonov was perhaps being a bit too adventurous, Nicolson complained, but it would not do to say so since Britain needed to keep on the best possible terms with Russia.[20]

International concern grew as it became clear that Bulgaria and Greece, long divided by their competing ambitions in Macedonia, were now also drawing closer. The new Greek Prime Minister, Eleutherios Venizelos, was committed to freeing his home island of Crete from Ottoman rule, and was prepared to sacrifice Greek interests in Macedonia, at least for the time being, in order to gain allies. In May a treaty between Bulgaria and Greece – again, of course, described as defensive only – brought a league of Balkan states against the Ottoman Empire a step closer. The Bulgarians and Montenegrins found occasion to talk the following month, ironically in the great Habsburg palace, the Hofburg, while both kings, Ferdinand and Nicholas, were paying visits to Franz Joseph. The agreement reached later in the summer dispensed with the pretence of defence and simply took a war against the Ottoman Empire for granted. At the end of September Serbia and Montenegro signed an alliance. The Balkan League was now complete, with Bulgaria at its centre.

The Ottoman Empire itself appeared to be in its last throes. In Constantinople, the Young Turks were turned out of office at the start of the summer by right-wing army officers who then proved unable to re-establish order. The revolt in Albania continued to gain strength and the cycle of unrest and violence in Macedonia went on. In August a bomb exploded at a market killing several innocent bystanders. The Ottoman police panicked and fired on the crowds that gathered. Over a hundred people, most of them Bulgars, were killed. In Bulgaria, the public demanded that its government intervene to liberate Macedonia. The Ottomans mobilised their forces on the southern border of Macedonia and the members of the Balkan League did the same a few days later. Russia was by now trying, ineffectually, to restrain its protégés. The other great powers had also awakened from their complacency and after a round of hasty discussions it was agreed that Russia and Austria-Hungary should act on behalf of what remained of the Concert of Europe to caution the Balkan states and the Ottoman Empire against war. The powers would not, they stated firmly, accept any territorial changes in the Balkans as a result of war. A French diplomat at St Petersburg was more realistic: 'For the first time in the history of the Eastern question the small states have acquired a position of such independence of the Great Powers that they feel able to act completely without them and even to take them in tow.'[21]

On 8 October, the day the warning from the Concert reached the

Balkan capitals, Nicholas of Montenegro, always a gambler, declared war on the Ottoman Empire. Although he had worked assiduously to stir up trouble in the Ottoman territories along his borders, he declared to the British ambassador in Cetinje that he had been left no choice: 'Above all continued massacres of Christian brothers on the frontier had struck him to the heart.'[22] (Rumours later suggested that his main motive had been to make a financial killing in Paris by using his advance knowledge of the timing of the outbreak of hostilities.)[23] On 18 October, after some unconvincing attempts to portray themselves as the innocent parties, the other members of the Balkan League joined in. Trotsky was in Belgrade as the ill-equipped Serbian peasant soldiers marched off to war, cheering as they went:

> Along with this shout there enters into one's heart a peculiar spontaneous feeling of tragedy, impossible to convey at a distance: a feeling, too, of helplessness in the face of the historical fate which is so closely approaching the peoples shut up in the Balkan triangle, and of anguish for all those hordes of men who are being led to destruction …[24]

Across the Balkans there was intense excitement with huge crowds demonstrating and singing patriotic songs. Old rivalries were briefly forgotten as newspapers talked about 'The Balkans for Balkan peoples'. Outside the Bulgarian embassy in Belgrade, Serbians shouted 'Long Live King Ferdinand!'[25]

The combined Balkan forces outnumbered the Ottomans by more than two to one and the Ottoman armies were demoralised and unprepared. Obliged to fight on several different fronts at once, they suffered a series of rapid defeats. (The French attributed the success of the Balkan armies to their use of artillery from the French firm of Creusot while the Ottomans were using guns made by the German firm of Krupp.)[26] By the end of October the Ottomans had lost almost all their remaining territory in Europe. Intoxicated by dreams of wearing the crown of old Byzantium and having a victory Mass sung in the great church of Santa Sophia, Ferdinand urged his Bulgarian troops on to attack Constantinople but they were held at a ridge north-east of the city. The Bulgarians had outrun their supply lines and the soldiers were short of ammunition, proper clothing and food, and an increasing number were falling ill. Additionally, the tensions in the Balkan League, never far below the surface, were becoming apparent. To the dismay of Bulgaria, Greece had seized the Macedonian port of Salonika (today Thessaloniki) while the Serbians and Montenegrins rushed to occupy the Sanjak of Novi Bazar, that piece of land south of Bosnia which separated them, and as much of Albania as they could. None of its allies liked the fact that Bulgaria had come up with by far the greatest share of Ottoman territory. On 3 December, under pressure from the great powers who were both shocked and worried by the dramatic changes in the Balkans, the members of the Balkan League and the Ottoman Empire agreed to sign an armistice and to start peace talks in London later that month.

What made the Balkans so dangerous was that a highly volatile situation on the ground mingled with great power interests and ambitions. Britain and France, who had the least at stake in the Balkans, did not want to see the equilibrium in Europe, so recently threatened by the second Moroccan crisis, challenged again. On the other hand, neither power wanted to see the Ottoman Empire disappear with a resulting scramble for its territory at the eastern end of the Mediterranean or in the largely Arab lands throughout the Middle East. If the Ottoman sultan – who was also caliph, the chief religious leader for the world's Sunni Muslims – was deposed, that might well stir up unrest among the large, mostly Sunni, Muslim population in British India who had hitherto been loyal supporters of the British Raj or among the millions of Muslims in France's North African colonies.[27] The French also worried about what would happen to the large sums of money they had lent to the Ottoman Empire (France was its biggest foreign lender). And both powers feared the consequences of a confrontation between Russia and Austria-Hungary in the Balkans. Poincaré, now President, made it clear to the Russians as early as August 1912 that France had no interest in getting dragged into a conflict between Russia and Austria-Hungary over the Balkans. The message from Paris was mixed, though: Poincaré also promised that France would fulfil its alliance obligations to Russia if Germany got involved on the side of Austria-Hungary.[28] In December 1912, when relations between Russia and Austria-Hungary were deteriorating rapidly, France apparently indicated that it would support Russia if war broke out.[29] And whether Poincaré actually believed it himself or was indulging in wishful thinking, he assured the Russians that Britain had given a verbal promise to send an expeditionary force to support France if it were attacked by Germany.[30]

Grey insisted as he always did that Britain had a free hand in deciding what to do in any crisis but in fact he offered Russia considerable support. While he offered to help bring about a peace settlement, he also reassured the Russians that Britain was sympathetic to its need to keep the Straits in friendly hands.[31] As the threat of a general war appeared to increase, Grey pointed out to the French yet again that Britain was under no obligation to support France if Germany then chose to support Austria-Hungary by attacking Russia's ally in the west. Nevertheless, as the First Balkan War raged on, there were discussions in London about how to get a British expeditionary force to France and Grey told the German ambassador that it was a 'vital necessity' for Britain to prevent France being crushed by Germany and that Britain would have no choice but to come to France's assistance.[32] If Britain and France felt that their options were increasingly limited, that was much truer of the two neighbouring powers which took the closest interest in the Balkans – Russia and Austria-Hungary.

Although Russia had little directly at stake in the Balkans in economic terms – Russian trade with and investment in the Balkans was tiny compared with other powers such as France – Russian attitudes to troubles there were shaped both by powerful ambitions and by fears.[33] If the Ottoman Empire collapsed, as looked increasingly likely, the issue of control of the Straits would at once become critical. Russia's economic prosperity and its future development were both tied up with its foreign trade. Most of its key export of grain went out through the Straits and the modern machinery Russia needed for its factories and mines came in the same way. Russians were reminded of how vulnerable geography made that trade when the Straits were temporarily closed in 1911 and again in 1912 because of the Italian war on the Ottomans. As grain piled up in Russia's Black Sea ports, its price fell, panicky merchants called on the government to do something, and, as the value of Russia's exports fell dramatically, interest rates went up.[34] The speed of the Bulgarian advance in the war that broke out in the autumn of 1912 caused real alarm in St Petersburg. At one point the government seriously considered sending a force to protect Constantinople, perhaps even to seize a strip of land along the shores of the Bosphorus, until it realised that Russia did not have the necessary shipping or proper amphibious forces.[35]

Russia had other reasons for fearing trouble in the Ottoman Empire. Up to this point the very backwardness of its southern neighbour had been convenient. The Anatolian plateau, which was undeveloped with only the beginnings of a railway system, had provided a convenient land barrier between the other continental powers and the Russian Empire in Central Asia and left Russia a relatively free hand to extend its rule still further, in particular into Persia. (Although this repeatedly produced friction with the British, Grey and his colleagues were prepared to put up with a lot to maintain the Russian friendship.) Since 1900, however, growing German penetration of the Ottoman lands and the much-publicised German project for a railway network stretching from Berlin to Baghdad had presented a new and unwelcome challenge to Russia's imperial ambitions.[36]

Finally, when it came to the Balkans themselves, Russia's leaders were affected by a determination not to be outmanoeuvred or humiliated again by Austria-Hungary as Russia had been over Bosnia-Herzegovina in 1908. From St Petersburg every move made by Austria-Hungary, its wooing of Montenegro and Bulgaria by offering loans, for example, or the activities of Catholic priests from the Austrian church throughout the Balkans, raised suspicions. Russian views on the Balkans were also shaped by Panslavism and the desire to protect fellow South Slavs, many of whom like the Russians themselves were Orthodox Christians. A set of emotions and attitudes rather than a coherent political movement or ideology, Panslavism generated much heated rhetoric in Russia and elsewhere in central Europe before the Great War. For Russian Panslavists it was about their 'historic mission', 'our Slavic brothers', or turning the great mosque of Hagia Sophia back into the church of Santa Sophia. There was much talk too of winning back 'the keys and gates to the Russian house' – the Straits between the Mediterranean and the Black Sea – so that Russian commerce and naval power could flow out into the world. (The Russians did not always seem to take into account that the Mediterranean was a bigger version of the Black Sea with its key exits at Suez and Gibraltar controlled by another power, in this case Britain.) If such rhetoric did not directly guide Russian policies in the Balkans, it served to limit Russia's options. Sazonov found himself under pressure to support the Balkan nations and not to work with Austria-Hungary even though Russia might have been wise to try to rebuild the old understanding to keep the status quo in the Balkans.[37] To be sure, Panslavism found in him a willing victim.

It was unfortunate for Russia, for the stability of the Balkans, and in the longer run for the peace of Europe that the man now in charge of its foreign policy was so easily swayed by emotion and prejudice. Russia's historic mission, Sazonov believed, was to liberate the South Slavs from Ottoman oppression. Although this great duty had almost been completed by the start of the twentieth century, Russia still needed to be on guard against threats to the Balkan nations, whether from a resurgent Ottoman Empire or Austria-Hungary and its German ally. He was deeply suspicious of Ferdinand of Bulgaria, whom he saw as a German cuckoo in the Balkan nest, and feared the Young Turks who, he believed, were under the leadership of Jewish Freemasons.[38] It was unfortunate too that Sazonov had little of the intelligence, experience, or strength of character of his predecessor. His main qualifications for the post seem to have been that he was not Izvolsky, who was widely discredited after the Bosnian crisis, and that he was the brother-in-law of Prime Minister Stolypin.

Like so many of the top officials in Russia, the new Foreign Minister came from an old noble family. Unlike some of his colleagues, he was upright and honest and even his enemies agreed that he was a thorough gentleman and a loyal servant of both the tsar and Russia. Sazonov was also profoundly religious and, in the opinion of Baron Taube, who worked with him in the Foreign Ministry, would have done well in the hierarchy of the Russian Orthodox Church. He was not, in Taube's view, cut out to be Foreign Minister: 'Sickly by nature, overly sensitive and a little sentimental, nervous and even neurotic, Sazonov was the type of womanly Slav par excellence, easy and generous but soft and vague, constantly changing because of his impressions and intuitions, resisting all sustained efforts at thinking, incapable of following through his reasoning to the logical end.'[39]

In 1911 and 1912, as the Balkan states circled around the carcass of the Ottoman Empire, Sazonov encouraged them. 'To have done nothing', he wrote in his memoirs, 'to further the attainment of their aim by Serbia and Bulgaria, would have meant, for Russia, not only a renunciation of her historic mission, but also a surrender, without resistance, to the enemies of the Slav nationalities, of a political position secured by age-long efforts.'[40] He promoted the formation of the Balkan League and appears, like the sorcerer's hapless apprentice, to have entertained the illusion that he could control it. When he told the Serbian and Bulgarian leaders that Russia did not want a war in the Balkans, they assumed that he did not really mean it. As the British chargé d'affaires in Sofia wrote on the eve of the First Balkan War:

> The danger of the situation really lies in the fact that neither Bulgaria nor Serbia can believe that Russia could abandon her policy of centuries in the Balkans without even an attempt at resistance. The Balkan States have been brought together by Russia – true for a defensive purpose – but defensive and offensive are terms much akin under certain conditions. They are now working together and, once they are quite ready and think the moment opportune, it is not the withholding of loans by France, nor the admonitions of Russia nor of the whole of Europe that will hold them back. They care little whether they bring about a European war or not.[41]

When Hartwig warmly supported the Serbians' ambitions for a Greater Serbia, Sazonov complained but did little to stop him. Nor was Sazonov prepared to stand up to his own strongly pro-Serbian public opinion even though he felt, as he admitted in his memoirs, 'a certain fear lest the Government should find itself unable to control the course of events'.[42] He also found Serbia difficult to deal with: 'I did not always find that self-control and sober estimate of the dangers of the moment which alone could avert a catastrophe.'[43] Russia was to find, as so often happens to great powers, that its much smaller and weaker client state was exigent, often with success, in demanding support from its patron. In November 1912, for example, during the First Balkan War, the Serbian leader Pašić, without consulting Russia, published a dramatic letter about Serbia's aims in the London *Times*. His country, Pašić declared, must have a coastline of some fifty kilometres along the Adriatic. 'For this minimum Serbia is prepared to make every sacrifice, since not to do so would be false to her national duty.' Even the smallest

Serbian presence on the Adriatic was, as Pašić knew well, anathema to Austria-Hungary. His letter was an attempt to put Russia into a position where it had no choice but to support Serbia.[44] On this occasion the Russians eventually refused to be drawn in but Sazonov and his colleagues were going to face a similar dilemma with Serbia two years later. If they abandoned it in the face of Austria-Hungary's aggression, Russia would appear weak; if Russia assured Serbia of its unwavering support, it might well encourage recklessness in Belgrade.

Austria-Hungary, the other great power most concerned about developments in the Balkans, shared Russia's fear of appearing weak, but where Russia wanted stronger Balkan states, Austria-Hungary regarded the prospect with horror, especially when it came to Serbia. The mere existence of Serbia was a danger to the existence of the old multinational monarchy, acting as it did as a magnet, a model, and an inspiration for the empire's own South Slavs. The ruling elites in Austria-Hungary, remembering all too well how the kingdom of Piedmont had taken the lead in uniting Italy and how Prussia had done the same with Germany, and at the expense in each case of Austria-Hungary, saw Serbia in the same dangerous role. (It did not help that Serbian nationalists felt much the same and that they called one of their more extreme newspapers *Piejmont*.) The activities of Serbia's nationalist leaders after the 1903 coup in encouraging nationalist sentiments throughout the peninsula and within the empire itself had done much to exacerbate Austrian-Hungarian fears.

In one of those inopportune coincidences which play their part in human affairs, Austria-Hungary also had a new Foreign Minister in 1912 and, as in Russia, one who was weaker and less decisive than his predecessor. Leopold von Berchtold was one of the Dual Monarchy's richest men and had married a Hungarian heiress. His family was old and distinguished and he was related to virtually everyone who counted in society. Although at least one of his ancestors had broken with convention to marry Mozart's sister, who came from the middle classes, Berchtold himself was a terrific snob and something of a prude who found Edward VII barely acceptable in society. '*Une royauté en décadence*', wrote Berchtold in his diary when the British king brought a former mistress to the elegant spa at Marienbad. 'Return to the loathsome and unworthy Georgian tradition after the Victorian epoch of moral greatness.'[45] Elegant and charming, with impeccable manners, Berchtold moved easily through society. 'The beautiful poodle', or so claimed one of his many critics, was more interested in his amusements and collecting exquisite objects than in high politics. Bad taste upset him; when he visited a new wing that Franz Ferdinand had constructed at one of his castles he found the marble 'looked like head cheese and reminds one of a butcher's'.[46] Next to his family, to whom he was devoted, Berchtold's great enthusiasm was for horse-racing. He had always wanted, he said, to be a government minister and win a great horse race. He achieved the former by catching Aehrenthal's attention, first as a promising young diplomat and then as his likely successor, and the latter by lavish spending. Berchtold built his own race track, imported the best English trainers, and bought the best horses.

When Aehrenthal died, Franz Joseph's choice for a successor was a limited one. It had to be someone of high social rank who was also acceptable to the heir to the throne and Franz Ferdinand's opposition had already eliminated two likely candidates. Berchtold, who was in favour with both the uncle and nephew, and who had enjoyed a good record as Austria-Hungary's ambassador in Russia, appeared the most suitable candidate and the dying Aehrenthal had begged him to take on his office.[47] Berchtold himself had doubts about his ability to fill it. (So did his colleagues, one of whom said he would have been excellent as a high court official responsible for its elaborate ceremonies but was a disaster as a Foreign Minister.[48]) In his interview with the emperor Berchtold listed his own deficiencies. He was not familiar with the inner workings of the Foreign Ministry and he had never dealt with the Austrian parliament. Furthermore, as someone who saw himself as both Austrian and Hungarian, he was likely to be despised by both nationalities. Finally, he was probably not up to the physical demands of the office. He nevertheless took the position out of a sense of duty to his emperor.[49]

Berchtold was an intelligent man and an experienced diplomat but he had spoken truthfully. He lacked both confidence and determination. He took forever to make decisions, going round and round with his officials, even sometimes asking his children for their views.[50] While he favoured peace, he found it difficult to stand up to the hawks, especially Conrad, who bombarded him with memoranda arguing for war, against Italy, or in 1912, 1913 and 1914, against Serbia.[51] Berchtold also lacked the depth of knowledge he needed. He knew little about South Slav issues or the Balkans or such matters as the details of the alliance between Austria-Hungary and Italy.[52] As a result he was intimidated by his more knowledgeable officials and tended, too much, to defer to their opinions. His own foreign policy views were simple and pessimistic: Austria-Hungary was menaced by hostile neighbours and had only one friend in Germany. Where he had once hoped for an understanding with Russia, he had become convinced since the crisis over Bosnia that there was little chance of that happening. Austria-Hungary must now see Russia, he believed, as 'an enemy, who could certainly wait, but did not want to forget'.[53]

As the tensions and talk of war spread in the Balkans in the late summer of 1912, Berchtold tried to maintain the status quo there, urging the great powers to act together as the old Concert of Europe. If they could put pressure on the Ottoman Empire to reform its treatment of the Christians under its rule, the Balkan states would no longer have an excuse for war. It was a sign of how far Europe was now dividing itself into hostile camps that the initial reaction from Russia and France in the Triple Entente was one of suspicion and a determination not to let the Triple Alliance take the lead.[54] Sazonov told the British ambassador in St Petersburg that Russia's prestige in the Balkans would be seriously damaged if Austria-Hungary were seen to be taking over as the protector of the Christians.[55]

When war finally broke out in the Balkans at the end of September, Austria-Hungary's leadership still seems to have been taken by surprise, with its military attachés in both Belgrade and Constantinople off on holidays.[56] The Balkan League's string of quick victories caused intense worry and much anxious debate in Vienna. The Common Ministerial Council, which gave Austria-Hungary what unity it had, had been dragging its feet on proposed new military expenditures; now it voted a large sum for new artillery and fortifications. As it became clear that the Ottoman Empire was going to lose most if not all of its remaining European territories and that the old order in the Balkans was dead, the pressing question for Austria-Hungary was what the new one would look like. A greater Bulgaria was acceptable and an independent Albanian state desirable because it would block Serbia from the Adriatic and was also likely to be a client state of Austria-Hungary. A much bigger

454 | THE WAR THAT ENDED PEACE

Serbia or Montenegro, however, and the resulting increase in Russia's influence in the Balkans were certainly not what Vienna wanted to see on its southern borders. Serbia's demands included the Sanjak, which would give it a common border with Montenegro, part of Kosovo, and access to the Adriatic. It was bad enough that Montenegro had a tiny piece of the Adriatic coast but if Serbia pushed westwards to the sea, Austria-Hungary's dominant position in the Adriatic, already challenged by Italy, would face a new threat. Its naval base at Pula which had already absorbed a good deal of Austria-Hungary's resources might well become useless and the very important port of Trieste, at the head of the Adriatic, could be strangled. Public opinion, already hostile to Serbia, was further inflamed by reports that the Serbians had captured an Austrian-Hungarian diplomat as they advanced into Ottoman territory and were treating him badly, even, it was rumoured, castrating him. (He turned out to be unharmed.)[57]

If his government failed to act to bring Serbia and Montenegro under control, warned General Blasius Schemua, Conrad's replacement for a brief period as chief of staff, Austria-Hungary could say goodbye to its great-power status.[58] Conrad, who was very depressed at Serbia's successes (the muscles in his face were twitching incessantly, said a friend),[59] sent his usual long memoranda, this time more vehement than ever, urging that Serbia be destroyed. Berchtold, with support from the emperor and, at first, from Franz Ferdinand, resisted but he set out Austria-Hungary's minimum aims to the other powers: the establishment of an independent and large Albania and Serbia to be blocked from acquiring a piece of the Adriatic coast. The latter, unfortunately for the peace of Europe, was a Serbian demand that Russia initially supported in order to demonstrate its firm backing for its client state.

Russia found itself in an awkward position. Its military leaders estimated that the country would not be ready for a major war for another couple of years, yet Russia could not stand by and see the Balkan states pushed around by Austria-Hungary.[60] In an effort to deter Austria-Hungary and its ally Germany, Russia used a tactic it was to use again in the summer of 1914. At the end of September 1912, at precisely the same moment that the Balkan states were mobilising their armies, the Russian military carried out what it described as a trial mobilisation in its westernmost Warsaw military district which bordered both Germany

and Austria-Hungary. The Russians also extended the service of conscript troops who had been due to be released, which had the effect of
increasing the number of active soldiers by some 270,000.[61]

The Russian actions brought a response from Austria-Hungary
where there was mounting gloom over the collapse of the status quo in
the Balkans and the growing power of Serbia, Montenegro and, to a
lesser extent, Bulgaria. At the end of October Berchtold had a long and
difficult meeting with his colleagues – the ministers for the Dual Monarchy's military and shared finances – in the Common Ministerial
Council. The meeting considered war with the Balkan League as a
serious possibility and it was agreed to ask the emperor to send considerable reinforcements to the forces already in Bosnia.[62] Shortly
afterwards, Berchtold visited Italy where he tried to persuade the Italians to support Austria-Hungary. (He also cheered himself up by
visiting antique stores and art galleries.)[63] In November, as the Balkan
League consolidated its victories over the Turks, Austria-Hungary
responded to Russia by putting its troops in Bosnia and Dalmatia on a
war footing. It also increased its garrisons in Galicia near the border
with Russia, something which caused panic among the locals, who
feared war was about to break out.[64]

Europe did indeed move closer to a general war. In Russia's ruling
circles, Sazonov later wrote in his memoirs, there was a firm conviction
that the time had come to settle accounts with Austria-Hungary and
get revenge for the Bosnian fiasco.[65] On 22 November, two days after
the measures by Austria-Hungary, the tsar chaired a meeting with his
top military commanders from the key western parts of Russia who had
been urging the government to strengthen their forces and arguing for
a military showdown with Austria-Hungary.[66] As for Nicholas, in the
opinion of the British ambassador, he was even more a Panslavist than
his government and had reportedly said that he would not endure a
second humiliation like the one Russia had suffered over Bosnia.[67] At
the meeting it was decided to mobilise the whole of the Kiev military
district which covered west Ukraine as well as a large part of the Warsaw
district in Russian Poland. And preparations were also to be made to
mobilise the Odessa district bordering on the Black Sea. Sukhomlinov,
as War Minister, did not bother to inform his civilian colleagues of this
dramatic and risky decision. It would be best, he told them, that they

should learn from the tsar himself what he had in mind. The following day, when the civilians including Sazonov and Kokovtsov, who was now Prime Minister, were summoned to the tsar's study at his palace outside St Petersburg they were appalled at what they heard. Nicholas told them he had taken his decision and that the telegrams for the mobilisation were ready to go out. Russia was, he pointed out, only mobilising against Austria-Hungary at this point and he had hopes that Wilhelm might support him in forcing Austria-Hungary to behave sensibly. Kokovtsov denounced the planned mobilisation; it meant risking a war with both Austria-Hungary and its ally Germany and Russia simply was not ready. Sazonov too, for all his enthusiasm for the Slav cause, also had cold feet and had become noticeably more restrained in his support of Serbia, telling the Austrians and the Italians, for example, that Russia no longer supported Serbia getting a port on the Adriatic. As the British ambassador said unkindly, 'Sazonov is so continually changing his ground that it is difficult to follow the successive phases of pessimism and optimism through which he passes.'[68] On this occasion, the civilians successfully resisted pressure from the military and the planned mobilisation was shelved, although the number of active troops was again increased by extending the term of military service.[69] Sukhomlinov, who by virtue of his office knew Russia's military weaknesses all too well, continued nevertheless to argue that war with Germany and Austria-Hungary was inevitable and that it might be best to get it over with. 'Tell them in Paris', he told the French military attachés in St Petersburg, 'that they can rest assured, everything is ready here, without fuss; you will see.'[70]

While the Russians were flirting with danger, another set of equally portentous meetings was going on in Berlin. Franz Ferdinand and Schemua, the then Austrian chief of staff, had arrived to ask for assurances of German support in case of Russian attack. The German Chancellor, Bethmann, and Kiderlen, the Foreign Secretary, initially hoped to strike a balance between working with Britain to calm the international tensions over the Balkans but showing support for Austria-Hungary. At the same time they intended to restrain their ally from going too far, for example in annexing the Sanjak which Austria-Hungary had renounced in 1908. Nor did the German leaders wish to see the destruction of the Ottoman Empire, where Germany had significant interests including the beginnings of the Berlin-to-Baghdad railway.[71] The Kaiser, as always unpredictable, had initially been hostile to the Ottomans, on the grounds that the present leadership had revolted against 'my friend the Sultan', and had been sympathetic to the Balkan League, even for a time referring to the man he called 'the sheep stealer of the Black Mountains' as 'His Majesty the King of Montenegro'.[72] By the time of Franz Ferdinand and Schemua's November visit, however, Wilhelm had swung round to outright support of Austria-Hungary. Indeed, in the conversations that took place, first in Berlin and then at his hunting lodge in the east, he went further than his own government would have liked and promised his visitors German support if a war broke out between Austria-Hungary and Russia over the Balkans. A week later Bethmann told the Reichstag that Germany would stand by its ally, although he carefully avoided going into specifics.[73] In Silesia, near the Russian border, German families made plans to move west, away from the expected invasion, while in Berlin high officials were said to be putting their money into Swiss banks for safety. Tirpitz asked his senior officers what preliminary steps could be taken before a complete naval mobilisation and, in a foreshadowing of what was to be his more complete psychological collapse in 1914, Moltke, the chief of the German general staff, was noticeably both nervous and lethargic.[74]

Across Europe the stock markets grew jittery and the press filled with reports of troop movements and other military preparations. 'The air is dense with rumours', reported the *Times* correspondent from Vienna, 'not all of which merit credence. Taken together they show, however, that the conflict in the Near East is approaching the stage when European Governments will need perspicacity and prudence if it is to be prevented from becoming a European conflict.'[75] Austria-Hungary ordered its diplomats in Belgrade, Cetinje and St Petersburg to pack up their most important papers and be ready to leave in case of war. (They were able to use the same orders two years later.)[76] On 7 December, shortly after the armistice in the Balkans, Conrad was reappointed as Austria-Hungary's chief of the general staff. He rushed to share the news with his beloved Gina but when he saw her he put his head in his hands and could not speak. Austria-Hungary now faced much greater problems than before in the Balkans, he told her; the Balkan states were much stronger.[77] He nevertheless continued to put

pressure on Berchtold for military action against Serbia and Montenegro and, for the time being, he had the support of Franz Ferdinand,
more usually, like Berchtold, a voice for moderation.[78]

At the start of December, as the armistice was being signed to end
the First Balkan War, Grey attempted to calm international tensions by
calling for a conference of the ambassadors of the great powers along
with a separate one for representatives of the Balkan nations, both to
meet in London to make peace. Speaking for the government, Haldane,
the Secretary of State for War, also warned the new German ambassador in London, Prince Karl Lichnowsky, that Britain was unlikely to
stand by if Austria-Hungary attacked Serbia and that, if a general war
broke out, was almost certain to intervene to prevent France being
crushed. Although the Kaiser was furious with the British – 'cowardly',
'a nation of shopkeepers', 'dog-in-the-manger attitude' – his government was prepared to co-operate with Britain to bring the crisis to a
conclusion. Both Kiderlen and Bethmann hoped for Britain's neutrality
in a future European war although they had given up on gaining its
friendship.[79] Austria-Hungary for its part resented what it saw as lukewarm support from its ally.[80]

The other powers also accepted Grey's invitation. France did not
want a war over the Balkans and Italy always jumped at the chance to
be treated as a great power. Both Austria-Hungary and Russia were
feeling the financial strain of their military preparations and on both
sides voices, particularly from conservative circles, called for a better
understanding between the two great monarchies. The Russian government had already made one decision in November to back away from
the brink. Sazonov, though, faced fierce public criticism for being
willing to compromise: it was, said one deputy in the Duma, 'a diplomatic Mukden', equivalent to one of Russia's key land defeats in the
Russo-Japanese War. On 11 December, Austria-Hungary's top leaders
met with Franz Joseph to decide between peace or war. Conrad vehemently made the case for war with Franz Ferdinand's support. (The
archduke was shortly afterwards to return to a more moderate position.) Berchtold and most of the civilian ministers opposed Conrad.
The emperor, 'unusually serious, composed and determined', gave his
decision for peace. In July 1914, he was going to decide the other way.[81]

The London conference of ambassadors met in the Foreign Office under Grey's chairmanship from late December 1912 until August 1913. Its proceedings, Grey later said, were 'protracted and sometimes intolerably wearisome'. Paul Cambon, who was representing France, joked that the conference would continue until there were six skeletons seated around the table.[82] (It was a mark of the old Europe with its interrelated aristocracy that Count Albert Mensdorff, the ambassador of Austria-Hungary, Lichnowsky from Germany, and Count Alexander Benckendorff, the Russian ambassador, were cousins.) The Italian ambassador, complained Mensdorff, talked more than the rest of them put together.[83] Although the powers were now agreed on avoiding war if at all possible, they found that it was not easy to bring the Balkan states to a settlement. The Balkan League was coming apart under national rivalries and the Ottoman Empire was again in turmoil. In January, Enver Pasha of the Young Turks, who had briefly been ousted, appeared at the head of a group of armed men at a Cabinet meeting in Constantinople to accuse the government of giving way to the other powers and to demand its resignation. To underline their demand, the Young Turks shot and killed the War Minister.

The main disagreement among the great powers was over the nature and shape of Albania. Austria-Hungary argued that the new state should be a monarchy. Cambon thought cynically that an incompetent ruler there would suit Austria-Hungary very well by getting himself killed and giving it reason to intervene and make Albania its protectorate.[84] Albania's borders also caused endless difficulties. Part of the problem was that the Albanians, who may well have been descended from the original inhabitants of the Balkans, were intermingled with South Slavs of various nationalities and religions. The Albanians were also divided by clan and by religion – those in south were mainly Muslim while the north was largely Christian – which further encouraged outside powers to meddle. In addition Austria-Hungary wanted a large Albania to balance against the Slav states and to block Serbia from the sea while Russia hoped to give as much Ottoman territory as possible to its Slav protégés.[85] As a result there were endless arguments over small villages which most had never heard of. It was, Grey complained, 'unreasonable and intolerable that the greater part of Europe should be involved in a war for a dispute about one or two towns on the Albanian frontier'.[86] (Neville Chamberlain made a similar complaint when he exclaimed in a broadcast about the crisis over Czechoslovakia in 1938: 'How horrible, fantastic, incredible it is that we should be digging trenches and trying on gas-masks here because of a quarrel in a far away country between people of whom we know nothing.')

The fate of the small town of Scutari (today Shkodër) led to particular tensions and renewed fears of war. Austria-Hungary wanted the town included in Albania since it was a centre of Catholic and therefore Austrian-Hungarian influence. Its inclusion in either Montenegro or Serbia would be, so Berchtold among others believed, damaging to Austria-Hungary's prestige and interests.[87] Franz Ferdinand, who by now had backed away from his earlier belligerence, wrote anxiously – and presciently – to Berchtold in mid February 1913:

> Without giving up everything, we should do anything to uphold peace! If we enter a great war with Russia, it would be a catastrophe, and who knows if your right and left flanks will function; Germany has to deal with France and Rumania makes excuses due to the Bulgarian threat. Therefore now is a very disadvantageous moment. If we wage a special war with Serbia, we will quickly overcome the hurdle, but what then? And what would we have? First all of Europe would fall on us and see us as disturber of the peace and God help us, that we annex Serbia.[88]

As tensions mounted again between Russia and Austria-Hungary, Franz Joseph sent a trusted emissary, Prince Gottfried von Hohenlohe-Schillingfürst, to St Petersburg to reassure the tsar that the civilians were still in control of the generals in Austria-Hungary. In yet another chilling example of how readily the top leadership in Europe was now taking the prospect of a large-scale war for granted, Hohenlohe warned that war was likely in the next six to eight weeks if the Albanian issues were not settled.[89] The two powers again pulled back from war, and by March this latest European crisis was winding down as Russia and Austria-Hungary cut back their troops along their common borders and came to an agreement that Scutari would be included in Albania in return for a handful of towns going to Serbia.

On the ground, however, the situation was far from being resolved as the Balkan states continued to play their own game. Montenegro and Serbia, who were temporarily friends, had attempted to pre-empt any peace settlement by seizing Scutari during the war itself but the Ottoman garrison had held out with remarkable determination. The Montenegrins and Serbians remained deaf to increasingly forceful demands from the great powers to end the siege. At the end of March, Austria-Hungary sent its Adriatic Fleet to blockade Montenegro's ports. Sazonov warned of 'the monstrous danger which this isolated act involved for the European peace' and the Russian government contemplated increasing its armed forces again.[90] Britain and Italy hastily suggested a common demonstration of naval power and dispatched ships of their own, and the Russians and French later added theirs. (Since Scutari was twelve miles inland, it was not entirely clear what the powers hoped to gain by this.) The Russians reluctantly also agreed to put pressure on Serbia, which ended its part in the siege at the start of April. Nicholas of Montenegro was not so easily swayed, however. He had bribed one of the defenders, an Albanian officer in the Ottoman army, to deliver the city to him. Essad Pasha Toptani, almost as much of a rogue as Nicholas himself, had first murdered the garrison's commander and then set his price at £80,000 by sending out a message that he had lost a suitcase containing that amount and asking that it be returned.[91]

On 23 April, Essad duly surrendered Scutari to the Montenegrins. In Montenegro's capital, Cetinje, there were wild celebrations with drunken revellers firing their guns in all directions. Some wits sent a donkey dressed in black carrying a large sign with rude messages to the embassy of Austria-Hungary. Across the Balkans and in St Petersburg crowds came out to show their enthusiasm for the victory of their South Slav brothers.[92] In Vienna and Berlin, the mood was grim. Conrad ordered his staff to prepare plans for a campaign against Montenegro if it refused to give up Scutari and at the end of April Gottlieb von Jagow, who had replaced Kiderlen as Foreign Secretary after the latter's sudden death, promised German support for Austria-Hungary. At the start of May, Austria-Hungary decided to issue an ultimatum to Montenegro and started military preparations, among other measures declaring emergency rule in Bosnia. Russia in turn stepped up its measures, among other things placing orders for horses for its armed forces.[93] By

3 May, Nicholas of Montenegro realised that Austria-Hungary meant business and on 4 May he announced that his troops would leave Scutari and let the great powers deal with it. Austria-Hungary and Russia yet again stood down their preparations for war. Europe's peace had been maintained, for the time being, but not everyone greeted this with pleasure. In Vienna Conrad regretted that Austria-Hungary had not acted: a victory over Montenegro would have at least bolstered its prestige. At a dinner party, a friend noticed that Conrad was very depressed. In addition Austria-Hungary now had to deal with a Serbia that had doubled in size.[94]

Under the Treaty of London, which was signed at the end of May, Albania became an independent state. It was subject to an international Control Commission, which never worked effectively because of Austria-Hungary's obstruction. The little state, which was poor and divided, duly got a king, an ineffectual and amiable German prince. William of Wied survived in his new kingdom for six months before Essad Pasha, who had his own designs on the throne, helped to drive him out. The treaty also confirmed the gains made by the Balkan League but that did not lead to peace. The Balkan League promptly fell to pieces. Both Serbia and Greece were infuriated that Bulgaria had come out by far the greatest winner, incorporating territory which they thought was rightfully theirs, and immediately pushed for a revision of the treaty. Rumania, which had stayed out of the first war, now saw an opportunity to seize part of Bulgaria while the Ottoman Empire hoped to push Bulgaria back in the south. On 29 June 1913, a month after the treaty had been signed, Bulgaria, where public opinion was strongly in favour of war, launched a pre-emptive attack on Serbia and Greece. Rumania and the Ottoman Empire joined in against Bulgaria, which then suffered a series of defeats. On 10 August 1913 the Balkan powers made the Peace of Bucharest under which Rumania, Greece, and Serbia all gained territory at the expense of Bulgaria. 'The peace bells of Bucharest', said Berchtold in his memoirs, 'had a hollow ring.'[95] For Austria-Hungary the two Balkan wars had delivered damaging blows to its honour and its prestige.

Unrest in the Balkans rumbled on. Serbia, which now controlled the Ottoman province of Kosovo and a part of Macedonia, immediately had to deal with a revolt among its new large population of Albanian

Muslims. Although the Serbian government crushed all resistance savagely, it stored up for Serbia a legacy of hatred and resentment among the Albanians which was still causing trouble at the end of the century. Albania's borders were disputed by Greece in the south and Serbia in the north and the Serbians, in particular, were determined not to back down in the face of the great powers.

Victory in both the Balkan wars had made the Serbians, both the public and their leaders, increasingly and excessively confident. 'They listened to nothing and were capable of all sorts of follies,' reported the *Times* correspondent in Belgrade.[96] The military and the extreme nationalist Black Hand complained bitterly when the government showed any signs of backing down but the civilian officials were generally equally intransigent. 'If Serbia is defeated on the battlefield', Pašić had exclaimed in early 1913 to his ambassador in St Petersburg, 'then at least it will not be despised by the world, for the world will esteem highly a people who would not living enter the servitude of Austria.' Serbia's appetites had also grown with its successes on the battlefields. In early 1914 Pašić had a meeting in St Petersburg with the tsar. Serbia's hopes of uniting all Serbs (something Pašić defined generously to include Croatians) now seemed closer to reality. There were some 6 million restless 'Serbocroats' inside Austria-Hungary, he told Nicholas, not including the Slovenes who were starting to wake up to the fact that they belonged with their South Slav kindred.[97]

Austria-Hungary remained the chief obstacle to this dream. In the autumn of 1913, it demanded that Serbia pull its troops out of the pieces of northern Albania which they had occupied. The Serbian government not only refused; it sent more troops in order, so it claimed, to protect fellow Serbs against the Albanians. At the start of October, Pašić, with his long grey beard looking like a benevolent Balkan sage, visited Vienna for discussions with the government. 'He is humble in person, anxious,' wrote Berchtold in his diary. 'Through his amiability he made us forget our fundamental differences that divide us, and also made us overlook his devious nature.' Pašić was full of goodwill but he refused to make any concrete agreements.[98] Although he did not know it, the Common Ministerial Council was meeting at the same time to discuss what steps to take against his country. Conrad, who, unusually, was attending this civilian meeting, urged that Austria-Hungary simply go ahead and annex its troublesome neighbour. The civilians were not yet ready to go so far but they had clearly come to accept that war was likely at some point in the future and, for some, it was even to be desired. Even Berchtold, who was usually a force for moderation, was now prepared to support an increase in armaments.[99]

Among the ministers attending was the Prime Minister of Hungary, István Tisza, who took a hard line and who, in the crisis of 1914, was going to play a crucial part in Austria-Hungary's decision to go to war with Serbia. His compatriots, even those who were his political enemies, regarded Tisza with awe for his courage, his determination, and his wilfulness. 'He is the smartest man in Hungary,' said a leading political opponent, 'smarter than all of us put together. He is like a Maria Theresa commode with many drawers. Each drawer is filled with knowledge up to the top. However, what is not in those drawers does not exist, as far as Tisza is concerned. This smart, headstrong, and proud man is a threat to our country. Mark my words, this Tisza is as dangerous as an uncovered razor blade.'[100] Franz Joseph liked him because he was able to deal firmly and effectively with the Hungarian extremists who thought only of Hungary's independence and who had been blocking all attempts in the Hungarian parliament to get increases in the military budget.

Tisza, who had been Prime Minister once before, was at once a strong Hungarian patriot and a supporter of the Habsburg monarchy. Hungary had an advantageous position, in his view, inside Austria-Hungary which protected it from its enemies such as Rumania and allowed the survival of the old Hungarian kingdom with its large territories. Deeply conservative, he was determined to maintain both the commanding position of his own landed class and the dominance of Hungarians over their non-Hungarian subjects including Croatians, Slovaks, and Rumanians. Universal suffrage, which would have given the minorities a say in Hungary's politics, would, he said, amount to 'castrating the nation'.[101]

In foreign policy, Tisza supported the alliance with Germany and regarded the Balkan states with suspicion. He would have preferred peace with them but was prepared for war, especially if any of them became too strong.[102] In the Common Ministerial Council he supported an ultimatum to Serbia to withdraw its forces from Albania. He wrote privately to Berchtold: 'Events on the Albanian-Serbian border make us confront the question whether we will remain a viable power or if we will give up and sink into laughable decadence. With every day of indecision we lose esteem and the chances of an advantageous and peaceful solution become more and more compromised.' If Austria-Hungary missed this chance to assert itself, Tisza went on, it would rightly lose its place among the great powers.[103]

On 18 October Austria-Hungary issued its ultimatum to Serbia and gave it eight days to comply. Among the great powers, only Italy and Germany had been informed ahead of time, yet another indication that the Concert of Europe was ceasing to exist and in the next months the Triple Entente and the Triple Alliance increasingly worked separately when it came to Balkan issues.[104] Neither of its allies opposed Austria-Hungary's move and Germany went further and gave its firm support. The Kaiser was especially vehement: 'Now or never!' he wrote on a letter of thanks from Berchtold. 'Some time or other peace and order must be established down there!'[105] On 25 October, Serbia capitulated and moved its troops out of Albania. The following day the Kaiser, who was on a visit to Vienna, had tea with Berchtold and told him that Austria-Hungary must continue to be firm: 'When His Majesty Emperor Francis Joseph demands something, the Serbian government must give way, and if it does not then Belgrade will be bombarded and occupied until the will of His Majesty is fulfilled.' And gesturing towards his sabre, Wilhelm promised that Germany was always ready to support its ally.[106]

The year of crises in the Balkans ended peacefully but it left behind a fresh crop of resentments and dangerous lessons. Serbia was a clear winner and on 7 November it gained yet more territory when it signed an agreement with Montenegro to divide the Sanjak of Novi Bazar. Serbia's national project was still, however, unfinished. There was now talk of union with Montenegro or the formation of a new Balkan League.[107] The Serbian government was incapable and largely unwilling to rein in the various nationalist organisations within Serbia which were agitating among the South Slavs within Austria-Hungary. In the spring of 1914 during the celebration of Easter, always a major festival in the Orthodox Church, the Serbian press was filled with references to Serbia's own resurrection. Their fellow Serbs, said a leading newspaper, were languishing within Austria-Hungary, longing for the freedom that only the bayonets of Serbia could bring them. 'Let us therefore stand closer together and hasten to the assistance of those who cannot feel with us the joy of this year's feast of resurrection.'[108] Russia's leaders were concerned about their headstrong small ally but showed little inclination to rein it in.

In Austria-Hungary, there was satisfaction that the government had finally taken action against Serbia. As Berchtold wrote to Franz Ferdinand shortly after Serbia bowed to the ultimatum: 'Europe now recognizes that we, even without tutelage, can act independently if our interests are threatened and that our allies will stand closely behind us.'[109] The German ambassador in Vienna had noticed, however, 'the feeling of disgrace, of restrained anger, the feeling of being mucked about by Russia and its own friends'.[110] There was relief that Germany had in the end remained true to the alliance but resentment at Austria-Hungary's growing dependency. Conrad complained: 'Now we are nothing more than a satellite of Germany.'[111] To the south, the continued existence of an independent Serbia, and one now more powerful than before, remained as a reminder of Austria-Hungary's failures in the Balkans. Berchtold was widely criticised by the political representatives of Austria and Hungary and in the press for his weakness. When he offered to resign at the end of 1913, Franz Joseph was unsympathetic: 'There is no reason, nor is it permissible to capitulate before a group of a few delegates and a newspaper. Also, you don't have a successor.'[112]

Like so many of his colleagues, Berchtold remained obsessed with the menace from Serbia and with Austria-Hungary's great-power status, which he saw as intertwined. In his memoirs he tellingly talks about how the empire had been 'emasculated' in the Balkan wars.[113] Increasingly, so it seemed, Austria-Hungary faced a stark choice between fighting for its existence or disappearing from the map. Although Tisza initially had floated improbable schemes to work with Russia to persuade Serbia to give up some of its gains, by this point most of the leadership in Austria-Hungary had abandoned hope that Serbia could be won over peacefully; it would only understand the language of force. Conrad, the new War Minister General Alexander Krobatin, and General Oskar Potiorek, the military governor of Bosnia, all were convinced hardliners. The Common Finance Minister, Leon von Biliński, who had tried to keep Austria-Hungary's finances on an even keel, now supported greatly increased military spending. 'A war would perhaps be cheaper', he said, 'than the present state of affairs. It was useless to say we have no money. We must pay until a change comes about and we no longer have almost all of Europe against us.'[114] It was also now widely accepted among the top leadership that a showdown with Serbia and possibly with Russia could not long be postponed, although Conrad continued to believe until the eve of the Great War that Russia might tolerate a limited Austrian-Hungarian attack on Serbia and Montenegro.[115] The one man who still hoped to avert war was Franz Ferdinand.

In the year from the outbreak of the First Balkan War to the autumn of 1913, Russia and Austria-Hungary had come close to war on several occasions, and the shadow of a more general conflict had fallen across Europe as a whole as their allies had waited in the wings. Although the powers had in the end been able to manage the crises, their peoples, leaders and publics alike had become accustomed to the idea of war, and as something that might happen sooner rather than later. When Conrad threatened to resign because he felt he had been snubbed by Franz Ferdinand, Moltke begged him to reconsider: 'Now, when we are moving towards a conflict, you must remain.'[116] Russia and Austria-Hungary had used preparations for war, especially mobilisation, for deterrence but also to put pressure on each other, and, in the case of Austria-Hungary, on Serbia. Threats had worked this time because none of the three countries had been prepared to call the bluffs of the others and because, in the end, the voices for maintaining the peace were stronger than those for war. What was dangerous for the future was that each of Austria-Hungary and Russia was left thinking that such threats might work again. Or, and this was equally dangerous, they decided that next time they would not back down.

The great powers drew a sort of comfort from the fact that they had muddled through yet again. Over the past eight years, the first and second Moroccan crises, the one over Bosnia, and now the Balkan wars, had all threatened to bring about a general war but diplomacy had always averted it. In these most recent months of tension, the Concert of Europe had more or less survived and Britain and Germany had worked well together to find compromises and to restrain their own alliance partners. When the next Balkan crisis came, in the summer of 1914, Grey at least expected that the same thing would happen again.[117]

The peace movement which had watched with apprehension also breathed a sigh of relief. The great emergency congress of the Second International at Basle in the late autumn of 1912 had seemed to mark a new high point in co-operation in the cause of peace across national boundaries. In February 1913, the French and German socialists issued a joint manifesto condemning the armaments race and pledging to work together. Surely, so pacifists thought, the anti-war forces were growing even within capitalism and better relations among the powers were just over the horizon.[118] To bring home the horrors of war, a German film maker took footage during the Second Balkan War. His film was just starting to be shown by peace societies across Europe in the summer of 1914.[119] The new Carnegie Endowment for International Peace, which had been generously endowed by the American millionaire Andrew Carnegie, sent a mission made up of Austrian, French, German, British, Russian, and American representatives to investigate the Balkan wars. The Commission's report noted with dismay the tendency of the warring peoples to portray their enemies as subhuman and the all too-frequent atrocities committed against both enemy soldiers and civilians. 'In the older civilizations', the report said, 'there is a synthesis of moral and social forces embodied in laws and institutions giving stability of character, forming public sentiment, and making for security.'[120] The report was issued early in the summer of 1914, just as the rest of Europe was about to learn how fragile its civilisation was.

CHAPTER 17

Preparing for War or Peace: Europe's Last Months of Peace

I n May 1913, in the brief interlude between the first two Balkan wars, the cousins George V of Britain, Nicholas II of Russia and Wilhelm II of Germany met in Berlin for the wedding of the Kaiser's only daughter to the Duke of Brunswick (who was also related to them all). Although the bride's mother reportedly cried the whole night of the wedding at being parted from her child, the occasion was, so Sir Edward Goschen, the British ambassador, told Grey, a 'splendid success'. The Germans had been extremely hospitable and the king and queen had enjoyed themselves thoroughly. 'His Majesty told me that He had never known a Royal visit at which politics had been so freely and thoroughly discussed, and He was glad to be able to inform me that He, the King and the Emperor of Russia had been in thorough agreement on all the points which they had had under review.' The cousins were in particular agreement that Foxy Ferdinand of Bulgaria – 'to whom His Majesty applied a strong epithet' – must be kept under control. 'My impression', Goschen concluded, 'is that the visit has done real good and that its effect will perhaps be more lasting than is usually the case with State visits of foreign Sovereigns.'[1]

17. The last years before the Great War brought an intensifying arms race. Although moderates and supporters of the peace movement pointed to the dangers of the increasing preparations for war and complained of the increasing costs, European nations were now so suspicious of each other that they dared not back down. The cartoon shows a prosperous row of houses, bearing different national flags, becoming more and more dilapidated while the caption reads 'The more the nations try to outdo their neighbours in the arms race, the more their own people suffer …'

His king was privately less enthusiastic. When he tried to talk alone with Nicholas, he complained, Wilhelm's ear 'was glued to the keyhole'. The Kaiser had also harangued George about Britain's support for France: 'There you are making alliances with a decadent nation like France and a semi-barbarous nation like Russia and opposing us, the true upholders of progress and liberty …'[2] Wilhelm apparently believed that he had made a deep impression and so weakened the Entente between Britain and France.[3] It was the last time the cousins were to meet. In shortly over a year their countries would be at war with each other.

Europe still had choices in that last period of peace. True there was much troubling its nations in 1913: fear of losing ground, fear of being outnumbered and outgunned by their neighbours, fear of unrest or revolution at home, or fear of the consequences of war itself. Such fears could have played out either way: to make the powers more cautious or to make them ready to gamble on war. Yet while Europe's leaders did not have to opt for war it was increasingly likely that they would. The naval race between Britain and Germany, rivalry between Austria-Hungary and Russia in the Balkans, the rift between Russia and Germany, France's anxieties about Germany had driven apart nations who had much to gain from working together. And the previous dozen or so years with their accumulated suspicions and memories weighed heavily in the minds of decision-makers and their publics. Whether defeat and isolation by Germany for France, the Boer War for Britain, the Moroccan crises for Germany, the Russo-Japanese War and Bosnia for Russia or the Balkan wars for Austria-Hungary, each power had its share of bitter experiences, ones it hoped not to repeat. Demonstrating that you are a great power and avoiding humiliation are powerful forces in international relations, whether for the United States or Russia or China today, or for the European powers a century ago. If Germany and Italy wanted their places in the sun, Britain hoped to avoid decline and hang on to its huge empire. Russia and France wanted to regain what they felt to be their rightful stature while Austria-Hungary was struggling for its survival. Military force was an option they all considered using but somehow, for all the tensions, Europe had always managed to pull back in time. In 1905, 1908, 1911, 1912 and 1913, the Concert of Europe, a much weakened one, had held. The dangerous moments were coming closer together, though, and in 1914, in a world which had become dangerously inured to crises, Europe's leaders were to face the choice, yet again, for war or for peace.

And yet again they had to deal with the gusts of fear and heightened nationalism that ran through their own publics, and the lobby and special-interest groups grew increasingly skilled in stirring up opinion. In Germany, for example, Major General August Keim, who had been active in the German Navy League, founded a similar organisation at the start of 1912 to agitate for a bigger army. The Wehrverein had 40,000 members by May and 300,000 by the following summer and funding from big industrialists such as Alfred Krupp. Keim supported each military bill that went to the Reichstag but invariably said they were completely inadequate.[4] In Britain the mass papers continued to circulate stories of German invasion plans and German waiters who were really serving officers. Sudden press wars between nations flared up. In 1913 the German press made a fuss when French actors appeared in German uniforms in a play called *Fritz le Uhlan* while in Berlin the following summer the aptly named Valhalla theatre planned to mount a melodrama, *The Terror of the Foreign Legion, or the Hell of Sidi-bel-Abbes*.[5] Early in 1914 a German paper published an article from its St Petersburg correspondent to say that hostility to Germany in official Russian circles was growing. The Russian press responded by accusing the Germans of preparing a preventive war against Russia. Sukhomlinov, the War Minister, gave a belligerent interview to a leading paper to say that Russia was ready.[6]

In the early summer of 1914 General Aleksei Brusilov, who was to lead one of Russia's few successful attacks in the Great War, was taking the waters at the south German resort of Bad Kissingen, where he and his wife were astounded by what they saw at the local festival. 'The central square, surrounded by banked masses of flowers, was surmounted by a superb set-piece representing the Kremlin at Moscow with its church, ramparts, and towers, and, in the foreground, the Cathedral of St. Basil.' Guns fired a salute and a magnificent display of fireworks lit up the night and while a band played the Russian and German national anthems followed by Tchaikovsky's 1812 Overture, the model of the Kremlin burned to the ground. The German crowd cheered happily while Brusilov, his wife, and a handful of fellow Russians stood by silently chagrined and resentful.[7]

Although the ruling classes across Europe often shared the nationalism of their publics they also worried about their reliability. Political
parties of the left were growing, and in some countries their leaders were
now openly revolutionary. In Italy initial enthusiasm for the war in
North Africa had quickly worn off among the socialists and their supporters; the young radical Benito Mussolini organised demonstrations
to protest as the troops left for the war and the moderate leaders of the
Socialist Party were expelled and replaced by more radical ones. In the
German elections of 1912, the Social Democrats gained sixty-seven new
seats, something that was viewed with near panic by the right. The
leader of the conservative and nationalist Agrarian League published *If
I Were Kaiser* to argue for a good victorious war which would give the
government an excuse to get rid of universal suffrage.[8] And workers
were both better organised and more militant. In the cities, towns and
countryside of northern Italy, the army had to be called in to suppress
strikes and demonstrations. In Britain the number of workers on strike
had risen sharply from 138,000 in 1899 to 1,200,000 in 1912. While the
numbers had dropped in 1913, the first seven months of 1914 saw almost
a thousand strikes, often about apparently trivial matters. Moreover, like
those on the Continent, the British working classes appeared to be
increasingly open to revolutionary ideas and ready to use direct action
such as strikes and sabotage for political goals. Early in 1914, three of the
most militant unions, representing railway and transport workers and
miners, joined forces in their own triple alliance. Since the alliance
could, if it chose, close down the coal mines, stop the trains and paralyse
the docks, it represented a threat to British industry and ultimately to
Britain's power which caused much unease among the ruling classes.

On the other side of Europe, Russia continued its fitful moves
towards the rest of the modern European world. The assassination of
Stolypin, though, in the autumn of 1911 had removed a man who might
have dragged the tsarist regime, over the objections of Nicholas and his
court, into making reforms before it was too late. The tsar, who was
increasingly under the influence of reactionaries in his court, did his
best to stall Russia's move towards constitutional government. He
appointed compliant and right-wing ministers and ignored the Duma
as much as possible. At the start of 1914 he dismayed moderate opinion
by suddenly dismissing his Prime Minister, Kokovtsov – 'like a

474 | THE WAR THAT ENDED PEACE

domestic' said one of the grand dukes – so removing one of the few remaining competent and reform-minded ministers.[9] Kokovtsov's successor was an elderly favourite of the tsar. Ivan Goremykin was charming, reactionary, and utterly incapable of leading Russia in the troubles already upon it, much less the ones about to come. Sazonov, the Foreign Minister, said of him: 'An old man who had long ago lost not only his capacity for interesting himself in anything but his own peace and well-being, but also the power of taking into account the activities in progress around him.'[10] Goremykin himself had no illusions about his own capacities for his new position. 'I completely fail to understand why I was needed,' he told a leading liberal politician. 'I resemble an old raccoon fur coat which has been packed away in the trunk long ago and sprinkled with camphor.'[11]

To make matters still worse, the scandal surrounding Rasputin was becoming increasingly public. Rumours swirled through Russian society that the priest had an unhealthy influence over the imperial family and was far too intimate with the tsarina and her daughters. The tsar's mother wept as she told Kokovtsov: 'My poor daughter-in-law does not perceive that she is ruining both the dynasty and herself. She sincerely believes in the holiness of an adventurer, and we are powerless to ward off the misfortune which is sure to come.'[12] The 300th anniversary of Romanov rule fell in 1913, and Nicholas and Alexandra travelled across Russia that spring on a rare excursion to show themselves to the people. Although the imperial couple and their courtiers still believed that the ordinary Russians, especially the peasants, loved and revered the Romanovs, Kokovtsov, who accompanied his master, was struck by the small size of the crowds and their noticeable lack of enthusiasm. The March winds were cold and the tsar did not always bother to come out at the different stops. In Moscow the crowds were again small and there were murmurs at the pitiful spectacle of the sickly heir to the throne as he was carried along in the arms of his Cossack bodyguard.[13]

In the Duma the divisions between the conservatives and the radicals had deepened, producing little but endless debates and recriminations, while the democratic parties of the middle were increasingly squeezed out by the extremes of left and right. The Council of State which was supposed to function as an upper house was dominated by elderly reactionaries who saw their role as blocking any liberal measures which came out of the Duma.[14] On the right there was talk of a coup to restore absolutist rule while for much of the left revolution seemed the only way to effect change. In the cities, the workers were falling under the influence of the far left, including the Bolsheviks. In the last two years before the war, strikes increased sharply in number and violence. Out in the countryside the mood among the peasants was increasingly sullen; in 1905 and 1906 in many parts of Russia they had tried to seize farms from the landed classes. They had failed that time but they had not forgotten. Russia's subject nationalities, whether in the Baltic, Ukraine, or the Caucasus, were stirring and organising, partly in response to government policies of Russification which produced absurd situations such as Polish students being forced to read their own literature in Russian translation and which left deep and growing resentments.

The reaction of the authorities to unrest within Russia was to blame agitators, whether revolutionaries or Freemasons and Jews, who were seen as amounting to much the same thing. In 1913 the reactionary Minister of the Interior and Minister of Justice had the approval of the tsar when they pandered to Russian anti-Semitism by allowing the trial of a Kiev Jew, Mendel Beilis, for allegedly carrying out the ritual murder of a Christian boy. The evidence was not only flimsy but, as became apparent, fabricated. Even the tsar and his ministers knew by the time of the trial that Beilis was innocent but they decided to go ahead on the grounds that Jews were known to carry out ritual murders, just not in this case. The trial raised outrage among liberal circles in Russia and abroad and the clumsy efforts of the government to ensure a conviction – which included arresting defence witnesses – undermined its credibility still further. Beilis was acquitted and emigrated to the United States, where he was to witness the collapse of the old order in 1917 from a position of safety.[15]

By 1914, Russians and foreigners alike had taken to describing the country as being on top of a volcano with the fires which had erupted in the aftermath of the war with Japan in 1905 and 1906 gathering force again under the surface. 'An unskilled hand', said Count Otto von Czernin of the Austrian-Hungarian embassy in St Petersburg, 'may fan the flames and start a conflagration if the nationalist hotheads, together with the extreme Right, bring about a union of the

oppressed nationalities and the socialist proletariat.'[16] Russian intellectuals complained of a feeling of helplessness and despair, of watching
the old society collapsing while a new one was not yet ready to be
born.[17] War increasingly came to be seen as a way out of Russia's
dilemma, a way to bring Russian society together. The Russian upper
and middle classes agreed with each other and the government on only
one thing – the glory of Russia's past and the need to reassert its role
as a great power. Defeat by Japan had been a terrible humiliation and
Russia's evident weakness in the Bosnian crisis of 1908 and more
recently in the Balkan wars brought the liberal opposition together
with the most passionate reactionaries to support the rebuilding of the
military and an assertive foreign policy.[18] There was much talk in the
press and the Duma of Russia's historic mission in the Balkans and its
rights to the Straits even if that meant war with Germany and Austria-
Hungary, or, as the more fervent Russian nationalists put it, the
inevitable struggle between the Slavs and the Teutonic races.[19]
Although its deputies spent the greater part of their time attacking the
government, the Duma always supported spending on the military.
'One must profit from the general enthusiasm,' the speaker of the
Duma told the tsar in the spring of 1913. 'The Straits must belong to
us. War will be accepted with joy and will serve only to increase the
prestige of the imperial power.'[20]

Austria-Hungary, Russia's adversary in the Balkans, was only in
somewhat better shape. Its economy, which had been badly hit by the
uncertainty and expense occasioned by the Balkan wars, was starting to
revive in early 1914 but increasing industrialisation brought with it a
larger and more militant working class. In the Hungarian half of the
Dual Monarchy the Social Democrats' demands for universal suffrage
met the resistance of the Hungarian upper classes who were not prepared to share their power. In the spring of 1912 massive worker
demonstrations in Budapest led to pitched battles with government
forces. In both halves of the Monarchy, too, nationality problems, like
forest fires, smouldered on, breaking out first here and then there into
open flames. In the Austrian part, the Ruthenians, who spoke a language closely linked to Ukrainian and belonged to their own churches,
were demanding greater political and language rights from their Polish
overlords while the Czechs and Germans were locked into a seemingly

unending battle for power. The parliament in Vienna became so unruly that the Austrian government suspended it in the spring of 1914; it did not meet again until 1916. In Hungary, the Rumanian National Party demanded concessions, including greater autonomy for the predominantly Rumanian parts, which the parliament, dominated as it was by Hungarian nationalists, would not accept. Under Tisza's influence the Hungarians were at least content to stay within the Dual Monarchy but it would almost certainly be different when Franz Ferdinand, who was notoriously anti-Hungarian, succeeded his uncle. In the spring of 1914 when the old emperor fell seriously ill the future of the monarchy looked grim. It was, said the German ambassador Heinrich von Tschirschky, who inclined to the gloomy view, 'falling apart at the seams'.[21] And, given the growth of Serbia's power, Austria-Hungary was going to have to divert more of its military resources southwards, something that disturbed Germany's military planners who counted on their ally for help against Russia.

Although Germany was doing well by many indicators, industry and trade for example, and its population continued to grow, its leadership and much of its public were strangely insecure in the last years of the peace. Fears of encirclement, the growth of Russian power, the revitalisation of France, Britain's refusal to concede in the naval race, the unreliability of its own allies, the marked growth in the votes for the SPD, all produced much pessimism about Germany's future. War was increasingly accepted as likely if not inevitable; France was deemed the most likely enemy but its entente partners would probably come to its defence (although Bethmann still hoped for better relations with Britain and Russia).[22] 'The resentment against Germany', said the former Chancellor, Bülow, early in 1914, 'might well be called the soul of French policy.' When a postcard appeared in France with '*merde pour le roi de Prusse*' written backwards German diplomats found their suspicions confirmed. The French military attaché in Berlin reported a growing warlike mood among the public which might produce 'an outburst of anger and national pride which could one day force the Kaiser's hand and lead the masses to war'.[23] Even the gentle composer Richard Strauss was carried away by anti-French feeling. He told Kessler in the summer of 1912 that he would go along when war broke out. What did he think he could do, his wife asked. Perhaps, Strauss said uncertainly, he could be a nurse. 'Oh, *you*, Richard!' snapped his wife, 'You can't stand the sight of blood!' Strauss looked embarrassed but insisted: 'I would do my best. But if the French get a thrashing, I want to be there.'[24]

Among Germany's top civilian leadership Bethmann and, usually, the Kaiser still were anxious to avoid a war. (The Kaiser had a new passion for archaeology and spent every spring digging in Corfu, which made Bethmann's life somewhat easier.) The Foreign Secretary Kiderlen, in spite of his fondness for belligerent talk, was also a force for moderation but he died suddenly at the end of 1912 of a heart attack. His successor Gottlieb von Jagow was too weak to stand up to the generals. 'That little squirt', as the Kaiser described him, Jagow was a small, unimpressive man from an aristocratic Prussian family. His main goal seems to have been to defend Germany's interests in whatever way he could.[25] What was dangerous was that the military were increasingly accepting war as inevitable, even desirable. Many of them had not forgiven Wilhelm for backing down in the Morocco crisis of 1911 or more recently during the First Balkan War. 'They reproach him', reported the well-connected Baroness Spitzemberg, 'with too "great a love of peace" and believe that Germany had let pass its chance when it could have overcome France while Russia was occupied in the Balkans.'[26]

The general staff took for granted that in the future it would have to fight a two-front war on land. Schlieffen died in January 1913, his last words apparently 'only keep the right wing strong', but his strategic ideas still shaped Germany's military planning. His successor as chief, Moltke, true to his pessimistic nature, remained doubtful as to whether Germany could prevail in a war against its enemies, especially if it had to fight alone without allies. Despite his earlier misgivings about conscripting members of the working classes, Moltke was now arguing for increasing the size of the army and he was joined by a rising generation of officers, among them Erich von Ludendorff, one of the ambitious and intelligent middle-class men who were now making their way into the general staff. While one army bill went through the Reichstag in the summer of 1912, the crisis of the First Balkan War in the autumn which showed Austria-Hungary's weakness as well as the willingness of Russia to mobilise, brought fresh demands, drafted for Moltke by Ludendorff, to the government for rapid increases in numbers of men and materiel and for the formation of special units such as for machine guns. The language was alarmist and spoke matter-of-factly of the 'coming world war'.[27]

On 8 December 1912, as the situation in the Balkans remained tense, there occurred what has since become one of the most controversial incidents on the way to the Great War: the Kaiser's War Council at his palace in Potsdam. That morning Wilhelm read a dispatch from his ambassador in London, who reported that Grey and the British War Minister, Haldane, had warned that if a general war on the Continent broke out Britain would almost certainly come in to prevent France being destroyed by Germany. While this likelihood cannot have been news to the Kaiser, he flew into a rage at Britain's impertinence. He also felt a sense of betrayal: in the final coming struggle between Teutons and Slavs the British would be on the wrong side along with the Gauls. He hastily summoned several of his most trusted advisers, all military men including Moltke, Tirpitz, and his naval aide Admiral George von Müller. According to Müller's diary which is the best record, the Kaiser held forth at considerable length. It was good, he felt, to get a clarification of Britain's position; from now on Germany would have to fight Britain and France together. 'The Fleet must naturally prepare itself for war against England.' Austria-Hungary, he went on, ought to deal with the Serbians, which would almost certainly bring Russia in and Germany would not be able to avoid a war on that front either. Germany therefore ought to gather what allies it could – he had hopes of Rumania and Bulgaria and possibly the Ottoman Empire. Moltke concurred that war was unavoidable (and none of the others disagreed) but said that the German press should be used get the public in the right frame of mind. Tirpitz, who never seems to have wanted his beloved navy to be used in combat, said that he would prefer to see the war postponed for a year and half. Moltke replied sardonically that 'the Navy will not be ready even then', and warned that the army's position would grow weaker over time as its enemies grew stronger. 'War the sooner the better.' While too much can be made of a hasty council summoned at a time of crisis, what is chilling is how readily those present accepted that war was coming.[28]

In a memorandum he wrote for Bethmann shortly after the Council, Moltke also warned that it was important to ensure that German public opinion was persuaded that a war was just and necessary:

If war occurs, there can be no doubt that the main weight of responsibility will be on Germany's shoulders, which will be gripped on
three sides by her opponents. Nonetheless we can, *under the current
conditions*, still face even the most difficult tasks with confidence, if
we manage to formulate the *casus belli* in such a way that the nation
will take up arms unitedly and enthusiastically.[29]

In the crisis of 1914 all the governments were to do their best to ensure
that their nations appeared as the innocent party.

Filled with enthusiasm after his Council, the Kaiser ordered the
preparation of new army and navy bills. Bethmann was horrified, partly
because he did not know how he was going to pay for them. 'The Kaiser
has held a war council with his paladins from the army and navy, of
course behind Kiderlen's back and mine, and has ordered the preparation of a new army *and navy* increase.' He managed to persuade
Wilhelm to back down on Tirpitz's demand to build three new battlecruisers a year. In his 1913 New Year's address to army corps
commanders, the Kaiser said proudly: 'The navy will surrender to the
army the major portion of available funds.'[30] The army was able to add
another 136,000 men to its ranks to give Germany a standing army of
890,000 by 1914. (To the east, though, lay Russia, which already had an
army of 1.3 million and, with a population three times greater than
Germany's, a much larger pool of potential soldiers.) According to the
Kaiser, Bethmann now accepted the idea of a war, and as Jules Cambon
reported to Paris in the autumn of 1913: 'The Kaiser has come to the
point of believing that war with France is inevitable and even necessary
one day or another.'[31]

Germany's increases in its military of course worried its enemies.
Russia was already increasing the size of its army by keeping conscripts
for several extra months and was carrying out trial mobilisations along
its expanding railway network. In 1913, in response to the German
moves and with encouragement and the offer of a major loan from
France, the tsar approved a new ten-year 'Great Programme' which
would raise the strength of the peacetime army by over 200,000 men
immediately, with more increases and more formations to come. The
final programme was approved on 7 July 1914.[32]

The French took their own steps to meet the German challenge.

Joffre's plans depended on having enough troops ready at the start of hostilities both to counter any German attack and to launch his own into Germany. Since Germany would be fielding a larger army by 1914, France would either have to change its plans and fight more defensively, which was contrary to the army's strategic doctrines, or increase the number of soldiers in its own army.[33] For the military and their supporters the second option was the more appealing but it ran up against France's demographic problem. The army could call up more conscripts every year – and was doing so by this point – but with a population of 39 million France had far fewer potential recruits than Germany with its 68 million people. The Ministry of War therefore brought forward a proposal to increase the size of the army by lengthening the term of service of the conscripts from two to three years. The Three Year Law awakened afresh the divisions in the Republic over the nature and role of the military. While the right wing and the military themselves tended to support a larger army, the socialists and many of the radicals jumped to attack the law as an attempt by the military to create a professional force with reactionary rather than good republican values. Jaurès made passionate speeches in favour of a citizens' militia. The military and the right pointed to the German menace and noted that the French army was already dangerously short of troops at home in Europe because it had been obliged to send a force to pacify Morocco where the locals were resisting French domination.[34] According to Joffre, the law would increase the available French soldiers to 700,000. Germany would still have 870,000 soldiers but enough would be on the Eastern Front facing Russia to tilt the balance in the west in France's favour.[35] A longer term also gave the army the opportunity to improve training, which had long been a concern.[36] Although the law was passed in July the debate continued on into 1914 in the French parliament and the press.

France also had one of those complex scandals so typical of the Third Republic rumbling on. What had started out in 1911 as a sordid story of financial corruption involving government ministers had developed into a concerted campaign against Joseph Caillaux, who had always been suspected by nationalists of being too willing to compromise with Germany, perhaps even of being in German pay. Rumour had it that the editor of the conservative *Figaro* had got his hands on damaging documents about Caillaux's complicated personal life as well as evidence that he had used his position as Justice Minister to block investigations into the corruption charges.

Nevertheless France, unusually given its recent history, seemed relatively calm and stable in the last two years of peace. The country, so both foreigners and the French themselves thought, was experiencing a revival of nationalist feeling and of confidence. The Morocco crisis of 1911 had persuaded much French opinion, on the left as much as on the right, that Germany was an implacable enemy which would never cease to bully France. (That France had done much to provoke the crisis was simply not considered; French commentators invariably assumed that their country was the innocent party.) In the summer months of 1911, when the crisis was at its height, the War Ministry received hundreds of requests from soldiers asking to be reinstated on the active list. 'I am told I am too old for a command,' wrote one general. 'I simply ask to be sent to the frontier as a cavalryman, to show the young soldiers of France an old division commander, *grand'-croix de la Legion d'Honneur*, knows how to die.'[37] Students who, only a decade before, might have been cynical and world-weary, suspicious of pride in the nation and in the French past, now talked about being willing to sacrifice their lives for France. In Latin Quarter 3,000 demonstrated, chanting *'Vive l'Alsace! Vive la Lorraine!'* and in the Parisian theatres patriotic plays were newly popular. From the countryside observers noted a new belligerence among peasant farmers.[38] Joan of Arc, who had been beatified in 1909, enjoyed a fresh popularity. This time the enemy was not the British, however. 'Wilma says that in her circles everyone is mad for war,' Harry Kessler reported in 1912 of his sister who lived in Paris. 'All are convinced that they will beat us.'[39] When a German Zeppelin had to make a forced landing in a French town in the spring of 1913, local crowds threw stones at the crew. The French government apologised for the 'lamentable' behaviour. Wilhelm wrote an angry note: 'this is really mild! It is simply plebeian and uncivilised, like in a land of barbarians! This is derived from anti-German agitation!'[40] The Zabern affair a few months later, when German officers treated the inhabitants of Alsace with contempt, received wide coverage in the French press which saw it as yet another example of Prussian militarism.[41] (Moltke found the belligerence in the French press useful as a further justification for increasing the size of the German army.)[42]

One man in particular epitomised the new mood in France, Raymond Poincaré, the leading conservative politician who became Prime Minister in January 1912 when Caillaux fell in the aftermath of the second Moroccan crisis. At the start of 1913, Poincaré was elected President, an office he was to hold until 1920. Perhaps because he came from Lorraine, so much of which had been lost to Germany after 1871, Poincaré was a passionate French nationalist, determined to heal the divisions within French society and restore France to its rightful place in the world. Although he lost his early fervent Catholic faith, he accepted the Church as an institution which was important to the majority of his compatriots. As Prime Minister he did much to defuse the long-standing conflicts between the Catholics and the anti-clericals over education by supporting secular schools while insisting on tolerance for religious ones.[43] The world, he believed, had much to gain from French influence. 'Wisdom, sangfroid and dignity', he said in a speech in 1912, were the marks of French policy. 'Let us therefore endeavour to preserve and enhance the vital energy of our country, and I am not only referring to her military and naval strength but above all to this political confidence and this unity of national feeling which endows a people with grandeur, glory and immortality.'[44] Although, as a man who valued reason, he opposed war he also believed in making France's armed forces stronger. He became something of a hero for French nationalists and there was a surge in the number of babies christened Raymond.

Poincaré himself was no Napoleon or, in a later age, Charles de Gaulle, although he was always conscious of appearing well in public opinion. The opposite of flamboyant, he was small, neat, fussy and precise. He was also clever and exceptionally hard working. It seems to have been a family tradition; on both sides he was descended from bourgeois families who produced judges, civil servants, professors or, like his own father, engineers. A first cousin was Henri Poincaré, one of France's leading mathematicians. Raymond for his part distinguished himself at his lycée in Paris and became the youngest lawyer in France in 1880 at the age of twenty. Although he followed the path of other ambitious young men and moved into journalism and politics, his legal training left him with a respect for forms and processes. In public Poincaré was unemotional and cool. The ferocious radical Georges Clemenceau, who could not bear him, said he was 'A lively little beast, dry, disagreeable, and not courageous.'[45] This, like so much of what Clemenceau said, was unfair. In politics before 1914 and in the dark days of the Great War, Poincaré showed both courage and fortitude. And even Clemenceau could never accuse him of being corrupt, as so many other political figures in the Third Republic were.

Poincaré, unusually for his time and class, was a feminist and a strong supporter of animal rights, refusing, for example, to join the customary hunting parties at the presidential country estate. He loved the arts, the theatre and concerts in particular and in 1909 became a member of the French Academy.[46] His copious diaries also reveal a man who was emotional and sensitive (he wept when he was elected President), and one who was frequently hurt by perceived slights and by the attacks of his enemies. When he announced just after Christmas in 1912 that he was standing for President he was attacked viciously by the radicals and the left. His wife, a divorcee, was said to have a chequered past, even, gossip had it, performing in a cabaret or a circus.[47] Clemenceau claimed that she had been married to a postman whom Poincaré had dispatched to North America. 'You wish to sleep with Madame Poincaré?' Clemenceau would say loudly, 'OK, my friend, it's fixed.'[48] The attacks so infuriated Poincaré that he once challenged Clemenceau to a duel. (Fortunately for the former it was never fought, for Clemenceau was an experienced dueller.)

When he became President, Poincaré was determined that he would use the powers of his office to the utmost and manage foreign affairs himself. He visited the Foreign Ministry every day, received ambassadors, often on his own, wrote dispatches and selected trusted friends for key foreign posts. As his Foreign Ministers he chose men who were content to play second fiddle. On 12 July 1914, shortly before Europe's final crisis erupted, René Viviani, a moderate socialist, assumed the office although he had no obvious qualifications unless patriotism and eloquence counted. He knew very little about foreign affairs and tended to blame his officials when he made mistakes while Poincaré simply intimidated him. For his part Poincaré was highly irritated by Viviani's ignorance of diplomacy, even such a basic detail as the name of the Austrian-Hungarian Foreign Office. 'When he is reading telegrams from Vienna', Poincaré complained, 'he cannot say the Ballplatz without making it the Bol-platz or the Baliplatz.'[49]

Poincaré's determination to control France's foreign policy did not always translate, however, into practical policies or leadership. From London Paul Cambon, who eventually came to have a grudging respect for him, accused him of 'clear speaking at the service of a confused mind'.[50] Poincaré did not want war but his goal was to make France stronger and more assertive, in Europe of course but also in the Middle East, where France already had strong interests in the Ottoman territories of Syria and Lebanon. In his inaugural address to the French parliament in February 1913 he said that peace was possible only if the country was always ready for war. 'A diminished France, a France exposed by its own fault to challenges, to humiliation, would no longer be France.'[51]

Poincaré was willing nevertheless to work for a limited détente with Germany. While he regretted the lost provinces of Alsace and Lorraine he did not want to use war to get them back.[52] France co-operated with Germany during the crises in the Balkans in 1912 and 1913 and in January 1914 Poincaré dined at the German embassy in Paris, the first French head of state to have done so since the war of 1870. Poincaré even seems to have hoped that the alliance system dividing Europe into two camps might somehow bring a sort of stability and allow the European powers to work out agreements in the wider world, over the division of the Ottoman Empire, for example.[53] At the same time, he believed, as did many of his compatriots, that Germans were bullies who had to be confronted with firmness. He gave Viviani one of his frequent tutorials: 'With Germany it is always necessary to be steadfast and decided, that its diplomacy is given very much to "bluffing" and that it always tests us in order to see whether we are determined to resist or whether we are inclined to give way.'[54] By 1914 Poincaré had grown more pessimistic about the possibilities of working with Germany. 'More and more', he wrote in his private diary, 'Germany imagines that it was predestined to dominate the world, that the alleged superiority of the German race, the always increasing number of inhabitants of the Reich and the continuing pressure of economic necessities creates for it exceptional rights among nations.' He also came to doubt that, in any future crisis, Germany would in fact back down.[55]

That made its friendships more than ever the key to maintaining France's greatness and its position in the world. France's military alliance with Russia needed to be nurtured and deepened. With Poincaré's approval France's loans for Russian railway building increased by some 500 million francs in the two years before the war.[56] He assured Izvolsky, still the Russian ambassador in Paris, that he would use his influence over France's foreign policy, to ensure 'the closest ties with Russia'.[57] He was as good as his word, appointing Delcassé, the staunch French nationalist who had been forced out of office by Germany in the first Morocco crisis, as his ambassador to St Petersburg. Poincaré also made a point of visiting Russia himself, the first time when he was still Prime Minister. 'The Emperor Nicholas,' said Sazonov, 'who often prized in others those qualities which he did not himself possess, was chiefly impressed by the determination and strength of will of the French Prime Minister.'[58]

Poincaré also shared the widespread view that the Triple Entente should be made even stronger with Britain tied in by military alliances with both France and Russia. The trouble was that Britain with Grey still firmly in charge of foreign policy showed little interest in moving beyond assurances of goodwill and support. Even more worrying were Britain's domestic politics, which were looking, well, rather like those of France in unhappier times. There was even a complicated financial scandal with Lloyd George and several other leading Liberals being charged very enthusiastically by the Conservatives with exploiting inside knowledge to buy shares in the Marconi company which was about to be awarded a contract to build government wireless stations throughout the British Empire. Although a parliamentary investigation found that the accused were innocent, in part because they had bought shares only in the American branch of the company, which did not benefit from the contract, the matter looked bad and damaged the reputation of Lloyd George and the others as well as that of the government as a whole. In 1913 and the first half of 1914, which was even more worrying for the British and their allies, Britain was experiencing deep and bitter social and political divisions with violent demonstrations, bombs, barricades, even armed militias. And the Irish question had again grown acute to the point where Britain faced, for the first time since the seventeenth century, the possibility of civil war.

The monarch who now presided over this suddenly turbulent Britain was George V, who had succeeded Edward VII in 1910. In many ways he was the opposite of his father. He had simple tastes, disliked foreign countries, and was bored by fashionable society. His court, as he said himself with pride, was dull but respectable. With this king, there would be no scandals about mistresses or unsuitable friends. In appearance he looked very like his cousin the tsar of Russia (the two men were some-times mistaken for each other) and in manner he remained very much the naval officer he had been. He ran his court as much like a ship as possible with attention to uniforms, routine, and punctuality. He was devoted to his wife but expected her to obey his orders; he liked the fashions she had worn when he first met her in the 1890s so she wore long dresses until she died in 1953. 'The Paris mob went mad about her', reported a courtier after the royal couple visited early in 1914, 'and it was rumoured that her out-of-date hats and early Victorian gowns would become next year's fashions!'[59] Although George found his office a burden and dreaded making his annual address from the throne, he did his work conscientiously. He also understood and accepted that he was a constitutional monarch, bound to take the advice of his ministers. His own politics were those of a Tory country squire with an instinctive aversion to anything that smacked of socialism and he suspected that many of the leading Liberal politicians were not really gentlemen – including his Prime Minister, although he came to like and respect Asquith.[60]

Herbert Asquith, who was in office as Britain went from peace to war, was a clever and ambitious man who came from a prosperous man-ufacturing family in the north of England. What had been a secure childhood was suddenly shattered when their father died leaving his young family dependent on the charity of his wife's brothers. Herbert and one of his brothers were taken in by an uncle and then farmed out to different families while they went to school in London. Unlike his sickly brother, Herbert flourished, winning a prestigious scholarship to Balliol, the most intellectual of all the colleges at Oxford University and one which was known for producing leading figures in public life.[61] There Asquith made a name for himself as a clever and hard-working scholar as well as a formidable debater, qualities which served him well as he launched his highly successful career as a lawyer. He had married young, for love, and by all accounts was a devoted father and husband. By the time his first wife died of typhoid in 1891, however, Asquith had already fallen in love with Margot Tennant, the vivacious and self-willed daughter of a very rich businessman. Margot, who was both an intellectual and social snob, had a reputation for being outspoken, often to the point of rudeness, physically brave – she adored riding to hounds – and unpredictable. Asquith sat next to her at a dinner party in the House of Commons a few months before his wife's fatal illness. 'The passion', he told a friend later, 'which comes, I suppose, to everyone once in life, visited and conquered me.' (He was to be conquered in that way again in 1914.) Margot found that he reminded her of Oliver Cromwell (who had led the Parliamentary forces against the king in the Civil War) and felt 'this was the man who could help me and who would understand everything'.[62] In fact she hesitated for over two years after Asquith first told her of his love, some few weeks after he buried his wife. In 1894, after Margot had reviewed her other suitors, she decided, abruptly as she often did, to marry him. She threw herself into managing her stepchildren (who did not invariably appreciate her domineering ways) and furthering Asquith's promising political career.

In 1886 he had been elected as a Liberal to Parliament and over the next years had risen steadily through the party and in British society, acquiring new and influential friends, including Margot herself, among the upper classes. When the Liberals returned to office at the end of 1905, Asquith became Chancellor of the Exchequer and then, in 1908, Prime Minister. He was a skilful leader, keeping together a disparate group of Liberals which included pacifists and radical reformers such as Lloyd George on the one hand and imperialists such as Grey on the other. When a prolonged battle broke out in the last years of the peace between Churchill and Lloyd George over the naval estimates for 1914–15, Asquith managed to contain it. Churchill, who became First Lord of the Admiralty in 1911, had now reversed himself and was pushing for more spending on the navy, while his old ally Lloyd George who was Chancellor of the Exchequer, was determined to hold the line. Their dispute was not finally settled until January 1914 when, with Asquith's backing, Churchill got the increases he wanted.

Asquith was also was capable on occasion of considerable political courage, in the prolonged political struggle between the Commons and the Lords over Lloyd George's Budget of 1909 or in the severe crises which were to follow. By 1914, however, he was clearly less interested than he had once been in the mundane but essential details of politics. His political enemies nicknamed him 'Wait and See' as his propensity for delaying decisions to get consensus turned into delay for its own sake. His great friend and fellow Liberal, Richard Haldane, who was Secretary of State for War between 1905 and 1912, commented: 'London Society came, however, to have a great attraction for him, and he grew by degrees diverted from the sterner outlook on life which he and I for long shared.'[63] Another old friend found him 'red and bloated – quite different from what he used to be'.[64]

It was unfortunate that, as his energies waned, Asquith's government faced increasingly intractable domestic problems. While the struggle between the British workers and their employers went on, a new conflict had broken out between women from all classes and all political persuasions who demanded the right to vote and their opponents who included, among others, Asquith himself. His own Cabinet was divided on the issue. While most of the suffragettes were peaceable and relatively law-abiding, a vociferous radical fringe led by the formidable Mrs Pankhurst and her equally intransigent daughter Christabel threw themselves into the fight using a variety of ingenious weapons. Their supporters disrupted meetings, spat at opponents of votes for women, chained themselves to railings, harassed government ministers, slashed paintings in art galleries, and smashed windows, even in Downing Street itself. 'I nearly vomited with terror,' Margot Asquith complained.[65] In 1913 a bomb destroyed a new house Lloyd George was having built on the outskirts of London, even though he supported votes for women. Between January and July 1914, militant suffragettes set over a hundred buildings, including churches and schools, on fire. When the women were caught and sentenced to prison, they responded by going on hunger strike. The movement got its first martyr in 1913 when a suffragette threw herself in front of King George V's horse at the Derby and the authorities seemed, for a time, determined to create even more by allowing the police to manhandle women marchers and demonstrators and by forcibly feeding the hunger strikers. By the summer of 1914 Asquith was ready to give up his opposition and bring a bill for female suffrage before Parliament but the Great War intervened and votes for women had to wait.

Most dangerous of all for Britain in those years was the Irish question. Demands for Home Rule for Ireland had been gathering strength, particularly in the Catholic South. One wing of the Liberals, following the example of their great leader Gladstone, was sympathetic, but political exigencies also played their part. After the elections of 1910, the Liberal government no longer had a majority and so depended on the votes of the Irish nationalists. At the beginning of 1912, the government brought in a Home Rule Bill which would have given Ireland its own parliament within a federal Britain. Unfortunately a significant minority in Ireland, mainly those Protestants who were in a majority in Ulster in the north part of the island, did not want Home Rule which, in their view, would leave them under Catholic domination, and they were supported in their resistance by a large part of the Conservative Party in Britain including its leader Bonar Law, himself from Ulster Protestant stock.

The question of Irish Home Rule divided British society; old friends cut each other dead and people refused to sit next to each other at dinner parties. This was, however, mere froth on what were much more sinister currents. In Ireland the Ulster Unionists, as they liked to call themselves, issued a programme in 1911 in which they declared that they were ready to set up their own government if Home Rule passed. At the start of 1912 the first paramilitary forces, the Volunteers, started drilling and acquiring arms, an example soon to be followed by Irish Home Rulers in the South. At the end of September nearly 300,000 men of Ulster signed a covenant, some apparently using their own blood, pledging to defeat Home Rule. From Britain, Bonar Law and senior Conservatives openly encouraged them, using recklessly emotive and provocative language. In July 1912, Law and many of his colleagues from the House of Commons along with a collection of Conservative peers, attended a large rally at the Duke of Marlborough's Blenheim Palace. In a long and passionate speech, Law declared that the government was behaving unconstitutionally in proposing Home Rule for Ireland and, in a threat he was to make repeatedly, accused it of risking civil war. 'I can imagine', he concluded, 'no length of resistance to which Ulster will go, in which I shall not be ready to support them, and in which they will not be supported by the overwhelming majority of the British people.'[66] While Law was throwing fuel on the fires he claimed to fear, another Ulsterman, Sir Henry Wilson, chief of military operations at the War

Office, who loathed Asquith ('Squiff'), and indeed most Liberals, was encouraging the wilder supporters of Ulster in their plans to seize power by force in the event of Home Rule.[67] (He could well have been cashiered, which would have presumably had a damaging effect on Britain's military deployment at the start of the Great War.) More, Wilson was feeding the Conservatives with confidential information about the army and its reactions to the crisis. Since many of the officers and enlisted men came from Ulster or from the Protestants of the South, the Home Rule crisis was causing considerable anxiety that they might be obliged to move against rebellious compatriots.

In March 1914 the crisis took an even more serious turn. The House of Commons had passed the Home Rule Bill twice and the House of Lords, dominated as it was by Unionist peers, rejected it each time. Asquith suggested a compromise – keeping the six counties of Ulster out of the area for Home Rule for the time being – but his opponents refused to consider it. Indeed, there was a move in the Lords to put pressure on the government by rejecting the bill to authorise the existence of the army, which had been passed without debate every year since 1688, and Law certainly toyed with the idea of supporting the 'Die-Hard peers', as they came to be known. (There is a parallel in recent American politics with the refusal of the Republicans to allow the customary approval of an increased debt ceiling for the government so that it can carry on borrowing the funds it needs for its operations.) That same month there then came the most worrying incident of all, the so-called Curragh Mutiny among British army officers stationed in the south of Ireland. As a result of stupidity, muddle and perhaps malevolence on the part of the Secretary of State for War, the incompetent Sir John Seely, and the commander-in-chief in Ireland, Sir Arthur Paget, officers at the base of Curragh were warned that they might be ordered to take military action against the Ulster Volunteers and that, if they did not want to, they could absent themselves or resign. Some dozens of officers made it clear that they would resign, at which point Seely allowed himself to be persuaded to send them an assurance that they would not be asked to force Home Rule on Ulster. Asquith preferred not to push the issue but he eased Seely out and took over the War Office himself.

As spring turned to summer in 1914, the Liberals and Conservatives remained as far apart as ever and on the ground, in Ireland, the arms continued to flow in to both sides and the drilling went on. In July, in a last attempt to get a compromise, the king called a conference at Buckingham Palace of the main leaders from both sides. The British ruling classes, the British public, and the British press were almost completely preoccupied by the Irish question and paid little attention to what was happening on the Continent, even when Franz Ferdinand, the heir to the Austrian throne was assassinated in Sarajevo on 28 June. Asquith, who had now fallen in love with the much younger Venetia Stanley, only mentioned the growing crisis on the Continent for the first time in his daily letters to her on 24 July, the day the Buckingham Palace conference ended in yet another failure. If the British were not noticing their neighbours, though, the European powers were for their part transfixed by the spectacle of British society apparently trembling on the edge of civil war. He found the situation in Britain difficult to understand, the tsar told the British ambassador, and he hoped it would not affect Britain's international position.[68] Germany and Austria-Hungary had a different view; with any luck Britain would be too divided internally to fight if war should come.[69]

At the start of 1914 that seemed to most Europeans no more or less likely than it had done for the past decade. Of course, there were the familiar tensions: Britain and Germany were still engaged in their naval race; France and Germany were no closer to being friendly; and Russia and Austria-Hungary still manoeuvred against each other in the Balkans. By 1914 Russian nationalists were also busily stirring up trouble among the Ruthenians in Austrian Galicia, something which both irritated and worried Vienna.[70] (It cut both ways; the Monarchy was also encouraging Catholic priests to go over the border to proselytise among Russia's own Ruthenians.) And there were strains as well within the alliances. After the Balkan wars, relations between Germany and Austria-Hungary worsened; the Germans felt that their allies had recklessly risked war with Russia while in Austria-Hungary there was resentment that Germany had been a poor friend. The Monarchy also deeply resented growing German investment and influence in the Balkans and the Ottoman Empire. Despite the Triple Alliance, Italy and Austria-Hungary continued to vie for influence in Albania and Italian public opinion continued to concern itself with the rights of Italian speakers within the Dual Monarchy. Relations between the two powers had reached such a low point by the summer of 1914 that neither the Italian king nor an official representative attended Franz Ferdinand's funeral.[71] In 1912 Germany and Austria-Hungary agreed to renew the Triple Alliance early, perhaps to reassure each other of their reliability, but also to try to keep Italy tied in.

'The Triple Entente', said the Russian ambassador in Germany, 'always are in agreement with themselves, on the other hand, the Triple Alliance is usually the complete opposite. If Austria-Hungary thinks of something, it hurries to carry out its thought. Italy sometimes takes the other side, and Germany, which announces its intentions in the last moment, is mostly forced to support its allies for better or worse.'[72] Within the Triple Entente, though, the rivalry between Britain and Russia over Central Asia and Persia had never really gone away and by the spring of 1914 Grey and his chief advisers were afraid that the deal where Russia had a sphere of influence in the north of Persia with Britain having the same in the south was about to break down.

The anticipated disintegration of the Ottoman Empire offered its own temptations to outside powers to vie with each other, over the Straits and Constantinople as well as in the largely Turkish-speaking Asia Minor and its vast Arab territories which included today's Syria, Iraq, Lebanon, Jordan, Israel and most of the Saudi peninsula. The Russian government may have recognised how limited its capacity to seize the Straits was, but Russian nationalists continued to agitate for Russia to take what they saw as its rightful heritage. Austria-Hungary, which had largely stayed out of the scramble for colonies, now showed an interest in establishing a presence in Asia Minor, partly to compensate for its recent string of disasters in the Balkans. That caused trouble with both of its allies; Germany and Italy had their own dreams of creating colonies in the Middle East when the Ottoman Empire vanished.[73] And the invalid itself showed some surprising signs of life. The Young Turks, by now firmly back in control, were trying to centralise and reinvigorate the government. They were strengthening their military and were buying three dreadnoughts from Britain which, once they were delivered, would shift the balance of power decisively against the Russian navy. Russia responded by starting to build its own dreadnoughts but the Ottoman Empire would have an advantage between 1913 and 1915.[74]

At the end of 1913 there was a ripple of concern among the Entente powers when news leaked out that the Germans were increasing their military mission to the Ottoman Empire and had sent as commander a senior general, Otto Liman von Sanders. Since he was to have extensive powers over training and promotion in the Ottoman forces as well as direct command of an army corps based in Constantinople, this would sharply increase German influence in the Ottoman Empire. Wilhelm, who had drawn up the plans in secret with his closest military advisers, told Liman dramatically: 'Either the German flag will soon fly over the fortifications on the Bosphorus or I shall share the sad fate of the great exile on St Helena.'[75] Yet again the German civilian leadership found themselves dealing with the unwelcome fallout from the actions of an irresponsible and independent emperor.

Up to this point Russia and Germany had in fact been co-operating fairly successfully in the Ottoman Empire. In November 1910 Tsar Nicholas had visited Wilhelm at Potsdam and the two had signed an agreement on the Ottoman Empire which removed at least one source of tension: Russia promised not to undermine the new Young Turk government and Germany undertook to support reforms in the Ottoman Empire. The Germans also recognised Russia's sphere of influence in the north of Persia and assuaged Russian apprehensions by moving the projected Berlin-to-Baghdad railway further south. Bethmann was pleased: 'The Russian visit went better than expected. Both sovereigns treated each other openly and relaxedly, in best, almost gay spirits.'[76] The two rulers met again on their yachts in the summer of 1912 at Russia's Baltic Port (today Paldiski in Estonia) just before the crisis in the Balkans blew up. Alexandra, according to Sazonov, 'displayed nothing but weariness, as she did on such occasions', but the meetings had 'a peaceful and friendly tone'. Kokovtsov and Bethmann, who were also in attendance, complained quietly to each other about how hard it was to resist pressures from the public for increased defence spending. Wilhelm told endless loud jokes. 'I must confess', said Sazonov, 'that not all of them were to my taste.' The Kaiser also advised the tsar to look eastwards and build up his strength against Japan. Nicholas listened with his usual reserve. 'Thank heaven!' he said to Kokovtsov after the meeting was over. 'Now one does not have to watch one's every word lest it be construed in a way one had not even dreamed.' Nicholas was relieved, though, because Wilhelm had repeatedly said he would not let the situation in the Balkans lead to a world war.[77]

The Liman von Sanders affair, as it rapidly became known, destroyed the co-operation between Germany and Russia in the Ottoman Empire and the reactions to it showed how jittery Europe's capitals had become by this point. The Russians, who were furious at the appointment, urged their French allies and the British to put pressure on the Young Turks to limit Liman's powers. Sazonov talked about seizing Ottoman ports to press the point home and yet again talk of a general war was in the air. The Russian Prime Minister, Kokovtsov, urged moderation and so did the French and the British, who did not want to be dragged into a war over the Ottoman Empire. (The British government was also embarrassed when it discovered that the admiral who headed a British naval mission in Constantinople had the same powers as Liman.) As before, though, they recognised – especially the French – the need to stand by Russia. Izvolsky reported to St Petersburg that Poincaré showed 'a calm determination not to dodge away from the duties which the alliance with us has imposed on them and Delcassé, the French ambassador there, assured the Russian government of unconditional support'.[78]

Fortunately Europe had a reprieve this time: the Russians and the Germans were unwilling to force the matter to a showdown and the Young Turks, who were becoming alarmed at the furore, were anxious for a settlement as well. In January, in a face-saving move, Liman was raised in rank so that he was now too senior to command a corps. (He was to stay in the Ottoman Empire until its defeat in 1918; one of his lasting legacies was to further the career of a promising Turkish officer, Mustafa Kemal Ataturk.) The affair served to heighten still more the Entente's suspicions of Germany and drove Russia and Germany even further apart. Within the Russian government, especially after Kokovtsov fell January 1914, it became accepted that Germany was planning a war. In an audience that month with Delcassé Nicholas talked calmly with the French ambassador about the coming conflict. 'We will not let them tread on our toes and, this time, it will not be like the war in the Far East: the national mood will support us.'[79] In February 1914, the Russian general staff gave to the government two secret German memoranda which its spies had gained in which the Germans talked of a two-front war and how German public opinion must be prepared well in advance. The same month the tsar approved preparations for an attack on the Ottoman Empire in the event of a general war.[80]

Nevertheless, the successful conclusion of the Liman von Sanders affair and the international management of the crises in the Balkans in 1912 and 1913 seemed to show that Europe could still keep its peace, that something of the old Concert of Europe where the great powers came together to broker and enforce settlements lingered on. In fact many observers felt that the mood in Europe by 1914 was better than it had been for some time. Churchill in his history of the Great War talked about the 'exceptional tranquillity' of those last months of the peace and Grey, again looking back, wrote: 'In the early months of 1914 the international sky seemed clearer than it had been. The Balkan clouds had disappeared. After the threatening periods of 1911, 1912, and 1913 a little calm was probable, and, it would seem, due.'[81] In June 1914 Oxford University awarded honorary degrees to Prince Lichnowsky, the German ambassador, and the composer Richard Strauss.

Europe was, it is true, divided into two alliance systems and after the Great War this was seen as one of the main causes of the war since a conflict between any two powers ran the risk of bringing their allies in. It could be argued, though, as it was at the time and has been since, that defensive alliances, which these were, act as a deterrent to aggression and can be a force for stability. The North Atlantic Treaty Organization (NATO) and the Warsaw Pact after all brought a balance, which was in the end a peaceful one, to Europe during the Cold War. As Grey said approvingly in the House of Commons in 1912, the powers were divided into 'separate groups not opposite' and many Europeans, Poincaré among them, agreed with him. In his memoirs, written after the Great War, Grey continued to insist on the value of the alliances: 'We wanted the Entente and Germany's Triple Alliance to live side by side in amity. That was the best that was practicable.'[82] And while France and Russia in the former and Germany, Austria-Hungary and Italy in the latter had signed military alliances, Britain still refused to do so, to keep, as Grey insisted, its free hand. Indeed, in 1911 Arthur Nicolson, now Permanent Undersecretary at the Foreign Office, complained that Britain had still not committed itself sufficiently to the Triple Entente: 'I do not think that people quite recognise that, if we are to assist in preserving the peace and the status quo, it is necessary for us to acknowledge our responsibilities, and to be prepared to afford our friends or our allies, in case of necessity, some assistance of a more material and efficient kind than we are at present in a position to offer them.'[83]

In reality, defensive though the alliances might have been and as much as Britain felt it was free to steer its own course, over the years the division of Europe had become an accepted fact. That was reflected even in the language of those statesmen who had always been cautious identifying too clearly with one side. By 1913 Sazonov, who only the year before had told the German ambassador in St Petersburg that he refused to use the term, was talking of the Triple Entente. Grey, who had shared Sazonov's reluctance, conceded the following year that there was no more hope of avoiding its use than of getting rid of split infinitives. In any case, he argued, the entente was good for Britain: 'The alternatives are either a policy of complete isolation in Europe, or a policy of definite alliance with one or the other group of European powers …'[84]

Inevitably expectations and understandings of mutual support accumulated within the two alliances as diplomats and the military grew accustomed to working with each other. The partners also found that they needed to reassure each other or run the risk of losing an ally. Even though Germany had no vital interests at stake in the Balkans, it found it increasingly difficult not to support Austria-Hungary there. For France, the Russian alliance was crucial to its great-power status yet the French always feared that once Russia had grown strong again it would not need France and that it might revert to an older alliance, the one with Germany.[85] That led the French to support Russian aims even when they felt they were dangerous; Poincaré apparently gave Russia the impression that France would enter a war between Russia and Austria-Hungary even over Serbia. 'The bottom line is', he told Izvolsky in Paris in 1912, 'that all this amounts to the same thing, that is to say that if Russia enters a war, France will also enter it as we know that in this question Germany will stand behind Austria.'[86] Although France's treaty with Russia was a defensive one, coming into effect only if either party was attacked, Poincaré went beyond its terms to suggest that France would feel obliged to enter a war even if Germany merely mobilised. By 1914, the alliances, rather than acting as brakes on their members, were too often pushing the accelerators.

The Triple Entente, despite Britain's caution, developed greater cohesion and depth than the Triple Alliance as the ties binding it together, whether financial, especially in the case of France and Russia, military, diplomatic, or even improved wireless and telegraph communications grew more numerous and stronger. The French not only encouraged Britain and Russia to enter into military discussions but themselves pressed Britain for a clearer commitment than it had yet been willing to give. Although the British Cabinet remained divided on the issue and Grey himself preferred to occupy the foggy ground between reassuring the French of his support and refusing to specify what that might consist of, France had a willing and active collaborator in Henry Wilson, who visited the country seven times alone in 1913 for discussions with his French counterparts.[87] By 1912, as well, the British and French navies were moving towards closer co-operation in the Mediterranean, the Atlantic and the Far East.

This was not just a result of French pressure but because the British faced a dilemma: their navy could no longer meet all the challenges facing it, in particular defending British interests in the Mediterranean, where Italy, Austria-Hungary and the Ottoman Empire were all building dreadnoughts, and outmatching the German navy on the high seas. If Britain could not bring the naval race with Germany under control – and by the end of 1912, with the failure of yet more talks, that looked highly unlikely – it would have to either spend a good deal more on its navy or work with the navies of friendly powers to share responsibilities for key areas. This posed a political problem for Asquith. Although the Conservatives generally supported increased naval spending, the radicals in his own party did not, and many Liberals were also wary of making further international commitments which might lead Britain into war.

Britain's new First Lord of the Admiralty was the ambitious, energetic and forceful young Winston Churchill, in those days a member of the Liberal Party. 'Winston talks about nothing but the Sea and the Navy and the wonderful things he is going to do,' his Naval Secretary noted.[88] Churchill took to his new post with boundless enthusiasm and self-confidence, mastering the details of ships, shipyards, docks, and equipment as well as thinking through Britain's strategic needs. 'These were great days,' he wrote in his account of the Great War. 'From dawn to midnight, day after day, one's whole mind was absorbed by the fascination and novelty of the problems which came crowding forward.'[89] In the three years before the war he spent eight months on board the Admiralty yacht, *Enchantress*, visiting every key ship and naval establishment in the Mediterranean and British home waters. ('Holiday at Govt. expense', noted Wilson of one of these trips.)[90] 'In the end', Churchill claimed with some exaggeration, 'I could put my hand on anything that was wanted and knew thoroughly the current state of our naval affairs.'[91] Although he infuriated many of the senior naval officers with his calm assumption that he could do their jobs better than they, he made much needed reforms. He created a proper general staff for the first time; he improved the working conditions of the ordinary sailors; and he converted the navy's ships from coal to the more efficient and less labour-intensive fuel of oil.[92] Although this last had long-term strategic implications by making oil fields in the Middle East of critical importance to Britain, it was Churchill's decision to reorganise and reposition the Mediterranean Fleet that added yet another element to the mix that made the Great War possible.

While the Mediterranean remained of great importance to the British, providing as it did access to the vital Suez Canal, the Atlantic especially around the British Isles was a matter of life and death, and Germany now could bring an equal number of battleships to its waters. Churchill and his naval advisers therefore decided early in 1912 to improve the odds by moving their battleships from their bases in the Mediterranean to Gibraltar at its entrance from the Atlantic and leave only a squadron of fast cruisers based at Malta. What that meant, although the implications were not recognised immediately, was that France was now primarily responsible for the security of the Mediterranean in the face of threats from the Italian and Austrian fleets and possibly, if matters turned out badly, that of the Ottoman Empire as well. To do this, the French would be obliged to move more of their own fleet from its Atlantic ports into the Mediterranean, which they soon did, and they could reasonably expect as a consequence that Britain would guarantee the safety of the French Atlantic coast and protect the vital shipping lanes of the Channel. As Churchill pointed out in a memorandum to Grey in August 1912, the French would have had to concentrate in the Mediterranean because of their North African colonies even if the British navy had not existed but the fact that the British had withdrawn their battleships left the French in a strong moral position if war came. Consider, he urged Grey, 'how tremendous would be the weapon which France would possess to compel our intervention, if she could say, "On the advice of and by arrangement with your naval authorities we have left our Northern coasts defenceless."' And he concluded, perfectly correctly, 'Every one must feel who knows the facts that we have the obligations of an alliance without its advantages, and above all without its precise definitions.'[93]

An alliance and precise definitions were what, of course, Paul Cambon, the French ambassador in London, and his government wanted, and just what Grey and the British government hoped to avoid. The conversations between the French and British armies had already encouraged the French to think that they could count on British military support on land, however much Grey waved his free hands about. Naval conversations had also been going on in a desultory and inconclusive fashion for some years but in July 1912 the British Cabinet gave them greater significance by formally authorising them to continue. By the end of 1913 the British and French navies had reached several understandings to co-operate if war should come. The British navy would look after the narrowest point of the Channel, the Straits of Dover, while the British and the French would share responsibility for the rest. In the Mediterranean, the French would patrol the western half while the British, with their fleet at Malta, looked after the eastern end. The two navies would also work together against Germany in the Far East. Detailed operational plans were drawn up, especially for the Channel.[94]

Cambon also pushed Grey for a written statement about Britain's and France's co-operation if either feared attack. He was not, he assured Grey, asking for an alliance or any binding agreement that their two nations would in fact take action together, merely for confirmation that they would consult. Grey, who would have much preferred to leave matters as they were, recognised that he had to do something to reassure the French or risk the Entente Cordiale falling to pieces. In November 1912 with approval from his Cabinet, he exchanged letters with Cambon. In his own letter, Grey referred to the conversations between the British and French military and naval experts and stressed that they did not constitute a promise to take action. He went on, though, to concede that in a crisis it might be essential for each power to know whether the other would come to its aid with armed force and that it would make sense, in such circumstances, to take into account the plans already made. 'I agree', he wrote, 'that, if either Government had grave reason to expect an unprovoked attack by a third Power, or something that threatened the general peace, it should immediately discuss with the other, whether both Governments should act together to prevent aggression and to preserve peace, and if so what measures they would be prepared to take in common.'[95]

Grey and his Prime Minister Asquith continued to insist right up to the outbreak of the war that Britain had kept a completely free hand as far as France was concerned. That was technically true but it was not the whole truth. The military and naval conversations had led the British and the French forces to make their arrangements in the confidence that the other would be there if war broke out. Lord Esher, courtier, defence expert and a superb backroom operator, wrote to a friend in 1913: 'Of course there is no treaty or convention, but how we can get out of the commitments of the General Staff with honour, I cannot understand. It all seems so shifty to me.'[96] The decade of naval and military conversations, the diplomatic co-operation, and the public acceptance in both countries of the Entente Cordiale created a web of links which would be difficult to ignore when the next crisis came. As Paul Cambon had reminded Grey when the latter said that there was no formal agreement between France and Britain: 'There was nothing but a moral "Entente", which might however be transformed into a formal "Entente" if the two Governments desired, when an occasion arose.'[97]

Grey himself, as he had always done, continued to send the French mixed signals. In April 1914 he chose to demonstrate the importance he attached to the relationship with France by making his first official trip abroad (after being Foreign Secretary for nine years) to accompany George V to Paris. Neither minister nor king liked foreign travel. Grey was also gloomy because he had just learned that he was losing his eyesight. He planned to go later that summer to visit a specialist in Germany.[98] The British were pleased, though, by the weather, which was lovely and mild, and by the warm French welcome. Grey even managed to have a conversation with Poincaré, who did not speak English. 'The Holy Ghost has descended upon Sir Edward Grey', said Paul Cambon, 'and he now speaks French!'[99] Although Grey assured the Austrian and German ambassadors that he spent most of his time sightseeing and that there had been 'nothing aggressive' in his discussions with the French,[100] he did in fact give way to French pressure and agree to start naval conversations with the Russians. When there were comments and questions in the press, Grey took the opportunity to postpone the talks until August. Although no naval agreements with the Russians had been or were ever reached, the Germans were alarmed by the possibility of co-ordinated attacks from the Baltic and the Atlantic and more persuaded than ever that Germany was encircled.[101]

What made the division of Europe even more dangerous was the intensifying arms race. Although no great power except Italy fought a war between 1908 and 1914 their combined spending on defence went up by 50 per cent. (The United States was also increasing its expenditure but by much less.)[102] Between 1912 and 1914 the Balkan wars helped to set off a new round of increased spending as the Balkan nations themselves and the powers expanded their armed forces and invested in the greatly improved weapons and the new ones such as submarines, machine guns, or aircraft that the wonders of European science and technology were producing. Among the great powers, Germany and Russia stood out: Germany's defence spending leapt from £88 million in 1911 to nearly £118 million in 1913 while Russia's went from £74 million to nearly £111 million in the same period.[103] Finance Ministers and others worried that expenditure was too high, that it was accelerating too fast and was not sustainable, and that it would lead to popular unrest. Increasingly, though, they were pushed to one side by worried statesmen and generals caught by a greater fear, that of being left behind in a world of enemies who were busy increasing their forces. Army intelligence in Vienna reported early in 1914: 'Greece is tripling, Serbia doubling, Rumania and finally even Bulgaria and Montenegro are strengthening their armies by significant amounts.'[104] Austria-Hungary responded with a new army bill that increased the size of its armed forces (although by much less than Germany or Russia). The German army and navy bills, the French Three Year Law, the Russian Great

Programme, and increased British naval spending were likewise responses to perceived threats, but that is not how they appeared to others. What seemed defensive from one perspective was a threat from another. And there were usually domestic lobbies and the press, sometimes backed by arms manufacturers, to raise the spectre of the nation in peril. Tirpitz, always inventive when it came to arguing for more resources for his navy, came up with a further reason for the new Navy Law of 1912: Germany must not waste its previous investments. 'Without an adequate defensive chance against an English attack our policy must always show consideration for England and our sacrifices would have been in vain.'[105]

Liberals and the left as well as the peace movement attacked the arms race and its 'merchants of death' at the time, and after the Great War, it was singled out as one of the main factors, perhaps indeed the key one, in bringing about the catastrophe. It was a view that had a particular resonance in the 1920s and 1930s in the United States, where disillusionment about American participation in the war had grown. In 1934 Senator Gerald Nye of North Dakota chaired a special Senate committee to investigate the role of the arms manufacturers in creating the Great War and promised to show 'that war and preparation for war is not a matter of national honor and national defense, but a matter of profit for the few.' The committee saw dozens of witnesses but not surprisingly was unable to prove its case. The Great War was not produced by a single cause but by a combination and, in the end, by human decisions. What the arms race did do was raise the level of tensions in Europe and put pressure on decision-makers to pull the trigger before the enemy did.

Ironically, in retrospect, decision-makers at the time tended to see military preparedness as a sound deterrent. In 1913 the British ambassador to Paris had an audience with George V. 'I suggest to the King that the best guarantee of peace between the Great Powers is that they are all afraid of each other.'[106] Since deterrence only works if the other side thinks you are prepared to use force, there is always the likelihood of going too far and starting a conflict by accident – or of losing credibility by failing to follow through on a threat. And honour, as nations called it then (we might say prestige today), was a part of that calculation. The great powers were conscious of their status as much as of their interests and being too willing to make concessions or appearing timid could be damaging to that. And the events of the decade before 1914 seemed to show that deterrence worked, whether it was Britain and France forcing Germany to back down over Morocco or Russia's mobilisation putting pressure on Austria-Hungary to leave Serbia alone during the Balkan wars. An English word which was used frequently in those days entered the German language as *der Bluff*. But what do you do when your bluff is called?

The prewar arms race also brought in considerations about timing: if war was coming, it was better to fight while you had the advantage. With a few exceptions – Italy, Rumania or the Ottoman Empire perhaps – European nations knew who they would be fighting in a war, and, thanks to their spies, usually had a good idea of the strength of the enemy forces and their plans. The Germans, for example, were well aware of the growth and modernisation of Russia's armed forces and of its railway building. The German general staff calculated that by 1917 it would not be able to fight Russia and win: Russia's mobilisation of its greatly increased army would take only three days longer than Germany's (unless Germany undertook major and costly railway building of its own in the east).[107] In a gloomy conversation with the banker Max Warburg, the Kaiser saw a war coming with Russia as early as 1916. 'Beset by his anxieties, the Kaiser even considered whether it would not be better to attack first instead of waiting.'[108] Looking west, the Germans also knew about France's current deficiencies such as its lack of heavy artillery even before the public criticisms by a French senator in July 1914. Finally, the Germans feared that Austria-Hungary could not survive much longer. All these considerations encouraged the key German decision-makers to think that, if they had to fight, 1914 was a good time. (The Japanese military made a similar calculation when they contemplated war with the United States in 1941.) While the Germans felt that time was running out for them, both the Russians and the French thought that things were moving in their favour and the French in particular felt they could afford to wait.[109] Austria-Hungary was not so sanguine. In March 1914 Conrad, the Monarchy's chief of staff, posed a question to a colleague, whether 'one should wait until France and Russia were prepared to invade us jointly or if it were more desirable to settle the inevitable conflict at an earlier date'.[110]

Too many Europeans, especially those like Conrad in crucial posts such as the upper ranks of the military and the governments, were now waiting for war to come. The Russian general Brusilov made haste to go with his wife to their German spa in the summer of 1914: 'I was absolutely certain that a World War would break out in 1915. We were therefore determined not to postpone our cure and rest, so as to be able to return home for the manoeuvres.'[111] While confidence in the power of the offensive still reassured many that any war would be brief, men such as Bethmann and Moltke regarded the prospect with deep pessimism. In April 1913, as Russia and Austria-Hungary faced each other in the aftermath of the First Balkan War, Bethmann warned the Reichstag: 'No person can imagine the dimensions of a world conflagration, of the misery and destruction, which it would bring to nations.'[112] Yet increasingly he, like Moltke, felt helpless to avert it. Grey on the other hand still believed on the eve of the Great War that the knowledge that a general war would be a catastrophe for all concerned must make Europe's statesmen more cautious. 'Was it not this that had, in the difficult years from 1905 till now, made the Great Powers recoil from pressing anything to the point of war?'[113]

As war seemed more likely, it became more important than ever to find new allies. The land forces of the two alliance systems were now so evenly balanced that even a small country such as Greece or Belgium could help to tip the balance. Although the Greeks wisely refused to commit themselves, the Kaiser was confident that its king, a member of the Hohenzollern family, would do the right thing when the time came. Belgium was another matter. All Wilhelm's blustering attempts to win over its king had only had the effect of making the Belgians determined to defend their neutrality as best they could. In 1913 Belgium introduced conscription and increased the size of its army. It also reorganised its armed forces to strengthen its great fortress at Liège near the German border, showing clearly which of the nations guaranteeing Belgium's neutrality it considered most likely violate it. German military planners still did not count, though, on resistance from the 'chocolate soldiers'.

The other key prizes still up for grabs were in the Balkans. The Ottoman Empire appeared to be tilting towards Germany. Wilhelm also placed his hopes on Rumania, another nation with a Hohenzollern ruler. King Carol had, moreover, made a secret agreement with Germany and Austria-Hungary. Perhaps the Dual Alliance should have been more suspicious that he never cared to acknowledge it publicly. Carol, whom Berchtold described as being like a 'clever, careful, leading civil servant', was not prepared to go against his own public opinion, which was increasingly hostile to the Monarchy because of the way the Hungarians treated the Rumanians under their rule. Tisza, the Hungarian Prime Minister, recognised the problem and tried to appease the Rumanian nationalists, who were mainly concentrated in Transylvania, by offering them autonomy in such areas as religion and education but this was not enough for the Rumanians within Hungary and negotiations broke off in February 1914. Russia in the meanwhile was laying itself out to be friendly. The tsar visited Rumania in June 1914 and there was talk of an engagement between one of his daughters and the heir to the Rumanian throne. Sazonov, who was accompanying the imperial party, travelled up to the border between Rumania and Austria-Hungary and, in a provocative act, went a few miles into Transylvania.

Although Berchtold described himself as walking on eggshells between Bulgaria and Rumania, who hated each other with a vengeance after the Second Balkan War, he also tried draw Bulgaria into the Triple Alliance.[114] Although he ran into strong resistance from Wilhelm, who loathed Foxy Ferdinand its king, Berchtold finally persuaded the German government to offer Bulgaria a substantial loan in June 1914. Berchtold's efforts also served to drive Rumania towards the Entente but in spite of many warning signs, he continued to place his trust in Carol until the eve of the Great War. Conrad, however, ordered his staff at the end of 1913 to prepare war plans against Rumania. He also asked Moltke for more troops to compensate for Rumania's likely enmity. Moltke, as always, carefully avoided making any promises but it was likely that Germany would have thirteen to fourteen divisions in the east. The worst case, Conrad estimated, was if the combined forces of Germany and Austria-Hungary (which could put forty-eight divisions into the field) had to take on the ninety Russian divisions along with Rumania's and Serbia's sixteen and a half apiece, and Montenegro's five, an overall balance of 128 in favour of the Triple Entente over some 62 for the Dual Alliance. That was what was going to happen.[115]

In that last period of the peace there were still attempts by the different sides to reach across the divide. In Russia, Germany, and Austria-Hungary, there were those who argued for an alliance of the three conservative monarchies. In February 1914 the conservative Russian and former Minister of the Interior, Peter Durnovo, presented a long memorandum to the tsar in which he urged that Russia should stay out of the quarrels between France and Germany or Britain and Germany. Russia had much to gain by being on good terms with Germany and everything to lose. A European war would shake Russian society even more than the Japanese one had. If Russia lost, he predicted, it would suffer 'a social revolution in its most extreme manifestation'.[116] In Austria-Hungary Baron Stephen von Burián, an old friend of Tisza's whom the Hungarian Prime Minister had appointed to keep an eye on things in Vienna for him, floated the possibility of an understanding in Europe and over the Straits with Russia. He had made little headway by June 1914 but remained optimistic.[117]

The most significant of all the attempts at détente and the one with the greatest potential for keeping Europe away from war was that between Germany and Britain. In the summer of 1913, with a breathtaking disregard of their oldest ally, the British offered Germany Portugal's African colonies in an attempt to satisfy German hunger for an empire. Terms for liquidating the Portuguese Empire were reached but still awaited signature in the summer of 1914. Britain and Germany also reached an agreement over the Berlin–Baghdad railway: Britain would no longer oppose its construction and the Germans agreed to respect British control of the area south of Baghdad including the sea coast. These were encouraging developments but the key to a better relationship was, as always, the naval race.

At the start of 1912, as the Germans readied a fresh naval bill, the British suggested that the two sides talk. From Britain's perspective the German increases represented an unacceptable threat to British home waters while for the Asquith government the prospect of trying to get more naval spending approved by Parliament was an unpalatable one. Sir Ernest Cassel, a leading British financier with good links in Germany, visited Berlin in late January 1912 with the approval of the Cabinet to sound out the Germans about some form of agreement. He saw his good friend, the shipping magnate Albert Ballin, who also wanted to end the naval race and had meetings with Bethmann and the Kaiser, to whom he presented a brief memorandum. It contained three key points. First and most important, Germany must accept that Britain's naval superiority was essential to the island empire and the German programme must therefore be frozen or cut back. Secondly and in return, Britain would do what it could to help Germany obtain colonies. Finally, the two countries should promise not to take part in aggressive plans or alliances against each other. Bethmann, reported Cassel, was pleased and Wilhelm was 'enchanted, almost childishly so'.[118] The Germans suggested that the British send a government minister to Berlin for discussions.

On 5 February 1912 the British Cabinet chose Richard Haldane, the Secretary of State for War, to be their emissary. Haldane, a tubby and self-important lawyer, had fallen in love with Germany and German philosophy as a young man and spoke the language impressively well. (This was to be a black mark against him during the Great War.) He was on the hawkish side of the Cabinet and particularly close to Grey, with whom he shared a house. Officially it was given out that Haldane was studying German education, but the real purpose of his trip was to sound out the Germans and suggest that if the two sides could reach an agreement Churchill or Grey himself would be willing to come to Berlin to finalise it. Haldane held two days of talks with Bethmann, the Kaiser and Tirpitz. He judged Tirpitz difficult, the Kaiser friendly – Wilhelm presented him with a bronze bust of himself – and Bethmann sincere in wanting peace.[119]

It was soon apparent that the two sides were, in fact, far apart. The British wanted an end to the naval race; the Germans wanted a guarantee that Britain would remain neutral in any war on the Continent. This would, of course, have given Germany a free hand to deal with Russia and France. The most that Germany would do was to slow the tempo of its ship-building if it got that guarantee whereas the most the British would promise was to remain neutral if Germany was attacked and was therefore the innocent party. Wilhelm was furious at what he saw as British insolence: 'I must as Kaiser in the name of the German Empire and as commander-in-chief in the name of my armed forces absolutely *reject* such a view as incompatible *with our* honour.'[120] Although negotiations continued after Haldane's return to London, it was clear they were going nowhere.[121] On 12 March the Kaiser approved the new naval bill after the empress, who hated the British with a passion, told him to stop being subservient to Britain. Tirpitz, who had strongly opposed the negotiations from the start, kissed her hand and thanked her in the name of the German people.[122] Bethmann, who had not been consulted, tried to submit his resignation but Wilhelm angrily accused him of being a coward and refused to accept it. Bethmann loyally remained in office. He later said sadly that he could have achieved a deal with Britain if only Wilhelm had not kept interfering.[123]

When Churchill presented his naval estimates for 1912–13 to Parliament shortly after the failure of the Haldane mission, he said openly that Britain was building only against Germany and must keep a decisive advantage. As a gesture of goodwill and in an attempt to keep expenditure under control, he also suggested a naval holiday, where the two sides would take a breather in their battleship building. It was an offer he was to repeat in the next two years. He seems to have been motivated by a desire to appease those members of his own party who objected to the great increase in defence spending and the recognition that a naval holiday at that point would freeze the balance of power in Britain's favour. The proposal was rejected out of hand by Germany's leaders and attacked by conservatives in Britain. The only country where it received a warm welcome was in the United States: the new President, Woodrow Wilson, was enthusiastic and the House of Representatives called for an international conference to discuss a freeze in naval building. In 1914 Wilson sent his closest confidant, the small enigmatic Colonel Edward House, to the capitals of Europe to see if the United States could help broker a naval disarmament agreement. House reported from Berlin in May: 'The situation is extraordinary. It is militarism run stark mad. Unless someone acting for you can bring about a different understanding there is some day to be an awful cataclysm.'[124]

Wilson's Secretary of State, William Jennings Bryan, also sent out a letter to other governments suggesting that the third of the Hague international peace conferences, which had started in 1899, take place in the autumn of 1915, and by 1914 a number of countries had started their preparations.[125] The international peace movement remained active as well. On 2 August an international peace conference, supported by the American philanthropist Andrew Carnegie, was due to take place in the German city of Constance and the Interparliamentary Union planned to meet later that month in Stockholm. While many of the pacifists remained confident that war was becoming increasingly impossible, one veteran was filled with gloom. Bertha von Suttner wrote in her diary: 'Nothing but mutual suspicions, accusations and agitation. Well, that is an adequate chorus for the increasing cannons, the airplanes which are testing dropping bombs and for war ministries which always demand more.'[126] She died a week before Franz Ferdinand was assassinated at Sarajevo.

As that fateful event drew near, Europe was an odd combination of unease and complacency. Jaurès, the great French socialist, put his finger on it: 'Europe has been afflicted by so many crises for so many years, it has been put dangerously to the test so many times without war breaking out that it has almost ceased to believe in the threat and is watching the further development of the interminable Balkan conflict with decreased attention and reduced disquiet.'[127] The statesmen had muddled through before. They had resisted the calls from their own generals to strike first. Why should they not do so again?

CHAPTER 18

Assassination at Sarajevo

———

The 28th of June 1914 was a Sunday and the weather was warm and sunny. Holidaymakers thronged Europe's amusements, its parks, and its beaches. Poincaré, the French President, was with his wife at the Longchamp races, just outside Paris. The crowds, he later wrote in his diary, were happy and carefree. The course with its expanse of green lawns looked beautiful and there were many elegant women to admire. For many Europeans the summer vacation had already started. Europe's cabinets, its foreign ministries and its military headquarters were half empty, their members scattered. Berchtold, the Chancellor of Austria-Hungary, was duck-hunting in Moravia; Kaiser Wilhelm was racing in his yacht *Meteor* at the annual summer regatta in the Baltic; and Moltke, the chief of his general staff was at a spa. The crisis that was about to come was made worse because so many of the key figures were hard to reach or simply did not take it sufficiently seriously until it was too late.

As Poincaré was enjoying the day with his guests from the diplomatic corps in the special presidential box, he was handed a telegram from the French news agency Havas. The archduke Franz Ferdinand and his morganatic wife Sophie had just been assassinated in Sarajevo, the capital of Austria-Hungary's recently acquired province of Bosnia. Poincaré immediately told the Austrian ambassador, who went white and left at once for his embassy. While the races went on below, the news spread among Poincaré's guests. Most thought it would make

18. The confrontation between Austria-Hungary and Serbia after the
assassination of Archduke Franz Ferdinand, heir to the Austrian throne,
risked drawing in other powers. Serbia, whose government probably knew
about the planned assassination, was emboldened to stand up to Austria-
Hungary because it had support from Russia. As the imperial eagle of
Austria-Hungary prepares to attack the chicken of Serbia, the Russian bear
lurks behind a rock preparing to defend its small Balkan friend.

little difference to Europe but the Rumanian ambassador was deeply
pessimistic. Austria-Hungary, he thought, would now have the excuse
it wanted to wage a war on Serbia.[1]

In the five weeks which followed Europe went from peace to a full-
scale war involving all the great powers except, at first, Italy and the
Ottoman Empire. The public, which had played its part over the decades
in pushing its leaders towards war or peace, now waited on the sidelines
as a handful of men in each of Europe's main capitals juggled with
fateful decisions. Products of their backgrounds and times, with deeply
engrained beliefs in prestige and honour (and such terms were going to
be used frequently in those hectic days), they based their decisions on

assumptions which they did not always articulate, even to themselves. They also were at the mercy of their own memories of past triumphs and defeats, and of their hopes and fears for the future.

As the news of the assassinations spread quickly across Europe, it was greeted with the same mixture of indifference and apprehension as in Poincaré's box. In Vienna, where the archduke had not been much loved, the rides and entertainments in the popular Prater park remained open. Among the upper classes, though, there was despair about the future of a monarchy which repeatedly lost its heirs and renewed animus against the Serbians who, it was widely assumed, were responsible. In the German university town of Freiburg most citizens, according to their diaries, were thinking about their own concerns, whether the state of the summer harvest or their holidays. Perhaps because he was an historian, the eminent scholar Friedrich Meinecke had a different reaction: 'Immediately it became black in front of my eyes. This means war, I told myself.'[2] When the news arrived in Kiel the authorities sent a launch out to find the Kaiser's yacht. Wilhelm, who had counted Franz Ferdinand as a friend, was shocked. 'Would it be better to abandon the race?' he asked. He decided to travel back to Berlin at once to take charge and let it be known that he intended to work for peace, though during the next few days he still managed to find the time for intense discussions over the interior decoration of his new yacht.[3] In Kiel itself flags were immediately lowered to half-mast and the remaining social events were cancelled. A British fleet, which had been paying a courtesy call, sailed away on 30 June. The Germans sent the signal 'Pleasant journey' and the British replied 'Friends in past and friends forever.'[4] Just over a month later they would be at war.

The act which was going to send Europe on the final leg of its journey towards the Great War was the work of fanatical Slav nationalists, the Young Bosnians, and their shadowy backers in Serbia. The assassins themselves and their immediate circle were mostly young Serb and Croat peasant boys who had left the countryside to study and work in the towns and cities of the Dual Monarchy and Serbia. While they had put on suits in place of their traditional dress and condemned the conservatism of their elders, they nevertheless found much in the modern world bewildering and disturbing. It is hard not to compare them to the extreme groups among Islamic fundamentalists such as Al

Qaeda a century later. Like those later fanatics, the Young Bosnians were usually fiercely puritanical, despising such things as alcohol and sexual intercourse. They hated Austria-Hungary in part because they blamed it for corrupting its South Slav subjects. Few of the Young Bosnians had regular jobs. Rather they depended on handouts from their families, with whom they had usually quarrelled. They shared their few possessions, slept on each other's floors, and spent hours over a single cup of coffee in cheap cafés arguing about life and politics.[5] They were idealistic, and passionately committed to liberating Bosnia from foreign rule and to building a new and fairer world. Strongly influenced by the great Russian revolutionaries and anarchists, the Young Bosnians believed that they could only achieve their goals through violence and, if necessary, the sacrifice of their own lives.[6]

The leader of the assassination plot was a Bosnian Serb, Gavrilo Princip, the slight, introverted and sensitive son of a hardworking farmer. Princip, who had longings to be a poet, had gone from one school to another without conspicuous success. 'Wherever I went, people took me for a weakling,' he told the police after he was arrested on 28 June, 'and I pretended that I was a weak person, even though I was not.'[7] In 1911 he was drawn into the subterranean world of revolutionary politics. He and several of his friends who were to become his co-conspirators dedicated themselves to acts of terror against important targets, whether the old emperor himself, or someone close to him. In the Balkan wars of 1912 and 1913 the victories of Serbia and the great increase in its territories inspired them afresh to think that the final triumph of the South Slavs was not far off.[8]

Within Serbia itself there was considerable support for the Young Bosnians and their activities. For a decade or more, parts of the Serbian government had encouraged the activities of quasi-military and conspiratorial organisations on the soil of Serbia's enemies, whether the Ottoman Empire or Austria-Hungary. The army provided money and weapons for armed Serbian bands in Macedonia and smuggled weapons into Bosnia much as Iran does today with Hezbollah in Lebanon. The Serbians also had their own secret societies. In 1903 a group made up largely of officers assassinated the unpopular king Alexander Obrenović and his wife and put King Peter on the throne. Over the next years, the new king found it expedient to tolerate the activities of the conspirators who remained highly influential within Serbia and who promoted

Serbian nationalism abroad. The key figure among them was the charming, ruthless, sinister, and immensely strong Dragutin Dimitrijević, nicknamed Apis after the Egyptian god who is always portrayed as a bull. Apis was prepared to sacrifice his own life and those of his family and friends in the cause of a Greater Serbia. In 1911 he and some of his fellow conspirators founded the Black Hand, dedicated to bringing all Serbs together by fair means and foul.[9] The Prime Minister, Pašić, who hoped to avoid conflict with Serbia's neighbours, knew of its existence and tried to bring it under control by pensioning off, for example, some of the more dangerous among the nationalistic army officers. In the early summer of 1914 his confrontation with Apis reached an acute stage. On 2 June he resigned, but returned to office on 11 June and on 24 June, as the archduke was preparing to travel to Bosnia, he announced that parliament was dissolved and that fresh elections would be held later that summer. King Peter also stepped down and made his son Alexander regent. As the Bosnian conspirators were putting the final touches to their plans to assassinate the archduke on 28 June, Pašić, who had no wish to provoke Austria-Hungary, was fighting for his political life and not yet capable of rooting out the Black Hand and bringing Apis down.

The news of Franz Ferdinand's impending trip had been widely publicised earlier that spring and the conspirators, several of whom were at that point in Belgrade, decided to assassinate him. A sympathetic major in the Serbian army provided them with six bombs and four revolvers from the army's arsenal and, at the end of May, Princip and two others, along with their weapons and capsules of cyanide with which to commit suicide after they had done their deed, were smuggled across the border from Serbia into Bosnia with the connivance of sympathetic Serbian officials. Pašić got wind of what was up but was either unable or unwilling to do anything. In any case it was probably too late; the conspirators had arrived safely in Sarajevo and linked up with local terrorists. In the next few weeks some were to have second thoughts and argue for postponing the attempt but not, apparently, Princip. 'I was not in agreement with the postponement of the assassination', he told the judge at his trial, 'because a certain morbid yearning for it had been awakened in me.'[10]

Their job was going to be made easier by incompetence and arrogance on the part of the Austrian-Hungarians. There had been rumours for years of plots against Austria-Hungary from South Slav nationalists as well actual attempts on the lives of high-ranking officials, even on the emperor himself. The authorities in Vienna and in the trouble spots of Bosnia and Croatia kept close watch on nationalist students, societies and newspapers. Yet a visit by the Habsburg heir to Bosnia, when memories of its annexation only six years before still rankled with Serbs, was bound to inflame nationalist sentiments. And he was coming, moreover, to watch manoeuvres by forces of the Dual Monarchy which might well be used against Serbia and Montenegro one day. The timing of the visit made matters still worse for it coincided with the Serbs' greatest national festival, the annual feast for their patron saint St Vitus, when they also commemorated their greatest national defeat at the hands of the Ottomans on 28 June 1389 at the Battle of Kosovo. In spite of the tensions surrounding the event security for the visit was lackadaisical at best. General Potiorek, the reactionary and stubborn governor of Bosnia, ignored the warnings that came in from several quarters that the archduke was putting himself in harm's way and refused to use the army to guard the streets of Sarajevo. He hoped to show off his own achievements in pacifying and ruling Bosnia and also to advance himself with Franz Ferdinand by receiving Sophie with full imperial honours, something she was always denied elsewhere in the Dual Monarchy. The special committee set up to look after arrangements for the visit spent most of its time and energy worrying about such matters as what kind of wine the archduke should have or whether he liked music played during meals.[11]

On the evening of 23 June, Franz Ferdinand and Sophie boarded a train in Vienna for Trieste. He apparently remarked to the wife of an aide before he left: 'This thing isn't especially secret and I wouldn't be surprised if there are a few Serbian bullets waiting for me!' The lights in his railway carriage were broken; the candles that had to be used gave it, so some thought, the appearance of a crypt. On Wednesday morning the imperial party boarded the dreadnought *Viribus Unitis* ('With United Forces') and sailed down the Dalmatian coast towards Bosnia. They landed the following day and went to the small resort town of Ilidze near Sarajevo, where they were to stay. That evening the archduke and his duchess made a quick impromptu visit to explore Sarajevo's well-known handicrafts. Princip was apparently in the crowd as the imperial couple went into a carpet shop.

On Friday and Saturday, the archduke took part in army manoeuvres in the mountains south of Sarajevo while the duchess visited local sights. On Saturday evening local dignitaries attended a banquet in Ilidze. Dr Josip Sunaric, a leading Croat politician who had been one of those who had sent warnings of plots against the imperial couple, was introduced to the duchess. 'You see', she said cheerfully to him, 'you have made a mistake. It really isn't the way you always say it is. We were all over the countryside, and without exception among the Serbian population, and greeted in such a friendly manner, with such sincerity and unrestrained warmth that we are really happy about it.' 'Your highness,' he replied, 'I ask God that – if I will have the honour tomorrow evening to see you again – you can tell me the same words again. Then a large burden will have fallen off my heart, a great stone.'[12] That night the imperial party did discuss whether to cancel the visit planned for Sarajevo the next day but it was decided to go ahead.

That Sunday morning of 28 June was fine in Sarajevo and the imperial couple descended from their train to take their seats in an open touring car, one of the few of its kind in Europe. The archduke was resplendent in the blue tunic and feathered hat of the dress uniform of an Austrian cavalry general and the duchess was all in white except for a red sash. The conspirators, seven in all, were already in place, dotted among the crowds that had gathered along the route of the visit. As the procession of cars drove along the Appel Quay beside the river that runs through the heart of Sarajevo, the young Nedeljko Čabrinović hurled a bomb at the archduke's car. Like suicide bombers in a later era he had said farewell to his family and friends and distributed his only possessions. The driver saw the bomb coming and accelerated, with the result that it exploded under the next car and several of the passengers as well as bystanders were wounded. The archduke sent an aide to find out what had happened and then ordered the programme to proceed as planned. The party, now shaken and angry, made its way to the town hall where the Lord Mayor was waiting to make a speech of welcome. He stumbled through it and the archduke brought out his notes to reply. They were damp with the blood of one of his staff. There was a hasty consultation and it was decided that the party would go to the military hospital to see the wounded. As the cars sped back along the Appel Quay, the two leading ones carrying the chief security detective and the mayor of Sarajevo suddenly turned right into a much narrower street. The archduke's driver was about to follow when Potiorek, the governor of Sarajevo, shouted 'Stop! You are going the wrong way.' As the driver put on the brakes, Princip, who had been standing in wait, stepped up on to the running board and shot the archduke and the duchess point blank. She collapsed on to her husband's legs as he called out 'Sophie, Sophie, don't die. Live for my children.' He then lost consciousness himself. The pair were taken to the governor's palace where they were pronounced dead.[13] Princip, who was trying to shoot himself, was seized by spectators and his fellow conspirators were rounded up by the police who belatedly swung into action.

When a courtier brought the news to the emperor at his favourite villa in the lovely little resort of Ischl, Franz Joseph closed his eyes and remained silent for a few moments. His first words, uttered with deep emotion, showed the depths of his estrangement from his heir who, in marrying Sophie, had not only defied him but, as the emperor saw it, damaged the honour of the Habsburgs. 'Horrible! The Almighty does not allow himself to be challenged with impunity ... A higher power has restored the old order which I unfortunately was unable to uphold.'[14] He said nothing more but gave orders for his return to Vienna. Whether he was thinking of how his empire might take its revenge on Serbia is not known. In the past he had opted for peace and Franz Ferdinand had supported him. Now the assassination had removed the one person close to the emperor who might have counselled restraint in those last weeks of Europe's long peace. The eighty-three-year-old emperor, whose health was failing – he had been seriously ill that spring – was left alone to face the hawks in his government and his military.

The funeral in Vienna on 3 July for the archduke and his wife was a low-key affair. The Kaiser gave out that an attack of lumbago had prevented him from travelling but the real explanation seems to have been that he and his government had heard rumours of plans to assassinate him too. In any case, the Dual Monarchy requested that no foreign heads of state attend, only their ambassadors in Vienna. Even in death, the rigid court etiquette held for the unfortunate couple: his coffin was bigger and placed on a higher dais than hers. The service, in the Habsburg chapel, lasted a brief fifteen minutes and the coffins were loaded on to hearses to be taken to the railway station. Since he had long known that his wife would not be allowed to lie beside him in the Habsburg crypt, the archduke had made arrangements that they would both be buried when the time came at one of their favourite castles at Artstetten in lower Austria, where they still rest. In a spontaneous expression of their resentment at the way in which the obsequies were conducted, members of the empire's great families walked behind the coffins to the station. Ordinary Viennese watched the cortège pass, the Russian ambassador reported, with curiosity rather than sadness and the roundabouts in the Prater continued to spin merrily. The coffins were loaded on to trains and then taken on a barge across the Danube in the midst of a storm so violent that they were nearly pitched into the river.[15]

Before the funeral took place the discussions had already started about what Austria-Hungary should do in the face of what was widely seen as an outrageous provocation by Serbia. Just as the tragedy of September 11 2001 gave the hardliners the opportunity to urge what they had advocated all along on President Bush and Prime Minister Blair – the invasions of Afghanistan and Iraq – so too the Sarajevo assassination opened the door wide for those in Austria-Hungary who wanted to settle the South Slav problem once and for all. That meant destroying Serbia – the country generally assumed to be behind the assassination – as a first step to asserting Austria-Hungary's dominance in the Balkans and bringing the empire's own South Slavs under control. The nationalist press described Serbia and the South Slavs in terms which owed much to Social Darwinism as Austria-Hungary's eternal enemy. 'It should now be clear to everyone', the leading conservative politician and intellectual Josef Redlich wrote in his diary on 28 June, 'that peaceful coexistence is impossible to achieve between this half-German monarchy with its sister-relationship to Germany, and Balkan nationalism with its fanatical bloodthirstiness.'[16] Even those in the ruling circles who mourned for Franz Ferdinand talked of revenge while his enemies heartlessly blamed him for preventing war on Serbia on earlier occasions.[17]

Conrad, who as chief of the general staff had been clamouring for war ever since the Bosnian crisis in 1908, heard the news as he changed trains in Zagreb. He wrote immediately to his beloved Gina. Serbia was clearly behind the assassinations and Austria-Hungary should have dealt with it long since. The future of the Dual Monarchy now looked grim, he went on: Russia would probably support Serbia and Rumania would have to be counted as an enemy as well. Nevertheless, he told Gina, war there must be: 'It will be a hopeless struggle, but it must be pursued, because so old a Monarchy and so glorious an army cannot go down ingloriously.' His message to his own staff and to the Chancellor the next day in Vienna was, so Berchtold noted, simply 'War. War. War.'[18] For Conrad it was out of the question to do anything less, such as mobilising the army as a means of applying pressure for a diplomatic solution. When that happened during the Balkan wars, Conrad told Berchtold, army morale had been badly damaged. 'A horse', as the general was fond of saying, 'that is brought three times before the hurdle and is stopped before jumping won't approach the hurdle again.'[19] When the crisis reached its acute point at the end of July, Conrad continued to firmly oppose a partial mobilisation against either Serbia or Russia for diplomatic purposes. Nor would he contemplate a limited war against Serbia with a halt in Belgrade as Grey and others were going to propose.[20] Conrad's belligerence had wide support from his fellow officers including General Alexander Krobatin, the War Minister, and Potiorek in Bosnia, who was adamant on revenge against Serbia partly out of embarrassment about his own failure to protect the archduke.

In the Foreign Office too, especially among younger officials, many of whom had admired Aehrenthal and his activist foreign policy, opinion was largely in favour of a hardline response to the assassination. Austria-Hungary, it was argued, did not want to fade into insignificance like its neighbour to the south, the Ottoman Empire. As Count Alexander Hoyos, who was to play a crucial role in the next few weeks, said to Redlich, 'We are still capable of resolve! We do not want to or ought to be a sick man. Better to be destroyed quickly.'[21] In the next weeks his subordinates urged Berchtold to act decisively and quickly against Serbia. Russia, it is true, might feel obliged to intervene but it was better to take it on now before it got any stronger. Or perhaps the old solidarity between the two conservative monarchies might just be enough to keep it on the sidelines. The argument that time was running out was also used with reference to the Dual Monarchy's domestic situation: its own South Slavs might still support their government but waiting was dangerous because Serbian propaganda was already making inroads among them.[22] With unfounded optimism, the Foreign Ministry also hoped that Rumania might be scared into remaining loyal by the threat of a closer friendship between Austria-Hungary and Bulgaria.[23]

The German ambassador Heinrich von Tschirschky, a headstrong, arrogant and belligerent man, added his voice: Austria-Hungary should stand up for itself and show Serbia who was master. Even before his superiors in Berlin had decided on their policy, Tschirschky was telling every official he met in Vienna that Germany would back the Dual Monarchy whatever it decided to do. If Austria-Hungary showed itself to be weak yet again, he warned, Germany might have to look elsewhere for allies.[24] Berchtold in fact needed little persuading; where he had held out against war in previous crises, he had been convinced since the end of the Second Balkan War in 1913 that Austria-Hungary would have to go to war with Serbia one day. Now the time had come.[25] On 1 July Berchtold had a meeting with a shaken Franz Joseph, who agreed that Austria-Hungary must reassert itself as a great power. 'We,' said the emperor, 'the most conservative power in Europe, were forced into this plight by the expansionary policies of Italy and the Balkan states.'[26]

The only serious opposition to those who were bent on war came from the Hungarians, in particular from the Prime Minister Tisza. Austria-Hungary did not have enough evidence against Serbia, he wrote to the emperor on 1 July, to persuade the world that the smaller state was guilty. Moreover, the Dual Monarchy's international position was already weak: Rumania, despite its secret treaty, was unlikely to stand by it and the possible support of Bulgaria was not sufficient compensation. Tisza's advice was that Austria-Hungary should continue to work for a peaceful settlement with Serbia.[27] In the next few weeks he was to be put under great pressure to join the war party. Without support from Hungary the government in Vienna would not be able to act.

The other matter that had to be settled was what Austria-Hungary's ally Germany was prepared to do. The signals coming from Tschirschky were encouraging and on 1 July Victor Naumann, an influential German journalist who was known to be close to Jagow, the German Foreign Secretary, visited Hoyos to say that Kaiser Wilhelm, if handled rightly, would stand firmly behind Austria-Hungary and so would German

public opinion. 'Austria-Hungary', Naumann went on, 'would be finished as a monarchy and a great power if it did not take advantage of
this moment.'[28] Berchtold decided to deal with Berlin directly on the
crucial question of what official German policy was going to be. His
emissary, not perhaps by coincidence, was Hoyos, who was known as a
leading hawk and who also had good connections in Germany (his
sister was married to Bismarck's son). When Conrad learned of the
mission, he asked Franz Joseph 'If the answer is to the effect that
Germany is on our side, do we then go to war against Serbia?' The old
emperor replied 'In that case, yes.'[29]

Hoyos set off on the evening of 4 July, carrying with him a long memorandum on the situation in the Balkans as well as a personal letter from
Franz Joseph to Wilhelm. Although neither document spoke of a decision for war, their tone was bellicose, talking for example of the
unbridgeable gulf between Austria-Hungary and Serbia and the need
for the Dual Monarchy to cut the strands of the net which its enemies
were throwing over it. The emperor's letter to Wilhelm concluded, 'You
must also have been convinced after the recent terrible events in Bosnia,
that the reconciliation of the antagonism, which divides us from Serbia,
can no longer be considered and that the long-term policy of peace of the
European monarchs is threatened so long as this furnace of criminal agitation in Belgrade continues to burn unpunished.'[30] Hoyos also carried a
verbal message from Berchtold to his elderly ambassador Count Ladislaus Szögyény-Marich in Berlin to say that Austria-Hungary felt that it
was the right time to deal with Serbia. In Berlin, Hoyos went beyond
even these instructions and told the Germans that Austria-Hungary
intended to occupy and partition Serbia.[31]

On 5 July, while the Foreign Ministry considered the meaning of the
messages from Vienna, Szögyény had lunch with the Kaiser. Wilhelm
read through the documents and, at first, temporised. It was all very
serious and he would have to consult his Chancellor, Bethmann. When
the ambassador pressed him, however, Wilhelm abandoned caution.
Franz Joseph, he promised, could rely on Germany's full support: even
if it came to war with Serbia and with Russia Germany would stand by
the side of its ally. That afternoon the Kaiser belatedly consulted his
officials: Bethmann gave his approval to the promise to Austria-
Hungary and Falkenhayn, the War Minister, said tersely that the army

was ready to fight. The following day Bethmann repeated the German assurances of support to Szögyény and Hoyos. The latter returned, delighted with the success of his mission, to Vienna. After the war he was to remark, 'No one today can imagine how strongly we at that time believed in German power, in the invincibility of the German army.' His government set about its next steps in bringing Serbia to heel.[32]

So it was, a week after the assassination, that Germany issued what came to be known as its 'blank cheque' and Europe took a giant step towards a general war. This does not mean, as some have argued, that Germany was determined to bring about such a war for its own ends. Rather its leaders were prepared to accept the possibility partly because, if war were going to come, the time was favourable for Germany and partly because Austria-Hungary had to be kept as an ally. And then there are those individuals, especially Wilhelm himself and Bethmann, who had the power to decide between war and peace and who in the end were persuaded that war was the better option for Germany – or they simply lacked the courage to resist the pressures on them and the arguments of those who wanted war. And perhaps they had simply grown tired, as so many Europeans had, of the tensions and the crises and wanted a resolution. A leap into the dark, as Bethmann described it to his private secretary Kurt Riezler, had its attractions.[33]

Germany's actions, like those of its friends and foes in this last period of peace, must be understood in the context of the preceding decades and the assumptions that underpinned the thinking of its leaders. In the end only a few men – in particular Bethmann, Moltke, and the Kaiser – determined Germany's policy. What influenced them and the subordinates who urged them on was that they tended to see threats rather than opportunities. They were fearful of the left at home and when they looked abroad their old fears of encirclement were more acute than ever. By 1914 the German military took it for granted that they would have to fight on land on two fronts. That May, Georg von Waldersee, the Quartermaster General of the German army, wrote a memorandum to argue that Germany faced determined enemies who were likely to attack simultaneously and who were arming at an increasing rate. Germany's leaders must not plump for peace at all costs; rather they must strengthen their armed forces, through conscripting all available young men if necessary, and be prepared to fight at any moment.[34]

It was ominous too that the Entente appeared to be stronger while the Triple Alliance grew weaker. The military alliance between France and Russia had deepened and now Britain and Russia appeared to be moving in the direction of greater military co-operation. Although the Anglo-Russian naval talks that summer never came to anything, they served to raise the German level of apprehension. The day after the assassination, Bethmann told his ambassador in London, Prince Max von Lichnowsky, that he had reliable reports that an agreement was being readied under which British freighters would transport Russian troops to Germany's Baltic coast.[35] A week later, as Austria-Hungary demanded and got its blank cheque, Bethmann said to a leading nationalist politician, 'If there is war with France, England will march against us to the last man.'[36] And to make the situation worse Germany and Austria-Hungary could not count on their other allies: Rumania was probably going to defect and Italy was unreliable. True, Pollio, the chief of its general staff, appeared to be both competent and eager to co-operate with Germany and Austria-Hungary, but as Waldersee asked that May, 'How long will his influence last?' It was a prescient question; Pollio died the same day as the assassination in Sarajevo and the Italian government did not get around to appointing his successor until near the end of July. Italy's willingness to fight with its allies remained as it had always been – doubtful.[37]

It was its great neighbour to the east that caused the most nightmares for Germany's leaders. Reflecting the Social Darwinist assumptions of their era, many Germans saw the Slavs, and especially Russia, as the natural opponent of the Teuton races. Wilhelm was by no means alone in fearing the Slavic hordes sweeping westwards. He frequently sounded like right-wing politicians in the United Kingdom today worried about eastern Europeans storming British ports or conservative US Republicans with similar worries about Mexicans. 'I hate the Slavs,' he said to the military attaché from Austria-Hungary with a striking lack of tact, given the large numbers of Slavs living within the Dual Monarchy. 'I know it's a sin but I cannot help myself.' Serbia, he was fond of saying, was 'the pig monarchy'. His senior generals such as Waldersee and Moltke talked in apocalyptic terms about the impending need for Germans to fight for their very existence as a people and a culture. They also found such arguments convenient as they pushed the government in the spring and early summer of 1914 for big increases in the army.[38]

It is curious in retrospect how little attention the German leadership paid to the alternatives to war as a way of breaking the encirclement. Bethmann, it is true, had hoped for a rapprochement with Britain but after the failure of the Haldane mission two years earlier that seemed increasingly unlikely. The Kaiser from time to time expressed the hope that the old alliance between the two conservative monarchies of Germany and Russia might be revived but it is doubtful that he really believed it was possible. In 1914 a prominent banker, Max Warburg, recorded a conversation with him: 'Russia's armaments, the great Russian railway constructions were in his opinion preparations for a war which could break out in the year 1916 ... Beset by his anxieties, the Kaiser even considered whether it would not be better to attack first instead of waiting.'[39] And the Kaiser, like others among the German leadership, thought that conflict with Russia was inevitable and seriously considered a preventive war. In the Foreign Office there were many including Jagow and his deputy Zimmermann who agreed and argued that the diplomatic and military situation in 1914 was particularly favourable for Germany.[40] They should have remembered that famous saying of Bismarck: 'Preventive war is like committing suicide out of fear of death.'

The top military leadership were, if anything, even more psychologically ready for war than the civilians. The Kiel Canal works were nearly complete and by 25 July German dreadnoughts would be able to go back and forth in safety between the North Sea and the Baltic. True, the army had not yet achieved its increases but Russia's new programme had only just started. At a memorial service in Berlin for Franz Ferdinand on 3 July, the military representative of Saxony fell into conversation with Waldersee. The general, he reported to his own government, felt that war could come at any moment. The German general staff was ready: 'I had the impression that they would regard it as quite convenient if it came to a war right now. The conditions and prospects would not get any better for us.'[41] What helped to give the German military leadership confidence was that they had their strategy all mapped out. 'Armed with the Schlieffen Plan as we were', Groener of the general staff later wrote, 'we believed that we could await the inevitable martial conflict with our neighbours in calmness ...'[42]

A few weeks before Sarajevo Moltke mused to Jagow that it would make sense for Germany to take Russia on while it still had a chance of winning. Jagow, the chief of staff suggested, should conduct his foreign policy 'with the aim of provoking a war in the near future'. Around the same time Moltke said to a German diplomat from the London embassy, 'If only things would finally boil over – we are ready; the sooner the better.'[43] And sooner was better for him as well. As he said to a niece in 1912, during the First Balkan War, 'If war is coming, I hope it will come soon before I am too old to cope with things satisfactorily.'[44] By 1914, his health appeared to be breaking down. He had to spend four weeks at the spa in Carlsbad between April and May receiving treatment for what was said to be bronchitis and he went back again for another extended stay on 28 June.[45] Nor was he as confident of Germany's success as he sounded. He was well aware of the dangers of a long-drawn-out war. When Conrad von Hötzendorf queried him in May 1914 about what he intended to do if Germany failed to win a quick victory over the French, Moltke was evasive: 'Well, I will do what I can. We are not superior to the French.' And while Bethmann continued to hope until the end that the British would opt for neutrality, Moltke also took for granted that Britain would enter the war on France's side. Yet he and his colleagues exuded confidence to the civilians that Germany could handily defeat France, Russia and Britain in a short war.[46]

By 1914 its partnership with Austria-Hungary assumed greater importance for Germany than ever before. Jagow put it with brutal honesty to Lichnowsky on 18 July: 'It is also arguable whether we are likely to find an alliance with that crumbling constellation of States on the Danube a good investment: but I say with the poet – I think it was Busch – "If you no longer like your company, try to find other, if other there be."'[47] That gave Austria-Hungary, as happens surprisingly often in international relations, power over its stronger partner. By 1914 Germany's leaders felt that they had little choice but to support their ally even as it pursued dangerous policies, much as the United States continues to support Israel or Pakistan today. Crucially, Bethmann, who in earlier crises had counselled Austria-Hungary to compromise, had now come round accepting that Germany would have to back its ally whatever it chose to do. 'We face our old dilemma over any Austrian actions in the Balkans,' he said to Riezler, to whom the Chancellor frequently unburdened himself. 'If we advise them to take action, they will say we had pushed them into it; if we advise against, they will say that we have abandoned them. Then they will approach the Western powers whose arms are open and we will lose our last powerful ally.'[48]

In those crisis weeks of July 1914, Bethmann was particularly melancholy, for his beloved wife Martha had died on 11 May after a painful illness. 'What was past and should have been future,' he wrote to his predecessor Bülow, 'all that was tied to our common life is now destroyed by death'.[49] Riezler kept a diary of his conversations with Bethmann in the weeks of the crisis. On 7 July, the day after the Chancellor had added his support to the blank cheque, the two men sat up late under the summer night sky at Bethmann's old castle at Hohenfinow east of Berlin. Riezler was shocked by the older man's pessimism as he lamented the state of the world and of Germany. German society, Bethmann felt, was in moral and intellectual decline and the existing political and social order seemed incapable of renewing itself. 'Everything', he said sadly, 'has become so very old.' The future too looked bleak: Russia, 'an increasingly heavy nightmare', would grow still stronger while Austria-Hungary declined to the point where it was no longer capable of fighting with Germany as an ally. (Recall that Bethmann had earlier decided not to plant trees on his estate because he assumed the Russians would be overrunning eastern Germany within in few years.)[50]

Germany's key leaders such as Bethmann may not have deliberately started the Great War, as has often been charged, by among others German historians such as Fritz Fischer. Nevertheless, by taking its coming for granted, as something desirable even, by issuing the blank cheque to Austria-Hungary, and by sticking to a war plan which made it inevitable that Germany would fight on two fronts, Germany's leaders allowed it to happen. At times in those last increasingly tense weeks they seemed to grasp the enormity of what they were risking and took comfort in what were mostly unlikely scenarios. If Austria-Hungary moved quickly to deal with Serbia, Bethmann said to Riezler, the Entente might just accept it. Or Germany and Britain might work together – after all they had done so before in the Balkans – to keep a war involving Austria-Hungary from dragging in other powers. That last Jagow consigned to 'the category of pious wishes'.[51] Yet the Foreign Secretary himself indulged in wishful thinking, writing for example to

Lichnowsky on 18 July, 'when all is said and done, Russia at present is not ready for war'. As for Russia's allies, Britain and France, did they really want to go war on its side? Grey always wanted to maintain the balance of power in Europe but if Russia destroyed Austria-Hungary and defeated Germany, Europe would have a new hegemonic ruler. France too might not be ready to fight: the divisive battle over the three-year military service could well be renewed in the autumn and it was well known that the French army had serious shortfalls in its equipment and training. On 13 July, revelations in the French Senate added further details, about France's lack of field artillery for example, which encouraged the Germans to think that France was unlikely to fight in the near future and that the Russians might conclude they could not rely on their ally. With any luck the Entente might fall apart.[52]

If war came, so Germany's leaders hoped in their more optimistic moments, perhaps they could localise it in the Balkans. Or perhaps the threat alone of military force could bring victory. Bluff after all had worked against Russia in the Bosnian crisis when it had backed down in the face of stepped-up military preparations by Austria-Hungary and an ultimatum from Germany. Bluff had worked again in the Balkan wars when Austria-Hungary had forced Serbia and Montenegro out of Scutari and Russia had chosen to stand by. Serbia and its patron Russia might back down again this time in the face of a resolute Dual Alliance. 'We hoped', said Bethmann's chief of press, Otto Hammann in October 1914, 'that we would humiliate Russia without war; this would have been a nice success.'[53]

What made it unlikely that Germany's leaders would be resolute in the pursuit of peace was the fear they had of appearing weak and unmanly, of not standing up for their honour and that of Germany. 'I do not desire a preventive war', said Jagow, 'but *if we are called upon to fight, we must not funk it*'.[54] The Kaiser, who had the final say in whether Germany went to war or not, wavered as he had done so often before between hoping that peace could be preserved and uttering the most belligerent sentiments – 'The Serbs must be disposed of, *and* that right *soon!*' he scribbled on 30 June for example in one of his marginal notes.[55] Like the younger George Bush nearly a century later, who blamed his father for not finishing off Saddam Hussein while he had the chance, Wilhelm had always wanted to distinguish himself from a father he held to be weak and indecisive. While Wilhelm took great pride in being Germany's supreme warlord he knew that many of his subjects, including army officers, held him responsible for the country's poor showing in previous crises. Although he insisted that he had worked for peace throughout his reign, the epithet 'Emperor of Peace' stung. In a conversation with his friend the industrialist Gustav Krupp von Bohlen und Halbach on 6 July, just after the blank cheque had been issued, the Kaiser said that he made his promise knowing that Austria-Hungary intended to take action against Serbia. 'This time I shall not give in,' he said three times. As Krupp noted in a letter to a colleague, 'The repeated Imperial assurance that this time nobody could again accuse him of irresolution had had an almost comic effect.'[56] Bethmann used what was perhaps the most revealing phrase of all when he said that for Germany to back down in the face of its enemies would be an act of self-castration.[57] Such attitudes came in part from the German leaders' social class and their times but Bismarck, who came out of the same world, had been strong enough to defy its code when he chose. He never allowed war to be forced upon him. It was Germany's tragedy and that of Europe that his successors were not the man he was.

Once the German leadership had made up its mind to back Austria-Hungary, they expected their ally to move quickly while opinion in Europe was still shocked and sympathetic. It was also important for domestic reasons, as the Germans frequently reminded Vienna, to make sure that Serbia was put in the wrong. (Right up to the outbreak of hostilities the German leaders feared that the working classes and their leaders in the unions and the Social Democratic Party would be true to their often-repeated word and oppose a war.) An ultimatum from Vienna to Belgrade followed up rapidly with a short victorious war if Serbia did not capitulate would leave the other great powers unable to intervene until it was too late.

The Germans found it impossible to hurry up their counterparts in Vienna. Like a great jellyfish with indigestion, the Dual Monarchy moved at its own stately and complicated pace. The army had let many of its soldiers off on 'harvest leave' and they would not be back in uniform until 25 July. 'We are above all an agrarian state', Conrad, whose policy it was, told the German military attaché, 'and must live on the result of the harvest for a whole year.' And if he tried to bring his sol-diers back early it might cause chaos on the railways and, worse, alert the rest of Europe that something was up. Yet another argument for waiting was that the French President Poincaré and his Prime Minister Viviani, who was also responsible for foreign relations, were going to be on a state visit to Russia until 23 July. Once they were on board ship on their way back to France, communications would be poor and they would have difficulty for several days in co-ordinating with Russia on a response to the ultimatum. The delay was costly to Austria-Hungary: in the almost four weeks between the assassinations and the presentation of the ultimatum much of the sympathy that Europeans had felt for it had dissipated and what might have looked like a natural reaction was to appear more like cold-blooded power politics.[58]

The most important reason of all for Austria-Hungary's dilatoriness was Tisza, who was still not convinced that a hard line towards Serbia was the right one. He feared, as he told the emperor in a letter on 1 July, that war would be damaging whatever the outcome: defeat could lead to loss of much territory or the end of Hungary while victory might see Serbia being annexed and so result in a much too strong South Slav component within the Dual Monarchy.[59] On 7 July the Common Min-isterial Council, the only body with responsibility for the whole of Austria-Hungary, met in Vienna. Tisza found himself isolated as his fellow ministers discussed how best to crush Serbia and what they should do with it once the war was over. Berchtold and Krobatin, the War Minister, dismissed the Hungarian's argument that they try first for a diplomatic victory over Serbia. They had enjoyed such successes in the past, said the Chancellor, but Serbia had not changed its ways and had continued to agitate for a Greater Serbia. The only way to deal with it was by force. Stürgkh, the Austrian Prime Minister, who had been a hardliner in the earlier crises in the Balkans, talked of 'a solution at the point of the sword'. Although the decision was Austria-Hungary's alone, he said, it was a great comfort to know that Germany stood so faithfully behind it. Conrad joined the meeting even though he was not a government minister to discuss what might happen if Russia came to Serbia's defence, something he thought likely. Everyone except Tisza agreed that the demands contained in the ultimatum should be designed so that Serbia would have to refuse them, thus giving Austria-Hungary grounds for war. Tisza accepted that the ultimatum had to be firm but asked to see the terms before it was sent.[60]

In the next week he was put under severe pressure from his colleagues and, indirectly, from Germany. For Tisza the alliance with Germany, 'the cornerstone of our entire policy', was essential for maintaining Austria-Hungary's great-power status and, to him, even more important, the status of Hungary itself. Nor was he any less hostile to Serbia than his colleagues; he disagreed rather on tactics. He also seems to have persuaded himself that Rumania would stay neutral (King Carol had sent an anodyne letter of reassurance to Franz Joseph) and Bulgaria could be drawn into the Triple Alliance now that Berlin had promised it a loan. On 14 July at a meeting with Berchtold he gave way and agreed that a severe ultimatum should be sent to Serbia with a deadline of forty-eight hours. If Serbia failed to comply with the conditions war would follow. The one concession he managed to get was that Austria-Hungary should make it clear that it did not intend to take Serbia's territory after the war was over.[61]

Later that afternoon he had a conversation with the German ambassador which Tschirschky reported back to Berlin. Tisza claimed that, although he had argued for caution in the past, each passing day had strengthened his conviction that the Dual Monarchy now must take action to show that it was still vital and, in Tschirschky's italics, '*to put an end to the intolerable conditions in the southeast*'. Austria-Hungary could no longer tolerate the insolent tone coming from Serbia. The time, Tisza now felt, had come for action. 'The note is being composed so that the possibility of its acceptance is *practically excluded*.' Austria-Hungary's mobilisation against Serbia would follow as soon as the deadline was reached. As he left, Tisza clasped Tschirschky's hand and said, 'Together we shall now look the future calmly and firmly in the face.' Wilhelm noted approvingly in the margins of the report, 'Well, a real man at last!'[62]

The main outlines of the ultimatum were already set by the second week of July. It would include a demand that nationalist officers be dismissed from the Serbian army and nationalist societies be dissolved. The Serbian king would have to issue a public declaration that his country would no longer promote a Greater Serbia. To ensure that Serbia fulfilled these and any other demands, Austria-Hungary would establish a special agency in Belgrade. The terms were already exceedingly difficult for an independent nation to accept and they were going to become more stringent still as Austria-Hungary's officials worked on them as well as on a dossier that was meant to prove that Serbia had been plotting against Austria-Hungary for years. To bolster its case the Foreign Ministry sent its legal adviser to Sarajevo to investigate the assassination; unfortunately he was unable to find evidence that the Serbian government was behind it. The dossier in the end proved to be full of errors and was not finished in time to be handed over to the powers along with a copy of the ultimatum. As a result Russia continued to believe the Serbian government when it claimed that it was completely innocent while France and Great Britain found Austria-Hungary had not proved its case.[63]

While there was intense activity behind the scenes in Vienna, the government did its best to give the impression that it was business as usual. Newspapers in both Vienna and Budapest were asked to tone down their comments on Serbia. Tschirschky reported to Berlin that Berchtold had sent Conrad and the War Minister off for their summer holidays to prevent any unease. ('Childish!' noted the Kaiser from his yacht to which he had returned, not suspecting that his own government wanted him out of the way in part for the same reason.)[64] Nevertheless rumours started to circulate that Austria-Hungary was planning something unpleasant for Serbia. The German ambassador in Rome told the Italian Foreign Minister about, among other things, the blank cheque and San Giuliano alerted his ambassadors in St Petersburg and Belgrade, not knowing that the Russians had broken Italy's diplomatic codes.[65] In Vienna the Russian ambassador asked what Austria-Hungary intended to do but was sufficiently reassured, being told that it would wait until its investigation was complete, that he left on his own holidays two days before the ultimatum was presented to Serbia.[66] On 17 July the British ambassador reported to London: 'There is only one topic in the Vienna press, even Albania in its throes being almost crowded out – namely, when will the protest against Serbia be put in, and what will it contain? That there will be a protest nobody doubts, and it will probably be coupled with demands intended to humiliate Serbia.' There was an 'ominous silence' from the Foreign Ministry but he had it on good authority that, if Serbia did not cave in at once, Austria-Hungary would use force and, moreover, that it was sure of Germany's support. He then added a postscript: 'I have just had a talk with Berchtold. He was charming, announced himself for a visit to our place in the country next Sunday, invited us to stay with him at Buchlau, the place of the famous interview between Aehrenthal and Izvolsky, told me he had some horses running in some races shortly, but never mentioned general politics or the Serbians.'[67]

The German government also presented a picture of summer calm, possibly deliberately as historians have later charged in order to lull any suspicions that it was contemplating a war. Jagow returned to Berlin from his honeymoon in the first week of July but the Kaiser toured the North Sea on his usual cruise and most senior civilians and military remained on holiday. The general staff kept to its usual peacetime routine. Waldersee, who was on his father-in-law's estate, wrote to Jagow on 17 July: 'I shall remain here, ready to jump; we are all prepared at the General Staff; in the meantime there is nothing to do.' Nevertheless the main leaders made sure that they were in contact with Berlin. Bethmann in fact had a special telegraph line run through to Hohenfinow.[68] The German government also kept a close eye on what was happening in Vienna. Arthur Zimmermann, the tough Deputy Foreign Secretary who felt the time was right for Austria-Hungary to take its revenge on Serbia, remained at his post in Berlin and repeatedly urged Vienna to speed up its slow pace. He had a pretty good idea of what terms Austria-Hungary intended to present to Serbia by 13 July although the German government claimed then and later that it knew nothing about the contents of any ultimatum.[69]

In Serbia, where the news of the assassination had initially been received with, according to the British chargé d'affaires, 'a sensation rather of stupefaction than of regret', the more rabid of the nationalist press hastened to justify the murders. Pašić, who was in the middle of a difficult election campaign, apparently said on hearing the news, 'It is very bad. It will mean war.' He ordered all hotels and cafés to close by 10 p.m. as a sign of mourning and sent his condolences to Vienna. In spite of pressure from Austria-Hungary, he refused, however, to hold an investigation and gave a defiant interview to a German newspaper denying that his government had anything to do with the assassination.[70]

Apprehension about Austria-Hungary's intentions nevertheless mounted in Serbia and on 10 July was further fuelled by a curious incident in Belgrade. Hartwig, the highly influential Russian ambassador who had done much over the years to fan Serbian ambitions, called in the evening on his counterpart from Austria-Hungary, Baron Wladimir Giesl von Gieslingen. The Russian, who was grossly overweight, was puffing from his exertion. He refused an offer of coffee but pulled out his favourite Russian cigarettes. He wanted to clear up, he said, the unfortunate rumour that he had held a bridge party the night of the assassination and refused to fly the legation's flags at half-mast. Giesl said he considered the matter settled. Hartwig then turned to the main purpose of his visit. 'I ask you', he said, 'in the name of our earnest friendship to answer as fully as you can: what will Austria-Hungary do with Serbia and what has been decided in Vienna?' Giesl followed his government's line: 'I can definitely assure you that the sovereignty of Serbia will not be infringed and that with the good will of the Serbian government, this crisis can find a solution that will please both parties.' Hartwig thanked him profusely and was struggling to his feet when he suddenly collapsed on to the floor and a few moments later died. His family at once blamed Giesl for poisoning him and even wilder rumours went around Belgrade that the Austrians had brought a special electrified chair from Vienna which could kill without leaving a trace. The matter did little to improve relations between Austria-Hungary and Russia, which were already deteriorating. More seriously still, Hartwig's death removed the one man who might have prevailed on the Serbian government to accept even the most outrageous of the demands in the ultimatum.[71]

Although he was by now very worried about what was likely to come, Pašić sent a message on 18 July to all Serbian embassies to say that Serbia would resist any demands from Austria-Hungary which infringed on its sovereignty.[72]

His worries would have become still more acute if he had been aware of a secret meeting that took place in Vienna the following day. Arriving in unmarked cars at Berchtold's house, Austria-Hungary's most powerful men took the decision they knew could lead to a general European war. Berchtold distributed a copy of the ultimatum which he and his officials in the Foreign Ministry had drawn up. Later that year when most of Europe was at war, Berchtold's wife apparently told a friend 'poor Leopold could not sleep on the day when he wrote his ultimatum to the Serbs, as he was so worried that they might accept it. Several times during the night he got up and altered or added some clause, to reduce the risk.'[73] Those present assumed that Serbia would reject the terms and most of the discussion was about Austria-Hungary's mobilisation and other necessary military measures. Conrad said the sooner action came the better and showed no concern at the prospect of Russia's intervention. Tisza insisted, as he had always done, that there should be no annexation of Serbian territory. The meeting agreed but Conrad said cynically to Krobatin, the War Minister, as they left, 'We will see.'[74] Tisza wrote shortly afterwards to his niece that he still hoped war could be avoided but he now put his trust in God. His own mood, he told her, was 'serious but not anxious or restless, because I am like the man on the street corner who could be hit over the head at any moment, but who is always prepared to make the big journey'.[75]

On 20 July, the day following the meeting, Berchtold sent copies of the ultimatum and a covering note to his embassies throughout Europe. The ambassador in Belgrade was to deliver his copy to the Serbian government on the evening of Thursday 23 July while the rest waited until the morning of 24 July. To the annoyance of the Germans, their ally did not get round to giving them a copy of the ultimatum until 22 July.[76] Nevertheless they were prepared to keep their promise of support. On 19 July the *Norddeutsche Allgemeine Zeitung*, which was generally seen as representing the views of the government, published a brief notice to the effect that Austria-Hungary was justified in wanting to set its relations with Serbia in order. Serbia, it went on, should give way and the other European powers should stay out so that any conflict between the two antagonists could remain localised. On 21 July Bethmann sent a telegram to his ambassadors in London, Paris, and St Petersburg asking them to make the same points to their host governments. The following day Jules Cambon, the French ambassador in Berlin, asked Jagow for details of what was in the ultimatum. Jagow replied that he had no idea. 'I was all the more astonished at this', Cambon reported mordantly to Paris, 'since Germany is about to take her stand at Austria's side with particular vigour.'[77]

Berchtold still needed formal approval from the old emperor and so on the morning of 20 July, accompanied by Hoyos, he travelled out to Ischl. Franz Joseph read the document through and commented that some of the conditions it contained were very harsh. He was right. The ultimatum accused the Serbian government of tolerating criminal activities on its soil and demanded that it take immediate steps to end them, including dismissing any civilian or military officials Austria-Hungary chose to name, closing down nationalist newspapers and reforming the education curriculum to get rid of anything that could be construed as propaganda directed against Austria-Hungary. More, the ultimatum infringed Serbia's sovereignty. In two clauses, which in the end were to be the sticking point for Serbia, it was ordered to accept the participation of the Dual Monarchy in suppressing subversion within Serbia's borders and in the investigation and trial of any Serbian conspirators responsible for the assassinations. The Serbian government was to be given forty-eight hours to respond. The emperor nevertheless approved the ultimatum as it stood. Berchtold and Hoyos stayed to lunch and returned to Vienna that evening.[78]

On 23 July Giesl, Austria-Hungary's ambassador in Belgrade, made an appointment to visit the Foreign Ministry late that afternoon. Pašić was away campaigning so Giesl was received by Laza Paču, the Finance Minister, who was chain-smoking. Giesl started to read out the ultimatum but the Serbian interrupted him after the first sentence, saying he did not have authority to receive such a document in Pašić's absence. Giesl was adamant; Serbia had until 6 p.m. on 25 July to make its response. He laid the ultimatum on a table and left. There was a deathly silence as the Serbian officials absorbed the contents. Finally, the Minister of the Interior spoke: 'We have no other choice than to fight it out.' Paču rushed to the Russian chargé d'affaires and begged him for Russia's support. The regent Prince Alexander said that Austria-Hungary would meet 'an iron fist' if it attacked Serbia and the Serbian Defence Minister took preliminary steps to prepare for the country's defence. For all the defiant rhetoric, however, Serbia was in a poor condition to fight. It was still recovering from the Balkan wars and a large part of its army was in the south holding down the unruly new territories it had acquired. Over the next two days its government desperately sought to escape the doom that hung over Serbia. It had faced Austria-Hungary's anger before in the Bosnian crisis and in the First and Second Balkan Wars yet it had always managed to survive through a combination of its own conces- sions and pressure on Austria-Hungary from the Concert of Europe.[79]

Pašić arrived back in Belgrade at 5 a.m. the next morning, 'very anxious and dejected' according to the British chargé d'affaires. Plans were being made for the government to leave the capital and to mine the bridges over the Sava which marked the border with Austria- Hungary. The Russian ambassador reported that funds from the national bank and government files were being shipped out and that the Serbian army had started to mobilise. The Serbian cabinet met for hours on 24 July trying to draft a response to the ultimatum; it ended by accepting all the demands except the two which gave Austria-Hungary the right to interfere in Serbia's internal affairs. The Serbians tried to buy time by asking Vienna to extend the deadline but Berchtold curtly told their ambassador that he expected a satisfactory reply – or else. Pašić also sent out urgent requests to Europe's capitals for support. He seems to have hoped that the other great powers, France, Britain, Italy and Russia but possibly even Germany, would come together as they had before in crises in the Balkans to impose a settlement. The responses, if they came at all, were discouraging. In Serbia's immediate neighbourhood, Greece and Rumania made it clear that they were unlikely to come its aid in a war with Austria-Hungary while Montenegro, true to form, made vague promises which could not be relied upon. Britain, Italy and France advised that Serbia do its best to compromise and in those early days showed little inclination to mediate.

The only power which offered anything stronger was Russia and even there the message it sent was mixed. On 24 July Sazonov told the Serbian ambassador in St Petersburg that he found the ultimatum dis- gusting and promised Russia's help, but said that he would have to consult with the tsar and with the French before he could offer any- thing concrete. If Serbia decided to fight, the Russian Foreign Minister added helpfully, it would be wise to go on the defensive and retreat southwards. On 25 July, as the deadline approached, Sazonov had a more robust message for the ambassador. Russia's key ministers had now met with the tsar and decided, so it was reported to Belgrade, 'to go to the limit in defense of Serbia'. While this still did not constitute a firm promise of military support, it may well have encouraged the Serbian government as it prepared its final reply to Austria-Hungary.

Belgrade was very hot that day and the city reverberated with the sound of drums beating to call up the conscripts.[80]

Among the Entente nations, whose leaders had not really focussed up to this point on the developing crisis in the Balkans, the reaction to the ultimatum was one of shock and dismay and they scrambled to work out their own positions. Poincaré and his Prime Minister Viviani were by now on board a ship in the Baltic and were having difficulties in communicating with Paris and with their allies. Separately Grey in London and Sazonov in Russia asked Austria-Hungary to extend the deadline. Berchtold refused to budge.

Reactions were different in Germany and Austria-Hungary, where nationalist and military circles greeted the news with enthusiasm. The German military attaché in Vienna reported, 'Today, a heightened mood dominates the war ministry. Finally a sign of awakening energy in the monarchy even if for now only on paper.' The main fear was that, yet again, Serbia would wriggle out of its punishment. From Sarajevo on the day the deadline was to expire the military commander wrote to a friend: 'With what pleasure and bliss would I sacrifice my old bones and my life, if it will successfully humble the assassin-state and put an end to this harbour for murderous children – God grant us only that we stay resolute and that today at 6 p.m. in Belgrade the die rolls in our favour!'[81]

The Serbian reply which Pašić brought to Giesl shortly before the deadline granted this wish. While its tone was conciliatory, the Serbian government refused to concede on the crucial points of Austria-Hungary's interference in Serbia's internal affairs. Saying, 'we place our hopes on your loyalty and chivalry as an Austrian general', Pašić shook Giesl's hand and left. The ambassador, who had already assumed the reply would be unsatisfactory, gave the document a cursory glance. His instructions from Berchtold were clear: if Serbia did not accept all the conditions, he must break off diplomatic relations. In fact he had already prepared the note doing so. While a messenger took it to Pašić, Giesl burned the embassy code books in his garden. He, his wife and his staff, with one small piece of hand luggage each, made their way by car to the railway station through streets jammed with crowds. A large part of the diplomatic corps had come to see them off. Serbian troops guarded the train and as it puffed out one shouted to the departing military attaché:

'Au revoir à Budapest.' At the first stop in Austria-Hungary, Giesl was called to the platform to take a phone call from Tisza. 'Must it really be like this?' the Hungarian asked. 'Yes', replied Giesl. In Ischl far to the north Franz Joseph and Berchtold were anxiously waiting for news. Just after 6 p.m. the War Ministry in Vienna phoned to say that relations with Serbia had been ruptured. The emperor's first reaction was 'So after all!' but after a silence he mused that breaking off relations need not necessarily lead to war. Berchtold also clutched briefly at that straw but he had now set in motion forces which he did not have the strength of character to resist.[82]

Conrad, who had been leading the hawks, suddenly demanded a delay in Austria-Hungary's formal declaration of war until the second week of August on the grounds that his armies would not be ready until then. Berchtold, who feared that any delay would give time for the other powers to insist on negotiations and who was also under pressure from Germany to move quickly, refused and on 28 July Austria-Hungary declared war on Serbia, although the serious fighting was not going to start until the second week of August. Austria-Hungary and Germany, with help from Serbia, had got Europe to this dangerous point. Much now depended on what the other powers did. In the next week Europe was to hang between war and peace.

CHAPTER 19

The End of the Concert of Europe: Austria-Hungary Declares War on Serbia

In the middle of July that indefatigable couple, Beatrice and Sidney Webb, were at a Fabian summer camp talking about Control of Industry and Insurance and complaining about an unruly group of Oxford students who sang revolutionary songs and drank too much beer. Troubles on the Continent caught their attention from time to time but, as Sidney said, war among the powers 'would be too insane'.[1] Indeed, the main issue that was worrying foreign offices and the press across Europe for most of the month was not Serbia but the deteriorating situation in Albania, where its new ruler, a hapless German prince called William of Wied, was facing widespread revolt and civil war. The Austrian ultimatum to Serbia on 23 July was the first indication for most Europeans that a much more serious confrontation was shaping up in the Balkans, and when Serbia's reply was rejected by Vienna on 25 July, concern started to turn to alarm. Harry Kessler who had been spending a pleasant few weeks visiting friends in London and Paris, among them Asquith, Lady Randolph Churchill, Diaghilev and Rodin, began to think seriously about heading back to Germany.[2]

Yet many of those close to the centres of power assumed that war could still be avoided, as it had been in other similar crises. On 27 July, Theodor Wolff, the editor of the *Berliner Tageblatt*, one of Germany's leading newspapers, took his family on their annual holiday to the Dutch seaside, although he himself returned to Berlin. Jagow, the Foreign Secretary, told him that the situation was not critical, that none of the major powers wanted war, and that Wolff was quite safe to leave his family in the Netherlands. Even those whose business was fighting found it difficult to believe that this time the crisis was a serious one; as a member of Germany's general staff wrote in his diary after the war had broken out, 'If anyone had told me then that the world would be ablaze a month later, I would have only looked at him with pity. For, after the various events of the last years, the Morocco-Algeciras crisis, the annexation crisis of Bosnia-Herzegovina, one had slowly but surely lost the belief in war.'[3]

Even in Russia, where trouble in the Balkans tended to raise alarms, reaction to the news of the assassination was marked at first more by indifference than apprehension. The Duma had already risen for the summer and there seemed no need to call it back. The Russian ambassador in Vienna assured his government, 'There is already reason to suppose that at least in the immediate future the course of Austro-Hungarian policy will be more restrained and calm.'[4] Nevertheless, like its ally France and its rivals Germany and Austria-Hungary the Russia of 1914 was apprehensive about the future. Britain did not seem anxious to conclude a naval agreement and Persia remained a source of tension. Russia was also engaged in a struggle with Austria-Hungary for influence over Bulgaria, which it appeared to be losing, and it faced challenges from both its own ally France and Germany in the Ottoman Empire. A 'Teutonic ring', an influential St Petersburg newspaper had warned at the end of 1913, 'threatens Russia and the whole of Slavdom with fatal consequences …'[5] In May the chief of Russia's police forces had passed on a warning to the Russian general staff that his spies were telling him that Germany was ready to find a pretext to strike while it still had a chance of winning.[6] For the Russian government the domestic situation was even more troubling than the international; in May and June the value of the rouble was going down and there were worries about a coming depression. There had been strikes and demonstrations all year across Russia and July was going to see more than in any previous month.[7]

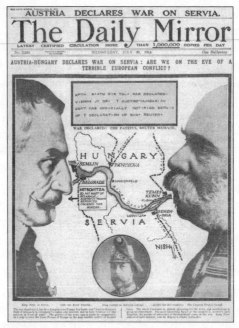

19. As the headline suggests – 'Are we on the eve of a terrible European conflict?' – the crisis unfolding in the Balkans in July 1914 took most of Europe by surprise. With the death of the Archduke, Austria-Hungary issued an ultimatum to Serbia, designed to be unacceptable. The Serbian government went a considerable way to accepting its terms but on 28 July Austria-Hungary declared war. Here King Peter I of Serbia faces the Emperor Franz Joseph while in the small insert, the British king George V appears dressed in the uniform of an Austrian colonel, a sign of older and now vanished friendships.

By that time the tsar and his family, who had spent much of the spring in the Crimea, partly for the sake of Alexandra's nerves, were back in their seclusion outside St Petersburg. The empress's condition did not improve when her haemophiliac son fell while aboard one of the imperial yachts early in July and bled badly. To make matters still worse for her, Rasputin was thousands of miles away. He had been stabbed in the stomach by a madwoman the same day the archduke was assassinated in Sarajevo. Although the tsar sent the imperial surgeon to care for him, Rasputin was too ill to travel until later in the summer. It was perhaps unfortunate that he was far from the centre of the events that were about to unfold for he was a committed pacifist and had counselled the tsar against going to war during the First Balkan Wars. From his sickbed, Rasputin sent a telegram which warned: 'A terrible storm cloud hangs over Russia. Disaster, grief, murky darkness and no light. A whole ocean of tears ... and so much blood. What can I say? I can find no words to describe the horror.'[8]

On the other side of Europe, in Britain, the Foreign Office initially took much the same calm attitude to the assassination as the Russian ambassador in Vienna. Nicolson, the Permanent Undersecretary, doubted that Austria-Hungary would take any action against Serbia. British opinion at first was quite sympathetic to the Dual Monarchy. King George V called unannounced on its embassy the morning after the assassinations to express his sorrow and Count Albert Mensdorff, its ambassador, was gratified to receive scores of letters from his many friends among the British upper classes. Grey and Asquith as well as leading Conservatives made speeches of commiseration in Parliament but it was another death – that of Joseph Chamberlain on 2 July – that caused a much greater sense of loss.[9] In a debate on foreign affairs in the House of Commons on 10 July, Grey mentioned the Balkans only briefly, spending most of his time on non-European matters. Asquith, who was by now in the grip of his passion for Venetia Stanley and writing her daily love letters, mentioned the assassinations in passing on 30 June and did not refer to them again until 24 July. His letters were mostly taken up with the Irish question, her pets, which included a penguin, and his longing to see her.[10]

For the British public and their leaders, the continuing crisis over Home Rule for Ireland and the accompanying threat of civil war was a far more immediate and pressing concern than events in a far-off part of Europe. In a last-ditch attempt to get agreement over which parts of Protestant Ulster should be exempted from the Home Rule Bill still making its way slowly through Parliament, the king postponed his summer holidays and called a conference at Buckingham Palace on 21 July. For four swelteringly hot days Asquith and John Redmond, the leader of the Irish nationalists, faced the Conservative leader Bonar Law and Carson, the spokesman for the Ulster Protestants, as they tried in vain to come to an agreement. On 24 July, as the conference broke up, news came in of Austria-Hungary's ultimatum to Serbia. George V decided that he would have to prolong his stay in London and cancelled his usual visit to the races with his friend the Duke of Richmond. 'The political crisis', he wrote to the duke, 'is so acute with regard to the Irish question and now the probability of a general European war necessitates my remaining in London for the present ... I hope you will have fine weather and that the racing will be good.'[11] Asquith took, at least at first, a more sanguine view of the growing European crisis 'This will take attention away from Ulster, which is a good thing,' he told a leading London hostess.[12]

The French were slow as well to awaken to the developing dangers. It was just a bit of trouble in the Balkans, thought Adolphe Messimy, who had just come back into office as War Minister. 'It would sort itself out just as the others had.'[13] At the Quai d'Orsay, the Foreign Ministry was taken up with plans for the forthcoming visit by the President, Poincaré, and his Prime Minister, Viviani, to St Petersburg. Most of the cables between Paris and the French ambassador to Russia, Maurice Paléologue, were more concerned with such matters as the exact wording of the toasts to be made than with the Balkans.

French politicians and the general public were largely preoccupied by a sensational scandal involving the wife of the leading Radical politician Joseph Caillaux. He was accused by his enemies of being corrupt, which was probably true, and friendly to Germany, which was certainly true. He was after all a realist who believed that Germany and France had much to gain from working together. As Prime Minister at the time of the second crisis over Morocco, he had done much to bring a peaceful solution. He was hated by French nationalists for this and for opposing the introduction of three years' compulsory military service designed to enlarge the French army. (Almost as bad, he had advocated the introduction of an income tax.) In the first months of 1914, Gaston Calmette, editor of the leading Paris daily *Figaro*, mounted a savage campaign against him with articles carrying such titles as 'Shady Financier' and 'Germany's Man'. In addition Calmette had managed to get his hands on some indiscreet love letters which Caillaux had written to his second wife Henriette while she was still married to someone else and was threatening to publish them. On 16 March Henriette, who was beautifully dressed as always, went to *Figaro*'s offices. When she was shown in to see Calmette, she pulled a Browning pistol out of her fur muff and emptied it into him. Saying to the horrified staff, 'There's no more justice in France. It was the only thing to do,' she waited calmly to be arrested for the murder. Her trial started on 20 July. Eight days later, as Austria-Hungary declared war on Serbia, the jury acquitted her on the grounds that she had committed a crime of passion. An unfortunate consequence of her action was that her husband, who might well have been a voice of moderation in France as Europe moved towards war, had been obliged to resign from the government.[14]

Towards the end of July the fresh trouble brewing in the Balkans began to move to the front pages of Europe's press. The stock exchanges grew jittery as rumours spread that Austria-Hungary intended to force a showdown with Serbia and that Russia was determined to back its little ally this time. Surely, though, people thought, the crisis would, in the end, play out as earlier ones had. There would be some back and forth of diplomatic notes, perhaps even military preparations by Austria-Hungary and Russia as a means of exerting pressure, but eventually the other powers would intervene and broker a settlement and the armies would stand down. The Concert of Europe would maintain the peace, as it had done for so long. 'Bluff, everything a bluff', Kiderlen the German Foreign Secretary had written in 1912 during the First Balkan War. 'I'll live to see it now for the third time: Algeciras, Morocco, and now this. Only now, one always attempts to trump the other with bluffs. War could only happen if one were so unfathomably foolish to bluff so badly as to be unable to go back down on it and had to shoot. I really consider none of the current coming statesmen an example of such oxen.'[15] Kiderlen did not live long enough to see how wrong he had been. His death is yet another example, like that of the archduke's assassination, Rasputin's stabbing or Caillaux's forced resignation, of the role of accident in history. If Kiderlen had been in office in the summer of 1914, he might just have been strong enough to stand up to the military and persuade Bethmann and the Kaiser to take the path of peace.

The crisis in July 1914 was initially created by the recklessness of Serbia, the vengefulness of Austria-Hungary and the blank cheque from Germany. Now it was increasingly the turn of the Entente powers to do what they could either to avert war or, if it came, to bring it about on favourable terms for themselves. While many of the historical debates have centred on the question of Germany's or Austria-Hungary's or even Serbia's culpability for the war, others have placed the blame on the Triple Entente, whether on France for following a policy of revenge against Germany, on Russia for the alliance with France and for backing Serbia, or on Britain for not recognising Germany's legitimate demands for a place in the sun and a greater share of the world's colonies or for not making it clear early in the crisis that it would intervene on the side of France and Russia. While these have fascinated and will continue to fascinate historians and political scientists, we may have to accept that there can never be a definitive answer because for every argument there is a strong counter. Was France really intent on revenge on Germany? Even nationalists such as Poincaré had resigned themselves to the loss of Alsace and Lorraine and were not prepared to risk war to regain the provinces. True, France's treaty with Russia led Germany to feel encircled but from both the French and Russian points of view the treaty was a defensive one, triggered only if Germany attacked. (As so often in international relations, though, what is defensive from one perspective may appear a threat from another, and that is certainly how Germany saw the treaty.) How much responsibility should Russia bear for encouraging Serbian nationalism? Sazonov should have done more to keep his ambassador Hartwig under control but for all the Panslav rhetoric in nationalist circles not all Russia's leaders wanted to come to Serbia's defence if it meant risking another major conflict so soon after the catastrophic defeat in the Russo-Japanese War. As for Britain, while an early declaration that it would unhesitatingly fight on France's side might have acted as a deterrent on Germany, that is not at all clear. The German military regarded the British Expeditionary Force as negligible and hoped to win in France long before naval power came into play. In any case, Britain could not have made such a declaration before the Cabinet approved it – and the Cabinet was deeply divided over what to do in the last weeks before the war broke out.

Of the three entente powers, France had the most straightforward policy in 1914 – to make sure that if war came France would enter it united, as the innocent party, and with Russia by its side. The French also hoped to restrain their ally from acting provocatively in ways which would allow Germany and Austria-Hungary to claim that they were merely defending themselves against Russian aggression. As an emergency meeting of the Cabinet on 30 July stressed, 'For the sake of public opinion, let the Germans put themselves in the wrong.'[16] This was important both domestically and internationally. French leaders were haunted by the memories of the defeats of the 1870–71 war and France's long isolation afterwards, by France's own internal divisions, by the knowledge of France's demographic weakness in comparison with Germany and by fears that its allies would not stand by it. The French hoped for but never completely counted on Britain's intervening even if Germany, as was widely suspected, intended to violate Belgium's neutrality. It was essential for France, however, that Russia moved quickly to attack German forces in the east when war broke out. In the years immediately before 1914, the French had done their utmost to get a firm commitment from Russia that it would attack Germany early to relieve the pressure of the expected German onslaught on France. With huge loans for Russia's railway building and industrial development, the French managed to extract promises from the Russian military but they were never entirely sure that these would be kept. Even Russia's growing power was a double-edged sword for France, which was in danger of becoming the junior partner. Worse still, Russia might become so strong that it no longer needed the French alliance.[17]

There was always the danger, too – and this also haunted the French – that the conservatives in Russia who continued to argue for a rapprochement with Germany would gain the upper hand. Paléologue, who sent alarmist reports back to Paris, told the British ambassador in May 1914, 'The Emperor is changeable and the Ministry is not stable. There has always been a party at court in favour of an understanding with Germany.'[18] Just as Germany backed Austria-Hungary for fear of losing it, so too France in the summer of 1914 was reluctant to rein Russia in as it moved towards a confrontation in the Balkans. Jaurès, the great socialist leader, whose grasp of foreign affairs was profound, said in the French parliament on 7 July as the forthcoming trip of Poincaré and Viviani to St Petersburg was being discussed, 'We find it inadmissible ... that France should become involved in wild Balkan adventures because of treaties of which she knows neither the text, not the sense, nor the limits, nor the consequences.'[19]

Despite opposition from the Socialists, Poincaré and Viviani duly set out on 15 July for Russia, travelling aboard the cruiser *France* to avoid crossing German territory. Although they could not know it, on the previous day Tisza had finally dropped his opposition to Austria-Hungary's ultimatum to Serbia and it was now being finalised in Vienna. As the French warship made its way through the North Sea and into the Baltic, the weather, as it was all over Europe, was glorious and Poincaré sat on the deck reading Ibsen and chatting to Viviani. Even though he was also responsible for foreign affairs, the French Prime Minister knew little about them but, it turned out, he was a walking compendium of literature and recited great chunks of both prose and poetry to his companion. Poincaré's thoughts occasionally turned to the Caillaux trial at home but he was not worried about the international situation, or so he claimed in the version of his diary he published later. He felt sure, he wrote, that he was sailing towards peace, to establishing good relations with other nations, and to reasserting France's alliance with Russia.[20] He was in fact more concerned about the alliance than he admitted; there was a strong possibility that the French parliament might in the autumn reverse the hard-won three-year military service law, something which could well add further to Russian doubts about France's value as an ally.[21]

When the French party landed in Russia on 20 July the tsar himself was there to greet them and they were housed at his great palace of Peterhof just to the west of St Petersburg. (In the city itself, the workers had called a general strike and there was fighting in the streets; Poincaré scandalised his hosts by inquiring about the causes.[22]) The next few days were packed with banquets, receptions, and military reviews. Viviani, who was longing to be back in Paris where the Caillaux trial had reached its climax and where his wayward mistress was enjoying herself, complained incessantly of being bored and tired. He had trouble with his liver and a local French doctor had to be hastily summoned. Poincaré found it impossible to feel much sympathy for his travelling companion: 'He is violent, timid and vulgar, wrapped in a gloomy silence.'[23]

The important part of the trip occurred behind the scenes, in the private conversations between the French and the Russians but unfortunately we know very little about what was said. The records are sketchy at best and it may well be that some were destroyed. The two sides talked, it is known, about the tensions between Russia and Britain over

Persia and the French urged the Russians to pursue a naval agreement with the British.[24] According to the British ambassador, he was reliably informed afterwards by Sazonov and the French ambassador that the conversations had dealt as well with Austria-Hungary and Serbia and that France and Russia intended to make a joint approach to Vienna to warn it against threatening Serbia's independence.[25] Certainly, the situation in the Balkans was much on the minds of both the Russian and the French leaders. At a reception for the diplomatic corps in St Petersburg on the evening of 21 June Poincaré told the ambassador from Austria-Hungary that no country could be held responsible for plots made on their territory. Serbia had 'friends' including Russia which would be 'astonished' if Austria-Hungary took any strong measures. The ambassador sent a warning to Berchtold in Vienna, who chose to ignore it.[26] While there is no evidence that the French and Russians plotted to provoke a war with Germany, they were talking openly of the possibility of a conflict by 22 July, something, according to a French attaché in St Petersburg, 'which no one had even dreamt of a few days earlier'.[27]

The Russians, who had become increasingly concerned by the rumours that were coming out of Vienna, were sending out their own warnings even before the French arrived. On 8 July Sazonov told the Austrian-Hungarian chargé d'affaires that any attempt by Vienna to interfere in Serbia's internal affairs would be a dangerous step which would make 'a very bad impression' in Russia.[28] A week later, at a summer party, a high-ranking official from the Russian Foreign Ministry asked the Italian ambassador to convey a message to Austria-Hungary that Russia would not stand for any threat to the independence of Serbia. Two days afterwards Sazonov made a point of talking to Baron Friedrich Szápáry, Austria-Hungary's ambassador, about Russia's concerns. Szápáry was most reassuring – 'gentle as a lamb', said Sazonov – saying that his government had a deep love of peace and did not want to make its relations with Serbia any more difficult than they were.[29] So for the time being the Russian government waited to see what would happen.

It was Russia's misfortune, and the world's, that its leadership was so inadequate as it was about to head into a major international storm. Sazonov himself as well as the tsar were inclined towards peace but both men were weak and easily swayed; both too had a strong sense of

Russia's honour and dignity and remembered with resentment how it had been forced to back down in earlier crises in the Balkans. Goremykin, the Prime Minister, was a nonentity and the dominant figures in the Council of Ministers were Alexander Krivoshein, the Minister of Agriculture, who was a hardliner when it came to Russia's prestige abroad, and Sukhomlinov, who was reckless and whose pride made him insist that Russia's armed forces were ready for any eventuality.[30] General Nicholas Yanushkevich, the chief of staff, had been in office for only five months and had few obvious qualifications for the post beyond having the tsar's favour. The British military attaché said the appointment 'excited general surprise. He gave the impression rather of a courtier than of a soldier.'[31] Among the other top military leaders, Grand Duke Nicholas Nikolaevich had both experience and common sense but he was to be an advocate of early mobilisation even at the risk of war as the crisis intensified. His wife, one of the many children of the king of Montenegro who had married well, was a passionate and uncritical supporter of Serbia. 'There's going to be war,' she exclaimed to Paléologue on 21 July during Poincaré's visit. 'There'll be nothing left of Austria … Our armies will meet in Berlin, Germany will be destroyed.'[32]

Another influential voice for war was the French ambassador in St Petersburg. Paléologue hated Germany and had long been convinced that a major conflict with it was inevitable. Clever, devious, emotional and vain, he had climbed steadily upwards in the French foreign service by attaching himself to powerful men, among them Delcassé and Poincaré, whom he had met when they were both students. With aspirations to be a writer as well as a statesman, Paléologue claimed to be descended from an ancient and noble Byzantine family, but his many enemies claimed that his parents – a Greek exile from Rumania and a Belgian musician mother – came from humble, even dubious backgrounds. When he was appointed to St Petersburg in January 1914 to replace Delcassé, the French Prime Minister, then Gaston Doumergue, told him that war could break out at any time and that France's safety depended on how quickly its allies came into the fight. Paléologue, who saw himself as an independent actor rather than a servant of his government, made it his duty to foster the Triple Entente and, when war came, bring Russia in on the side of France.[33] On 24 July, as news of the

Austrian ultimatum to Serbia became known and when Poincaré and Viviani had already sailed homewards, he had the British ambassador Sir George Buchanan and Sazonov to lunch. The Russian Foreign Minister was angry about Austria-Hungary's move, which he described as 'immoral and provocative'. He hoped, Buchanan reported to London, that Britain would immediately proclaim its solidarity with France and Russia. Paléologue was even more vehement: 'From French Ambassador's language it almost looked as if France and Russia were determined to make a strong stand even if we declined to join them. Language of Minister for Foreign Affairs, however, was not so decided on this subject.'[34] In the next days Paléologue repeated the assurances of France's support for Russia, to Sazonov himself but also to the Italian ambassador who may well have passed news of this French position to Austria-Hungary and Germany.[35]

Paléologue may have exceeded his instructions but he was close to Poincaré who himself had assured the Russians of French support in the crisis. In his parting meeting with the tsar, Poincaré told him that their two countries must work closely together if Austria-Hungary and Germany attacked Serbia. 'The more difficult the situation gets, the more united and close we will have to be'. The two men apparently also talked at length about how Russia and France might co-operate militarily.[36] This was not, of course, the first time such discussions had taken place; for over a decade the Russian and the French military had made plans together for a war against Germany and their links, including direct wireless communication, had become tighter with time.[37] In July 1914, given their anger with Austria-Hungary, the Russians would have made up their own minds about going to war but the French did not want to deter them. Indeed, like their German counterparts, many French leaders thought that, if war were to come, the present was the best time. In June 1914, a general staff report noted that Rumania was now a potential enemy for Austria-Hungary and Russia was more of a threat to Germany.[38]

Sazonov's first reaction on the morning of 24 July when he learned of the ultimatum was 'This means a European war'. The tsar, who was attending summer army manoeuvres at the village of Krasnoye Selo, south of St Petersburg, said merely 'This is disturbing'. Initially he at least believed Wilhelm's assurances that Germany did not know anything about the ultimatum and took comfort in the Kaiser's reminder that Germany and Russia had always managed to come to an agreement in previous crises. The Council of Ministers met in emergency meeting at Krasnoye Selo that afternoon. While Sazonov still hoped war might be avoided, he took the position that Russia could not allow Austria-Hungary to destroy its influence in the Balkans by crushing Serbia. Privately, as he commented later, surprisingly to the ambassador of Austria-Hungary, he resented the demands that Serbia made on Russia and the way in which it dragged its larger ally into conflicts but he saw no alternative now but to offer support. Russia's prestige and Russian public opinion would demand no less.[39] Krivoshein, in a speech that was significant in swaying the others, said Russia had to take a firm stand even at the risk of war. His colleague Peter Bark, who was usually a voice of caution, agreed: 'When it comes to honour and dignity of Russia and its whole existence as a great power the Finance Minister should join the majority of the Cabinet.' The Council decided to work with the other powers including Germany to try to persuade Austria-Hungary to allow time for a diplomatic solution by extending the deadline for Serbia's reply to the ultimatum. To add pressure, however, the Council also authorised the mobilising of the Baltic and Black Sea Fleets and a partial mobilisation of Russia's army in four military districts. While this mobilisation posed more of a threat to Austria-Hungary than Germany, it was still a highly risky move for it challenged the Dual Alliance to respond. As it turned out, it was also militarily impractical for the army had no developed plans for a mobilisation against Austria-Hungary alone. As Goremykin summed up Russia's policy at the end of the meeting, 'We do not want a war, but do not fear it.' That evening Sazonov told the visibly upset German ambassador of Russia's extreme displeasure with the ultimatum.[40]

The following day, as the deadline for Serbia's reply to the Austrian ultimatum was approaching, the Russian attitude was hardening. 'Russia', Sazonov told Buchanan, who duly cabled to London, 'cannot allow Austria to crush Serbia and become predominant Power in the Balkans, and, secure of support of France, she will face all the risks of war.' Paléologue, who was also present when the two men met, declared that France was ready to fight at Russia's side and demanded to know whether Britain would stand by its friends. The British would have to choose, Sazonov added, between giving Russia active support or losing its friendship.[41] The Russian Council of Ministers, which had met again that morning, had already approved further warlike measures. All fortresses were to be placed on a war footing, frontier posts fully manned, and the preliminary measures for mobilisation in the remaining military districts undertaken. Russia's most senior generals apparently saw this at the time as a step towards general mobilisation and war.[42] Although the Russians continued to deny for several days that they were doing anything out of the ordinary – Sukhomlinov gave the German military attaché his word of honour on 26 July – observers crossing Russia's western border saw signs of increased military activity everywhere.[43]

That night a retired Russian diplomat was having dinner with a friend at his villa on the road between Peterhof and Krasnoye Selo when they heard a regiment marching past towards St Petersburg: 'We all rushed out to the garden gate and stood there looking at the giant forms of the guardsmen tramping silently on the dusty road in the summer twilight. I shall never forget the sinister impression of impending doom this sight produced on me.'[44] Whether or not that doom came depended ultimately on one man, just as it did in Germany and Austria-Hungary. Despite the new constitution of 1906 the tsar still controlled foreign policy and the military. As Jules Cambon, the French ambassador in Berlin, told a colleague just after Austria-Hungary's ultimatum to Serbia, 'Today the fate of France and the conservation of the peace of Europe depend upon a foreign will, that of the Tsar. What will he decide and on what advice?'[45]

While the Russian government was stepping towards war, Poincaré and Viviani, as the government of Austria-Hungary had intended, were at sea, from 24 July onwards able to communicate only intermittently with Paris and French embassies abroad. When news of the ultimatum reached the *France* as it sailed towards Stockholm, Viviani hastily sent a cable, probably written by Poincaré, to St Petersburg with a request that it then be forwarded on to Paris and London. It recommended that Serbia accept all the conditions in the ultimatum compatible with its honour and independence. The cable also suggested that the Triple Entente internationalise the issue by asking for an international inquiry into Serbia's complicity rather than allowing Austria-Hungary to conduct one on its own.[46] The hope that somehow the moribund Concert of Europe might come to life again and settle yet another European crisis was one that the French, the Italians, and in particular the British were to grasp at in the next few days.

Poincaré and Viviani also discussed abandoning their scheduled visits to the Scandinavian countries and setting course immediately for France but they decided that this might cause offence to their hosts and unnecessary alarm at home. So they continued around the Baltic, growing increasingly worried as the news from the Balkans worsened. Since the Germans were now jamming all radio transmissions between the *France* and Paris (as well as those between France itself and Russia), it was difficult to send and receive messages. In Paris their colleagues decided on their own initiative to take precautionary measures. Staff officers were called back from leave and troops sent to guard railways and other key sites. General Joffre, chief of the general staff, later claimed that he had no illusions about the gravity of the situation: 'We were headed straight for war and Russia was going to find herself drawn in at the same time as ourselves.' He and the War Minister assured the Russian military attaché that France stood ready to fulfil its alliance. By the end of the month France had gone a considerable way towards preparing itself for war and in the towns and cities shops that sold men's clothing were starting to display heavy boots and thick socks.[47]

While the French government had been playing a largely passive role in the period between Austria-Hungary's ultimatum to Serbia and its declaration of war on 28 July, Britain had finally directed its attention away from Ireland to the Continent and started to take action. Grey had been slow – too slow – to grasp the extent of the danger that was looming in the Balkans and unwilling to admit to himself that Britain was in any way constrained by its membership of the Triple Entente. On 9 July the German ambassador Prince Karl von Lichnowsky found him cheerful and optimistic that the situation could be sorted out. Britain would of course, Grey insisted, exercise its customary free hand but, he added, it was very close to France and Russia. He did admit that there had been some 'conversations' with the French on military issues but gave the impression that they amounted to very little. In a meeting a week later he warned Lichnowsky that if public opinion in Russia grew aroused about Serbia, Britain would have to 'humour Russian sensibilities'.[48] He did not choose to explain to the German just how concerned he and the Foreign Office were about relations with Russia. A new source of tension had arisen over control of oil in Mesopotamia (now part of Iraq); the struggle for influence in Persia continued; and the government of India was making worried noises about Russian intrigues in Afghanistan. Nicolson and his colleagues in the Foreign Office were not at all confident that the Anglo-Russian Convention of 1907 could be renewed when that came up in 1915. 'I am also haunted by the same fear as you', Nicolson wrote to Buchanan in St Petersburg earlier that spring, '– lest Russia should become tired of us and strike a bargain with Germany.'[49] As the crisis worsened in July 1914 Grey and his officials were reluctant to pressure Russia too strongly to back down in its confrontation with Austria-Hungary for fear that they would drive Russia into Germany's arms. (Germany, of course, had a similar fear: that it had to back Austria-Hungary or risk losing its only significant ally.) On 28 July, the day Austria-Hungary declared war on Serbia, Nicolson wrote privately to Buchanan, 'I foresaw as well as you did that this crisis might be taken by Russia as a test of our friendship, and that were we to disappoint her all hope of a friendly and permanent understanding with her would disappear.'[50]

Grey's hope, as the crisis worsened, was for Britain to avoid making hard choices. The powers acting one more time as the Concert of Europe must somehow bring about a settlement, whether through a conference of ambassadors in London, as they had done with success during the First and Second Balkan Wars, or by exerting pressure on those powers most directly involved to negotiate with each other. Perhaps, he suggested, Russia could put pressure on Serbia and Germany on Austria-Hungary? When it became clear that Russia was taking Serbia's part, Grey grasped at the possibility that France, Britain, Germany, and Italy might persuade Russia and Austria-Hungary to talk directly to each other. When Europe passed the milestone of Austria-Hungary's declaration of war on Serbia on 28 July, Grey floated the idea of a halt in Belgrade for Austria-Hungary's forces in order to give time for negotiations. (Wilhelm, who shrank from war when he had actually to confront its reality, came up with a similar suggestion at the same time.) As Grey put forth one proposal after another, however, he also told the French and his own colleagues that, despite all the military and naval conversations over the years, Britain was not bound to France by any obligations or secret treaties and would exercise its own judgement. He was never completely frank with either his colleagues, the British public, or perhaps even with himself about how much he and the military had actually committed Britain to working with France. On the other hand, as he had done so often before, he warned Germany that Britain could not stand by and see France crushed and that it would regard any violation of Belgium's neutrality with strong disfavour.

On 23 July Mensdorff, Austria-Hungary's ambassador in London, gave Grey an indication of the nature of the ultimatum that was about to be presented to Serbia. Apparently, Grey was shocked. That night he and Haldane, the Secretary of State for War, had dinner with the German industrialist Albert Ballin, who had been sent to London by the German government on an unofficial mission to sound out possible British reactions if war broke out on the Continent. As with so many other moments in those last frantic days, recollections differed after the event: Haldane remembered that he and Grey warned Ballin that if Germany attacked France, he should not count on Britain's remaining neutral; Ballin, however, took another message back to Berlin: in his view Britain was concerned mainly with the balance of power on the Continent so that as long as Germany undertook not to swallow up France after any war (perhaps only taking a few French colonies) Britain would not intervene.[51]

The following day Grey read the full text of the ultimatum. 'The note seemed to me', he told Mensdorff, 'the most formidable document I had ever seen addressed by one State to another that was independent.' On Berchtold's instructions, Mensdorff made an unconvincing attempt to play down the document's significance; it was really not so much an ultimatum as a démarche with a time limit, and while Austria-Hungary intended to start military preparations after the deadline, those were not the same thing as military action.[52] At a Cabinet meeting later that day, which was meeting to discuss the failure of the Irish conference at Buckingham Palace, Grey brought up the crisis in the Balkans for the first time and said he was sure that if Russia attacked Austria-Hungary, Germany would defend its ally. While a majority of his colleagues were still firmly opposed to Britain becoming involved in a war, that balance was going to shift over the next week largely as a result of Germany's actions. Grey said sombrely that the ultimatum was bringing them closer to Armageddon than at any time since the First Balkan Wars. His solution was considerably less dramatic: he was going to suggest that Germany, France, Italy and Britain join forces to urge Austria-Hungary and Russia not to take action. The same day, though, Britain also started its first, tentative preparations for war. The whole of the British fleet in home waters had been on summer naval manoeuvres the week before and the government now ordered it to remain mobilised. Like the Russian and French preparatory moves, and the ones about to start in Germany, such manoeuvres may have been defensive in intent but they did not necessarily appear so from outside and so yet another factor came into play to raise the already high levels of tension in Europe.

In the evening of 24 July Grey summoned Lichnowsky and asked that the ambassador tell his government that Britain would be willing to make a joint request with Germany for Austria-Hungary to extend the time limit. The other powers would then have time to defuse the growing quarrel between Austria-Hungary and Russia. 'Useless', scribbled the Kaiser when he read Lichnowsky's report the next day. 'I will not join in it unless Austria expressly asks me to, which is not likely. In *vital* questions and those of honour, one does not consult others.'[53]

On Saturday 25 July, Grey saw Lichnowsky again to discuss the whole situation. The German ambassador was finding it increasingly difficult to defend the position of his own government. A great admirer of Britain and its institutions, he had long advocated a better understanding between London and Berlin. He had been called out of retirement in 1912 to take up his post by the Kaiser, who told him to go and be 'a jolly good fellow'. Bethmann and the Foreign Office disliked the appointment because they felt he lacked experience and was too naïve about the British.[54] In fact, Lichnowsky in the crisis gave consistently good advice: that Germany was following a dangerous course in its encouragement of Austria-Hungary and that, if a general war broke out, Britain would be drawn in. His superiors, he informed them, were dreaming if they really thought that any conflict could be localised in the Balkans.[55] (And, as Nicolson wrote acerbically to Buchanan, 'I think the talk about localising the war merely means that all the Powers are to hold the ring while Austria quietly strangles Serbia.'[56])

That afternoon, as the urgent telegrams continued to fly about Europe, Grey chose to go as usual to his country retreat near Winchester for the weekend.[57] Although he could be reached by telegram, it seems a curious decision in such a rapidly developing situation. Back in London, he learned on Monday 27 July that Germany had abruptly rejected the suggestion of four-power mediation on the grounds, so Jagow claimed, that it would amount to an international court of arbitration and so it could happen only if Russia and Austria-Hungary, the two parties directly concerned, requested it.[58] Britain was by now also under increasing pressure from Russia and France to make its support clear. Buchanan, who had met Sazonov on the Sunday to urge him to work with Austria-Hungary to resolve the situation and to delay Russia's mobilisation in the cause of peace, cabled to London on the Monday that the Russian position had hardened: 'Minister for Foreign Affairs replied that he did not believe that we should succeed in winning over Germany to cause of peace unless we publicly proclaimed our solidarity with France and Russia.'[59] In Paris, Izvolsky told a British diplomat at a dinner party that war was certainly coming and that it was Britain's fault. If only the British had made it clear when the crisis started that they would fight with the Russians and the French, Austria-Hungary and Germany would have hesitated. It was not like the Bosnian crisis, he added ominously, when a weak Russia had been obliged to back down. This time Russia was in a position to fight.[60] On Tuesday 28 July, Paul Cambon, who had rushed back from Paris where he had been advising the government in the absence of Poincaré and Viviani, warned Grey that 'if once it were assumed that Britain would certainly stand aside from a European war, the chance of preserving peace would be very much imperilled'.[61] Cambon, who had devoted his time in London to turning the Entente Cordiale into something more substantial than a warm friendship, had feared from the outset of the crisis that Grey would 'wobble and hesitate' and that Germany would therefore be emboldened to go ahead. 'England is sure to join us in the end,' he nevertheless assured a colleague in Paris, 'but too late.'[62] Cambon was going to suffer agonies in the next week as he tried to get a firm commitment out of Grey.

Across the Continent there were reports of unusual activities. On the weekend of 25–26 July German spies reported increased radio traffic between the Eiffel Tower in Paris and a major Russian military base in western Russia. Russian frontier guards were said to be on full alert and railway rolling stock being moved to Russian towns close to the border with East Prussia.[63] On 26 July Wilhelm, whose government had hoped to keep him safely away in the North Sea, suddenly ordered the German fleet to escort his yacht back to Germany. He feared, apparently, that Russia was planning to torpedo it in a surprise attack. He also felt that Bethmann did not have the proper understanding of military matters.[64] The following day Poincaré and Viviani abruptly cancelled their planned visit to Copenhagen and steamed back towards France. Ripples of nationalist feeling started to disturb the summer calm. In St Petersburg, crowds, small at first but growing in size as the week went on, paraded carrying portraits of Tsar Nicholas and the national flag and singing 'Save Thy people, Lord'.[65] When Nicholas himself attended a local theatre in Krasnoye Selo, the audience gave him several spontaneous standing ovations and army officers who were present broke into song. In Paris crowds demonstrated outside the embassy of Austria-Hungary and in Vienna, 'wildest enthusiasm prevails', reported the British ambassador, as locals tried to demonstrate outside the Russian embassy while officers in uniform received rousing cheers. In Berlin, when the news came of the Serbian response to the Austrian ultimatum, large crowds gathered to sing patriotic songs and the Austrian national anthem. University students marched up and down Unter den Linden singing and chanting patriotic slogans.[66]

In Italy, however, the streets were quiet and the British ambassador reported that opinion condemned both Serbia's role in the assassination and what was seen as an overly harsh reaction by Austria-Hungary. The Italian public was waiting, he noted, in an 'attitude of somewhat anxious expectancy'. The government, in his view, was looking for a plausible reason to evade the obligations of its membership of the Triple Alliance.[67] The dilemma for the Italian government was that it did not want to see Austria-Hungary destroy Serbia and so be supreme in the Balkans but, on the other hand, it did not want to antagonise its alliance partners and particularly Germany. (The Italians like many other Europeans had a healthy, even exaggerated respect for German military power.) An actual European war presented a further problem still: if Germany and

Austria-Hungary won, Italy would be left even more at their mercy and become a sort of vassal state. War on the side of the Dual Alliance would also be unpopular at home, where public opinion still tended to view Austria-Hungary as the traditional enemy which had bullied and oppressed Italians just as it was now doing with Serbians. A final consideration was Italy's own weakness. Its navy would be decimated if it had to fight the British and French navies and its army badly needed a period of recovery after the war with the Ottoman Empire over Libya. Indeed, Italian forces were still fighting a strong resistance in their new North African territories.[68]

San Giuliani, Italy's wise and experienced Foreign Minister, was spending July in Fiuggi Fonte in the hills south of Rome in a vain attempt to cure his debilitating gout. (The local waters were famous for curing kidney stones as well and had a testimonial from Michelangelo, who said it cured him of 'the only kind of stone I couldn't love'.) The German ambassador to Italy visited him there on 24 July to pass on the details of the ultimatum. Despite considerable pressure from both Germany and Austria-Hungary, San Giuliani took the position then and in the ensuing weeks that Italy was not obliged to enter any war which was clearly not a defensive one but that it might decide to join in under certain circumstances – the offer of territory inhabited by Italian speakers from Austria-Hungary in particular. And if Austria-Hungary made gains in the Balkans Italy would have to be compensated as well. On 2 August the government of Austria-Hungary, which rudely referred to Italians as unreliable rabbits, reluctantly gave way to pressure from Germany and made a vague offer of compensation of territory, not including, however, any from Austria-Hungary itself and only if Italy entered the war. The following day, Italy declared that it would remain neutral.[69]

In Britain during that last week of July, public opinion was also deeply divided with both the strong radical wing of the Liberal Party and the Labour Party opposed to war. When the Cabinet met on the afternoon of Monday 27 July it was split down the middle. Grey, equivocating, did not propose a clear course of action. On the one hand, he said, if Britain failed to join France and Russia,

we should forfeit naturally their confidence for ever, and Germany would almost certainly attack France while Russia was mobilising.

If on the other hand we said we were prepared to throw our lot in with the *Entente*, Russia would at once attack Austria. Consequently our influence for peace depended on our apparent indecision. Italy, dishonest as usual, was repudiating her obligations to the Triplice on the ground that Austria had not consulted her before the ultimatum.[70]

After the meeting Lloyd George, the influential Chancellor of the Exchequer, who was still in the camp of those who wanted peace, told a friend 'there could be no question of our taking part in any war in the first instance. He knew of no Minister who would be in favour of it.'[71]

Across the Channel some of those decision-makers who had been so bellicose were briefly having second thoughts. Now back in Berlin, on 27 July the Kaiser thought that the Serbian reply to the ultimatum was acceptable. Falkenhayn, the War Minister, wrote in his diary, 'He makes confused speeches. The only thing that emerges clearly is that he no longer wants war, even if it means letting Austria down. I point out that he no longer has control over the situation.'[72] The tsar sent Sazonov a note suggesting that Russia join forces with France and Britain, and perhaps Germany and Italy, for an attempt to preserve the peace by persuading Austria-Hungary and Serbia to take their dispute to the Permanent Court of Arbitration in The Hague: 'Maybe time is not lost yet before fatal events.'[73] Sazonov also undertook to have direct conversations with Austria-Hungary and from Berlin Bethmann advised Germany's ally to take part, more it seems to have the opportunity to put Russia in the wrong before domestic opinion in the Dual Alliance than for peace.

Although the Kaiser and perhaps Bethmann continued to grasp at straws as they whirled past on the strong currents that were now running, the prevailing mood among the German leadership by this point was that war was inevitable. They were also persuading themselves that Germany was the innocent party. Moltke in a grim memorandum he wrote on 28 July said Russia was bound to mobilise when Austria-Hungary attacked Serbia and Germany would then be bound to come to the aid of its ally with its own mobilisation. Russia would respond by attacking Germany and France would come in. 'Thus the Franco-Russian alliance, so often held up to praise as a purely defensive compact, created only in order to meet the aggressive plans of Germany, will become active, and the mutual butchery of the civilised nations of Europe will begin.'[74] The talks between Russia and Austria-Hungary duly started on 27 July only to be broken off again the next day when Austria-Hungary, under pressure from Germany to move quickly, declared war on Serbia.[75]

Austria-Hungary's declaration of war on Serbia would have been amusing if it had not had such tragic consequences. Since he had melo-dramatically closed his embassy in Belgrade, Berchtold found himself at a loss as to how to deliver the news to Serbia. Germany refused to be the emissary since it was still trying to give the impression that it did not know what Austria-Hungary was planning and so Berchtold resorted to sending an uncoded telegram to Pašić, the first time that war had been declared that way. The Serbian Prime Minister, suspecting that someone in Vienna might be trying to trick Serbia into attacking first, refused to believe it until confirmation had come in from Serbian embassies in St Petersburg, London and Paris.[76] In Budapest Tisza gave a passionate speech of support for the declaration in the Hungarian parliament and the leader of the opposition cried out, 'At Last!'[77] When Sukhomlinov heard the news at a dinner party in St Petersburg, he said to his neighbour, 'This time we will march.'[78] On the night of 28 July Austrian guns on the north shore of the Sava fired shots at Belgrade. Europe had a week of peace left.

CHAPTER 20

Turning Out the Lights:
Europe's Last
Week of Peace

Austria-Hungary's declaration of war on Serbia on 28 July turned what had been Europe's increasingly firm march towards war into a run over the precipice. Russia, which made no secret of its support for Serbia, was likely to threaten Austria-Hungary in response. If that were to happen, Germany might well come to the aid of its ally and so find itself at war with Russia. Then, given the nature of the alliance systems, France might be obliged to enter on Russia's side. In any case, although the German war plans were secret, the French already had a fairly clear understanding that Germany had no intention of waging a war on Russia alone but would attack in the west as well. What Britain and Italy as well as smaller powers such as Rumania and Bulgaria would do was still an open question, although all had existing friendships and ties to the potential belligerents.

The Austrian writer Stefan Zweig was taking a holiday near the Belgian port of Ostend, where he remembered the mood was as carefree as every other summer. 'Visitors enjoying their holiday lay on the beach in brightly coloured tents or bathed in the sea, the children flew kites, young people danced outside the cafés on the promenade laid out on the harbour wall. All imaginable nations were gathered companionably

NO THOROUGHFARE

BRAVO, BELGIUM!

20. The German plan, usually known as the Schlieffen, assumed that Germany would fight a two-front war against France and Russia. To knock its enemy in the west out quickly, the German military planned a quick advance into Belgium and northern France. Although Germany called on Belgium to let the German armies pass through peacefully, the Belgian government decided to resist. This both slowed down the German advance and, even more importantly, persuaded the British to enter the war to defend brave little Belgium.

together there.' Occasionally the mood darkened when the newspaper sellers shouted out their alarming headlines of threats of mobilisation further to the east or the visitors noticed more Belgian soldiers about, but the holiday spirit soon returned. Overnight, though, it became impossible to ignore the clouds that were gathering over Europe. 'All of a sudden', Zweig recalled, 'a cold wind of fear was blowing over the beach, sweeping it clean.' He packed up hastily and rushed homewards by train. By the time he reached Vienna the Great War had started. Like thousands upon thousands of his fellow Europeans he had trouble believing that Europe's peace had ended so quickly and so finally.[1]

The sudden deterioration in Europe's international relations set off a round of frantic last-minute manoeuvres in Europe's capitals. Cabinets held emergency meetings around the clock; lights burned all night in foreign offices; even rulers and the most eminent of statesmen were dragged out of their beds as telegrams came in and were decoded; and junior officials slept on camp beds by their desks. Not everyone in a position of authority wanted to avoid war – think of Conrad in Austria or Moltke in Germany – but as exhaustion crept up on the decision-makers so did a dangerous feeling of helplessness in the face of doom. And all were concerned to demonstrate that their own country was the innocent party. This was necessary both for domestic consumption, in order to bring the nation united into any conflict, but also to win over the uncommitted powers, such as Rumania, Bulgaria, Greece or the Ottoman Empire in Europe, and, further away, the great prize of the United States with its manpower, its resources and its industries.

The morning after the Austrian declaration of war, on 29 July, Poincaré and Viviani landed at Dunkirk and immediately made their way to Paris, where they were greeted by a large and enthusiastic crowd which shouted 'Vive la France! Vive la République! Vive le Président!' and, occasionally 'To Berlin.' Poincaré was thrilled. 'Never I have I been so overwhelmed', he wrote in his diary. 'Here was a united France.'[2] He immediately took charge of the government and relegated Viviani, whom he found ignorant and unreliable, to a minor role.[3] Rumours – true as it turned out – were coming in that the Russian government had ordered a partial mobilisation. Paléologue, perhaps hoping to present his own government with a fait accompli or for fear that it might try to deter Russia, had not bothered to warn Paris or the France ahead of time that Russia was mobilising. He also repeatedly assured Sazonov of the 'complete readiness of France to fulfil her obligations as an ally in case of necessity'.[4] Later that day the German ambassador called on Viviani to warn him that Germany would take the first steps towards its own mobilisation unless France stopped its military preparations. That evening word came in from St Petersburg that Russia had refused German demands to stop its mobilisation. The French Cabinet, calm and serious according to an observer, met the next day and decided that it would not make any attempt to persuade Russia to comply with Germany. Messimy, the War Minister, took steps to move French forces up to the frontier but these were to be held back ten kilometres from the border in order to avoid provoking any incidents with the Germans. The need to show that both to the French public and, crucially to Britain, which still had not declared itself, that France was not the aggressor remained uppermost in the minds of the French leadership.[5]

Far to the east the pace towards war was accelerating. The military plans with their built-in bias towards the offensive now became an argument for mobilisation, to get the troops into place and be ready to launch an attack over the frontiers before the enemy was ready. Whatever reservations they had, the commanders and their general staffs spoke confidently of victory to the civilians, who found it increasingly difficult to resist the pressure. In Russia, with its great distances, Sukhomlinov and the military argued that a general mobilisation against both partners in the Dual Alliance was imperative: Austria-Hungary was already starting its mobilisation and Germany had taken preliminary steps such as calling back soldiers who were on leave. By 29 July his colleagues had managed to persuade Sazonov that it was dangerous to delay any longer. The Foreign Minister agreed to speak to Nicholas, who was unable to make up his mind.

The tsar feared that war, once started, would be difficult to stop and could lead to disaster, and he still had faith in Wilhelm's peaceful intentions.[6] He signed two decrees, at the insistence of his ministers, one for partial mobilisation mainly along Russia's frontiers with Austria-Hungary and one for general mobilisation against Germany as well, but he still held back on deciding which to use. On 29 July Nicholas sent Wilhelm a cable (in English, as their communications usually were). 'Am glad you are back', he wrote, and begged for his German cousin's help in maintaining the peace. He warned, though, that he and his people were furious at the attack on Serbia: 'I foresee that very soon I shall be *overwhelmed* by the *pressure* brought upon me, and be *forced* to take extreme measures which will *lead to war*.'[7] Wilhelm was unmoved and wrote in a marginal note: 'A confession of his own weakness, and an attempt to put the responsibility on my own shoulders.' In a telegram of his own which he had sent at Bethmann's suggestion and which crossed with that of Nicholas, Wilhelm defended Austria-Hungary's actions but said that he, as a friend, was doing his best to bring about an understanding between Austria-Hungary and Russia.[8] The two rulers were to exchange ten telegrams before 1 August as the chasm between their two countries deepened irreparably.

On the evening of 29 July, Sazonov, who was with Sukhomlinov and Yanushkevich, the chief of staff, telephoned Nicholas to say that his ministers recommended a general mobilisation. There was enthusiasm at their end of the line when the tsar agreed.[9] Later that evening, though, as an officer stood by at the Central Telegraph Office in St Petersburg to send out the necessary orders, Yanushkevich phoned to say that Nicholas had changed his mind, perhaps as a result of reading Wilhelm's message, and would only allow a partial mobilisation against Austria-Hungary, saying, 'I will not be responsible for a monstrous slaughter.'[10] Nicholas still seems to have been thinking of mobilisation as a tool of diplomacy and not as a prelude to war. In a telegram the next day to Wilhelm he explained that Russia's moves were purely defensive measures against its southern neighbour and that he still counted on Wilhelm to put pressure on Austria-Hungary to talk to Russia. 'So it is almost a *week ahead* of us,' the Kaiser scribbled angrily. 'I cannot agree to any more mediation, since the tsar who requested it has at the same time secretly mobilised behind my back. It is only a manoeuvre, in order to hold us back and to increase the start they already have!'[11]

Nicholas's government greeted the news of his decision with dismay. Austria-Hungary showed little inclination to back down on Serbia and Germany appeared to be moving towards general mobilisation. A partial mobilisation would leave Russia dangerously exposed. Indeed, as General Yuri Danilov, the quartermaster general, argued forcefully, it would introduce 'germs of hesitation and disorder in a domain in which all must be based on preestablished calculations of the greatest precision'.[12] On the morning of 30 July, Sukhomlinov and Yanushkevich begged the tsar over the phone to order a general mobilisation instead. Nicholas was adamant that he would not change his mind. Sazonov then came on the line to request that the tsar see him in person that afternoon. Nicholas replied that his diary was already full but that he could fit the Foreign Minister in at 3 p.m. In the event the two men talked for almost an hour. Nicholas, who looked haggard, was irritable and nervous and at one point snapped, 'The decision is mine alone.' Sazonov, so it was said in St Petersburg society, finally broke his ruler's resistance by saying that, given the state of public opinion in Russia, war with Germany was the only means for Nicholas to save his own life and preserve his throne to hand on to his son. The tsar agreed to a general mobilisation to start the next day. Sazonov telephoned Yanushkevich to give him the news and then told him, 'Smash your phone.'[13]

From Berlin the German government had been watching developments in Russia closely. The Kaiser was furious at the news of Russian military preparations, which he saw as an act of betrayal even when they were still only directed against Austria-Hungary. He blamed France and Britain, and his dead uncle Edward VII, for seducing the tsar away from his rightful alliance. He would, Wilhelm declared, destroy the British Empire and call up his friends in the Muslim world to wage a jihad against it. (In this last at least he was true to his word.) 'For if we are to bleed to death, England shall at least lose India.'[14] While some in the high command, Falkenhayn for example, were pressing for mobilisation – which in Germany's case would lead inexorably to combat – they met resistance. Moltke did not initially think the situation was serious enough and Bethmann was for delay in order to portray Germany as the victim of aggression. It was Russia's military measures, so Bethmann told the British ambassador on 28 July, that were becoming an insuperable obstacle to attempts to get a peaceful settlement between Austria-Hungary in the Balkans as well as a threat to Germany itself. On 29 July, as the Russian government was wrestling with whether or not to go for a general mobilisation, Bethmann sent a telegram to his ambassador in St Petersburg: 'Kindly impress on M. Sazonov very seriously that further progress of Russian mobilisation measures would compel us to mobilise and that then European war would scarcely be prevented.'[15]

The British Cabinet met at 11.30 on the morning of 29 July to discuss Austria-Hungary's declaration of war on Serbia and it also spent considerable time on Britain's obligations to Belgium as one of the parties to the 1839 Treaty of London which guaranteed the neutrality and independence of the little country. (The other signatories were France, Austria, Russia and Prussia and in the last case Germany had assumed the obligations after 1871.) John Burns, the President of the Board of Trade and among those radical Liberals firmly against war, noted in his diary: 'Situation seriously reviewed from all points of view. It was decided not to decide.' Grey was asked to tell both Cambon and Lichnowsky that 'at this stage we were unable to pledge in ourselves in advance, either under all conditions to stand aside, or in any conditions to join in'.[16] The Cabinet did make two important decisions, however. First, Churchill was given permission to send out cables for a preliminary mobilisation of the navy. That night the fleet sailed northwards without its lights through the Channel to its battle stations in the North Sea. Second, the government would put a 'Precautionary Stage' into effect for the armed forces in Britain as provided for in their new War Book. There was confusion briefly when it was realised that no one knew exactly how to start the process and consternation when it became known that a section of the Territorials had been called up for guard duty, something that was most unusual in peacetime. The government hastily put a notice in the newspapers to say Britain was not mobilising: 'the only orders that have been given are purely precautionary and of a defensive character'.[17]

Grey met with both Paul Cambon and Lichnowsky immediately after the Cabinet meeting. To Cambon he stressed the free hand but with Lichnowsky he went further than the Cabinet might have approved and gave a warning: the British government still hoped for mediation of the conflict between Austria-Hungary and Serbia but if Russia and Germany got drawn in the British government would have to make up its mind quickly. 'In such an event', Grey went on, '*it would not be practicable to stand aside and wait for any length of time.*' Wilhelm's pen erupted with marginal notes when he read the ambassador's dispatch later that evening; 'The common cheat!'"Common cur!"Scoundrels.' 'That mean crew of shopkeepers.'[18]

In the last stage of the crisis both the Kaiser and Bethmann, both of whom had come down on the side of peace in previous crises, were showing the nervous strain they were under as they faced towards war. France had begun preparations; Belgium was calling up its reservists and strengthening its defences, particularly around the crucial fortress of Liège, and the British navy had gone to its battle stations. Most dangerously of all, Russia was moving rapidly towards full mobilisation. On 29 July, Bethmann instructed his cousin, Pourtalès, the German ambassador in St Petersburg, to warn Sazonov that if Russia continued to mobilise Germany would have no choice but to do the same. Pourtalès, a rich and amiable man who was a great favourite of the Kaiser, had been sending reassuring reports back to Berlin to the effect that Russia was only bluffing. He now found himself in the uncomfortable position of calling the bluff. When Sazonov heard the threat, which Pourtalès preferred to call merely a friendly opinion, he exclaimed angrily, 'Now I have no doubt about the real reasons for Austria's intransigence.' Pourtalès protested vehemently against such a hurtful remark. Sazonov curtly responded that the German still had the opportunity to prove him wrong.[19]

The same day Bethmann, who had to this point refused British or Russian requests to put pressure on Austria-Hungary to compromise, reversed himself and urged it to accept mediation. How sincere an attempt to maintain the peace this was is still a matter of debate; Bethmann also had an eye to opinion in Germany and elsewhere. Much of the nationalist right was openly for war, even a preventive one, while many moderates were prepared to support a defensive war. The right wing and liberal press increasingly used the language of honour and sacrifice and painted the horrors of Russian despotism and its 'Asiatic' barbarism sweeping into Germany, with women and children at the mercy of bestial Cossacks.[20] Anti-war sentiment still seemed to be powerful, however, among the working classes. That week there were big demonstrations for peace all over the country involving some 750,000 people and in Berlin alone 100,000 took to the streets, more than had turned out in patriotic marches.[21] Nevertheless Bethmann hoped, rightly as it turned out, that the workers and their leaders in the SPD would rally around their homeland if it were attacked by Russia. As a consequence he strongly resisted the calls from the Kaiser and those on the right to take advantage of the crisis and use the army to crack down on the SPD.[22]

Bethmann did, however, ask Tschirschky, his ambassador in Vienna, to recommend strongly to the government there that it accept mediation. By this point Bethmann had seen the warning sent by Lichnowsky that Britain might well intervene and his mood was sombre. He had little hope, however, of prevailing on the government of Austria-Hungary. On the morning of 30 July Berchtold simply said that military operations against Serbia were now too far along and that any attempt to freeze them in place, with a halt in Belgrade, was out of the question given the state of public opinion and the feeling among the military.[23] A direct appeal from Wilhelm to Franz Joseph echoing Bethmann's proposal for a halt in Belgrade and mediation had as little impact. What the Kaiser and Bethmann may not have known was that the German military were sending a very different message, urging their counterparts in Austria-Hungary to make their mobilisation a general one and to move forces up to the Russian border. Late in the evening of 30 July, Moltke sent an emotional telegram to Conrad which read in part: 'Austria-Hungary must be preserved, mobilise at once against Russia. Germany will mobilise.'[24]

The mixed messages coming from Berlin shook the government of Austria-Hungary, which was under intense international pressure to accept mediation and which feared that Germany would back away from support, as it had done in the Bosnian crisis and more recently in the First and Second Balkan Wars. 'Who rules in Berlin? Moltke or Bethmann?' a shaken Berchtold asked his colleagues. He chose to believe that it was Moltke and said, 'I had the impression that Germany was beating a retreat; but now I have the most reassuring pronouncement from responsible military quarters.'[25] At its meeting on the morning of 31 July, the Common Ministerial Council dismissed out of hand the proposals which were coming from Britain as well for a halt in Belgrade and international mediation. Russia, said Berchtold, would only emerge as Serbia's saviour; Serbia's army would remain intact; and Austria-Hungary would be left in a weaker position to deal with Serbia in the future. Count Joseph Stürgkh, the Austrian Prime Minister, and Bilinski, the Common Finance Minister, both referred bitterly to the previous mediation in the First and Second Balkan Wars when Austria-Hungary had been obliged to back down. 'The entire public', said Bilinski, 'would revolt at a replay of this political theatre.'[26] With Franz Ferdinand no longer there to help him resist the calls for war and Conrad telling him 'The Monarchy is at stake', the old emperor signed the order for a general mobilisation of Austria-Hungary's forces the same day.[27] Berchtold described this to the world as 'defensive military counter measures in Galicia to which we have been compelled by Russian mobilisation' and said that Austria-Hungary would stop as soon as Russia did.[28] Another giant step had been taken to a European war.

Bethmann in those couple of days at the end of July may not have really intended Austria-Hungary to negotiate but he still entertained hopes that he could persuade Britain to remain neutral; as he said to

Falkenhayn, who recorded it in his diary, 'The latter was desirable because in the Chancellor's opinion, England would not be able to side with Russia if the latter unleashed a general war by attacking Austria.'[29] The Germans were encouraged to believe this might be possible because the Kaiser's brother Prince Heinrich had breakfasted with George V earlier in the week and the king, it was reported back to Berlin, had said, 'We shall do all we can to keep out of this and shall remain neutral.'[30] On 29 July Bethmann also made a bid for British neutrality in what again can be seen as either a genuine effort to avert a general war or merely a further attempt to show Germany as the innocent party. Late in the evening, he had a meeting with the British ambassador in Berlin, Sir Edward Goschen. Goschen immediately reported the conversation to London. War might be inevitable between Russia on the one hand and Germany and Austria-Hungary on the other, the Chancellor said, but he hoped that Britain would remain neutral. After all, its main interest on the Continent was in not seeing France crushed. In return for a guarantee of neutrality from Britain, Germany was therefore willing to promise that it would not take any territory from France, although it might take some of its colonies. Nor would Germany invade the Netherlands. 'As regards Belgium', Goschen informed London, 'his Excellency could not tell to what operations Germany might be forced by the action of France, but he could state that, provided that Belgium did not take sides against Germany, her integrity would be respected after the conclusion of the war.' Bethmann concluded by saying that he hoped that such an agreement between Britain and Germany might lead to the better relations which had always been his goal.

His offer was met with derision in London when Goschen's telegram was read the next morning. Reflecting the strongly anti-German bias of the Foreign Office, Crowe noted, 'The only comment that need be made on these astounding proposals is that they reflect discredit on the statesman who makes them ... It is clear that Germany is practically determined to go to war, and that the one restraining influence so far has been the fear of England joining in the defence of France and Belgium.'[31] Grey went white with anger when he learned of Bethmann's overture and the language of the reply which he sent to the British ambassador in Berlin later that afternoon was as strong as he ever allowed himself to use. The proposal that Britain acquiesce in Germany's violation of

Belgian neutrality and undertake to stay neutral while Germany beat France was 'unacceptable'. And, Grey went on, 'for us to make this bargain with Germany at the expense of France would be a disgrace from which the good name of this country would never recover'.[32]

The pressures on the British to declare themselves mounted. In Paris Poincaré told Bertie, the British ambassador, that if war broke out on the Continent Britain would almost certainly be drawn in to protect its interests – and if it were to say so now, Germany would almost certainly be deterred from attacking its neighbours. An increasingly desperate Paul Cambon haunted his friends in the Foreign Office and visited Grey to remind him that they had exchanged letters in November 1912 promising that their two countries would consult in a major crisis over what steps they might take together. The British Cabinet, however, was still unable to come to a firm decision about the policy it would adopt if war broke out on the Continent. The Liberals' Foreign Affairs Committee, which had long been critical of Grey and suspicious of his secrecy on commitments to France, threatened Asquith with the withdrawal of its support if a decision were taken that Britain would intervene. One of its members wrote to Asquith to claim that up to nine-tenths of Liberal MPs would oppose the government. On the other hand, Grey and his fellow Liberal imperialists would probably refuse to serve in a government which did not support France. The Liberal leaders feared, with good reason, that the government could fall, leaving the way open for the Conservatives to take power.[33]

On 31 July, a Friday, the Cabinet met again and decided only that it could not give Cambon any promises. Russia was already mobilising and, although they could not know it, Austria-Hungary was about to declare its general mobilisation and Germany was to take the first steps towards its own. In the meeting Grey continued to insist that Britain remained perfectly free to decide what it would do.[34] Eyre Crowe disagreed. In a forceful memorandum the same day he argued:

> The theory that England cannot engage in a big war means her abdication as an independent State. She can be brought to her knees and made to obey the behests of any Power or group of Powers who *can* go to war, of whom there are several … The whole policy of the *Entente* can have no meaning if it does not signify that

in a just quarrel England would stand by her friends. This honourable expectation has been raised. We cannot repudiate it without
exposing our good name to grave criticism.[35]

Outside the small circle of those who now controlled Britain's fate,
public opinion also remained divided but it appeared to be shifting
towards intervention. *The Times*, for example, now argued that Britain
had a moral obligation to France and Russia and that, moreover, it
could not stand by while the balance of power on the Continent shifted
in Germany's favour.[36]

While Britain was grappling with the dilemmas before it, Germany
was making its own fateful decision to start mobilising. This was particularly dangerous to Europe's peace because German mobilisation
was unlike all others. Its beautifully co-ordinated and seamless steps –
from declaring a state of siege or 'imminent threat of war', to ordering
full mobilisation and organising the men into their units with their
supplies, to finally launching its armies over the borders – made it
almost impossible to stop once started. And the army was always ready,
even in peacetime, to move at a moment's notice; the communications
office of the general staff was manned around the clock, had its own
telephone exchange and was wired directly into the main post office and
telegraph office.[37] For Germany mobilisation was not a diplomatic tool;
it was war itself. Although Bethmann and the Kaiser had resisted the
army pressures to set the process going, by 31 July the military were
starting to take over. Bethmann accepted this shift in power with resignation; the representative of Saxony in Berlin reported him saying:
'The control has slipped out of the hands of the responsible monarchs
and statesmen so that the mad European war would happen without
the rulers or their people wanting it.'[38]

Crucially Moltke, who had earlier agreed that mobilisation could
still wait, had suddenly shifted ground the evening before. Falkenhayn
wrote in his diary, 'His changes of mood are hardly explicable, or not at
all.'[39] In fact, though, Moltke had good reason: Germany needed to be
ready to take Liège before war was declared and he had received reports
that the Belgians were hastily reinforcing it. (He had never informed
the civilians of this part of the German war plans.)[40] It may be too that
he simply could no longer bear the tension of indecision. After 'endless

negotiations' on 30 July between Bethmann and Falkenhayn the decision was taken to announce the 'state of imminent threat of war', the necessary preliminary stage of mobilisation, at noon the following day whether Russia had mobilised or not. At midnight one of his adjutants found a visibly agitated Moltke busy drafting a proclamation for the Kaiser. He feared, the chief of the general staff said, that Britain would intervene and that the conflict would be worldwide. 'Few can have an idea of the extent, the duration and the end of this war.'[41]

When confirmation of Russian mobilisation came in just before noon on 31 July Bethmann telephoned Wilhelm and obtained his permission to proclaim the 'state of imminent threat of war'. At the War Ministry in Berlin, the military attaché from Bavaria wrote in his diary, 'Everywhere beaming faces, shaking of hands in the corridors; one congratulates oneself for having taken the hurdle.' The Bavarian ambassador cabled Munich to say 'General Staff looks ahead to war with France with great confidence, expects to defeat France within four weeks.'[42] The German public learned of the decision around 4 p.m. in the old Prussian way: a detachment of soldiers marched out from the palace in Berlin and stopped in the Unter den Linden, the great thoroughfare. The drummers beat their drums in each direction of the compass and an officer read out a proclamation. The German government also sent an ultimatum to Russia, which it knew would almost certainly be rejected, demanding that it stop all war preparations against both Germany and Austria-Hungary within twelve hours. When Bethmann met the representatives of all the German states the next morning to ask them to approve a war if Russia refused to back down, he assured them that he had worked to the very end for peace: 'But we cannot bear Russia's provocation, if we do not want to abdicate as a Great Power in Europe.'[43] A second ultimatum went to France, giving it eighteen hours to promise that it would remain neutral in any conflict. As proof of its willingness to keep such a promise, France was to hand over its key frontier fortresses at Toul and Verdun. (Germany promised to hand them back in good order at the end of its war with Russia.) Germany also sent out telegrams to Greece, Rumania, and the Ottoman Empire to ask them what it would take to get them to join with the Triple Alliance in the coming war.

As Germany prepared for war on two fronts, the actions of its most important ally caused it concerns as Austria-Hungary moved that part of its army already mobilised, some two-fifths of the total, towards Serbia in spite of reports coming in from 27 July onwards of increasing Russian military activity.[44] Even after the general mobilisation order of 31 July substantial Austrian-Hungarian forces continued to go south-wards into the Balkans. Conrad, with the wishful thinking that marked so many of his decisions, seems to have hoped that Russia would bring its forces up to Austria-Hungary's frontiers and merely sit there while he defeated Serbia quickly.[45] This was not how Germany saw it or what Germany needed.

As often happens in alliances, war had brought to the fore the diver-gent interests of the partners. Austria-Hungary, while it had promised in peacetime to attack Russia as soon as possible, was obsessed with destroying Serbia. Germany, for its part, had little intention of diverting forces from the west to protect Austria-Hungary until France was defeated. It was essential from the German point of view that Austria-Hungary send as many forces northwards as possible against Russia. Moltke was already urging Conrad, his Austrian counterpart, to move his forces north and east, and on 31 July the Kaiser sent a strong tele-gram to Franz Joseph to say, 'In this great struggle it is of primary importance that Austria should mobilise her main forces against Russia and not fragment herself through any simultaneous offensive on Serbia.' And, the Kaiser went on, 'Serbia plays, in this gigantic struggle where we stand shoulder to shoulder, a quite subsidiary role, requiring only a necessary minimum of defensive measures.'[46] Conrad did not, however, redeploy his troops from south to north until 4 August, a decision which was to lead to military disaster for Austria-Hungary.

By the afternoon of 1 August, a Saturday, still no reply had come from Russia to the German ultimatum. The patriotic demonstrations of earlier in the week had been dying down and the German public was waiting for developments with apprehension, even depression. A journalist reported that, in Frankfurt, 'Over everything lies an enormous seriousness, a frightening peace and quiet. Inside their quiet rooms wives and young women sit with their serious thoughts concerning the new future. Sepa-ration, a great fear of the horrible, a fear of what may come.' Housewives started to hoard food and there were runs on banks as people withdrew their savings. The Kaiser was now under great pressure to declare a general mobilisation from his generals who saw time slipping away while Russia's armies grew, and from his own wife who told him to be a man. He signed the order at 5 p.m.[47] Shortly afterwards he made a speech from the balcony of his Berlin palace: 'From the depths of my heart I thank you for the expressions of your love, of your faithfulness. In the battle now lying ahead of us, I see no more parties in my *Volk*. Among us there are only Germans ...' He was cheered, far more than he usually was; Germans of all political persuasions were now ready to defend their homeland against the Russians who, at this point, were singled out as the main enemy. In spite of later nationalist mythmaking about a huge upsurge in patriotic enthusiasm as the war became reality, the public mood seems to have been one of resignation as much as anything else.[48]

Shortly after the Kaiser signed the general mobilisation order, a telegram arrived from Lichnowsky. According to the ambassador, Britain had promised to remain neutral if Germany did not attack France. The news, said one observer, was 'like a bomb'. The Kaiser and perhaps Bethmann were relieved. Turning to Moltke, Wilhelm said cheerfully, 'So we simply deploy the whole army in the East!' The mood in the room rapidly turned stormy. Moltke refused to contemplate the possibility of deploying only against Russia. The deployment in the west could not be stopped without disrupting the plans and so ending any chance of success in the coming war against France. 'Besides,' he added, 'our patrols have already entered Luxembourg and the Division from Trier is to follow immediately.' And he bluntly told the Kaiser, 'If his Majesty insisted on leading the entire army to the East then he would not have an army that was ready to strike but a messy heap of disorderly, armed men without supplies.' Wilhelm replied, 'Your uncle would have given me a different answer.'[49]

There has been a debate ever since over whether Moltke was right, that it was too late for Germany to go to war on one front alone. General Groener, head of the general staff's Railway Department at the time, maintained afterwards that it would have been feasible.[50] In the event, a compromise was patched up; deployment on both fronts would continue as planned but the German armies in the west would halt just before the French border until France's position was clearer. Moltke never really recovered from the psychological battering he received that day. When he returned home, recalled his wife, after the Kaiser's request for a partial mobilisation, 'I saw immediately something terrible had happened here. He was purple in the face, his pulse hardly countable. I had a desperate man in front of me.'[51]

Later that night a second telegram from Lichnowsky came in to say that his earlier one had been mistaken; the British were insisting that there be no German invasion of Belgium nor an attack on France and, furthermore, German troops designated for an attack on France in the west must not be moved to the east to be used against Russia. When Moltke went back to the royal palace in Berlin to get permission to resume the movement against Belgium and France, the Kaiser, who was already in bed, said curtly, 'Now do as you please; I don't care either way,' and turned over to go to sleep.[52] There was still no sleep on that fateful day for the Kaiser's ministers who sat up to the early hours of the next morning in a debate over whether going to war with Russia required a formal declaration. Moltke and Tirpitz did not see the necessity but Bethmann, who argued 'otherwise I cannot pull the Socialists along', won what was to be one of his last victories over the military.[53] A declaration of war was to be prepared and cabled to Pourtalès in St Petersburg. With Germany's decision to mobilise, three of the five great European powers had now begun their general mobilisations and were either already formally at war, as in Austria-Hungary's case, or about to be so in the case of Russia and Germany. Of the remaining three, Italy was choosing neutrality, France had decided to ignore the German ultimatum and start its own general mobilisation on 2 August, and Britain still had not decided what to do.

The 1st of August was the start of a bank holiday weekend for the British. Many families had gone to the seaside and in London Madame Tussaud's was advertising new waxworks exhibitions for the holiday-makers: 'The European Crisis. Lifelike Portrait Models of H.I.M. the Emperor of Austria, King Peter of Servia, and other reigning Sovereigns of Europe. The Home Rule Crisis. Sir Edward Carson, Mr. John Redmond, and other Celebrities. Naval and Military Tableaux. Delightful Music. Refreshments at Popular Prices.'[54] There was little holiday mood in the corridors of power in Whitehall and this time an increasingly morose Grey was not able to slip away to his country cottage.

One piece of bad news followed another. The City of London was panicking. The bank rate had doubled overnight and hundreds of people had queued in the courtyard of the Bank of England to change their paper notes for gold. The management of the Stock Exchange had decided to close until further notice (and it was to remain closed until the following January). Lloyd George, as Chancellor of the Exchequer, and Asquith had held a meeting with leading businessmen in an attempt to reassure them that the government would intervene if necessary to stabilise the economy. From the Continent came reports of armies on the move and stories, false as it turned out, that German troops were already crossing the French frontier. In a private letter to Nicolson at the Foreign Office, Goschen, the British ambassador in Berlin, wrote plaintively, 'It's all very terrible! All my servants will have to go I suppose and I shall remain with my English valet and Swiss *aide-cuisinier.* I hope you're not as tired as I am.'[55]

The Cabinet met in the late morning of Saturday 1 August. 'I can honestly say that I have never had a more bitter disappointment,' wrote Asquith to Venetia Stanley afterwards – but he was talking about not being able to meet her during the week. The international crisis, he went on, was no closer to being resolved and the Cabinet remained undecided on what to do. One group that morning still took what Asquith described in his letter as 'the *Manchester Guardian* tack' – that Britain should declare that it would not join a continental war under any circumstances – and on the other side were Grey and his supporters such as Churchill and Asquith himself who refused to rule out war. Grey had hinted again at resignation if the Cabinet adopted a firm policy of nonintervention. In the middle and as yet undecided was the pivotal figure of Lloyd George, who was temperamentally inclined towards peace but who had a lively sense of Britain's need to maintain its position as a great power. The meeting could only agree that it would not ask Parliament to approve sending the British Expeditionary Force to France.[56]

After the Cabinet meeting Grey saw Cambon, who had been waiting anxiously at the Foreign Office for news of Britain's intentions. The French ambassador pointed out the grave peril that his country now faced from German armies on land and with the German navy able to threaten its Atlantic coasts which France had left bare, so Cambon claimed with a certain amount of exaggeration, as a result of its agreement with Britain which had undertaken to protect them. Grey gave him little comfort, waving, yet again, the free hand in front of him.

Belgium's neutrality was important to the British, however, and the Foreign Secretary intended to ask the House of Commons on Monday, if the Cabinet agreed, to affirm that Britain would not allow a violation of that neutrality. Cambon pointed out that French opinion was going to be very disappointed at Britain's delayed response and, according to Grey's account of the meeting, gave a warning: 'If we did not help France, the *entente* would disappear; and, whether victory came to Germany or to France and Russia, our situation at the end of the war would be very uncomfortable.'[57] Afterwards Cambon staggered into Nicolson's office white in the face and able to say only, 'They are going to abandon us, they are going to abandon us [Ils vont nous lâcher, ils vont nous lâcher].'[58] To a friendly British journalist who visited him at the French embassy, he said, 'I wonder whether the word "honour" should be stripped from the English vocabulary.' Nicolson rushed upstairs to ask Grey whether Cambon was speaking the truth about their meeting. When Grey said that he was, Nicolson said bitterly, 'You will render us ... a by-word among nations,' and protested that the Foreign Secretary had always given Cambon the impression that if Germany were the aggressor Britain would take France's side. 'Yes,' replied Grey, 'but he has nothing in writing.'[59] That night, Crowe, who was a strong advocate in the Foreign Office for intervention, wrote to his wife: 'The government has finally decided to run away, and desert France in her hour of need. The feeling in the office is such that practically everyone wants to resign rather than serve such a government of dishonourable cowards.'[60]

On the other side of Europe that same day, Russia and Germany were breaking off relations. (Austria-Hungary, still dreaming of crushing Serbia, did not make its own declaration of war on Russia until 6 August.) At 6 p.m. an emotional Pourtalès, the German ambassador, asked Sazonov three times whether Russia would accede to Germany's demand to stop mobilising. Sazonov replied each time that Russia was still willing to negotiate but that the orders could not be revoked. 'I have', he said, 'no other reply to give you.' Pourtalès then drew a deep breath and said with difficulty, 'In that case, sir, I am instructed by my Government to hand you this note.' With trembling hands he passed over the declaration of war and went to the window and wept. 'I never could have believed', he said to Sazonov, 'that I should quit Petersburg under these conditions.' The two men embraced. The next morning the German embassy staff along with representatives of the separate German states left by a special train from the same Finland station Lenin was to arrive at three years later to make his revolution.[61] Sazonov phoned the tsar to inform him that the break had been made. Nicholas said only, 'My conscience is clear – I did my utmost to avoid war.'[62] His family had been waiting anxiously for him to come into dinner. He arrived, very pale, and told them that Russia and Germany were now at war. 'Hearing the news,' recalled one of the children's tutors, 'the Empress started to cry, and the grand duchesses, seeing their mother's despair, also burst into tears.'[63] There were many other tears in Europe that day, although nothing by comparison with what was to come, as the fact of war sank in and the conscripts marched off to join their regiments.

The international peace movement had watched the rapid slide towards war with horror and there had been demonstrations for peace in several European cities, to little effect. Jean Jaurès, the great French socialist, had worked tirelessly as the crisis unfolded to keep Europe's working classes united in the fight against the war. 'Their hearts must beat as one to prevent this horrible disaster!' he said on 25 July in his last speech in France.[64] On 29 July he joined representatives of Europe's socialist parties in Brussels in a last attempt to hold the Second International together. They still called each other comrade and the leader of the German Social Democratic Party embraced Jaurès, but it was becoming clear that the nationalism, which had always threatened the unity of the Second International, was now about to tear it apart as the working classes in each country swung to the defence of their homelands and their parties prepared to vote with the governments for war credits. After a lot of debate, it was decided only to move the full Congress scheduled for later that summer up to 9 August and to hold it in Paris rather than Vienna as planned. British delegates complained that there would not be enough time for Australians to get there. Jaurès was worried and sad and had a dreadful headache. Nevertheless he made a speech that evening at a huge assembly in the Cirque Royale, the largest concert hall in Brussels. Yet again he warned of the dreadful fate with death, destruction, and disease that lay in store for Europe unless they all worked to avert war. The next morning he was more cheerful and said to a Belgian socialist friend: 'There will be ups and downs. But it is impossible that things won't turn out all right. I've got two hours before catching the train. Let's go to the Museum and see your Flemish primitives.'[65]

Back in Paris by 30 July, Jaurès fought on as he had always done, writing his columns for the left-wing newspaper *Humanité*, organising meetings and trying to see government ministers. When Jaurès snatched a drink with friends late that evening, at his favourite café, no one noticed the bearded young man who stalked up and down on the pavement outside. Raoul Villain, a passionate and fanatical nationalist, had decided Jaurès was a traitor because of his internationalism and pacifism. He had brought a revolver with him but did not use it that night. The next day, Jaurès managed to get a meeting with Abel Ferry, the Undersecretary for Foreign Affairs, who told him bluntly there was nothing to be done to avert war. Jaurès reacted as though he had been hit by a sledgehammer but he said that he would continue the struggle for peace. 'You will be assassinated on the nearest street corner,' Ferry warned. That evening Jaurès and a few friends stopped by the café again for supper before continuing their work. They sat by a window which had been opened to get some air on the stiflingly hot night. Villain suddenly appeared outside and fired twice; Jaurès died almost at once. A plaque still marks the spot at the Café du Croissant in the rue du Montmartre.[66]

The news of his death reached the French Cabinet on the evening of 31 July as it met yet again in emergency session. The ministers were all feeling the strain. Germany's and Austria-Hungary's general mobilisations had been confirmed and Joffre, the chief of the general staff, was bombarding them with demands for France's own general mobilisation with warnings that every day of delay put France in a more dangerous position. Poincaré tried to maintain a strong facade for the others, he wrote in his diary, but underneath he was deeply troubled. His only respite from the endless meetings came when he took a walk in the grounds of the Elysée Palace with his wife. As their two dogs gambolled around them, Poincaré wrote, 'I asked myself anxiously if Europe is really going to fall victim to a general war because Austria is wilfully determined in wanting to make a row with Wilhelm II's sword.'[67] The German ambassador had just been to ask the French Prime Minister whether France would remain neutral in a war between Russia and

Germany. Viviani said that he would give a definite reply in the morning. The ambassador also asked if it was true that Russia had ordered a general mobilisation and Viviani had replied that he had not been informed of this. Controversy continues to surround the question of how much the French leadership knew at this point. A telegram from Paléologue with news of Russia's decision sent that morning took some twelve hours in transmission (a sign of how communications were starting to break down across Europe) so may not have arrived in time for the Cabinet's meeting. In any case the policy of the French government had remained the same since the start of the crisis: to ensure that both Russia and France were seen as the innocent parties in the face of German aggression. In the preceding days, Poincaré and Viviani had repeatedly urged Russia to move cautiously and avoid provocative actions.[68] Although no record exists of the Cabinet's discussions that evening, when it broke up at midnight it had decided to make a decision on mobilisation the next day. It also agreed to promise Britain, in response to a request from London, that France would respect Belgian neutrality. Messimy, the War Minister, also saw Izvolsky, the Russian ambassador, to assure him that France would fight alongside Russia.[69]

When the Cabinet met again on the morning of 1 August, Poincaré said they could no longer delay a general mobilisation of French troops and his colleagues, some reluctantly, agreed. The telegrams, which were already prepared, went out that afternoon and in cities and towns around France people gathered to read the little blue notices that were posted in shop windows. In Paris a huge crowd filled the Place de la Concorde. Some rushed to the statue representing Strasbourg, the capital of the lost province of Alsace, and tore off the black mourning it had worn since 1871. In a message to the French people which called for national unity, Poincaré assured them that the French government continued to bend all its efforts towards maintaining the peace. He promised that mobilisation did not mean war. 'To tell the truth,' said an astute observer, 'no one believed him. If it was not war, it was certainly something terribly near to it.'[70] In the following days trains rumbled across the country gathering up France's young men to take them to the frontiers. The general staff had feared that perhaps as many as 10 per cent of the reserves would refuse the mobilisation orders; less than 1.5 per cent failed to show up.[71]

By Sunday 2 August, Russia, Germany, Austria-Hungary and France had all mobilised; Russia and Germany were officially at war with each other; and Austria-Hungary was at war with Serbia. That day Russian cavalry troops crossed the border into Germany and German troops had moved into Luxembourg, just to the south of Belgium, although the neutrality of the tiny duchy had been guaranteed by the great powers, Germany among them. Italy, it was increasingly clear, intended to proclaim its neutrality. From across the Atlantic, where the Americans watched with a mixture of amazement and horror, President Wilson, who was spending much of his time at the bedside of his dying wife, sent offers through his ambassadors of mediation but it was too late and the Europeans were not prepared to listen. One major last step remained before Europe's path to war was finished: Britain's entry.

That Sunday morning a tearful Lichnowsky, his hopes of a British–German rapprochement in ruins, visited Asquith while he was having breakfast to beg that Britain not side with France, but it was now nearly too late. British public opinion was hardening against Germany. As Lord Morley, former Secretary of State for India and one of those in the Cabinet most firmly opposed to a war, wrote that day to a friend, 'the high-handed action of Germany was weakening the efforts of the peacemakers in the Cabinet'.[72] More importantly the unfolding threat to Belgium was swaying opinion in the Cabinet in a way which German war preparations against France or Russia had not. Geography meant that, down through the centuries, Britain could never stand by unconcerned while another power took over the Low Countries with their crucial waterways by which goods (and often armies) funnelled back and forth from the Continent to Britain. The Conservative Party now brought its own pressure to bear on Asquith in the form of a letter from the Conservative leader Bonar Law which argued that it would be 'fatal to the honour and security of the United Kingdom to hesitate in support for France and Russia' and promised the party's full support to the government.[73]

At 11 a.m. the Cabinet broke all precedent by meeting on a Sunday. It was a difficult session and showed how deeply the ministers were still divided. A majority was starting to form, however, of those for whom a German violation of Belgian neutrality would be a cause for war. All that was agreed that morning, though, was that Grey could tell Cambon that Britain would not allow the German fleet to attack the northern French coast. The Cabinet also ratified Churchill's decision, taken the previous evening, to mobilise the naval reserves and it was agreed to hold another meeting at 6.30 p.m. Several of the pacifists as well as Lloyd George, who was still uncommitted, had lunch together. Grey went to the London zoo for an hour to look at birds while Asquith snatched a moment to write to Venetia Stanley. 'I got no letter from you this morning,' he complained, 'which is the saddest blank in my day.'[74] The British Cabinet met again at 6.30 p.m. as arranged. Although Morley and the Board of Trade's John Burns, both of whom would subsequently resign, still opposed war outright, Lloyd George was now swinging round to support for Belgium. He was also well aware of British strategic interests in keeping the Continent free from German domination. A tentative majority now existed for intervention if there were a 'substantial' violation of Belgian neutrality. What would solidify that majority was if Belgium decided to resist Germany and appeal for help.[75]

At 7 p.m. British time, while the British were still debating what to do about the European crisis, the German ambassador in Brussels called on the Belgian Foreign Minister with an ultimatum which had been sitting in his office since 29 July. It had been drafted by Moltke, rather than Bethmann, yet another indication of how the military were taking charge of German policy. Germany, the document claimed, had 'reliable information' that the French were planning to advance into Belgium en route to attacking Germany. (In fact the French government had expressly told Joffre that he could not go into Belgium before the Germans invaded.) The German government could not help but be concerned that Belgium would not be able to defend itself, leaving Germany at the mercy of the French. In self-preservation Germany might be obliged to take action against this French aggression. 'It would therefore', the document went on, 'fill the German government with the deepest regret, should Belgium view as an act of hostility to herself the entrance of Germany upon Belgian soil, should she be forced by the measures of her opponents to do so in self-protection'. Germany demanded of Belgium 'benevolent neutrality' and free passage for German troops through its territory. In return, Germany would guarantee Belgium's integrity and independence after the war. The Belgian government was given twelve hours to answer.[76]

Belgium had always guarded its neutrality with determination, refusing to consider military alliances with its neighbours but preparing itself to fight any if necessary. Even in 1914, as German troops were advancing into the country, some Belgian troops were still stationed in the south and along the coast to show that Belgium intended to defend its neutrality against all enemies, even an unlikely attack from France or Britain. Belgian public opinion, at least until 1914, had fixed on no single enemy, or friend. There was a long-standing resentment of Britain for leading the international campaign at the turn of the century against the hideous abuses of their avaricious king, Leopold II, in the Congo. The Belgian Foreign Office and conservative and Catholic circles tended to be pro-German but France exerted the greatest cultural influence.[77] The Belgians were proud of their independence and cherished their freedom. The military reforms and increased spending of 1913 were intended to protect these. As the likelihood of war between France and Germany grew ever closer, the Belgian government called up more conscripts on 29 July and instructed the commander at Liège to strengthen the defences of the great fortress and to sabotage its approaches on the east side, in the direction of Germany. On 31 July the government ordered full mobilisation of the Belgian army.

When the ultimatum had been translated from German into French, the Belgian government took very little time to make up its mind. The Prime Minister, Baron Charles de Broqueville, and the king, Albert I, decided immediately that the German demands must be rejected. The government ministers who were assembled hastily in the middle of the night agreed unanimously. Perhaps to their own surprise, the Belgians also decided without hesitation that they would offer as much resistance as they could to the German advance. 'Oh, the poor fools!' said a German diplomat in Brussels when he heard. 'Why don't they get out of the way of the steamroller?' When the news of the rejection of the ultimatum, leaked to the papers by a French diplomat, appeared on the morning of 3 August, the Belgian public showed its approval. The Belgian flag flew everywhere and there was much talk of Belgium's national pride. As the king himself said in his proclamation to the nation, 'We refused to forfeit our honour.'[78] It helped that Albert was widely respected. He was unlike his uncle, the late, unlamented, Leopold, in almost every respect: the new king was honest, lived modestly in domestic bliss with his German wife and three children, and loved reading and mountain climbing rather than teenage mistresses. When the king and queen left the palace the following day, for a special session of parliament, they were cheered by huge crowds. In the chamber the royal couple received a standing ovation; all the measures proposed by the government including war credits passed unanimously. The Socialist Party issued a statement to say that their members were defending themselves against 'militarist barbarism' and fighting for liberty and democracy.[79]

On the morning of Monday 3 August, the British Cabinet met to consider what Grey should say to Parliament that afternoon, and it also decided to mobilise the army. Although the details were not yet available, word of the German ultimatum to Belgium had arrived as well as a telegram from Albert to George V asking for British help. From the British point of view, as Asquith later wrote to Venetia Stanley, Germany's aggression against Belgium 'simplifies matters'.[80] Lloyd George, whose support was essential to keep the left wing of the Liberal Party with the government, was now firmly in the camp advocating intervention in support of Belgian neutrality and on the side of France. Grey went back to the Foreign Office around 2 p.m., hoping to take a hasty lunch and work on his speech. He found the German ambassador waiting for him to ask what the Cabinet had decided. 'Was it a declaration of war?' Grey said that it was rather a 'statement of conditions'. He could not tell Lichnowsky what these were until he had informed Parliament. Lichnowsky begged Grey not to make Belgian neutrality one of the conditions. Grey merely repeated that he could not say anything.[81]

At 4 p.m. a pale and tired Grey stood up before the House of Commons. 'His voice was clear,' said one observer, 'with no warm tones in it, his language wholly unadorned, precise, simple, accurate, austerely dignified.'[82] The benches and gangways were jammed and the galleries were filled with onlookers including the Archbishop of Canterbury and the Russian ambassador. Grey claimed, as he always did, that he had kept Britain's hands completely free. Yet its friendship with France ('and with Germany', shouted one member) and its pledge to respect Belgium's neutrality had created 'obligations of honour and interest'. France, he said, had so trusted in Britain that it had left its Atlantic shores defenceless. 'Let every man look into his own heart and his own feelings', he went on, 'and construe the extent of the obligation for himself. I construe it myself as I feel it, but I do not wish to urge upon any one else more than their feelings dictate as to what they should feel about the obligation.' He knew where he stood. Britain was now in a position, he said, where it had either to accept its obligations of honour and interest or run away. And even if Britain stood aside from the war, it would come out the worse with its vital lifelines of trade and commerce with the Continent and its own shores menaced by the rise of a dominant power in Europe. 'I am quite sure', he concluded, 'that our moral position would be such as to have lost us all respect.' His last words were drowned out by loud cheers. Bonar Law for the Conservatives and John Redmond for the Irish nationalists pledged their support. Ramsay MacDonald, speaking for the small Labour Party, said that Britain should have remained neutral. There was no vote that day or later that Britain should declare war on Germany but it was clear that the government now had overwhelming support if it decided to intervene.

When Nicolson later came into Grey's office to congratulate him on the success of his speech a miserable Grey did not reply but only banged his fists on a table, saying, 'I hate war ... I hate war.' Sometime later that evening Grey made the remark which for so many Europeans came to sum up what the war meant. As he looked out the window into St James's Park where the lamplighters were lighting up the gas lamps, he said, 'The lamps are going out all over Europe; we shall not see them lit again in our life-time.'[83] Although Grey later said modestly that he was 'only the mouthpiece of England', he had done much to bring Britain to intervention in the war.[84] Lloyd George, who had played such a key role in swinging the Cabinet towards war, wrote to his wife in North Wales: 'I am moving through a nightmare world these days. I have fought hard for peace & succeeded so far in keeping the Cabinet out of it but I am driven to the conclusion that if the small nationality of Belgium is attacked by Germany all my traditions & even prejudices will be engaged on the side of war. I am filled with horror at the prospect.' Asquith was more prosaic; at his customary bridge game he said that 'the one bright spot in this hateful war, upon which we were about to enter, was the settlement of Irish strife and the cordial union of forces in Ireland in aiding the Government to maintain our supreme National interests'.[85] It is possible, or so many thought at the time, that the Great War saved Britain from a civil war.

In Paris that same Monday evening Wilhelm Schoen, the German ambassador, was struggling to decipher a badly mangled telegram from Bethmann. He made out enough to be able to go immediately to the French Prime Minister with Germany's declaration of war. The German government claimed that it had been driven to this measure by French advances across the border into Alsace and by vicious attacks by French aviators. One, it said, had even thrown a bomb on a German railway line. (Hitler was to use a similar excuse with as little basis in the truth when he attacked Poland in 1939.) Schoen had a last request – that Germans remaining in Paris be placed under the protection of the American ambassador – and a complaint – that a man using threatening language had jumped into his car on his way to the meeting. The two men parted courteously and in a sombre mood.[86] Poincaré later wrote in his diary:

> It is a hundred times better that we were not led to declare war ourselves even on account of repeated violations of our frontier. It was imperative that Germany, fully responsible for the aggression, should be forced to admit her interests publicly. If France had declared war, the alliance with Russia would have become controversial and French unity and spirit broken, and Italy might have been obliged by the Triple Alliance to come in against France.[87]

The following day, Tuesday 4 August, amidst repeated cheers, a message from Poincaré was read to the French parliament. Germany was entirely to blame for the war, he stated, and would have to defend itself before the judgement of history. All French would come together in a sacred union, and this *union sacrée* would never be shattered. There were no dissenting voices; the Socialist Party had already decided to support the war. When a leading opponent of the left paid tribute to Jaurès, who was being buried that day, saying, 'There are no longer adversaries; there are only French,' the chamber erupted into prolonged shouts of 'Vive la France'.[88]

The same day the British government sent an ultimatum to Germany that it provide an assurance that it would respect Belgium's neutrality. There was a deadline of 11 p.m. that evening British time. Since no one expected Germany to agree, a declaration of war was readied to be given to Lichnowsky. Printed telegrams to warn British embassies and consulates around the world that Britain was about to go to war had been in the Foreign Office files for years with only the name of the enemy left out. Clerks spent the day writing in 'Germany'.

Meanwhile in Berlin that same day, Bethmann was addressing the German parliament to explain that Germany was only defending itself. True, he admitted, Germany was invading the neutral countries of Belgium and Luxembourg, but that was only because of the French threat. When the war was over, Germany would make good any damage. The Socialist Party, which had for so long promised to lead its millions of members in opposition to a capitalist war, joined the other parties in voting for war credits. Bethmann had worked hard to win them over but they had been moving in his direction. On 3 August at a long and difficult meeting of Socialist deputies, a majority had decided to vote for war credits, partly on the grounds that they could not betray their rank and file who were going off to war and partly because they saw Germany as the victim of Russian aggression. For the sake of party unity the rest agreed to go along.[89]

On the evening of 4 August, even before the British deadline for Germany's reply had passed, Goschen, the British ambassador, called on Bethmann to request his passport. 'Oh, this is too terrible!' exclaimed Goschen as he asked in vain whether Germany could not respect Belgium's neutrality. Bethmann harangued the ambassador. Britain was taking a dreadful step and all for a mere word, 'neutrality'. The treaty with Belgium, Bethmann said in words which cost Germany dearly in world opinion, was just a 'scrap of paper'. Britain, he went on, could have reined in France's desire for revenge and Russian Panslavism but instead it had encouraged them. The war was Britain's fault. Goschen burst into tears and left.[90] Bethmann could not see that Germany bore any responsibility. He later wrote to a friend, 'It remains highly questionable whether with reasonable actions we could have prevented the natural French, Russian, and British antagonisms from uniting against us.'[91] The Kaiser ranted at Britain's betrayal and accused Nicholas of 'unscrupulous wantonness' in ignoring all Germany's and Wilhelm's attempts to keep the peace. Moltke thought that the British had planned the war all along and wondered whether Germany could persuade the United States to come in as its ally by promising the Americans Canada.[92]

In London the British waited for their 11 p.m. deadline to approach. There was a brief panic in the Foreign Office when someone realised they had made a mistake in the declaration of war on Germany and sent it prematurely to Lichnowsky. An amended declaration was hurriedly drawn up and a junior official delegated to retrieve the wrong document. The Cabinet ministers gathered at Downing Street, most looking anxious and drawn except for Churchill, who looked alert and confident with a large cigar in his mouth. Secretaries waited outside the Cabinet room. 'At any rate the war can't last long,' someone said. Just before 11 p.m. a junior official phoned the Foreign Office to ask if there were any news. 'No news here or at the German Embassy,' came the answer. Big Ben started to chime and Britain was at war. Outside, crowds in Whitehall and the Mall linked arms and sang patriotic songs. Churchill dispatched a telegram to the fleet: 'COMMENCE HOSTILITIES AGAINST GERMANY.'[93]

The ties that had bound a peaceful and prosperous Europe over the nineteenth century now broke rapidly. Rail and telegraph lines were cut; shipping slowed down; bank reserves were frozen and international currency exchanges stopped; and trade dwindled away. Ordinary citizens scrambled desperately to get home in a world that had suddenly become different. In the German embassy in Paris there was chaos as mothers clutched their crying babies and hundreds of suitcases littered the floor. Perhaps as many as 100,000 Americans were caught on the Continent, often without money because the banks were closed. Many managed to make their way to Britain where Walter Page, the American ambassador, and his staff did their best to cope. 'God save us!' he wrote to President Woodrow Wilson:

What a week it has been! ... Those first two days, there was, of course, great confusion. Crazy men and weeping women were imploring and cursing and demanding – God knows it was bedlam turned loose. I have been called a man of greatest genius for an emergency by some, by others a damned fool, by others every epithet between these extremes.

The American government dispatched the *Tennessee* with gold to finance its citizens; the warship also ferried Americans across the Channel from France.[94] The ambassadors from the belligerent countries were treated more gently, leaving in special trains, protected by the troops of their enemy. Jules Cambon and the Russian ambassador had already left Berlin on the weekend and now on 5 August a shattered Lichnowsky prepared to leave London. 'I feared he might literally go mad,' Page wrote to Wilson after seeing him. 'He is of the anti-war party and utterly failed. This interview was one of the most pathetic experiences of my life …'[95]

In 1914 Europe's leaders failed it either by deliberately opting for war or by not finding the strength to oppose it. Over half a century later a young and inexperienced American president faced his own crisis and his own choices. In 1962 when the Soviet Union placed military forces on Cuba, including missiles capable of striking the eastern seaboard of the United States with nuclear warheads, John F. Kennedy was under intense pressure from his own military to take action even at the risk of an all-out war with the Soviet Union. He resisted, partly because he had learned from the previous year's fiasco of the Bay of Pigs that the military were not always right but also because he had just read *The Guns of August*, Barbara Tuchman's extraordinary account of how Europe had blundered into the Great War. He choose to open negotiations with the Soviet Union and the world backed away from the brink.

Shock, exhilaration, gloom, resignation: Europeans greeted the coming of the war in many ways. Some found comfort, even inspiration, in the way in which their nations seemed to be as one. Friedrich Meinecke, the great German historian, described it as 'one of the great moments of my life which suddenly filled my soul with the deepest confidence in our people and the profoundest joy'.[96] Henry James, by contrast, wrote in anguish to a friend:

> The intense unthinkability of anything so blank and so infamous in an age that we have been living in and taking for our own as if it were of a high refinement of civilisation – in spite of all conscious incongruities; finding it after all carrying this abomination in its blood, finding this to have been what it *meant* all the while, is like suddenly having to recognise in one's family circle or group of best friends a band of murderers, swindlers and villains – it's just such a similar shock.[97]

Europe's steps could have gone in other directions but in August 1914 they led it to the end of the path and now destruction faced it.

Epilogue:
The War

On 4 August what Theodore Roosevelt called 'that great black tornado' broke over Europe.[1] Like a sudden summer storm the war caught many by surprise, but there was little attempt, at first, to escape from it. For some Europeans there was relief that the waiting was over, comfort even as their societies pulled together. The European peace movement fell apart along the national lines that had always been there, and across the Continent the socialists joined forces with the middle- and upper-class parties to vote overwhelmingly for war credits. A German socialist felt 'the terrible tension was resolved ... one could, for the first time in almost a quarter-century, join with a full heart, a clean conscience and without a sense of treason in the sweeping, stormy song: "Deutschland, Deutschland, über alles"'.[2] Winston Churchill was by no means alone in feeling exhilaration at the drama itself. 'My darling one', he wrote to his wife, 'Everything tends towards catastrophe and collapse. I am interested, geared up and happy. Is it not horrible to be built like that?'[3] The majority of Europeans, as far as it is possible to tell, were simply stupefied at the speed and finality with which Europe's long peace had ended. They accepted the coming of war with resignation and a sense of obligation, persuaded that their nations were the innocent parties under attack from menacing foreign forces.

Although there are many myths about the Great War, in August 1914 the soldiers did indeed tell their families that they would be home for Christmas. At the British Staff College at Camberley where the graduating students waited amidst the usual garden parties, cricket matches and picnics for their orders, word came at last that they were to take up their appointments, most with the British Expeditionary Force that was going to the Continent. The college itself was closed until further notice and its instructors were also given staff posts; the authorities thought there was no need to carry on training more officers for a short war.[4] The warnings of experts such as Ivan Bloch and Moltke himself or of pacifists such as Bertha von Suttner and Jean Jaurès that offensives would end in stalemates with neither side strong enough to overcome the other, while societies were drained of their resources, from men to munitions, were forgotten, at least for the time being, as the European powers marched into war. Most people, from those in command to the ordinary citizen, assumed that it would be short, like the Franco-Prussian War, for example, where it took the armies of the German alliance less than two months to force the surrender of France. (That the fighting then dragged on because the French people took up the struggle was another matter.) Financial experts, whether bankers or finance ministers, took it for granted that the war would have to be short: the disruption of trade and the inability of governments to borrow money as the international capital markets dried up would mean that impending bankruptcy would make it impossible for the belligerents to carry on fighting. As Norman Angell, in his *Great Illusion*, warned, even if Europe was so foolish as to go to war, the resulting economic chaos and domestic misery would rapidly force the warring nations to negotiate a peace. What few realised – although Bloch had – was that Europe's governments had an untested but great capacity to squeeze resources out of their societies, whether through taxation, managing their economies or freeing up men for the front by using the labour of women, and that Europeans themselves had a stoicism and doggedness which could keep them fighting through the long years to come even as the terrible losses mounted. What is surprising about the Great War is not that European societies and individuals eventually buckled under the strain – and not all did, or not completely – but that Russia, Germany and Austria-Hungary endured for so long before they collapsed into revolution or mutiny or despair.

In those first weeks of the war, it looked as though Europe might just be spared its doom. If Germany defeated France quickly, Russia might well decide to make peace in the east and Britain might reconsider its commitment to fight. Even if the French people decided to fight on as they had done in 1870–71, they would in the end be obliged to capitulate. As the German forces poured through Belgium and Luxembourg on their way into northern France, the German war plans appeared to be unfolding as they should. Not quite, however. Belgium's decision to resist slowed the pace of the German advance. The main fortress at Liège fell on 7 August but twelve more had to be taken one by one. Belgian resistance also meant that Germany had to leave troops behind as it advanced. The German army on the great right wing which was to swoop across the Meuse towards the Channel and then swing south towards Paris and so bring a stunning victory was both weaker and slower than had been planned. On 25 August Moltke, alarmed at the speed of Russia's advance in the east – with Russian troops overrunning Junker estates and burning the Kaiser's favourite hunting lodge at Rominten – had ordered two army corps amounting to some 88,000 men to move from the west to East Prussia.[5] And the British Expeditionary Force had arrived earlier than expected to reinforce the French.

The German advance slowed and then stopped in the face of Allied resistance. By the start of September the balance was tilting against Germany and the Allies were far from defeat. On 9 September Moltke ordered the German armies in France to withdraw to the north and regroup and two days later he gave a general order for a retreat all along the line. This, although he could not know it at the time, was the end of the Schlieffen Plan and Germany's chance to defeat France quickly. On 14 September the Kaiser relieved him of his duties on the grounds of health.

The Germans and the Allies each made desperate last attempts to outmanoeuvre the other that autumn. The losses mounted but victory remained elusive. By the end of 1914 265,000 French soldiers were dead and the British had lost 90,000 men. Some German regiments had taken 60 per cent casualties; the German army had lost 80,000 men in the fighting around the Flemish town of Ypres in October alone.[6] As winter approached, the armies on each side dug in expecting to resume their attacks in the spring. Little did they know that the temporary trenches they dug from the Swiss border across the eastern and northern frontiers of France and into Belgium would grow deeper, stronger, and more elaborate and would last until the summer of 1918.

On the Eastern Front, because the distances were so much greater, the network of trenches never developed to the same extent or grew as impermeable, but again the power of the defence to blunt attacks was all too clearly apparent in the opening months of the war. Austria-Hungary suffered major reverses but Russia proved unable to win a decisive victory. In the first four months of the war Austria-Hungary had suffered a total of nearly a million casualties. Although Germany, contrary to what Schlieffen and his successors had expected, had gone on the attack to defeat two Russian armies in the Battle of Tannenberg, victory on the battlefield did not bring the end of the war. Both Russia and its enemies had the resources and the determination to fight on.

There is a story, which may even be true. Ernest Shackleton, the great polar explorer, set off for the Antarctic in the autumn of 1914. When he finally made his way back to the whaling station on South Georgia Island in spring of 1916 he reportedly asked who had won the European war and was amazed to be told that it was still going on. Industries, national wealth, labour, science, technology, even the arts had all been harnessed to the war effort. Europe's progress, which it had celebrated so proudly at the Paris Exposition of 1900, had enabled it to perfect the means to mobilise its great resources in order to destroy itself.

The opening stages set the dreadful pattern for the next years: attacks were blunted time and again, as the defenders' guns poured out their lethal fire. The generals tried repeatedly to break the deadlock with massive offensives which led to equally massive casualties; fronts, especially in the west, where the terrain was churned up by explosives, were pitted with shell holes and criss-crossed by barbed wire, and the lines scarcely moved. And as the war dragged on, it consumed lives on a scale we find hard to imagine. In 1916 alone Russia's summer offensive produced 1.4 million casualties; 400,000 Italians were taken prisoner in Conrad's offensive in the Dolomites against Italy; and there were 57,000 British casualties on 1 July, the first day of the Somme, and by the battle's end in November 650,000 Allied dead, wounded or missing along with 400,000 Germans. At Verdun, the struggle between France and Germany for control of the fortress may have cost the French defenders over 500,000 casualties and the German attackers more than 400,000. By the time the war ended on 11 November 1918, sixty-five million men had fought and eight and a half million had been killed. Eight million were prisoners or simply missing. Twenty-one million had been wounded and that figure only included the wounds that could be measured; no one will ever know how many were damaged or destroyed psychologically. By comparison, 47,000 American soldiers were killed in Vietnam and 4,800 coalition troops in the invasion and occupation of Iraq.

The war, initially European, soon became global. From the start the empires had automatically been involved. No one stopped to ask the Canadians or the Australians, the Vietnamese or the Algerians whether they wanted to fight for the imperial powers. To be fair, many did. In the 'white' dominions, where many still had family ties to Britain, it was simply assumed that the mother country must be defended. More surprisingly, Indian nationalists, many of them, rallied to Britain's support. The young radical lawyer Mahatma Gandhi helped the British authorities recruit Indians for the war effort. Other powers gradually chose sides. Japan declared war on Germany at the end of August 1914 and took the opportunity to seize German possessions in China and the Pacific. The Ottoman Empire threw in its lot with Germany and Austria-Hungary two months later and Bulgaria joined them in 1915. That was the last ally the Central Powers acquired. Rumania, Greece, Italy, several Latin American countries and China eventually joined the Allies.

In the United States there was initially no strong support for either side in a conflict which seemed to have little to do with American interests. 'Again and ever I thank God for the Atlantic Ocean', wrote Walter Page, the American ambassador in London. The elites, liberals and those on the eastern seaboard or with family ties to Britain inclined towards the Allies but a significant minority, perhaps as much as a quarter of Americans, were of German descent. And the large Irish Catholic minority had strong reason to hate Britain. As the war started Wilson tore himself from his wife's deathbed to give a press conference at which he proclaimed the United States would remain neutral. 'I want', he said, 'to have the pride of feeling that America, if nobody else, has her self-possession and stands ready with calmness of thought and steadiness of purpose to help the rest of the world.' It took German policies, or more specifically those of the high command, to goad Americans out of their neutrality. In 1917 the United States, infuriated by German submarine attacks on its shipping and by the news, which the British obligingly passed on to Washington, that Germany was trying to persuade Mexico and Japan to attack the United States, entered the war on the Allied side.

By 1918, the combined forces of their enemies were too much for the Central Powers and one by one they sued for peace until Germany at last made its request for an armistice. When the guns fell silent on 11 November, it was in a very different world from that of 1914. Across Europe the old fissures in society which had been temporarily papered over at the start of the conflict had re-emerged as the war had dragged on, imposing its increasingly heavy burdens. As social and political unrest spread, old regimes floundered, unable to maintain the trust of their publics or meet their expectations. In February 1917 the tsarist regime finally collapsed and the weak provisional government which succeeded it was in turn ousted ten months later by a new type of revolutionary force, Vladimir Lenin's Bolsheviks. To save his regime, which was under attack by his political rivals and the remnants of the old order, Lenin made peace with the Central Powers at the start of 1918, ceding them huge swathes of Russian territory in the west. While Russians fought Russians in a bitter civil war, the peoples subjugated to the Russian Empire took the opportunity to escape. Poles, Ukrainians, Georgians, Azerbaijanis, Armenians, Finns, Estonians and Latvians, all enjoyed, some only briefly, their independence.

Austria-Hungary fell to pieces in the summer of 1918, its nationality problems finally too much for it. Its Poles joined with those who were suddenly freed from Russia and Germany to create, for the first time in over a century, a Polish state. Czechs and Slovaks came together in an uneasy marriage to form Czechoslovakia while the Dual Monarchy's South Slavs in Croatia, Slovenia, and Bosnia joined with Serbia to form a new state that would be known as Yugoslavia. Hungary, much reduced by the loss of Croatia and by the peace settlements after the war, became an independent state while what was left of the Habsburg territories became the little state of Austria. Of the other Central Powers, Bulgaria too had its revolution and Ferdinand, foxy to the last, abdicated in favour of his son. The Ottoman Empire also collapsed; the victorious Allies stripped it of its Arab territories and most of what was left in Europe, leaving only the Turkish heartland. The last of the Ottoman sultans slipped quietly away into exile in 1922 and a new secular ruler, Kemal Ataturk, set about creating the modern state of Turkey.

As Germany's armies met defeat in the summer of 1918, the German public, which had been kept in the dark by Hindenburg and Ludendorff, who now dominated the civilian government, reacted angrily against the whole regime. For a time, as sailors and soldiers mutinied and workers' councils seized control of local governments, it looked as though Germany might follow Russia's path. A reluctant Kaiser was forced to abdicate at the start of November 1918 and a new republic was proclaimed by the socialists who, it turned out, managed to check the revolution.

Although the victorious powers had their share of upheavals – there were violent strikes and demonstrations in France, Italy, and Britain by 1918 – the old order held there, for the time being. But Europe collectively was no longer the centre of the world. It had spent down its great wealth and exhausted its power. The peoples of its empires who had largely acquiesced in rule from outside were stirring, their confidence that their foreign masters knew best shaken irremediably by the four years of savagery on Europe's battlefields. New nationalist leaders, many of them soldiers who had witnessed for themselves what European civilisation could produce, demanded self-government now and not in some far-off future. Britain's 'white' dominions were content to stay within the empire but only on the condition that they had increased autonomy. New players from outside Europe were taking a greater part in world affairs. In the Far East, Japan had grown in both power and confidence and dominated its neighbourhood. Across the Atlantic the United States was now a major world power, its industries and farms stimulated to even more growth by the war and with New York increasingly the centre of world finance. Americans saw Europe as old, decadent and finished – and many Europeans agreed with them.

The war had not just destroyed much of Europe's heritage and millions of its people but it had brutalised many of those who survived. The nationalist passions which sustained Europeans during the war had also led to the wanton killing of civilians, whether by Germans in Belgium, the Russians in Galicia or the Austrians in Bosnia. Occupying armies had rounded up civilians for forced labour and driven out those of the 'wrong' ethnicity. After the war, in much of Europe politics were marked by violence, with frequent assassinations and pitched battles between opposing parties. And the new intolerant and totalitarian ideologies of fascism and Russian-style communism drew their organisation and discipline from the military and, in the case of fascists, their inspiration from war itself.

The Great War marked a break in Europe's history. Before 1914, Europe for all its problems had hope that the world was becoming a better place and that human civilisation was advancing. After 1918 that faith was no longer possible for Europeans. As they looked back at their lost world before the war, they could feel only a sense of loss and waste. In the late summer of 1918, as the extent of Germany's defeat was becoming clear, Count Harry Kessler returned to his old house in Weimar which he had not visited for many years. Although Kessler had been caught up in the nationalist fervour in 1914, he had long since come to regret that the war had ever started. His old coachman and his dog were waiting for him at the train station and greeted him as though he had only been away for a few days. His house, he recalled, like the Sleeping Beauty, was waiting unchanged for him:

> The impressionist and neo-impressionist paintings, the rows of books in French, English, Italian, Greek, and German, the figures of Maillol, his somewhat too strong, lusty women, his beautiful naked youth after the little Colin, as if it were still 1913 and the many people who were here and are now dead, missing, scattered, or enemies could return and begin European life anew. It seemed to me like a little palace out of *A Thousand and One Nights*, full of all kinds of treasures and half-faded symbols and memories that someone thrust from another age could only sip. I found a dedication from d'Annunzio; Persian cigarettes from Isfahan brought by Claude Anet; the bonbonnière from the baptism of the youngest child of Maurice Denis; a program of the Russian Ballet from 1911 with pictures of Nijinsky; the secret book by Lord Lovelace, the grandchild of Byron, about his incest, sent to me by Julia Ward; books by Oscar Wilde and Alfred Douglas with a letter from Ross;

and – still unpacked – Robert de Montesquiou's comic-serious masterpiece from the years before the war on the beautiful Countess of Castiglione, whom he affected to love posthumously – her nightshirt lay in a jewel case or little glass coffin in one of his reception rooms. How monstrously did fate rear up from this European life – precisely from it – just like the second bloodiest tragedy of history arose from the playing at shepherds and the light spirit of Boucher and Voltaire. That the age was heading not toward a more solid peace but toward war we all actually knew, but didn't know at the same time. It was a kind of a floating feeling that like a soap bubble suddenly burst and disappeared without a trace when the hellish forces that were bubbling up in its lap were ripe.[7]

Of those who had played their part in taking Europe down the path to the Great War some did not live to see its end. Moltke never returned from his sick leave to resume his duties as Germany's chief of staff. He died of a stroke in 1916 as his successor Falkenhayn was throwing the German army into repeated, costly and futile attacks at Verdun. Princip, who had set the fatal train of events in motion when he assassinated Franz Ferdinand in Sarajevo, was found guilty in an Austrian-Hungarian court but could not be executed because he was under age. He died of tuberculosis in an Austrian prison in the spring of 1918, unrepentant to the last about what his act had unleashed.[8] The emperor, Franz Joseph, died in 1916, leaving his tottering throne to a young, inexperienced great nephew, Karl, who held on to power only until 1918. István Tisza, who finally decided to approve Austria-Hungary's decision to force a war on Serbia, was murdered in front of his wife by revolutionary Hungarian soldiers in 1918. Rasputin was assassinated in St Petersburg in 1916 by aristocratic conspirators who hoped in vain that his removal would save the regime. Nicholas abdicated the following year. He and Alexandra and their children were murdered in Ekaterinburg by the Bolsheviks in the spring of 1918. The bodies were buried in an unmarked grave but rediscovered after the fall of the Soviet Union. The remains were identified using DNA including a sample from the Duke of Edinburgh, Alexandra's grand-nephew, and the Russian Orthodox Church has now made the parents and the children saints.

Some of Nicholas's ministers were more fortunate. Izvolsky never returned from Paris to Russia and lived on in France with a small allowance from the French government. Sazonov, the Foreign Minister, was dismissed early in 1917. He joined the anti-Bolshevik forces of Admiral Kolchak in the civil war and ended in exile in France, dying in Nice in 1927. Sukhomlinov was blamed for Russia's failures in the war and in 1916 the tsar abandoned his War Minister and allowed him to be tried on the charges of corruption, neglect of Russia's armies, and spying for Germany and Austria-Hungary. The corruption was no doubt true but the government was able to produce only the feeblest evidence to support the other charges. The new provisional government which took power early in 1917 threw him and his beautiful wife, Ekaterina, into jail and resumed the trial in the late summer. Ekaterina was acquitted but Sukhomlinov was sentenced to life imprisonment, although in May 1918 the Bolsheviks, who were now in power, released him as part of a general amnesty. He escaped from Russia into Finland that autumn and made his way to Berlin, where he wrote the almost inevitable memoirs and tried to survive in extreme poverty. Ekaterina, who had by now found a new rich protector, stayed on; the Bolsheviks apparently shot her in 1921. One morning in February 1926 policemen in Berlin found the body of an old man on a park bench. Sukhomlinov, who was once one of the richest and most powerful men in Russia, had frozen to death overnight.[9]

At the war's end Hoyos, the hawk who had helped to obtain Germany's blank cheque for Austria-Hungary, briefly contemplated suicide as he contemplated his own responsibility for the war and the end of the Dual Monarchy but thought better of it and died peacefully in 1937. Berchtold, the Chancellor, resigned during the early stages of the war in protest against the short-sighted refusal of the emperor and his colleagues to give Italy pieces of the Austrian territory it desired in order to ensure its neutrality. He lived until 1942, on one of his estates in Hungary, and is buried at his castle at Buchlau, scene of the fateful meeting between his predecessor Aehrenthal and Izvolsky which set off the Bosnian crisis of 1908. Conrad, the chief of staff of Austria-Hungary who had finally got Franz Joseph's permission to marry Gina von Reininghaus in 1915, was dismissed by the new emperor 1917. After the war he and Gina lived simply in the Austrian mountains and he passed the time by studying English – his ninth language – going for walks with ex-King Ferdinand of Bulgaria and writing a huge self-justifying memoir in five volumes. (There was to be a flood of such memoirs in the 1920s as the key players tried to exonerate themselves and cast the blame on others for the war.) Conrad died in 1925 and was given a state funeral by the government of the new republic of Austria. Gina lived to see Austria absorbed into the Third German Reich and the Nazis always treated her with great deference. She died in 1961.

Asquith came under increasing criticism for his lackadaisical handling of the war effort and was forced to resign at the end of 1916. His successor was Lloyd George, who, despite his antipathy to war, proved to be a strong wartime leader. The rivalry between the two men split the Liberal Party, which has never recovered its former strength. Grey, who was nearly blind, also went into opposition but agreed to be British ambassador to the United States at the end of the war. In his memoirs he continued to deny that he had ever made any commitments to France. Shortly before he died he published a book on the charm of birds. Sir Henry Wilson, who had done so much to build the relationship between Britain and France, ended the war as a field marshal. In 1922 he became security adviser to the government of Northern Ireland which had remained part of the United Kingdom when the South became independent. He was assassinated shortly afterwards by two Irish nationalists on the steps of his house in London.

Poincaré remained in office throughout the war to preside over France's victory and the restoration to it of Alsace and Lorraine. His term as President ended in 1920 but he came back as Prime Minister twice in the 1920s. He retired because of ill health in the summer of 1929 but survived to see Hitler and the Nazis take power in 1933, dying the following year. Dreyfus volunteered to fight in the army which had disgraced him when war broke out and served throughout; he died in 1935 and his funeral passed through the Place de la Concorde which was lined with troops.

In Germany, Bethmann was forced out of office in the summer of 1917 by the duo of Hindenburg and Ludendorff when he tried to oppose their resumption of unrestricted submarine warfare against merchant shipping and their expansionist war aims. Bethmann retreated to his beloved estate at Hohenfinow and spent the few remaining years of his life trying to justify himself and his policies as well as denying German responsibility for the war. He died in 1920 aged sixty-four. His rival for the Kaiser's ear, Tirpitz, dabbled in right-wing politics after the war and maintained to his death in 1930 that his naval policy had been right and blamed everyone else from the Kaiser to the army for Germany's defeat.

Wilhelm survived for years, bombastic, bossy, and self-righteous to the last. During the war he had become 'the Shadow Kaiser'; his generals did all in his name but paid him little attention in reality. Wilhelm set up his headquarters in the little Belgian town of Spa behind the lines on the Western Front and passed his days in a routine of early morning rides, a couple of hours' work (which consisted largely of awarding decorations and sending telegrams of congratulation to his officers), visits to hospitals, sightseeing and walks in the afternoons, and then dinner with his generals and bed at eleven. He liked going close enough to the front to hear the gunfire and would proudly say back at Spa that he had been in the war. As Hitler would in a later war, he liked to dream about what he would do after the conflict had ended. Wilhelm was full of plans for encouraging motor racing and for reforming society in Berlin. There were to be no more parties in hotels; the aristocracy must all build their own palaces.[10] As the war went on his staff noticed that he looked lined and was easily depressed. They took to keeping the increasingly bad news from him.[11]

As Germany's defeat became clear in the autumn of 1918, his military made plans for their Kaiser to die heroically in a last charge onto the battlefield. Wilhelm would have none of this and continued to hope, in vain, that he could keep his throne. As the situation deteriorated in Germany, he was finally persuaded on 9 November to go to the Netherlands by special train and Germany became a republic the same day. Wilhelm's first request when he arrived at the estate of a Dutch aristocrat who had agreed to take him in was 'a cup of real good English tea'.[12] In spite of pressure from the Allies, the Dutch refused to extradite him and he lived out his days in a small palace at Doorn. He kept himself busy by chopping down trees – 20,000 by the end of the 1920s; writing his memoirs, which, not surprisingly, showed no remorse for the war or for the policies leading up to it; reading long extracts in English from P. G. Wodehouse to his staff; fulminating against the Weimar Republic, socialists and Jews; and blaming the German people for letting him down while still believing they would one day call him back.

He took note of the rise of Hitler and the Nazis with mixed feelings; he found Hitler lower class and vulgar but agreed with many of his ideas, especially where they meant restoring Germany's greatness. He warned, though: 'It will run away with him, as it ran away with me.'[13] Wilhelm welcomed the start of the Second World War and the string of early German victories with delight. He died on 4 June 1941, less than three weeks before Hitler invaded Russia, and is buried at Doorn.[14]

Was he to blame for the Great War? Was Tirpitz? Grey? Moltke? Berchtold? Poincaré? Or was no one to blame? Should we look instead at institutions or ideas? General staffs with too much power, absolutist governments, Social Darwinism, the cult of the offensive, nationalism? There are so many questions and as many answers again. Perhaps the most we can hope for is to understand as best we can those individuals, who had to make the choices between war and peace, and their strengths and weaknesses, their loves, hatreds and biases. To do that we must also understand their world, with its assumptions. We must remember, as the decision-makers did, what had happened before that last crisis of 1914 and what they had learned from the Moroccan crises, the Bosnian one, or the events of the First Balkan Wars. Europe's very success in surviving those earlier crises paradoxically led to a dangerous complacency in the summer of 1914 that, yet again, solutions would be found at the last moment and the peace would be maintained. And if we want to point fingers from the twenty-first century we can accuse those who took Europe into war of two things. First, a failure of imagination in not seeing how destructive such a conflict would be and second, their lack of courage to stand up to those who said there was no choice left but to go war. There are always choices.

Acknowledgements

Yet again I have been extremely fortunate in the help I have had from many people in the writing of this book. They deserve credit for what is good about it and I will take responsibility for its shortcomings.

I start, as I should, with my wonderful research assistants who have been indefatigable, highly organised and helpful to the point where I see them as essential collaborators. Dawn Berry, Yulia Naumova, Rebecca Snow, Katharina Uhl, and Troy Vettese unearthed and analysed wonderful materials in several languages and showed an unerring instinct for what was important and interesting. In the last stages, Dawn stepped in to read through the manuscript, sort out the endnotes and wrestle my bibliography into shape. In Toronto, Mischa Kaplan also contributed useful work.

Over the past few years I have had the great pleasure and benefit of being part of Oxford and of St Antony's College. While there have been times when I have felt like the character in the Monty Python sketch who complained loudly that his brain hurt, I have never ceased to be amazed and deeply grateful for the extraordinary intellectual and social life here. I have learned much and keep learning from my colleagues and students. I have benefited greatly too from being able to use the resources of the Bodleian and the College Library.

The Governing Body of St Antony's College generously gave me a leave of absence for the academic year 2012–13 and I owe a particular thanks to Professor Rosemary Foot, who selflessly took on the role of Acting Warden, which, to no one's surprise, she did with her customary integrity and efficiency. I am also grateful to my colleagues who kept the considerable work involved in the administration of the College flowing smoothly in my absence. They include the Sub Warden, Alex Pravda, the Estates Bursars, Alan Taylor and his successor Kirsten Gillingham, the Domestic Bursar, Peter Robinson, the Development Director, Ranjit Majumdar, the Registrar, Margaret Couling, my Personal Assistant Penny Cooke, and their colleagues.

While I have been in Oxford I have also remained part of another great institution, the University of Toronto and I have continued to benefit from contact with my colleagues and students there and by being able to use its excellent library. I am particularly grateful to the Munk Centre of Global Affairs, its founder Peter Munk and its Director Janice Stein, for giving me a fellowship there for the year that I was in Toronto writing this book and who made me part of its lively and stimulating academic community.

Five years ago I did not intend to write a book on the outbreak of the Great War; the path had been too well-trodden and I had other projects underway. When Andrew Franklin of Profile Books put the idea to me, I resisted – and then found that I spent a summer thinking about it. So I owe him perhaps a small grudge but a much bigger thanks for getting me involved in an enthralling subject. Without him and his wonderful team at Profile – including Penny Daniel, Daniel Crewe and the late and much-missed Peter Carson – this book could not have taken shape. And I owe an equal debt of gratitude to my publishers in the United States at Random House and in Canada at Penguin. Kate Medina in New York and Diane Turbide in Toronto are model publishers whose constructive comments and suggestions have made this book much better than it would have been. Cecilia Mackay is an outstanding picture researcher and Trevor Horwood is her equal as a copy-editor. I am also lucky to have had as cheerleaders on what has sometimes seemed like a long journey Caroline Dawnay, agent and friend, and, in Canada, the endlessly enthusiastic Michael Levine.

I would like to thank the curators of the Bodleian Library and Sir Brian Crowe for permission to quote from the Eyre Crowe papers. Thanks too to Professor Laird Easton and Knopf Doubleday Publishing Group for permission to use his translations of Count Harry Kessler's diaries. Extracts from Queen Victoria's journals were used by kind permission of Her Majesty Queen Elizabeth II.

Henry Kissinger, Alistair Horne, Norman Davies, Michael Howard, Eugene Rogan, Avi Shlaim, Paul Betts, Alan Alexandroff, Hartmut Pogge von Strandmann and Liaquat Ahamed all kindly took the time from their own work to discuss my ideas with me and give their advice. Many friends and family have offered encouragement as well as hot meals throughout, including Thomas Barcsay, David Blewett, Robert Bothwell, Gwyneth Daniel, Arthur Sheps, and Andrew Watson. I am always grateful that I have a large and friendly family who kept an eye on me and prevented me from becoming a complete hermit living only with the ghosts of Austrian archdukes, Russian counts, German generals or British Cabinet ministers. Ann MacMillan and Peter Snow, Thomas and Catharina MacMillan, Margot Finley and Daniel Snow also read parts of the manuscript and, as they always do, made invaluable comments and criticisms. My best and most painstaking reader is my mother Eluned MacMillan who, yet again, read every word. Although it pains her to criticise her children, she was both honest and very helpful. My deepest thanks to you all.

Notes

Abbreviations: BD – Gooch, G. P. and Temperley, H., eds., *British Documents on the Origins of the War*; DDF – France. Ministère des Affaires Étrangères, *Documents diplomatiques français, 1871–1914*, 3rd series; RA – Royal Archives, Windsor Castle, available at http://www.royal.gov.uk/. Full entries for these and all other sources will be found in the Bibliography.

Introduction: War or Peace?
1. Kramer, *Dynamic of Destruction*, 8–9. **2.** *New York Times*, 29 September 1914. **3.** Kramer, *Dynamic of Destruction*, 30. **4.** Lloyd George, *War Memoirs*, vol. I, 52.

1 Europe in 1900
1. All references to Hachette's guide to the Exposition, *Paris Exposition, 1900: guide pratique du visiteur de Paris et de l'exposition*, are taken from the online version at http://archive.org/details/parisexpositionoopari **2.** *The Times*, 24 May 1900. **3.** *New York Observer and Chronicle*, 25 October 1900. **4.** *The Times*, 18 April 1900. **5.** Lieven, *The Aristocracy in Europe, 1815–1914*, 7. **6.** Zweig, *The World of Yesterday*, 215. **7.** Addison and O'Grady, *Diary of a European Tour, 1900*, 30. **8.** Zweig, *The World of Yesterday*, 26. **9.** Dowler, *Russia in 1913*, ch. 1, passim. **10.** Kennedy, *The Rise and Fall of the Great Powers*, ch. 4, passim. **11.** Tylor, *Primitive Culture*, 2. **12.** Blom, *The Vertigo Years*, 8. **13.** *New York Observer and Chronicle*, 27 December 1900. **14.** *New York Observer and Chronicle*, 11 October 1900. **15.** Herring, *From Colony to Superpower*, 345. **16.** Cronin, *Paris on the Eve*, 37. **17.** Zweig, *The World of Yesterday*, 216. **18.** Weber, *France: Fin de Siècle*, 230–31. **19.** Blom, *The Vertigo Years*, 265–8. **20.** *New York Observer and Chronicle*, 18 October 1900. **21.** Kessler, *Journey to the Abyss*, 81. **22.** Hewitson, 'Germany and France', 580. **23.** Weber, *France: Fin de Siècle*, 243–4. **24.** Cronin, *Paris on the Eve*, 36. **25.** Weber, *France: Fin de Siècle*, 243. **26.** Andrew, *Théophile Delcassé*, 136; *New York Observer and Chronicle*, 1 November 1900. **27.** Ridley, *Bertie*, 338.

2 Great Britain and Splendid Isolation
1. *New York Times*, 24 June 1897; *Spectator*, 26 June 1897. **2.** RA VIC/MAIN/QVJ (W) 22 June 1897 (Princess Beatrice's copies). **3.** Massie, *Dreadnought*, xviii. **4.** Rüger, *The*

Great Naval Game, 200, 74. **5.** Massie, *Dreadnought*, xx. **6.** Roberts, *Salisbury*, 664–5; Rüger, *The Great Naval Game*, 184–5; Massie, *Dreadnought*, xviii–xx. **7.** Kipling and Pinney, *The Letters of Rudyard Kipling*, vol. II, 303. **8.** Massie, *Dreadnought*, xxx; Rüger, *The Great Naval Game*, 191–2; Roberts, *Salisbury*, 661. **9.** Cannadine, *The Decline and Fall of the British Aristocracy*, 9–11; Lieven, *The Aristocracy in Europe, 1815–1914*, 205; Cecil, *Life of Robert, Marquis of Salisbury*, 159. **10.** Roberts, *Salisbury*, 8–12, 28.
11. Tuchman, *The Proud Tower*, 9. **12.** Roberts, *Salisbury*, 714–15; Tuchman, *The Proud Tower*, 6. **13.** Cecil, *Life of Robert, Marquis of Salisbury*, 176. **14.** Roberts, *Salisbury*, 111. **15.** Cecil, *Life of Robert, Marquis of Salisbury*, 3–4, 6, 8. **16.** Gilmour, *Curzon*, 125. **17.** Massie, *Dreadnought*, 195. **18.** Roberts, *Salisbury*, 6. **19.** Ibid., 34. **20.** Bánffy, *They Were Divided*, Kindle version, loc. 6086. **21.** Cannadine, *The Decline and Fall of the British Aristocracy*, 36–9. **22.** Hamilton, *Parliamentary Reminiscences and Reflections, 1886–1906*, 253. **23.** Roberts, *Salisbury*, 624, 651. **24.** Ibid., 626. **25.** Ibid., 65. **26.** Ibid., 647; Gilmour, *Curzon*, 125. **27.** Cecil, *Life of Robert, Marquis of Salisbury*, 247. **28.** Roberts, *Salisbury*, 44. **29.** Ibid., 46–50. **30.** Ibid., 628. **31.** Howard, 'The Policy of Isolation', 82. **32.** Cecil, *Life of Robert, Marquis of Salisbury*, 90. **33.** Ibid. **34.** Howard, 'The Policy of Isolation', 81. **35.** Ibid., 79–80. **36.** Beesly, *Queen Elizabeth*, 107. **37.** Burrows, *The History of the Foreign Policy of Great Britain*, 34; Otte, 'Almost a Law of Nature?', 75–6. **38.** Rüger, *The Great Naval Game*, 179. **39.** Steiner and Neilson, *Britain and the Origins*, 19. **40.** Kennedy, *Rise of the Anglo-German Antagonism*, 229. **41.** Roberts, *Salisbury*, 495–6. **42.** Ibid., 692. **43.** Ibid., 615–16; Herring, *From Colony to Superpower*, 307–8. **44.** Cecil, *Life of Robert, Marquis of Salisbury*, 3, 218. **45.** Gilmour, *Curzon*, 128. **46.** Mansergh, *The Commonwealth Experience*, vol. II, 27. **47.** Tuchman, *The Proud Tower*, 46–7. **48.** Ibid., 56. **49.** Spender, *The Public Life*, 81. **50.** Massie, *Dreadnought*, 233–9. **51.** Spender, *The Public Life*, 89. **52.** Kennedy, *Rise of the Anglo-German Antagonism*, 230–32. **53.** Roberts, *Salisbury*, 748. **54.** Taylor, *The Struggle for Mastery in Europe*, 396. **55.** Neilson, 'The Anglo-Japanese Alliance', 52. **56.** Kennedy, *Rise of the Anglo-German Antagonism*, 230–31; Roberts, *Salisbury*, 745. **57.** Bond, *The Victorian Army and the Staff College*, 191. **58.** Taylor, *The Struggle for Mastery in Europe*, 376. **59.** Ibid., 395. **60.** Massie, *Dreadnought*, 306. **61.** Neilson, 'The Anglo-Japanese Alliance', 49. **62.** Steiner and Neilson, *Britain and the Origins*, 29. **63.** Massie, *Dreadnought*, 308; Balfour, *The Kaiser and His Times*, 235–6; Eckardstein and Young, *Ten Years at the Court of St. James*, 227. **64.** Nish, 'Origins of the Anglo-Japanese Alliance', 12. **65.** Ibid., 13. **66.** *The Times*, 4 January 1902. **67.** Balfour, *The Kaiser and His Times*, 240.

3 Wilhelm II and Germany

1. Benson and Esher, *Letters: A Selection from Her Majesty's Correspondence*, vol. III, 414. **2.** Kennedy, *Rise of the Anglo-German Antagonism*, 119. **3.** Ibid., 104. **4.** *The Times*, 4 January 1896. **5.** Roberts, *Salisbury*, 624. **6.** Balfour, *The Kaiser and His Times*, 195. **7.** Steiner and Neilson, *Britain and the Origins*, 21. **8.** Ibid., 195. **9.** Kennedy, 'German World Policy', 614. **10.** Kennedy, *Rise of the Anglo-German Antagonism*, 234. **11.** Massie, *Dreadnought*, 358. **12.** Ibid., 259. **13.** Kröger, 'Imperial Germany and the Boer War', 38. **14.** Balfour, *The Kaiser and His Times*, 222–3. **15.** Kennedy, *Rise of the Anglo-German Antagonism*, 246–7. **16.** Ibid., ch. 14. **17.** Steiner and Neilson, *Britain and the Origins*, 22. **18.** Eckardstein and Young, *Ten Years at the Court of St. James*, 112. **19.** Kennedy, *Rise of the Anglo-German Antagonism*, 238. **20.** Balfour, *The Kaiser and*

His Times, 231. **21.** Carter, *The Three Emperors*, 267–71; *The Times*, 6 February 1901.
22. Lerchenfeld-Koefering, *Kaiser Wilhelm II*, 65, 58, 34. **23.** Beyens, *Germany before the War*, 14–15. **24.** Ibid., 14. **25.** Balfour, *The Kaiser and His Times*, 82, 138–9.
26. Hopman, *Das ereignisreiche Leben*, 125. **27.** Hull, *The Entourage of Kaiser Wilhelm II*, 17. **28.** Balfour, *The Kaiser and His Times*, 162. **29.** Lerchenfeld-Koefering, *Kaiser Wilhelm II*, 11. **30.** Zedlitz-Trützschler, *Twelve Years at the Imperial German Court*, 58–9. **31.** Hopman, *Das ereignisreiche Leben*, 140. **32.** Epkenhans, 'Wilhelm II and "His" Navy', 12. **33.** Balfour, *The Kaiser and His Times*, 143, 142. **34.** Cecil, *German Diplomatic Service*, 212. **35.** Zedlitz-Trützschler, *Twelve Years at the Imperial German Court*, 36. **36.** Lerchenfeld-Koefering, *Kaiser Wilhelm II*, 33. **37.** Balfour, *The Kaiser and His Times*, 82, 139, 148; Röhl, *The Kaiser and His Court*, 15–16. **38.** Zedlitz-Trützschler, *Twelve Years at the Imperial German Court*, 69. **39.** Röhl, *The Kaiser and His Court*, 15–16; Balfour, *The Kaiser and His Times*, 148. **40.** Beyens, *Germany before the War*, 58–9.
41. Kessler, *Journey to the Abyss*, 199. **42.** Röhl, *The Kaiser and His Court*, 13.
43. Wilhelm II, *Reden des Kaisers*, 32–3. **44.** Lerchenfeld-Koefering, *Kaiser Wilhelm II*, 19. **45.** Wilhelm II, *Reden des Kaisers*, 44. **46.** Balfour, *The Kaiser and His Times*, 226–7.
47. Hull, *The Entourage of Kaiser Wilhelm II*, 15–16. **48.** Schoen, *Memoirs of an Ambassador*, 138. **49.** Röhl, *The Kaiser and His Court*, 23–4. **50.** Ibid., 25–6; Balfour, *The Kaiser and His Times*, 73–4. **51.** Balfour, *The Kaiser and His Times*, 75–6. **52.** Clark, *Kaiser Wilhelm II*, 1–2, 16–18. **53.** Carter, *The Three Emperors*, 22. **54.** Zedlitz-Trützschler, *Twelve Years at the Imperial German Court*, 233. **55.** Bülow, *Memoirs of Prince von Bulow*, vol. II, 22. **56.** See, for example, Zedlitz-Trützschler, *Twelve Years at the Imperial German Court*, 184, 235, 272. **57.** Craig, *Germany, 1866–1945*, ch. 2; Clark, *Iron Kingdom*, 558–62. **58.** Wilhelm II, *Reden des Kaisers*, 51. **59.** Balfour, *The Kaiser and His Times*, 126. **60.** Hull, *The Entourage of Kaiser Wilhelm II*, 31–3. **61.** Herwig, '*Luxury*' *Fleet*, 23. **62.** Zedlitz-Trützschler, *Twelve Years at the Imperial German Court*, 37–8, 67; Clark, *Kaiser Wilhelm II*, 120. **63.** Fesser, *Reichskanzler Fürst von Bülow*, 46–7.
64. Rüger, *The Great Naval Game*, 93. **65.** Zedlitz-Trützschler, *Twelve Years at the Imperial German Court*, 233. **66.** Balfour, *The Kaiser and His Times*, 119. **67.** Wilhelm II, *Reden des Kaisers*, 56. **68.** Holstein et al., *The Holstein Papers*, 175. **69.** Clark, *Iron Kingdom*, 564. **70.** Craig, *Germany, 1866–1945*, 228; Cecil, *German Diplomatic Service*, 211–12. **71.** Lerchenfeld-Koefering, *Kaiser Wilhelm II*, 23. **72.** Herwig, '*Luxury*' *Fleet*, 17.

4 *Weltpolitik*: Germany's Place on the World Stage

1. Hull, *The Entourage of Kaiser Wilhelm II*, 31. **2.** Langsam, 'Nationalism and History', 242–3. **3.** Herwig, '*Luxury*' *Fleet*, 18. **4.** Epkenhans, 'Wilhelm II and "His" Navy', 15.
5. Ibid., 16. **6.** Balfour, *The Kaiser and His Times*, 232. **7.** Craig, *Germany, 1866–1945*, 244–5. **8.** Ibid., 246. **9.** Cecil, *German Diplomatic Service*, 282. **10.** Lerman, *The Chancellor as Courtier*, 1. **11.** Cecil, *German Diplomatic Service*, 281–2. **12.** Balfour, *The Kaiser and His Times*, 201. **13.** Lerman, *The Chancellor as Courtier*, 86–90. **14.** Cecil, *German Diplomatic Service*, 283. **15.** Berghahn, 'War Preparations and National Identity', 315. **16.** Kennedy, 'German World Policy', 617. **17.** Kennedy, *Rise of the Anglo-German Antagonism*, 226. **18.** Ibid., 235. **19.** Massie, *Dreadnought*, 126.
20. Eckardstein and Young, *Ten Years at the Court of St. James*, 33. **21.** Massie, *Dreadnought*, 129–30; Cecil, *German Diplomatic Service*, 294–5. **22.** Massie, *Dreadnought*, 124; Craig, *Germany, 1866–1945*, 127. **23.** Hewitson, *Germany and the Causes*, 146–7. **24.** Ibid., 147. **25.** Craig, *Germany, 1866–1945*, 249. **26.** Winzen, 'Prince

Bulow's Weltmachtpolitik', 227–8. **27.** Bülow, *Memoirs of Prince von Bulow*, vol. III, 100. **28.** Winzen, 'Treitschke's Influence', 155. **29.** Cecil, *Wilhelm II*, 51. **30.** Epkenhans, 'Wilhelm II and "His" Navy', 17. **31.** Winzen, 'Treitschke's Influence', 160–61. **32.** Wilson, *The Policy of the Entente*, 4. **33.** Kennedy, *Rise of the Anglo-German Antagonism*, 209. **34.** Epkenhans, 'Wilhelm II and "His" Navy', 13. **35.** Ritter, *The Sword and the Sceptre*, 110. **36.** Kennedy, 'German World Policy', 622. **37.** McMeekin, *The Berlin–Baghdad Express*, 14. **38.** Cecil, *Albert Ballin*, 152–3. **39.** Winzen, 'Treitschke's Influence', 159. **40.** Kennedy, *Rise of the Anglo-German Antagonism*, 241. **41.** Carter, *The Three Emperors*, 105. **42.** Balfour, *The Kaiser and His Times*, 140. **43.** Ibid., 84. **44.** Pless and Chapman-Huston, *Daisy, Princess of Pless*, 263–4. **45.** Balfour, *The Kaiser and His Times*, 180. **46.** Eckardstein and Young, *Ten Years at the Court of St. James*, 55. **47.** Balfour, *The Kaiser and His Times*, 265. **48.** Massie, *Dreadnought*, 106. **49.** Balfour, *The Kaiser and His Times*, 296. **50.** Ibid., 265. **51.** Roberts, *Salisbury*, 485–6. **52.** Massie, *Dreadnought*, 107. **53.** Clark, *Kaiser Wilhelm II*, 184. **54.** Tuchman, *The Proud Tower*, 131–4. **55.** Ibid., 132. **56.** Mahan, *The Influence of Sea Power upon History*, 28. **57.** Rüger, *The Great Naval Game*, 205–6. **58.** Clark, *Kaiser Wilhelm II*, 184. **59.** Bülow, *Memoirs of Prince von Bulow*, vol. II, 36–7. **60.** Epkenhans, *Tirpitz*, Kindle version, loc. 345. **61.** Ibid., loc. 375–6. **62.** Ibid., loc. 391–5. **63.** Beyens, *Germany before the War*, 129. **64.** Massie, *Dreadnought*, 165. **65.** Steinberg, *Yesterday's Deterrent*, 69. **66.** Epkenhans, *Tirpitz*, Kindle version, loc. 93–4. **67.** Balfour, *The Kaiser and His Times*, 203. **68.** Epkenhans, *Tirpitz*, Kindle version, loc. 383–7. **69.** Ibid., loc. 427–31. **70.** Herwig, 'From Tirpitz Plan to Schlieffen Plan', 53–5. **71.** Epkenhans, *Tirpitz*, Kindle version, loc. 592–5; Lambi, *The Navy and German Power Politics*, 147. **72.** Kennedy, *Rise of the Anglo-German Antagonism*, 239. **73.** Steinberg, 'The Copenhagen Complex', passim. **74.** Tirpitz, *Politische Dokumente*, vol. I, 1. **75.** Herwig, '*Luxury*' Fleet, 35. **76.** Epkenhans, *Tirpitz*, Kindle version, loc. 598–601. **77.** Ibid., loc. 438–43, 465–77; Herwig, '*Luxury*' Fleet, 35; Rüger, *The Great Naval Game*, 37–43. **78.** Epkenhans, *Tirpitz*, Kindle version, loc. 479–83. **79.** Ibid., loc. 529–48. **80.** Zedlitz-Trützschler, *Twelve Years at the Imperial German Court*, 183–4. **81.** Kennedy, 'German World Policy', 620. **82.** Fesser, *Der Traum vom Platz*, 184.

5 *Dreadnought*: The Anglo-German Naval Rivalry

1. *The Times*, 16 August 1902. **2.** Williams, 'Made in Germany', 10. **3.** Ibid., 11. **4.** Geppert, 'The Public Challenge to Diplomacy', 134. **5.** Ibid., 143–4. **6.** Thompson, *Northcliffe*, 45. **7.** Steiner and Neilson, *Britain and the Origins*, 178–81. **8.** Roberts, *Salisbury*, 666. **9.** Kennedy, *Rise of the Anglo-German Antagonism*, 247. **10.** Ibid., 237. **11.** Ibid., 248. **12.** Steiner and Neilson, *Britain and the Origins*, 33. **13.** Rüger, *The Great Naval Game*, 12, 98. **14.** Rüger, 'Nation, Empire and Navy', 162. **15.** Offer, *The First World War*, 82. **16.** French, 'The Edwardian Crisis and the Origins of the First World War', 208–9. **17.** Thompson, *Northcliffe*, 296. **18.** Kennedy, *Rise of the Anglo-German Antagonism*, 416. **19.** Offer, *The First World War*, 222. **20.** Ibid., 223–4. **21.** Ibid., ch. 15. **22.** French, 'The Edwardian Crisis and the Origins of the First World War', 211–12. **23.** Thompson, *Northcliffe*, 134. **24.** O'Brien, 'The Costs and Benefits of British Imperialism, 1846–1914', 187. **25.** Wilson, *The Policy of the Entente*, 11. **26.** Roberts, *Salisbury*, 109. **27.** Gardiner, *Pillars of Society*, 53. **28.** Massie, *Dreadnought*, 404. **29.** Gardiner, *Pillars of Society*, 54. **30.** Ibid., 56. **31.** Massie, *Dreadnought*, 408. **32.** Marder, *From the Dreadnought to Scapa Flow*, 14. **33.** Gardiner, *Pillars of Society*, 57.

34. Ibid., 57. **35.** Marder, *From the Dreadnought to Scapa Flow*, 15. **36.** Ibid., 18.
37. Gardiner, *Pillars of Society*, 55–6. **38.** Massie, *Dreadnought*, 410. **39.** Marder, *From the Dreadnought to Scapa Flow*, 7–9. **40.** Ibid., 33. **41.** Ibid., 36. **42.** Herwig, *'Luxury' Fleet*, 55. **43.** Ibid., 54–5. **44.** Massie, *Dreadnought*, 485. **45.** Herwig, 'The German Reaction to the Dreadnought Revolution', 276. **46.** Marder, *From the Dreadnought to Scapa Flow*, 107. **47.** Herwig, *'Luxury' Fleet*, 50. **48.** O'Brien, 'The Titan Refreshed', 153–6. **49.** Rüger, 'Nation, Empire and Navy', 174. **50.** Gordon, 'The Admiralty and Dominion Navies, 1902–1914', 409–10. **51.** O'Brien, 'The Titan Refreshed', 150.
52. Ibid., 159. **53.** Steiner, 'The Last Years', 77. **54.** Ibid., 76, 85. **55.** Otte, 'Eyre Crowe and British Foreign Policy', 27. **56.** BD, vol. III, Appendix, 397–420, p. 417. **57.** Ibid., 403–4. **58.** Ibid., 415–16. **59.** Ibid., 419. **60.** Stevenson, *Armaments*, 101. **61.** Epkenhans, *Tirpitz*, Kindle version, loc. 695–9. **62.** Herwig, 'The German Reaction to the Dreadnought Revolution', 278. **63.** Epkenhans, *Tirpitz*, Kindle version, loc. 831–5.
64. Herwig, *'Luxury' Fleet*, 8–9. **65.** Ibid., 62. **66.** Herwig, 'The German Reaction to the Dreadnought Revolution', 279. **67.** Ibid., 281. **68.** Steinberg, 'The Copenhagen Complex', 38. **69.** Steinberg, 'The Novelle of 1908', 28. **70.** Marder, *From the Dreadnought to Scapa Flow*, 112–13. **71.** Berghahn, *Germany and the Approach of War*, 57–8. **72.** Herwig, *'Luxury' Fleet*, 62; Epkenhans, *Tirpitz*, Kindle version, loc. 764–7.
73. Massie, *Dreadnought*, 701. **74.** Epkenhans, *Tirpitz*, Kindle version, loc. 813–17.
75. Ritter, *The Sword and the Sceptre*, 298n76. **76.** Steinberg, 'The Novelle of 1908', 26, 36. **77.** Ibid., 39. **78.** Epkenhans, *Tirpitz*, Kindle version, loc. 749–56. **79.** Marder, *From the Dreadnought to Scapa Flow*, 140–42. **80.** Epkenhans, *Tirpitz*, Kindle version, loc. 758–61. **81.** Bülow, *Memoirs of Prince von Bulow*, vol. I, 357. **82.** Thompson, *Northcliffe*, 153. **83.** BD, vol. VI, 117, pp. 184–90; Bülow, *Memoirs of Prince von Bulow*, vol. I, 358–60.
84. Steinberg, 'The Novelle of 1908', 41–2. **85.** Hopman, *Das ereignisreiche Leben*, 152.
86. Otte, 'An Altogether Unfortunate Affair', 297–301. **87.** Ibid., 301–2. **88.** Ibid., 305–7, 314. **89.** Clark, *Kaiser Wilhelm II*, 239–40. **90.** Otte, 'An Altogether Unfortunate Affair', 329. **91.** Balfour, *The Kaiser and His Times*, 291. **92.** Einem, *Erinnerungen eines Soldaten*, 122. **93.** Wilson, *The Policy of the Entente*, 7. **94.** Marder, *From the Dreadnought to Scapa Flow*, 156. **95.** Cannadine, *The Decline and Fall of the British Aristocracy*, 48–9; Grigg, *Lloyd George*, 203–8, 223. **96.** Kennedy, *Rise of the Anglo-German Antagonism*, 423.

6 Unlikely Friends: The Entente Cordiale between France and Britain

1. Eubank, 'The Fashoda Crisis Re-examined', 145–8. **2.** Andrew, *Théophile Delcassé*, 45.
3. Tombs and Tombs, *That Sweet Enemy*, 428–9; Roberts, *Salisbury*, 702; Eubank, 'The Fashoda Crisis Re-examined', 146–7. **4.** Tombs, 126. **5.** Thompson, *Northcliffe*, 55–7.
6. Roberts, *Salisbury*, 706–8. **7.** Mayne et al., *Cross Channel Currents*, 5. **8.** BD, vol. I, 300, p. 242. **9.** Mayne et al., *Cross Channel Currents*, 5. **10.** Kennedy, *Rise of the Anglo-German Antagonism*, 234. **11.** Eckardstein and Young, *Ten Years at the Court of St. James*, 228. **12.** Rich, *The Tsar's Colonels*, 88. **13.** Weber, *France: Fin de Siècle*, 105–6.
14. Ousby, *The Road to Verdun*, 168–9. **15.** Weber, *France: Fin de Siècle*, 106. **16.** Joly, 'La France et la Revanche', passim. **17.** Porch, *The March to the Marne*, 55. **18.** Ousby, *The Road to Verdun*, 169. **19.** Ibid., 122–4. **20.** Barclay, *Thirty Years*, 135. **21.** Weber, *France: Fin de Siècle*, 121–4. **22.** Ousby, *The Road to Verdun*, 120. **23.** Hayne, *French Foreign Office*, 28–40; Keiger, *France and the Origins*, 25–9. **24.** Hayne, *French Foreign Office*, 38–9. **25.** Porch, *The March to the Marne*, 83, 218–21, 250–52 and passim. **26.** Tombs and

Tombs, *That Sweet Enemy*, 426. **27.** Ibid., 426–7. **28.** Barclay, *Thirty Years*, 140–41. **29.** Lincoln, *In War's Dark Shadow*, 17. **30.** Keiger, *France and the Origins*, 11–12; Fuller, *Strategy and Power in Russia*, 353–4. **31.** Sanborn, 'Education for War and Peace', 213–14. **32.** BD, vol. II, 35, pp. 285–8. **33.** Andrew, *Théophile Delcassé*, 1–10. **34.** Hayne, 'The Quai d'Orsay', 430. **35.** Andrew, *Théophile Delcassé*, 67. **36.** Ibid., 90. **37.** Ibid., 18–19. **38.** Ibid., 54. **39.** Ibid., 24, 91. **40.** Ibid., 191. **41.** Monger, *The End of Isolation*, 104–5. **42.** Andrew, *Théophile Delcassé*, 190, 196–7. **43.** Ibid., 181. **44.** Hayne, *French Foreign Office*, 109. **45.** Eubank, *Paul Cambon*, 65. **46.** Hayne, *French Foreign Office*, 103. **47.** Eubank, *Paul Cambon*, 95. **48.** Ibid., 209. **49.** Ibid., 65, 68; Hayne, *French Foreign Office*, 103. **50.** Andrew, *Théophile Delcassé*, 186–7. **51.** Nicolson, *Portrait of a Diplomatist*, 86. **52.** Ibid., 84. **53.** Andrew, *Théophile Delcassé*, 186. **54.** Monger, *The End of Isolation*, 772. **55.** Andrew, *Théophile Delcassé*, 207–8. **56.** Cronin, *Paris on the Eve*, 63; Tombs and Tombs, *That Sweet Enemy*, 439–41; Mayne et al., *Cross Channel Currents*, 14–16. **57.** Andrew, *Théophile Delcassé*, 209. **58.** Hayne, *French Foreign Office*, 94. **59.** Andrew, *Théophile Delcassé*, 212–14; Williamson, *Politics of Grand Strategy*, 10–13. **60.** Eubank, *Paul Cambon*, 87. **61.** Williamson, *Politics of Grand Strategy*, 27; Weinroth, 'The British Radicals', 657–8. **62.** Clark, *Kaiser Wilhelm II*, 192. **63.** Fischer, *War of Illusions*, 52–4. **64.** Sharp, *Anglo-French Relations*, 18. **65.** Lloyd George, *War Memoirs*, vol. I, 3.

7 The Bear and the Whale Russia and Great Britain

1. *Scarborough Evening News*, 24 October 1904. **2.** Neilson, *Britain and the Last Tsar*, 255–8. **3.** Herring, *From Colony to Superpower*, 360–61. **4.** McDonald, *United Government*, 70–71. **5.** Kleinmikhel', *Memories of a Shipwrecked World*, 176. **6.** Lincoln, *In War's Dark Shadow*, 224. **7.** McDonald, *United Government*, 71; Lincoln, *In War's Dark Shadow*, 225. **8.** McDonald, *United Government*, 71, 73. **9.** Lieven, *Nicholas II*, 144. **10.** Figes, *A People's Tragedy*, 179–86. **11.** Lieven, *Nicholas II*, 149. **12.** Airapetov, *Generalui*, 12. **13.** Figes, *A People's Tragedy*, 16. **14.** Lieven, *Nicholas II*, 39. **15.** McDonald, *United Government*, 16n39. **16.** Ibid., 16. **17.** Izvol'skii and Seeger, *The Memoirs of Alexander Iswolsky*, 270n. **18.** Carter, *The Three Emperors*, 64–71; Lieven, *Nicholas II*, 40–42, 58–9, 166–7. **19.** Carter, *The Three Emperors*, 69. **20.** Steinberg, *All the Tsar's Men*, 29–31. **21.** Ibid., 30. **22.** Lincoln, *In War's Dark Shadow*, 33. **23.** Lieven, *Nicholas II*, 42. **24.** Neklyudov, *Diplomatic Reminiscences*, 4. **25.** McDonald, *United Government*, 65–6. **26.** Neilson, *Britain and the Last Tsar*, 70. **27.** Carter, *The Three Emperors*, 225. **28.** Lieven, *Nicholas II*, 64. **29.** Ibid., 71. **30.** Ibid., 141. **31.** Neilson, *Britain and the Last Tsar*, 62. **32.** Lieven, *Nicholas II*, 102. **33.** McDonald, *United Government*, 70. **34.** Ibid., 70. **35.** Ibid., 73 and chs 2 and 3. **36.** Ibid., 40–41. **37.** Radziwill, *Behind the Veil*, 226. **38.** Lieven, *Nicholas II*, 65–6. **39.** Kleinmikhel', *Memories of a Shipwrecked World*, 211–12. **40.** Radziwill, *Behind the Veil*, 230. **41.** Lieven, *Nicholas II*, 227. **42.** Ibid., 55n8. **43.** Carter, *The Three Emperors*, 221. **44.** Neilson, *Britain and the Last Tsar*, 55. **45.** Lieven, *Nicholas II*, 149; Figes, *A People's Tragedy*, 191. **46.** Radziwill, *Behind the Veil*, 357; Lincoln, *In War's Dark Shadow*, 343. **47.** Figes, *A People's Tragedy*, 230; Radziwill, *Behind the Veil*, 361. **48.** Lieven, *Russia and the Origins*, 23–4. **49.** Fuller, *Strategy and Power in Russia*, 415. **50.** Szamuely, *The Russian Tradition*, 19. **51.** Quoted in Robert Chandler, 'Searching for a Saviour', *Spectator* (London), 31 March 2012. **52.** Kennan, *Siberia and the Exile System*, 55. **53.** Dowler, *Russia in 1913*, 198. **54.** Vinogradov, '1914 God: Byt' Ili ne Byt' Vojne?', 162. **55.** Fuller, *Strategy and Power in Russia*, 378. **56.** Neilson, *Britain and the Last Tsar*, 86 and ch. 3. **57.** Weinroth,

'The British Radicals', 665–70. **58.** Gilmour, *Curzon*, 201. **59.** Hinsley, *British Foreign Policy under Sir Edward Grey*, 135–6. **60.** Fuller, *Strategy and Power in Russia*, 364–5; Neilson, *Britain and the Last Tsar*, 113–15. **61.** Jusserand, *What Me Befell*, 203. **62.** Lieven, *Russia and the Origins*, 6. **63.** Stevenson, *Armaments*, 53. **64.** Lieven, 'Pro-Germans and Russian Foreign Policy', 38. **65.** Airapetov, *Generalui*, 10–11. **66.** Fuller, *Strategy and Power in Russia*, 379–82. **67.** Ibid., 404. **68.** Lieven, 'Pro-Germans and Russian Foreign Policy', 41–2. **69.** Spring, 'Russia and the Franco-Russian Alliance', passim. **70.** Ibid., 569. **71.** Soroka, 'Debating Russia's Choice', 14. **72.** Hantsch, *Leopold Graf Berchtold*, 33. **73.** Taube, *La Politique russe d'avant-guerre*, 15. **74.** Ibid., 43. **75.** Soroka, 'Debating Russia's Choice', 11. **76.** Ibid., 4. **77.** Carter, *The Three Emperors*, 138. **78.** Albertini, *The Origins of the War*, vol. I, 159. **79.** Lieven, 'Pro-Germans and Russian Foreign Policy', 43–5. **80.** Levine and Grant, *The Kaiser's Letters to the Tsar*, 118, 120. **81.** Andrew, *Théophile Delcassé*, 250–52. **82.** Carter, *The Three Emperors*, 130. **83.** Cecil, *Wilhelm II*, 14. **84.** Carter, *The Three Emperors*, 185; Bülow, *Memoirs of Prince von Bulow*, vol. II, 146. **85.** Balfour, *The Kaiser and His Times*, 248. **86.** Albertini, *The Origins of the War*, vol. I, 159–60; Bülow, *Memoirs of Prince von Bulow*, vol. II, 152–3; McDonald, *United Government and Foreign Policy in Russia*, 78–9. **87.** Levine and Grant, *The Kaiser's Letters to the Tsar*, 191–4. **88.** Lerman, *The Chancellor as Courtier*, 128–30. **89.** Bülow, *Memoirs of Prince von Bulow*, vol. I, 161. **90.** Hopman, *Das ereignisreiche Leben*, 144. **91.** Lieven, *Nicholas II*, 192. **92.** BD, vol. IV, 205, pp. 219–20. **93.** Neilson, *Britain and the Last Tsar*, 102–3. **94.** Taube, *La Politique russe d'avant-guerre*, 90. **95.** Ibid., 101. **96.** Soroka, 'Debating Russia's Choice', 15. **97.** Hantsch, *Leopold Graf Berchtold*, 49. **98.** Csáky, *Vom Geachteten zum Geächteten*, 67. **99.** In the original 'Je l'ai regretté tous les jours, mais je m'en félicité toutes les nuits'. Bülow, *Memoirs of Prince von Bulow*, vol. II, 325. **100.** Radziwill, *Behind the Veil*, 380. **101.** Taube, *La Politique russe d'avant-guerre*, 105. **102.** BD, vol. IV, 219, 235–6. **103.** Fuller, *Strategy and Power in Russia*, 416. **104.** Soroka, 'Debating Russia's Choice', 3. **105.** Taube, *La Politique russe d'avant-guerre*, 103. **106.** Nicolson, *Portrait of a Diplomatist*, 183–5. **107.** Hinsley, *British Foreign Policy under Sir Edward Grey*, 158. **108.** Bülow, *Memoirs of Prince von Bulow*, vol. II, 352. **109.** Menning and Menning, '"Baseless Allegations"', 373. **110.** Grey, *Twenty-five Years*, vol. I, 154. **111.** Spring, 'Russia and the Franco-Russian Alliance', 584. **112.** Albertini, *The Origins of the War*, vol. I, 189.

8 The Loyalty of the Nibelungs: The Dual Alliance of Austria-Hungary and Germany

1. Geiss, 'Deutschland und Österreich-Ungarn', 386. **2.** Angelow, 'Der Zweibund zwischen Politischer', 58; Snyder, *The Ideology of the Offensive*, 107. **3.** Bülow, *Memoirs of Prince von Bulow*, vol. II, 367. **4.** Ibid., 362. **5.** Stevenson, *Armaments*, 4. **6.** Stone, *Europe Transformed*, 315. **7.** Redlich, *Emperor Francis Joseph*, 40. **8.** Palmer, *Twilight of the Habsburgs*, 23. **9.** Margutti, *The Emperor Francis Joseph*, 26–7. **10.** Ibid., 50. **11.** Palmer, *Twilight of the Habsburgs*, 230–31. **12.** Margutti, *The Emperor Francis Joseph*, 35–50; Redlich, *Emperor Francis Joseph*, 17–18, 188. **13.** Palmer, *Twilight of the Habsburgs*, 172. **14.** Margutti, *The Emperor Francis Joseph*, 45–6. **15.** Ibid., 52. **16.** Palmer, *Twilight of the Habsburgs*, 265. **17.** Ibid. **18.** RA VIC/MAIN/QVJ (W) 4 August 1874 (Princess Beatrice's copies). **19.** Margutti, *The Emperor Francis Joseph*, 48. **20.** Leslie, 'The Antecedents', 309–10; Williamson, 'Influence, Power, and the Policy Process', 419.

21. Lukacs, *Budapest 1900*, 49–50, 108–12. **22.** Deák, *Beyond Nationalism*, 69.
23. Vermes, *Istv'an Tisza*, 102. **24.** Freud, *Civilization and Its Discontents*, 61. **25.** Steed,
Through Thirty Years, vol. I, 196. **26.** Wank, 'Pessimism in the Austrian Establishment',
299. **27.** Ibid.; Johnston, *The Austrian Mind*, 47. **28.** Boyer, 'The End of an Old
Regime', 177–9; Stone, *Europe Transformed*, 304; Johnston, *The Austrian Mind*, 48;
Urbas, *Schicksale und Schatten*, 77; Bridge, *From Sadowa to Sarajevo*, 254. **29.** Boyer,
'The End of an Old Regime', 174–7; Palmer, *Twilight of the Habsburgs*, 291; Stone,
Europe Transformed, 316; Stevenson, *Armaments*, 4; Williamson, *Austria-Hungary*,
44–6. **30.** Palmer, *Twilight of the Habsburgs*, 293. **31.** Czernin, *In the World War*, 46;
Macartney, *The Habsburg Empire*, 746; Steed, *Through Thirty Years*, 367; Wank, 'The
Archduke and Aehrenthal', 86. **32.** Ibid. **33.** Steed, *Through Thirty Years*, vol. I, 367;
Bridge, *The Habsburg Monarchy*, 7. **34.** Czernin, *In the World War*, 48. **35.** Ibid., 50;
Afflerbach, *Der Dreibund*, 596–7. **36.** Hantsch, *Leopold Graf Berchtold*, 389.
37. Aehrenthal, *Aus dem Nachlass*, 179–80. **38.** Bridge, 'Tarde Venientibus Ossa',
passim. **39.** Sondhaus, *Franz Conrad von Hötzendorf*, 82–4; Ritter, *The Sword and the
Sceptre*, 229. **40.** Hoetzendorf, *Mein Leben mit Conrad von Hötzendorf*, 174–5.
41. Sondhaus, *Franz Conrad von Hötzendorf*, 73–4. **42.** Hoetzendorf, *Mein Leben mit
Conrad von Hötzendorf*, 66; Sondhaus, *Franz Conrad von Hötzendorf*, 89, 104.
43. Hoetzendorf, *Mein Leben mit Conrad von Hötzendorf*, 30. **44.** Ibid., 210. **45.** Ibid.,
31; Sondhaus, *Franz Conrad von Hötzendorf*, 111; Williamson, *Austria-Hungary*, 49–50.
46. Bridge, *From Sadowa to Sarajevo*, 440. **47.** Ibid., 267. **48.** Bosworth, *Italy and the
Approach*, 55–7. **49.** Herwig, 'Disjointed Allies', 271; Angelow, 'Der Zweibund zwischen
Politischer', 34; Margutti, *The Emperor Francis Joseph*, 220–28; Williamson, *Austria-
Hungary*, 36. **50.** Bridge, *From Sadowa to Sarajevo*, 254–5, 427–8; Margutti, *The Emperor
Francis Joseph*, 127, 228. **51.** Musulin, *Das Haus am Ballplatz*, 80; Stevenson, *Armaments*,
38–9; Williamson, *Austria-Hungary*, 114. **52.** Bridge, 'Austria-Hungary and the Boer
War', 79. **53.** Bridge, *From Sadowa to Sarajevo*, 260; Steiner, *The Foreign Office and
Foreign Policy*, 182–3; Williamson, *Austria-Hungary*, 112. **54.** Wank, 'Foreign Policy and
the Nationality Problem in Austria-Hungary', 45. **55.** Bridge, *From Sadowa to
Sarajevo*, 232–4; Jelavich, *Russia's Balkan Entanglements*, 212–13.

9 What Were They Thinking? Hopes, Fears, Ideas, and Unspoken Assumptions

1. Kessler, *Journey to the Abyss*, xxi. **2.** Schorske, *Fin-de-siècle Vienna*, 213–19. **3.** Ibid.,
346–8. **4.** Kessler, *Journey to the Abyss*, 230. **5.** Lukacs, *Budapest 1900*, 129–32. **6.** Offer,
The First World War, 121–7. **7.** Ibid., 128. **8.** Wank, 'The Archduke and Aehrenthal',
83n33. **9.** Sondhaus, *Franz Conrad von Hötzendorf*, 84–5. **10.** Förster, 'Der deutschen
Generalstab', 95. **11.** Offer, *The First World War*, 129. **12.** Deák, *Beyond Nationalism*,
128–9, 134–6. **13.** Lukacs, *Budapest 1900*, 184n. **14.** Weber, *France: Fin de Siècle*, 218–20.
15. Offer, 'Going to War in 1914', 217. **16.** Kronenbitter, *Krieg im Frieden*, 33.
17. Lieven, *Russia and the Origins*, 22. **18.** Neklyudov, *Diplomatic Reminiscences*, 5.
19. Bernhardi, *Germany and the Next War*, 28. **20.** Offer, 'Going to War in 1914', 216.
21. Rathenau, *Briefe*, 147. **22.** Rathenau and von Strandmann, *Walther Rathenau*,
142–3. **23.** Stromberg, 'The Intellectuals', 115, 119. **24.** Tanner, *Nietzsche*, 4 and passim.
25. Blom, *The Vertigo Years*, 354. **26.** Kessler, *Journey to the Abyss*, 128. **27.** Cronin, *Paris
on the Eve*, 43–6. **28.** Ibid., 47. **29.** Wohl, *The Generation of 1914*, 6–7. **30.** Blom, *The
Vertigo Years*, ch. 8. **31.** Tuchman, *The Proud Tower*, 88–97. **32.** Ibid., 106. **33.** De Burgh,
Elizabeth, 326–7. **34.** Butterworth, *The World that Never Was*, 323. **35.** Barclay, *Thirty*

Years, 142. **36.** Gooch, 'Attitudes to War', 95; Hynes, *The Edwardian Turn of Mind*, 24–7. **37.** Hynes, *The Edwardian Turn of Mind*, 26–7. **38.** Weber, *France: Fin de Siècle*, 224. **39.** Ibid., 12. **40.** Tuchman, *The Proud Tower*, 32; Blom, *The Vertigo Years*, 184–5. **41.** Travers, 'Technology, Tactics, and Morale', 279. **42.** Miller et al., *Military Strategy*, 14n28. **43.** Steiner and Neilson, *Britain and the Origins*, 171. **44.** Hull, *The Entourage of Kaiser Wilhelm II*, 133–5. **45.** Hynes, *The Edwardian Turn of Mind*, 201. **46.** Ibid., 199. **47.** Gildea, *Barricades and Borders*, 268–7. **48.** Ousby, *The Road to Verdun*, 155–6. **49.** Bourdon, *The German Enigma*, 170. **50.** Hynes, *The Edwardian Turn of Mind*, 286–7. **51.** Blom, *The Vertigo Years*, 334 and ch. 13. **52.** Leslie, 'The Antecedents', 312. **53.** I am grateful to Brigadier David Godsal for his permission to quote this extract from the unpublished diary of Captain Wilmot Caulfeild. **54.** Gooch, 'Attitudes to War', 94. **55.** Bernhardi, *Germany and the Next War*, 26. **56.** Joll and Martel, *The Origins of the First World War*, 276–7. **57.** Lukacs, *Budapest 1900*, 130–32. **58.** Schorske, *Fin-de-Siècle Vienna*, 133–46. **59.** Bernhardi, *Germany and the Next War*, 57–8. **60.** Berghahn, 'War Preparations and National Identity', 311ff. **61.** Nolan, *The Inverted Mirror*, 25. **62.** Steiner and Neilson, *Britain and the Origins*, 165. **63.** Hewitson, *Germany and the Causes*, 92. **64.** Eby, *The Road to Armageddon*, 6. **65.** Martel, *The Origins of the First World War*, 280–81. **66.** Cannadine et al., *The Right Kind of History*, 19–20, 23–4. **67.** Langsam, 'Nationalism and History', 250–51. **68.** Joll and Martel, *The Origins of the First World War*, 274–5. **69.** Bernhardi, *Germany and the Next War*, 57. **70.** Ibid., 20. **71.** Berghahn, 'War Preparations and National Identity', 316. **72.** Cannadine et al., *The Right Kind of History*, 53. **73.** Roberts, *Salisbury*, 799. **74.** Kennedy, 'German World Policy', 616–18. **75.** Fischer, 'The Foreign Policy of Imperial Germany', 26. **76.** Joll, *1914*, 18. **77.** Hewitson, *Germany and the Causes*, 95. **78.** Thompson, *Northcliffe*, 155–6. **79.** Steiner, 'The Last Years', 76. **80.** Ousby, *The Road to Verdun*, 154–6. **81.** Hewitson, 'Germany and France', 574–5, 580–81. **82.** Nolan, *The Inverted Mirror*, 56. **83.** Herwig, *The Marne*, 32–3. **84.** Nolan, *The Inverted Mirror*, 30. **85.** Bourdon, *The German Enigma*, 163–4. **86.** Nolan, *The Inverted Mirror*, 58. **87.** Ibid., 61. **88.** Gooch, 'Attitudes to War', 96. **89.** Förster, 'Facing "People's War"', 223–4. **90.** Ritter, *The Sword and the Scepter*, 102. **91.** Joll, *The Second International*, 196. **92.** Stevenson, *Armaments*, 38. **93.** Ferguson, *The Pity of War*, 31–3. **94.** Förster, 'Im Reich des Absurden', 213–14; Feldman, 'Hugo Stinnes', 84–5. **95.** Steed, *Through Thirty Years*, 359. **96.** Lieven, *Russia and the Origins*, 16–17; Bushnell, 'The Tsarist Officer Corps', passim. **97.** Airapetov, *Poslednyaya Voina Imperatorskoi Rossii*, 44–58. **98.** Ritter, *The Sword and the Sceptre*, 102–3. **99.** Bourdon, *The German Enigma*, 207. **100.** Eby, *The Road to Armageddon*, 4. **101.** Howard, 'Men Against Fire', 17. **102.** Rohkrämer, 'Heroes and Would-be Heroes', 192–3. **103.** Steiner and Neilson, *Britain and the Origins*, 169. **104.** Hynes, *The Edwardian Turn of Mind*, 28–9. **105.** Linton, 'Preparing German Youth for War', 177–8. **106.** Ibid., 167. **107.** Ibid., 180–83. **108.** Weber, *France: Fin de Siècle*, 215–17; Porch, *The March to the Marne*, 207–10. **109.** Porch, *The March to the Marne*, 92–3. **110.** Ibid., ch. 5, 106–7; Harris, *The Man on Devil's Island*, 365–6. **111.** Porch, *The March to the Marne*, ch. 7. **112.** Ibid., 189. **113.** Clark, *Iron Kingdom*, 596–9. **114.** Balfour, *The Kaiser and His Times*, 333. **115.** Berghahn, *Germany and the Approach of War*, 174–8. **116.** Gooch, 'Attitudes to War', 97. **117.** Rohkrämer, 'Heroes and Would-be Heroes', 199–203. **118.** Stromberg, 'The Intellectuals', 109. **119.** Urbas, *Schicksale und Schatten*, 67–8. **120.** Kessler, *Journey to the Abyss*, 581. **121.** Stromberg,

'The Intellectuals', 117–18n37. **122.** Ibid., 120; Weber, *The Nationalist Revival in France*, 108–9.

10 Dreaming of Peace

1. Laurence, 'Bertha von Suttner', 184–5. **2.** Ibid., 196. **3.** Blom, *The Vertigo Years*, 192. **4.** Laurence, 'Bertha von Suttner', 186–7; Joll and Martel, *The Origins of the First World War*, 260–61; LaFeber, *The Cambridge History of American Foreign Relations*, 43. **5.** Kennedy, *Rise of the Anglo-German Antagonism*, 293. **6.** Rotte, 'Global Warfare', 483–5. **7.** Bloch, *The Future of War*, xxx. **8.** Ibid., lxxi. **9.** Ibid., ix. **10.** Ibid., xix. **11.** Travers, 'Technology, Tactics, and Morale', 266. **12.** Bloch, *The Future of War*, xvi. **13.** Ibid., xi. **14.** Dungen, 'Preventing Catastrophe', 456–7. **15.** Ceadel, *Living the Great Illusion*, 4, 20–21. **16.** Angell, *The Great Illusion*, Kindle version, loc. 4285. **17.** Ibid., loc. 947–9. **18.** Ibid., loc. 633–4. **19.** Ibid., loc. 1149. **20.** Steiner and Neilson, *Britain and the Origins*, 142; Ceadel, *Living the Great Illusion*, 8–12, 22. **21.** Offer, *The First World War*, 250. **22.** Laity, *The British Peace Movement*, 189. **23.** Cooper, 'Pacifism in France', 360–62. **24.** Bülow, *Memoirs of Prince von Bulow*, vol. II, 383. **25.** Chickering, 'Problems of a German Peace Movement', 46, 52. **26.** Chickering, *Imperial Germany*, 239–53. **27.** Wank, 'The Austrian Peace Movement', 42–3; Dülffer, 'Efforts to Reform the International System', 28. **28.** Herring, *From Colony to Superpower*, 358–60. **29.** Patterson, 'Citizen Peace Initiatives', 187–92. **30.** Herring, *From Colony to Superpower*, 357–8. **31.** Chickering, *Imperial Germany*, 345. **32.** Cooper, 'Pacifism in France', 366–7. **33.** Morris, 'The English Radicals' Campaign', passim. **34.** Weinroth, 'The British Radicals', 661–2. **35.** Kessler, *Journey to the Abyss*, 336, 368–9. **36.** Zweig, *The World of Yesterday*, 226. **37.** Cooper, 'Pacifism in France', 363. **38.** Anderson, *The Rise of Modern Diplomacy*, 253–5. **39.** Ibid., 255. **40.** Morrill, 'Nicholas II and the Call', 296–313. **41.** Dülffer, 'Chances and Limits of Arms Control', 98. **42.** Dülffer, 'Citizens and Diplomats', 30–31. **43.** Joll and Martel, *The Origins of the First World War*, 258. **44.** Massie, *Dreadnought*, 429. **45.** Chickering, *Imperial Germany*, 225. **46.** Dülffer, 'Citizens and Diplomats', 25. **47.** Laurence, 'The Peace Movement in Austria', 55. **48.** Andrew, *Théophile Delcassé*, 121. **49.** BD, vol. I, 274, pp. 224–5; 276, p. 226. **50.** White, *The First Hague Conference*, 114. **51.** Tuchman, *The Proud Tower*, 252. **52.** BD, vol. I, 282, pp. 229–31. **53.** White, *The First Hague Conference*, 8. **54.** Ibid., 18–19. **55.** Dülffer, 'Citizens and Diplomats', 24. **56.** Dülffer, 'Chances and Limits of Arms Control', 102. **57.** Chickering, *Imperial Germany*, 227. **58.** Ibid., 228. **59.** Aehrenthal, *Aus dem Nachlass*, 388. **60.** Stevenson, *Armaments*, 109. **61.** Laity, *The British Peace Movement*, 171–2. **62.** Laurence, 'The Peace Movement in Austria', 29. **63.** Stevenson, *Armaments*, 109–10. **64.** Ceadel, *Semi-Detached Idealists*, 166. **65.** Charykov, *Glimpses of High Politics*, 261. **66.** Marder, *From the Dreadnought to Scapa Flow*, 133. **67.** Chickering, *Imperial Germany*, 229–30. **68.** Steiner, 'Grey, Hardinge and the Foreign Office', 434–5. **69.** Dülffer, 'Efforts to Reform the International System', 40. **70.** Howorth, 'French Workers and German Workers', 85. **71.** Chickering, *Imperial Germany*, 269. **72.** Laurence, 'Bertha von Suttner', 194. **73.** Joll, *The Second International*, 107. **74.** Craig, *Germany, 1866–1945*, 267–9; Joll, *The Second International*, 89–90. **75.** Groh, 'The "Unpatriotic Socialists"', 153–5. **76.** Chickering, *Imperial Germany*, 272. **77.** Joll, *The Second International*, 100–105; Goldberg, *Life of Jean Jaurès*, 329–30. **78.** Goldberg, *Life of Jean Jaurès*, 13. **79.** Ibid., 63–5. **80.** Ibid., 15, 375; Heinrich, *Geschichte in Gesprächen*, 327–8. **81.** Goldberg, *Life of*

Jean Jaurès, 385. **82.** Porch, *The March to the Marne*, 247–9. **83.** Joll, *The Second International*, 126–43, 197. **84.** Chickering, *Imperial Germany*, 275; Haupt, *Socialism and the Great War*, 90–91, 107. **85.** Haupt, *Socialism and the Great War*, 67–8. **86.** Ibid., 64. **87.** Ibid., 91–2; Joll, *The Second International*, 152–7. **88.** Haupt, *Socialism and the Great War*, 102–3. **89.** Joll, *The Second International*, 70. **90.** Howorth, 'French Workers and German Workers', 75; Chickering, 'War, Peace, and Social Mobilization', 16–17. **91.** Joll, *The Second International*, 49–54; Howorth, 'French Workers and German Workers', 78–81. **92.** Haupt, *Socialism and the Great War*, 68–9. **93.** Ibid., 69–70. **94.** Joll, *The Second International*, 123–4. **95.** Haupt, *Socialism and the Great War*, 64–6. **96.** Ibid., 77. **97.** Ibid., 114; Goldberg, *Life of Jean Jaurès*, 435–8. **98.** Cooper, *Patriotic Pacifism*, 171. **99.** Ibid., 165–7. **100.** Chickering, *Imperial Germany*, 317. **101.** Weinroth, 'The British Radicals', 676; Chickering, *Imperial Germany*, 118. **102.** Cooper, 'Pacifism in France', 365. **103.** Angell, *The Great Illusion* Kindle version, loc. 2928–30.

11 Thinking about War

1. Howard, 'The Armed Forces', 217. **2.** Stevenson, 'War by Timetable?', 167–8; Herwig, 'Conclusions', 232. **3.** Howard, *The Franco-Prussian War*, 14. **4.** Stevenson, 'War by Timetable?', 167. **5.** Bucholz, *Moltke, Schlieffen*, 146–7, 229, 232. **6.** Ibid., 150. **7.** Stevenson, 'War by Timetable?', 171. **8.** Craig, *The Politics of the Prussian Army*, 197n3. **9.** Bucholz, *Moltke, Schlieffen*, 64–6. **10.** Craig, *The Politics of the Prussian Army*, 216. **11.** Moltke, *Erinnerungen*, 11. **12.** Herwig, 'Conclusions', 231. **13.** Showalter, 'Railroads', 40. **14.** Stevenson, 'War by Timetable?', 192–3. **15.** Evera, 'The Cult of the Offensive', 73–6. **16.** Hamilton, 'War Planning', 13. **17.** Herwig, 'Imperial Germany', 90. **18.** Herwig, 'From Tirpitz Plan to Schlieffen Plan', 57. **19.** Tirpitz, *My Memoirs*, vol. II, 290. **20.** Bond, *The Victorian Army and the Staff College*, 133. **21.** Kronenbitter, *Krieg im Frieden*, 88. **22.** Echevarria, 'Heroic History', 573–90. **23.** Echevarria, 'On the Brink of the Abyss', 31–3. **24.** Howard, 'The Armed Forces', 206–9. **25.** Travers, 'Technology, Tactics, and Morale', 268. **26.** Welch, 'The Centenary', 273–94. **27.** Bloch, 'The Wars of the Future', 307. **28.** Ibid., 314–15. **29.** Cairns, 'International Politics', 280–81. **30.** Bloch, 'The Wars of the Future', 314. **31.** Travers, 'Technology, Tactics, and Morale', 273–4. **32.** Burkhardt, 'Kriegsgrund Geschichte?', 72–4. **33.** Mombauer, 'German War Plans', 52n10. **34.** Snyder, *The Ideology of the Offensive*, 26–30; Evera, 'The Cult of the Offensive', passim. **35.** Travers, 'Technology, Tactics, and Morale', 271n22. **36.** Doughty, *Pyrrhic Victory*, 25. **37.** Howard, 'Men Against Fire', 10–11. **38.** Messimy, *Mes Souvenirs*, 119. **39.** Porch, 'The French Army', 120. **40.** Ibid., 118. **41.** Gooch, 'Attitudes to War', 95. **42.** Echevarria, 'On the Brink of the Abyss', 27–8, 30–31. **43.** Foley, *German Strategy*, 41. **44.** Howard, 'Men Against Fire', 8–10. **45.** Cairns, 'International Politics', 282. **46.** Foley, *German Strategy*, 28–9. **47.** Kießling, *Gegen den 'Großen Krieg'?*, 43–50, 139; McDonald, *United Government*, 199–201; Kronenbitter, *Krieg im Frieden*, 139. **48.** Kronenbitter, *Krieg im Frieden*, 126–31. **49.** Förster, 'Dreams and Nightmares', 345, 360. **50.** Maurer, *The Outbreak of the First World War*; see, for example, ch. 1. **51.** Förster, 'Der deutschen Generalstab', 61–95. **52.** Csáky, *Vom Geächteten zum Geächteten*, 137. **53.** Mombauer, 'German War Plans', 59.

12 Making the Plans

1. Steinberg, *Bismarck*, 57–60; Bucholz, *Moltke, Schlieffen*, 110–13. **2.** Bucholz, *Moltke, Schlieffen*, 120–21. **3.** Ibid., 127. **4.** Snyder, *The Ideology of the Offensive*, 134. **5.** Bucholz,

Moltke, Schlieffen, 130–31. **6.** Ibid., 124, 129–31. **7.** Craig, *The Politics of the Prussian Army*, 277. **8.** Echevarria, 'Heroic History', 585; Mombauer, 'German War Plans', 52n10. **9.** Snyder, 'Civil–Military Relations', 35. **10.** Förster, 'Dreams and Nightmares', 359–60. **11.** Craig, *The Politics of the Prussian Army*, 277. **12.** Herwig, *The Marne*, 33. **13.** Mombauer, *Helmuth von Moltke*, 100–105; Snyder, *The Ideology of the Offensive*, 117. **14.** Bucholz, *Moltke, Schlieffen*, 301–2. **15.** Foley, *German Strategy*, 6–7. **16.** Herwig, 'From Tirpitz Plan to Schlieffen Plan', 55. **17.** Craig, *Germany, 1866–1945*, 317. **18.** Ritter, *The Sword and the Sceptre*, 206. **19.** Ibid. **20.** Mombauer, *Helmuth von Moltke*, 46. **21.** Ibid., 42–6. **22.** Craig, *The Politics of the Prussian Army*, 300. **23.** Bülow, *Memoirs of Prince von Bulow*, vol. II, 201–2. **24.** Maurer, *The Outbreak of the First World War*, 37. **25.** Herwig, 'From Tirpitz Plan to Schlieffen Plan', 59. **26.** Mombauer, *Helmuth von Moltke*, 59. **27.** Bucholz, *Moltke, Schlieffen*, 223–5. **28.** Kronenbitter, *Krieg im Frieden*, 311. **29.** Hull, *The Entourage of Kaiser Wilhelm II*, 240. **30.** Kessler, *Journey to the Abyss*, 658; Foley, 'Debate – the Real Schlieffen Plan', 222. **31.** Snyder, *The Ideology of the Offensive*, 203. **32.** Groener, *Lebenserinnerungen*, 84. **33.** Fischer, *War of Illusions*, 55. **34.** Hull, *The Entourage of Kaiser Wilhelm II*, 258–9; Afflerbach, *Falkenhayn. Politisches*, 79. **35.** Mombauer, *Helmuth von Moltke*, 165. **36.** Bucholz, *Moltke, Schlieffen*, 263–4. **37.** Mombauer, 'German War Plans', 57. **38.** Craig, *The Politics of the Prussian Army*, 280. **39.** Showalter, 'From Deterrence to Doomsday Machine', 696. **40.** Snyder, *The Ideology of the Offensive*, 152. **41.** Bülow, *Memoirs of Prince von Bulow*, vol. II, 88–9. **42.** Fischer, *War of Illusions*, 390. **43.** Bülow, *Memoirs of Prince von Bulow*, vol. II, 84–5. **44.** Fischer, *War of Illusions*, 225–9; Beyens, *Germany before the War*, 36–8. **45.** Mombauer, 'German War Plans', 48–79. **46.** Fischer, *War of Illusions*, 390. **47.** Hewitson, *Germany and the Causes*, 118. **48.** Herrmann, *The Arming of Europe*, 96–7. **49.** Mombauer, *Helmuth von Moltke*, 210. **50.** Hewitson, *Germany and the Causes*, 131–3; Hewitson, 'Images of the Enemy', passim. **51.** Herrmann, *The Arming of Europe*, 132–3. **52.** Ibid., 84. **53.** Ibid., 91–5. **54.** Mombauer, 'German War Plans', 57. **55.** Herwig, 'Imperial Germany', 71. **56.** Herwig, 'Disjointed Allies', 273. **57.** Herrmann, *The Arming of Europe*, 101. **58.** Gooch, 'Italy before 1915', 211–22; Mombauer, *Helmuth von Moltke*, 167–9. **59.** Maurer, *The Outbreak of the First World War*, 33; Herwig, 'Disjointed Allies', 271–2; Ritter, 'Zusammenarbeit', 535. **60.** Herwig, 'Disjointed Allies', 271n9. **61.** Williamson, *Austria-Hungary*, 87–8. **62.** Kronenbitter, *Krieg im Frieden*, 282. **63.** Stone, 'V. Moltke–Conrad', 201–2 and passim. **64.** Sondhaus, *Franz Conrad von Hötzendorf*, 85. **65.** Stevenson, 'War by Timetable?', 181–2. **66.** Stone, 'V. Moltke–Conrad', 204n7. **67.** Kronenbitter, '"Nur los lassen"', 39. **68.** Herrmann, *The Arming of Europe*, 234, 237. **69.** Stone, 'V. Moltke–Conrad', 213–14. **70.** Herwig, 'Disjointed Allies', 278. **71.** Menning, 'The Offensive Revisited', 226. **72.** Armour, 'Colonel Redl: Fact and Fantasy', 175–6. **73.** Ibid., 179–80; Sondhaus, *Franz Conrad von Hötzendorf*, 124–7. **74.** Stevenson, 'War by Timetable?', 177–8; Heywood, 'The Most Catastrophic Question', 46, 54. **75.** Menning, 'The Offensive Revisited', 224. **76.** Menning, 'Pieces of the Puzzle', 782. **77.** Fuller, 'The Russian Empire', 109, 122–4. **78.** Shatsillo, *Ot Portsmutskogo*, 199. **79.** Fuller, 'The Russian Empire', 110. **80.** Stevenson, *Armaments*, 151–6. **81.** Fuller, *Strategy and Power in Russia*, 427–33. **82.** Brusilov, *A Soldier's Notebook*, 11. **83.** Fuller, *The Foe Within*, 46–8. **84.** Turner, 'Role of the General Staffs', 317; Paléologue, *Ambassador's Memoirs*, vol. I, 83. **85.** Rich, *The Tsar's Colonels*, 221. **86.** Fuller, 'The Russian Empire', 100–101. **87.** Spring, 'Russia and the Franco-Russian Alliance', 568–9, 578–9 and passim.

88. Menning, 'The Offensive Revisited', 219. **89.** Airapetov, *Poslednyaya Voina Imperatorskoi Rossii*, 174–5; Shatsillo, *Ot Portsmutskogo*, 65–7. **90.** Menning, 'Pieces of the Puzzle', 788. **91.** Fuller, 'The Russian Empire', 111–12, 118–21. **92.** Snyder, *The Ideology of the Offensive*, 178. **93.** Fuller, 'The Russian Empire', 111–13; Menning, 'The Offensive Revisited', 225. **94.** Fuller, *Strategy and Power in Russia*, 440–41. **95.** Menning, 'Pieces of the Puzzle', 796. **96.** Menning, 'War Planning', 121. **97.** Airapetov, 'K voprosu o prichinah porazheniya russkoi armii'; Snyder, *The Ideology of the Offensive*, 189–94. **98.** Fuller, 'The Russian Empire', 110–11. **99.** Airapetov, 'K voprosu o prichinah porazheniya russkoi armii'; Menning, 'War Planning', 122–5. **100.** Andrew, 'France and the German Menace', 147. **101.** Ignat'ev, *50 Let v Stroyu*, 390–91. **102.** Schmidt, *Frankreichs Aussenpolitik*, 182–3. **103.** Ignat'ev, *50 Let v Stroyu*, 392. **104.** Messimy, *Mes Souvenirs*, 118n1; Porch, *The March to the Marne*, 184–5. **105.** Porch, *The March to the Marne*, 216–23. **106.** Tanenbaum, 'French Estimates', 163. **107.** Doughty, 'France', 160. **108.** Doughty, *Pyrrhic Victory*, 26. **109.** Doughty, 'France', 159. **110.** Becker, *1914, Comment les Français*, 43n174. **111.** Tanenbaum, 'French Estimates', 164. **112.** Porch, *The March to the Marne*, 129–32. **113.** Tanenbaum, 'French Estimates', 137. **114.** Doughty, 'France', 154. **115.** Ibid., 154; Tanenbaum, 'French Estimates', 156. **116.** Doughty, 'France', 153. **117.** Herwig, 'Imperial Germany', 70. **118.** Schmidt, *Frankreichs Aussenpolitik*, 165–7. **119.** Tanenbaum, 'French Estimates', 163. **120.** Ibid., 159. **121.** Ibid., 166. **122.** Snyder, *The Ideology of the Offensive*, 102–3. **123.** Tanenbaum, 'French Estimates', 170–71. **124.** Doughty, 'France', 163. **125.** Williamson, *Politics of Grand Strategy*, 226. **126.** Doughty, 'France', 165–8; Doughty, 'French Strategy in 1914', 434. **127.** Doughty, 'France', 165. **128.** Porch, *The March to the Marne*, 232–3. **129.** Messimy, *Mes Souvenirs*, 179.

13 The Crises Start: Germany, France and Morocco

1. Schoen, *Memoirs of an Ambassador*, 20; Rich, *Friedrich von Holstein*, vol. II, 694. **2.** Schoen, *Memoirs of an Ambassador*, 22–3. **3.** BD, vol. III, 71, p. 62. **4.** Balfour, *The Kaiser and His Times*, 255. **5.** Rich, *Friedrich von Holstein*, vol. II, 695. **6.** Hewitson, 'Germany and France', 579. **7.** Rich, *Friedrich von Holstein*, vol. II, 691–3. **8.** Ibid., 702n1. **9.** Hewitson, 'Germany and France', 585–6. **10.** Rich, *Friedrich von Holstein*, vol. II, 680–81. **11.** Ibid., 683, 684. **12.** Morris, *Theodore Rex*, 334–5. **13.** Andrew, *Théophile Delcassé*, 269–70. **14.** Ibid., 272. **15.** Kaiser, 'Germany and the Origins', 453. **16.** Bülow, *Memoirs of Prince von Bulow*, vol. II, 162. **17.** Kaiser, 'Germany and the Origins', 453. **18.** Craig, *The Politics of the Prussian Army*, 285. **19.** Lee, *Edward VII*, vol. II, 340. **20.** *The Times*, 31 March 1905. **21.** Marder, *From the Dreadnought to Scapa Flow*, 116. **22.** Monger, *The End of Isolation*, 192. **23.** Ibid., 187. **24.** Ibid., 190. **25.** Andrew, *Théophile Delcassé*, 287–8. **26.** Ibid., 281, 283, 285. **27.** Ibid., 286. **28.** Balfour, *The Kaiser and His Times*, 265. **29.** Monger, *The End of Isolation*, 224 and n2. **30.** Nicolson, *Portrait of a Diplomatist*, 119. **31.** Andrew, *Théophile Delcassé*, 291–2. **32.** Ibid., 299. **33.** Ibid., 292–3. **34.** Ibid., 296–7. **35.** Ibid., 289. **36.** Ibid., 276–8, 278–9. **37.** Ibid., 296–301. **38.** Weber, *The Nationalist Revival in France*, 31. **39.** Monger, *The End of Isolation*, 202. **40.** Bülow, *Memoirs of Prince von Bulow*, vol. II, 135, 138. **41.** Rich, *Friedrich von Holstein*, vol. II, 707. **42.** Nicolson, *Portrait of a Diplomatist*, 122. **43.** Andrew, *Théophile Delcassé*, 303. **44.** Weber, *The Nationalist Revival in France*, 32. **45.** Williamson, *Politics of Grand Strategy*, 40–41. **46.** Ibid., 42. **47.** Marder, *From the Dreadnought to Scapa Flow*, 117. **48.** Rich, *Friedrich von Holstein*, vol. II, 731. **49.** Grey, *Twenty-five Years*, vol.

I; see for example his letter of 31 January 1906, 176–9. **50.** Otte, 'Almost a Law of Nature?', 82–3. **51.** Wilson, *The Policy of the Entente*, 13. **52.** Grey, *Twenty-five Years*, vol. I, 128. **53.** Lloyd George, *War Memoirs*, vol. I, 91. **54.** Gilmour, *Curzon*, 26n. **55.** Robbins, *Sir Edward Grey*, 23–4, 29. **56.** Massie, *Dreadnought*, 585. **57.** Steiner and Neilson, *Britain and the Origins*, 41–2. **58.** Wilson, *The Policy of the Entente*, 35. **59.** Steiner and Neilson, *Britain and the Origins*, 42–3. **60.** Otte, 'Almost a Law of Nature?', 79. **61.** BD, vol. III, 200, p. 162. **62.** Grey, *Twenty-Five Years*, vol. I, 98. **63.** Rich, *Friedrich von Holstein*, vol. II, 733. **64.** Oppel, 'The Waning of a Traditional Alliance', 324. **65.** Bridge, *From Sadowa to Sarajevo*, 281–2. **66.** Herring, *From Colony to Superpower*, 363. **67.** BD, vol. III, 401, pp. 337–8. **68.** Lerman, *The Chancellor as Courtier*, 147–8. **69.** Balfour, *The Kaiser and His Times*, 262; Lerman, *The Chancellor as Courtier*, 144. **70.** Balfour, *The Kaiser and His Times*, 264. **71.** Otte, 'Almost a Law of Nature?', 83. **72.** Foley, 'Debate – the Real Schlieffen Plan', 44–5. **73.** Craig, *The Politics of the Prussian Army*, 284–5. **74.** Joll and Martel, *The Origins of the First World War*, 197. **75.** Oppel, 'The Waning of a Traditional Alliance', 325–6. **76.** Dumas, *The Franco-British Exhibition*, 4. **77.** Williamson, *Politics of Grand Strategy*, 38–40. **78.** BD, vol. III, 299, pp. 266–8. **79.** Williamson, *Politics of Grand Strategy*, 76. **80.** Lloyd George, *War Memoirs*, vol. I, 49–50. **81.** Wilson, *The Policy of the Entente*, 85–7. **82.** Ibid., 93–6. **83.** Williamson, *Politics of Grand Strategy*, 90–92. **84.** Kennedy, 'Great Britain before 1914', 173. **85.** Wilson, *The Policy of the Entente*, 125. **86.** Offer, *The First World War*, 303. **87.** Doughty, *Pyrrhic Victory*, 39. **88.** Marder, *From the Dreadnought to Scapa Flow*, 384–8. **89.** Wilson, *The Policy of the Entente*, 126; Fisher and Marder, *Fear God and Dread Nought*, vol. II, 232. **90.** Marder, *From the Dreadnought to Scapa Flow*, 246–7. **91.** Williamson, *Politics of Grand Strategy*, 106–7. **92.** Steiner and Neilson, *Britain and the Origins*, 213. **93.** Neilson, 'Great Britain', 183–5; Williamson, *Politics of Grand Strategy*, 187–93. **94.** Jeffery, *Field Marshal Sir Henry Wilson*, 96–7. **95.** Williamson, *Politics of Grand Strategy*, 196. **96.** Porch, *The March to the Marne*, 228. **97.** Eubank, *Paul Cambon*, 114, 123, 155 and passim. **98.** Doughty, 'French Strategy in 1914', 435. **99.** Schmidt, *Frankreichs Aussenpolitik*, 138–41. **100.** Jeffery, *Field Marshal Sir Henry Wilson*, 37. **101.** Williamson, 'General Henry Wilson', 91. **102.** Ibid., 94–6. **103.** Callwell, *Field-Marshal Sir Henry Wilson*, vol. I, 89. **104.** Ibid., 78–9. **105.** Andrew, 'France and the German Menace', 137. **106.** Callwell, *Field-Marshal Sir Henry Wilson*, vol. I, 105. **107.** Keiger, 'Jules Cambon', 642.

14 The Bosnian Crisis: Confrontation between Russia and Austria-Hungary in the Balkans

1. Aehrenthal, *Aus dem Nachlass*, 196. **2.** Diószegi, *Hungarians in the Ballhausplatz*, 197–200. **3.** Hoetzendorf, *Mein Leben mit Conrad von Hötzendorf*, 63, 237. **4.** Bülow, *Memoirs of Prince von Bulow*, vol. I, 372. **5.** Kronenbitter, *Krieg im Frieden*, 248–51. **6.** Bridge, *From Sadowa to Sarajevo*, 290. **7.** Wank, 'Aehrenthal's Programme', 520–22. **8.** Aehrenthal, *Aus dem Nachlass*; see, for example, 385–8. **9.** Bülow, *Memoirs of Prince von Bulow*, vol. II, 371. **10.** Jelavich, *Russia's Balkan Entanglements*, 217. **11.** Musulin, *Das Haus am Ballplatz*, 57. **12.** Williamson, *Austria-Hungary*, 95. **13.** Czernin, *In the World War*, 50. **14.** Williamson, 'Influence, Power, and the Policy Process', 431. **15.** Williamson, *Austria-Hungary*, 97. **16.** Bridge, *From Sadowa to Sarajevo*, 279; Bridge, *The Habsburg Monarchy*, 189–90. **17.** Diószegi, *Hungarians in the Ballhausplatz*, 200. **18.** Macartney, *The Habsburg Empire*, 597–8; Bridge, *From Sadowa to Sarajevo*,

149–50. **19.** Stevenson, *Armaments*, 82. **20.** Jelavich, *Russia's Balkan Entanglements*, 240; Jelavich and Jelavich, *The Establishment*, 255–6. **21.** Jelavich, *Russia's Balkan Entanglements*, 239n53. **22.** Macartney, *The Habsburg Empire*, 774. **23.** Williamson, *Austria-Hungary*, 65. **24.** Baernreither and Redlich, *Fragments*, 21–2. **25.** Ibid., 35, 44. **26.** Ibid., 43–4. **27.** Aehrenthal, *Aus dem Nachlass*, 449–52. **28.** Ibid., 599. **29.** Bridge, 'Isvolsky, Aehrenthal', 326. **30.** Bridge, 'The Entente Cordiale', 341. **31.** Bridge, *From Sadowa to Sarajevo*, 433. **32.** Baernreither and Redlich, *Fragments*, 37. **33.** Bridge, 'Isvolsky, Aehrenthal', 326. **34.** Bridge, *From Sadowa to Sarajevo*, 298–9. **35.** Lee, *Europe's Crucial Years*, 326. **36.** McDonald, *United Government*, 127. **37.** Cooper, 'British Policy in the Balkans', 262. **38.** Taube, *La Politique russe d'avant-guerre*, 185–7; Nicolson, *Portrait of a Diplomatist*, 200; Lee, *Europe's Crucial Years*, 184–5.
39. Margutti, *The Emperor Francis Joseph*, 225. **40.** Hopman, *Das ereignisreiche Leben*, 147–8. **41.** Reynolds, *Shattering Empires*, 22. **42.** Schoen, *Memoirs of an Ambassador*, 77; Bridge, 'Isvolsky, Aehrenthal', 332–3. **43.** Fuller, *Strategy and Power in Russia*, 419.
44. Bülow, *Memoirs of Prince von Bulow*, vol. I, 373. **45.** Bridge, 'Isvolsky, Aehrenthal', 334; Hantsch, *Leopold Graf Berchtold*, 121–2. **46.** Bridge, 'Isvolsky, Aehrenthal', 335.
47. Fuller, *Strategy and Power in Russia*, 419. **48.** Bridge, 'Isvolsky, Aehrenthal', 334.
49. Ibid., 339. **50.** McMeekin, *The Russian Origins*, 225. **51.** Bridge, *From Sadowa to Sarajevo*, 437. **52.** Hantsch, *Leopold Graf Berchtold*, 144. **53.** McDonald, *United Government*, 136–51. **54.** Bridge, *From Sadowa to Sarajevo*, 435–6. **55.** Bülow, *Memoirs of Prince von Bulow*, vol. I, 373, 379–80; Balfour, *The Kaiser and His Times*, 287.
56. Bridge, *The Habsburg Monarchy*, 296. **57.** Steed, *Through Thirty Years*, 308–14.
58. Aehrenthal, *Aus dem Nachlass*, 624. **59.** Sweet, 'The Bosnian Crisis', 178–9. **60.** Eby, *The Road to Armageddon*, 151. **61.** Otte, 'Almost a Law of Nature?', 92. **62.** Marder, *From the Dreadnought to Scapa Flow*, 149–50. **63.** Menning, 'Dress Rehearsal for 1914?', 8. **64.** Ibid., 11–15. **65.** Bülow, *Memoirs of Prince von Bulow*, vol. I, 374.
66. Boghitschewitsch, *Die auswärtige Politik Serbiens*, vol. III, 78. **67.** Stevenson, *Armaments*, 115–16. **68.** Boghitschewitsch, *Die auswärtige Politik Serbiens*, vol. III, 93; Jelavich, *Russia's Balkan Entanglements*, 241–2. **69.** Hantsch, *Leopold Graf Berchtold*, 137.
70. Herrmann, *The Arming of Europe*, 123–5; Stevenson, *Armaments*, 116. **71.** Heinrich, *Geschichte in Gesprächen*, 124–5, 221–2. **72.** Aehrenthal, *Aus dem Nachlass*, 628.
73. Musulin, *Das Haus am Ballplatz*, 168. **74.** Stevenson, *Armaments*, 117–18, 125–6.
75. Turner, 'Role of the General Staffs', 306; Aehrenthal, *Aus dem Nachlass*, 629.
76. Bülow, *Memoirs of Prince von Bulow*, vol. II, 439. **77.** Wilson, *The Policy of the Entente*, 91. **78.** Herrmann, *The Arming of Europe*, 118–19. **79.** Hantsch, *Leopold Graf Berchtold*, 142. **80.** McDonald, *United Government*, 141–4; Lee, *Europe's Crucial Years*, 193–4. **81.** Sweet, 'The Bosnian Crisis', 183–4; Nicolson, *Portrait of a Diplomatist*, 215.
82. Sweet, 'The Bosnian Crisis', 182–3; Heinrich, *Geschichte in Gesprächen*, 169.
83. Menning, 'Dress Rehearsal for 1914?', 7. **84.** BD, vol. V, 576, p. 603. **85.** Berghahn, *Germany and the Approach of War*, 81. **86.** Zedlitz-Trützschler, *Twelve Years at the Imperial German Court*, 263. **87.** Afflerbach, *Der Dreibund*, 655. **88.** Jelavich, *Russia's Balkan Entanglements*, 224. **89.** Fuller, 'The Russian Empire', 99. **90.** Bridge, *From Sadowa to Sarajevo*, 438. **91.** Hantsch, *Leopold Graf Berchtold*, 174. **92.** Carter, *The Three Emperors*, 371. **93.** Palmer, *Twilight of the Habsburgs*, 305. **94.** Epkenhans, *Tirpitz*, Kindle version, loc. 755–64. **95.** Sondhaus, *Franz Conrad von Hötzendorf*, 96.
96. Stevenson, *Armaments*, 122; Bridge, *The Habsburg Monarchy*, 295. **97.** Aehrenthal, *Aus dem Nachlass*, 726. **98.** Fellner, 'Die "Mission Hoyos"', 115. **99.** Herrmann, *The*

Arming of Europe, 131. **100.** Lieven, *Nicholas II*, 193–4. **101.** Herrmann, *The Arming of Europe*, 131. **102.** Grey, *Twenty-five Years*, vol. I, 182. **103.** Lieven, *Russia and the Origins*, 37. **104.** Goldberg, *Life of Jean Jaurès*, 470. **105.** Stevenson, *Armaments*, 136. **106.** Cooper, 'British Policy in the Balkans', 261. **107.** Stevenson, *Armaments*, 131–3; Boghitschewitsch, *Die auswärtige Politik Serbiens*, vol. III, 77. **108.** Jelavich, *Russia's Balkan Entanglements*, 244; Hantsch, *Leopold Graf Berchtold*, 33; Neklyudov, *Diplomatic Reminiscences*, 46–50; Gieslingen, *Zwei Jahrzehnte im Nahen Orient*, 253. **109.** Cooper, 'British Policy in the Balkans', 279.

15 1911: The Year of Discords – Morocco Again

1. Barraclough, *From Agadir to Armageddon*, 1–2. **2.** Mortimer, 'Commercial Interests and German Diplomacy', 454. **3.** Barraclough, *From Agadir to Armageddon*, 2; Cecil, *Albert Ballin*, 178; Massie, *Dreadnought*, 725–7. **4.** Fesser, *Der Traum vom Platz*, 141; Fischer, *War of Illusions*, 74–5. **5.** Barraclough, *From Agadir to Armageddon*, 31–2. **6.** Keiger, 'Jules Cambon', 642–3; Keiger, *France and the Origins*, 31–3. **7.** Hewitson, 'Germany and France', 591. **8.** Berghahn, *Germany and the Approach of War*, 94. **9.** Bülow, *Memoirs of Prince von Bulow*, vol. III, 12. **10.** Cecil, *Albert Ballin*, 122–3. **11.** Jarausch, *The Enigmatic Chancellor*, 16. **12.** Ibid., 43. **13.** Ibid., 29n34. **14.** Bülow, *Memoirs of Prince von Bulow*, vol. III, 19. **15.** Cecil, *Albert Ballin*, 122–3. **16.** Jarausch, *The Enigmatic Chancellor*, 68. **17.** Ibid., 25–7. **18.** Ibid., 27–9. **19.** Ibid., 122. **20.** Fuller, *Strategy and Power in Russia*, 422. **21.** Kessler, *Journey to the Abyss*, 509. **22.** Rathenau and von Strandmann, *Walther Rathenau*, 134. **23.** Jarausch, *The Enigmatic Chancellor*, 121. **24.** Spitzemberg, *Das Tagebuch*, 545. **25.** Bülow, *Memoirs of Prince von Bulow*, vol. II, 464. **26.** Cecil, *German Diplomatic Service*, 310–12. **27.** Jarausch, *The Enigmatic Chancellor*, 123. **28.** Herrmann, *The Arming of Europe*, 160. **29.** Allain, *Joseph Caillaux*, 371–7. **30.** Hewitson, 'Germany and France', 592–4. **31.** Williamson, *Politics of Grand Strategy*, 143. **32.** Barraclough, *From Agadir to Armageddon*, 127–8. **33.** Stevenson, *Armaments*, 183. **34.** Jarausch, *The Enigmatic Chancellor*, 124; Mommsen, 'Domestic Factors', 23. **35.** Crampton, 'August Bebel and the British', 221–2. **36.** Keiger, *France and the Origins*, 35. **37.** Messimy, *Mes Souvenirs*, 64–5. **38.** Ibid., 60. **39.** Ibid. **40.** Keiger, 'Jules Cambon', 646; Keiger, *France and the Origins*, 35. **41.** Herrmann, *The Arming of Europe*, 153. **42.** Steiner and Neilson, *Britain and the Origins*, 75. **43.** Neilson, *Britain and the Last Tsar*, 321. **44.** Rose, *King George V*, 165–6. **45.** Weinroth, 'The British Radicals', 664. **46.** Neilson, *Britain and the Last Tsar*, 318. **47.** Wilson, 'The Agadir Crisis', 514–15; Dockrill, 'British Policy', 274–5. **48.** BD, vol. VII, 392, pp. 371–3. **49.** *The Times*, 22 July 1911. **50.** Redlich, *Schicksalsjahre Österreichs*, 95–6. **51.** Fesser, *Der Traum vom Platz*, 145; Balfour, *The Kaiser and His Times*, 313–14. **52.** Callwell, *Field-Marshal Sir Henry Wilson*, vol. I, 97–8. **53.** Marder, *From the Dreadnought to Scapa Flow*, 244–6. **54.** Eubank, *Paul Cambon*, 139; Messimy, *Mes Souvenirs*, 61. **55.** Jeffery, *Field Marshal Sir Henry Wilson*, 99–100. **56.** Riezler, *Tagebücher, Aufsätze, Dokumente*, 180. **57.** Mombauer, *Helmuth von Moltke*, 124. **58.** Barraclough, *From Agadir to Armageddon*, 135. **59.** Fischer, *War of Illusions*, 83. **60.** Andrew, *Théophile Delcassé*, 70n1. **61.** Rathenau and von Strandmann, *Walther Rathenau*, 157. **62.** Eubank, *Paul Cambon*, 141. **63.** Grey, *Twenty-five Years*, vol. I, 233. **64.** Stieve, *Der diplomatische Schriftwechsel Iswolskis*, 194–5. **65.** Steiner and Neilson, *Britain and the Origins*, 79–80. **66.** Ibid., 80–81. **67.** Messimy, *Mes Souvenirs*, 68. **68.** Krumeich, *Armaments and Politics*, 21–9. **69.** Schmidt, *Frankreichs Aussenpolitik*, 217–21. **70.** Jarausch, *The Enigmatic Chancellor*,

124. **71.** Beyens, *Germany before the War*, 61. **72.** Fesser, *Der Traum vom Platz*, 148.
73. Craig, *The Politics of the Prussian Army*, 291. **74.** Mombauer, *Helmuth von Moltke*,
125. **75.** Ritter, *The Sword and the Sceptre*, 172. **76.** Epkenhans, *Tirpitz*, Kindle version,
loc. 852–9. **77.** Röhl, 'Admiral von Müller', 656. **78.** Herwig, 'Imperial Germany', 81–2;
Mombauer, *Helmuth von Moltke*, 131. **79.** Herrmann, *The Arming of Europe*, 161–6.
80. Bosworth, *Italy and the Approach*, 57. **81.** Albertini, *The Origins of the War*, vol. I,
342. **82.** Bosworth, 'Britain and Italy's Acquisition', 683. **83.** Bosworth, *Italy and the
Approach*, 10. **84.** Ibid., 38–9. **85.** Gooch, 'Italy before 1915', 222. **86.** Ibid., 225–8.
87. Ibid., 206. **88.** Bosworth, *Italy and the Approach*, 6–8; Gooch, 'Italy before 1915',
216–17. **89.** Bosworth, *Italy and the Approach*, 34. **90.** Ibid., 36. **91.** Gooch, 'Italy before
1915', 209. **92.** BD, vol. IX, part 1, 257, pp. 289–91. **93.** BD, vol. IX, part 1, 241, pp. 278–9.
94. Barraclough, *From Agadir to Armageddon*, 143–4. **95.** Haupt, *Socialism and the
Great War*, 58–62. **96.** BD, vol. IX, part 1, 250, p. 284. **97.** Rossos, *Russia and the
Balkans*, 35. **98.** Albertini, *The Origins of the War*, vol. I, 346; Barraclough, *From Agadir
to Armageddon*, 144–5. **99.** BD, vol. VII, 763, pp. 788–9.

16 The First Balkan Wars

1. Cambon, *Correspondance*, vol. III, 7. **2.** Albertini, *The Origins of the War*, vol. I, 357.
3. Trotsky, *The Balkan Wars*, 360–61. **4.** Hoetzendorf, *Mein Leben mit Conrad von
Hötzendorf*, 105. **5.** Aehrenthal, *Aus dem Nachlass*, 232. **6.** Trotsky, *The Balkan Wars*, 72.
7. Dedijer, *The Road to Sarajevo*, 179–80. **8.** Jelavich, *History of the Balkans*, 110.
9. Rossos, *Russia and the Balkans*, 34–5. **10.** Trotsky, *The Balkan Wars*, 80. **11.** BD, vol.
IX, part 1, 249, pp. 283–4. **12.** Helmreich, *The Diplomacy*, 29–30. **13.** Ibid., 32–3.
14. Ibid., 33. **15.** Thaden, *Russia and the Balkan Alliance*, 27–8. **16.** Neklyudov,
Diplomatic Reminiscences, 38–9. **17.** Ibid., 45. **18.** Ibid., 80–81. **19.** Helmreich, *The
Diplomacy*, 62–4, 67. **20.** BD, vol. IX, part 1, 570, p. 568. **21.** Fischer, *War of Illusions*, 150.
22. BD, vol. IX, part 2, 5, pp. 3–4. **23.** Helmreich, *The Diplomacy*, 141–5. **24.** Trotsky, *The
Balkan Wars*, 65–6. **25.** Rossos, *Russia and the Balkans*, 79. **26.** Helmreich, *The
Diplomacy*, 203–4. **27.** Wilson, *The Policy of the Entente*, 92. **28.** Thaden, *Russia and the
Balkan Alliance*, 116–17; Jelavich, *Russia's Balkan Entanglements*, 231. **29.** Thaden, *Russia
and the Balkan Alliance*, 118; Albertini, *The Origins of the War*, vol. I, 412–13. **30.** Ignat'ev,
Vneshniaia Politika Rossii, 1907–1914, 141. **31.** Neilson, *Britain and the Last Tsar*, 328–9.
32. Wilson, *The Policy of the Entente*, 92. **33.** Jelavich, *Russia's Balkan Entanglements*,
203. **34.** Bodger, 'Russia and the End', 84. **35.** Thaden, *Russia and the Balkan Alliance*,
132. **36.** Bodger, 'Russia and the End', 79. **37.** Rossos, *Russia and the Balkans*, 85.
38. Sazonov, *Fateful Years*, 49–50; Hantsch, *Leopold Graf Berchtold*, 234n. **39.** Taube, *La
Politique russe d'avant-guerre*, 225–7. **40.** Sazonov, *Fateful Years*, 54. **41.** BD, vol. IX,
part 1, 711, pp. 683–5; Helmreich, *The Diplomacy*, 154–5. **42.** Sazonov, *Fateful Years*, 78.
43. Ibid., 80. **44.** Rossos, *Russia and the Balkans*, 102. **45.** Hantsch, *Leopold Graf
Berchtold*, 119. **46.** Ibid., 484–5. **47.** Musulin, *Das Haus am Ballplatz*, 178. **48.** Vermes,
Istv'an Tisza, 199. **49.** Hantsch, *Leopold Graf Berchtold*, 246. **50.** Csáky, *Vom Geächteten
zum Geächteten*, 129; Leslie, 'Osterreich-Ungarn', 663. **51.** Albertini, *The Origins of the
War*, vol. I, 385. **52.** Ibid., 383–4. **53.** Hantsch, *Leopold Graf Berchtold*, 176. **54.** See for
example, Bertie to Grey, 29 August 1912, BD, vol. IX, part 1, 671, pp. 653–5. **55.** BD, vol.
IX, part 1, 695, pp. 671–3. **56.** Heinrich, *Geschichte in Gesprächen*, 380. **57.** Helmreich,
The Diplomacy, 214–15. **58.** Boghitschewitsch, *Die auswärtige Politik Serbiens*, vol. III,
159. **59.** Sondhaus, *Franz Conrad von Hötzendorf*, 124. **60.** Helmreich, *The Diplomacy*,

153. **61.** Williamson, *Austria-Hungary*, 132; Bucholz, *Moltke, Schlieffen*, 276.
62. Hantsch, *Leopold Graf Berchtold*, 323; Afflerbach, *Der Dreibund*, 731–3; Williamson, *Austria-Hungary*, 127. **63.** Hantsch, *Leopold Graf Berchtold*, 328. **64.** Williamson, *Austria-Hungary*, 132. **65.** Sazonov, *Fateful Years*, 78. **66.** Herrmann, *The Arming of Europe*, 178. **67.** BD, vol. IX, part 2, 303, pp. 227–8. **68.** Ibid. **69.** Rossos, *Russia and the Balkans*, 104–5. **70.** Herrmann, *The Arming of Europe*, 178. **71.** Fischer, *War of Illusions*, 155–6. **72.** Röhl, 'Admiral von Müller', 659. **73.** Fischer, *War of Illusions*, 157–8. **74.** Röhl, 'Admiral von Müller', 664; Bucholz, *Moltke, Schlieffen*, 276–7. **75.** *The Times*, 22 November 1912. **76.** Helmreich, *The Diplomacy*, 216. **77.** Sondhaus, *Franz Conrad von Hötzendorf*, 120–21. **78.** Williamson, *Austria-Hungary*, 130–31. **79.** Fischer, *War of Illusions*, 158–61. **80.** Hantsch, *Leopold Graf Berchtold*, 388. **81.** Williamson, *Austria-Hungary*, 130–31. **82.** Grey, *Twenty-Five Years*, vol. I, 256. **83.** Helmreich, *The Diplomacy*, 250. **84.** Eubank, *Paul Cambon*, 161. **85.** Crampton, 'The Decline', 393–4. **86.** BD, vol. IX, part 2, 626, p. 506. **87.** Hantsch, *Leopold Graf Berchtold*, 377. **88.** Ibid., 381. **89.** Williamson, *Austria-Hungary*, 134; Helmreich, *The Diplomacy*, 282–4. **90.** Williamson, *Austria-Hungary*, 136; Helmreich, *The Diplomacy*, 296–7. **91.** Crampton, 'The Decline', 395 and fn 12. **92.** Helmreich, *The Diplomacy*, 313–14. **93.** Williamson, *Austria-Hungary*, 139–40. **94.** Sondhaus, *Franz Conrad von Hötzendorf*, 123. **95.** Hantsch, *Leopold Graf Berchtold*, 471. **96.** Cambon, *Correspondance*, vol. III, 27. **97.** Jelavich, *Russia's Balkan Entanglements*, 246–8. **98.** Williamson, *Austria-Hungary*, 151. **99.** Vermes, *Istv'an Tisza*, 203. **100.** Ibid., p. 131. **101.** Stone, 'Hungary and the July Crisis', 157. **102.** Leslie, 'The Antecedents', 323–4. **103.** Hantsch, *Leopold Graf Berchtold*, 498; Williamson, *Austria-Hungary*, 133–4. **104.** Crampton, 'The Decline', 417–19. **105.** Albertini, *The Origins of the War*, vol. I, 483–4. **106.** Helmreich, *The Diplomacy*, 428. **107.** Bridge, *From Sadowa to Sarajevo*, 366–7. **108.** Ibid., 442. **109.** Williamson, *Austria-Hungary*, 154–5. **110.** Afflerbach, *Der Dreibund*, 748. **111.** Sondhaus, *Franz Conrad von Hötzendorf*, 129. **112.** Hantsch, *Leopold Graf Berchtold*, 513. **113.** Ibid., 312. **114.** Herrmann, *The Arming of Europe*, 179. **115.** Williamson, *Austria-Hungary*, 135; Leslie, *The Antecedents*, 352–3. **116.** Albertini, *The Origins of the War*, vol. I, 483–4. **117.** Crampton, *The Hollow Detente*, 172. **118.** Haupt, *Socialism and the Great War*, 107. **119.** Cooper, *Patriotic Pacifism*, 159–60. **120.** Kennan, *The Other Balkan Wars*, 271.

17 Preparing for War or Peace Europe's Last Months of Peace

1. BD, vol. X, part 2, 476, pp. 702–3. **2.** Rose, *King George V*, 166–7. **3.** McLean, *Royalty and Diplomacy*, 197. **4.** Craig, *Germany, 1866–1945*, 295; Herwig, 'Imperial Germany', 84. **5.** Kießling, *Gegen den 'Großen Krieg'?*, 195–6. **6.** Rosen, *Forty Years of Diplomacy*, 154. **7.** Brusilov, *A Soldier's Notebook*, 3–4. **8.** Gildea, *Barricades and Borders*, 419. **9.** Rogger, 'Russia in 1914', 96. **10.** Sazonov, *Fateful Years*, 80. **11.** Miliukov and Mendel, *Political Memoirs*, 284. **12.** Kokovtsov, *Out of My Past*, 296. **13.** Ibid., 361. **14.** Figes, *A People's Tragedy*, 216. **15.** Ibid., 241–5. **16.** Rogger, 'Russia in 1914', 95–6. **17.** Ibid., 101–2. **18.** Geyer, *Russian Imperialism*, 249–54. **19.** Ibid., 274–5. **20.** Lieven, *Nicholas II*, 168. **21.** Bridge, *From Sadowa to Sarajevo*, 371. **22.** Hewitson, 'Germany and France', 578; Kießling, *Gegen den 'Großen Krieg'?*, 196. **23.** Tanenbaum, 'French Estimates', 167–8. **24.** Kessler, *Journey to the Abyss*, 609. **25.** Bülow, *Memoirs of Prince von Bulow*, vol. III, 33; Cecil, *German Diplomatic Service*, 317. **26.** Spitzemberg, *Das Tagebuch*, 563. **27.** Stevenson, *Armaments*, 286–9. **28.** Röhl, *The Kaiser and His Court*, 173–4; Röhl,

'Admiral von Müller', 661; Stevenson, *Armaments*, 252–3. **29.** Mombauer, *Helmuth von Moltke*, 145. **30.** Herwig, 'Imperial Germany', 84. **31.** Röhl, 'Admiral von Müller', 665; Balfour, *The Kaiser and His Times*, 339–40; Tanenbaum, 'French Estimates', 169. **32.** Stevenson, *Armaments*, 316–20. **33.** Krumeich, *Armaments and Politics*, ch. 2. **34.** Stevenson, *Armaments*, 221. **35.** Doughty, 'France', 163. **36.** Ibid., 162. **37.** Weber, *The Nationalist Revival in France*, 97. **38.** Ibid., 94–5, 102. **39.** Kessler, *Journey to the Abyss*, 580. **40.** German Foreign Office, *Die grosse Politik*, vol. XXXIX, 292. **41.** Nolan, *The Inverted Mirror*, 40, 82–3. **42.** Stevenson, *Armaments*, 222. **43.** Keiger, *Raymond Poincaré*, 122–3, 130–31. **44.** Ibid., 145. **45.** Williams, *Tiger of France*, 286. **46.** Ibid., 11–14, 24–7, 154. **47.** Ibid., 147. **48.** Adamthwaite, *Grandeur and Misery*, 8; Hughes, *Policies and Potentates*, 223–7. **49.** Hayne, *French Foreign Office*, 274. **50.** Cambon, *Correspondance*, vol. III, 39. **51.** Keiger, *Raymond Poincaré*, 151. **52.** Hayne, *French Foreign Office*, 238. **53.** Keiger, *Raymond Poincaré*, 155–7. **54.** Schmidt, *Frankreichs Aussenpolitik*, 236–7. **55.** Ibid., 238–40. **56.** Williamson, 'German Perceptions', 206. **57.** Goldberg, *Life of Jean Jaurès*, 439. **58.** Sazonov, *Fateful Years*, 56. **59.** Rose, *King George V*, 80. **60.** Ibid., 71. **61.** Clifford, *The Asquiths*, 2–3. **62.** Ibid., 13–14. **63.** Haldane, *An Autobiography*, 111. **64.** Clifford, *The Asquiths*, 186. **65.** Ibid., 145. **66.** Adam, *Bonar Law*, 107–9. **67.** Jeffery, *Field Marshal Sir Henry Wilson*, 115–16. **68.** BD, vol. X, part 2, 537, pp. 780–83. **69.** Churchill, *The World Crisis*, vol. I, 185; Dangerfield, *The Strange Death*, 366. **70.** Leslie, 'Osterreich-Ungarn', 669–70. **71.** Afflerbach, *Der Dreibund*, 793–4, 806–8, 810–11. **72.** Angelow, *Der Weg in die Katastrophe*, 26. **73.** Wandruszka and Urbanitsch, *Die Habsburgermonarchie*, 331–2; Bridge, *From Sadowa to Sarajevo*, 364–5. **74.** Bodger, 'Russia and the End', 88. **75.** Herwig, 'Imperial Germany', 87. **76.** Jarausch, *The Enigmatic Chancellor*, 117. **77.** Sazonov, *Fateful Years*, 43–4; Kokovtsov, *Out of My Past*, 321–3. **78.** Stieve, *Der diplomatische Schriftwechsel Iswolskis*, 17–18. **79.** McLean, *Royalty and Diplomacy*, 67–8. **80.** Shatsillo, *Ot Portsmutskogo*, 272–4; Stevenson, *Armaments*, 343–9. **81.** Churchill, *The World Crisis*, vol. I, 178; Grey, *Twenty-Five Years*, vol. I, 269. **82.** Grey, *Twenty-Five Years*, vol. I, 195. **83.** Wilson, *The Policy of the Entente*, 68. **84.** Spring, 'Russia and the Franco-Russian Alliance', 584; Robbins, *Sir Edward Grey*, 271. **85.** Schmidt, *Frankreichs Aussenpolitik*, 266–76. **86.** Ibid., 252–3, 258–9. **87.** Jeffery, *Field Marshal Sir Henry Wilson*, 103. **88.** Marder, *From the Dreadnought to Scapa Flow*, 253. **89.** Churchill, *The World Crisis*, vol. I, 118. **90.** Williamson, *Politics of Grand Strategy*, 274. **91.** Churchill, *The World Crisis*, vol. I, 119. **92.** Marder, *From the Dreadnought to Scapa Flow*, 254–6, 265–6. **93.** Churchill, *The World Crisis*, vol. I, 113. **94.** Williamson, *Politics of Grand Strategy*, 320–25. **95.** BD, vol. X, part 2, 416, pp. 614–15. **96.** Esher, *Journals and Letters*, vol. III, 331. **97.** BD, vol. X, part 2, 400, pp. 601–2. **98.** Robbins, *Sir Edward Grey*, 285. **99.** Rose, *King George V*, 164. **100.** Bridge, 'The Entente Cordiale', 350. **101.** Angelow, *Der Weg in die Katastrophe*, 60–61. **102.** Stevenson, *Armaments*, 2–9. **103.** Ibid., 4. **104.** Herrmann, *The Arming of Europe*, 207. **105.** Epkenhans, *Tirpitz*, Kindle version, loc. 862. **106.** Kießling, *Gegen den 'Großen Krieg'?*, 67–8. **107.** Heywood, 'The Most Catastrophic Question', 56. **108.** Förster, 'Im Reich des Absurden', 233. **109.** Stevenson, *Armaments*, 358–9; Schmidt, *Frankreichs Aussenpolitik*, 208–11, 242–4. **110.** Herwig, 'Imperial Germany', 88. **111.** Brusilov, *A Soldier's Notebook*, 1. **112.** Kießling, *Gegen den 'Großen Krieg'?*, 43–4. **113.** Grey, *Twenty-Five Years*, vol. I, 292. **114.** Hantsch, *Leopold Graf Berchtold*, 458. **115.** Sondhaus, *Franz Conrad von Hötzendorf*, 134; Hantsch, *Leopold Graf Berchtold*, 252–3; Kronenbitter, '"Nur los lassen"', 39. **116.** McDonald, *United Government*,

199–201. **117.** Leslie, 'The Antecedents', 334–6, 338–9. **118.** Churchill, *The World Crisis*, vol. I, 95. **119.** Haldane, *Before the War*, 33–6. **120.** Cecil, *Wilhelm II*, 172. **121.** Cecil, *Albert Ballin*, 182–96. **122.** Hopman, *Das ereignisreiche Leben*, 209–10. **123.** Cecil, *Wilhelm II*, 172–3. **124.** House and Seymour, *The Intimate Papers*, vol. I, 249. **125.** Marder, *From the Dreadnought to Scapa Flow*, 283–4; Maurer, 'Churchill's Naval Holiday', 109–10. **126.** Brinker-Gabler, *Kämpferin für den Frieden*, 167. **127.** Haupt, *Socialism and the Great War*, 108.

18 Assassination at Sarajevo

1. Poincaré, *Au Service de la France*, vol. IV, 173–4. **2.** Geinitz, *Kriegsfurcht und Kampfbereitschaft*, 50–53. **3.** Cecil, *Wilhelm II*, 198. **4.** Massie, *Dreadnought*, 852–3; Cecil, *Wilhelm II*, 198; Geiss, *July 1914*, 69. **5.** Smith, *One Morning in Sarajevo*, 40. **6.** Dedijer, *The Road to Sarajevo*, 175–8, 208–9, 217 and ch. 10, passim. **7.** Ibid., 197. **8.** Ibid. **9.** Ibid., 373–5; Jelavich, *What the Habsburg Government Knew*, 134–5. **10.** Dedijer, *The Road to Sarajevo*, 294–301, 309; Jelavich, *What the Habsburg Government Knew*, 136. **11.** Leslie, 'The Antecedents', 368; Funder, *Vom Gestern ins Heute*, 483; Dedijer, *The Road to Sarajevo*, 405–7, 409–10. **12.** Kronenbitter, *Krieg im Frieden*, 459; Dedijer, *The Road to Sarajevo*, 312; Funder, *Vom Gestern ins Heute*, 484. **13.** Dedijer, *The Road to Sarajevo*, 11–16, 316. **14.** Margutti, *The Emperor Francis Joseph*, 138–9. **15.** Smith, *One Morning in Sarajevo*, 214; Hopman, *Das ereignisreiche Leben*, 381; Albertini, *The Origins of the War*, vol. II, 117–19; Hoetzsch, *Die internationalen Beziehungen*, 106–7. **16.** Stone, 'Hungary and the July Crisis', 159–60. **17.** Kronenbitter, *Krieg im Frieden*, 460–62. **18.** Sondhaus, *Franz Conrad von Hötzendorf*, 140; Hantsch, *Leopold Graf Berchtold*, 558–9. **19.** Musulin, *Das Haus am Ballplatz*, 226. **20.** Leslie, 'The Antecedents', 320. **21.** Wank, 'Desperate Counsel', 295; Leslie, 'Osterreich-Ungarn', 664. **22.** Leslie, 'Osterreich-Ungarn', 665. **23.** Stone, 'Hungary and the July Crisis', 161. **24.** Albertini, *The Origins of the War*, vol. II, 150–55. **25.** Leslie, 'The Antecedents', 375–80. **26.** Hantsch, *Leopold Graf Berchtold*, 559. **27.** Bittner and Ubersberger, *Österreich-Ungarns Aussenpolitik*, 248. **28.** Fellner, 'Die "Mission Hoyos"', 122; Albertini, *The Origins of the War*, vol. II, 129–30. **29.** Turner, 'Role of the General Staffs', 308. **30.** Bittner and Ubersberger, *Österreich-Ungarns Aussenpolitik*, 252; Albertini, *The Origins of the War*, vol. II, 133–5. **31.** Fellner, 'Die "Mission Hoyos"', 125–6, 137. **32.** See for example: Albertini, *The Origins of the War*, vol. II, 137–48; Geiss, *July 1914*, 70–80; Kronenbitter, '"Nur los lassen"', 182. **33.** Sösemann, 'Die Tagebücher Kurt Riezlers', 185. **34.** Mombauer, *Helmuth von Moltke*, 168–9, 177. **35.** Jarausch, *The Enigmatic Chancellor*, 153–5. **36.** Mommsen, 'The Debate on German War Aims', 60n16. **37.** Mombauer, *Helmuth von Moltke*, 168–9. **38.** Cecil, *Wilhelm II*, 172; Dülffer, 'Kriegserwartung und Kriegsbild', 785; Joll and Martel, *The Origins of the First World War*, 274; Förster, 'Im Reich des Absurden', 251–2; Mombauer, *Helmuth von Moltke*, 177, 181. **39.** Förster, 'Im Reich des Absurden', 233. **40.** Wolff, *Tagebücher 1914–1919*, 63–5. **41.** Bach, *Deutsche Gesandtschaftsberichte*, 63. **42.** Groener, *Lebenserinnerungen*, 140. **43.** Stevenson, *Armaments*, 363–4; Mombauer, *Helmuth von Moltke*, 182. **44.** Mombauer, *Helmuth von Moltke*, 135. **45.** Ibid., 173. **46.** Herwig, 'From Tirpitz Plan to Schlieffen Plan', 58; Mombauer, *Helmuth von Moltke*, 159–60, 212–13. **47.** Lichnowsky and Delmer, *Heading for the Abyss*, 379–80n. **48.** Sösemann, 'Die Tagebücher Kurt Riezlers', 183. **49.** Jarausch, *The Enigmatic Chancellor*, 105. **50.** Herwig, 'Imperial Germany', 80; Sösemann, 'Die Tagebücher Kurt Riezlers',

183–4. **51**. Sösemann, 'Die Tagebücher Kurt Riezlers', 184–5; Lichnowsky and Delmer, *Heading for the Abyss*, 392. **52**. Mombauer, *Helmuth von Moltke*, 195n44; Lichnowsky and Delmer, *Heading for the Abyss*, 381; Sösemann, 'Die Tagebücher Kurt Riezlers', 184. **53**. Fesser, *Der Traum vom Platz*, 181. **54**. Lichnowsky and Delmer, *Heading for the Abyss*, 381. **55**. Turner, 'Role of the General Staffs', 312; Geiss, *July 1914*, 65. **56**. Fischer, *War of Illusions*, 478; Cecil, *Wilhelm II*, 193–6. **57**. Joll, *1914*, 8. **58**. Kronenbitter, 'Die Macht der Illusionen', 531; Williamson, *Austria-Hungary*, 199–200. **59**. Bittner and Ubersberger, *Österreich-Ungarns Aussenpolitik*, 248. **60**. Geiss, *July 1914*, 80–87; Sondhaus, *Franz Conrad von Hötzendorf*, 141; Williamson, *Austria-Hungary*, 197–9.
61. Stone, 'Hungary and the July Crisis', 166–8; Vermes, *Istv'an Tisza*, 226; Leslie, 'The Antecedents', 343. **62**. Geiss, *July 1914*, 114–15. **63**. Jelavich, *What the Habsburg Government Knew*, 133. **64**. Williamson, *Austria-Hungary*, 200–201; Geiss, *July 1914*, 90–92. **65**. Williamson, *Austria-Hungary*, 201. **66**. Jelavich, *Russia's Balkan Entanglements*, 256. **67**. BD, vol. XI, 56, pp. 44–5. **68**. Turner, 'Role of the General Staffs', 312; Fischer, *War of Illusions*, 478–9; Geiss, *July 1914*, 89–90. **69**. Hoetzsch, *Die internationalen Beziehungen*, vol. IV, 301–2; Jarausch, *The Enigmatic Chancellor*, 161–2; Hertling and Lerchenfeld-Köfering, *Briefwechsel Hertling-Lerchenfeld*, 307. **70**. BD, vol. XI, 27, pp. 19–20; 45, p. 37; Albertini, *The Origins of the War*, vol. II, 272–5.
71. Gieslingen, *Zwei Jahrzehnte im Nahen Orient*, 257–61; Albertini, *The Origins of the War*, vol. II, 276–9. **72**. Williamson, *Austria-Hungary*, 201. **73**. Macartney, *The Habsburg Empire*, 808n. **74**. Austro-Hungarian Gemeinsamer Ministerrat, *Protokolle des Gemeinsamen Ministerrates*, 150–54; Williamson, *Austria-Hungary*, 203. **75**. Vermes, *Istv'an Tisza*, 232–3. **76**. Albertini, *The Origins of the War*, vol. II, 265. **77**. Geiss, *July 1914*, 142, 149–50, 154. **78**. Macartney, *The Habsburg Empire*, 808n; Hantsch, *Leopold Graf Berchtold*, 602–3. Complete text in Albertini, *The Origins of the War*, vol. II, 286–9.
79. Gieslingen, *Zwei Jahrzehnte im Nahen Orient*, 267–8; Albertini, *The Origins of the War*, vol. II, 346; Bittner and Ubersberger, *Österreich-Ungarns Aussenpolitik*, 659–63; Cornwall, 'Serbia', 72–4. **80**. BD, vol. XI, 92, p. 74; 107, p. 85; Stokes, 'Serbian Documents from 1914', 71–4; Cornwall, 'Serbia', 75–9, 82. **81**. Kronenbitter, 'Die Macht der Illusionen', 536; Kronenbitter, '"Nur los lassen"', 159. **82**. Albertini, *The Origins of the War*, vol. II, 373–5; Gieslingen, *Zwei Jahrzehnte im Nahen Orient*, 268–72.

19 The End of the Concert of Europe: Austria-Hungary Declares War on Serbia

1. MacKenzie and MacKenzie, *The Diary of Beatrice Webb*, vol. III, 203–5. **2**. Kessler, *Journey to the Abyss*, 631–40. **3**. Mombauer, 'A Reluctant Military Leader?', 422.
4. Lieven, *Nicholas II*, 198. **5**. Bestuzhev, 'Russian Foreign Policy February–June 1914', 100–101. **6**. Lieven, *Russia and the Origins*, 49. **7**. Rogger, 'Russia in 1914', 98–9. **8**. Shukman, *Rasputin*, 58. **9**. Bridge, 'The British Declaration of War', 403–4.
10. Brock and Brock, *H. H. Asquith*, 93, 122–3. **11**. Rose, *King George V*, 157–8.
12. Hazlehurst, *Politicians at War*, 31. **13**. Messimy, *Mes Souvenirs*, 126–7. **14**. Cronin, *Paris on the Eve*, 427–9. **15**. Afflerbach, 'The Topos of Improbable War', 179.
16. Doughty, 'France', 149. **17**. Schmidt, *Frankreichs Aussenpolitik*, 271–2, 278–83.
18. Ibid., 265–8. **19**. Goldberg, *Life of Jean Jaurès*, 460. **20**. Poincaré, *Au Service de la France*, 224–6, 230. **21**. Krumeich, *Armaments and Politics*, 217; Schmidt, *Frankreichs Aussenpolitik*, 283. **22**. Figes, *A People's Tragedy*, 232; Ignat'ev, *50 Let v Stroyu*, 423.
23. Poincaré, *Au Service de la France*, 259, 269–70; Krumeich, *Armaments and Politics*, 291n153. **24**. Poincaré, *Au Service de la France*, 246–7. **25**. BD, vol. IX, 101, pp. 80–82.

26. Ibid., 253–5; Williamson, *Austria-Hungary*, 203. 27. Schmidt, *Frankreichs Aussenpolitik*, 78. 28. Hoetzsch, *Die internationalen Beziehungen*, vol. IV, 128.
29. Bridge, *How the War Began*, 27. 30. Lieven, *Nicholas II*, 201; Lieven, *Russia and the Origins*, 108–9. 31. Turner, 'The Russian Mobilization', 74. 32. Ibid., 78. 33. Hayne, *French Foreign Office*, 116–21; Schmidt, *Frankreichs Aussenpolitik*, 227–8; Cairns, 'International Politics', 285. 34. BD, vol. IX, 101, pp. 80–2. 35. Turner, 'The Russian Mobilization', 81, 83. 36. Schmidt, *Frankreichs Aussenpolitik*, 89–91. 37. Doughty, 'France', 146–7. 38. Schmidt, *Frankreichs Aussenpolitik*, 202–4. 39. Bittner and Ubersberger, *Österreich-Ungarns Aussenpolitik*, 805. 40. Bark, 'Iul'skie Dni 1914 Goda', 32–4; Bridge, *How the War Began*, 30–32; Ignat'ev, *Vneshniaia Politika Rossii, 1907–1914*, 213–14. 41. BD, vol. IX, 125, pp. 93–4. 42. Turner, 'The Russian Mobilization', 76–7. 43. Ibid., 77, 80. 44. Rosen, *Forty Years of Diplomacy*, 163. 45. Stengers, 'Belgium', 158. 46. Schmidt, *Frankreichs Aussenpolitik*, 335–42; Poincaré, *Au Service de la France*, 288; Krumeich, *Armaments and Politics*, 219–20. 47. Turner, 'The Russian Mobilization', 82–3; Poincaré, *Au Service de la France*, 302; Doughty, 'French Strategy in 1914', 443. 48. Lichnowsky and Delmer, *Heading for the Abyss*, 375. 49. Nicolson, *Portrait of a Diplomatist*, 295. 50. Ibid., 301. 51. Bridge, 'The British Declaration of War', 407; Haldane, *An Autobiography*, 288–9; Cecil, *Albert Ballin*, 205–9. 52. Bridge, 'The British Declaration of War', 408; Wilson, *The Policy of the Entente*, 135–6; BD, vol. XI, 91, pp. 73–4; 104, pp. 83–4. 53. Geiss, *July 1914*, 183–4. 54. Bülow, *Memoirs of Prince Von Bulow*, vol. III, 122–3. 55. Lichnowsky and Delmer, *Heading for the Abyss*, 368–469.
56. Nicolson, *Portrait of a Diplomatist*, 301. 57. Hobhouse, *Inside Asquith's Cabinet*, 176–7; Robbins, *Sir Edward Grey*, 289–90. 58. BD, vol. IX, 185, p. 128. 59. BD, vol. IX, 170, pp. 120–1. 60. BD, vol. IX, 216, p. 148. 61. Eubank, *Paul Cambon*, 171. 62. Ibid., 169. 63. Trumpener, 'War Premeditated?', 66–7; Bittner and Ubersberger, *Österreich-Ungarns Aussenpolitik*, 739, 741. 64. Cecil, *Wilhelm II*, 202–3. 65. Bridge, *Russia*, 52. 66. BD, vol. IX, 135, p. 99; 147, p. 103; *The Times*, 27 July 1914; Bark, 'Iul'skie Dni 1914 Goda', 26; Bittner and Ubersberger, *Österreich-Ungarns Aussenpolitik*, 759; Verhey, *Spirit of 1914*, 28–31. 67. BD, vol. XI, 162, p. 116; 245, pp. 160–61. 68. Renzi, 'Italy's Neutrality', 1419–20. 69. Ibid., 1421–2. 70. Hobhouse, *Inside Asquith's Cabinet*, 177. 71. Williamson, *Politics of Grand Strategy*, 345. 72. Afflerbach, 'Wilhelm II as Supreme Warlord', 432. 73. Ignat'ev, *Vneshniaia politika Rossii, 1907–1914*, 218–19. 74. Geiss, *July 1914*, 283. 75. Jarausch, *The Enigmatic Chancellor*, 171. 76. Albertini, *The Origins of the War*, vol. II, 460–61. 77. Vermes, *Istv'an Tisza*, 234. 78. Rosen, *Forty Years of Diplomacy*, 163.

20 Turning Out the Lights: Europe's Last Week of Peace

1. Zweig, *The World of Yesterday*, 243–5. 2. BD, vol. XI, 270, p. 174; Poincaré, *Au Service de la France*, 368. 3. Keiger, *Raymond Poincaré*, 171. 4. Schmidt, *Frankreichs Aussenpolitik*, 335–42; Turner, 'The Russian Mobilization', 83. 5. Schmidt, *Frankreichs Aussenpolitik*, 345–7; Herwig, *The Marne*, 17. 6. Lieven, *Nicholas II*, 199–200. 7. Geiss, *July 1914*, 260–61. 8. Ibid. 9. Bridge, *Russia*, 50; Turner, 'The Russian Mobilization', 86. 10. Ibid., 87–8. 11. Ibid., 78; Geiss, *July 1914*, 291. 12. Cimbala, 'Steering through Rapids', 387. 13. Bridge, *How the War Began*, 65–6; Bark, 'Iul'skie Dni 1914 Goda', 31–2; Kleinmikhel', *Memories of a Shipwrecked World*, 202–3. 14. Cecil, *Wilhelm II*, 204–5. 15. Geiss, *July 1914*, 284–5; Fuller, *Strategy and Power in Russia*, 447; Jarausch, *The Enigmatic Chancellor*, 168–9. 16. Ekstein and Steiner, 'The Sarajevo Crisis', 404;

Williamson, *Politics of Grand Strategy*, 347. 17. Hankey, *The Supreme Command*, 154–6.
18. Geiss, *July 1914*, 288–90. 19. Albertini, *The Origins of the War*, vol. II, 300–302;
Geiss, *July 1914*, 296–7; Turner, 'The Russian Mobilization', 86. 20. Verhey, *Spirit of 1914*, 17–20. 21. Ibid., 53–6. 22. Jarausch, *The Enigmatic Chancellor*, 151–2, 164, 168–9.
23. Geiss, *July 1914*, 291–2, 308–9. 24. Turner, 'Role of General Staffs', 315. 25. Ibid.
26. Austro-Hungarian Gemeinsamer Ministerrat, *Protokolle des Gemeinsamen Ministerrates*, 156–7. 27. Albertini, *The Origins of the War*, vol. II, 669–70. 28. Geiss,
July 1914, 323. 29. Mombauer, *Helmuth von Moltke*, 199–200; Hewitson, *Germany and the Causes*, 197; Turner, 'Role of General Staffs', 314–15. 30. Cecil, *Wilhelm II*, 204.
31. BD, vol. XI, 293, pp. 185–6. 32. BD, vol. XI, 303, p. 193; Robbins, *Sir Edward Grey*, 293–4. 33. Wilson, *The Policy of the Entente*, 140–3; Hazlehurst, *Politicians at War*, 84–7.
34. Williamson, *Politics of Grand Strategy*, 349. 35. BD, vol. XI, 369, pp. 228–9. 36. *The Times*, 29, 30 and 31 July 1914. 37. Bucholz, *Moltke, Schlieffen*, 280–81. 38. Bach,
Deutsche Gesandtschaftsberichte, 107. 39. Mombauer, *Helmuth von Moltke*, 205. 40. Ibid.,
208. 41. Ibid., 206. 42. Herwig, 'Imperial Germany', 95; Fischer, *War of Illusions*,
502–4. 43. Jarausch, *The Enigmatic Chancellor*, 174; Verhey, *Spirit of 1914*, 59–60.
44. Stone, 'V. Moltke–Conrad', 216–17. 45. Albertini, *The Origins of the War*, 670–71;
Williamson, *Austria-Hungary*, 206–8. 46. Stone, 'V. Moltke–Conrad', 217.
47. Afflerbach, 'Wilhelm II as Supreme Warlord', 433n22. 48. Verhey, *Spirit of 1914*,
46–50, 62–4, 68, 71; Stargardt, *The German Idea of Militarism*, 145–9. 49. Mombauer,
Helmuth von Moltke, 216–20. 50. Groener, *Lebenserinnerungen*, 141–2, 145–6.
51. Mombauer, *Helmuth von Moltke*, 219–24. 52. Ibid., 223–4. 53. Jarausch, *The Enigmatic Chancellor*, 174–5. 54. *The Times*, 1 August 1914. 55. BD, vol. XI, 510, pp.
283–5. 56. Robbins, *Sir Edward Grey*, 295; Wilson, *The Policy of the Entente*, 136–7;
Brock and Brock, *H. H. Asquith*, 38. 57. DDF, 3rd series, 532, pp. 424–5; BD, vol. IX,
447, p. 260. 58. Nicolson, *Portrait of a Diplomatist*, 304. 59. Williamson, *Politics of Grand Strategy*, 353n34; Nicolson, *Portrait of a Diplomatist*, 304–5; Hazlehurst,
Politicians at War, 88. 60. Bodleian Libraries Oxford, Papers of Sir Eyre Alexander
Barby Wichart Crowe, MS Eng. E. 3020, 1–2. 61. Bridge, *Russia*, 76–9. 62. Voeikov, *S Tsarem I Bez Tsarya*, 110. 63. Lieven, *Nicholas II*, 203. 64. Goldberg, *Life of Jean Jaurès*,
463–4. 65. Ibid., 465–7; Joll, *The Second International*, 162–6. 66. Goldberg, *Life of Jean Jaurès*, 469–72. 67. Poincaré, *Au Service de la France*, 432–3. 68. Keiger, *Raymond Poincaré*, 174–7; Albertini, *The Origins of the War*, vol. III, 88–91. 69. Albertini, *The Origins of the War*, vol. III, 85, 89; Krumeich, *Armaments and Politics*, 227. 70. Albertini,
The Origins of the War, vol. III, 106–7; Keiger, *Raymond Poincaré*, 180–82. 71. Keiger,
Raymond Poincaré, 189. 72. Wilson, *The Policy of the Entente*, 147n82; Lichnowsky and
Delmer, *Heading for the Abyss*, 422. 73. Adam, *Bonar Law*, 170. 74. Hazlehurst,
Politicians at War, 96–7; Brock and Brock, *H. H. Asquith*, 145; Wilson, *The Policy of the Entente*, 136ff. 75. Hankey, *The Supreme Command*, 161–2; Hazlehurst, *Politicians at War*, 97–100. 76. Geiss, *July 1914*, 231. 77. Stengers, 'Belgium', 152–5. 78. Ibid., 161–3.
79. BD, vol. XI, 670, pp. 349–50; Tuchman, *The Guns of August*, 107–8; *The Times*, 4
August 1914. 80. Brock and Brock, *H. H. Asquith*, 150. 81. Grey, *Twenty-Five Years*,
vol. II, 12–13. 82. Robbins, *Sir Edward Grey*, 296. 83. Grey, *Twenty-Five Years*, vol. II,
20; Nicolson, *Portrait of a Diplomatist*, 305–6. 84. Grey, *Twenty-Five Years*, vol. II,
321–2; Wilson, *The Policy of the Entente*, 145–6; Great Britain, Parliamentary Debates,
Commons, 5th series, vol. LXV, 1914, cols 1809–34; *The Times*, 4 August 1914.
85. Hazlehurst, *Politicians at War*, 32; Grigg, *Lloyd George*, 154. 86. BD, vol. IX, 147,

pp. 240–41; Schoen, *Memoirs of an Ambassador*, 200–201, 204. 87. Krumeich, *Armaments and Politics*, 229. 88. *The Times*, 5 August 1914. 89. Joll, *The Second International*, 171–6. 90. Hollweg, *Reflections on the World War*, 158n; Jarausch, *The Enigmatic Chancellor*, 176–7; BD, vol. XI, 671, pp. 350–54. 91. Jarausch, *The Enigmatic Chancellor*, 181. 92. Cecil, *Wilhelm II*, 208–9. 93. Williamson, *Politics of Grand Strategy*, 361. 94. Gregory, *Walter Hines Page*, 51–2. 95. Ibid., 151. 96. Joll, *1914*, 15. 97. Lubbock, *Letters of Henry James*, 389.

Epilogue: War

1. Morison, *Letters of Theodore Roosevelt*, 790. 2. Bosworth, *Italy and the Approach*, 78. 3. Brock and Brock, *H. H. Asquith*, 130n2. 4. Bond, *The Victorian Army and the Staff College*, 294–5, 303. 5. Strachan, *The First World War*, vol. I, 239–42. 6. Ibid., 278–9. 7. Kessler, *Journey to the Abyss*, 857–8. 8. Smith, *One Morning in Sarajevo*, 264–8. 9. Fuller, *The Foe Within*, ch. 8, passim. 10. Craig, *Germany, 1866–1945*, 368. 11. Cecil, *Wilhelm II*, 210–12. 12. Ibid., 296. 13. Joll, *1914*, 6. 14. For a good description of Wilhelm's last years, see Cecil, *Wilhelm II*, chs 14–16.

List of Illustrations

13. 'At the Moroccan Conference', cartoon by J. H. W. Dietz in *Der Wahre Jacob*, 6 February, 1906. Photo: akg-images, p. 355
14. Bulgaria and Austria whip parts of the Ottoman Empire from beneath the feet of Abdul Hamid II of Turkey, *Le Petit Journal*, 18 October, 1908. Photo: Mary Evans, p. 379
15. An Italian soldier grabs the green standard of the Prophet during the annexation of Tripoli, *Le Petit Journal*, 12 November, 1911. Photo: akg-images, p. 413
16. 'Fire in the Balkans', cartoon by Thomas Theodor Heine, from *Simplicissimus*, 28 October, 1912. Photo: akg-images. © DACS, 2013, p. 438
17. 'The more the nations try to outdo their neighbours in the arms race, the more their own people suffer', cartoon by Rata Langa, *Der Wahre Jacob*, 1909. Photo: Mary Evans, p. 470
18. 'The Power Behind', cartoon by L. Raven Hill, *Punch*, 29 July, 1914. Photo: Mary Evans, p. 512
19. Austria-Hungary declares war on Serbia, front page of the *Daily Mirror*, 29 July, 1914. Photo: John Frost Newspapers/Mary Evans, p. 542
20. 'Bravo, Belgium!', cartoon by F. H. Townsend, *Punch*, 12 August, 1914. Photo: Mary Evans, p. 564

Black and white illustrations

1. View of the Alexandre III bridge and of the Grand and Petit Palais (respectively left and right on the image) during the Paris Exposition, 1900. Photo: Brown University Library, Providence, RI
2. Royal group at the Palais Edinburgh, Coburg, 1894. Private Collection. Photo: Bernard Platman Antiquarian Collection/The Bridgeman Art Library
3. Kaiser Wilhelm II with Edward VII. Photo: Mary Evans/SZ Photo
4. Otto von Bismarck, 1890. Photo: akg-images
5. Franz Joseph I. Photo: *Illustrated London News Ltd*/Mary Evans
6. Robert Gascoyne-Cecil, 3rd Marquess of Salisbury, *c*.1900. Photo: IAM/akg-images
7. Jean de Bloch. Photo: New York Public Library/The Bridgeman Art Library
8. Admiral Alfred von Tirpitz, *c*.1910. Photo: akg-images
9. Vice-Admiral Sir John Arbuthnot Fisher, *c*.1896. Photo: Robert Hunt Library/Mary Evans
10. Théophile Delcassé. Photo: Roger-Viollet/Topfoto
11. Tsar Nicholas II and his family. Photo: Library of Congress Prints and Photographs Division Washington, D.C.
12. Bloody Sunday on Nevsky Prospekt, St Petersburg, 9 January 1905. Photo: ullstein bild/Topfoto
13. Jean Jaurès, making a speech, 1914. Photo: akg-images
14. Bertha von Suttner, 1908. Photo: Imagno/akg-images
15. Greek boy scouts training in first aid, 1912. Photo: Roger Viollet/Topfoto
16. The Feast of Joan of Arc, Orléans, May 1909. Photo: Roger-Viollet/Topfoto
17. President Raymond Poincaré and General Joseph Joffre, observe French army manoeuvres, Toulouse, 1913. Photo: Roger Viollet/Topfoto
18. Helmuth von Moltke, 1908. Photo: Roger Viollet/Topfoto

Bibliography

Adam, R. J. Q., *Bonar Law* (London, 1999)

Adamthwaite, A., *Grandeur and Misery: France's Bid for Power in Europe 1914–1940* (New York, 1995)

Addison, M. and O'Grady, J., *Diary of a European Tour, 1900* (Montreal, 1999)

Aehrenthal, A. L. v., *Aus dem Nachlass Aehrenthal. Briefe und Dokumente zur Österreichisch-Ungarischen Innen- und Aussenpolitik 1885–1912* (Graz, 1994)

Afflerbach, H., *Der Dreibund. Europäische Großmacht- und Allianzpolitik vor dem Ersten Weltkrieg* (Vienna, 2002)

———, *Falkenhayn. Politisches Denken und Handeln im Kaiserreich* (Munich, 1994)

———, 'The Topos of Improbable War in Europe before 1914', in H. Afflerbach and D. Stevenson (eds.), *An Improbable War? The Outbreak of World War I and European Political Culture before 1914* (New York, 2007), 161–82

———, 'Wilhelm II as Supreme Warlord in the First World War', *War in History*, vol. 5, no. 4 (1998), 427–9

Airapetov, O. R. (ed.), *Generalui, Liberalui i Predprinimateli: Rabota Na Front i Na Revolyutsiyu 1907–1917* (Moscow, 2003)

———, *Poslednyaya Voina Imperatorskoi Rossii: Sbornik Statei* (Moscow, 2002)

———, 'K voprosu o prichinah porazheniya russkoi armii v vostochno-prusskoi operatsii', zapadrus.su/rusmir/istf/327-2011-04-26-13-04-00.html

Albertini, L., *The Origins of the War of 1914* (London, 1957)

Allain, J., *Joseph Caillaux: Le Défi victorieux, 1863–1914* (Paris, 1978)

Anderson, M. S., *The Rise of Modern Diplomacy, 1450–1919* (London, 1993)

Andrew, C., 'France and the German Menace', in E. R. May (ed.), *Knowing One's Enemies: Intelligence Assessments before the Two World Wars* (Princeton, 1986), 127–49

———, *Théophile Delcassé and the Making of the Entente Cordiale: A Reappraisal of French Foreign Policy 1898–1905* (London, 1968)

Angell, N., *The Great Illusion* (Toronto, 1911)

Angelow, J., *Der Weg in die Katastrophe: Der Zerfall des alten Europa, 1900–1914* (Berlin, 2010)

————, 'Der Zweibund zwischen Politischer auf- und militärischer Abwertung', *Mitteilungen des Österreichischen Staatsarchivs*, vol. 44 (1996), 25–74

Armour, I. D., 'Colonel Redl: Fact and Fantasy', *Intelligence and National Security*, vol. 2, no. 1 (1987), 170–83

Austro-Hungarian Gemeinsamer Ministerrat, *Protokolle des Gemeinsamen Ministerrates der Österreichisch-Ungarischen Monarchie (1914–1918)* (Budapest, 1966)

Bach, A. (ed.), *Deutsche Gesandtschaftsberichte zum Kriegsausbruch 1914. Berichte und Telegramme der Badischen, Sächsischen und Württembergischen Gesandtschaften in Berlin aus dem Juli und August 1914* (Berlin, 1937)

Baernreither, J. M. and Redlich, J., *Fragments of a Political Diary* (London, 1930)

Balfour, M. L. G., *The Kaiser and His Times* (New York, 1972)

Bánffy, M., *They Were Divided: The Writing on the Wall* (Kindle version, 2010)

Barclay, T., *Thirty Years: Anglo-French Reminiscences, 1876–1906* (London, 1914)

Bark, P. L., 'Tul'skie Dni 1914 Goda: Nachalo Velikoy Voinui. Iz Vospominany P. L. Barka, Poslednego Ministra Finansov Rossiiskogo Imperatorskogo Pravitel'Stva', *Vozrozhdenie*, no. 91 (1959), 17–45

Barraclough, G., *From Agadir to Armageddon: Anatomy of a Crisis* (London, 1982)

Becker, J. J., *1914, Comment les Français sont entrés dans la Guerre: Contribution à l'étude de l'opinion publique printemps-été 1914* (Paris, 1977)

Beesly, E. S., *Queen Elizabeth* (London, 1906)

Berghahn, V., *Germany and the Approach of War in 1914* (London, 1973)

————, 'War Preparations and National Identity in Imperial Germany', in M. F. Boemeke, R. Chickering, and S. Förster (eds.), *Anticipating Total War: The German and American Experiences, 1871–1914* (Cambridge, 1999), 307–26

Bernhardi, F. v., *Germany and the Next War* (London, 1914)

Bestuzhev, I. V., 'Russian Foreign Policy February–June 1914', *Journal of Contemporary History*, vol. 1, no. 3 (1966), 93–112

Bethmann Hollweg, T. v., *Reflections on the World War* (London, 1920)

Beyens, H., *Germany before the War* (London, 1916)

Bittner, L. and Ubersberger, H. (eds.), *Österreich-Ungarns Aussenpolitik von der Bosnischen Krise 1908 bis zum Kriegsausbruch 1914. Diplomatische Aktenstücke des Österreichisch-Ungarischen Ministeriums des Äussern* (Vienna, 1930)

Bloch, I. S., *The Future of War in its Technical Economic and Political Relations: Is War Now Impossible?* (Toronto, 1900)

————, 'The Wars of the Future', *Contemporary Review*, vol. 80 (1901), 305–32

Blom, P., *The Vertigo Years: Change and Culture in the West, 1900–1914* (London, 2008)

Bodger, A., 'Russia and the End of the Ottoman Empire', in M. Kent (ed.), *The Great Powers and the End of the Ottoman Empire* (London, 1996), 76–110

Boemeke, M. F., Chickering, R., and Förster, S. (eds.), *Anticipating Total War: The German and American Experiences, 1871–1914* (Cambridge, 1999)

Boghitschewitsch, M. (ed.), *Die auswärtige Politik Serbiens 1903–1914* (Berlin, 1931)

Bond, B., *The Victorian Army and the Staff College 1854–1914* (London, 1972)

Bosworth, R., 'Britain and Italy's Acquisition of the Dodecanese, 1912–1915', *Historical Journal*, vol. 13, no. 4 (1970), 683–705

————, *Italy and the Approach of the First World War* (London, 1983)

Bourdon, G., *The German Enigma* (Paris, 1914)

Boyer, J. W., 'The End of an Old Regime: Visions of Political Reform in Late Imperial Austria', *Journal of Modern History*, vol. 58, no. 1 (1986), 159–93

Bridge, F. R., 'Austria-Hungary and the Boer War', in K. M. Wilson (ed.), *The International Impact of the Boer War* (Chesham, 2001), 79–96

———, 'The British Declaration of War on Austria-Hungary in 1914', *Slavonic and East European Review*, vol. 47, no. 109 (1969), 401–22

———, 'The Entente Cordiale, 1904–14: An Austro-Hungarian Perspective', *Mitteilungen des Österreichischen Staatsarchivs*, vol. 53 (2009), 335–51

———, *The Habsburg Monarchy among the Great Powers, 1815–1918* (New York, 1990)

———, 'Isvolsky, Aehrenthal, and the End of the Austro-Russian Entente, 1906–8', *Mitteilungen des Österreichischen Staatsarchivs*, vol. 20 (1976), 315–62

———, *From Sadowa to Sarajevo: The Foreign Policy of Austria-Hungary, 1866–1914* (London, 1972)

———, 'Tarde Venientibus Ossa: Austro-Hungarian Colonial Aspirations in Asia Minor 1913–14', *Middle Eastern Studies*, vol. 6, no. 3 (1970), 319–30

Bridge, W. C., *How the War Began in 1914* (London, 1925)

Brinker-Gabler, G. (ed.), *Kämpferin für den Frieden: Bertha von Suttner. Lebenserinnerungen, Reden und Schriften: Eine Auswahl* (Frankfurt am Main, 1982)

Brock, Michael and Brock, Eleanor (eds.), *H. H. Asquith: Letters to Venetia Stanley* (Oxford, 1982)

Brusilov, A. A., *A Soldier's Notebook 1914–1918* (London, 1930)

Bülow, B., *Memoirs of Prince von Bulow* (Boston, 1931)

Burkhardt, J., 'Kriegsgrund Geschichte? 1870, 1813, 1756 – historische Argumente und Orientierungen bei Ausbruch des Ersten Weltkriegs', in J. Burkhardt, J. Becker, S. Förster, and G. Kronenbitter (eds.), *Lange und kurze Wege in den Ersten Weltkrieg: Vier Augsburger Beitraeger zur Kriesursachenforschung* (Munich, 1996), 9–86

Burkhardt, J., Becker, J., Förster, S., and Kronenbitter, G. (eds.), *Lange und kurze Wege in den Ersten Weltkrieg: Vier Augsburger Beitraeger zur Kriesursachenforschung* (Munich, 1996)

Burrows, M., *The History of the Foreign Policy of Great Britain* (London, 1895)

Bushnell, J., 'The Tsarist Officer Corps, 1881–1914: Customs, Duties, Inefficiency', *American Historical Review*, vol. 86, no. 4 (1981), 753–80

Butterworth, A., *The World that Never Was: A True Story of Dreamers, Schemers, Anarchists and Secret Agents* (London, 2010)

Cairns, J. C., 'International Politics and the Military Mind: The Case of the French Republic, 1911–1914', *Journal of Modern History*, vol. 25, no. 3 (1953), 273–85

Callwell, C. E., *Field-Marshal Sir Henry Wilson: His Life and Diaries* (London, 1927)

Cambon, P., *Correspondance, 1870–1924*, vol. III: *1912–1924* (Paris, 1940–46)

Cannadine, D., *The Decline and Fall of the British Aristocracy* (New Haven, CT, 1990)

Cannadine, D., Keating, J., and Sheldon, N., *The Right Kind of History: Teaching the Past in Twentieth-Century England* (New York, 2012)

Carter, M., *The Three Emperors: Three Cousins, Three Empires and the Road to World War One* (London, 2009)

Ceadel, M., *Living the Great Illusion: Sir Norman Angell, 1872–1967* (Oxford, 2009)

————, *Semi-Detached Idealists: The British Peace Movement and International Relations, 1854–1945* (Oxford, 2000)

Cecil, G., *Life of Robert Marquis of Salisbury*, 4 vols (London, 1921–32)

Cecil, L., *Albert Ballin: Business and Politics in Imperial Germany, 1888–1918* (Princeton, 1967)

————, *The German Diplomatic Service, 1871–1914* (Princeton, 1976)

————, *Wilhelm II*, vol. II: *Emperor and Exile, 1900–1941* (Chapel Hill, 1989)

Chandler, R., 'Searching for a Saviour', *Spectator*, 31 March 2012

Charykov, N. V., *Glimpses of High Politics: Through War & Peace, 1855–1929* (London, 1931)

Chickering, R., *Imperial Germany and a World without War: The Peace Movement and German Society, 1892–1914* (Princeton, 1975)

————, 'Problems of a German Peace Movement, 1890–1914', in S. Wank (ed.), *Doves and Diplomats: Foreign Offices and Peace Movements in Europe and America in the Twentieth Century* (London, 1978), 42–54

————, 'War, Peace, and Social Mobilization in Imperial Germany', in C. Chatfield and P. Van den Dungen (eds.), *Peace Movements and Political Cultures* (Knoxville, 1988), 3–22

Churchill, W. S., *The World Crisis, 1911–1918*, vol. I: *1911–1914* (London, 1923)

Cimbala, S. J., 'Steering through Rapids: Russian Mobilization and World War I', *Journal of Slavic Military Studies*, vol. 9, no. 2 (1996), 376–98

Clark, C., *Iron Kingdom: The Rise and Downfall of Prussia, 1600–1947* (London, 2007)

————, *Kaiser Wilhelm II* (Harlow, 2000)

————, *The Sleepwalkers: How Europe Went to War in 1914* (London, 2012)

Clifford, C., *The Asquiths* (London, 2002)

Cooper, M. B., 'British Policy in the Balkans, 1908–1909', *Historical Journal*, vol. 7, no. 2 (1964), 258–79

Cooper, S. E., 'Pacifism in France, 1889–1914: International Peace as a Human Right', *French Historical Studies*, vol. 17, no. 2 (1991), 359–86

————, *Patriotic Pacifism: Waging War on War in Europe, 1815–1914* (Oxford, 1991)

Cornwall, M., 'Serbia', in K. M. Wilson (ed.), *Decisions for War, 1914* (London, 1995)

Craig, G. A., *Germany, 1866–1945* (Oxford, 1978)

————, *The Politics of the Prussian Army, 1640–1945* (Oxford, 1964)

Crampton, R. J., 'August Bebel and the British Foreign Office', *History*, vol. 58, no. 193 (1973), 218–32

————, 'The Balkans as a Factor in German Foreign Policy, 1912–1914', *Slavonic and East European Review*, vol. 55, no. 3 (1977), 370–90

————, 'The Decline of the Concert of Europe in the Balkans, 1913–1914', *Slavonic and East European Review*, vol. 52, no. 128 (1974), 393–419

————, *The Hollow Detente: Anglo-German Relations in the Balkans, 1911–1914* (London, 1979)

Cronin, V., *Paris on the Eve, 1900–1914* (London, 1989)

Csáky, I., *Vom Geachteten zum Geächteten: Erinnerungen des k. und k. Diplomaten und k. Ungarischen Aussenministers Emerich Csaky (1882–1961)* (Weimar, 1994)

Czernin, C. O., *In the World War* (London, 1919)

Dangerfield, G., *The Strange Death of Liberal England, 1910–1914* (New York, 1961)

De Burgh, E., *Elizabeth, Empress of Austria: A Memoir* (London, 1899)

Deák, I., *Beyond Nationalism: A Social and Political History of the Habsburg Officer Corps, 1848–1918* (Oxford, 1992)

Dedijer, V., *The Road to Sarajevo* (London, 1967)

Diószegi, I., *Hungarians in the Ballhausplatz: Studies on the Austro-Hungarian Common Foreign Policy* (Budapest, 1983)

Dockrill, M. L., 'British Policy during the Agadir Crisis of 1911', in F. H. Hinsley (ed.), *British Foreign Policy under Sir Edward Grey* (Cambridge, 1977), 271–87

Doughty, R., 'France', in R. F. Hamilton and H. H. Herwig (eds.), *War Planning, 1914* (Cambridge, 2010), 143–74

———, 'French Strategy in 1914: Joffre's Own', *Journal of Military History*, vol. 67 (2003), 427–54

———, *Pyrrhic Victory: French Strategy and Operations in the Great War* (London, 2005)

Dowler, W., *Russia in 1913* (DeKalb, 2010)

Dülffer, J., 'Chances and Limits of Arms Control 1898–1914', in H. Afflerbach and D. Stevenson (eds.), *An Improbable War: The Outbreak of World War I and European Political Culture before 1914* (Oxford, 2007), 95–112

———, 'Citizens and Diplomats: The Debate on the First Hague Conference (1899) in Germany', in C. Chatfield and P. Van den Dungen (eds.), *Peace Movements and Political Cultures* (Knoxville, 1988), 23–39

———, 'Efforts to Reform the International System and Peace Movements before 1914', *Peace & Change*, vol. 14, no. 1 (1989), 24–45

———, 'Kriegserwartung und Kriegsbild in Deutschland vor 1914', in W. Michalka (ed.), *Der Erste Weltkrieg: Wirkung, Wahrnehmung, Analyse* (Munich, 1994), 778–98

Dumas, F. G. (ed.), *The Franco-British Exhibition: Illustrated Review, 1908* (London, 1908)

Dungen, P. v. d., 'Preventing Catastrophe: The World's First Peace Museum', *Ritsumeikan Journal of International Studies*, vol. 18, no. 3 (2006), 449–62

Eby, C., *The Road to Armageddon: The Martial Spirit in English Popular Literature, 1870–1914* (Durham, NC, 1987)

Echevarria, A. J., 'Heroic History and Vicarious War: Nineteenth-Century German Military History Writing', *The Historian*, vol. 59, no. 3 (1997), 573–90

———, 'On the Brink of the Abyss: The Warrior Identity and German Military Thought before the Great War', *War & Society*, vol. 13, no. 2 (1995), 23–40

Eckardstein, H. F. v. and Young, G., *Ten Years at the Court of St. James', 1895–1905* (London, 1921)

Einem, K. v., *Erinnerungen eines Soldaten*, 4th edn (Leipzig, 1933)

Ekstein, M. and Steiner, Z., 'The Sarajevo Crisis', in F. H. Hinsley (ed.), *British Foreign Policy under Sir Edward Grey* (Cambridge, 1977), 397–410

Epkenhans, M., *Tirpitz: Architect of the German High Seas Fleet* (Washington, DC, 2008)

———, 'Wilhelm II and "His" Navy, 1888–1918', in A. Mombauer and W. Deist (eds.), *The Kaiser: New Research on Wilhelm II's Role in Imperial Germany* (Cambridge, 2003), 12–36

Esher, R., *Journals and Letters of Reginald, Viscount Esher* (London, 1934–8)

Eubank, K., *Paul Cambon: Master Diplomatist* (Norman, OK, 1960)

—— , 'The Fashoda Crisis Re-Examined', *The Historian*, vol. 22, no. 2 (1960), 145–62

Evera, S. V., 'The Cult of the Offensive and the Origins of the First World War', in
S. E. Miller, S. M. Lynn-Jones, and S. Van Evera (eds.), *Military Strategy and the
Origins of the First World War* (Princeton, 1991), 59–108

Exposition Universelle Internationale de 1900, *1900 Paris Exposition: Guide pratique de
visiteur de Paris et de l'Exposition* ... (Paris, 1900)

Feldman, G. D., 'Hugo Stinnes and the Prospect of War before 1914', in M. F.
Boemeke, R. Chickering, and S. Förster (eds.), *Anticipating Total War: The
German and American Experiences, 1871–1914* (Cambridge, 1999), 77–95

Fellner, F., 'Die "Mission Hoyos"', in H. Maschl and B. Mazohl-Wallnig (eds.), *Vom
Dreibund zum Völkerbund. Studien zur Geschichte der internationalen Beziehungen,
1882–1919* (Vienna, 1994), 112–41

Ferguson, N., *The Pity of War* (New York, 1999)

Fesser, G., *Reichskanzler Fürst von Bülow. Architekt der Deutschen Weltpolitik* (Leipzig,
2003)

—— , *Der Traum vom Platz an der Sonne. Deutsche 'Weltpolitik' 1897–1914* (Bremen,
1996)

Figes, O., *A People's Tragedy: The Russian Revolution, 1891–1924* (London, 1996)

Fischer, F., 'The Foreign Policy of Imperial Germany and the Outbreak of the First
World War', in G. Schöllgen (ed.), *Escape into War? The Foreign Policy of Imperial
Germany* (New York, 1990), 19–40

—— , *Germany's Aims in the First World War* (London, 1967)

—— , *War of Illusions: German Policies from 1911 to 1914* (New York, 1975)

Fisher, J. A. F. and Marder, A. J., *Fear God and Dread Nought: The Correspondence of
Admiral of the Fleet Lord Fisher of Kilverstone* (London, 1952)

Foley, R. T., 'Debate – the Real Schlieffen Plan', *War in History*, vol. 13, no. 1 (2006),
91–115

—— , *German Strategy and the Path to Verdun: Erich von Falkenhayn and the
Development of Attrition, 1870–1916* (Cambridge, 2005)

Förster, S., 'Der Deutschen Generalstab und die Illusion des kurzen Krieges, 1871–
1914', *Militärgeschichtliche Mitteilungen*, vol. 54 (1995), 61–95

—— , *Der doppette Militarismus. Die deutsche Heeresrüstungpolitik zwischen Status-
quo-Sicherung und Aggression. 1890–1913* (Stuttgart, 1985)

—— , 'Dreams and Nightmares: German Military Leadership and Images of
Future Warfare, 1871–1914', in M. F. Boemeke, R. Chickering, and S. Förster
(eds.), *Anticipating Total War: The German and American Experiences, 1871–1914*
(Cambridge, 1999), 343–76

—— , 'Facing "People's War": Moltke the Elder and Germany's Military Options
after 1871', *Journal of Strategic Studies*, vol. 10, no. 2 (1987), 209–30

—— , 'Im Reich des Absurden. Die Ursachen des Ersten Weltkriegs', in B. Wegner
(ed.), *Wie Kriege entstehen. Zum historischen Hintergrund von Staatskonflikten*
(Munich, 2000), 211–52

France. Ministère des Affaires Étrangères, *Documents diplomatiques français, 1871–1914*,
3rd series

French, D., 'The Edwardian Crisis and the Origins of the First World War',
International History Review, vol. 4, no. 2 (1982), 207–21

Freud, S., *Civilization and its Discontents* (New York, 1962)

Fuller, W. C., *The Foe Within: Fantasies of Treason and the End of Imperial Russia* (Ithaca, 2006)

———, 'The Russian Empire', in E. R. May (ed.), *Knowing One's Enemies: Intelligence Assessment before the Two World Wars* (Princeton, 1986), 98–126

———, *Strategy and Power in Russia, 1600–1914* (New York, 1992)

Funder, F., *Vom Gestern ins Heute. Aus dem Kaiserreich in die Republik* (Vienna, 1953)

Gardiner, A. G., *Pillars of Society* (London, 1916)

Geinitz, C., *Kriegsfurcht und Kampfbereitschaft. Das Augusterlebnis in Freiburg. Eine Studie zum Kriegsbeginn 1914* (Essen, 1998)

Geiss, I., 'Deutschland und Österreich-Ungarn beim Kriegsausbruch 1914. Eine machthistorische Analyse', in M. Gehler (ed.), *Ungleiche Partner? Österreich und Deutschland in ihrer gegenseitigen Wahrnehmung. Historische Analysen und Vergleiche aus dem 19. und 20. Jahrhundert* (Stuttgart, 1996), 375–95

Geiss, I. (ed.), *July 1914: The Outbreak of the First World War: Selected Documents* (London, 1967)

Geppert, D., 'The Public Challenge to Diplomacy: German and British Ways of Dealing with the Press, 1890–1914', in M. Mösslang and T. Riotte (eds.), *The Diplomats' World: A Cultural History of Diplomacy, 1815–1914* (Oxford, 2008), 133–64

German Foreign Office, *Die grosse Politik der Europäischen Kabinette 1871–1914. Sammlung der diplomatischen Akten des auswärtigen Amtes*, vol. XXXIX: *Das Nahen des Weltkrieges, 1912–1914* (Berlin, 1926)

Geyer, D., *Russian Imperialism: The Interaction of Domestic and Foreign Policy, 1860–1914* (Leamington Spa, 1987)

Gieslingen, W. G. v., *Zwei Jahrzehnte im Nahen Orient: Aufzeichnungen des Generals der Kavallerie Baron Wladimir Giesl* (Berlin, 1927)

Gildea, R., *Barricades and Borders: Europe, 1800–1914* (Oxford, 1996)

Gilmour, D., *Curzon* (London, 1994)

Goldberg, H., *The Life of Jean Jaurès* (Madison, 1968)

Gooch, G. P. and Temperley, H. W. (eds.), *British Documents on the Origins of the War, 1898–1914*, vols. I–XI (London, 1926–38)

Gooch, J., 'Attitudes to War in Late Victorian and Edwardian England', in B. Bond and I. Roy (eds.), *War and Society: A Yearbook of Military History* (New York, 1975), 88–102

———, 'Italy before 1915', in E. R. May (ed.), *Knowing One's Enemies: Intelligence Assessments before the Two World Wars* (Princeton, 1986), 205–33

Gordon, D. C., 'The Admiralty and Dominion Navies, 1902–1914', *Journal of Modern History*, vol. 33, no. 4 (1961), 407–22

Gregory, R., *Walter Hines Page: Ambassador to the Court of St. James's* (Lexington, 1970)

Grey, E., *Twenty-Five Years, 1892–1916* (London, 1925)

Grigg, J., *Lloyd George: The People's Champion, 1902–1911* (Berkeley, 1978)

———, *Lloyd George: From Peace to War, 1912–1916* (London, 1985)

Groener, W., *Lebenserinnerungen. Jugend, Generalstab, Weltkrieg* (Göttingen, 1957)

Groh, D., 'The "Unpatriotic Socialists" and the State', *Journal of Contemporary History*, vol. 1, no. 4 (1966), 151–77

Haldane, R. B. H., *An Autobiography* (London, 1929)

———, *Before the War* (London, 1920)

Hamilton, G. F., *Parliamentary Reminiscences and Reflections, 1886–1906* (London, 1922)

Hamilton, R. F., 'War Planning: Obvious Needs, Not so Obvious Solutions', in R. F. Hamilton and H. H. Herwig (eds.), *War Planning: 1914* (Cambridge, 2009)

Hamilton, R. F. and Herwig, H., *Decisions for War, 1914–1917* (Cambridge, 2005)

———, *The Origins of World War I* (Cambridge, 2003)

———, *War Planning 1914* (Cambridge, 2010)

Hankey, M. P. A. H., *The Supreme Command, 1914–1918* (London, 1961)

Hantsch, H., *Leopold Graf Berchtold: Grandseigneur und Staatsmann* (Graz, 1963)

Harris, R., *The Man on Devil's Island: Alfred Dreyfus and the Affair that Divided France* (London, 2010)

Haupt, G., *Socialism and the Great War: The Collapse of the Second International* (Oxford, 1972)

Hayne, M. B., *The French Foreign Office and the Origins of the First World War, 1898–1914* (Oxford, 1993)

———, 'The Quai d'Orsay and Influences on the Formulation of French Foreign Policy, 1898–1914', *French History*, vol. 2, no. 4 (1988), 427–52

Hazlehurst, C., *Politicians at War, July 1914 to May 1915: A Prologue to the Triumph of Lloyd George* (London, 1971)

Heinrich, F., *Geschichte in Gesprächen. Aufzeichnungen, 1898–1919* (Vienna, 1997)

Helmreich, E., *The Diplomacy of the Balkan Wars, 1912–1913* (London, 1938)

Herring, G., *From Colony to Superpower: US Foreign Relations since 1776* (Oxford, 2008)

Herrmann, D. G., *The Arming of Europe and the Making of the First World War* (Princeton, 1997)

Hertling, G., Graf von, and Lerchenfeld-Köfering, H., Graf, *Briefwechsel Hertling-Lerchenfeld 1912–1917. Dienstliche Privatkorrespondenz Zwischen dem Bayerischen Ministerpräsidenten Georg Graf von Hertling und dem Bayerischen Gesandten in Berlin Hugo Graf von und zu Lerchenfeld* (Boppard am Rhein, 1973)

Herwig, H., 'Conclusions', in R. F. Hamilton and H. Herwig (eds.), *War Planning, 1914* (Cambridge, 2010), 226–56

———, 'Disjointed Allies: Coalition Warfare in Berlin and Vienna, 1914', *Journal of Military History*, vol. 54, no. 3 (1990), 265–80

———, 'The German Reaction to the Dreadnought Revolution', *International History Review*, vol. 13, no. 2 (1991), 273–83

———, 'Imperial Germany', in E. R. May (ed.), *Knowing One's Enemies: Intelligence Assessment before the Two World Wars* (Princeton, 1986), 62–97

———, *'Luxury' Fleet: The Imperial German Navy, 1888–1918* (London, 1987)

———, *The Marne, 1914: The Opening of World War I and the Battle that Changed the World* (New York, 2009)

———, 'From Tirpitz Plan to Schlieffen Plan: Some Observations on German Military Planning', *Journal of Strategic Studies*, vol. 9, no. 1 (1986), 53–63

Hewitson, M., *Germany and the Causes of the First World War* (New York, 2004)

———, 'Germany and France before the First World War: A Reassessment of Wilhelmine Foreign Policy', *English Historical Review*, vol. 115, no. 462 (2000), 570–606

————, 'Images of the Enemy: German Depictions of the French Military, 1890–1914', *War in History*, vol. 11, no. 4 (2004), 4–33

Heywood, A., '"The Most Catastrophic Question": Railway Development and Military Strategy in Late Imperial Russia', in T. G. Otte and K. Neilson (eds.), *Railways and International Politics: Paths of Empire, 1848–1945* (New York, 2006), 45–67

Hinsley, F. H. (ed.), *British Foreign Policy under Sir Edward Grey* (Cambridge, 1977)

Hobhouse, C., *Inside Asquith's Cabinet: From the Diaries of Charles Hobhouse* (London, 1977)

Hoetzendorf, Gina Agujari-Kárász Conrad von, *Mein Leben mit Conrad von Hötzendorf: Sein geistiges Vermächtnis* (Leipzig, 1935)

Hoetzsch, O. (ed.), *Die Internationalen Beziehungen im Zeitalter des Imperialismus. Dokumente aus den Archiven der Zarischen und der provisorischen Regierung*, vol. IV: *28. Juni Bis 22. Juli 1914* (Berlin, 1932)

Holstein, F. v., *The Holstein Papers*, ed. N. Rich et al. (Cambridge, 1955)

Hopman, A., *Das Ereignisreiche Leben eines 'Wilhelminers'. Tagebücher, Briefe, Aufzeichnungen 1901 bis 1920* (Munich, 2004)

House, E. M. and Seymour, C., *The Intimate Papers of Colonel House* (New York, 1926)

Howard, C., 'The Policy of Isolation', *Historical Journal*, vol. 10, no. 1 (1967), 77–88

Howard, M., 'Men against Fire: Expectations of War in 1914', in S. E. Miller, S. M. Lynn-Jones, and S. van Evera (eds.), *Military Strategy and the Origins of the First World War* (Princeton, 1991), 3–19

————, *The Franco-Prussian War: The German Invasion of France, 1870–1871* (London, 1961)

Howorth, J., 'French Workers and German Workers: The Impossibility of Internationalism, 1900–1914', *European History Quarterly*, vol. 85, no. 1 (1985), 71–97

Hughes, W. M., *Policies and Potentates* (Sydney, 1950)

Hull, I., *The Entourage of Kaiser Wilhelm II, 1888–1918* (Cambridge, 2004)

Hynes, S. L., *The Edwardian Turn of Mind* (Princeton, 1968)

Ignat'ev, A. A., *50 Let v Stroyu* (Moscow, 1986)

Ignat'ev, A. V., *Vneshniaia Politika Rossii 1907–1914: Tendentsii, Liudi, Sobytiia* (Moscow, 2000)

Izvol'skii, A. P. and Seeger, C., *The Memoirs of Alexander Iswolsky, Formerly Russian Minister of Foreign Affairs and Ambassador to France* (London, 1920)

Jarausch, K., *The Enigmatic Chancellor: Bethmann Hollweg and the Hubris of Imperial Germany* (New Haven, CT, 1973)

Jeffery, K., *Field Marshal Sir Henry Wilson: A Political Soldier* (Oxford, 2006)

Jelavich, B., *History of the Balkans*, vol. I: *Eighteenth and Nineteenth Centuries* (Cambridge, 1983)

————, *Russia's Balkan Entanglements 1806–1914* (Cambridge, 1991)

————, 'What the Habsburg Government Knew about the Black Hand', *Austrian History Yearbook*, vol. XXII (Houston, 1991), 131–50

Jelavich, C. and Jelavich, B., *The Establishment of the Balkan National States, 1804–1920* (Seattle, 1977)

Johnston, W. M., *The Austrian Mind: An Intellectual and Social History, 1848–1938* (Berkeley, 1972)

Joll, J., *1914: The Unspoken Assumptions: An Inaugural Lecture Delivered 25 April 1968 at the London School of Economics* (London, 1968)

——, *The Second International, 1889–1914* (New York, 1966)

Joll, J. and Martel, G., *The Origins of the First World War* (Harlow, 2007)

Joly, B., 'La France et la Revanche (1871–1914)', *Revue d'Histoire Moderne et Contemporaine*, vol. 46, no. 2 (2002), 325–47

Jusserand, J. J., *What Me Befell: The Reminiscences of J. J. Jusserand* (London, 1933)

Kaiser, D. E., 'Germany and the Origins of the First World War', *Journal of Modern History*, vol. 55, no. 3 (1983), 442–74

Keiger, J., *France and the Origins of the First World War* (Basingstoke, 1983)

——, 'Jules Cambon and Franco-German Detente, 1907–1914', *Historical Journal*, vol. 26, no. 3 (1983), 641–59

——, *Raymond Poincaré* (Cambridge, 1997)

Kennan, G., *Siberia and the Exile System* (New York, 1891)

Kennan, G. F., *The Other Balkan Wars: A 1913 Carnegie Endowment Inquiry in Retrospect* (Washington, DC, 1993)

Kennedy, P. M., 'German World Policy and the Alliance Negotiations with England, 1897–1900', *Journal of Modern History*, vol. 45, no. 4 (1973), 605–25

——, 'Great Britain before 1914', in E. R. May (ed.), *Knowing One's Enemies: Intelligence Assessment before the Two World Wars* (Princeton, 1986), 172–204

——, *The Rise of the Anglo-German Antagonism, 1860–1914* (London, 1982)

——, *The Rise and Fall of the Great Powers: Economic Change and Military Conflict from 1500 to 2000* (New York, 1987)

——, *The War Plans of the Great Powers, 1860–1914* (London, 1979)

Kennedy, P. M., Nicholls, A. J., *Nationalist and Racialist Movements in Britain and Germany before 1914* (London, 1981)

Kessler, H., *Journey to the Abyss: The Diaries of Count Harry Kessler, 1880–1918* (New York, 2011)

Kießling, F., *Gegen den 'Grossen Krieg'?: Entspannung in den internationalen Beziehungen 1911–1914* (Munich, 2002)

Kipling, R. and Pinney, T., *The Letters of Rudyard Kipling* (Houndmills, 1990)

Kissinger, Henry, *Diplomacy* (New York, 1994)

——, 'The White Revolutionary: Reflections on Bismarck', *Daedalus*, vol. 97, no. 3 (1968), 888–924

——, *A World Restored: Metternich, Castlereagh and the Problems of Peace, 1812–1822* (Boston, 1957)

Kleinmikhel', M., *Memories of a Shipwrecked World: Being the Memoirs of Countess Kleinmichel* (London, 1923)

Kokovtsov, V. N., *Out of My Past: The Memoirs of Count Kokovtsov, Russian Minister of Finance, 1904–1914, Chairman of the Council of Ministers, 1911–1914*, ed. H. H. Fisher (London, 1935)

Kramer, A., *Dynamic of Destruction: Culture and Mass Killing in the First World War* (Oxford, 2008)

Kröger, M., 'Imperial Germany and the Boer War', in K. M. Wilson (ed.), *The International Impact of the Boer War* (London, 2001), 25–42

Kronenbitter, G., 'Die Macht der Illusionen. Julikrise und Kriegsausbruch 1914 aus
    der Sicht des Militärattachés in Wien', *Militärgeschichtliche Mitteilungen*, vol. 57
    (1998), 519–50
———, '"Nur los lassen". Österreich-Ungarn und der Wille zum Krieg', in J.
    Burkhardt, J. Becker, S. Förster, and G. Kronenbitter (eds.), *Lange und kurze
    Wege in den Ersten Weltkrieg. Vier Augsburger Beitraeger zur Kriesursachenforschung*
    (Munich, 1996), 159–87
Krumeich, G., *Armaments and Politics in France on the Eve of the First World War: The
    Introduction of Three-Year Conscription, 1913–1914* (Leamington Spa, 1984)
LaFeber, W., *The Cambridge History of American Foreign Relations*, vol. II: *The
    American Search for Opportunity, 1865–1913* (Cambridge, 1993)
Laity, P., *The British Peace Movement, 1870–1914* (Oxford, 2001)
Lambi, I. N., *The Navy and German Power Politics, 1862–1914* (Boston, 1984)
Langsam, W. C., 'Nationalism and History in the Prussian Elementary Schools under
    William II', in E. M. Earle and C. J. H. Hayes (eds.), *Nationalism and
    Internationalism: Essays Inscribed to Carlton J. H. Hayes* (New York, 1950)
Laurence, R., 'Bertha von Suttner and the Peace Movement in Austria to World War
    I', *Austrian History Yearbook*, vol. 23 (1992), 181–201
———, 'The Peace Movement in Austria, 1867–1914', in S. Wank (ed.), *Doves and
    Diplomats: Foreign Offices and Peace Movements in Europe and America in the
    Twentieth Century* (Westport, 1978), 21–41
Lee, D. E., *Europe's Crucial Years: The Diplomatic Background of World War One, 1902–
    1914* (Hanover, 1974)
Lee, S., *King Edward VII: A Biography* (London, 1925)
Lerchenfeld-Koefering, Hugo Graf von und zu, *Kaiser Wilhelm II. Als Persönlichkeit
    und Herrscher* (Regensburg, 1985)
Lerman, K., *The Chancellor as Courtier: Bernhard von Bülow and the Governance of
    Germany, 1900–1909* (Cambridge, 1990)
Leslie, J., 'The Antecedents of Austria-Hungary's War Aims: Policies and Policy-
    Makers in Vienna and Budapest before and during 1914', *Wiener Beiträge zur
    Geschichte der Neuzeit*, vol. 20 (1993), 307–94
———, 'Österreich-Ungarn vor dem Kriegsausbruch', in R. Melville (ed.),
    *Deutschland und Europa in der Neuzeit: Festschrift für Karl Otmar Freiherr von
    Aretin zum 65. Geburtstag* (Stuttgart, 1988), 661–84
Levine, I. D. and Grant, N. F., *The Kaiser's Letters to the Tsar, Copied from the
    Government Archives in Petrograd, and Brought from Russia by Isaac Don Levine*
    (London, 1920)
Lichnowsky, K. and Delmer, F. S., *Heading for the Abyss: Reminiscences* (London, 1928)
Lieven, D. C. B., *Nicholas II: Twilight of the Empire* (New York, 1993)
———, 'Pro-Germans and Russian Foreign Policy 1890–1914', *International History
    Review*, vol. 2, no. 1 (1980), 34–54
———, *Russia and the Origins of the First World War* (Basingstoke, 1987)
Lincoln, W. B., *In War's Dark Shadow: The Russians before the Great War* (Oxford, 1994)
Linton, D. S., 'Preparing German Youth for War', in M. F. Boemeke, R. Chickering,
    and S. Förster (eds.), *Anticipating Total War: The German and American
    Experiences, 1871–1914* (Cambridge, 1999), 167–88
Lloyd George, D., *War Memoirs of David Lloyd George* (London, 1933)

Lubbock, P. and James, H., *The Letters of Henry James* (London, 1920)

Lukacs, J., *Budapest 1900: A Historical Portrait of a City and its Culture* (New York, 1990)

Macartney, C. A., *The Habsburg Empire, 1790–1918* (London, 1968)

MacKenzie, N. and MacKenzie, J. (eds.), *The Diary of Beatrice Webb*, vol. III: *1905–1924* (Cambridge, MA, 1984)

Mahan, A. T., *The Influence of Sea Power upon History, 1660–1805* (Boston, 1890)

Mansergh, N., *The Commonwealth Experience: From British to Multiracial Commonwealth* (Toronto, 1983)

Marder, A., *From the Dreadnought to Scapa Flow: The Royal Navy in the Fisher Era, 1904–1919* (Oxford, 1961)

Margutti, A., *The Emperor Francis Joseph and His Times* (London, 1921)

Martel, G., *The Origins of the First World War*, 3rd edn (Harlow, 2003)

Massie, R. K., *Dreadnought: Britain, Germany, and the Coming of the Great War* (New York, 1992)

Maurer, J., 'Churchill's Naval Holiday: Arms Control and the Anglo-German Naval Race, 1912–1914', *Journal of Strategic Studies*, vol. 15, no. 1 (1992), 102–27

———, *The Outbreak of the First World War: Strategic Planning, Crisis Decision Making and Deterrence Failure* (Westport, 1995)

May, E. R. (ed.), *Knowing One's Enemies: Intelligence Assessment before the Two World Wars* (Princeton, 1986)

Mayne, R., Johnson, D., and R. Tombs (eds.), *Cross Channel Currents: 100 Years of the Entente Cordiale* (London, 2004)

McDonald, D. M., *United Government and Foreign Policy in Russia, 1900–1914* (Cambridge, 1992)

McLean, R. R., *Royalty and Diplomacy in Europe, 1890–1914* (Cambridge, 2001)

McMeekin, S., *The Berlin–Baghdad Express: The Ottoman Empire and Germany's Bid for World Power, 1898–1918* (London, 2010)

———, *The Russian Origins of the First World War* (Cambridge, Mass., 2011)

Menning, B., 'The Offensive Revisited: Russian Preparation for Future War, 1906–1914', in David Schimmelpenninck van der Oye, and B. Menning (eds.), *Reforming the Tsar's Army: Military Innovation in Imperial Russia from Peter the Great to the Revolution* (Cambridge, 2004), 215–31

———, 'Pieces of the Puzzle: The Role of Lu. N. Danilov and M. V. Alekseev in Russian War Planning before 1914', *International History Review*, vol. 25, no. 4 (2003), 775–98

———, *Bayonets before Bullets: the Imperial Russian Army, 1861–1914* (Bloomington, Ind., 1992)

———, 'War Planning and Initial Operations in the Russian Context', in R. F. Hamilton and H. H. Herwig (eds.), *War Planning 1914* (Cambridge, 2010), 80–142

Menning, R., 'Dress Rehearsal for 1914? Germany, the Franco-Russian Alliance, and the Bosnian Crisis of 1909', *Journal of the Historical Society*, vol. 12, no. 1 (2012), 1–25

Menning, R. and Menning, C. B., '"Baseless Allegations": Wilhelm II and the Hale Interview of 1908', *Central European History*, vol. 16, no. 4 (1983), 368–97

Messimy, A., *Mes Souvenirs: Jeunesse et Entrée au Parlement. Ministre des Colonies et de la Guerre en 1911 et 1912: Agadir. Ministre de la Guerre du 16 Juin au 16 Août 1914: La Guerre. Avec un Frontispice et une Introduction* (Paris, 1937)

Miliukov, P. N. and Mendel, A. P., *Political Memoirs, 1905–1917* (Ann Arbor, 1967)

Miller, S. E., Lynn-Jones, S. M., and Van Evera, S. (eds.), *Military Strategy and the Origins of the First World War* (Princeton, 1991)

Moltke, H. v., *Erinnerungen, Briefe, Dokumente 1877–1916. Ein Bild vom Kriegsausbruch und Persönlichkeit des ersten militärischen Führers des Krieges*, 2nd edn (Stuttgart, 1922)

Mombauer, A., 'German War Plans', in R. F. Hamilton and H. H. Herwig (eds.), *War Planning: 1914* (Cambridge, 2009), 48–79

——, *Helmuth von Moltke and the Origins of the First World War* (Cambridge, 2001)

——, 'A Reluctant Military Leader? Helmuth von Moltke and the July Crisis of 1914', *War in History*, vol. 6, no. 1 (1999), 417–46

——, 'Of War Plans and War Guilt: the Debacle Surrounding the Schlieffen Plan', *Journal of Strategic Studies*, vol. 28, no. 5 (2008), 857–85

Mommsen, W., 'The Debate on German War Aims', *Journal of Contemporary History*, vol. 1, no. 3 (1966), 47–72

——, 'Domestic Factors in German Foreign Policy before 1914', *Central European History*, vol. 6, no. 1 (1973), 3–43

Monger, G., *The End of Isolation: British Foreign Policy, 1900–1907* (London, 1963)

Morison, E. E. (ed.), *The Letters of Theodore Roosevelt*, 7 vols (Cambridge, 1954)

Morrill, D. L., 'Nicholas II and the Call for the First Hague Conference', *Journal of Modern History*, vol. 46, no. 2 (1974), 296–313

Morris, A. J. A., 'The English Radicals' Campaign for Disarmament and the Hague Conference of 1907', *Journal of Modern History*, vol. 43, no. 3 (1971), 367–93

Morris, E., *Theodore Rex* (New York, 2001)

Mortimer, J. S., 'Commercial Interests and German Diplomacy in the Agadir Crisis', *Historical Journal*, vol. 10, no. 3 (1967), 440–56

Musulin, A. v., *Das Haus am Ballplatz. Erinnerungen eines Österreich-Ungarischen Diplomaten* (Munich, 1924)

Neilson, K., 'The Anglo-Japanese Alliance and British Strategic Foreign Policy, 1902–1914', in P. P. O'Brien (ed.), *The Anglo-Japanese Alliance* (New York, 2004), 48–63

——, *Britain and the Last Tsar: British Policy and Russia, 1894–1917* (Oxford, 1995)

——, 'Great Britain', in R. F. Hamilton and H. H. Herwig (eds.), *War Planning, 1914* (Cambridge, 2009), 175–97

Neklyudov, A. V., *Diplomatic Reminiscences before and during the World War, 1911–1917* (London, 1920)

Nicolson, H. G., *Portrait of a Diplomatist: Being the Life of Sir Arthur Nicolson, Bart., First Lord Carnock: A Study in the Old Diplomacy* (London, 1930)

Nish, I., 'Origins of the Anglo-Japanese Alliance: In the Shadow of the Dreibund', in P. P. O'Brien (ed.), *The Anglo-Japanese Alliance* (New York, 2004), 8–25

Nolan, M., *The Inverted Mirror: Mythologizing the Enemy in France and Germany, 1898–1914* (New York, 2005)

O'Brien, P. P., 'The Costs and Benefits of British Imperialism 1846–1914', *Past and Present*, no. 120 (1988), 163–200

————, 'The Titan Refreshed: Imperial Overstretch and the British Navy before the First World War', *Past and Present*, vol. 172, no. 1 (2001), 146–69

O'Brien, P. P. (ed.), *The Anglo-Japanese Alliance* (New York, 2004)

Offer, A., *The First World War: An Agrarian Interpretation* (Oxford, 1991)

————, 'Going to War in 1914: A Matter of Honor?', *Politics & Society*, vol. 23, no. 2 (1995), 213–41

Oppel, B., 'The Waning of a Traditional Alliance: Russia and Germany after the Portsmouth Peace Conference', *Central European History*, vol. 5, no. 4 (1972), 318–29

Otte, T. G., '"Almost a Law of Nature?": Sir Edward Grey, the Foreign Office, and the Balance of Power in Europe, 1905–12', in E. Goldstein and B. J. C. McKercher (eds.), *Power and Stability: British Foreign Policy, 1865–1965* (London, 2003), 75–116

————, '"An Altogether Unfortunate Affair": Great Britain and the Daily Telegraph Affair', *Diplomacy and Statecraft*, vol. 5, no. 2 (1994), 296–333

————, 'Eyre Crowe and British Foreign Policy: A Cognitive Map', in T. G. Otte and C. A. Pagedas (eds.), *Personalities, War and Diplomacy: Essays in International History* (London, 1997), 14–37

Ousby, I., *The Road to Verdun: France, Nationalism and the First World War* (London, 2003)

Paléologue, M. and Holt, F. A., *An Ambassador's Memoirs, 1914–1917* (London, 1973)

Palmer, A. W., *Twilight of the Habsburgs: The Life and Times of Emperor Francis Joseph* (London, 1994)

Patterson, D. F., 'Citizen Peace Initiatives and American Political Culture, 1865–1920', in C. Chatfield and P. van den Dungen (eds.), *Peace Movements and Political Culture* (Knoxville, 1988), 187–203

Pless, D. F. v. and Chapman-Huston, D., *Daisy, Princess of Pless* (New York, 1929)

Poincaré, R., *Au Service de la France: Neuf Années de Souvenirs*, 11 vols (Paris, 1926–74)

Porch, D., 'The French Army and the Spirit of the Offensive, 1900–1914', in B. Bond and I. Roy (eds.), *War and Society: A Yearbook of Military History* (New York, 1975), 117

————, *The March to the Marne: The French Army, 1871–1914* (Cambridge, 1981)

Radziwill, C., *Behind the Veil at the Russian Court, by Count Paul Vassili* (London, 1913)

Rathenau, W. and Pogge von Strandmann, H., *Walther Rathenau, Industrialist, Banker, Intellectual, and Politician: Notes and Diaries, 1907–1922* (Oxford, 1985)

Rathenau, W. (ed.), *Briefe* (Dresden, 1926)

Redlich, J., *Emperor Francis Joseph of Austria: A Biography* (New York, 1929)

————, *Schicksalsjahre Österreichs, 1908–1919: Das politische Tagebuch Josef Redlichs* (Graz, 1953)

Renzi, W. A., *In the Shadow of the Sword: Italy's Neutrality and Entrance into the Great War, 1914–1915* (New York, 1987)

Reynolds, M. A., *Shattering Empires: The Clash and Collapse of the Ottoman and Russian Empires, 1908–1918* (Cambridge, 2011)

Rich, D. A., *The Tsar's Colonels: Professionalism, Strategy, and Subversion in Late Imperial Russia* (Cambridge, 1998)

Rich, N., *Friedrich von Holstein, Politics and Diplomacy in the Era of Bismarck and Wilhelm II* (Cambridge, 1965)

Ridley, J., *Bertie: A Life of Edward VII* (London, 2012)

Riezler, K., *Tagebücher, Aufsätze, Dokumente* (Göttingen, 1972)

Ritter, G., *The Sword and the Scepter: The Problem of Militarism in Germany*, vol. II: *The European Powers and the Wilhelminian Empire, 1890–1914* (Coral Gables, 1970)

———, 'Zusammenarbeit der Generalstäbe Deutschlands und Österreichs', in C. Hinrichs (ed.), *Zur Geschichte und Problematik der Demokratie. Festgabe für Hans Herzfeld, Professor der Neueren Geschichte an der Freien Universität Berlin, Anlässlich seines fünfundsechzigsten Geburtstages Am 22. Juni 1957* (Berlin, 1958), 523–50

Robbins, K., *Sir Edward Grey: A Biography of Lord Grey of Fallodon* (London, 1971)

Roberts, A., *Salisbury: Victorian Titan* (London, 1999)

Rogger, H., 'Russia in 1914', *Journal of Contemporary History*, vol. 1, no. 4 (1966), 95–119

Rohrkrämer, T., 'Heroes and Would-be Heroes: Veterans' and Reservists' Associations in Imperial Germany', in M. F. Boemeke, R. Chickering, and S. Förster (eds.), *Anticipating Total War: The German and American Experiences, 1871–1914* (Cambridge, 1999), 189–215

Röhl, J. C. G., 'Admiral von Müller and the Approach of War, 1911–1914', *Historical Journal*, vol. 12, no. 4 (1969), 651–73

———, *The Kaiser and His Court: Wilhelm II and the Government of Germany* (Cambridge, 1996)

Rose, K., *King George V* (London, 1983)

Rosen, R. R., *Forty Years of Diplomacy* (London, 1922)

Rossos, A., *Russia and the Balkans: Inter-Balkan Rivalries and Russian Foreign Policy, 1908–1914* (Toronto, 1981)

Rotte, R., 'Global Warfare, Economic Loss and the Outbreak of the Great War', *War in History*, vol. 5, no. 4 (1998), 481–93

Rüger, J., *The Great Naval Game: Britain and Germany in the Age of Empire* (Cambridge, 2007)

———, 'Nation, Empire and Navy: Identity Politics in the United Kingdom, 1887–1914', *Past and Present*, vol. 185, no. 1 (2004), 159–87

Sanborn, J., 'Education for War, Peace, and Patriotism in Russia on the Eve of World War I', in H. Afflerbach and D. Stevenson (eds.), *An Improbable War? The Outbreak of World War I and European Political Culture before 1914* (New York, 2007), 213–29

Sazonov, S. D., *Fateful Years, 1909–1916: The Reminiscences of Serge Sazonov* (London, 1928)

Schmidt, S., *Frankreichs Aussenpolitik in der Julikrise 1914. Ein Beitrag zur Geschichte des Ausbruchs des Ersten Weltkrieges* (Munich, 2009)

Schoen, W., *The Memoirs of an Ambassador: A Contribution to the Political History of Modern Times* (London, 1922)

Schorske, C., *Fin-de-Siècle Vienna: Politics and Culture* (New York, 1981)

Sharp, A., *Anglo-French Relations in the Twentieth Century: Rivalry and Cooperation* (London, 2000)

Shatsillo, K. F., *Ot Portsmutskogo Mira k Pervoi Mirovoi Voine* (Moscow, 2000)

Showalter, D., 'From Deterrence to Doomsday Machine: The German Way of War, 1890–1914', *Journal of Military History*, vol. 64, no. 3 (2000), 679–710

———, 'Railroads, the Prussian Army, and the German Way of War in the Nineteenth Century', in T. G. Otte and K. Neilson (eds.), *Railways and International Politics: Paths of Empire, 1848–1945* (New York, 2006), 21–44

Shukman, H., *Rasputin* (Stroud, 1997)

Smith, D., *One Morning in Sarajevo: 28 June 1914* (London, 2008)

Snyder, J., 'Civil–Military Relations and the Cult of the Offensive, 1914 and 1984', in S. E. Miller, S. M. Lynn-Jones, and S. van Evera (eds.), *Military Strategy and the Origins of the First World War* (Princeton, 1991), 20–58

———, *The Ideology of the Offensive: Military Decision Making and the Disasters of 1914* (Ithaca, 1984)

Sondhaus, L., *Franz Conrad von Hötzendorf: Architect of the Apocalypse* (Boston, 2000)

Soroka, M., 'Debating Russia's Choice between Great Britain and Germany: Count Benckendorff versus Count Lamsdorff, 1902–1906', *International History Review*, vol. 32, no. 1 (2010), 1–24

Sösemann, B., 'Die Tagebücher Kurt Riezlers. Untersuchungen zu Ihrer Echtheit und Edition', *Historische Zeitschrift*, vol. 236 (1983), 327–69

Spender, J. A., *The Public Life* (London, 1925)

Spitzemberg, H. v., *Das Tagebuch der Baronin Spitzemberg. Aufzeichnungen aus der Hofgesellschaft des Hohenzollernreiches* (Göttingen, 1960)

Spring, D. W., 'Russia and the Franco-Russian Alliance, 1905–14: Dependence or Interdependence?', *Slavonic and East European Review*, vol. 66, no. 4 (1988), 564–92

Stargardt, N., *The German Idea of Militarism: Radical and Socialist Critics, 1866–1914* (Cambridge, 1994)

Steed, H. W., *Through Thirty Years, 1892–1922: A Personal Narrative* (London, 1924)

Steinberg, J., *Bismarck: A Life* (Oxford, 2011)

———, 'The Copenhagen Complex', *Journal of Contemporary History*, vol. 1, no. 3 (1966), 23–46

———, 'The Novelle of 1908: Necessities and Choices in the Anglo-German Naval Arms Race', *Transactions of the Royal Historical Society*, vol. 21 (1971), 25–43

———, *Yesterday's Deterrent: Tirpitz and the Birth of the German Battle Fleet* (New York, 1965)

Steinberg, J. W., *All the Tsar's Men: Russia's General Staff and the Fate of the Empire, 1898–1914* (Baltimore, 2010)

Steiner, Z., *The Foreign Office and Foreign Policy, 1898–1914* (Cambridge, 1969)

———, 'Grey, Hardinge and the Foreign Office, 1906–1910', *Historical Journal*, vol. 10, no. 3 (1967), 415–39

———, 'The Last Years of the Old Foreign Office, 1898–1905', *Historical Journal*, vol. 6, no. 1 (1963), 59–90

Steiner, Z. and Neilson, K., *Britain and the Origins of the First World War* (London, 2003)

Stengers, J., 'Belgium', in K. M. Wilson (ed.), *Decisions for War, 1914* (London, 1995), 151–74

Stevenson, D., *Armaments and the Coming of War: Europe, 1904–1914* (Oxford, 1996)

———, 'Militarization and Diplomacy in Europe before 1914', *International Security*, vol. 22, no. 1 (1997), 125–61

————, 'War by Timetable? The Railway Race before 1914', *Past and Present*, vol. 162, no. 2 (1999), 163–94

Stieve, F. (ed.), *Der diplomatische Schriftwechsel Iswolskis, 1911–1914* (Berlin, 1924)

Stone, N., *Europe Transformed, 1878–1919* (Glasgow, 1983)

————, 'Hungary and the Crisis of July 1914', *Journal of Contemporary History*, vol. 1, no. 3 (1966), 153–70

————, 'V. Moltke–Conrad: Relations between the Austro-Hungarian and German General Staffs, 1909–14', *Historical Journal*, vol. 9, no. 2 (1966), 201–28

Strachan, H., *The First World War*, vol. I: *To Arms* (Oxford, 2001)

Stromberg, R. N., 'The Intellectuals and the Coming of War in 1914', *Journal of European Studies*, vol. 3, no. 2 (1973), 109–22

Sweet, D. W., 'The Bosnian Crisis', in F. H. Hinsley (ed.), *British Foreign Policy under Sir Edward Grey* (Cambridge, 1977), 178–92

Szamuely, T., *The Russian Tradition* (London, 1988)

Tanenbaum, J. K., 'French Estimates of Germany's Operational War Plans', in E. R. May (ed.), *Knowing One's Enemies: Intelligence Assessment before the Two World Wars* (Princeton, 1986), 150–71

Tanner, M., *Nietzsche: A Very Short Introduction* (Oxford, 2000)

Taube, M. d., *La Politique russe d'avant-guerre et la fin de l'empire des tsars (1904–1917): Mémoires du Baron M. de Taube ...* (Paris, 1928)

Taylor, A. J. P., *The Struggle for Mastery in Europe* (London, 1998)

Thaden, E. C., *Russia and the Balkan Alliance of 1912* (University Park, PA, 1965)

Thompson, J. L., *Northcliffe: Press Baron in Politics, 1865–1922* (London, 2000)

Tirpitz, A. v., *My Memoirs* (London, 1919)

————, *Politische Dokumente*, vol. I: *Der Aufbau der deutschen Weltmacht* (Stuttgart, 1924)

Tombs, R. and Tombs, I., *That Sweet Enemy: The French and the British from the Sun King to the Present* (New York, 2008)

Travers, T. H. E., 'Technology, Tactics, and Morale: Jean de Bloch, the Boer War, and British Military Theory, 1900–1914', *Journal of Modern History*, vol. 51, no. 2 (1979), 264–86

Trotsky, L., *The Balkan Wars, 1912–13: The War Correspondence of Leon Trotsky*, ed. G. Weissman and D. Williams (New York, 1991)

Trumpener, U., 'War Premeditated? German Intelligence Operations in July 1914', *Central European History*, vol. 9, no. 1 (1976), 58–85

Tuchman, B., *The Guns of August* (New York, 1963)

————, *The Proud Tower: A Portrait of the World before the War, 1890–1914* (London, 1967)

Turner, L. C. F., 'The Role of the General Staffs in July 1914', *Australian Journal of Politics and History*, vol. 11, no. 3 (1965), 305–23

————, 'The Russian Mobilization in 1914', *Journal of Contemporary History*, vol. 3, no. 1 (1968), 65–88

Tylor, E. B., *Primitive Culture: Researches into the Development of Mythology, Philosophy, Religion, Art, and Custom* (London, 1873)

Urbas, Emanuel [Ernest U. Cormons], *Schicksale und Schatten* (Salzburg, 1951)

Verhey, J., *The Spirit of 1914: Militarism, Myth, and Mobilization in Germany* (Cambridge, 2000)

Vermes, G., *Istv'an Tisza: The Liberal Vision and Conservative Statecraft of a Magyar Nationalist* (New York, 1985)

Victoria, Queen of Great Britain, *The Letters of Queen Victoria: A Selection from Her Majesty's Correspondence between the Years 1837 and 1861*, vol. III: *1854–1861* (London, 1908)

——, *Queen Victoria's Journals*, www.queenvictoriasjournals.org

Vinogradov, V. N., '1914 God: Byt' Ili Ne Byt' Vojne?', in anon. (ed.), *Poslednjaja Vojna Rossijskoj Imperii: Rossija, Mir Nakanune, v Hode i Posle Pervoj Mirovoj Vojny Po Dokumentam Rossijskih i Zarubezhnyh Arhivov* (Moscow, 2004), 161–4

Voeikov, V. N., *S Tsarem I Bez Tsarya: Vospominaniya Poslednego Dvortsovogo Komendanta Gosudarya Imperatora Nikolaya II* (Moscow, 1995)

Wandruszka, A. and Urbanitsch, P. (eds.), *Die Habsburgermonarchie 1848–1918* (Vienna, 1989)

Wank, S., 'Aehrenthal's Programme for the Constitutional Transformation of the Habsburg Monarchy: Three Secret "Mémoires"', *Slavonic and East European Review*, vol. 41, no. 97 (1963), 513–36

——, 'The Archduke and Aehrenthal: The Origins of a Hatred', *Austrian History Yearbook*, vol. 38 (2002), 77–104

——, 'The Austrian Peace Movement and the Habsburg Ruling Elite', in C. Chatfield and P. van den Dungen (eds.), *Peace Movements and Political Cultures* (Knoxville, 1988), 40–63

——, 'Desperate Counsel in Vienna in July 1914: Berthold Molden's Unpublished Memorandum', *Central European History*, vol. 26, no. 3 (1993), 281–310

——, 'Foreign Policy and the Nationality Problem in Austria-Hungary, 1867–1914', *Austrian History Yearbook*, vol. 3, no. 3 (1967), 37–56

——, 'Pessimism in the Austrian Establishment at the Turn of the Century', in S. Wank, H. Maschl, B. Mazohl-Wallnig, and R. Wagnleitner, *The Mirror of History: Essays in Honor of Fritz Fellner* (Santa Barbara, 1988)

Weber, E., *France: Fin de Siècle* (London, 1986)

——, *The Nationalist Revival in France, 1905–1914* (Berkeley, 1968)

Weinroth, H. S., 'The British Radicals and the Balance of Power, 1902–1914', *Historical Journal*, vol. 13, no. 4 (1970), 653–82

Welch, M., 'The Centenary of the British Publication of Jean de Bloch's Is War Now Impossible? (1899–1999)', *War in History*, vol. 7 (2000), 273–94

White, A. D., *The First Hague Conference* (Boston, 1912)

Wilhelm II, *Reden des Kaisers. Ansprachen, Predigten und Trinksprüche Wilhelms II* (Munich, 1966)

Williams, E. E., 'Made in Germany' (London, 1896)

Williams, W., *The Tiger of France: Conversations with Clemenceau* (Berkeley, 1949)

Williamson, S. R. J., *Austria-Hungary and the Origins of the First World War* (Basingstoke, 1991)

——, 'General Henry Wilson, Ireland, and the Great War', in W. R. Louis (ed.), *Resurgent Adventures with Britannia: Personalities, Politics and Culture in Britain* (London, 2011), 91–105

——, 'German Perceptions of the Triple Entente After 1911: Their Mounting Apprehensions Reconsidered', *Foreign Policy Analysis*, vol. 7 (2011), 205–14

————, 'Influence, Power, and the Policy Process: The Case of Franz Ferdinand, 1906–1914', *Historical Journal*, vol. 17, no. 2 (1974), 417–34

————, *The Politics of Grand Strategy: Britain and France Prepare for War, 1904–1914* (London, 1990)

Williamson, S. and May, E., 'An Identity of Opinion: Historians and 1914', *The Journal of Modern History*, vol. 79, no. 2 (2007), 335–387

Wilson, K. M., 'The Agadir Crisis, the Mansion House Speech, and the Double-Edgedness of Agreements', *Historical Journal*, vol. 15, no. 3 (1972), 513–32

————, *The Policy of the Entente: Essays on the Determinants of British Foreign Policy, 1904–1914* (Cambridge, 1985)

Winzen, P., 'Prince Bulow's Weltmachtpolitik', *Australian Journal of Politics and History*, vol. 22, no. 2 (1976), 227–42

————, 'Treitschke's Influence on the Rise of Imperialism and Anti-British Nationalism in Germany', in P. M. Kennedy and A. J. Nicholls (eds.), *Nationalist and Racialist Movements in Britain and Germany before 1914* (London, 1981), 154–71

Wohl, R., *The Generation of 1914* (Cambridge, MA, 1979)

Wolff, T., *Tagebücher 1914–1919. Der Erste Weltkrieg und die Entstehung der Weimarer Republik in Tagebüchern, Leitartikeln und Briefen des Chefredakteurs am „Berliner Tagblatt" und Mitbegründer der „Deutschen Demokratischen Partei". Erster Teil* (Boppard am Rhein, 1984)

Zedlitz-Trützschler, R. v., *Twelve Years at the Imperial German Court* (New York, 1924)

Zuber, T., *Inventing the Schlieffen Plan: German War Planning, 1871–1914* (Oxford, 2002)

Zweig, S., *The World of Yesterday* (London, 2009)

Index